Lecture Notes in Computer Science   16334

Founding Editors

Gerhard Goos
Juris Hartmanis

The series Lecture Notes in Computer Science (LNCS), including its subseries Lecture Notes in Artificial Intelligence (LNAI) and Lecture Notes in Bioinformatics (LNBI), has established itself as a medium for the publication of new developments in computer science and information technology research, teaching, and education.

LNCS enjoys close cooperation with the computer science R & D community, the series counts many renowned academics among its volume editors and paper authors, and collaborates with prestigious societies. Its mission is to serve this international community by providing an invaluable service, mainly focused on the publication of conference and workshop proceedings and postproceedings. LNCS commenced publication in 1973.

Don Harris · Wen-Chin Li · Norbert A. Streitz ·
Shin'ichi Konomi

Editors

HCI International 2025 – Late Breaking Papers

27th International Conference on
Human-Computer Interaction, HCII 2025
Gothenburg, Sweden, June 22–27, 2025
Proceedings, Part IV

 Springer

Editors
Don Harris
Coventry University
Coventry, UK

Norbert A. Streitz ⓘ
Smart Future Initiative
Frankfurt am Main, Germany

Wen-Chin Li
Cranfield University
Cranfield, UK

Shin'ichi Konomi ⓘ
Kyushu University
Fukuoka, Japan

ISSN 0302-9743   ISSN 1611-3349 (electronic)
Lecture Notes in Computer Science
ISBN 978-3-032-12391-6   ISBN 978-3-032-12392-3 (eBook)
https://doi.org/10.1007/978-3-032-12392-3

Foreword

The HCI International (HCII) conference was founded in 1984 by Gavriel Salvendy (Purdue University, USA, Tsinghua University, P.R. China, and University of Central Florida, USA) and the first event of the series, "1st USA-Japan Conference on Human-Computer Interaction", was held in Honolulu, Hawaii, USA, on 18–20 August. Since then, HCI International has been held jointly with several Thematic Areas and Affiliated Conferences, with each one under the auspices of a distinguished international Program Board and under one management and one registration. Twenty-seven HCI International Conferences have been organized so far (every two years until 2013, and annually thereafter).

Last year, we celebrated 40 years since the establishment of the HCII conference, which has been a hub for presenting groundbreaking research and novel ideas and collaboration for people from all over the world. Over the years, this conference has served as a platform for scholars, researchers, industry experts, and students to exchange ideas, connect, and address challenges in the ever-evolving HCI field. The conference has evolved itself, adapting to new technologies and emerging trends, while staying committed to its core mission of advancing knowledge and driving change.

The 27th International Conference on Human-Computer Interaction, HCI International 2025 (HCII 2025), was held as an 'on-site' conference at the Gothia Towers Hotel and Swedish Exhibition & Congress Centre, in Gothenburg, Sweden, on June 22–27, 2025, with the additional option for 'on-line' participation. It incorporated the 21 thematic areas and affiliated conferences listed below.

A total of 7972 individuals from academia, research institutes, industry, and government agencies from 92 countries submitted contributions. 1430 papers and 355 posters (as short research papers) were included in the volumes of the proceedings published just before the start of the conference. Additionally, 439 papers and 104 posters were included in the volumes of the proceedings published after the conference, as "Late Breaking Work". The contributions thoroughly cover the entire field of human-computer interaction, highlight the evolving role of computers in diverse contexts, and demonstrate how HCI research is shaping and improving user experiences across a wide range of domains, influencing technological progress and its effective integration into various sectors. The volumes constituting the full set of the HCII 2025 conference proceedings are listed on the following pages.

I would like to thank the Program Board Chairs and the members of the Program Boards of all thematic areas and affiliated conferences for their contribution towards the high scientific quality and overall success of the HCI International 2025 conference. Their manifold support including paper reviews (via a single-blind review process, with a minimum of two reviews per submission), session organization, and their willingness to act as goodwill ambassadors for the conference is most highly appreciated.

This conference would not have been possible without the continuous and unwavering support and advice of Gavriel Salvendy, founder, General Chair Emeritus, and Scientific Advisor. For his outstanding efforts, I would like to express my sincere appreciation to Abbas Moallem, Communications Chair and Editor of HCI International News.

September 2025

Constantine Stephanidis

HCI International 2025 Thematic Areas and Affiliated Conferences

- HCI: Human-Computer Interaction Thematic Area
- HIMI: Human Interface and the Management of Information Thematic Area
- EPCE: 22nd International Conference on Engineering Psychology and Cognitive Ergonomics
- AC: 19th International Conference on Augmented Cognition
- UAHCI: 19th International Conference on Universal Access in Human-Computer Interaction
- CCD: 17th International Conference on Cross-Cultural Design
- SCSM: 17th International Conference on Social Computing and Social Media
- VAMR: 17th International Conference on Virtual, Augmented and Mixed Reality
- DHM: 16th International Conference on Digital Human Modeling & Applications in Health, Safety, Ergonomics & Risk Management
- DUXU: 14th International Conference on Design, User Experience and Usability
- C&C: 13th International Conference on Culture and Computing
- DAPI: 13th International Conference on Distributed, Ambient and Pervasive Interactions
- HCIBGO: 12th International Conference on HCI in Business, Government and Organizations
- LCT: 12th International Conference on Learning and Collaboration Technologies
- ITAP: 11th International Conference on Human Aspects of IT for the Aged Population
- AIS: 7th International Conference on Adaptive Instructional Systems
- HCI-CPT: 7th International Conference on HCI for Cybersecurity, Privacy and Trust
- HCI-Games: 7th International Conference on HCI in Games
- MobiTAS: 7th International Conference on HCI in Mobility, Transport and Automotive Systems
- AI-HCI: 6th International Conference on Artificial Intelligence in HCI
- MOBILE: 6th International Conference on Human-Centered Design, Operation and Evaluation of Mobile Communications

Conference Proceedings – Full List of Volumes

1. LNCS 15766, Human-Computer Interaction — Part I, edited by Masaaki Kurosu and Ayako Hashizume
2. LNCS 15767, Human-Computer Interaction — Part II, edited by Masaaki Kurosu and Ayako Hashizume
3. LNCS 15768, Human-Computer Interaction — Part III, edited by Masaaki Kurosu and Ayako Hashizume
4. LNCS 15769, Human-Computer Interaction — Part IV, edited by Masaaki Kurosu and Ayako Hashizume
5. LNCS 15770, Human-Computer Interaction — Part V, edited by Masaaki Kurosu and Ayako Hashizume
6. LNCS 15771, Human-Computer Interaction — Part VI, edited by Masaaki Kurosu and Ayako Hashizume
7. LNCS 15772, Human-Computer Interaction — Part VII, edited by Masaaki Kurosu and Ayako Hashizume
8. LNCS 15773, Human Interface and the Management of Information: Part I, edited by Hirohiko Mori and Yumi Asahi
9. LNCS 15774, Human Interface and the Management of Information: Part II, edited by Hirohiko Mori and Yumi Asahi
10. LNCS 15773, Human Interface and the Management of Information: Part III, edited by Hirohiko Mori and Yumi Asahi
11. LNAI 15776, Engineering Psychology and Cognitive Ergonomics: Part I, edited by Don Harris and Wen-Chin Li
12. LNAI 15777, Engineering Psychology and Cognitive Ergonomics: Part II, edited by Don Harris and Wen-Chin Li
13. LNAI 15778, Augmented Cognition, Part I, edited by Dylan D. Schmorrow and Cali M. Fidopiastis
14. LNAI 15779, Augmented Cognition, Part II, edited by Dylan D. Schmorrow and Cali M. Fidopiastis
15. LNCS 15780, Universal Access in Human-Computer Interaction: Part I, edited by Margherita Antona and Constantine Stephanidis
16. LNCS 15781, Universal Access in Human-Computer Interaction: Part II, edited by Margherita Antona and Constantine Stephanidis
17. LNCS 15782, Cross-Cultural Design: Part I, edited by Pei-Luen Patrick Rau
18. LNCS 15783, Cross-Cultural Design: Part II, edited by Pei-Luen Patrick Rau
19. LNCS 15784, Cross-Cultural Design: Part III, edited by Pei-Luen Patrick Rau
20. LNCS 15785, Cross-Cultural Design: Part IV, edited by Pei-Luen Patrick Rau
21. LNCS 15786, Social Computing and Social Media: Part I, edited by Adela Coman and Simona Vasilache

22. LNCS 15787, Social Computing and Social Media: Part II, edited by Adela Coman and Simona Vasilache
23. LNCS 15788, Virtual, Augmented and Mixed Reality: Part I, edited by Jessie Y. C. Chen and Gino Fragomeni
24. LNCS 15789, Virtual, Augmented and Mixed Reality: Part II, edited by Jessie Y. C. Chen and Gino Fragomeni
25. LNCS 15790, Virtual, Augmented and Mixed Reality: Part III, edited by Jessie Y. C. Chen and Gino Fragomeni
26. LNCS 15791, Digital Human Modeling and Applications in Health, Safety, Ergonomics and Risk Management: Part I, edited by Vincent G. Duffy
27. LNCS 15792, Digital Human Modeling and Applications in Health, Safety, Ergonomics and Risk Management: Part II, edited by Vincent G. Duffy
28. LNCS 15793, Digital Human Modeling and Applications in Health, Safety, Ergonomics and Risk Management: Part III, edited by Vincent G. Duffy
29. LNCS 15794, Design, User Experience, and Usability: Part I, edited by Martin Schrepp
30. LNCS 15795, Design, User Experience, and Usability: Part II, edited by Martin Schrepp
31. LNCS 15796, Design, User Experience, and Usability: Part III, edited by Martin Schrepp
32. LNCS 15797, Design, User Experience, and Usability: Part IV, edited by Martin Schrepp
33. LNCS 15798, Design, User Experience, and Usability: Part V, edited by Martin Schrepp
34. LNCS 15799, Design, User Experience, and Usability: Part VI, edited by Martin Schrepp
35. LNCS 15800, Culture and Computing; Part I, edited by Matthias Rauterberg
36. LNCS 15801, Culture and Computing; Part II, edited by Matthias Rauterberg
37. LNCS 15802, Distributed, Ambient and Pervasive Interactions: Part I, edited by Norbert A. Streitz and Shin'ichi Konomi
38. LNCS 15803, Distributed, Ambient and Pervasive Interactions: Part II, edited by Norbert A. Streitz and Shin'ichi Konomi
39. LNCS 15804, HCI in Business, Government and Organizations: Part I, edited by Fiona Fui-Hoon Nah and Keng Leng Siau
40. LNCS 158045, HCI in Business, Government and Organizations: Part II, edited by Fiona Fui-Hoon Nah and Keng Leng Siau
41. LNCS 15806, Learning and Collaboration Technologies: Part I, edited by Brian K. Smith and Marcela Borge
42. LNCS 15807, Learning and Collaboration Technologies: Part II, edited by Brian K. Smith and Marcela Borge
43. LNCS 15808, Learning and Collaboration Technologies: Part III, edited by Brian K. Smith and Marcela Borge
44. LNCS 15809, Human Aspects of IT for the Aged Population: Part I, edited by Qin Gao and Jia Zhou

45. LNCS 15810, Human Aspects of IT for the Aged Population: Part II, edited by Qin Gao and Jia Zhou
46. LNCS 15811, Human Aspects of IT for the Aged Population: Part III, edited by Qin Gao and Jia Zhou
47. LNCS 15812, Adaptive Instructional System: Part I, edited by Robert A. Sottilare and Jessica Schwarz
48. LNCS 15813, Adaptive Instructional System: Part II, edited by Robert A. Sottilare and Jessica Schwarz
49. LNCS 15814, HCI for Cybersecurity, Privacy and Trust: Part I, edited by Abbas Moallem
50. LNCS 15815, HCI for Cybersecurity, Privacy and Trust: Part II, edited by Abbas Moallem
51. LNCS 15816, HCI in Games, edited by Xiaowen Fang
52. LNCS 15817, HCI in Mobility, Transport and Automotive Systems: Part I, edited by Heidi Krömker
53. LNCS 15818, HCI in Mobility, Transport and Automotive Systems: Part II, edited by Heidi Krömker
54. LNAI 15819, Artificial Intelligence in HCI: Part I, edited by Helmut Degen and Stavroula Ntoa
55. LNAI 15820, Artificial Intelligence in HCI: Part II, edited by Helmut Degen and Stavroula Ntoa
56. LNAI 15821, Artificial Intelligence in HCI: Part III, edited by Helmut Degen and Stavroula Ntoa
57. LNAI 15822, Artificial Intelligence in HCI: Part IV, edited by Helmut Degen and Stavroula Ntoa
58. LNCS 15823, Human-Centered Design, Operation and Evaluation of Mobile Communications: Part I, edited by June Wei and George Margetis
59. LNCS 15824, Human-Centered Design, Operation and Evaluation of Mobile Communications: Part II, edited by June Wei and George Margetis
60. CCIS 2522, HCI International 2025 Posters — Part I, edited by Constantine Stephanidis, Margherita Antona, Stavroula Ntoa and Gavriel Salvendy
61. CCIS 2523, HCI International 2025 Posters — Part II, edited by Constantine Stephanidis, Margherita Antona, Stavroula Ntoa and Gavriel Salvendy
62. CCIS 2524, HCI International 2025 Posters — Part III, edited by Constantine Stephanidis, Margherita Antona, Stavroula Ntoa and Gavriel Salvendy
63. CCIS 2525, HCI International 2025 Posters — Part IV, edited by Constantine Stephanidis, Margherita Antona, Stavroula Ntoa and Gavriel Salvendy
64. CCIS 2526, HCI International 2025 Posters — Part V, edited by Constantine Stephanidis, Margherita Antona, Stavroula Ntoa and Gavriel Salvendy
65. CCIS 2527, HCI International 2025 Posters — Part VI, edited by Constantine Stephanidis, Margherita Antona, Stavroula Ntoa and Gavriel Salvendy
66. CCIS 2528, HCI International 2025 Posters — Part VII, edited by Constantine Stephanidis, Margherita Antona, Stavroula Ntoa and Gavriel Salvendy

67. CCIS 2529, HCI International 2025 Posters — Part VIII, edited by Constantine Stephanidis, Margherita Antona, Stavroula Ntoa and Gavriel Salvendy
68. LNCS 16331, HCI International 2025 — Late Breaking Papers: Part I, edited by Masaaki Kurosu and Ayako Hashizume
69. LNCS 16332, HCI International 2025 — Late Breaking Papers: Part II, edited by Masaaki Kurosu and Ayako Hashizume
70. LNCS 16333, HCI International 2025 — Late Breaking Papers: Part III, edited by Hirohiko Mori, Yumi Asahi, Dylan D. Schmorrow and Cali M. Fidopiastis
71. LNCS 16334, HCI International 2025 — Late Breaking Papers: Part IV, edited by Don Harris, Wen-Chin Li, Norbert A. Streitz and Shin'ichi Konomi
72. LNCS 16335, HCI International 2025 — Late Breaking Papers: Part V, edited by Margherita Antona and Constantine Stephanidis
73. LNCS 16336, HCI International 2025 — Late Breaking Papers: Part VI, edited by Pei-Luen Patrick Rau and Heidi Krömker
74. LNCS 16337, HCI International 2025 — Late Breaking Papers: Part VII, edited by Adela Coman, Simona Vasilache and Abbas Moallem
75. LNCS 16338, HCI International 2025 — Late Breaking Papers: Part VIII, edited by Jessie Y. C. Chen, Gino Fragomeni and Xiaowen Fang
76. LNCS 16339, HCI International 2025 — Late Breaking Papers: Part IX, edited by Vincent G. Duffy
77. LNCS 16340, HCI International 2025 — Late Breaking Papers: Part X, edited by Vincent G. Duffy, Qin Gao and Jia Zhou
78. LNCS 16341, HCI International 2025 — Late Breaking Papers: Part XI, edited by Martin Schrepp
79. LNCS 16342, HCI International 2025 — Late Breaking Papers: Part XII, edited by Martin Schrepp and Matthias Rauterberg
80. LNCS 16343, HCI International 2025 — Late Breaking Papers: Part XIII, edited by Fiona Fui-Hoon Nah and Keng Leng Siau
81. LNCS 16344, HCI International 2025 — Late Breaking Papers: Part XIV, edited by Brian K. Smith, Marcela Borge, Robert A. Sottilare and Jessica Schwarz
82. LNCS 16345, HCI International 2025 — Late Breaking Papers: Part XV, edited by Helmut Degen and Stavroula Ntoa
83. LNCS 16346, HCI International 2025 — Late Breaking Papers: Part XVI, edited by June Wei, George Margetis, Helmut Degen and Stavroula Ntoa
84. CCIS 2771, HCI International 2025 — Late Breaking Posters: Part I, edited by Constantine Stephanidis, Margherita Antona, Stavroula Ntoa, George Margetis and Gavriel Salvendy

85. CCIS 2772, HCI International 2025 — Late Breaking Posters: Part II, edited by Constantine Stephanidis, Margherita Antona, Stavroula Ntoa, George Margetis and Gavriel Salvendy
86. CCIS 2773, HCI International 2025 — Late Breaking Posters: Part III, edited by Constantine Stephanidis, Margherita Antona, Stavroula Ntoa, George Margetis and Gavriel Salvendy

https://2025.hci.international/proceedings

27th International Conference on Human-Computer Interaction (HCII 2025)

The full list with the Program Board Chairs and the members of the Program Boards of all thematic areas and affiliated conferences of HCII 2025 is available online at:

http://www.hci.international/board-members-2025.php

HCI International 2026 Conference

The 28th International Conference on Human-Computer Interaction, HCI International 2026, will be held jointly with the affiliated conferences at the Montréal Convention Centre (Palais des congrès de Montréal), in Montreal, Canada, 26–31 July 2026. It will cover a broad spectrum of themes related to Human-Computer Interaction, including theoretical issues, methods, tools, processes, and case studies in HCI design, as well as novel interaction techniques, interfaces, and applications. The proceedings will be published by Springer (part of Springer Nature) in a multi-volume set. More information will become available on the conference website: https://2026.hci.international/.

General Chair
Constantine Stephanidis
University of Crete and ICS-FORTH
Heraklion, Crete, Greece
Email: general_chair@2026.hci.international

https://2026.hci.international/

Contents

Human Performance and Safety in Aviation

Methods for Measuring Pilot Startle Effect: Novel Application
of Frequency Analysis on Flight Controls 3
   George Clayton and James Blundell

A Review of Unmanned Aircraft Systems Safety Reporting and Analysis
of Incidents 14
   Ryker Davis and Neelakshi Majumdar

Enhancement of Risk Control Measures to Mitigate Aircraft Maintenance
Errors in Critical Tasks 35
   Raj De

Safe Return-to-Land Operations in Future Cockpits: An Analysis of Cases
and Mitigation Technologies 54
   Andrew Fuchs, Carmen Bejarano, Adrien Metge, Sara Ruano,
   Jose Manuel Cordero, Andrés Perillo, Paris Vaiopoulos,
   Ginevra Fedrizzi, and Anna Giulia Vicario

Assessing the Mediating Role of Safety Communication Between Safety
Leadership and Safety Performance of Civil Aviation Pilots 73
   Chen Lin, Xie Di, Deng Hao, Yanqing Wang, Hua Sicheng, and Li Nan

What Does Cabin Crew Need During Inflight Emergencies?
A SHELL-Model Analysis 100
   Elizabeth Manikath, Wen-Chin Li, and Pawel Piotrowski

Datamining and Modeling Tacit Knowledge of Air Accident Investigators:
Research Aimed at Improving Efficiency and Quality of Investigations
Through AI 115
   Miwa Nakanishi and Mako Ono

Correlating Human Operator Risk Profiles and Intel Gain/Loss (IGL)
Assessments: An ISR Study 126
   Justin Nelson, Samuel Johnston, Anna Maresca, Erica Curtis,
   Justin Morgan, Timothy Heggedahl, and Jenna Cotter

Cognitive and Operational Challenges During Go-Arounds: Insights
from Airline Pilots   137
   İbrahim Sarıkaya and Fuat Ücrak

Quantitative Study on the Impact of Fatigue on Air Traffic Controllers'
Performance   147
   Lili Wang and Mincong Zhu

Human-Automation Teaming

HAT-TIME: Human Automation Teaming - Trust Interaction Measurement
Environment   163
   James Blundell, Christopher Burns, and Jaume Perello March

Toward a Neurophysiological Approach to Assess Optimal
Human-Machine Teaming in the Critical Environment of Air Traffic Control . . .   181
   Christophe Hurter, Alexandre Veyrie, Sara Kebir, Guillaume Truong,
   Stefano Bonelli, Gianluca Borghini, Pietro Aricò, Fabio Babiloni,
   Marc Baumgartner, Juan Alberto Besada, Luca Bergesio,
   Almudena Calatrava, Jose J. Cañas Delgado, Lidia Garcia,
   Raquel Garcia Lasheras, Brais Iglesias, Martina Jadronova,
   Florencia Lema, Alfonso Levantesi, Patricia Maria Lopez De Fruto,
   Hossein Mapar, Laurie Marsman, Job Smeltink, Anthony Smoker,
   Maykel van Miltenburg, Anna Giulia Vicario, Chen Xia, and Rolf Zon

Evaluation of a Plan and Goal Recognition System for Inferring the Pilot's
Intent in Helicopter Operations   200
   Dominik Künzel and Axel Schulte

CAAD: A Cognitive-Aware Framework for AI Agent Design in Complex
Tasks   213
   Jieyu Luo and Xinxiong Liu

Decoding Societal Acceptance of Innovative Air Mobility (IAM)
via Virtual Reality Simulations   231
   Sofia Samoili, Panagiotis-Eleftherios Eleftherakis, Margarida Lopes,
   Helena Filipe Almeida, James Lindsay Afonso de Brito Mcleod,
   George Anagnostopoulos, Konstantinos Iliakis, Sotirios Xydis,
   and Sofia Kalakou

The Future Impact of AI on the Human Role in Aviation: A Case Study
of Pilots   243
   Veronika Klara Takacs, Vanessa Arrigoni, Nicola Cavagnetto,
   and Simone Pozzi

Agent Transparency and Human Performance in the Context
of Autonomous Collision Avoidance 262
*Koen van de Merwe, Salman Nazir, Steven Mallam,
and Øystein Engelhardtsen*

Eye Tracking, Cognition, and Situation Awareness

Comparative Analysis of the Effects of Age on Cognitive Performance
in European and Asian Populations 277
*Mickaël Causse, Ami Ogawa, Damien Mouratille, Pauline Eder,
and Jean-Paul Imbert*

Do Our Eyes Behave Differently When Automation Increases? The
Influence of Automation on the Eye-Tracking Strategies During Ground
Movement Management 293
*Maik Friedrich, Meilin Schaper, Lennard Nöhren, Lukas Tyburzy,
Kathleen Muth, Florian Rudolph, Olga Gluchshenko, and Lisa Liepe*

A Study of Eye Movement Behavioral Differences Among Air Traffic
Controllers 306
Qiuli Gu and Lili Wang

Analysis of Air Traffic Controllers' Situation Awareness Based on Eye
Movement Characteristics 318
Yanqing Wang, Xiaolei Zhang, Siyu Wu, and Jingrui Ren

A Transformer-Enabled Method for Identifying Air Traffic Controllers'
Situation Awareness Using Eye Tracking 331
Xiaoqing Yu, Xing Yao, Hu Li, and Chun-Hsien Chen

Innovations in Adaptive and Responsive Environments

Ear Haptics: A Preliminary Suitability Study of a Novel Auricular Haptic
Human-Machine Interface 345
Chris Bodsworth, James Blundell, Stewart Birrell, and William Payre

Exploring Family Engagements with Smart Home Devices: A Multi-case
Study from a Distributed Cognition Perspective 364
Zixiang Feng

Designing Metaverse Environments to Enhance Creativity in Discussion:
The Impact of Avatar Gender Swapping on Male-Female Discussions   383
   Atsushi Hiyama, Katsuomi Kobayashi, Yuki Abe, Yuta Yoshino,
   Feby Juana Candra, Haruki Kitagawa, Yingting Chen,
   Yohsuke Ohtsubo, and Taro Kanno

CalmaStep: Designing Playful Interaction for Managing Collective Stress   397
   Yunyin Lou and Jun Hu

A Survey on Data Interoperability: Progress and Future Directions   413
   JunJie Su, GuoChao Peng, WeiZhen Lin, Xiao Cheng, and Yue Zhao

Dream Immersive Interactive Image Visualisation Based on Multimodal
Emotion Recognition - An Example from the Design of Dream   429
   Yuxiao Yi and Yiqi Liu

Research on Immersive and Interactive Prototype Design for Farming
and Weaving Pictures in Ancient China in Virtual Reality Environment   445
   Ruiqi Zhang, Zhenyu Zhan, Wei Li, and Ning Zhang

Author Index   459

Human Performance and Safety in Aviation

Methods for Measuring Pilot Startle Effect:
Novel Application of Frequency Analysis
on Flight Controls

George Clayton[(⊠)] and James Blundell

Cranfield University, Bedfordshire, UK
`george.clayton@cranfield.ac.uk`

Abstract. Startle is a significant contributor to aviation accidents and has been the subject of human factors research for several years. In addition to commonly used methods for measuring pilot startle - such as NASA-TLX and heart rate variability - this study applied frequency analysis to the control inputs of 16 participants. Half of these participants (n = 8) were exposed to a loud (90 db), startling sound during a simulated approach flying task, while the other half (n = 8) were not. The study found no significant difference between groups on either NASA-TLX or HRV metrics. However, a trend was observed indicating that exposure to the startle stimulus increased the quantity of high-power frequency control inputs made by participants. The current findings establish a foundation for frequency metrics as an objective, non-invasive marker of pilot startle. Future research is encouraged to incorporate frequency metrics into a broader set of physiological and performance measurements to better analyse the effects of startle in pilot populations.

Keywords: Startle · Frequency Analysis · Motor Reaction · Flight Safety

1 Introduction

The startle effect is a naturally occurring reflexive neurological and physiological response to an unexpected stimulus [1, 2]. Sensory signals, processed within the amygdala, may provoke a startle reflex if they are overly stimulating, for example a starting gun at a race or a sudden reveal of a shocking image in a film [3, 4]. The extent of the reaction varies between people, dependent primarily upon the expectedness of the stimuli and its intensity [5]. The initial development of the startle reflex elicits a rapid motor reaction, accompanied by activation of the autonomic nervous system's stress response, commonly known as the "fight-or-flight" response [6]. This physiological reaction is marked by increases in heart rate, blood pressure, and muscle tension. The startle response encompasses not only the basic reflex but also emotional (e.g., fear) and cognitive components, such as heightened attention and the disruption of ongoing tasks. Notably, the magnitude of the startle response can be amplified following exposure to aversive stimuli or in threatening contexts. This heightened reaction, known as fear-potentiated startle, tends to be more intense and longer-lasting, often resulting in a fully developed stress response [7–9].

D. Harris et al. (Eds.): HCII 2025, LNCS 16334, pp. 3–13, 2026.
https://doi.org/10.1007/978-3-032-12392-3_1

Pilot exposure to startling stimuli within aviation has been shown to be high. In recent survey studies, over 95% of pilots reported having encountered being startled during their career [10, 11]. More concerning is that the startle effect has been widely recognised as a contributing factor in aviation accidents [12]. In accident cases involving startle, 37% were triggered by highly intense stimuli, such as loud noises, which elicited a protective "fight-or-flight" reaction [13]. Startle has been attributed as a likely probable cause to accidents such as Colgan Air Flight 3407, where the pilot's reactions to pull back the flight controls, a reactive response to a stick shaker warning, were indicative of a startle response [14]. In this case, it is presumed that the pilot's inexperience with stick shakers led to a reflexive protective reaction to pull back the flight controls resulting in an accident. Another example of a startle induced air incident commonly referenced is the Air France Flight 447 crash which illustrates an example of a pilot who is so induced by startle that they instinctively hold back the flight stick preventing a stall recovery [15].

It is also worth noting that the startle effect in aviation may not always lead to negative outcomes, for example the autopilot disengage warning can 'jolt' the pilot into taking manual control of the aircraft. Regardless, due to its relevance in aviation, research has been conducted into understanding: 1) the negative effects of startle on pilot stress, decision making and performance [11, 16, 17], 2) examining the different ways to objectively detect the occurrence of startle based pilot's neurological and physiological states [16, 17], and 3) how to enhance the recovery of startled pilots through the development of targeted training [16, 18] and the introduction of adaptive cockpit systems [19]. Together, these three research aims strive to enhance pilot resilience and operational safety. However, the focus of the current study is upon the first and second dimensions – the description and detection of pilot startle.

1.1 Detection of Startle

There are multiple studies that have explored the physiological responses to startle, manifesting from the 'fight-or-flight' response which can in turn also provide insight into the neurological response of the pilot. Heart rate variation (HRV) is widely used as a monitoring method of the startle effect, representing sympathetic stress reactions in pilots and has also been used as an indicator of pilot mental workload [20]. However, there remains some conflicting findings in the literature as to whether HRV can adequately capture startle responses. For example, Landman et al. [16] found HRV, measured via ECG, could sufficiently detect startle in commercial airline pilots during an upset recovery scenario in a full-motion simulator, whilst Kinney and O'Hare [18] failed to detect startle using PPG with general aviation pilots who experienced an engine failure in a desktop simulator. Possible reasons for these conflicting findings could be attributed to the fidelity of the simulated aviation tasks, HRV sensor sensitivity, differences in the intensity and expectancy of startling stimuli, the flying experience of participants, or a combination of these factors. Interestingly, recent research by Duchevet et al. [17] found PPG could detect startle in a group of non-pilot participants within a simplified simulated cockpit environment (MAT-B).

Blood pressure, electrodermal activity, eye movement, pupillary dilation, breathing rate, electroencephalography, and electromyography are other methods of measurement that have been found to correlate with the startle response [21]. Recent studies [18, 19] have used a range of these methods in combination to investigate the physical effects of startle on pilots. However, there remains a gap in the literature regarding the use of frequency metrics applied directly to control input data, a novel and promising approach [22]. Frequency based metrics have been shown to be effective in assessing manual flying performance in large jet transport aircraft [23]. Specifically, pilots with fewer recent flying hours (i.e. in the past week) exhibited increased high-frequency control inputs, reflecting a more 'aggressive' control strategy by the pilot characterised by them 'over controlling' the aircraft. It is possible that similar observations of acute high-frequency control strategy may also be indicative of pilot startle. Notably, the neuro-muscular 'flinching' effects of startle, commonly measured with EMG in other studies, could be captured using this approach. In addition, their relevance to startle research lies in their ability to capture motor responses at a critical interface, the flight controls. Several studies have demonstrated how startle can impact pilot performance in the form of increased tracking task error, such as deviation from an ILS [17]. However, because of potential lags between control input and aircraft flight path error, particularly in larger aircraft, examining pilot performance based on control inputs represents a far more direct measurement approach that should be more sensitive to the acute nature of the startle response. Furthermore, performance-based approaches circumvents the necessity for pilots to be burdened with wearable sensors, which encompass their own set of usability and pilot acceptance issues.

The current study employs a desktop experiment simulating an approach task in a single jet light aircraft to detect and characterise the effects of pilot startle according to HRV, pilot control input and subjective workload. Addressing conflicting findings in previous research that are potentially driven by the expectancy value of startling stimuli and differences in participant flying experience, the experiment concerns an *expected* startle event in the form of a thunder clap auditory signal, that is presented to sample of pilot and non-pilot participants.

It is hypothesised that:

- The power of participant's high frequency control inputs will be significantly greater during startling conditions compared to non-startling conditions.
- There will be significant differences in HRV metrics between startling and non-startling conditions.
- There will be a difference in self-perceived workload, measured via the NASA-TLX, between startling and non-startling conditions.

2 Methodology

2.1 Participants

There were 18 participants recruited for the study. Of the 18 participants that took part in the experiment, 16 participants produced usable measurements for all recorded aspects of the study. Two participants did not produce usable HRV data, and another participant did not complete the NASA-TLX. Of the remaining 16 participants, 10 identified themselves as male and 6 as female. All participants were between the ages of 20 and 51 (M = 27.6, SD = 7.9).

Ethical approval was granted through the institutions CURES system and all participants completed a consent and information sheet prior to the experimental flight.

2.2 Procedure and Research Design

Prior to the experimental trials, participants were equipped with an ear worn PPG device and completed a resting-state HRV recording to establish a baseline reference measure. Each participant undertook a single landing task in Xplane™ 11 involving a manual approach in single-engine jet aircraft (the Cirrus Vision SF50). To accommodate the inclusion of participants with limited flight experience, a current jet was selected for its stable handling characteristics rather than demanding the operation of a more demanding aircraft - such as a fighter jet as used in similar trials.

The approach scenario began at an altitude of 1,184 ft, with the aircraft laterally aligned to the runway and positioned below the glideslope. Therefore, the participants were instructed to fly straight and level, intercept the glideslope, and commence a decent to the runway. Participants flew without the use of autopilot or flight director systems. A simulated storm included a cloud base that allowed sufficient visibility for participants to clearly observe the PAPI lights throughout the approach. A researcher acted as the co-pilot and managed the throttle, maintaining a consistent approach speed, while participants controlled only the flight stick and rudder pedals, as seen in Fig. 1. The researcher would ensure that participants were comfortable with the flight control setup, brief them on the different ways they can control the flight path, and clearly instruct them to use the PAPI lights to support their landing.

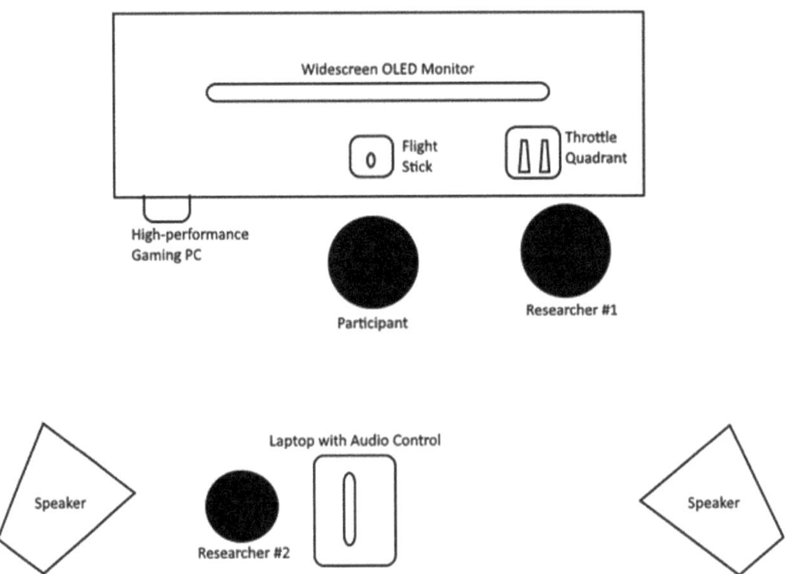

Fig. 1. Top-Down View of the Experimental Design.

Participants were exposed to a loud thunderclap sound effect, manually activated by a secondary researcher located behind the participant. The thunderclap was chosen due to its contextual appropriateness in a storm setting, where the presence of thunder would be expected. This ensured that participants were more likely to experience startle rather than surprise. The thunderclap was triggered at the researcher's discretion once the aircraft had descended below 500 ft but before reaching 100 ft.

A between-subjects design was employed, with participants randomly assigned to one of two groups. One group was exposed to the expected thunderclap intended to induce a startle response – *Startle Condition* - while the other group was not – *Non-Startle Condition*. 8 (50%) of the recorded participants experienced the *Startle Condition* and 8 experienced the *Non-Startle Condition* (50%).

2.3 Dependent Variables

Heart rate data was recorded continuously at 125 Hz throughout flights using an ear worn Inner Balance™ PPG device. The collected data were processed by EmWave software® to export as the raw moment-to-moment inter-beat interval (IBI) data. The raw IBI data were further imported into Kubios software. The R-wave time instants were autonomically detected using the Kubios Pan–Tompkins based QRS detection algorithm. RR interval data was subsequently processed to produced two HRV metrics: average heart rate/beats per minute (HR) and stress index. The latter stress index is a geometric measure of HRV reflecting cardiovascular system stress calculated by the variation scope of RR intervals [24]. The measure has been used in recent aviation-based research to capture pilot stress response [25, 26].

Control input frequency data were based on the longitudinal stick inputs during final 500 ft of the approach, which was recorded at 10 Hz. Based on the method of Ebbatson et al. [17], a moving average was first applied to smooth the data, followed by using the Matlab™ FFT function (MathWorks Inc., Natick, MA, USA) to compute the power spectral density (PSD) distribution of the control input time series data. From these distributions, based on visual inspection, high frequency control inputs were classified as above .05 Hz. The sum of power spectra within the high frequency bands were analysed.

Finally, the NASA-TLX was used to measure self-perceived mental workload. Participants completed the NASA-TLX after completing their approach.

3 Results

Results were drawn from three different data sources: HRV, control input and self-perceived workload. For all statistical tests, $p < 0.05$ (1-tailed) was considered significant. Data was organised using Microsoft Excel and analysed in IBM SPSS 25.

3.1 Flight Control Frequency Analysis

Independent samples t-tests were conducted to compare the high-frequency power input between the participant groups. Between the two groups, Fig. 2 shows that the power of high-frequency inputs were greater in the *Startle Condition* ($M = .21$, $SD = .15$) compared to participants in the *non-Startle Condition* ($M = .12$, $SD = .06$). Though this difference was not significant ($t\,(14) = -1.5$, $p = .080$.) the results were near significant ($p < .1$) and were indicative of a trend.

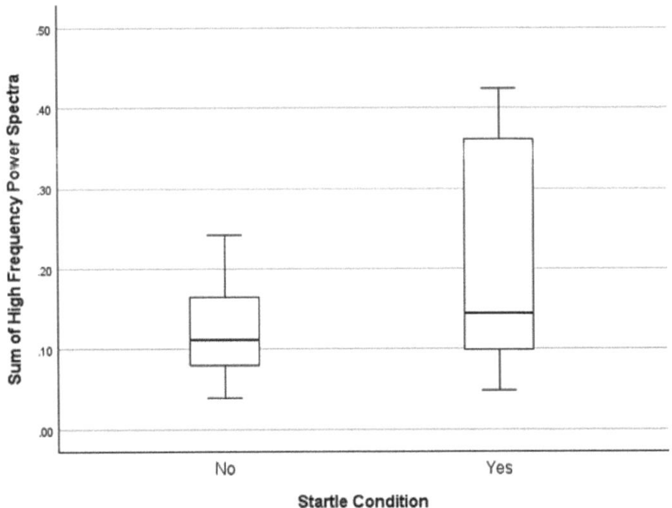

Fig. 2. High Frequency Power Comparison Between Participants.

3.2 Heart Rate Variability

To account for participants differences in resting HR, their experimental HR was subtracted from the baseline resting recording to produce a relative HR measurement indicating the change between the two states. Differences between experimental HR ($M = 78.14$, $SD = 8.21$) and resting HR ($M = 93.41$, $SD = 18.85$) was significant ($t\,(15) = 4.83$, $p < .001$).

The relative difference between the experimental and the resting HR in the *Startle Condition* ($M = 16.96$, $SD = 15.32$) was found to be larger than the *Non-Startle Condition* ($M = 13.59$, $SD = 10.13$), see Fig. 3. However, no significant difference was found, $t(14) = 0.52$, $p = .306$.

The relative stress index difference between resting and experimental conditions was calculated for each participant by subtracting the resting score from the experimental score ($M = 7$, $SD = 6.4$). No significant difference was found between participants who experienced the loud sound ($M = 4.3$, $SD = 2.9$) and those who did not ($M = 12.4$, $SD = 5.2$), $t(20) = -2.8$, $p = .006$.

3.3 NASA-TLX

An un-weighted score for each participant's NASA-TLX was calculated by averaging the individual scores from the six different factors ($M = 46.1$, $SD = 17.38$). There was

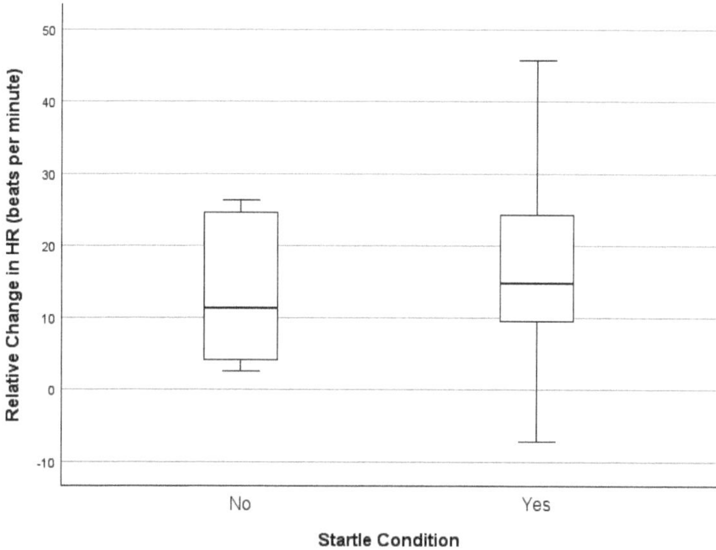

Fig. 3. Relative Difference in Participant HRV Between Resting and Experimental States.

no significant difference between the 8 participants that experienced the loud sound ($M = 53.7$, $SD = 18.6$) and the 8 participants that did not ($M = 51.1$, $SD = 11.8$), $t(14) = -.33$, $p = .377$.

4   Discussion

This study aimed to examine how frequency-based metrics can be utilised as a measure of startle using pilot control inputs. The study also contributes to the growing body of literature that has documented how pilot physiological responses, HRV in this case, are influenced by various experimental conditions that are intended to simulate startling scenarios. Specifically, non-pilot participants were evaluated in a 'pure' startle scenario (i.e., a briefed startle event that was dissociated from the effects of surprise) using a mid-fidelity desktop simulation environment. Overall, the results of the study reveal promising early trends that frequency-based measurement of pilot control inputs could form part of future applications that are intended for pilot startle detection. The remaining parts of the discussion section of this paper examines each of the three hypothesis statements in relation to the current findings in turn.

The first hypothesis '*The power of participant's high frequency control inputs will be significantly greater during startling conditions compared to non-startling conditions*' was not rejected. However, the relevant hypothesis test neared significance ($p < .1$) with there being a respective tread of indicating that high-frequency control inputs were in more prevalent in the startle condition compared to the non-startle condition. This observation supports recent startle findings by Duchevet et al. [17] who, again with non-pilots, found that startle increased tracking error in a MATB experiment. Indeed, the current findings likely offer insight into why increased tracking error might occur during startle; a more erratic inner control loop strategy leads to subsequent problems with closing of the outer control loop (flight path). However, it is noteworthy that participants in the startle conditions expressed substantial between-subject variability in the amount of high-frequency inputs. This could be reflective of the flying inexperience of the current sample of participants, encompassing a wide spectrum of manual flying proficiency. It could, however, be also due to variation in the way that individuals respond to startling stimulus. In simple terms, some participants may respond in a 'jolting'/'flight' response whilst others other responds might be characterised by a 'freezing'/'flight' response. It is feasible that these two states would lead to qualitatively different control input responses – represented by an increase and decrease of high-frequency input respectively.

The second hypothesis, *'There will be significant differences in HRV metrics between startling and non-startling conditions'*, and third hypothesis, *'There will be a difference in self-perceived workload, measured via the NASA-TLX, between startling and non-startling conditions'*, were not rejected and largely concerned changes in participant workload caused by exposure to an expected startling stimulus. These HRV findings corroborate Kinney and O'Hare [18], where HRV did not differ significantly between GA pilots exposed to either an expected or unexpected engine failure in a desktop simulator. However, the current HRV results do disagree with both Landman et al. [16] and Duchevet et al. [17]. Reasons for this vary. For instance, Landman et al. [16] findings came from a full-motion flight simulator capable of producing starling events (change of mass) with greater physical fidelity that can sufficiently elicit stress related HRV changes. Duchevet et al. [17], on the other hand, used a lower fidelity MAT-B experiment which involved greater cognitive demand imposed by a multitasking environment. Such cognitive demands would be lacking in the current study. Finally, the absence of an effect of startle upon self-perceived workload echoes the findings of Duchevet et al. [17], but not Landman et al. [16]. Simulation fidelity differences between these studies could partly explain these conflicting findings, as well as the higher physical workload demand of the tasks used in Landman et al. compared to Duchevet et al. and the current findings.

4.1 Limitations and Future Research

Several limitations of the study should be considered. Firstly, the large variation in high-frequency control inputs within the current study could be attributed to having a sample lacking manual flying proficiency. In this case, a sample of certified pilots would likely ascertain whether this variation is driven by flying experience or through individual variation in startle response – 'flight or fight'. Relatedly, the current between-group experimental design diminished the statistical power of the current study and a within-group design approach is advised in future work.

Future research would also benefit from examining how frequency-based measures could be integrated with more traditional outer control loop metric of pilot manual flying performance, such as flight path deviation. Finally, it is important to recognise that the role of typical 'stick and throttle' manual flying in large commercial airline operations is limited and is likely to diminish further as the industry moves closer towards more autonomous flight. This does suggest that the current results will have greater relevance to flight operations that carry a larger manual flying component (e.g. GA, rotary-wing, military fast-jet). It is possible, however, that a variation of pilot input monitoring in the form of aircraft system interaction within commercial flight deck operations could be explored in future startle research.

5 Conclusions

In conclusion, frequency metrics can be used in conjunction with other more commonly used methods of measuring the effect of startle such as NASA-TLX and HRV. This paper establishes a foundation for frequency metrics to observe how aircraft control is affected through pilots induced by startle. Future research could explore the inclusion of more aspects of flight data, such as flight stick deviation or altitude variance, as simulator environments can offer high levels of control of experimental conditions to allow for fair comparison between pilots who are exposed to startle and those that are not.

Acknowledgments. This study was supported by the University of Cranfield. Dr James Blundell is a recipient of an EPSRC New Investigator grant (EP/Y00194X/1) used to support this research.

Disclosure of Interests. The authors have no competing interests to declare that are relevant to the content of this article.

References

1. Simons, R.C.: Boo! Culture, Experience, and the Startle Reflex. Oxford University Press, Oxford (1996)
2. Yeomans, J.S., Li, L., Scott, B.W., Frankland, P.W.: Tactile, acoustic and vestibular systems sum to elicit the startle reflex. Neurosci. Biobehav. Rev. **26**(1), 1–11 (2002). https://doi.org/10.1016/S0149-7634(01)00057-4
3. Huang, W., Cano, J.C., Fénelon, K.: Deciphering the role of brainstem glycinergic neurons during startle and prepulse inhibition. Brain Res. **1836**, 148938 (2024). https://doi.org/10.1016/j.brainres.2024.148938
4. LeDoux, J.: The emotional brain, fear, and the amygdala. Cell. Mol. Neurobiol. **23**, 727–738 (2003). https://doi.org/10.1023/A:1025048802629
5. Martin, W.L., Murray, P.S., Bates, P.R., Lee, P.S.: Fear-potentiated startle: a review from an aviation perspective. Int. J. Aviat. Psychol. **25**(2), 97–107 (2015). https://doi.org/10.1027/2192-0923/a000092
6. Bradley, M.M., Moulder, B., Lang, P.J.: When good things go bad: the reflex physiology of defense. Psychol. Sci. **16**(6), 468–473 (2005). https://doi.org/10.1111/j.0956-7976.2005.01558.x
7. Davis, M.: The role of the amygdala in fear-potentiated startle: implications for animal models of anxiety. Trends Pharmacol. Sci. **13**, 35–41 (1992). https://doi.org/10.1016/0165-6147(92)90014-W
8. Grillon, C., Ameli, R., Woods, S.W., Merikangas, K., Davis, M.: Fear-potentiated startle in humans: effects of anticipatory anxiety on the acoustic blink reflex. Psychophysiology **28**(5), 588–595 (1991). https://doi.org/10.1111/j.1469-8986.1991.tb01999.x
9. Schupp, H.T., Cuthbert, B.N., Bradley, M.M., Birbaumer, N., Lang, P.J.: Probe P3 and blinks: two measures of affective startle modulation. Psychophysiology **34**(1), 1–6 (1997). https://doi.org/10.1111/j.1469-8986.1997.tb02409.x

10. Ko, K.Y., Vlaskamp, D., Landman, A., Blundell, J.: Evaluation of fixed-wing pilot strategies in startle and surprise events: a survey study. In: Harris, D., Li, W.-C. (eds.) HCII 2025. LNCS, vol. 15777, pp. 61–74 (2025). Springer, Cham. https://doi.org/10.1007/978-3-031-93721-7_5

11. Vlaskamp, D., Landman, A., van Rooij, J., Blundell, J.: Recovery from startle and surprise: a survey of airline pilots' operational experience using a startle and surprise management method. Int. J. Ind. Ergon. **107**, 103733 (2025). https://doi.org/10.1016/j.ergon.2025.103733

12. Landman, A., Groen, E.L., van Paassen, M.M., Bronkhorst, A.W., Mulder, M.: Dealing with unexpected events on the flight deck: a conceptual model of startle and surprise. Hum. Factors J. Hum. Factors Ergon. Soc. **59**(8), 1161–1172 (2017). https://doi.org/10.1177/0018720817723428

13. Diarra, M., Marchitto, M., Christine-Bressolle, M., Baccino, T.: A narrative review of the interconnection between pilot acute stress, startle, and surprise effects in the aviation context: contribution of physiological measurements. Front. Neuroergon. **4**, 1059476 (2023). https://doi.org/10.3389/fnrgo.2023.1059476

14. NTSB: Loss of Control on Approach, Colgan Air, Inc., Operating as Continental Connection Flight 3407, Bombardier DHC 8 400, N200WQ. NTSB Accident Report AAR1001 (2010). http://www.ntsb.gov/doclib/reports/2010/AAR1001.pdf

15. BEA: Final report on the accident on 1st June 2009 to the Airbus A330-203 registered F-GZCP operated by Air France flight AF 447 Rio de Janeiro – Paris. Accident Report f-cp090601.en (2012). http://www.bea.aero/docspa/2009/f-cp090601.en/pdf/f-cp090601.en.pdf

16. Landman, A., Groen, E.L., (René) van Paassen, M.M., Bronkhorst, A.W., Mulder, M.: The Influence of surprise on upset recovery performance in airline pilots. Int. J. Aerosp. Psychol. **27**(1–2), 2–14 (2017). https://doi.org/10.1080/10508414.2017.1365610

17. Duchevet, A., Imbert, J.-P., Garcia, J., Lamirault, B., Causse, M.: Investigating the independent and combined effects of startle and surprise in a simulated flight task. Hum. Factors (2025). https://doi.org/10.1177/00187208251342100

18. Kinney, L., O'Hare, D.: Responding to an unexpected in-flight event: physiological arousal, information processing, and performance. Hum. Factors **62**(5), 737–750 (2020). https://doi.org/10.1177/0018720819854830

19. Duchevet, A., et al.: FOCUS: an intelligent startle management assistant for maximizing pilot resilience. In: ICCAS24, May 2024. https://doi.org/10.5220/0012915600004562

20. Mansikka, H.P., Simola, P., Virtanen, K., Harris, D., Oksama, L.: Fighter pilots' heart rate, heart rate variation and performance during instrument approaches. Ergonomics **59**(10), 1344–1352 (2016). https://doi.org/10.1080/00140139.2015.1136699

21. Romano, F., Tritto, M., Cesare, M.G.D., Nocco, S., Cardone, D.: Evaluating startle in aviation: a focus on instrumentation and measurement techniques. In: 2024 IEEE International Workshop on Technologies for Defense and Security (TechDefense), Naples, Italy, pp. 19–24 (2024). https://doi.org/10.1109/TechDefense63521.2024.10863269

22. Deniel, J., Dupuy, M., Duchevet, A., Matton, N., Imbert, J.-P., Causse, M.: An in-depth examination of mental incapacitation and startle reflex: a flight simulator study. In: Harris, D., Li, W.-C. (eds.) HCII 2023. LNCS, vol. 14018, pp. 46–59. Springer, Cham (2023). https://doi.org/10.1007/978-3-031-35389-5_4

23. Ebbatson, M., Huddlestone, J., Harris, D., Sears, R.: The application of frequency analysis based performance measures as an adjunct to flight path derived measures of pilot performance. Hum. Factors Aerosp. Saf. **6**(4), 383–394 (2007). https://www.researchgate.net/publication/258107133_The_Application_of_Frequency_Analysis_Based_Performance_Measures_as_an_Adjunct_to_Flight_Path_Derived_Measures_of_Pilot_Performance

24. Baevsky, R.M., Chernikova, A.G.: Heart rate variability analysis: physiological foundations and main methods. Cardiometry (10) (2017). https://scholar.archive.org/work/6de6pr3t5bh2fbt3x74dpgsz6q/access/wayback//www.cardiometry.net/issues/no10-may-2017/item/download/316_88e37a72e8ffeee25c25d7665b7774d1

25. Li, W.C., Zhang, J., Braithwaite, G., Kearney, P.: Quick coherence technique facilitating commercial pilots' psychophysiological resilience to the impact of COVID-19. Ergonomics **66**(8), 1176–1189 (2022). https://doi.org/10.1080/00140139.2022.2139416
26. Zhang, J., Li, W.C., Braithwaite, G., Blundell, J.: Practice effects of a breathing technique on pilots' cognitive and stress associated heart rate variability during flight operations. Stress **27**(1) (2024). https://doi.org/10.1080/10253890.2024.2361253

A Review of Unmanned Aircraft Systems Safety Reporting and Analysis of Incidents

Ryker Davis and Neelakshi Majumdar[(✉)] [iD]

University of Arkansas, Fayetteville, AR 72701, USA
`{rgd004,neelm}@uark.edu`

Abstract. Unmanned Aircraft Systems (UASs) are rapidly integrating into civil airspace, raising new safety concerns regarding their design, training, and operations. This study aims to bridge the knowledge gap in civilian unmanned aircraft systems (UAS) safety reporting by reviewing existing UAS safety reporting sources and conducting an analysis of reported incidents. We reviewed the status of UAS safety reporting to compare the recorded information and discuss limitations of the databases. We then focus on the NASA Aviation Safety Reporting System (ASRS) database to identify contributing factors in UAS incidents. Using an enhanced classification framework, we identify key categories influencing the incidents. Our analysis identified trends and contributing factors in reported incidents, ultimately informing safety decisions and highlighting potential challenges in the current reporting system. We found that human error accounts for most incidents, followed by hardware/software failures. Results contribute to a better understanding of operational risks in UAS systems and the effectiveness of using a voluntary reporting system such as the ASRS database.

Keywords: Unmanned Aircraft Systems (UAS) · Aviation Safety Reporting · Human Factors

1 Introduction

Unmanned Aerial Vehicles (UAVs), commonly known as drones, have rapidly transformed various industries, from agriculture and logistics to surveillance and recreation. The Federal Aviation Administration (FAA) mandates registration of drones that weigh 0.55 lb or more (over 250 g) with the authorities, except for those flown under the Exception for Limited Recreational Operations (14 CFR Part 48) [1]. As of March 2024, the commercial drone registrations currently stand at around 375,226 [2]. The number of drones registered for recreational flying in the U.S. has reached around 400,858 units [2]. This figure excludes drones flown under the Exception for Limited Recreational Operations, which typically involve hobbyist use that do not require registration. With the popularity of unmanned aircraft systems (UAS) operations, more concerns rise regarding their design, training, and operation safety and risk. While a lot of research has been conducted on causation analysis for manned aircraft incidents, studies on UAS incidents remain limited [3–5]. To ensure safer integration into the National Airspace System (NAS), it is crucial to understand the potential risks associated with UAS operations.

D. Harris et al. (Eds.): HCII 2025, LNCS 16334, pp. 14–34, 2026.
https://doi.org/10.1007/978-3-032-12392-3_2

To address these safety concerns, a systematic analysis of UAS incidents is essential to identify common factors and potential risks. There are various sources that record UAS safety events such as accidents and incidents. Analyzing these safety events to identify their causes and contributing factors may help in developing improved design and operations and thereby implementing mitigation strategies for safety events [6]. Early studies of UAS safety have analyzed military incidents and found that most accidents were caused by latent failures involving organizational factors and the technological environment [6–9]. Civilian-focused studies, such as those by Clothier and Wu (2012), argue that traditional aviation safety standards are not directly transferable to UAS due to unique operational and safety challenges like the absence of onboard pilots [10]. Authors suggested a need for UAS-specific regulations to manage these unique safety challenges. Fern (2012) highlighted the challenges of integrating UAVs into the NAS, especially regarding human factors and situational awareness for UAS pilots [11].

Joslin (2015) used the Aviation Safety Information and Analysis Sharing system database to examine environmental situation awareness issues in civil and public use unmanned aircraft systems [12]. Another study by Joslin (2015) included reports from the National Transportation Safety Board (NTSB), Near Mid-Air Collision System (NMACS), and voluntary reports submitted through the National Aeronautics and Space Administration (NASA) Aviation Safety Reporting System (ASRS) [13]. The study included 18 NTSB reports from 1982–2014, 11 NMACS reports from 1987–2014, and 24 ASRS reports from 1988–2014. Most anomalous events were related to equipment failures, primarily lost link, distantly followed by a variety of non-equipment-related events involving pilot/operator errors, such as near-mid-air collisions, altitude deviations, airspace violations, and procedural deviations.

Grindley et al. (2024) analyzed UAV incidents using databases from countries, such as UK (AAIB—Air Accident Investigation Branch), US (Air Force Aircraft Investigation Board and NTSB), Australia (ATSB—Australian Transport Safety Bureau), Canada (Canadian Air Force and Transportation Safety Board of Canada), New Zealand (Transport Accident Investigation Commission), and Europe (EASA—European Union Aviation Safety Agency) [14]. The findings revealed that human factors contributed to 54% of the reported accidents and incidents, particularly during operational phases such as pre-flight checks, planning, and flight execution.

Williams (2004) reviewed unmanned aircraft accidents and incidents by gathering data from various U.S. military safety centers, including those of the Army, Navy, and Air Force. The analysis highlighted specific human factors such as alarm and display failures, procedural errors, and skill-based mistakes [9].

Sun and Hubbard (2025) used 2019–2024 ASRS UAS incidents recorded under Federal Aviation Regulations (FAR) Part 107 operations for UAS and recreational UAS use. Using a framework like the Software, Hardware, Environment, Livewire (SHELL) model, the study showed that human factors were the leading cause of incidents (37%), followed by equipment problems (27%), and policy issues (24%) [15]. Although the dataset used was sufficiently large, the paper provided limited detail on the classification process and the reliability of the qualitative analysis.

While recent studies have expanded civilian UAS safety analyses, there remains a need for a more comprehensive integration of available safety report sources and a broader examination of incidents across the U.S. This study helps bridge this knowledge gap by providing a comprehensive review of UAS safety report sources in the U.S. We then conducted an in-depth analysis of UAS incidents reported to the NASA ASRS database to identify trends and contributing factors. Due to the qualitative nature of the narrative analyses, we also used inter-rater reliability analysis by including multiple raters to ensure the reliability of the findings.

We specifically aim to address the following research questions:

1. What are the types of sources and databases available in the U.S. for UAS safety reports and what kind of information is recorded in these databases?
2. What type of findings can we collect from NASA's ASRS database for UAS safety reports?
3. How can the ASRS findings be effective in informing safety decisions?
4. Are there any limitations in the current UAS safety reporting system in the U.S.?

The remainder of this paper is laid out as follows. Section 2 reviews different sources used for UAS safety reporting and the type of information recorded. In Sect. 3, we discuss our method for analyzing UAS incidents using NASA's ASRS database. Section 4 presents our results from the ASRS data analysis. Section 5 discusses the results and addresses the last two research questions. Section 6 concludes the paper.

2 UAS Safety Reporting Sources and Database

Several databases focus on UAS safety reporting and record UAS-related accidents and incidents. According to the Code of Federal Regulations 49 CFR section 830.2, an unmanned aircraft accident is an occurrence associated with the operation of any public or civil unmanned aircraft system in which any person suffers death or serious injury, or the aircraft holds an airworthiness certificate or approval and sustains substantial damage [16]. An incident is an occurrence other than an accident, which affects or could affect the safety of operations. We identified eight major database sources used worldwide that record UAS accidents and incidents. The sources include (1) NASA's Aviation Safety Reporting System (ASRS), (2) National Transportation Safety Board (NTSB), (3) FAA's Preliminary Reports of Unmanned Aircraft System Accidents and Incidents (FAA UAS A&I), (4) Near Mid-Air Collision (NMAC), (6) Aviation Safety Network (ASN), (7) Transport Canada—Drone Incident Reports, (8) United Kingdom (UK) Air Accidents Investigation Branch (AAIB), and the (9) Australian Transport Safety Bureau (ATSB). We compared the type of information that is recorded in these databases. We based the information categories on the NASA ASRS online reporting form and the NTSB reports [17, 18].

Table 1 shows a summary of the type of information grouped into different categories in the above-mentioned databases. The different categories of information recorded in the databases are listed below:

1. **Pilot Information:** Pilot's personal details such as age and gender.

2. **Investigation Occurred:** This category indicates whether an agency investigated an incident or if the incident was filed as a report without further investigation.
3. **UAS Flying Experience:** Total flight time experience of the operator (applicable if the reporter is a pilot) with the unmanned aircraft system (UAS).
4. **Pilot Certificates/Ratings:** Certifications and/or ratings held by the operator (applicable if the reporter is a pilot), including experience in both manned and unmanned flight.
5. **Weather and Visibility:** Flight conditions at the time of the incident or accident, including visibility and weather conditions, e.g., visual meteorological conditions (VMC) and instrumental meteorological conditions (IMC).
6. **Classification of Airspace:** Airspace is a defined portion of the atmosphere regulated for aviation activities, classified by type (e.g., Class A, Class B, restricted) and level of ATC service provided based on its classification. This category represents the type of airspace where the incident or accident occurred. Recreational UAS flyers can operate in uncontrolled airspace (Class G) up to 400 feet AGL and must follow safety guidelines, with FAA authorization required for access to controlled airspace. Commercial operators have broader permissions, including streamlined access to controlled airspace [19].
7. **Authorization Provider:** Entity that authorized the use of airspace (i.e., FAA, third party, other, and not applicable, such as class G which is an uncontrolled airspace where ATC authorization is not required for UAS operations).
8. **Aircraft Information:** Details of the UAS involved, including make, model, weight, and other specifications.
9. **Incident Location:** Location of the incident or accident, including altitude and proximity to the nearest airport, if applicable.
10. **Near Miss Conflicts:** Estimated separation distance between the UAS and other aircraft during the event, if the incident was a type of near-miss conflict.
11. **Contributing Factors:** Factors that contributed to the incident or accident, such as environmental conditions, human error, or software issues.
12. **Narrative:** An open-ended section where the reporter provides a detailed account of the incident, addressing the who, what, when, where, and why.

The below sub-section discusses each database with the type of information it records.

1. NASA Aviation Safety Reporting System (ASRS)

The NASA Aviation Safety Reporting System (ASRS) database is the world's largest repository of voluntary, confidential safety information provided by aviation's frontline personnel, including pilots, controllers, mechanics, flight attendants, and dispatchers [20]. The FAA's Aviation Safety Reporting Program (ASRP) enables operators, personnel, and witnesses to report incidents to NASA via the ASRS system [21]. The FAA extended the ASRP to include UAS operations [22]. As shown in Table 1, of the twelve categories reviewed, NASA ASRS includes all except pilot information and investigation. However, the ASRS does provide some pilot information (e.g., pilot location, pilot certifications) if the pilot is the one submitting the report. Since ASRS is a voluntary reporting system with anonymized incident reports, the incidents are not subject to investigation.

Table 1. Comparison of type of information recorded in the databases. Red indicates that the database does not record specific information, while green indicates that the information is recorded in the database. The investigation status is marked as "NA" for the ASN database since it stores both investigated and uninvestigated reports.

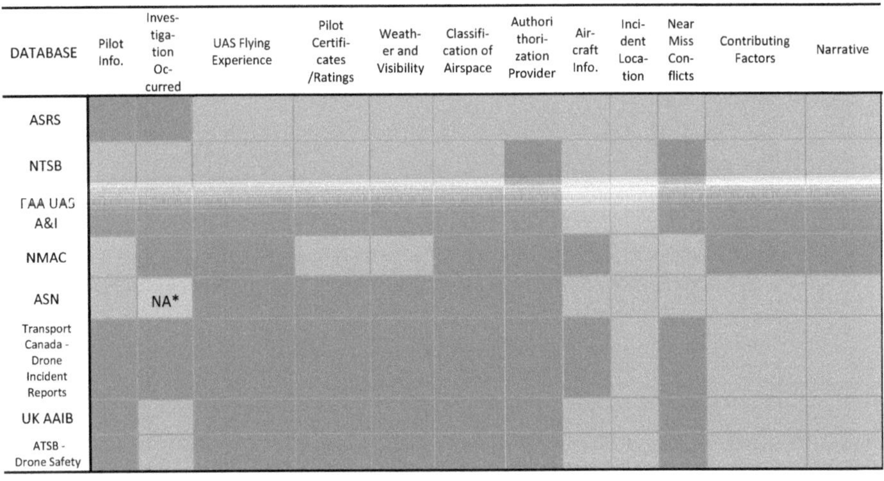

2. National Transportation Safety Board (NTSB)

The National Transportation Safety Board (NTSB) is an independent federal agency mandated by Congress to investigate all civil aviation accidents in the United States [23]. It is important to note that the NTSB requires a certain level of severity for an incident to be reported [24]. A civil UAS operator must immediately notify the NTSB of an accident or incident. After the completion of an accident or incident investigation, the NTSB provides any relevant safety recommendations to prevent similar accidents in the future. The NTSB records ten out of twelve information categories reviewed in Table 1, except for "authorization provider" and "near miss conflicts".

3. Federal Aviation Administration Preliminary Unmanned Aircraft System Accidents and Incidents (FAA UAS A&I)

The FAA Preliminary UAS Accidents and Incidents (A&I) database is integrated into the FAA's Aviation Safety Information Analysis and Sharing (ASIAS) system. The ASIAS system enables users to search across multiple databases for accident and incident reports [25]. The FAA Preliminary UAS A&I reports detailed accidents and incidents involving UAS. Each event is classified as either an incident or an accident, where an accident refers to a UAS operation resulting in complete loss of control and the aircraft, while an incident involves a UAS operation that does not comply with Federal Aviation Regulations (FARs) [26]. The FAA UAS A&I only records "aircraft info" and "incident location" information categories.

4. Near Mid-Air Collision (NMAC)

Near Mid-Air Collision (NMAC) database is also part of the FAA Aviation Safety Information Analysis and Sharing (ASIAS) system that records near mid-air collision incidents. NMAC occurs when an aircraft comes within 500 feet or less of another aircraft, or when a pilot or crew member reports a potential collision hazard between two or more aircraft [27]. The primary objective of the NMAC reporting program is to enhance the safety and efficiency of the National Airspace System (NAS). The FAA uses the data from the NMAC reports to improve airspace services and develop targeted programs, policies, and procedures to reduce NMAC incidents. Each report is rigorously investigated through collaboration between Flight Standards Facilities and Air Traffic Facilities. Findings from these investigations help the FAA to inform the development of safety initiatives and strategic recommendations [27]. No legal requirements or regulations mandate pilots or flight crews to report Near Mid-Air Collision (NMAC) incidents. Consequently, the data contained in NMAC reports are inherently subjective, necessitating careful and judicious evaluation of each report. Additionally, the dataset is incomplete, as it does not encompass all potential NMAC occurrences [26]. The NMAC reporting system includes five out of the twelve categories: pilot info, pilot certificates/ratings, weather and visibility, incident location, and near-miss conflicts.

5. Aviation Safety Network (ASN)

The Aviation Safety Network (ASN) is an exclusive service provided by Flight Safety Foundation and gives up-to-date, complete, and reliable authoritative information on airliner accidents and safety issues. The ASN consists of three accident/incident databases: the ASN accident database, the ASN Wikibase, and the ASN Drone database [28].

The Aviation Safety Network (ASN) drone database is updated at least four times a year and contains reports from pilots and reported airprox occurrences [28]. An airprox is a situation in which the pilot or air traffic services personnel, the distance between aircraft as well as their relative positions and speed, have been such that the safety of the aircraft involved may have been compromised [29]. The ASN drone database primarily derives its information from official government agencies like air accident investigation boards and civil aviation authorities [28]. The ASN database records six information categories: pilot info, aircraft info, incident location, near-miss conflicts, contributing factors, and narratives. Since the ASN database contains incident reports from multiple sources, it includes both investigated and uninvestigated reports. Due to the lack of a clear distinction between these categories, we have marked the investigation status as "NA" for ASN in Table 1.

6. Transport Canada – Drone Incident Reports

Transport Canada – Drone Incident Reports is a voluntary online reporting platform in Canada enabling users or observers to submit reports when they observe drones being operated in an irresponsible manner without a permit (e.g., flying close to other aircraft, near aerodromes, or at high altitude) [30]. Transport Canada's Drone Incident Reports are like the ASRS, as both rely on voluntary reporting to collect incident data and identify safety trends and hazards. The database records three information categories: incident location, contributing factors, and narrative.

7. United Kingdom (UK) Air Accidents Investigation Branch (AAIB)

The UK Air Accidents Investigation Branch (AAIB) investigates civil aircraft accidents and serious incidents within the UK [31]. Air accident investigation teams conduct thorough and independent investigations and produce detailed reports that explain circumstances, causes, and contributing factors. Investigations adhere to the standards outlined in International Civil Aviation Organization (ICAO) Annex 13 and comply with statutory obligations [31]. These teams also assist with international investigations, improve aviation safety by sharing lessons learned, and provide educational outreach. The AAIB records five categories in their reports: investigation occurred, aircraft info, incident location, contributing factors, and narrative.

8. Australian Transport Safety Bureau (ATSB)

The Australian Transport Safety Bureau (ATSB) improves safety and public confidence in aviation through the independent investigation of transport accidents and safety occurrences. It contributes to safety improvements by recording, analyzing, and researching safety data [32]. The Australian Transport Safety Bureau (ATSB) manages the Aviation Confidential Reporting Scheme (REPCON), which allows individuals to report safety concerns related to aviation, rail, and marine transport [33]. The ATSB also uses the Aviation Self Reporting Scheme (ASRS) to strengthen aviation human factors safety research, identify deficiencies and problems, and provide data for planning and improvement to the Australian aviation safety system [34]. The ATSB records similar information as the AAIB and includes five categories: investigation occurred, aircraft info, incident location, contributing factors, and narrative.

3 UAS Incident Analysis

For a detailed review of UAS incidents and safety status, we analyzed UAS incidents recorded in NASA's ASRS system. Since ASRS is a voluntary reporting system, it provides valuable insights into safety concerns and potential hazards that might not be captured through mandatory reporting channels. The confidential and non-punitive nature of ASRS encourages UAS operators, personnel, and witnesses to report incidents where aviation safety may have been compromised, without fear of repercussions. The ASRS database includes incidents involving collision or near midair collision with another UAS, aircraft, or object, equipment issues (such as hardware, software, and automation), procedural errors, operational errors, environmental hazards, and injuries [12]. Figure 1 and 2 show snippets of the ASRS UAS safety reporting online form [12]. Figure 1 shows the beginning of the form, which includes reporter details. As stated in the form, reporter's identity is removed to ensure complete anonymity. Figure 2 displays two sections of the UAS form: one that collects reporter information, such as their role at the time of the event, and another that records UAS details, including make, model, and weight. The full version of the form also includes fields for pilots' unmanned and manned flying experience, certificates, and ratings, as well as additional UAS details, such as FAR operations, mission, flight phase, and near-miss conflicts. The report also contains sections on weather, lighting conditions, and airspace, along with a list of contributing factors for the reporter to select and space to enter a narrative detailing the incident.

UAS FORM

For immediate action of UNSAFE or UNAUTHORIZED drone operations contact local authorities.

DO NOT REPORT UAS ACCIDENTS AND CRIMINAL ACTIVITIES ON THIS FORM.
ACCIDENTS AND CRIMINAL ACTIVITIES ARE NOT INCLUDED IN THE ASRS PROGRAM AND SHOULD NOT BE SUBMITTED TO NASA.
ALL IDENTITIES CONTAINED IN THIS REPORT WILL BE REMOVED TO ASSURE COMPLETE REPORTER ANONYMITY.

IDENTIFICATION STRIP: *Please fill in all blanks to ensure return of strip.*
NO RECORD WILL BE KEPT OF YOUR IDENTITY. This section will be returned to you.

TELEPHONE NUMBERS where we may reach you for further details of this occurrence.

HOME   HOURS

OTHER   HOURS

NAME (required)

ADDRESS/PO BOX (required)

TYPE OF EVENT / SITUATION (select all that apply)
Airspace Incursion / Excursion
Collision (aircraft, person, object)
Deviation (altitude, procedure)
Equipment Issue
(Use Command/Ctrl to multi-select)

Other: Event / Situation

Fig. 1. Snippet of the beginning section of the ASRS UAS safety reporting form.

REPORTER Reset

How were you involved in the UAS operation?

Single Person Crew   Multi-Person Crew   Not Involved (e.g. eyewitness)

If part of a Multi-Person crew tell us:

Crew Size: (total including reporter)

Role at time of event: (select all that apply)

Person Manipulating Controls (ground control station / remote control transmitter)

Remote Pilot in Command (RPIC)

UAS INVOLVED IN EVENT Reset

UAS Make / Model / Series
(or write "Homebuilt")   (do not include registration or serial number)

Weight Category   (Select Weight Category)   (at takeoff with payload)

Configuration   (Select Configuration)   Other

Fig. 2. Snippets of the "reporter" and "UAS" sections of the ASRS UAS safety reporting form.

For our analysis, we studied the narratives and factors recorded for each UAS incident in the ASRS database.

For this paper, we analyzed UAS incident narratives over two years and four months, from April 2021 to August 2023. This start date was chosen because the FAA officially introduced the new ASRS UAS reporting form on April 2, 2021, according to the FAA advisory circular 00-46F [21, 35]. To filter only UAS incidents, we selected "Public Aircraft Operations (UAS) or Recreational Operations/Section 44809 (UAS)" under Federal Aviation Regulations (FAR). The filter produced a total of 57 UAS incidents. These reports are usually submitted by UAS pilots or other witnesses of the event.

To analyze the incident data and the narratives, we created three classifications with additional categories and subcategories, partially based on the Human Factors Analysis and Classification System (HFACS) framework [36]. Inspired by Reason's [37] Swiss Cheese model, Wiegmann and Shappell [36] developed a Human Factors Analysis and

Classification System (HFACS) framework that defines the holes in the Swiss Cheese Model and describes different kinds of active and latent failures. The HFACS framework includes most aspects of human errors and latent conditions such as operator conditions, unsafe supervision, environmental factors, and organizational influences. See Majumdar and Marais (2022 and 2023) for a detailed discussion of the HFACS framework and its categories [38, 39]. The taxonomic nature of the HFACS framework provides a systematic approach for analyzing accidents. HFACS has been widely applied in the aviation industry and is a popular tool to identify causes and factors in accidents and incidents.

Table 2 shows the categories that we used for identifying issues in the UAS incidents. We used three main classifications: (1) Human Factors; (2) Hardware/Software; and (3) Environmental. Each classification has its own categories and sub-categories. Table 2 shows the description of the categories and sub-categories used for our analysis.

Table 2. Classification used to identify and map causes and contributing factors in the ASRS UAS incidents.

Classification	Category	Sub-category	Description
Human Factors	Organizational Influences	NA	Organizational issues with the working atmosphere and management (e.g., inadequate training programs)
	Errors	Decision	Errors that happen due to poor decision (e.g., decision to fly through poor visibility)
		Skill-Based	Errors that happen due to inadequate operator skills (e.g., improper maneuvering)
		Perceptual	Errors that happen when operator's sensory inputs are degraded (e.g., errors made during disorientation)
	Violations	Routine	Violations that are habitual by nature and often tolerated by a governing authority (e.g., operating UAV in an unsafe manner)

(continued)

Table 2. (*continued*)

Classification	Category	Sub-category	Description
		Exceptional	Violations that are rare, not typical for the person, and not approved by management (e.g., operating UAV without registration or in a prohibited area)
	Preconditions	Conditions of Operator	Operator's mental and psychological states, along with their physical limitations (e.g., fatigued operator)
		Practices of Operator	Communication between crew members and pilot's personal readiness (e.g., operator not certified)
Hardware/Software	Malfunction	Controls	Malfunction in the UAS controls (e.g., disconnection between the controller and the aircraft)
		Software	Malfunction in the UAS software (e.g., aircraft fails to run a preprogrammed code)
Environmental	Collisions	Aircraft	Collision between aircraft (e.g., midair)
		Other Objects	Collision of UAV with non-aircraft (e.g., birds, trees)
	Weather/Light	Ceiling/Visibility	Vertical altitude and distance of the UAV from pilot
		Weather Conditions	Description of the weather (e.g., wind, clear, rain)
		Light Conditions	Period of event day (e.g., daylight, night, dusk)

For the analysis, we used the following steps to categorize each incident: (1) summarize the event narrative, (2) map the findings from the narrative to a classification, and (3) map the appropriate category and sub-category to the findings. Table 3 shows an example of an incident report and our classification method.

Table 3. Method of classifying event findings to the sub-categories.

Narrative	Summary	Key Findings	Category	Sub-Category
I was flying my DJI aircraft recreationally […] I was unaware that I had missed steps to safely and legally fly over the water in that area	The pilot was not flying the drone with the correct licenses and approval	Unregistered drone, incorrect authorization, flying in a restricted zone	Error/Violation	Decision Error/Exceptional Violation

4   Results

The ASRS database includes 30 UAS incidents from 2021, 11 from 2022, and 16 incidents from January 2023–August 2023. We analyzed a total of 57 UAS incidents recorded in this timeframe to identify different contributing factors and the types of human factors, environmental conditions, and mechanical aspects involved in the incidents. We omitted four incidents from our analysis that did not fit with any of our classification categories and had external factors involved. One incident that we omitted involved a drone being shot down during its operation. Three other reports did not involve an incident and were caused by a manned aircraft and not the pilot of the UAS. Two of these reports involved a pilot flying in an approved location who experienced a near mid-air collision (NMAC) with a helicopter because the helicopter pilot did not see the UAV. The other report had a similar experience but with a C-130 aircraft.

4.1   Overview of Reported Incidents

Of the 53 incidents analyzed, most (41) UAS operators were recreational/hobbyist, seven were related to government, two were commercial, and one was military. Remaining two operators were tagged as "other" (specified as "personal" and "other school" respectively). 49 incidents occurred during visual meteorological conditions (VMC). VMC are the meteorological conditions during the flight, e.g., visibility, distance from cloud, and ceiling equal to or better than specified minima. One report indicated a "mixed" condition, which typically means a combination of different types of weather, such as snow and rain. Three reports did not include the flight condition information. Figure 3 shows the altitudes at which the incidents happened. Most incidents occurred below 51 feet AGL and above 300 feet AGL. Thirteen reports did not include altitude information.

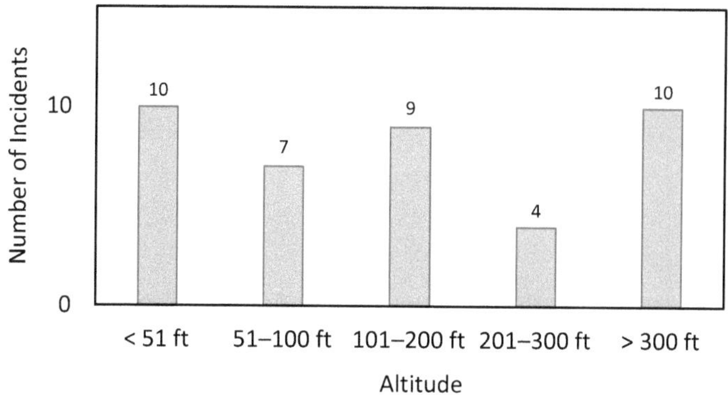

Fig. 3. Number of the incidents above ground level (AGL) altitude.

Daylight was the most common lighting condition (in 37 reports), followed by night (7 reports), and dusk (5 reports). Three reports did not include the lighting information.

Figure 4 shows the distribution of incidents across different phases of flight, with cruise being the most common, occurring in 18 reports. Notably, reporters can select multiple flight phases for each incident Ten flight phases were recorded, six of which are standard ASRS categories. The categories "return to home (UAS)" and "initial approach" were stated under "other". No additional details were provided for the two other reports grouped with "other." One report was labeled as "parked," which could correspond to the ASRS category "ground/preflight."

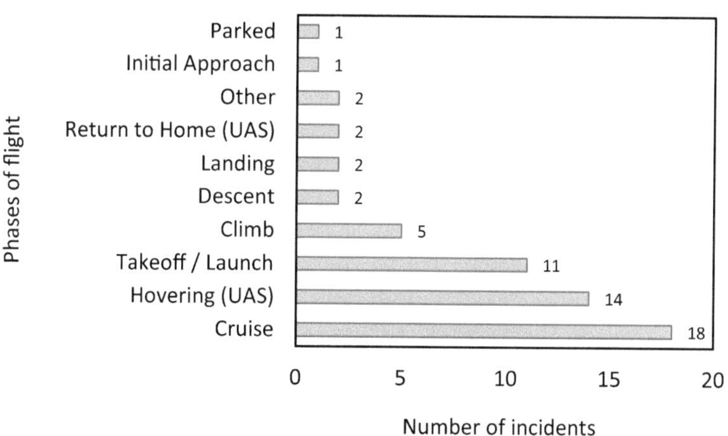

Fig. 4. Categories of different phases of flight.

Figure 5 presents the distribution of reported incidents across different types of airspaces. Class G (uncontrolled) airspace was the most frequently reported, associated with 14 incidents. Reporters could select multiple airspace types for each incident, and 13 reports did not include airspace information. TFR in Fig. 5 stands for Temporary Flight Restriction. These airspace restrictions are issued by the FAA, that prohibit or limit aircraft operations in a designated area for a specific period. Special use airspace has restricted or limited aircraft operation activities to accommodate national security, national welfare, and military activities, e.g., military operations area (MOA).

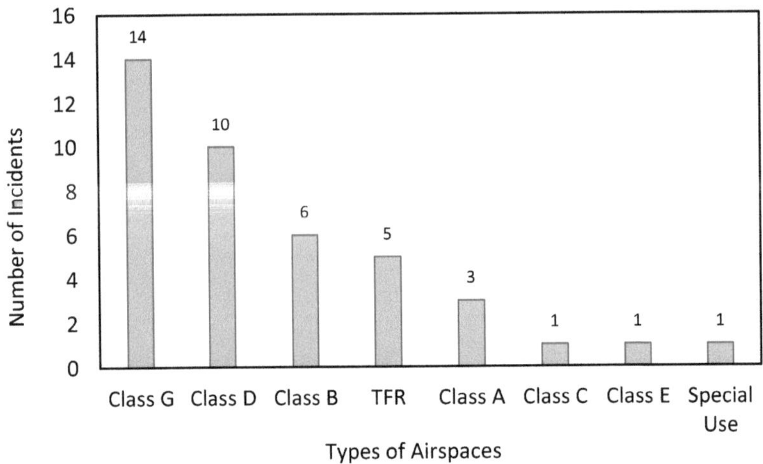

Fig. 5. Different airspaces where incidents were reported.

Figure 6 illustrates the distribution of UAS flying locations, based on responses to location-related questions such as "flying in," "flying near," or "flying over". Open space/field was the most frequently reported location, appearing in 20 incidents, followed by private property and airport/aerodrome/heliport. Reporters could select multiple locations per incident, and two reports did not include this information.

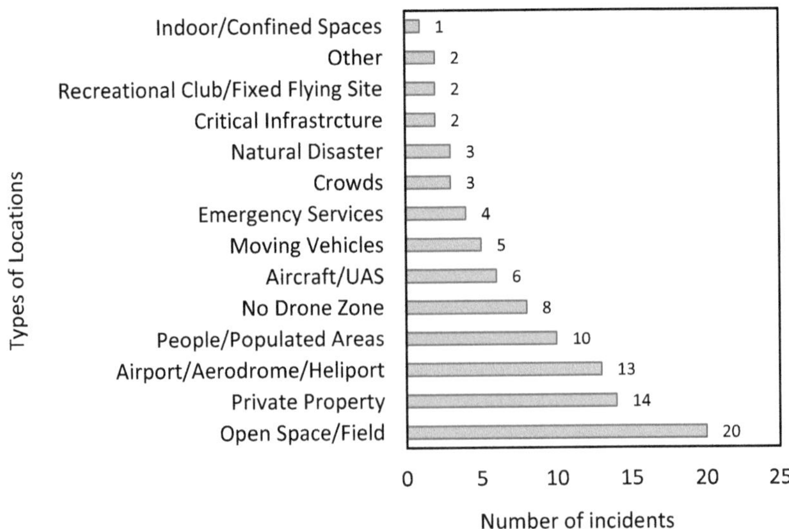

Fig. 6. Categories of flying locations reported.

4.2   Insights from Incident Narratives

Next, we analyzed the narratives of the UAS incidents, as submitted by the reporters to identify factors contributing to these incidents. We used the classification taxonomy, as shown in Table 1 by assigning categories and their sub-categories: (1) Human Factors; (2) Hardware/Software; and (3) Environmental.

Inter-rater Reliability Analysis (IRR) of Incident Classification.
To limit subjectivity and bias in categorizing the incident narratives, we assigned the analysis to two raters. Both the raters were undergraduate students who were trained on using the HFACS framework to analyze the narratives. We conducted an inter-rater reliability (IRR) assessment to evaluate the consistency between the two raters. Inter-rater reliability is a measure of the degree of agreement or consistency between multiple raters for a given dataset. A higher IRR value indicates greater agreement and coding consistency between the raters. A low IRR value means that there is a low level of agreement or consistency among the raters in their evaluations. We used the percentage agreement method for the IRR analysis. Percent agreement method gives the average percentage of agreement between raters [38].

Table 4 presents an example of the comparison of the classifications assigned by Rater 1 and Rater 2. In the comparison column, green indicates full agreement (FA) on the factors sub-categories, red denotes complete disagreement (DA) of the sub-categories, and yellow represents partial agreement (PA), where at least one sub-category matched, but not all. The raters fully agreed on more than half of incidents (27 incidents, i.e., 51%), partially matched on 6 incidents (11%), and disagreed on 20 incidents (38%). After comparing the results from Rater 1 and Rater 2, an analysis was conducted by reviewing both sets of classifications. In some cases, one rater assigned more contributing factors than the other, as illustrated by report record number 1803127 in Table 4. During the revision process, if both raters provided accurate but differing classifications, both were included in the final analysis. However, if one rater's classification was found to be inaccurate, only the correct classification was included in the revised analysis.

Table 4. Example of Inter-Rater Reliability (IRR) Comparison Between Raters. Green denotes full agreement, yellow denotes partial agreement, and red denotes disagreement.

Report/Accession Number (ACN)	Sub-Category		Comparison
	Rater 1	Rater 2	
1808986	Human Factors: Decision Error	Human Factors: Decision Error	FA
1803127	Human Factors: Decision Error & Exceptional Violation	Human Factors: Decision Error	PA
1807873	Human Factors: Exceptional Violation	Human Factors: Routine Infractions	DA

Table 5 shows examples of incidents for each of the sub-categories as mentioned in Table 2.

Table 5. Examples of incidents for each factor category

Factors Categories	Narrative summary
Human: Decision error	ACN 1808986: The operator flew their drone from a stadium parking lot, unaware that the area was within Class B airspace and near both airport and stadium authorization zones, which require special clearance
Human: Skill-based error	ACN 1817997: While level at altitude, the operator experienced wind shear, and the aircraft dropped from 2,300 ft. The operator tried to communicate, but the radio did not work
Human: Perceptual error	ACN 1841415: A trainer aircraft passed closely over a UAS in class G airspace in the woods resulting in a near-miss encounter. The drone operator missed detecting the aircraft before the incident happened, possibly due to the obstruction in the woods
Human: Routine infraction violation	ACN 1850466: The operator had previously lost full control of the UAS previously but chose to fly it again despite known deficiencies, in violation of FAR Part 107, which requires all damages to be repaired before flight
Human: Exceptional violation	ACN 1807873: The reporter observed a drone flying at about 400 ft at a university campus which is at/near an airport. Drone operations are limited to 100 ft at the campus, unless special permission is granted to fly up to 300 ft
Hardware/ software: Controls malfunction	ACN 1828128: A UAS experienced a "Center board failure" during the flight. The drone flew off on its own, got disconnected at 1,250 ft, and the Return to Home failed
Hardware/ software: Software malfunction	ACN 1948927: Due to a software malfunction in the geofencing system, the UAS exceeded 400 ft limit, reaching 774 ft after crossing a geofence that had no action configured
Environmental: Collision	ACN 2026233: A hawk collided with a UAS, causing it to crash and become completely damaged

Figure 7 presents the findings from the analysis of the 53 incidents. Note that each incident may have multiple factors. 78% of the total factors contributing to the 53 incidents were attributed to human factors, specifically errors, with decision errors being the most prevalent. In total, 42 (79%) incidents involved human factors. Although this dataset is limited, these findings are consistent with previous studies and causation analyses in aviation and other domains, where studies have shown that human error contributes to most accidents and incidents [40, 41]. 20% of the factors involved hardware/software issues. We found one incident that had environmental factors, i.e., collision with a bird during flight. The analysis highlights decision errors as the leading cause, often stemming from inadequate authorization.

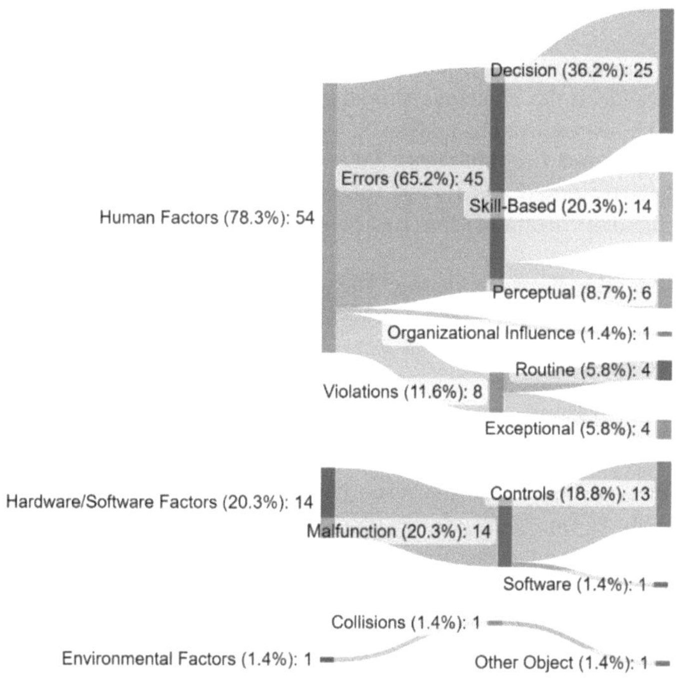

Fig. 7. Factors contributing to UAS incidents

5   Discussion

The increasing integration of UAS into national airspace necessitates robust safety reporting mechanisms. As a voluntary and confidential reporting system, ASRS encourages candid reporting from UAS users, which highlights operational challenges that might otherwise go undocumented. The richness of narrative data in ASRS provides insights into operational errors. The findings of this study may inform safety recommendations. For example, many decision errors stemmed from inadequate authorization or misjudgment of airspace regulations. Addressing inadequate authorization to the public may help inform the stakeholders and operators about the necessity of proper authorization in specific airspaces. Clearer guidelines and more awareness programs for operators may help prevent such operational failures.

However, there are certain limitations in comprehensive data collection and analysis. Some key challenges in UAS safety reporting that directly impacted this study are:

1. **Underreporting:** Many UAS operators may be unaware of the anonymous ASRS reporting or the importance of documenting safety incidents, leading to incomplete datasets within safety reporting databases.

2. **Voluntary Reporting:** Since the ASRS database relies on voluntary reporting, many incidents, including near-misses, may go undocumented, restricting the availability of data for safety analysis.
3. **Data Fragmentation:** UAS safety data is often dispersed across multiple independent reporting systems maintained by different agencies and organizations. A cross-database analyses of safety data becomes challenging to identify consistent safety trends. To address this challenge, this study relied exclusively on the ASRS database for a more consistent safety analysis.
4. **Data Quality and Completeness:** Incomplete or inconsistent reporting within the ASRS database posed a challenge for this study. Missing critical details, such as altitude, lighting conditions, or airspace classification can limit the scope and accuracy of the analysis.
5. **Lack of Standardized Reporting:** The absence of a standardized reporting format across different databases further complicates UAS safety analysis. Variability in data structures and categorization makes it difficult to perform comparative studies across different datasets. Although our analysis was only based on the ASRS data, the challenge became apparent when comparing various safety reporting databases (see Table 1).

While this study provides insights into UAS safety incidents, there are several limitations in its analysis. One of the primary limitations is the sample size. The study analyzed 53 incidents over two years and four months, which may not reflect recent trends given the rapid growth of UAS operations. Additionally, the ASRS database relies on voluntary reporting, leading to underreporting. While the ASRS maintains confidentiality for reporters, reducing concerns about legal consequences, many operators may be unaware of the system or may not report minor incidents. Consequently, the dataset may over-represent safety-conscious users and underrepresent severe or diverse incident types. Reports missing key variables, such as altitude (13 cases), lighting conditions (3 cases), and airspace classification (13 cases), limited the depth of these specific findings.

Although this study employed the enhanced HFACS framework to analyze incident narratives, the classification process remains subjective. To improve reliability, two independent raters conducted separate analyses and compared their results for consistency. Despite these limitations, this study enhances understanding of UAS safety risks and provides a foundation for future research.

Compared to previous studies, our results show a similar causation pattern of factors contributing to UAS incidents, concluding human factors as the primary cause, followed by hardware/software, and environmental factors as the least common. However, the percentage of incidents linked to human factors in our study is much higher. Grindley (2024) found that 54% of incidents were due to human factors, and Sun (2025) reported 37%, while our results show a significantly larger share [14, 15]. This difference may be because each study used different data. Grindley (2024) even notes that their percentage is on the lower end of what is usually found in safety-related fields, where human factors often account for 50% to 90% of cases.

6 Conclusion

In this paper, we addressed the following research questions:

1. What are the types of sources and databases available in the U.S. for UAS safety reports and what kind of information is recorded in these databases? We reviewed eight databases across multiple countries and compared the types of information recorded, as summarized in Table 1.
2. What type of findings can we collect from NASA's ASRS database for UAS safety reports? We analyzed UAS incident data from NASA's ASRS database to identify contributing factors, as detailed in the Results section.
3. How can the ASRS findings be effective in informing safety decisions? We discussed the utility of ASRS data for informing safety recommendations in the Discussion section, highlighting its value in identifying trends and underlying causes of incidents.
4. Are there any limitations in the current UAS safety reporting system in the U.S.? We examined the limitations of existing UAS reporting systems through a comparative review of available databases and a focused discussion of ASRS's reporting and database challenges in the Discussion section.

The findings from this study show that human factors account for most UAS incidents (78%), with decision errors being the most prevalent. This finding may suggest that many operators may not fully understand or follow airspace restrictions and may need better awareness and enforcement of those regulations. Hardware/software issues contributed to 20% of incidents, which highlights the need for more reliable control systems and software improvements in UAS. Only one incident in our dataset involved environmental factors, which could indicate that remote pilots are generally effective at avoiding or mitigating environmental risks such as wind, obstruction, or wildlife. Most incidents also occurred during daylight and under VMC, which indicates that remote pilots tend to avoid operating in poor weather. However, it is also possible that some environmental factors go unreported or are disregarded by the reporter for more immediate human or equipment-related issues.

Although this study analyzed a limited dataset of 53 UAS incidents from 2021 to 2023, a structured classification approach using an enhanced HFACS framework provides a classification methodology that can be applied to larger datasets, as more incident reports become available to identify trends and develop targeted safety interventions. The findings from this research may help in guiding future studies for UAS safety analysis and help stakeholders improve UAS safety status.

From this preliminary research into UAS safety reporting and incident analysis, there are recommendations for how future studies in this area could be enhanced. One of the primary challenges in this study was the limited number of available UAS reports under the "Public Aircraft Operations (UAS) or Recreational Operations/Section 44809 (UAS)" category at the time of analysis. As more reports become available, future studies may benefit from using machine learning tools to analyze the report narratives. These tools can eliminate the chances of subjectivity or bias in analyses. Additionally, future studies that focus on why pilots are making certain mistakes or violations may help prevent such incidents. For example, violations or mistakes that stem from inadequate training or awareness of the rules and regulations suggest enhanced training/awareness efforts and stronger enforcement of the rules that may help reduce such incidents in the future.

References

1. Code of Federal Regulations (CFR): Title 14, Chapter I, Subchapter C, Part 48 (2023). https://www.ecfr.gov/current/title-14/chapter-I/subchapter-C/part-48. Accessed 15 May 2024
2. Federal Aviation Administration: Drones by the Numbers (n.d.). https://www.faa.gov/node/54496. Accessed 01 May 2024
3. Majumdar, N., Marais, K., Rao, A.: Analysis of general aviation fixed-wing aircraft accidents involving inflight loss of control using a state-based approach. Aviation **25**(4), 283–294 (2021). https://doi.org/10.3846/aviation.2021.15837
4. Majumdar, N., Bhargava, D., El Khoury, T., Marais, K., Duffy, V.G.: An analysis and review of maintenance-related commercial aviation accidents and incidents. In: Duffy, V.G. (eds.) HCII 2023. LNCS, vol. 14029, pp. 531–547. Springer, Cham (2023). https://doi.org/10.1007/978-3-031-35748-0_36
5. Majumdar, N., Marais, K.: Human factors in general aviation loss of control: survey of pilot experiences. J. Air Transp. **33**(1), 57–68 (2025). https://doi.org/10.2514/1.D0432
6. Merlin, P.W.: Crash Course: Lessons Learned from Accidents Involving Remotely Piloted and Autonomous Aircraft. NASA AFRC-E-DAA-TN5128 (2013). https://ntrs.nasa.gov/api/citations/20180007590/downloads/20180007590.pdf
7. Manning, S.D., Rash, C.E., Leduc, P.A., Noback, R.K., McKeon, J.: The role of human causal factors in U.S. army unmanned aerial vehicle accidents (2004). https://doi.org/10.21236/ada421592
8. Tvaryanas, A.P., William, T.T.: Recurrent error pathways in HFACS data: analysis of 95 mishaps with remotely piloted aircraft. Aviat. Space Environ. Med. **79**(5), 525–532 (2008). https://doi.org/10.3357/asem.2002.2008
9. Williams, K.W.: A summary of unmanned aircraft accident/incident data: human factors implications. In: 2005 International Symposium on Aviation Psychology (2005). https://corescholar.libraries.wright.edu/isap_2005/95/. Accessed 15 May 2024
10. Clothier, R., Wu, P.: A review of system safety failure probability objectives for unmanned aircraft systems. In: 11th International Probabilistic Safety Assessment and Management Conference and the 2012 Annual European Safety and Reliability Conference, pp. 5132–5147. Curran Associates (2012). https://eprints.qut.edu.au/51232/
11. Fern, L., Kenny, C.A., Shively, R.J., Johnson, W.: UAS integration into the NAS: an examination of baseline compliance in the current airspace system. In: Proceedings of the Human Factors and Ergonomics Society Annual Meeting, vol. 56, no. 1, pp. 41–45. SAGE Publications, Los Angeles (2012). https://doi.org/10.1177/1071181312561029
12. Joslin, R.E.: Situation awareness issues in unmanned aircraft systems accidents and incidents. In: Proceedings of the Human Factors and Ergonomics Society Annual Meeting, vol. 59, no. 1. SAGE Publications, Los Angeles (2015). https://doi.org/10.1177/1541931215591009
13. Joslin, R.E.: Synthesis of unmanned aircraft systems safety reports. J. Aviat. Technol. Eng. **5**(1), 2 (2015). https://doi.org/10.7771/2159-6670.1117
14. Grindley, B., Phillips, K., Parnell, K.J., Cherrett, T., Scanlan, J., Plant, K.L.: Over a decade of UAV incidents: a human factors analysis of causal factors. Appl. Ergon. **121**, 104355 (2024). https://doi.org/10.1016/j.apergo.2024.104355
15. Sun, J., Hubbard, S.: An examination of UAS incidents: characteristics and safety considerations. Drones **9**(2) (2025). https://doi.org/10.3390/drones9020112
16. Code of Federal Regulations (CFR): Title 49, Subtitle B, Chapter VIII, Part 830.2 (2025). https://www.ecfr.gov/current/title-49/subtitle-B/chapter-VIII/part-830. Accessed 18 Feb 2025
17. National Aeronautics and Space Administration (NASA): UAS Safety Reporting (n.d.). https://asrs.arc.nasa.gov/uassafety.html. Accessed 12 May 2024

18. National Transportation Safety Board (NTSB): Aviation Accident and Incident Query (n.d.). https://www.ntsb.gov/Pages/AviationQueryv2.aspx. Accessed 28 Mar 2025
19. Federal Aviation Administration (FAA): Aeronautical Information Manual (AIM): Chapter 11: Unmanned Aircraft Systems (UAS) Section 4. Airspace Access for UAS (n.d.). https://www.faa.gov/air_traffic/publications/atpubs/aim_html/chap11_section_4.html. Accessed 12 May 2024
20. National Aeronautics and Space Administration: Aviation Safety Reporting System (n.d.). https://asrs.arc.nasa.gov/search/database.html. Accessed 22 May 2024
21. Federal Aviation Administration (FAA): Advisory Circular 00–46F. Aviation Safety Reporting Program (2021). https://www.faa.gov/documentLibrary/media/Advisory_Circular/AC_00-46F.pdf. Accessed 22 May 2024
22. Federal Aviation Administration (FAA): Aviation Safety Reporting Program (ASRP) for UAS (2022). https://www.faa.gov/uas/getting_started/asrp. Accessed 22 June 2024
23. National Transportation Safety Board (NTSB): Home (n.d.). https://www.ntsb.gov/Pages/home.aspx. Accessed 28 Mar 2025
24. National Transportation Safety Board (NTSB): Advisory to Operators of Civil Uncrewed Aircraft Systems in the United States (2022). https://www.ntsb.gov/investigations/process/Documents/NTSB-Advisory-Drones.pdf. Accessed 19 Feb 2025
25. Federal Aviation Administration (FAA): Aviation Safety Information Analysis and Sharing (ASIAS) (n.d.). https://www.asias.faa.gov/apex/f?p=100:1:::NO:::. Accessed 28 Mar 2025
26. Sharma, R.S.: Investigation into unmanned aircraft system incidents in the national airspace system. Int. J. Aviat. Aeronaut. Aerosp. 3(4) (2016). https://doi.org/10.15394/ijaaa.2016.1146
27. Federal Aviation Administration (FAA): Aeronautical Information Publication (AIP): Part 2, ENR Section 1.14 (n.d.). https://www.faa.gov/air_traffic/publications/atpubs/aip_html/part2_enr_section_1.14.html . Accessed 28 Mar 2025
28. Flight Safety Foundation: About the Aviation Safety Network (ASN) (n.d.). https://asn.flightsafety.org/about/. Accessed 28 Mar 2025
29. SKYbrary: Airprox (n.d.). https://skybrary.aero/articles/airprox. Accessed 28 Mar 2025
30. Transport Canada: Report a Drone Incident (n.d.). https://tc.canada.ca/en/aviation/drone-safety/report-drone-incident. Accessed 28 Mar 2025
31. Air Accidents Investigation Branch (AAIB): About the Air Accidents Investigation Branch (n.d.). https://www.gov.uk/government/organisations/air-accidents-investigation-branch/about. Accessed 28 Mar 2025
32. Australian Transport Safety Bureau (ATSB): Overview (n.d.). https://www.atsb.gov.au/about_atsb/overview. Accessed 28 Mar 2025
33. Australian Transport Safety Bureau (ATSB): REPCON – Confidential Reporting Scheme (n.d.). https://www.atsb.gov.au/voluntary. Accessed 28 Mar 2025
34. Australian Transport Safety Bureau (ATSB): Aviation Self Reporting Scheme (n.d.). https://www.atsb.gov.au/voluntary/asrs/asrs_more. Accessed 28 Mar 2025
35. NASA Aviation Safety Reporting System: Unmanned Aircraft Systems (UAS). CALLBACK 496 (2021). https://asrs.arc.nasa.gov/publications/callback/cb_496.html
36. Wiegmann, D.A., Shappell, S.A.: A Human Error Approach to Aviation Accident Analysis: The Human Factors Analysis and Classification System. Routledge (2017). https://doi.org/10.4324/9781315263878
37. Reason, J.T.: Human Error. Cambridge University Press, Cambridge (1990). https://doi.org/10.1017/CBO9781139062367. Accessed 23 Aug 2021
38. Majumdar, N.: State-based analysis of general aviation loss of control accidents using historical data and pilots' perspectives. Doctoral Dissertation, Purdue University, West Lafayette (2023). https://www.proquest.com/docview/2806444500. Accessed Jan 2025

39. Majumdar, N., Marais, K.: A survey of pilots' experiences of inflight loss of control incidents and training. In: AIAA AVIATION 2022 Forum, Chicago, IL & Virtual, p. 3778 (2022). https://doi.org/10.2514/6.2022-3778
40. Shappell, S.A., Wiegmann, D.A.: The Human Factors Analysis and Classification System – HFACS. Office of Aviation Medicine, Federal Aviation Administration, DOT/FAA/AM-00/7 (2000). https://commons.erau.edu/publication/737
41. Dul, J., et al.: Towards a systems ergonomics approach to the design of complex sociotechnical systems. Ergonomics **64**(11), 1435–1447 (2021). https://doi.org/10.1080/00140139.2021.1953615

Enhancement of Risk Control Measures to Mitigate Aircraft Maintenance Errors in Critical Tasks

Raj De[1,2]([✉]) [iD]

[1] Safety and Accident Investigation Centre, Cranfield University, Cranfield, UK
raj.de@easyJet.com, rajibde@yahoo.com
[2] EasyJet, Luton, UK
http://www.linkedin.com/in/raj-de-mba-cmgr-fcmi-0605ba24

Abstract. Aviation safety is critical to ensuring the well-being of passengers, crew, and other stakeholders. Aircraft maintenance plays a key role in preventing accidents and operational failures. Proper maintenance ensures the reliability and performance of aircraft systems, helping to minimize risks and maintain high safety standards in an increasingly complex and regulated industry. While most errors during maintenance activities are minor, a small percentage significantly threaten aviation safety. Maintenance mistakes can be hard to detect and may remain unnoticed, jeopardizing aircraft safety over time. Studies show that maintenance errors account for 12–15% of commercial aviation accidents. The research aims to identify common causes of aircraft maintenance errors, assess the effectiveness of current risk controls, review organizational factors impacting these controls, explore best practices for enhancing risk management, and develop guidelines to improve the implementation of risk control measures for critical maintenance tasks. The research method used has been qualitative analysis of interviews, using NVIVO software for the analysis. The research found that procedure deviation, including incomplete tasks and incorrect part usage, accounted for 85% of maintenance errors. Key contributing factors include complacency (33%) and night shifts (21%). Although 77% of participants viewed risk controls as effective, gaps persist in areas like technology application, task feedback, and engineer shortages.

Keywords: Aircraft Maintenance · Human Factors · Risk Control · Safety Management System · Technological Solution

1 Introduction

Aircraft maintenance is a critical aspect of aviation safety, ensuring that aircraft are in an airworthy condition for a safe flight. However, despite rigorous protocols and procedures, maintenance errors still occur, leading to potential safety risks. Maintenance and inspection deficiencies have been identified as the cause of 12% of major aviation accidents in the past [1]. Lee and Truong argue that maintenance errors are contributing

D. Harris et al. (Eds.): HCII 2025, LNCS 16334, pp. 35–53, 2026.
https://doi.org/10.1007/978-3-032-12392-3_3

to 35% of aircraft accidents, pose significant risks to aviation safety and air traffic flow [2]. The errors made by maintenance staff can be harder to identify than many other dangers to aviation safety, and they may also remain dormant for extended periods of time, impairing aircraft safety [3].

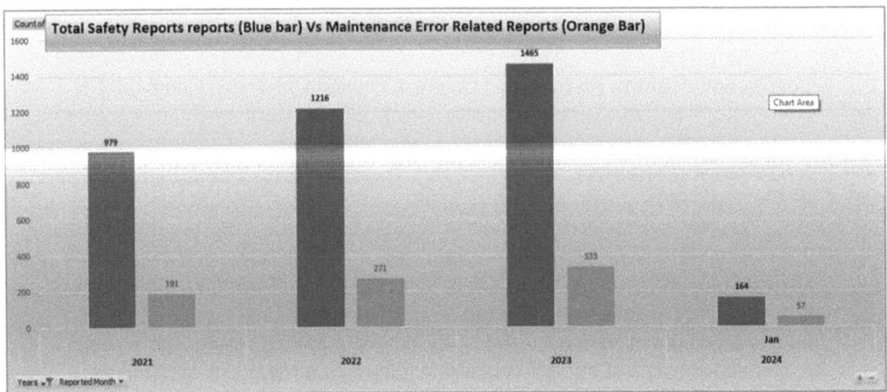

Fig. 1. Safety reports related to maintenance errors in relation to the Total Reports (*source easyJet Safety Reports*) shows Maintenance errors account for 25–30% of total Eng. reports.

Analysis of Engineering and Maintenance (E&M) safety reports in easyJet (Fig. 1) show that 25–30% of reports are related to maintenance errors. On August 5th, 2020, an easyJet aircraft departing Stansted experienced an in-flight engine shutdown due to a missing borescope plug after overnight maintenance. The missing plug led to hot gas leakage, causing significant engine damage. Investigation identified distraction as the root cause, with similar incidents occurring three more times in easyJet's operations. The failure of both primary and independent inspections highlighted gaps in error capture methods. Similarly, in October 2021, an aircraft departing Erfurt (ERF) experienced pressurization failure during climb, forcing the crew to descend with oxygen masks deployed. Post-landing inspection revealed an incorrectly installed aft cargo door seal, replaced during maintenance. This was not an isolated incident, with four similar occurrences in easyJet's experience. Despite the task being subject to independent inspection, the investigation identified procedural failures, non-compliance with guidelines, and communication lapses. While corrective actions were taken, including seal restoration and enhanced inspections, the incident highlights ongoing complacency and weaknesses in task completion feedback. These examples demonstrate significant operational safety consequences due to maintenance errors. These errors have occurred at different maintenance organizations. These errors can be attributed to various factors, with human factors being one of the key contributors. Human factors encompass a range of psychological, social, and organizational factors that can influence individual performance and decision-making [4]. In the context of aircraft maintenance, human factors can include fatigue, stress, lack of communication, and inadequate training. Understanding these factors is crucial in identifying the root causes of maintenance errors and implementing effective preventive measures. In recent years, there has been a surge in the development of human error frameworks and accident investigation schemes. However, this proliferation has led to a situation where there are numerous models, potentially as many as there are individuals interested in the topic [5]. A significant challenge lies in the fact that many of these models are either too academically complex and abstract for practitioners to grasp, or they are overly simplistic and lack theoretical depth, making it difficult to uncover the fundamental causes of human error in aviation operations. The Human Factors Analysis and Classification System (HFACS) framework is rooted in James Reason's widely recognized "Swiss cheese" model of accident causation, established in 1990 [6]. HFACS serves as a link between theory and practical application, facilitating enhancements in both the quantity and quality of information collected during aviation accidents and incidents.

The research question therefore this study tries to answer is – How can the effectiveness of the risk controls be enhanced to reduce the possibility of maintenance errors for critical maintenance tasks? The aviation industry, guided by the FAA (Federal Aviation Administration), CAA (Civil Aviation Authority), and EASA (European Union Aviation Safety Agency), classifies critical tasks based on their impact on aircraft safety and operational integrity, focusing on flight controls, engines, and landing gear. Regulations require sign-off of maintenance work only after completion, clear identification of critical steps, and supervision of personnel. A certificate of release to service (CRS) must be issued before flight post-maintenance. Critical tasks impacting flight safety, require thorough review. Independent inspections serve as an error-capture method, ensuring correct assembly, system functionality, and software compatibility.

Human factor contributors to aircraft maintenance errors-Aircraft have manuals detailing performance and operational procedures, but no such guides exist for people, who can act unpredictably [7]. Maintenance issues arise from three main causes: errors in executing correct plans, errors from inadequate plans, and intentional deviations from rules, procedures, or norms [8]. The 'Swiss Cheese' model [4] shows that accidents often result from operational actions influenced by local conditions like communication, environment, and equipment [6]. Risk controls and organizational factors, such as policies and management decisions, also affect safety. The HFACS, based on 'Swiss cheese' model, highlights that both active failures (immediate errors) and latent failures (systemic issues from management) weaken defenses, with organizational-level decisions often contributing to accidents [9]. In aircraft maintenance, errors are categorized into three primary taxonomies: skill-based errors, decision errors, and perceptual errors, each reflecting distinct cognitive failures [8].

Risk control measures in aircraft maintenance focus on reducing errors and enhancing safety. Standard Operating Procedures (SOPs) guide technicians with clear instructions, ensuring consistency. Redundancy systems, including independent inspections, catch errors missed in initial maintenance. Training programs, including human factors training, keep engineers updated on best practices. Supervision and independent inspections provide additional oversight, especially for critical tasks. However, there is limited empirical data on the effectiveness of these existing risk controls. Figure 2 below shows an analysis of maintenance errors from 2021 to 2024, covering both easyJet bases and contracted AMOs. The most significant categories shown in Fig. 2 are: Maintenance errors (429) are the most common, highlighting procedural lapses and human factors.

Incomplete maintenance (340) suggests the need for better oversight, while damage incidents (261) point to handling or procedural issues.

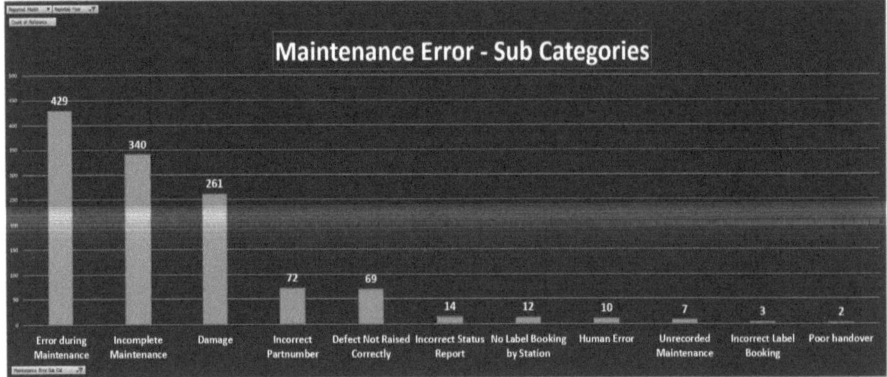

Fig. 2. Maintenance errors sub categories (*source easyJet period 2021–2024*)

Less frequent errors also indicate areas for improvement. Implementing risk controls [10] in aircraft maintenance is complex, with challenges such as a shortage of skilled labor, the complexity of modern systems, human error, changing regulations, and data management issues. Budget constraints often lead to inadequate risk controls, while resistance to change can hinder safety improvements. Overcoming these challenges requires training, effective communication, and investment in technology. Investigations into catastrophic events like Chernobyl, Tenerife, and Challenger often reveal that organizational issues play a key role in the causal chain. [11] highlighted that organizational culture shapes behaviors, standards, and responses to challenges [12]. Strong management commitment to safety is linked to better safety records, emphasizing the need for ongoing monitoring and support for safety practices. The HFACS framework analyzes organizational factors, but time gap between maintenance error taking place and the safety incident leading to investigations, results often in relying on guesses and faded memories, for establishing contributory factors, thereby reducing effectiveness in learning from the investigations.

1.1 A Lesson Learnt from Flight Data Monitoring and Analysis

The research examined how the introduction of mandatory FDM analysis (easyJet FDM Manager) in relation to flying an aircraft has helped to proactively identify pilots' skill errors. Crew training routinely incorporates the learnings from skill gaps, proactively training and enhancing risk controls before any aircraft incident occurs.

Pre-FDM (Flight Data Monitoring): A discrepancy between assumptions and the actual data, indicating that a significant number of unstable approaches were still being continued to land.

The implementation of the FDM at EasyJet Airlines has significantly reduced unstable approaches over time, as shown in Fig. 3 above.

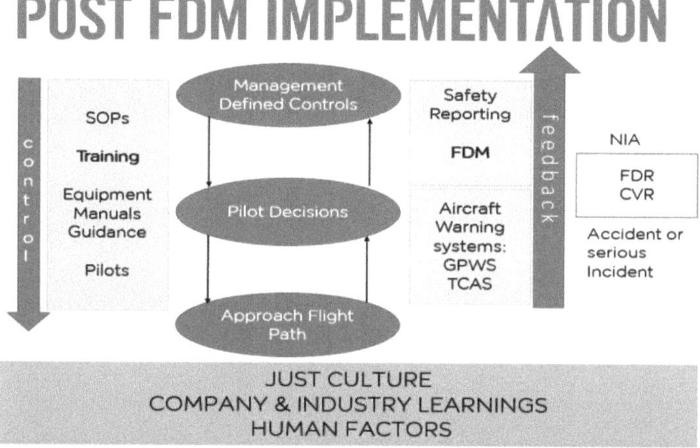

Fig. 3. Post FDM Analysis process implementation *(source easyJet).*

Relevance of the Lessons from FDM Implementation for Aircraft Maintenance. Unlike the FDM analysis, Aircraft maintenance activities lack an action feedback loop, post task completion, as this is confirmed only by a CRS. Therefore, proactive intervention in relation to skill errors is reliant on safety reporting, which in-turn relies on individuals to proactively raise a 'self' safety report when an error takes place. This is almost non-existent, similar to the 'pre FDM' period for the flight crew. Over 28000 tasks underwent independent inspections in 2023, however, not a single proactive safety report in relation to any related error capture was raised. In the same period, (Sect. 1) some reactive examples of independent inspection failures were experienced. An unfinished task may go unnoticed if a CRS is issued incorrectly. While maintenance efficiency relies on an engineer's knowledge and skill, training and competency assessments do not specifically identify skill gaps, unlike the FDM analysis for flight crews, which ensures errors are reported, analyzed, and used for continuous improvement.

Systems Perspective-Weakness/Gap in the Current Efforts in Reducing Maintenance Errors Using Only HFACS Analysis. Studies [13] highlighted the difficulty in obtaining data on latent factors from incident reports, and critiqued the HFACS framework for its limited focus on the work environment and its lack of clarity in analysis. They argued that the framework shifts human errors to higher organizational levels without offering effective solutions. Interventions at these higher levels, particularly in 'organizational processes' and 'resource management' at HFACS level-4, are more cost-effective and can significantly improve safety [9]. However, from a system engineering perspective [14], the lack of feedback on maintenance task completion weakens control processes, potentially affecting consistent maintenance standards.

1.2 Research Objectives

1) To identify, what factors are causal towards maintenance errors 2) In relation to critical aircraft maintenance, to review the effectiveness of the existing risk controls 3) Review

how organizational factors impact risk controls in against threat of maintenance errors 4) Explore best practices for enhancing risk controls in aircraft maintenance 5) Make recommendations to support the implementation of improved risk control measures for critical maintenance tasks.

2 Method

2.1 Participants

13 participants from different roles in the Engineering and Maintenance departments of easyJet Airline were selected. Both the Managers and Leaders group possess engineering and maintenance background. The sample size selection of the participants was based on various roles in the engineering and maintenance departments, so selected to capture the perspectives from different role-based viewpoints. An ethics council at Cranfield University approved a research proposal before any interviews were carried out (CURES/21510/2024). The participants were explained about the background of this study, the objectives of the project and the research question. The consent form was explained and was signed by the respective participant. Each of the questions was asked, and the interview was recorded and transcribed using Microsoft Teams software. The transcript was compared to the recording, and a sanitized transcript was uploaded to NVIVO qualitative data analysis software.

2.2 Research Framework

The research process commenced with an in-depth literature review in the three broad categories - The number of maintenance error related safety incidents, the available literature relating to the human factor contributors towards the maintenance errors; and the Systems view of managing the risks. This was followed by a qualitative research process to acquire a profound understanding on the subject. Qualitative approach was used, as it allows to investigate various subjects, although some researchers may argue that quantitative method is better [15] "While quantitative research methods usually focus on the frequency, intensity, or duration of a behaviour, qualitative research methodologies allow us to investigate the beliefs, values, and reasons that underpin the conduct" [16]. As qualitative techniques are descriptive, they enable the researcher to construct a thorough, multilayered image in an organic environment, and hence this method has been used for the research.

2.3 Data Collection Process

The data collection involved conducting interviews with the participants. The purpose of the interview questions was to find the views of the participants on the following 3 subjects: What are the different types and causal factors for the maintenance errors? Questions 1 and 2 relate to this theme.

How do the organizational factors, like Safety culture, leadership and communications, affect the safety risk controls? Question 4 has been structured around this theme.

From the participant's experience, how would they assess the current risk controls, especially for the critical tasks, and what would they recommend for enhancing the risk controls relating to those tasks? Questions 3, 5, 6, 7, 8 and 9 relate to this theme.

2.4 Interview Questions

1) From your experience, what are some common types of aircraft maintenance errors encountered? 2) What do you believe are the causal factors to these maintenance errors? 3) How effective do you perceive the current risk controls in mitigating maintenance errors? 4) How do the following organizational factors influence the effectiveness of the risk controls in aircraft maintenance, in your view? 5) Safety culture b. Leadership support c. Safety communication 6) Are there any specific challenges or barriers you encounter when implementing or adhering to risk control measures in critical tasks? 7) Have you observed any best practices or innovative strategies that have been successful in enhancing risk controls for reducing maintenance errors? 8) What recommendations or improvements would you suggest enhancing the effectiveness of risk controls for critical tasks in aircraft maintenance? 9) How do you think technology and automation could be leveraged to improve risk control measures in critical tasks? 10) Do you have anything that you would like to suggest to improve maintenance?

2.5 Analysis Process

Thematic analysis technique has been used, which effectively identifies consistent themes by coding and categorizing the content. However, pure textual thematic analysis may miss the intended meaning due to its lack of context and nuances. The research questions, therefore, have been set so that there is an overlap of the context between questions, to identify any inconsistencies in the answers. NVivo [17] software has been used, as it can process the data to draw conclusions [18] and quantify qualitative data as much as possible from documents, audio files, videos, and images [19, 20] The imported transcripts were coded by identifying key themes and patterns. This helped to categorize the information, explore relationships between themes, and generate insights. The data visualization tools that were used, like data maps, and data matrix, helped in enhancing the analysis and interpretation of the research findings.

3   Results

The study found different kinds of mistakes made in aircraft maintenance, like not following approved data, wrong data interpretation, unfinished tasks, and installing parts incorrectly (Fig. 4 below). The most common mistake (85%) was not following the procedure. The main causal factors included complacency (85%), working overnight (54%), and perception of time pressure (54%). Ineffective training and poor task instructions were also significant contributors. While 77% of participants found existing risk controls effective, challenges such as a shortage of experienced engineers post-COVID and resistance to change were also noted. Participants suggested enhancing risk controls through better task completion feedback, and leveraging technology for (maintenance) error capture and safety communications.

Fig. 4. Overview of the results, created from NVivo Mind map function.

Participant 4 stated "maybe someone skips a step in a maintenance procedure, especially if it's procedure they're not familiar with and especially if it's something like a test that involves lots of steps, pressing lots of buttons, put in lots of circuit Breakers, stuff like that." Similarly Participant 13 stated- "actually there's been like a surge of reports for independent inspections that have not been done according to our procedure and clearly that highlighted a lack of knowledge or something along the lines of a lack of knowledge of the procedure." of Maintenance Errors

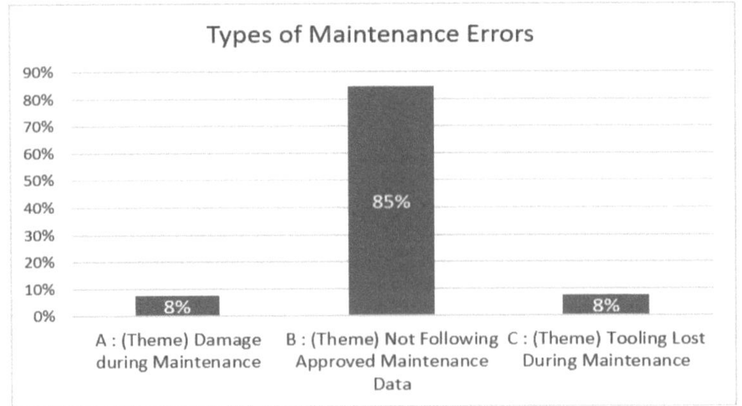

Fig. 5. Maintenance Error types & details on not following approved data.

Figure 5 above shows that the most common maintenance errors involve deviations from approved procedures, accounting for 85% of cases. Understanding the types of errors in this category is shown in Fig. 6, which reveals incorrect part fitting contributes to 27%, while incomplete procedures account for 18%, indicating a lack of thoroughness. Both data interpretation errors and incorrect torque application make up 9% each. The findings emphasize the need for stricter adherence to procedures and improved training to address these critical errors effectively.

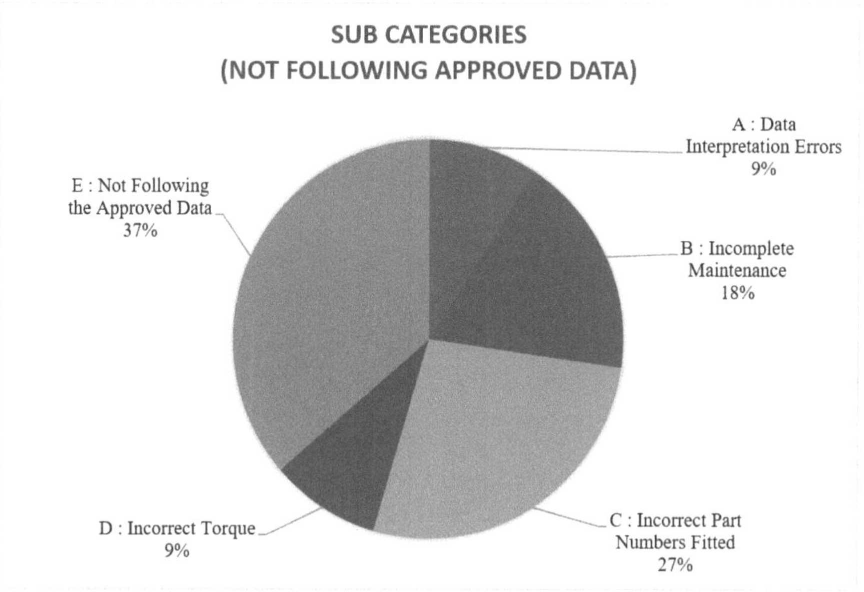

Fig. 6. Subcategories of 'Not Following Approved Data'.

3.1 Causal Factors

Understanding the causes of maintenance errors is critical for developing effective mitigation strategies. Participant 3 stated in relation to complacency- "So then that goes back down to that would go down to experience. OK, you might have a duly qualified. Licenced guy who's gone to do the inspection and he hasn't picked it up, OK? Whereas an experienced guy would have picked it up. Secondly, you've got somebody who's done the job, one person's gone and inspected it, a licenced guy, then the second guy will go and he might not have done it as thorough because he knows you know, the first guy's already done it. So, then that could be, yeah. And it can be complacency there as well."

On Consequences of working overnight, Participant 2 said-"I mean, one of the big things for me is tiredness. We're still in industry where people work a lot of hours. But working night shifts I mean, we have to get away from working, you know, sort of 12-hour night shifts."

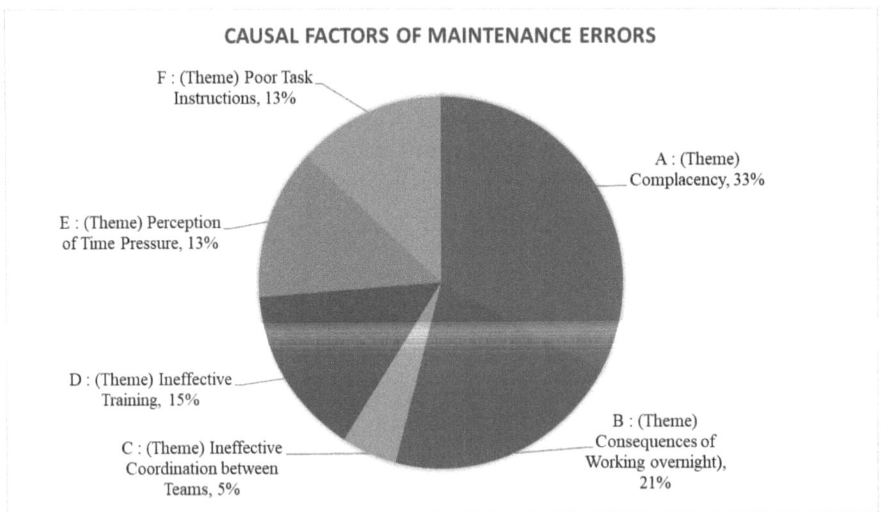

Fig. 7. Causal Factors for Maintenance Errors.

The study discovered (see Fig. 7) that causal factors often stem from a combination of human, organizational, and procedural deficiencies, such as inadequate training, lack of task recency, poor communication, and insufficient risk awareness. 85% of the participants cited complacency as the main theme for the causal factor, with 33% of total references to this theme. 54% of the participants identified working during the night as the next causal factor, accounting for 21% of all references. The next theme, Perception of Time Pressure, garnered the attention of 54% of participants and 13% of references. The fourth causal factor, cited by 38% of the participants was ineffective training. Poor task instructions, cited by 38% of participants, and ineffective coordination between teams, cited by 23% of participants, accounted for 5% of the total references.

3.2 Effectiveness of Risk Controls and Organisational Factors Influencing the Same

Figure 8 shows, 77% of the participants said that the existing risk controls are effective. 23% of participants expressed that the current risk controls are only partially effective due to the partial utilization of the AMOS system and the occasional ambiguity in the approved maintenance manuals. Participant 3 said- "some of the good things that have come out is where we finally creep back into the 20th century and look at electronic solutions like the electronic control of tools has been when you see it done well."

Participant 1 commented- …" I think it's more procedural and there's a more, a lot more checks and balances going on."

On the partial effectivity of the risk controls, Participant 7 said "Amos will allow you to book a part (after replacement on the aircraft) without necessarily using the correct batch number."

The majority of participants (42%) commented that smarter ways of communicating safety information will help to enhance the risk controls. These findings suggest

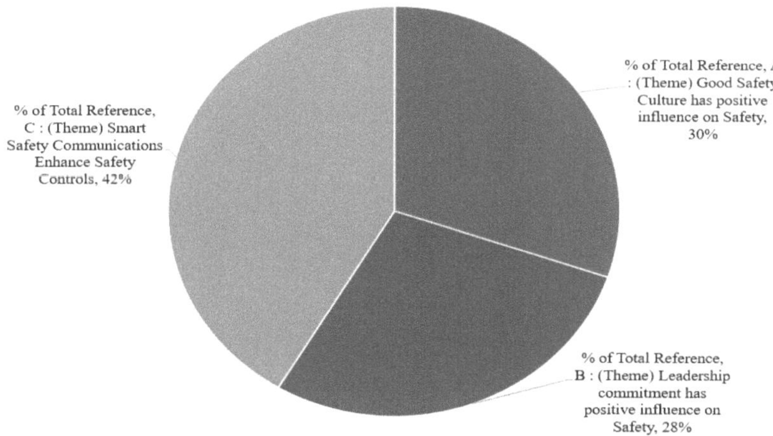

Fig. 8. Organisational factors affecting Risk Control effectivity.

that while all three factors are important, communication and leadership are viewed as more actionable and direct levers for improving safety in maintenance operations. This aligns with the research's broader emphasis on organizational dynamics and the role of technology in enhancing safety risk controls. The participants considered that easyJet has a particularly good Safety Culture, due to the transparency and commitment of the leadership towards this goal.

Challenges and barriers in risk control implementation - The primary theme emerging from the interviews was the scarcity of experienced engineers, which can be attributed to two factors: the departure of experienced engineers from the industry following the Covid pandemic, and the early stages of skill development for newly trained engineers. The other theme under this subject was a resistance to change by the more experienced engineers, when new measures are applied to enhance risk controls.

However, a crucial point raised by 15% of the participants was the absence of positive feedback following task completion. The feedback is only through a task certification method and this can be a weakness in the control cycle. Figure 9 illustrates the barriers to the effectiveness of risk controls based on the percentage of references attributed to each theme. The most significant barrier, accounting for 65%, is the shortage of competent engineers, suggesting a critical gap in available expertise. 18% of experienced engineers resist change, indicating cultural resistance to new procedures or technologies. Errors in task completion feedback make up 12%, pointing to a lack of accurate or timely information exchange. At 6%, inadequate ground time for maintenance is the smallest barrier, but it still highlights time constraints as a factor affecting maintenance quality. Overall, the chart underscores the need for both workforce development and better communication systems.

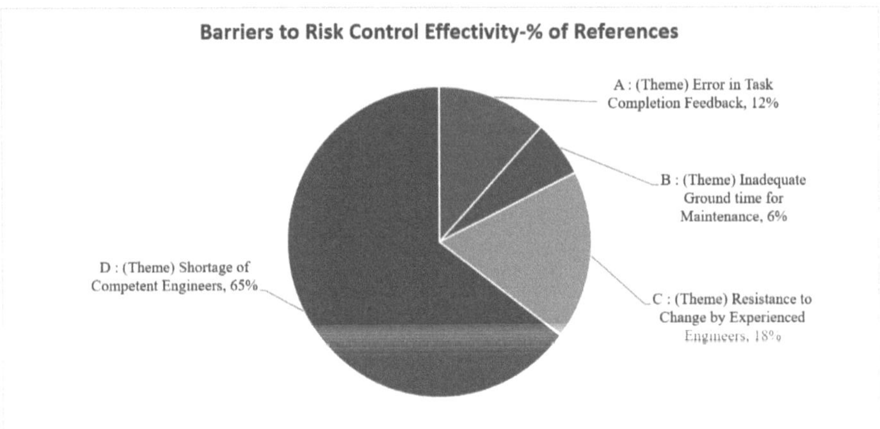

Fig. 9. Challenges and Barriers in Risk Control Implementation

3.3 Suggestions on Best Practices and Recommendations

The two themes that came out strongly were (Fig. 10), a better control of critical task maintenance, with 27% participants responding to the question; the other key theme was using smarter technologies for safety communications and handovers between shifts.

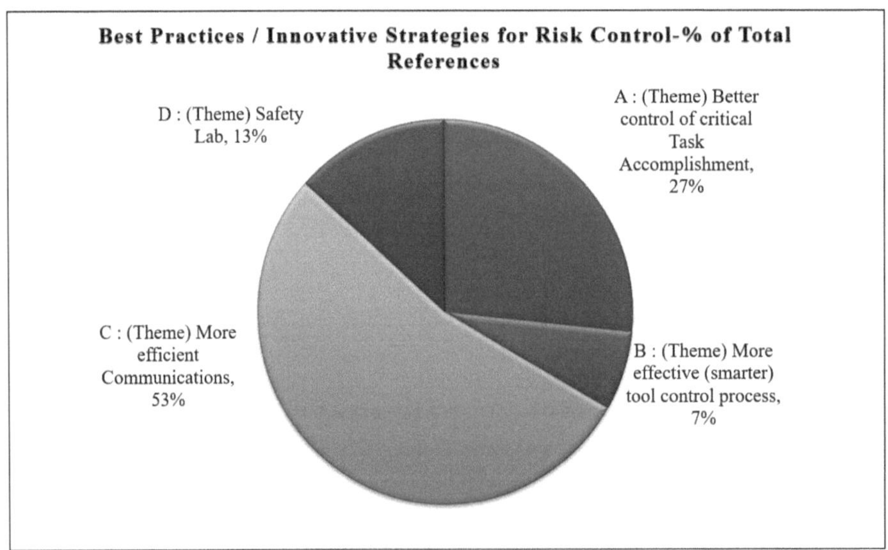

Fig. 10. Best Practices and Innovative Strategies.

Figure 11 below, shows the suggestions and improvement recommendations that the participants made. 62% of the participants recommended improving skill gaps using training, with the highest number of references (48%). Recommendations of using artificial intelligence for maintenance planning and improving communications were the next highest categories, with 23% of the participants.

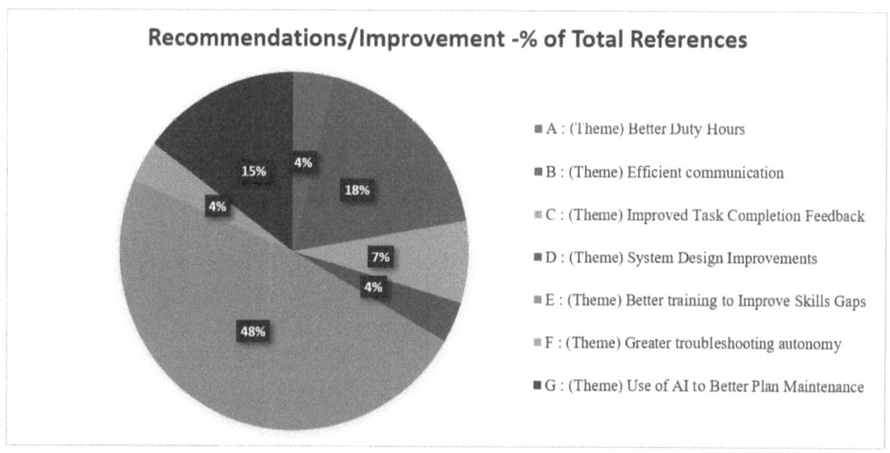

Fig. 11. Suggested improvements and recommendations.

3.4   Leveraging Technology and Automation to Enhance Risk Control

Figure 12, emphasises two key points: the lack of effective methods for capturing maintenance errors, and the potential enhancement of risk control effectiveness through increased use of technology for feedback on the completion of critical tasks. 79% of the references recommended using technology to positively confirm the correct completion of the critical task and training, indicating that these tools are integral to improving safety and operational efficiency.

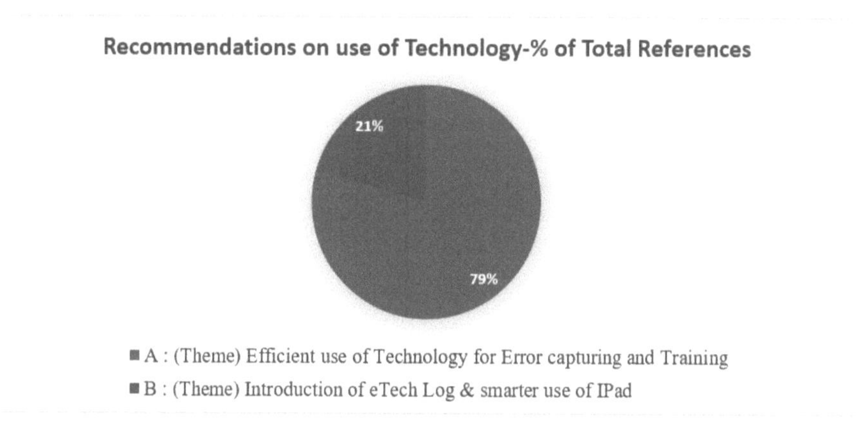

Fig. 12. Leveraging Technology and Automation to Enhance Risk Controls

4 Discussion

The study investigated ways to improve risk control effectiveness to lower the likelihood of maintenance errors for critical aircraft maintenance tasks.

The research findings identify key types of maintenance errors, such as deviations from approved procedures, and highlight procedure deviation as the most dominant error type, accounting for 85% of the observed instances. The participants' testimonies underscore the complexity of these errors, particularly emphasizing the challenges posed by incomplete maintenance, incorrect torque application, and the fitment of incorrect components.

A deeper examination into the causal factors reveals that maintenance errors are often rooted in a combination of human, organizational, and procedural deficiencies. The study identifies complacency as the primary causal factor, cited by 85% of the participants, with significant contributions from other factors such as night shifts, perceived time pressure, and ineffective training. These insights are further corroborated by participant narratives, which illustrate how these factors manifest in real-world scenarios, particularly highlighting the impact of complacency and fatigue during night shifts.

The effectiveness of current risk controls is a crucial aspect of this discussion. While 77% of participants believe the existing risk controls are effective, there is a notable concern about their partial effectiveness, particularly due to underutilization of systems like AMOS and ambiguities in maintenance manuals. Organizational factors also play a significant role in the effectiveness of risk controls, with participants emphasizing the importance of smarter communication of safety information and strong leadership commitment to fostering a robust safety culture.

However, the implementation of risk controls faces challenges, primarily due to a shortage of experienced engineers and resistance to change among more seasoned personnel. The post-COVID landscape has exacerbated these challenges, with a significant reduction in the number of experienced engineers available. Additionally, and importantly, the lack of positive feedback mechanisms after a maintenance task completion is identified as a weakness in the current control cycle.

In response to these problems, the discussion focuses on best practices and new ideas put forward by participants. For example, better ways of planning tasks and getting feedback on when they are done, as well as using smarter technologies for safety communication and handing off shifts. The role of technology and automation in enhancing risk controls is also emphasized, with participants advocating for the use of technology to ensure the correct completion of critical tasks and to capture maintenance errors more effectively. It was considered that better feedback of task completion will also enable timely identification of skill errors. Learning from skill errors could feed into the training cycle to address skill gaps.

The following section outlines how the research results align with or differ from previous research:

The research found that 85% of maintenance errors were due to deviations from approved procedures, such as incomplete maintenance, incorrect torque application, and incorrect part fitment. The research therefore, supports the literature by highlighting procedural deviations as key maintenance error sources, aligning with Reason's Model [8] and studies by [21] and [22] errors to slips, lapses, and violations, emphasizing their systemic nature rather than solely individual responsibility). Additionally, the emphasis on complacency, fatigue, time pressure, and inadequate training resonates with findings from [23] HFACS and [24]reinforcing these systemic issues. Similarly, [21] and [25] identified procedural violations and communication breakdowns as leading causes of maintenance errors. This supports the current findings, where deviations from standard procedures were the most common error type, reflecting broader challenges in adherence to established protocols. 85% of participants cited complacency as a key factor in maintenance errors, followed by working at night, time pressure, and ineffective training. This aligns with [23] HFACS framework, which identifies complacency as a latent condition that contributes to errors, along with fatigue and time pressure—factors noted by participants in this study.

On the subject of the effectiveness of the risk controls, while 77% of participants believe current risk controls are generally effective, underutilization of systems (like AMOS) and ambiguities in maintenance manuals reduce their effectiveness. This aligns with [22] who found a gap between the perceived effectiveness of risk controls and their practical application, with issues like underuse of error management tools. Similarly, systems (like AMOS) are designed to minimize errors, but their impact is often compromised due to improper use or lack of full integration into daily practices, reflecting participants' concerns in this study [26].

The barriers towards the effectiveness of the risk control are partly related to the challenges faced in the post covid aviation industry. The highlighted the shortage of experienced engineers following the pandemic and this is consistent with the European Union Aviation Safety Agency (EASA) Report on Post-COVID Aviation (EASA, 2021b), which warned of skill gaps and a decline in the availability of skilled personnel. This shortage poses significant risks for effective aircraft maintenance, as highly experienced engineers are crucial for handling complex and critical tasks. Additionally, resistance to change among seasoned engineers has been a persistent barrier in safety management, as Gerede identified [10]. This study echoes those findings, showing that resistance to adopting new safety protocols and risk control measures continues to hinder progress in the aviation industry. Together, these findings emphasize the need for focused strategies on training and change management to overcome workforce-related challenges and improve risk control effectiveness in aircraft maintenance.

79% of participants in the study, recommended using technology for error capture and task completion feedback, and this view aligns with existing research on automation and AI in maintenance. [27] highlighted the benefits of automation in reducing human error, a point supported by the participants in this study. However, the caution against over-reliance on automation is also reflected in the participants' preference for technology that enhances, rather than replaces, human oversight. Additionally, [28] emphasized the role of AI and machine learning in improving accuracy and efficiency, which aligns with participants' suggestions for AI-enhanced planning and communication in maintenance tasks. A similar view supported for training by the use of AI [29].

The research provides new perspectives in several critical areas of aviation safety and maintenance, particularly post-COVID challenges, the evolving role of technology, and specific insights into organizational dynamics. These insights contribute to the broader understanding of maintenance errors and risk management in the industry.

4.1 Impact of Post Covid Conditions on Maintenance Operations

The study highlights the significant impact of the COVID-19 pandemic on the availability of experienced engineers, with 46% of respondents noting a drop in experienced personnel. This is a relatively new area of concern that has not been extensively covered in earlier research, as most studies predate the pandemic. The pandemic has created a unique situation where the combination of experienced staff leaving the industry and a lack of seasoned replacements has exacerbated existing maintenance challenges. This finding adds a contemporary layer to the discussion on workforce challenges, suggesting that the aviation industry must adapt its risk control strategies to address the current skills gap. It also underscores the importance of retaining experienced personnel and developing rapid upskilling programs for newer engineers.

4.2 Need for Technological Solutions for Error Capture and Feedback for Training

The research underscores the growing importance of leveraging technology, particularly in error capture and providing real-time feedback on critical maintenance tasks. While the aviation industry has long recognized the potential of technology, the findings emphasize the specific need for automation and AI-driven tools to confirm the correct completion of tasks, as recommended by 79% of the references. This focus on proactive feedback systems represents a forward-looking approach to enhancing maintenance safety. This perspective contributes to the ongoing discourse by advocating for a more proactive use of technology, moving beyond traditional (reactive) systems to more interactive and immediate feedback mechanisms (see Sect. 1). It suggests a shift towards a more integrated use of AI and systems safety approach in maintenance activities, which could set new industry standards for error prevention, training feed and risk management.

4.3 Challenges in Implementing Risk Controls

The study sheds light on the specific challenges faced in implementing risk controls, such as the resistance to change among experienced engineers and the lack of positive feedback mechanisms after task completion. The identification of these barriers, particularly the task completion feedback issue, is a novel contribution as it highlights a gap in the control cycle that has not been widely recognized in previous studies. This research offers new avenues for improving risk control implementation by pinpointing these challenges. It suggests that addressing resistance to change and enhancing feedback loops could be crucial steps in ensuring that risk controls are not only effective on paper but also in practice.

4.4 Limitations of This Research

The reliance on self-reported data introduces biases such as social desirability and recall bias, which may affect the accuracy of the findings. The study's sample size may also limit the generalizability of the results, potentially skewing conclusions if certain subgroups are underrepresented. Additionally, the focus on qualitative data, while rich in detail, can be subjective and harder to generalize across different contexts. However, the sample size selected has tried to use a mix from various roles in engineering and maintenance from the airline, thereby potentially reducing the risk of a bias. The time-sensitive nature of findings related to the post-COVID landscape may diminish in relevance as the industry evolves, potentially limiting the recommendations' long-term applicability. Moreover, the emphasis on technological solutions may not fully account for varying levels of technological readiness across organizations, and the complexity of human factors like resistance to change may be oversimplified. However, the technological solutions could be staged, and simpler solutions, like using mobile phones to capture pictures of the last stage of a completed task (example for correct locking, torque values etc.), could be simpler to incorporate in the process. Successful implementation can then pave the way for the integration of advanced technological solutions. Lastly, regional differences in cultural attitudes towards maintenance and safety might limit the applicability of the findings across different geographical contexts. These limitations suggest a need for further research with a more diverse and quantitative approach.

5 Recommendations

The research has identified critical areas that require further exploration and offers actionable recommendations to enhance the effectiveness of risk controls in aviation maintenance. By addressing workforce challenges, leveraging advanced technologies, identifying skill gaps for training, fostering a culture of acceptance, and continuously evaluating risk controls, the aviation industry can significantly reduce the incidence of maintenance errors and improve overall safety. These efforts are particularly important in the post-COVID landscape, where the industry must adapt to new realities and ensure that safety remains a top priority.

The study identified that the pandemic has led to a shortage of experienced engineers, creating a critical gap in maintenance safety. This issue has not been extensively explored in pre-pandemic research. The recommendation is to investigate the long-term effects of the COVID-19 pandemic on the aviation maintenance workforce, particularly focusing on the availability and effectiveness of experienced engineers.

The research highlights the need for more immediate and interactive feedback systems to confirm task completion and capture errors, particularly using AI-driven tools. The recommendation is to assess the impact of implementing real-time feedback mechanisms on the reduction of maintenance errors in critical aircraft tasks. Any identified gaps in skill to be addressed through training.

The study emphasizes the potential of smarter technologies to enhance safety communication, but further research is needed to evaluate their practical application and effectiveness. As a result, the recommendation is to investigate the role of advanced technologies, such as AI and machine learning, in improving safety communication and shift handovers in aviation maintenance.

6 Conclusions

Aircraft maintenance is vital to aviation safety, but errors still occur, contributing to 12% of major accidents. Despite a 55% flight increase over the past decade, maintenance-related accidents have doubled. In easyJet, 22–30% of safety reports involve maintenance errors, often unnoticed until subsequent inspections or flight incidents. This study researched on the factors contributing to maintenance errors, exploring traditional and systems engineering models. It also examined Leveson's Systems-Theoretic Accident Model and Processes (STAMP), which addresses the limitations of conventional causality models. The research question focused on enhancing risk controls to reduce maintenance errors in critical tasks. This paper makes a significant contribution by identifying a current weakness in the process of providing feedback on the completion of maintenance tasks. Consequently, the paper recommends that there is a need to identify a better feedback of critical task completion, using technology. Key recommendations include smarter communication, improved training, and leveraging technology for error capture and task confirmation, particularly for critical maintenance tasks. Additionally, addressing organizational challenges and resistance to change is crucial for enhancing risk control effectiveness.

Acknowledgements. I sincerely thank my research guide, Professor Wen-Chin Li, for his invaluable guidance and support throughout this journey. I am also deeply grateful to my family for their constant support and inspiration. This thesis is a result of collective effort, and I am truly blessed for the support I have received.

References

1. Marx, D.A., Graeber, R.C.: Human error in aircraft maintenance (1997)
2. Lee, S.A., Truong, D.: Effects of aviation maintenance- related flight incidents on air traffic in national airspace system. In: ICNS (2024)
3. ICAO, Human Factors Training Manual International Civil Aviation Organization (1998)
4. James, R.: Managing the risks of organisational accidents (1997)
5. Moray, N., Senders, J.W.: Human error: cause, prediction, and reduction (1991)
6. Reason, J.: Culpability Model (1997)
7. Hobbs, A.: ATSB transport safety report aviation research and analysis an overview of human factors in aviation maintenance (2008)
8. Reason, J., Hobbs, A.: Managing Maintenance Error: A Practical Guide. Managing Maintenance Error (2017)
9. Harris, D., Li, W.C.: Using neural networks to predict HFACS unsafe acts from the preconditions of unsafe acts (2019)
10. Gerede, E.: A qualitative study on the exploration of challenges to the implementation of the Safety Management System in aircraft maintenance organizations in Turkey. J. Air Transp. Manag. (2015)
11. Schein, E.H.: Organisation culture and leadership (1985)
12. Richter, A., Koch, C.: Integration, differentiation and ambiguity in safety cultures. Saf. Sci. **42**(8), 703–722 (2004)

13. Beaubien, J.M., Baker, D.P.: A review of selected aviation human factors taxonomies, accident/incident reporting systems and data collection tools. Int. J. Appl. Aviation Stud. **2**(2), 11–36 (2002). Taxonomies, Reporting Systems, and Data Collection Tools 1 Running Head
14. Leveson, N., Daouk, M., Dulac, N., Marais, K.: Applying STAMP in accident analysis **1** (2003)
15. Chin, Z.: Qualitative research on the challenges and coping strategies of aviation maintenance engineers and mechanics (2019)
16. Castleberry, A., Nolen, A.: Thematic analysis of qualitative research data: is it as easy as it sounds? Curr. Pharm. Teach. Learn. **10**(6), 807–815 (2018)
17. Welsh, E.: Dealing with data: using NVivo in the qualitative data analysis process (2002)
18. Zamawe, F.C.: The implication of using NVivo software in qualitative data analysis: evidence-based reflections. Malawi Med. J. **27**(1), 13–15 (2015)
19. Lewis, R.B.: NVivo 2.0 and ATLAS.ti 5.0: a comparative review of two popular qualitative data-analysis programs. Field Methods **16**(4), 439–464 (2004)
20. Rich, M., Patashnick, J.: Narrative research with audio visual data: video intervention/prevention assessment (VIA) and NVivo. Int. J. Soc. Res. Methodol. **5**(3), 245–261 (2002)
21. Baron, R.: Failure to follow procedures: deviations are a significant factor in maintenance errors (2009)
22. Hobbs, A., Williamson, A.: Skills, rules and knowledge in aircraft maintenance: errors in context. Ergonomics **45**(4), 290–308 (2002)
23. D.A., Shappell, S.A.: A human error approach to aviation accident analysis (2003)
24. Chaparro, J.: Classification and analysis of errors reported in aircraft maintenance manuals. Int. J. Appl. Aviat. Stud. (2008)
25. Hobbs, A.: Maintenance mistakes and system solutions (2002)
26. Shanmugam, A., Paul Robert, T.: Human factors engineering in aircraft maintenance: a review. J. Qual. Maint. Eng. **21**(4), 478–505 (2015)
27. Straunch, B.: Investigating Human Error Incidents, Accidents, and Complex Systems, 2nd edn. (2017)
28. Ward, M., McDonald, N., Morrison, R., Gaynor, D., Nugent, T.: A performance improvement case study in aircraft maintenance and its implications for hazard identification. Ergonomics **53**(2), 247–267 (2010)
29. De Crescenzio, F., Fantini, M., Persiani, F., Di Stefano, L., Azzari, P., Salti, S.: Augmented reality for aircraft maintenance training and operations support (2003)
30. Leveson, N.: Engineering a Safer World: Systems Thinking Applied to Safety (2012)
31. Leveson, N.G.: An Introduction to System Safety Engineering (2021)

Safe Return-to-Land Operations in Future Cockpits: An Analysis of Cases and Mitigation Technologies

Andrew Fuchs[1]([envelope]) [ORCID], Carmen Bejarano[1], Adrien Metge[1], Sara Ruano[2],
Jose Manuel Cordero[2], Andrés Perillo[2], Paris Vaiopoulos[3], Ginevra Fedrizzi[3],
and Anna Giulia Vicario[3]

[1] Applied Research and Technology, Collins Aerospace Ireland Ltd., Cork, Ireland
`andrew.s.fuchs@collins.com`
[2] Centro de Referencia de Investigación, Desarrollo e Innovación ATM, A.I.E. (CRIDA),
Madrid, Spain
[3] Deep Blue S.r.l., Rome, Italy

Abstract. As air travel grows, increasing demand for pilots and ATC operators requires greater automation. Autonomous systems can help manage traffic, reduce crew sizes, and enable a transition from dual pilot operations (DPO) to reduced crew (RCO), single pilot (SiPO), or full autonomy. A major challenge is ensuring effective human-autonomy teaming. Depending on the scenario, humans may delegate tasks, work alongside automation, or interact with artificial pilots. Independent of the scenario, autonomous systems should help reduce workload and avoid increases in pilot stress. Similarly, trust and reliability are essential—without them, automation may be underutilized, leading to errors. Further, clear communication and decision-making are crucial, and autonomy levels must align with operational needs, balancing automation efficiency with human oversight. With respect to SiPO, support systems must address pilot incapacitation due to workload, fatigue, or health issues to ensure safety. This paper explores the transition from current operations to future autonomous paradigms, considering cases of partial and full autonomy. It examines key technologies, human-autonomy teaming, and cognitive methods to assess different models. The review provides insights into automation's role in future operations, analysing various configurations, autonomy levels, and their impact on human operators to determine optimal aviation strategies.

Keywords: Air-to-ground CONOPS · Reduced Crew Operations · Single Pilot Operations Enabled · Pilot incapacitation · Autonomous Systems

1 Introduction

As global air travel continues to steadily grow, the skies and airports grow busier as well, putting pressure on the systems and operators for both air and ground [1]. The scale of traffic managed by air traffic control (ATC) and ATC operators (ATCO) as well as the demand for pilots therefore grows in turn. As such, advancements will be needed to help

© The Author(s) 2026
D. Harris et al. (Eds.): HCII 2025, LNCS 16334, pp. 54–73, 2026.
https://doi.org/10.1007/978-3-032-12392-3_4

minimize the impacts of the growing demand and anticipated pilot shortages. These advancements will include broader support for, and integration of, autonomous systems. Further, the increase in autonomous system performance as well as their usage for the ground and air support/operation can be investigated in the context of supporting reduced crew and operator numbers. Combined, future frameworks could support a transition from dual pilot operations (DPO) to reduced crew operations (RCO) [2], single pilot operations (SiPO) [3] and even beyond to the case of fully autonomous operation.

The future of aerospace operations will involve a shift towards smaller crews, reduced human operators, and greater integration of autonomous systems. This change will include a transition from dual pilot operations (DPO) to reduced crew operations (RCO), single pilot operations (SiPO), and potentially full autonomy. To ensure successful integration, autonomous systems must support human operators through effective communication and collaboration. Depending on the use case, this could involve humans delegating tasks to autonomous systems, autonomous systems augmenting human actions, or air traffic controllers interacting with artificial pilots as they would with human pilots. The level of autonomy and its corresponding authority must align with operational needs to ensure that autonomous systems are both effective and appropriately supervised. In SiPO, systems must also account for situations where a pilot is incapacitated due to workload, fatigue, or health issues, ensuring continued safe operation. These support systems must mitigate risks and ensure effective control in such scenarios.

Autonomous systems should aim to reduce human workload and stress rather than increase it, improving overall performance and supporting operators in challenging situations. However, trust and reliability in these systems are critical. Without them, human operators may struggle to effectively utilize automation, which could increase task complexity and the risk of errors. The success of these future operations will depend on seamless interaction between humans and autonomous systems, ensuring safety and efficiency in increasingly complex air and ground operations.

1.1 Scope and Objectives

In this paper, we are considering the potential transition from the current concept of operations (CONOPS) for commercial dual pilot operations to future operation paradigms. We will not restrict the expectations regarding the future CONOPS to a particular outcome but will instead consider the anticipated impact and key technologies required with respect to cases such as RCO, SiPO, or full autonomy, which we differentiate in two study cases: *Partial Autonomy* and *Full Autonomy*. As will be demonstrated, several aspects are transversal while others necessitate key distinctions. For instance, SiPO implies a human-in-the-loop scenario in the cockpit while full autonomy clearly does not. Finally, the intention of this review is to provide insights into some of the key considerations when identifying which CONOPS paradigm is desired.

1.2 Structure of the Paper

In the remaining sections of the paper, we will present topics across multiple domains which present relevant investigations such as automation, cognitive methods, human-autonomy teaming (HAT), and more. These topics provide numerous examples of various teaming configurations, expectations regarding the level and performance of the autonomy, and the interactions/impact of the humans and autonomous systems. Following this discussion, we will provide a summary and analysis of the presented topics to indicate aspects we find key to the various potential CONOPS paradigms.

2 Related Topics and Relevant Technologies

In this section, we will discuss relevant topics investigated in related industries and research. These topics serve to both indicate the significance of these problems across multiple domains while also indicating some of the existing methods for overcoming aspects of the challenges observed. First, we will introduce prior investigations in the aerospace domain, automotive applications, and the area of robotics. Then, we will discuss several research topic areas of note.

2.1 Related Topics

Automotive. The introduction of autonomous systems in driving provides mechanisms to support, augment, or replace human operation, focusing on human interactions with the systems, safety, risk mitigation, and determining the appropriate driver (human or autonomous) for the situation. As with aerospace, the addition of a secondary decision-maker requires careful consideration to enable effective collaboration between humans and autonomous systems. This can be the representation of the human and autonomy team in a hierarchical representation to indicate roles and responsibilities [4]. Under such a structure, the level in the hierarchy and type of role dictates the expectations for the decision-maker (e.g., adherence to laws, level of control, etc.). With respect to safety, the riskiness of the driving conditions/context, models of performance, and more can be considered to recognize dangerous scenarios and mitigate risks [5–9]. Extending the previous concepts, a further key aspect in the case of human-autonomy teaming (HAT) in the context of driving is the alignment of decision-makers to the scenario to recognize suitability when delegating control [10]. If control needs to shift, factors such as the driver's readiness, awareness, and transition time must be considered. These topics highlight the importance of human-autonomous system interactions, the roles of each in a hybrid decision-making team, and the necessary safety and risk considerations.

Robotics. As with the automotive case, there have been considerations with respect to the safe and effective operation of robots aside humans. These include aspects such as the interaction type(s), safety, effectiveness, and more [11–13]. In the case of interaction and interaction type, a key aspect is the expectations with respect to the nature of the combined operation. More specifically, [11] indicates three human-robot roles and interaction types: 1) active (i.e., dominant decision-maker); 2) supportive (i.e., aided operations performed which are indicated by the teammate); and 3) inactive (remain idle and trust other's decisions). The role of a robot depends on the use case and the decisions it needs to make. For example, in a supportive role on an assembly line, a robotic arm could assist by recognizing the required part and positioning it appropriately. The human operator can also provide guidance, further emphasizing the robot's supportive role. Beyond the role expected of a robot, consideration is also made for the impact made with respect to the workload and cognitive burden for the human as well as the robot's ability to anticipate/comprehend the actions or needs of the human [11]. Extending this concept, a further consideration is the risk and safety impact of a robot operating in the environment with humans [13]. These can be impacted by the performance of the robot, its ability to anticipate the behaviour of the human, and external factors such as the environment state (e.g., weather/lighting impacting sensor readings). Again, these topics indicate the importance of key aspects relating to the safe operation and optimal interaction for humans and autonomous systems.

Aerospace. Regarding the aerospace sector, it is well known that the introduction of automation has been slower compared to others. This reduced pace is mainly due to the increased complexity of the environment, the high technology development costs, and the strict certification standards and regulations to guarantee the safety of operations. Although AI-based systems and highly automated architectures are starting to be developed for urban air mobility and ATC, and modern (commercial) aircraft are increasingly reliant on automation for safe and efficient operations, pilots remain essential for decision-making. As such, full automation is said to still be far in the horizon [14]. Alternatively, automation has brought significant advantages for flight safety and operations and is in fact required for certain types of operations and precise navigation.

Based on the advanced statistics of EASA Annual Safety Review 2024 [15] for the different aircraft categories in terms of human factors and human performances, analysis suggests that regardless of the type of aircraft (and number of pilots onboard), issues related to psychological and task performance events are the most common in commercial aviation. Additionally, regarding the areas that are raising more safety concerns for operations in complex aeroplanes, events related to alertness and fatigue are the most common. Therefore, being able to rely on monitoring technologies to evaluate mental fatigue and alertness as well as automated systems to support the tasks execution will contribute to increase the overall safety of future operations. However, relying on automated systems may be challenging for (senior) pilots who may be less comfortable with automation while skill degradation or inexperience could be a risk when the automation disconnects, fails, or must be reverted to a lower automation level, including hand flying the aircraft [16].

2.2 Relevant Technologies and Methods

Automation. In the context of automation, the prescribed level of authority guides considerations regarding the proficiency and responsibilities of an autonomous systems. In [17], the levels of automation are ordered as follows, where the computer:

1. Offers no human assistance: human must take all decisions and actions
2. Offers a complete set of decision/action alternatives
3. Narrows the selection of actions to a few
4. Suggests a single alternative action
5. Executes a suggestion given human approval
6. Automatically executes an action if the human does not veto before allotted time window expires

7. Automatically executes an action and informs the human
8. Operates without requesting approval but informing the human when prompted
9. Operates without requesting approval and decides when to inform the human
10. Operates entirely independently (i.e., full autonomy) and ignores human

For the aerospace domain, as outlined in [18], artificial intelligence (AI) levels are classified according to three levels with two sub-levels each. In level 1, the AI assists a human user via augmentation (level 1A) or cognitive assistance in decision-making or action selection (level 1B). For level, 2, the role of AI is extended to cases of cooperation (level 2A) or collaboration (level 2B) with a human for a teaming scenario. Lastly, level 3 indicates an advanced automation level with AI decisions which can be either overridable (level 3A) or non-overridable (level 3B) by the human. Like the previous levels, the EASA classifications indicate both the level of authority afforded and the expectations with respect to responsibility for the decisions made and actions taken.

Clearly, with either of the above classification schemes, the levels indicate the degree of freedom the autonomy has with respect to making decisions with or without human insights. Implicitly, this also indicates where the responsibility lies for a decision. In cases where the human must/will be informed, there is a clear reliance on the human for ensuring the operation conforms to their view of valid operation. The significance of the human input varies from levels 1–6, or 1A-3A for EASA, but a critical aspect is the ability for the human to use, guide, or override the decisions of the autonomous system. Therefore, the human maintains sufficient control to retain authority and responsibility.

In cases of automation level at or exceeding level 6/3A, the responsibilities shift to the autonomous system. Level 6 is included as the time window for human veto affords cases where the autonomy's decision will be executed without human override. Likewise, level 3A provides a similar assumption of a veto/override mechanism for the human. For levels 7–10/3B, there is a much clearer delineation, and the responsibility of a single action falls on the autonomous system. One key consideration is the fact that the human could still intervene after a single decision. However, intervention after the fact still requires ascribing responsibility to the autonomous system for the decision which motivated human intervention.

The connection between autonomous systems and action execution involves ensuring that the system can translate decisions into actions. For example, in autonomous driving, the system must control the steering, braking, and acceleration. Similarly, in aviation, autonomous systems need access to controls for action execution. The specific roles of humans and autonomous systems will determine how these controls are implemented.

Cognitive Methods. Methods like EEG, fNIRS, and eye tracking can monitor a pilot's mental and physiological states, helping track their health and suitability for tasks. Eye tracking, for example, can identify what the pilot is observing, linking their attention to situational awareness. These techniques provide valuable insights into the pilot's mental state and readiness for the task. First, identifying the information capturing the pilot's attention gives a clear indication of their awareness [19] regarding the aircraft state and environmental context. Next, the frequency with which they update and reinforce their awareness provides a measure recall strength for a memory [20], indicating how likely they are to forget an item or how likely another item is to take priority in their recall.

Lastly, these aspects support a model of mental state which supports the estimation of pilot perspective [21].

A mental model of the pilot (e.g., Theory of Mind [21–24]) can provide an estimation representing the perspective or beliefs of the pilot regarding their environment. Further, the representation can be used to estimate the significance of information, reminders, etc. to optimize the feedback and interactions and increase the accuracy of the pilot's world view. As such, reminders and notifications can be optimized to provide the most desirable impact. Relatedly, models can be used to replicate the decision-making of a human to provide support/augmentation/prediction (e.g., cognitive architectures [25] or kinetic models [26]) and help identify patterns of decisions. Further, a model of the pilot can help with providing assistance or indicating when intervention is needed [27]. Lastly, models which can also account for human skill level, and how it may impact performance and cognitive burden, would serve to indicate how best to tailor the pilot-specific considerations [28, 29]. As demonstrated in [29], the experience/skill level of a pilot impacts the brain regions utilized and overall usage. A pilot with more experience will typically require lower effort and have more refined control inducing lower levels of cognitive burden. Hence, skill level is a key indicator of necessary considerations when tailoring support for a specific user.

From another perspective, monitoring methods like EEG, fNIRS, etc. provide estimation methods for the mental state of a pilot with respect to awareness and perspective [19, 30–33] to recognize increased levels of load/burden that have been shown to lead to a degradation of performance and suboptimal or risky behaviour. By tracking these factors, the risk of continued pilot operation can be measured (e.g., how likely it is that key information or a task is overlooked, or a mistake is made [31]). As the load/burden increases, the autonomous system must recognize the significance of the increase. For example, the pilot's mental workload can be correlated to situational awareness, with excessive workload leading to poor performance [32]. Hence, the kind of intervention will be guided by the estimation of the human's workload and its impact on performance. Given these estimates regarding pilot performance, and beyond simply replacing pilot operation, the provided autonomous assistance needs to support reducing pilot workload through independent action or reducing the complexity of the pilot's task(s). Regarding pilot ability, as noted in [34], pilots may view their level of supported workload in terms of "spare capacity" and so we can view capacity as both perceived and actual ability [33]. Hence, assistance provided by autonomous systems should increase the pilot's spare capacity and reduce the likelihood of overburdening. In other words, solutions must take both the burden of the pilot and the current capacity to relate decisions to these two aspects. For example, [35] considers a model which accounts for task load, situational awareness, human error, decision-making speed/accuracy, and more to identify effective balances and alignments when managing the allocation of tasks and resolution of conflicts between humans and autonomous systems.

Human-Autonomy Teaming (HAT). The inclusion of several decision-makers necessitates aligning how the tasks are shared and the prioritization of the selected decision-maker according to the task(s). On one hand, tasks and team configuration might support parallel/concurrent operation (e.g., multi-agent systems, requiring a "complementary combination of human and/or machine autonomy" [36]. Appropriate in this context refers to aspects such as suitability, available resources, possible conflicting goals, etc. Additionally, the impact of multiple agents on each other can be considered with respect to emergent behaviour and "co-learning" [36]. Aside from the multi-agent setting, teams can share responsibility by offloading tasks to a decision-maker (e.g., autonomous driving) or augmenting performance via coordinated efforts. By merging responsibilities/tasks, the modelling of the team dynamics shifts and aligns better with single agent scenarios, enabling improved performance by utilization/hybridization of desirable decision-makers [37].

The inclusion of multiple agents also supports hierarchical models of teaming, which helps introduce structure to the team and support the decomposition of problems. However, considerations must be made with respect to the suitability of the domain to a hierarchical structure [38]. Additionally, effective teaming relies on effective sharing of knowledge to maintain transparency in situational awareness [39]. The hierarchical composition can be defined in two ways: one where a manager assigns decision-makers to tasks, and another where the manager also teaches or provides feedback to the decision-makers. In the latter case, the manager and decision-makers learn together, creating an interdependency between their selection and learning capabilities.

Behaviour Reasoning and Coordination. For multi-agent teams operating without centralized oversight or control, researchers have investigated effective management and sharing of knowledge. via dissemination of information within a sub-group (i.e., team) as well as between the various sub-groups [39]. Sharing knowledge in this manner reduces the cost of message passing as the number of team members communicating is reduced. Beyond decentralizing the knowledge, a team can extend coordination via similarly defined voting methods for the various decision-makers [40–44]. This can support resource allocation, identifying tasks to complete, etc. and reduce the complexity and cost of communications. This is achieved as communication again is typically reduced to a smaller local group of neighbours. Further, in some cases, this can be aligned with hierarchical models with representatives chosen for each group.

An additional aspect of teaming scenarios is understanding the behaviour of others. Extending this concept, autonomous system could attempt to replicate the decision/behavioural model of the human to more effectively identify the motivations of the human decisions (e.g., Imitation Learning/Inverse Reinforcement Learning [24]). At the base level, it is essential to consider mechanisms which support accurate interpretation of human behaviour and recognition of when that behaviour is either undesirable or abnormal (e.g., safety-critical domains where there are strict guidelines regarding actions). Therefore, the conversion of regulations, expectations, and past observations into a model of normative behaviour would enable recognizing potentially risky, prohibited, or abnormal human performance [45, 46]. A further interesting aspect is the ability to model and replicate human performance and learn to recognize or predict human goals [47], which could enable predicting future decisions or recognizing surprising behaviour. Essentially, a model which accurately replicates the human's linking of context to desirable decisions could better comprehend motivations and anticipate needs or likely decisions, improving team effectiveness.

Human Factors. Understanding the human factors implications of increasing automation is essential for designing safe and efficient next-generation cockpit and ATC environments. As commercial aviation moves toward higher levels of automation, including partially and fully automated operational paradigms, it is critical to examine how these changes affect human performance and decision-making. A key consideration is that as the level of automation (LoA) increases, manual control and decision-making responsibilities shift progressively from human operators to automated systems [48]. This transition redefines the role of human operators, shifting their focus from direct control to supervisory and monitoring tasks, while automation assumes a growing share of operational functions [17]. However, reduced human involvement can lead to passivity, as operators become less engaged in processing environmental cues, planning, and making decisions [49].

Extensive research has explored the impact of LoA on human performance, identifying several key challenges that must be addressed to ensure safe and effective human-machine collaboration. The most critical challenges include:

- Skill degradation: Increased automation leads to humans becoming passive monitors, causing a gradual loss of manual dexterity, slower response times, and difficulty handling automation failures [50].
- Reduced situation awareness: Passive monitoring limits the operator's ability to process environmental cues, hindering the development of accurate mental models, and making it harder to respond effectively to system changes or perform critical tasks [51].
- Workload complications: Poorly designed automation systems can create cycles of underload and overload, leading to higher stress, cognitive effort, and perceived workload, as operators struggle to understand automation behaviors or input data [52].
- Non-calibrated trust: Operators may not fully understand the systems they work with, leading to either over-reliance or distrust in automation, which can undermine safety and efficiency [53, 54]. Either scenario can undermine the intended role of automation or compromise the safety and efficiency of manual intervention.
- Reduced vigilance: Prolonged passive monitoring reduces operator engagement, impairing their ability to update mental models and decreasing reaction times and decision-making accuracy during critical events [49].
- Decompensation and automation surprises: Automated systems can obscure issues until control fails critically, leaving operators to respond to safety-critical events without full context, increasing the likelihood of catastrophic outcomes [55, 56].

The Adding-On Effect of AI in Automation. The human factors challenges above remain valid regardless of the type of automation integrated into the system, whether rule-based or AI-enabled. However, certain intrinsic characteristics of AI-based automation can amplify these challenges, primarily due to the following reasons [57]:

- AI perceptual limitations: AI systems process datasets and identify patterns within them to guide decision-making. However, their perceptual capabilities are inherently limited by the quality, scope, and representation of the data they are trained on and can lead to errors. As a result, AI systems may exhibit unpredictable or safety-critical behaviours, undermining their reliability and performance [58].

- Lack of causal reasoning and analytical interpretation: unlike human operators, AI does not reason or act based on causal understanding or analytical interpretations of the system it controls. Consequently, AI behaviour can appear unexplainable or unpredictable to human operators, who may also struggle to identify the underlying cause of such decisions. This mismatch severely impacts human-machine collaboration and the ability to achieve effective co-agency [51, 59].
- Bias: AI systems are trained on vast datasets that are collected, curated, and preprocessed by humans. These datasets inevitably contain biases, which become encoded in the behaviour of the resulting AI models. Such biases can impair the generalisation ability of AI, limiting its capacity to apply the correct course of action in situations or scenarios that were underrepresented—or entirely absent—in the training data [60].
- Goals and norm alignment: Aligning human and AI goals, norms, and control principles is challenging due to the context-dependent, individual nature of human norms, making it difficult to translate them into AI decision-making frameworks [61].
- Opacity and lack of explainability: the internal processes and decision-making mechanisms of AI systems are often difficult to explain, even for their developers. The lack of explainability stems from the complex architecture of many AI models, making their decisions and underlying data patterns opaque to human operators. This increased opacity, relative to rule-based automation, exacerbates challenges related to comprehension, communication, and trust, further complicating human-machine interaction [62].
- Brittleness: AI systems have shown a tendency toward brittleness, failing suddenly and significantly when exposed to scenarios absent or underrepresented in their training datasets. Since AI primarily learns patterns through repeated exposure during training, it often struggles to respond appropriately to entirely new or unexpected conditions. This can lead to marginal or unsafe decision-making, escalating into uncontrollable situations. Such failures intensify issues like automation surprises and decompensation patterns, forcing human operators to manage complex and critical scenarios with little context or preparation. In these situations, the time required to regain situational control can be dangerously short, increasing the likelihood of adverse outcomes [55, 56].

2.3 Assumptions and Interaction Cases Defined

To assess the feasibility and implementation of safe-return-to-land operations, several key assumptions must be established. These assumptions define the operational constraints, technological requirements, and human factors that will influence future cockpit automation and decision-making frameworks. The following points outline the foundational considerations that guide this study.

Regarding the Autonomous Systems, they will be designed to either support pilots in cases of partial incapacitation or perform tasks autonomously if the pilot is fully incapacitated. These systems will be capable of interpreting aircraft state and environmental factors, such as fuel levels and aircraft characteristics, to make decisions. Clear rules will define the operational domain and permitted actions. The authority level of autonomous systems will be well-defined, ensuring decision-making deference to the highest authority when needed. The level of automation must align with the technological ecosystem to ensure compatibility and integration with existing systems.

Additionally, effective communication between humans and autonomous systems is essential for accurate and understandable information exchange. Communication channels must meet aviation standards to ensure reliability. In cases where ground operators are involved, communication will be limited to instructions and aircraft status updates, with reduced channels for remote control. Autonomous systems will incorporate features to ensure compatible human-machine communication.

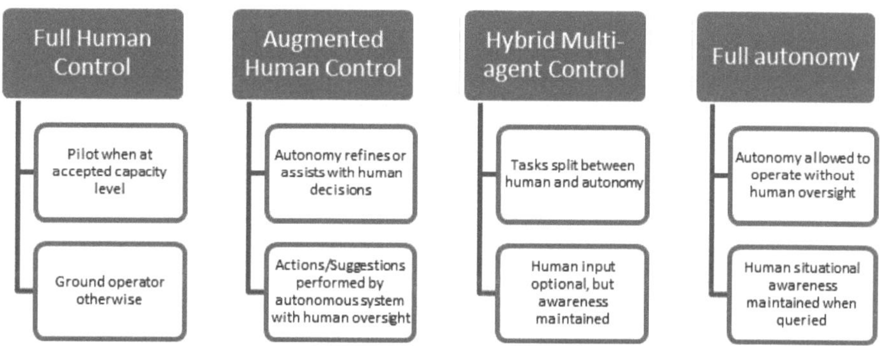

Fig. 1. Spectrum of interaction cases with the level of independent autonomous decisions and actions increasing from left to right.

Interaction Cases. Given the varying cases of CONOPS and interaction paradigms possible, we will present two cases of note which can highlight many of the key aspects. In these cases, we will consider the relationship between the air and ground sides with respect to the roles and responsibilities of the decision-makers. Additionally, we will discuss how the team dynamic and composition varies between the cases. These variations include the level of autonomy assumed, the prescribed level of authority for the ground and air decision-makers, and the overall interaction method anticipated.

With respect to the autonomy levels and interaction scenarios, we can break them down into a representation of autonomy level and interaction models (see Fig. 1). Further, we can relate these to the levels outlined in the Automation. Section. At the most restrictive level –roughly the one in place in current operations–, there is the expectation of full control via a human operator (either onboard pilot or ground assistance/control), aligning with levels 1/2 and possible EASA level 1A. In such a level, there must always be a mechanism enabling human input for the controls and information output by the systems to ensure proper situational awareness for the human. At this level, there is of course the least restrictive assumption regarding the level of proficiency for any autonomous systems. As a human is expected to always remain in control, the role of any integrated autonomous systems will be that of an assistant (i.e. levels 1/2 or EASA 1A) and only serve to provide information or perform non-critical activities. Again, the possibility of remote operation would indicate the need to ensure sufficient communication and support for remote operator control inputs [1–3, 63].

Moving one level higher with respect to the autonomous system(s), the expectation would shift to that of autonomous systems capable of augmenting the performance of the human. This can include aspects such as recommending courses of action, proposing actions to be taken by the autonomous system on the human's behalf, etc. In this case, aligning with levels 1–6 or EASA levels 2A-3A, there is again a reliance on human input, but we now see an increase in the expected proficiency of the autonomous systems. In this case, there must be sufficient understanding of the pilot/ATCO's goals, the current context, etc. by the autonomous systems to ensure the decisions proposed fit the current scenario. If there is not sufficient awareness, the autonomous system(s) would likely propose unsuitable courses of action and instead serve as a distraction. A further key aspect is the scenario in which there is a ground operator attempting to assist in the event of pilot incapacitation. As with the previous level, the ground operator must have sufficient means to provide the necessary input and maintain accurate situational awareness. With respect to the second level of interaction, the expectation would then be that the autonomous system(s) can interact with the ground operator as well as if interacting with the pilot. Again, this would require sufficient communication mechanisms and bandwidth to support the remote interaction.

For the next level, there is a shift/gap from the previous level in that the autonomy and decision-making must increase to that of independent identification of actions or decisions (i.e., levels 6–8, EASA 2B/3A). Such an advancement supports the offloading of tasks from the human to the autonomous system(s) while maintaining support for human input. The key distinction is therefore the removal of reliance on the human's input and instead expecting independence from the autonomous system component of the team. While this still ensures there are systems in place which can operate with a pilot, there is the extension of this concept to enable independent and concurrent operation. As such, the level of proficiency of the autonomous systems must support such an operational context to ensure effective coordination of activities/resources. More specifically, the inclusion of multiple decision-makers (i.e. cockpit automation as well as ATC automation) will require the consideration of the impact each of their decisions has on the others in the team. The consequences of their actions and their impact on the outcomes will now be intertwined, increasing the complexity of the air-ground teaming dynamics.

Extending the previous level, we can consider the case where human operation is completely replaced by autonomous systems in suitable scenarios (i.e., levels 8–10, EASA 3B). As demonstrated in aerospace, automotive domains, and robotics, there are tasks which can be successfully performed within acceptable safety constraints. For example, algorithms have been implemented in vehicles to enable automated parallel parking, aircraft have autopilot systems, etc. In such a paradigm, the autonomous system(s) are assumed to operate with little or no need for oversight from a human. While this does not exclude the possibility of the human intervening (e.g., human driving regaining control of a self-driving car), the key distinction is that the autonomous system(s) must serve as a suitable replacement where desired. For scenarios with a human which can regain control, there must be considerations regarding the take-over process. For instance, the human might not have sufficient situational awareness to immediately take control in a safe manner [63]. Further, the human may need further insight into the past decisions of the autonomous system(s) to have sufficient context for future decisions. Critically, this level of interaction indicates a case in which the human can rely to a prescribed degree on the independent operation of an autonomous system's decisions. This serves to enable both the reduction in human workload as well as provide a suitable alternative to human operation in cases of incapacitation or unpreparedness.

Extending across all the levels described, we can see a clear indication what scenarios involving human pilots or interactions between an autonomous cockpit and human ground operators there will be need for safe and effective teaming. The expected level of interaction and autonomy will dictate the framework necessary and human-machine communication mechanisms desired. Further, the level of interaction will dictate which responsibilities fall to any of the decision-makers and which regulations they are subject to in their operation.

Case 1: Partial Autonomy. As a first case, aligning best with the lower levels of interaction outline in Fig. 1 we can consider the case of partial autonomy with human oversight. Such a case of course implies several key distinctions and assumptions. First and foremost, there must be support for the effective communication between humans and the autonomous system(s). More specifically, the communications between the two must ensure accurate and comprehensible information is passed between the human and the machine. This requires both a sufficient representation of knowledge as well as suitable human-machine interface design.

With respect to the application in an aerospace scenario, we can consider several cases. First, in the event of either a pilot incapacitation in DPO or in the case of SiPO, there will be an opportunity, and possibly a need, to support the pilot with autonomous systems. The inclusion of these support systems allows for the offloading of tasks, assistance in maintaining effective levels of situational awareness, collaborative/joint operation, and an autonomous backup in case of significant incapacitation in a SiPO case. A further aspect is the support for interactions between the air and ground in these scenarios. The autonomous system(s) can assist a pilot in their interactions with the ground, maintain and summarize knowledge communicated, or work with a ground operator to maintain safe remote operation in the event of pilot incapacitation. Combined, at least three scenarios are supported: 1) pilot operations augmented by digital assistant aid; 2) pilot/ground hybrid input with digital assistant aid; 3) full ground-based control with digital assistant support and action execution. Each of these applies to the desired use case (e.g., SiPO, reduced crew, autonomous cockpit, etc.) and will indicate the relevant assumptions.

In addition to cockpit automation, there is also an opportunity to introduce autonomous systems within ATC to enhance operational support, particularly in managing the aforementioned pilot incapacitation scenarios. In a partial autonomy case, automation could assist controllers by identifying and highlighting affected traffic, detecting potential conflicts, and recognizing necessary adjustments, such as sequencing changes in the approach phase. Furthermore, autonomous systems could aid in representing the incapacitated aircraft's likely intentions, improving situational awareness for human operators.

The partial autonomy case indicates critical assumptions regarding the level of autonomy expected, the authority which can be afforded to the autonomy, and the overall interaction dynamic between humans and autonomy. By optimizing the roles and responsibilities of each, the best features of either can be utilized. Further, the cognitive burden and overall workload levels can be reduced through the effective utilization of proficient autonomous systems. As such, the risk of increased levels of intervention can be reduced and the pilot's duties can be made easier.

Phases and Roles in Air and Ground Interactions. Regarding the transition between the above human-machine teaming scenarios, the key aspect is the pilot's state. Critically, as outlined in Cognitive Methods., both the workload (or cognitive burden) and the physiological factors (e.g., fatigue) can be tracked to determine key aspects of the pilot's state. In cases of pilot incapacitation, partial or full, workload and cognitive burden will indicate how severely pilot performance is impacted and to what degree intervention is required. At the lowest degrees of incapacitation, the digital assistant can assist the pilot to reduce the effects of excess workload via reduced task complexity. To mitigate physiological factors and maintain situational awareness, steps should be taken to ensure the systems help maintain pilot focus and attention (e.g., altering the brightness of displays). These aspects can integrate concepts outlined in Human-Autonomy Teaming (HAT). and Behaviour Reasoning and Coordination. to support the effective interaction and coordination of the two decision-makers. Further, comprehension of the human's goals/tasks will ensure better alignment of human and machine goals.

Extending the expectations regarding HAT, considerations must be made with respect to any ground operators. As with the pilot-autonomy interactions, there will also be air-ground interactions. Based on the use case and role of autonomous systems, this will include a corresponding degree of HAT for air-ground coordination. As with the pilot-autonomy case, the ground operator must receive effective support from any air/ground-based autonomous support. Further, the various configurations and transitions of the human state will shift the key aspects of each team member. As the pilot's incapacitation level increases, the autonomy must both increase pilot support while also supporting augmentation from the ground side. The ground operator's role will be to ensure continued safety in lieu of full pilot operation. Therefore, coordination beyond the cockpit will also be essential in all levels of pilot state. In the lowest/no incapacitation level, the autonomy will still serve to improve pilot effectiveness. As incapacitation grows, the autonomy must enable effective ground-based support. Based on the use case, this will include aspects such as communicating aircraft state/health, environmental conditions, etc. Further, the autonomous systems must support the remote operation or execution of ground-based guidance for a safe return-to-land outcome. Therefore, the human-machine interfaces for both air and ground must ensure effective bidirectional communication and maintenance of situational awareness (see Human Factors. for more details). This remains true for cases where the pilot regains sufficient capacity and can regain control, requiring efficient access to information.

Case 2: Full Autonomy. Transitioning from the previous case, we must also consider operational paradigms including fully autonomous operations of an aircraft. These can either be cases where there are not human pilots or cases of complete pilot incapacitation.

Further, the other key discrepancy to Case 1: Partial Autonomy. is the assumption of air-based operation of the aircraft rather than external control from a ground operator. Clearly, such a paradigm relies on sufficient performance of autonomous systems and a correspondingly high level of afforded autonomy. The level of autonomy and interaction will need to align with the two highest cases in Fig. 1 to support collaboration and complete control cases. With respect to collaboration, a pilot with sufficient capacity can still operate the aircraft with the assistance of the autonomous system(s). The level of assistance will of course depend on the needs of the pilot, but concurrent and collaborative operation is expected. Again, the expectation is that full transfer of control is made once the pilot reaches the critical threshold for incapacitation. At this point, the autonomous systems take control and interact with the ground side in lieu of the pilot. With respect to ground operations, the fidelity of the interactions must be sufficient to enable operations and interactions consistent with a human pilot.

The above assumptions indicate several critical factors. First, the use of fully autonomous operation requires sufficient reliability with respect to the autonomous systems. Without suitable proficiency, there would be no justification for reliance on autonomous systems for operation of the aircraft. The proficiency will rely on the system's ability to maintain accurate models of the aircraft and environmental states as well as the input provided by the ground side. Therefore, systems must be trained to operate the aircraft, align their decisions with regulations and procedures, and comprehend the significance of contextual details (e.g., aircraft state, weather conditions, etc.). The understanding of these features must then enable autonomous system decisions and selection of suitable courses of action. Such systems will rely on modelling techniques which can either incorporate representations of decisions based on domain knowledge or learn an effective model of behaviour according to feedback and a learning process (e.g., Behaviour Reasoning and Coordination.).

With the introduction of full autonomy in the cockpit, there would also be an opportunity to further advance automation within the ATC systems. As the automation gets fully adopted in the air, ATC systems could adopt higher levels of automation to assist ATCO in handling complex scenarios, such as a full pilot incapacitation. Automated tools could propose resolution strategies for conflicting aircraft, optimize sequencing, and aid in workload management by handling routine tasks. This evolution in ATC automation would not replace human responsibility but rather support decision-making, ensuring seamless coordination between autonomous and human-operated aircraft.

Phases and Roles in Air and Ground Interactions. As with Case 1: Partial Autonomy., the roles for the humans and autonomous systems must account for the intentions regarding the reliance on autonomous systems and ground support. Diverging from the previous case, we do not see any intention for a significant shift or increase in responsibility for the ground operations. As the role for operating the aircraft remains on the air side, the ground operator (e.g., ATCO) should only expect to have interactions consistent with current methods. While there may still be some changes as the general CONOPS may still evolve, the expectations for this case are not such that additional training, responsibilities, or roles are anticipated.

Given the assumption of normative ground operations, we focus instead on the air side. First and foremost, there must be support for varying levels of support provided by the autonomous systems. As with the previous case, including autonomous decision-makers for human pilot support can help mitigate the cognitive burdens and excess workloads which can contribute to pilot incapacitation. As the system recognizes symptoms of these factors, efforts should be made to alleviate the pilot's workload and reduce the risk of more severe incapacitation/impact. Unlike the previous case, the expectation is that the autonomous system(s) are proficient enough to allow for operation without human intervention. With this level of proficiency, tasks can be directly offloaded from the pilot and the autonomy can transition to an active role. In the event of extreme pilot incapacitation, as with the previous phase, the autonomy must have an accurate understanding of the current state. One key distinction would be the exclusion of the pilot in this case. Unlike the previous phase, the autonomous system(s) and pilot are not expected to make decisions concurrently. As such, the dynamics of the decision problem are not the same as the previous phase. On the other hand, there is the potential for the pilot to regain sufficient capacity to all for transferring control back to the pilot. In this case, as with the previous case, the autonomous system(s) must provide accurate and appropriate updates to align pilot awareness. Consistent with all the phases is the need for the autonomous system(s) to interact and communicate with humans. This applies to both the human pilots and the ground operators. In either phase, the communications must be comprehensible and provide sufficient detail to maintain accurate knowledge. For this case, there is an increased expectation in this regard as the air-based autonomy must be able to interact with the ground side to reach the safe return-to-land outcome.

3 Conclusion

In our CONOPS proposition we will examine how increased automation can enhance operational efficiency and safety in future commercial aviation. A key focus is the integration of digital assistants to support coordination between human operators and automation in both the cockpit and ATC environments. These digital assistants will be architecture-agnostic, meaning they may be based on rule-based automation, AI/ML models, or a combination of both. We will investigate how tasks and functions currently performed by human operators can be redistributed within a more automated operational setting. This includes defining frameworks and procedures that ensure effective task allocation between humans and intelligent agents while maintaining high levels of human oversight and system reliability.

The need to redesign operational procedures and reallocate tasks and functions between humans and advanced automation introduces significant human factor challenges. The increased involvement of automation capable of performing tasks or functions with greater autonomy transforms its role from a decision-support tool to an effective teammate. Pilots and ATCOs will need to share control and cooperate with intelligent agents that are not human. For this reason, both onboard and ground procedures must be rethought to ensure humans remain engaged and "in-the-loop" while maintaining the highest standards of safety.

The challenges also extend to the design of the digital assistants themselves, as their operation must support human teamwork by enabling clear communication, dynamic adaptation to situations, transparency, and compatibility with situational context. This introduces specific requirements for how intelligent agents exert system control, make decisions, and collaborate with humans in setting goals and devising strategies. Defining CONOPS for significant changes in commercial aviation requires a gradual approach, identifying and analyzing incremental changes due to increased automation. These changes must be tailored to onboard and ground operations, with a focus on human factors, including decision-making and situational awareness. Tasks suitable for delegation to digital assistants must be identified, ensuring human operators stay engaged. New processes must be designed for safe and gradual integration of digital assistants, ensuring clear coordination among all actors. Finally, these procedures must be validated and refined based on feedback from pilots and ATCOs.

While we do not advocate for a particular configuration of roles in this review, it is worth considering the impact the various scenarios would have on the current ground and air roles. For instance, the use of a ground operator to remotely complete all/part of the duties of the pilot would indicate the need to either extend the role of an ATC operator or further increment the automation provided in their systems. As noted, the role will determine what information must be communicated and what aspects of the decision-making will align with the pilot, autonomy, or ground operator. Further, the intended use case with respect to cockpit configuration will also impact the roles. With respect to DPO and SiPO, both will have the potential for varying levels and conditions of pilot incapacitation. As such, the roles of the ground and interactions with the pilots will need to account for these cases. To mitigate the risks associated with reduced access to pilots (RCO, SiPO, incapacitation, etc.), we outlined several research topic areas in Sect. 2.2, which can motivate the use cases and methodologies for the implemented autonomous systems.

Acknowledgments. This project has received funding from the SESAR 3 Joint Undertaking under grant agreement No. 101166998 under European Union's Horizon Europe research and innovation programme.

References

1. Koltz, M.T., et al.: An investigation of the harbor pilot concept for single pilot operations. Procedia Manuf. **3**, 2937–2944 (2015)
2. Matessa, M., Strybel, T., Vu, K., Battiste, V., Schnell, T.: Concept of operations for RCO SPO (No. ARC-E-DAA-TN44254). National Aeronautics and Space Administration, United States (2017)
3. Lachter, J., Brandt, S.L., Battiste, V., Ligda, S.V., Matessa, M., Johnson, W.W.: Toward single pilot operations: developing a ground station. In: Proceedings of the International Conference on Human-Computer Interaction in Aerospace (2014)
4. Gillespie, T., Hailes, S.: Assignment of legal responsibilities for decisions by autonomous cars using system architectures. IEEE Trans. Technol. Soc. **1**, 148–160 (2020)
5. Li, X., Wu, X., Zhao, Y., Li, Y.: Perceptual risk-aware adaptive responsibility sensitive safety for autonomous driving. In: Indulska, M., Reinhartz-Berger, I., Cetina, C., Pastor, O. (eds.) CAiSE 2023, pp. 33–49. LNCS, vol. 13901. Springer, Cham (2023). https://doi.org/10.1007/978-3-031-34560-9_3

6. Huang, W., Liu, H., Huang, Z., Lv, C.: Safety-aware human-in-the-loop reinforcement learning with shared control for autonomous driving. IEEE Trans. Intell. Transp. Syst. **25**, 16181–16192 (2024)

7. Gao, F., Luo, C., Shi, F., Chen, X., Gao, Z., Zhao, R.: Online safety verification of autonomous driving decision-making based on dynamic reachability analysis. IEEE Access **11**, 93293–93309 (2023)

8. Thomas, S., Groth, K.M.: Toward a hybrid causal framework for autonomous vehicle safety analysis. Proc. Inst. Mech. Eng. Part O J. Risk Reliab. **237**, 367–388 (2023)

9. Boujezza, H., Boubakri, A.: A new redundant intelligent architecture to improve the operational safety of autonomous vehicles. In: Barolli, L. (ed.) AINA 2024. LNDECT, vol. 199, pp. 140–152. Springer, Cham (2024). https://doi.org/10.1007/978-3-031-57840-3_13

10. Morales-Alvarez, W., Sipele, O., Léberon, R., Tadjine, H.H., Olaverri-Monreal, C.: Automated driving: a literature review of the take over request in conditional automation. Electronics **9** (2020)

11. Mukherjee, D., Gupta, K., Chang, L.H., Najjaran, H.: A survey of robot learning strategies for human-robot collaboration in industrial settings. Robot. Comput. Integr. Manuf. **73**, 102231 (2022)

12. Li, S., et al.: Proactive human–robot collaboration: mutual-cognitive, predictable, and self-organising perspectives. Robot. Comput. Integr. Manuf. **81**, 102510 (2023)

13. Valori, M., et al.: Validating safety in human–robot collaboration: standards and new perspectives. Robotics **10** (2021)

14. EASA: EASA Artificial Intelligence Roadmap 2.0. EASA (2023)

15. EASA: Annual Safety Review 2024. EASA (2024)

16. E. I. G. o. P. T. (IGPT): EASA Automation Policy: Bridging Design and Training Principles. EASA (2013)

17. Parasuraman, R., Sheridan, T.B., Wickens, C.D.: A model for types and levels of human interaction with automation. IEEE Trans. Syst. Man Cybern. Part A Syst. Hum. **30**, 286–297 (2000)

18. EASA: EASA Concept Paper: Guidance for Level 1 & 2 machine learning applications. A deliverable of the EASA AI Roadmap. EASA (2024)

19. Klaproth, O.W., Vernaleken, C., Krol, L.R., Halbruegge, M., Zander, T.O., Russwinkel, N.: Tracing pilots' situation assessment by neuroadaptive cognitive modeling. Front. Neurosci. **14** (2020)

20. Chen, H., Liu, S., Pang, L., Wanyan, X., Fang, Y.: Developing an improved ACT-R model for pilot situation awareness measurement. IEEE Access **9**, 122113–122124 (2021)

21. Rabinowitz, N., Perbet, F., Song, F., Zhang, C., Eslami, S.A., Botvinick, M.: Machine theory of mind. In: International Conference on Machine Learning (2018)

22. Leslie, A.M., Friedman, O., German, T.P.: Core mechanisms in 'theory of mind.' Trends Cogn. Sci. **8**, 528–533 (2004)

23. Premack, D., Woodruff, G.: Does the chimpanzee have a theory of mind? Behav. Brain Sci. **1**, 515–526 (1978)

24. Fuchs, A., Passarella, A., Conti, M.: Modeling, replicating, and predicting human behavior: a survey. ACM Trans. Auton. Adapt. Syst. **18** (2023)

25. Tchio, G.C.T., Courtemanche, MA., Tato, A.A.N., Nkambou, R., Psyché, V.: Integrating an ontological reference model of piloting procedures in ACT-R cognitive architecture to simulate piloting tasks. In: Frasson, C., Mylonas, P., Troussas, C. (eds.) ITS 2023. LNCS, vol. 13891, pp. 183–194. Springer, Cham (2023). https://doi.org/10.1007/978-3-031-32883-1_16

26. Roth, W.-M., Mavin, T.J., Munro, I.: How a cockpit forgets speeds (and speed-related events): toward a kinetic description of joint cognitive systems. Cogn. Technol. Work **17**, 279–299 (2015)

27. Tamkodjou Tchio, G.C., Nkambou, R., Tato Nyamen, A.A., Psyché, V.: Handling of abnormal aircraft takeoff procedures: cognitive modeling of an ACT-R synthetic pilot integrating an ontological reference model. In: Mylonas, P., Kardaras, D., Caro, J. (eds.) NiDS 2024. LNNS, vol. 1170, pp. 448–461. Springer, Cham (2024). https://doi.org/10.1007/978-3-031-73344-4_38

28. Zheng, Z., Gao, S., Su, Y., Chen, Y., Wang, X.: Cognitive load-induced pupil dilation reflects potential flight ability. Curr. Psychol. **42**, 24871–24881 (2023)

29. Brams, S., Ziv, G., Levin, O., Wagemans, J., Williams, A.M., Helsen, W.F.: Brain, gaze behavior and perceptual-cognitive skills in aviation: what is yet to be studied? In: Proceedings of the 1st International Workshop on Eye-Tracking in Aviation (ETAVI 2020) (2020)

30. van Weelden, E., Alimardani, M., Wiltshire, T.J., Louwerse, M.M.: Aviation and neurophysiology: a systematic review. Appl. Ergon. **105**, 103838 (2022)

31. Vogl, J., Delgado-Howard, C., Plummer, H., McAtee, A., Hayes, A., Aura, C., Onge, P.S.: A literature review of applied cognitive workload assessment in the aviation domain. US Army Aeromedical Research Laboratory (2023)

32. Martinez-Marquez, D., Pingali, S., Panuwatwanich, K., Stewart, R.A., Mohamed, S.: Application of eye tracking technology in aviation, maritime, and construction industries: a systematic review. Sensors **21** (2021)

33. Wilson, J.C., Nair, S., Scielzo, S., Larson, E.C.: Objective measures of cognitive load using deep multi-modal learning: a use-case in aviation. Proc. ACM Interact. Mob. Wearable Ubiquitous Technol. **5** (2021)

34. Roscoe, A.H., Ellis, G.A.: A subjective rating scale for assessing pilot workload in flight: a decade of practical use (1990)

35. Zhang, X., Sun, Y., Zhang, Y.: Evolutionary game and collaboration mechanism of human-computer interaction for future intelligent aircraft cockpit based on system dynamics. IEEE Trans. Hum. Mach. Syst. **52**, 87–98 (2022)

36. Boy, G.A., Morel, C.: The machine as a partner: Human-machine teaming design using the PRODEC method. Work **73**, S15–S30 (2022)

37. Dormoy, C., André, J.-M., Pagani, A.: A human factors' approach for multimodal collaboration with cognitive computing to create a human intelligent machine team: a review. IOP Conf. Ser. Mater. Sci. Eng. **1024**, 012105 (2021)

38. Kolbjørnsrud, V.: Designing the intelligent organization: six principles for human-AI collaboration. Calif. Manag. Rev. **66**, 44–64 (2024)

39. Caldwell, S., et al.: An agile new research framework for hybrid human-AI teaming: trust, transparency, and transferability. ACM Trans. Interact. Intell. Syst. **12** (2022)

40. Ogunsina, K., DeLaurentis, D.: Enabling integration and interaction for decentralized artificial intelligence in airline disruption management. Eng. Appl. Artif. Intell. **109**, 104600 (2022)

41. Xu, H., Fan, Y., Li, W., Zhang, L.: Wireless distributed consensus for connected autonomous systems. IEEE Internet Things J. **10**, 7786–7799 (2022)

42. Hashemi, S.M., Botez, R.M., Ghazi, G.: Blockchain PoS and PoW consensus algorithms for airspace management application to the UAS-S4 Ehécatl. Algorithms **16** (2023)

43. Paul, S., Patterson, S., Varela, C.A.: Collaborative situational awareness for conflict-aware flight planning. In: 2020 AIAA/IEEE 39th Digital Avionics Systems Conference (DASC) (2020)

44. Xu, Z., Li, Y., Feng, C., Zhang, L.: Exact fault-tolerant consensus with voting validity. In: 2023 IEEE International Parallel and Distributed Processing Symposium (IPDPS) (2023)

45. Hung, F., et al.: Intention-based behavioral anomaly detection (2019)

46. Oh, M.-h., Iyengar, G.: Sequential anomaly detection using inverse reinforcement learning. In: Proceedings of the 25th ACM SIGKDD International Conference on Knowledge Discovery & Data Mining, New York, NY, USA (2019)

47. Suck, S., Fortmann, F.: Aircraft pilot intention recognition for advanced cockpit assistance systems. In: Schmorrow, D., Fidopiastis, C. (eds.) AC 2016, Part II. LNCS, vol. 9744, pp. 231–240. Springer, Cham (2016). https://doi.org/10.1007/978-3-319-39952-2_23

48. Endsley, M.R.: Toward a theory of situation awareness in dynamic systems. Hum. Factors J. Hum. Factors Ergon. Soc. **37**, 32–64 (1995)

49. Endsley, M.R., Kiris, E.O.: The out-of-the-loop performance problem and level of control in automation. Hum. Factors J. Hum. Factors Ergon. Soc. **37**, 381–394 (1995)

50. Rose, A.M.: Acquisition and retention of skills. In: McMillan, G.R., Beevis, D., Salas, E., Strub, M.H., Sutton, R., Van Breda, L. (eds.) Applications of Human Performance Models to System Design, pp. 419–426. Springer, Boston (1989). https://doi.org/10.1007/978-1-4757-9244-7_30

51. Kaber, D.B., Endsley, M.R.: The effects of level of automation and adaptive automation on human performance, situation awareness and workload in a dynamic control task. Theor. Issues Ergon. Sci. **5**, 113–153 (2004)

52. Kirlik, A.: Modeling strategic behavior in human-automation interaction: why an "aid" can (and should) go unused. Hum. Factors J. Hum. Factors Ergon. Soc. **35**, 221–242 (1993)

53. Chen, J.Y.C., Barnes, M.J., Harper-Sciarini, M.: Su-pervisory control of multiple robots: human-performance issues and user-interface design. IEEE Trans. Syst. Man Cybern. Part C (Appl. Rev.) **41**, 435–454 (2011)

54. Parasuraman, R., Sheridan, T.B., Wickens, C.D.: Situation awareness, mental workload, and trust in automation: viable, empirically supported cognitive engineering constructs. J. Cogn. Eng. Decis. Mak. **2**, 140–160 (2008)

55. Woods, D.D., Cook, R.I.: Incidents – markers of resilience or brittleness? In: Hollnagel, E., Woods, D.D., Leveson, N. (eds.) Resilience Engineering, 1st edn., pp. 69–76. CRC Press (2017)

56. Woods, D.D., Sarter, N.B., Sarter, I.N., Amalberti, R.: Learning from automation surprises and "going sour" accidents"

57. Endsley, M.R.: Supporting human-AI teams: transparency, explainability, and situation awareness. Comput. Hum. Behav. **140**, 107574 (2023)

58. Alcorn, M.A., et al.: Strike (with) a pose: neural networks are easily fooled by strange poses of familiar objects. arXiv (2019)

59. Pearl, J., Mackenzie, D.: The Book of Why: The New Science of Cause and Effect, First Trade Paperback Edition ed. Basic Books, New York (2020)

60. Howard, A., Borenstein, J.: The ugly truth about ourselves and our robot creations: the problem of bias and social inequity. Sci. Eng. Ethics **24**, 1521–1536 (2018)

61. Littman, M.L., et al.: Gathering strength, gathering storms: the one hundred year study on artificial intelligence (AI100) 2021 study panel report. arXiv (2022)

62. Chen, J.Y., Procci, K., Boyce, M., Wright, J., Garcia, A., Barnes, M.: Situation Awareness-Based Agent Transparency: Fort (2014)

63. Brandt, S.L., Lachter, J., Battiste, V., Johnson, W.: Pilot situation awareness and its implications for single pilot operations: analysis of a human-in-the-loop study. Procedia Manuf. **3**, 3017–3024 (2015)

64. Endsley, M.R., Farley, T.C., Jones, W.M., Midkiff, A.H., Hansman, R.J.: Situation awareness information requirements for commercial airline pilots

65. Endsley, M.R., Rodgers, M.D.: Situation awareness information requirements for en route air traffic control (406512004-001) (1994)

Assessing the Mediating Role of Safety Communication Between Safety Leadership and Safety Performance of Civil Aviation Pilots

Chen Lin[1]([✉]) [iD], Xie Di[2], Deng Hao[3], Yanqing Wang[4], Hua Sicheng[5], and Li Nan[5]

[1] Flight Technology Branch, Civil Aviation University of China, Tianjin 300300, China
l-chen@cauc.edu.cn
[2] Chongqing Airlines, Chongqing 400000, China
[3] Air China Southwest Branch, Chengdu 610000, China
[4] School of Safety Science and Engineering, Civil Aviation University of China, Tianjin 300300, China
[5] Chaoyang Flight Technology Branch, Civil Aviation University of China, Liaoning 122000, China

Abstract. The study explores the mediating role of safety communication between safety leadership and safety performance among civil aviation pilots. The research is set against the backdrop of the post-pandemic recovery phase of the aviation industry, where flight safety remains a critical concern. 336 valid replies to a survey were obtained, and SEM (structural equation modeling) and PLS-SEM (partial least squares structural equation modeling) were used to evaluate the data. The findings show that safety leadership significantly improves safety performance and safety communication. Furthermore, safety communication mediates the link between safety leadership and safety performance in addition to having a direct impact on safety performance. This study emphasizes how crucial it is to strengthen pilots' communication and leadership abilities in order to raise overall flight safety.

Keywords: Safety Leadership · Safety Communication · Safety Performance · Civil Aviation Pilots · Structural Equation Modeling (SEM)

1 Introduction

The COVID-19 pandemic in 2019 had a profound impact on the civil aviation industry, delivered an unprecedented blow to airlines worldwide, resulted in numerous flight cancellations, a significant decline in passenger numbers, and drastic reductions in staff income. The entire industry faced severe challenges [1]. After the pandemic, the civil aviation sector gradually resumed operations, however, airlines encountered greater operational pressure and safety challenges [2]. The technical skills and proficiency of pilots were affected, while employee psychological stress increased due to new policies and management regulations. These factors made safety management within airlines more complex, highlighting the critical importance of ensuring the safety performance of civil aviation pilots [3].

© The Author(s), under exclusive license to Springer Nature Switzerland AG 2026
D. Harris et al. (Eds.): HCII 2025, LNCS 16334, pp. 74–100, 2026.
https://doi.org/10.1007/978-3-032-12392-3_5

The initial improvement in civil aviation safety performance has been driven by technological advancements that have reduced aircraft system failure [4]. With these advancements and the strengthening of safety regulations, aviation accidents have significantly decreased, making air travel a safer mode of transportation. However, human factors account for 80% of aviation accidents [5], prompting civil aviation to shift its safety focus to pilots. This shift led to the introduction of CRM (Crew Resource Management) training programs and LOFT (Line Oriented Flight Training) to pilots' training. Since the release of Doc 9995, ICAO (International Civil Aviation Organization) has further implemented CBTA (Competency-Based Training and Assessment) methods aimed at enhancing the competency of aviation professionals, thereby ensuring a qualified workforce for a safe and efficient air transportation system [6].

Competency is a dimension of human performance used to reliably predict successful job performance. A pilot's competency encompasses technical and non-technical skills, both of which are crucial for assessing safety performance [7]. Having strong technical skills alone is insufficient for pilots to handle various flight operations [8]. As well as a complete set of non-technical skills such as workload management, situational awareness, decision making, communication, leadership and teamwork, pilots also need to ensure flight safety [9]. In fact, pilots must keep training continuously in order to keep a high level of competency [10], which guarantees high level of safe operations and emergency response effectiveness.

Safety leadership is one of the essential elements in pilot proficiency and has a major influence on pilots' decision making and teamwork [11], which is one element that is responsible for the occupation of pilots being regarded as the highest risk occupation. Lack of effective leadership in historical aviation accidents like the crash of Air France Flight 447, has exhibited the potential that historical critical decision making failures can arise from during critical moments [12]. Like 2015 when the co-pilot of Germanwings Flight 9525, on purpose caused the plane to crash which lead to the death of 150 [13]. Flight safety has been severely affected by these incidents because true safety leadership is being ignored, and there are numerous mental health/cognitive problems in the work force. They emphasize that airlines should better train pilots to make better decisions during crises relying more on teamwork and improving safety leadership amongst other things.

When discussing safety performance, we must not overlook the importance of communication [14]. When safety is well communicated in an organization it enables organizational safety management and poor communication could be a cause for disasters. A misunderstood phrase caused the deadliest aviation accident in history [15], and the crash of American Airlines Flight 965 was caused by confused and ambiguous phrasing in communication [16]. As with many tragic incidents in civil aviation [17], miscommunication and errors, including those in language, point to the importance of safety communication in maintaining aviation safety performance.

While previous research has examined the importance of safety leadership, safety performance, and safety communication in high-risk industries including natural gas, petrochemicals, and construction, [18, 20], but research that assesses the interactions between these three constructs in civil aviation is still lacking. The levels of safety performance of pilots, safety leadership, and safety communication directly influence the overall safety of civil aviation operations, and are particularly important for them, as direct participants and guardians of aviation transport.

The research problem addressed in this study includes mediating the role of safety communication in the relationship of safety leadership to safety performance in civil aviation pilots. We try to show how safety communication is critical for improving the safety performance of pilots by analyzing the impact of safety leadership on safety communication and the role of safety communication in improving safety performance.

Our goal is to improve safety leadership and communication among pilots to improve overall safety performance and decrease the risks posed to aviation from human factors. For continued safety and reliability of civil aviation operations and recovery and sustainable development of the industry, such a participation is essential.

2 Conceptual Framework and Research Hypothesis

2.1 Safety Performance

Safety Performance is results and achievements organizations earned through safety management and accident prevention [21]. It shows how well a company can provide a secure workplace, lower occupational risks, and lower the number of accidents [22].

In the civil aviation sector, safety performance is typically reflected in the quality and quantity of the crew's work across various components of the flight operation system. It involves implementing measures to reduce the risk of flight accidents and create a hazard-free safety environment. Additionally, airlines must comply with infrastructure requirements, regulations, and aviation safety standards [23, 24]. High levels of safety and performance in flight operations can provide companies with a competitive advantage [25]. Moreover, safety performance in civil aviation is crucial for preventing accidents and minimizing casualties and property damage [26].

Performance evaluation is a fundamental task for assessing the implementation of safety management measures, which is particularly crucial in the civil aviation system related to national security [27]. The ICAO requires a safety management system (SMS), which includes safety performance management as a core element [28]. The safety performance management indicators of airlines play an increasingly vital role in enhancing the safety management efficiency of civil aviation service providers [29]. Airline safety performance indicators are assessed through accident/event occurrence indicators, basic indicators, management indicators, and operational indicators. By collecting relevant risk data and establishing risk assessment models, it is possible to predict risk trends, which are also reflected in specific safety performance indicators. This allows for the formulation of targeted control measures to reduce operational risks [29]. A significant proportion of aviation accidents—approximately 80%—are attributed to human factors [30], making human factors a primary focus of safety performance [31]. As the most active participants in flight operations, pilots' performance directly impacts flight safety [32]. The evaluation of pilot performance is based on competency indicators, where competency is considered a key factor in achieving high performance. Technical and non-technical abilities are the main criteria for assessing pilot competency [33]. The professional flight program at Purdue University's SATT (School of Aviation and

Transportation Technology) adopts a competency-based training and assessment approach guided by SATT performance training, identifying six competency assessment indicators: technical skills, communication, leadership, decision-making, teamwork, and resilience [34]. These competency indicators enable the prediction of pilots' performance levels and the enhancement of their performance through training, ultimately ensuring the safety performance of the organization.

2.2 Safety Leadership

In order to ensure workplace safety, safety leadership is crucial [35] and it also has a big impact on improving organizational safety performance [36, 37]. It refers to leadership behaviors that positively influence employees' safety behaviors within the organization [38].

As safety performance becomes widely accepted and the relationship between safety performance and leadership is explored, the leadership being discussed is not specifically referred to as 'safety leadership'. Instead, transformational leadership within leadership styles is more prominently highlighted [39]. The 4 dimensions of transformational leadership positively influence many work-related factors [40]. But according to a meta-analysis, transformational leadership does not directly contribute to workplace safety [41]. Although safety leadership has historically been thought to revolve on transformational leadership, new research contradicts this idea, showing that using a variety of leadership philosophies is more successful in enhancing workplace safety [41, 42]. Safety leadership encompasses not only transformational leadership but also a combination of various leadership styles [43]. A good leader may exhibit characteristics of transformational, transactional, or leader-follower exchange styles, and when they focus on safety, they are regarded as safety leaders [44, 45].

At the same time, the concept of collective leadership further expands the connotation of leadership, moving beyond reliance on a single leader. Collective leadership emphasizes achieving team goals through collaboration and interaction among team members. All members share responsibility, thereby enhancing overall safety performance [46]. The multi-level leadership development emphasized by collective leadership helps teams flexibly respond to emergencies in complex flight environments [47]. The application of collective leadership is becoming increasingly common through crew resource management (CRM) training, where leader roles within teams are no longer singular, resulting in improved adaptability and flexibility of the team [48]. The collective leadership effectively extends individual pilot's leadership, enabling team to better address dynamic challenges during flight [49]. In the complex aviation environment, collective leadership in the cockpit is particularly important, as each member of the flight crew can assume leadership roles in specific situations. Through collective leadership, decision-making authority is more decentralized, and team members collaborate to reduce the occurrence of human errors and thereby enhance overall flight safety [50]. Future research should delve into how collective leadership can enhance safety performance in aviation, particularly through multi-level leadership development mechanisms that optimize team decision-making and communication. Combining collective leadership with safety leadership can better explain how team collaboration improves aviation safety performance [51].

Safety leadership primarily reflects the degree of emphasis and control that leaders place on safety. Leaders should integrate safety as a core value within the organizational culture to create a successful occupational safety team. Safety leadership is responsible for establishing and achieving operational and strategic goals related to safety, providing resources, and continuously emphasizing the importance of safety for both employees and the organization [52]. In civil aviation, leadership can be categorized into two main types: the captain leading the crew and leadership within the airline [53]. The focus for airline executives is on safety management practices, such as dedication to safety management, feedback-based safety communication, safety regulations, safety incentives, and safety training [54]. Commitment to safety reflects leaders' attitudes and the importance they place on safety, which plays a critical role in developing and implementing effective safety programs [55]. By establishing clear safety policies, creating efficient communication mechanisms, and implementing appropriate incentive and training measures, airline leadership can effectively enhance employees' safety behaviors, thereby improving overall safety performance [56]. Among civil aviation pilots, the captain is the primary leader responsible for the crew. Their leadership behavior directly influences and breeds the crew's atmosphere and plays a critical role in enhancing flight safety [57]. A responsible captain fulfills a vital leadership role, using demonstration and management to shape the safety climate among crew members and improve flight safety [58]. As emphasized in crew resource management (CRM), effective leadership is essential for optimizing teamwork and reducing human errors in high-risk environments such as civil aviation [59].

2.3 Safety Communication

One such strategy for addressing employees' risky conduct is safety communication [60]. It encompasses more than just the practice of sharing knowledge and safety information at work. [61], but also the influence on worker behaviors and safety perception [62]. In order to improve safety performance across different industries, safety communication is essential [20]. When organizations view safety communication as a key value, it not only enhances employee morale but also benefits the business [63]. Safety communication plays a critical role in mitigating hazards and strengthening risk management [64]. Effective safety communication can significantly promote organizational safety management, while poor safety communication can potentially lead to disasters [65].

Effective team communication and feedback are crucial for the success of teamwork [66]. Research indicates that informal safety communication significantly impacts safety compliance and participation, highlighting the importance of fostering effective communication and collaboration within teams to enhance safety performance [67]. Communication also plays a vital role in evaluating pilot's performance [68]. Effective communication is essential in teamwork and crew decision-making. Poor communication can lead to severe consequences, including accidents and risks, the Tenerife disaster serves as a stark example, where miscommunication between crew members and pilots resulted in the deadliest aviation accident in history [69]. ICAO has established language proficiency requirements for pilots to mitigate such risks, emphasizing the need for clear and standardized communication [70]. Effective communication ensures flight safety, and high-quality communication provides employees with the necessary information for a safe working environment, thereby safeguarding their safety [71, 72].

Feedback communication helps enhance professionals' experiences and raise safety awareness [73]. The workplace safety climate can also be enhanced by managers and staff communicating on a regular basis [74]. According to research, organizational safety performance is greatly impacted by safety communication combined with feedback [75, 76]. Feedback communication plays a positive role in strengthening internal team collaboration among crew members, preventing errors arising from leadership interference with crew coordination, and providing recommendations for improvement to airline management [77].

2.4 The Relationship Between the Variables

Safety leadership plays a crucial role in enhancing safety performance. In the shipping industry, effective captain safety leadership includes building strong interpersonal relationships, promoting teamwork, conducting safety training and boosting crew morale [78], all of which significantly improve safety performance. The complexity and high-risk nature of the civil aviation industry also demand high standards for effective safety leadership. Safety leadership not only directly influences safety management behaviors but also enhances overall safety performance in civil aviation by shaping pilots' safety culture, improving morale and encouraging safe behaviors. Effective safety leadership can influence safety culture, thereby enhancing safety performance [79]. The captain's active control and leadership within the crew team ensure flight safety [80]. The captain's leadership behaviors directly affect the crew's atmosphere and coordination abilities, they can influence safety culture and performance through Safety Based Dynamic Uncertainty Reduction (SDUR) [56]. Additionally, captains effectively lead by encouraging team members to adopt safe behaviors and attitudes, which lowers the risk of mishaps and accidents [81], which further ensures flight safety.

We put out the following hypothesis in light of the analysis above:

H1: Safety leadership has a positive impact on the safety performance of civil aviation pilots.

Leaders' communication skill can effectively solve ambiguities in management situations [82]. Situational awareness issues pose potential dangers in the aviation industry, which influence decision-making and safety outcomes. Effective communication by leaders is particularly critical in high-risk environments such as aviation, where it can enhance safety commitments and reduce the likelihood of accidents. Leaders' effective safety communication increases employees' knowledge and awareness of safety practices, fostering a safer work environment [83]. In the complex and dynamic flight operations environment of the cockpit, coordination and effective communication among pilots become even more crucial [84]. Safety leadership can enhance pilots' safety awareness and operational standards through safety communication, enabling pilots to stay informed about the latest safety information and preventive measures, thus promoting greater caution and compliance in actual operations.

We put out the following hypothesis in light of the analysis above:

H2: Safety leadership has a positive impact on safety communication.

To improve safety performance in a variety of businesses, safety communication is essential [20, 67]. Within airlines, effective safety communication conveys company policies and operational standards, ensuring the compliance and safety of flight operations. Communication encompasses not only interactions between pilots and crew members but also feedback and information transfer between managers and employees [85]. By establishing efficient communication mechanisms, airlines can promptly identify and address potential safety hazards, implement corresponding control measures to reduce operational risks. Pilots' safety performance is also influenced by safety communication, with 70% to 80% of safety incidents attributed to communication issues [86]. In the context of international radio telephony communication, pilots can address language and cultural barriers through training, ultimately improve the safety performance of civil aviation operations [87].

We put out the following hypothesis in light of the analysis above:

H3: Safety communication has a positive impact on the safety performance of civil aviation pilots.

Safety communication acts as a bridge between safety leadership and safety performance [83], ensuring that team members effectively understand and adhere to the safety protocols and guidelines established by leaders. When leaders communicate safety measures clearly and consistently, it fosters a safety culture [88], which makes employees feel more responsible and committed to following safety practices, thereby enhancing overall safety performance. ICAO emphasizes the importance of safety risk management within airlines [89], which necessitates strict regulations in policy formulation, internal controls and standards setting by civil aviation authorities and airlines. To ensure these safety standards are upheld, leadership must convey policies and minimum requirements through effective safety communication and create a positive atmosphere [90]. Many airlines develop this atmosphere into their safety culture. Both safety climate and safety culture are significant factors to influence safety performance [22].

As the leader in the cockpit, the captain directs crew decision-making and impacts flight safety. The ICAO highlights the crew resource management (CRM) to embody this characteristic, successfully reduce human errors by promoting effective communication and teamwork among crew members [91]. With advancements in aircraft automation, CRM has evolved from cockpit resource management to a comprehensive training system that includes all flight operations team members, such as pilots, maintenance personnel, dispatchers, and air traffic controllers [92]. The captain's leadership behavior affects not only cockpit management attitudes but also individual performance under pressure, as well as communication and teamwork effectiveness. Effective leadership behaviors can manage complexity and uncertainty, thereby ensuring flight safety and impacting safety performance [93].

The association between safety leadership and safety performance is somewhat mediated by safety communication, according to the analysis above. Consequently, we put up the following theory:

H4: Safety communication moderates the relationship between safety leadership and safety performance.

The purpose of this study is to elucidate the connections between civil aviation pilots' safety leadership, safety communication, and high safety performance. Safety leadership will be regarded as an independent variable in this study since it is thought to have an impact on safety performance (the dependent variable). Safety communication will act as a mediator in the relationship between safety leadership and safety performance. Figure 1 shows how the independent and dependent variables relate to one another:

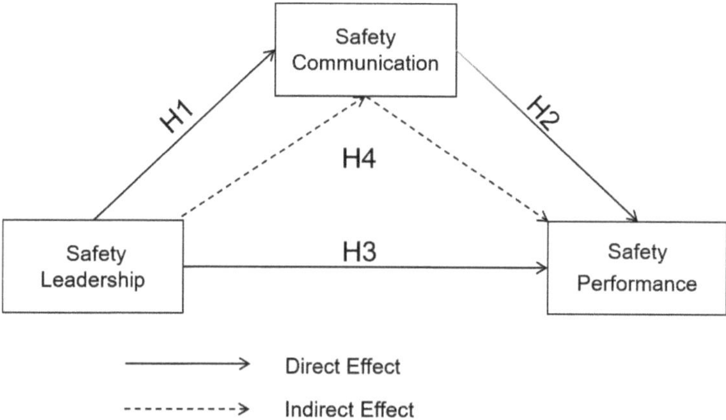

Fig. 1. Hypothesis Model of Relationships.

3 Methodology

To obtain relevant research data, this study collected data through an online questionnaire targeting civil aviation pilots in China. The questionnaire utilized a Likert 5-point scale, with questions designed around the three core elements: safety leadership, safety communication and safety performance. Data analysis was conducted using software SPSS 27.0 and AMOS 24.0 for structural equation modeling (CB-SEM), with further validation of the model's predictive capability and path relationships performed through PLS-SEM.

Ultimately, a total of 347 questionnaires were distributed via WJX (https://www.wjx.cn/), resulting in 336 valid responses, yielding an effective response rate of 96.82%. The sample comprised 31 flight inspectors, 47 flight instructors, 81 captains, 134 co-pilots and 43 flight trainees.

3.1 Questionnaire Instructions

This study employed a Likert 5-point scale consisting of 14 items for the survey. This scale has five possible scores: 1 for "strongly disagree," 2 for "disagree," 3 for "neutral," 4 for "agree," and 5 for "strongly agree". The three primary variables addressed in the questionnaire are safety performance, safety communication, and safety leadership. The dimensional classifications and sources for these key elements are grounded in a review of existing literature, with all corresponding questionnaire items have been previously utilized or theoretically supported in the literature.

Safety performance includes four dimensions. The first dimension is procedural compliance, which assesses respondents' ability to adhere to regulations and identify and execute operational procedures [4, 11, 35, 94–97]. The second dimension is safety training, focusing on respondents' participation in flight safety-related training and their application of the knowledge gained [98–101]. The third dimension is safety behavior, primarily examining respondents' capability to ensure the highest level of safety during flights [95, 97, 102]. Lastly, risk assessment evaluates respondents' ability to analyze issues from a risk perspective and to mitigate critical risks [4, 94, 97, 103].

Safety communication encompasses four dimensions as well. Effective communication aims to evaluate respondents' ability to convey information accurately and clearly [4, 94, 104]. Feedback communication emphasizes respondents' capacity to provide timely feedback on safety issues encountered during flights [35, 105]. The technical terminology dimension examines respondents' proficiency in using standard radio communication terms and in accurately interpreting data communication information [4, 94, 106]. Open communication assesses the internal discussion atmosphere within the team and the respondents' ability to offer constructive suggestions and effective solutions when necessary [96, 104, 107, 108].

Safety leadership consists of six dimensions. Leadership ability evaluates respondents' capacity to take charge during critical moments and to devise plans that engage team members [4, 94, 109, 110]. Team management focuses on respondents' ability to resolve conflicts and to respect different opinions [4, 94, 110]. Decision-making assesses respondents' capability to make timely decisions and implement control measures in response to unexpected issues [4, 94, 96, 110]. Responsibility pertains to respondents' willingness to accept accountability for decisions and actions [35, 96, 97]. Foresight examines respondents weather consider potential changes and emergencies when planning flight operations [110–112]. Finally, lifelong learning evaluates respondents' commitment to actively acquiring knowledge of new regulations and flight technical requirements [101, 113–115].

3.2 Reliability and KMO Test

By using software SPSS 27.0, the reliability of each scale was assessed, alongside an evaluation of the scales' suitability through the significance levels of the KMO and Bartlett's test of sphericity. The results for all items on the scales were analyzed using SPSS 27.0, as presented in Table 1. The Cronbach's α value for this study was 0.879, which exceeds the threshold of 0.8 ($\alpha > 0.8$), indicating good reliability. This suggests that the scales used in this research possess adequate reliability for further investigation. The data are appropriate for factor analysis, as shown by the KMO value of 0.89 and the significance level of $p < 0.001$ obtained from Bartlett's test of sphericity.

Table 1. Reliability and Bartlett spherical test results

Statistical Item	Result
Cronbach's Alpha	0.879
Number of Items	14
KMO Sampling Adequacy Measure	0.896
Bartlett's Sphericity Test	Approx. Chi-Square: 2658.190
	Degrees of Freedom: 91
	Significance: 0.000

3.3 Exploratory Factor

To explore the underlying factor structure of the variables in the questionnaire, this study employed Exploratory Factor Analysis (EFA) by using SPSS 27.0. The primary aim of EFA is to identify potential factors within the data, simplify the multivariate data structure, and provide a theoretical foundation for subsequent Confirmatory Factor Analysis (CFA). Given that safety performance, safety communication and safety leadership encompass multiple measurement items, EFA can assist in determining how these items are associated with specific factors.

In order to quantify each variable clearly, we assigned specific item numbers to the variables and dimensions in the questionnaire for ease of subsequent analysis. Safety performance is denoted as SP, with four measurement items numbered from SP1 to SP4, representing procedural compliance (SP1), safety training (SP2), safety behavior (SP3), and risk assessment (SP4). Safety communication is designated as SC, with four measurement items numbered from SC1 to SC4, corresponding to effective communication (SC1), feedback communication (SC2), standard terminology (SC3), and open communication (SC4). Safety leadership is labeled SL, with six measurement items numbered from SL1 to SL6, reflecting leadership ability (SL1), team management (SL2), decision-making (SL3), responsibility (SL4), foresight (SL5), and lifelong learning (SL6).

The study employed principal component analysis (PCA) as the method for factor extraction, using varimax orthogonal rotation to simplify the factor structure and enhance interpretability. We applied the criterion of eigenvalues greater than 1 to determine the number of factors to extract.

The results of the exploratory factor analysis are presented in revealing the extraction of three main factors corresponding to safety performance (SP), safety communication (SC), and safety leadership (SL), which account for 71.4% of the total variance together. The loading values for each factor are all above 0.60, indicating a strong correlation between the measurement items and their corresponding factors, while the three factors provide an ideal explanation of the original data.

Based on the rotated component matrix in Table 3, we can determine the factor assignments for each item. This aligns with the structure of the questionnaire used in this study. Overall, the safety performance factor includes four measurement items: procedural compliance, safety training, safety behavior, and risk assessment. The safety

Table 2. Total Variance Explained.

Components	Initial Eigenvalues			Extraction Sums of Squared Loadings			Rotation Sums of Squared Loadings		
	Total	variance percentage	accumulate%	Total	variance percentage	accumulate%	Total	variance percentage	accumulate%
1	5.497	39.265	39.265	5.497	39.265	39.265	4.121	29.434	29.434
2	2.563	18.305	57.569	2.563	18.305	57.569	3.014	21.526	50.96
3	1.945	13.896	71.466	1.945	13.896	71.466	2.871	20.506	71.466
4	0.516	3.686	75.152						
5	0.438	3.126	78.278						
6	0.413	2.949	81.227						
7	0.404	2.887	84.114						
8	0.368	2.628	86.742						
9	0.361	2.579	89.322						
10	0.344	2.455	91.776						
11	0.335	2.393	94.169						
12	0.303	2.167	96.336						
13	0.275	1.967	98.303						
14	0.238	1.697	100						

Extraction Method: Principal Component Analysis.

communication factor comprises four measurement items: effective communication, feedback communication, standard terminology, and open communication. The safety leadership factor includes six measurement items: leadership ability, team management, decision-making, responsibility, foresight, and lifelong learning.

3.4 Confirmatory Factor Analysis

Structural Validity. After assessing the reliability and conducting exploratory factor analysis on each scale, we found that it is suitable for confirmatory factor analysis to subsequent evaluate validity. By using AMOS 24.0, a structural equation model was first constructed based on the three factors extracted from the principal component analysis to examine the structural validity of the variables in the hypothesis model. The specific results are illustrated in Fig. 2.

Table 3. Rotated Component Matrix.

Rotated Component Matrix[a]			
Component			
	1	2	3
SP1			.824
SP2			.838
SP3			.794
SP4			.825
SC1		.843	
SC2		.854	
SC3		.838	
SC4		.856	
SL1	.820		
SL2	.826		
SL3	.819		
SL4	.808		
SL5	.792		
SL6	.811		

Extraction method: Principal Component Analysis.

Rotation method: Varimax with Kaiser normalization.

a. The rotation converged after 5 iterations.

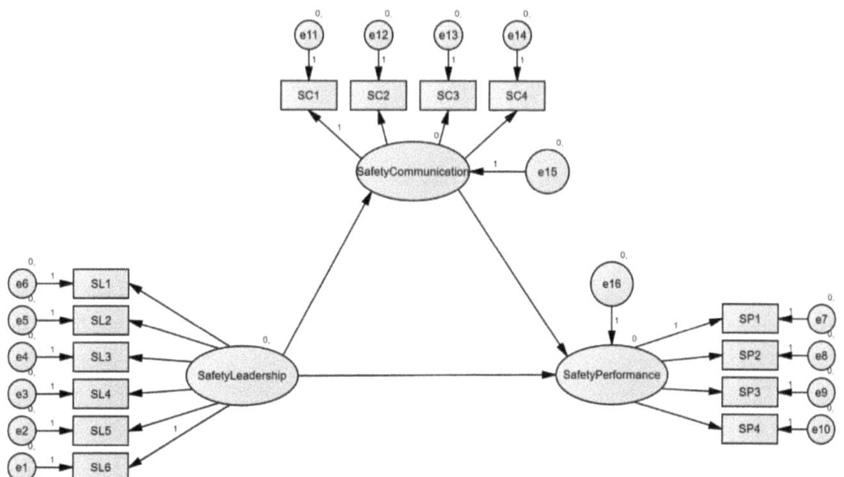

Fig. 2. Structural Equation Model (SEM).

To assess how well the measurement model fits the three elements of safety performance, safety communication, and safety leadership, we employ confirmatory factor analysis (CFA). Table 4 presents the results, which show that all of the model's fit indices are satisfactory: The RMSEA value is 0.014, under 0.05, showing a tiny error and great fit; the SRMR value is 0.031, also below 0.05, indicating close proximity between predicted values and actual data; and the χ^2/DF value is 1.069, below 3, indicating a strong model fit. The NFI is 0.971 and the RFI is 0.964, both exceeding 0.9, demonstrating a good fit between the model and the data. Additionally, the values for IFI, TLI, AGFI, CFI, and GFI are 0.998, 0.954, 0.998, 0.998 and 0.968 respectively, all near 1, indicating a high degree of match between the model and the data. The PRATIO, PNFI, and PCFI values are 0.813, 0.789 and 0.812, all above 0.5, further confirming the model's simplicity and good fit. The results of the confirmatory factor analysis indicate that the model meets fit and adequacy criteria, demonstrating satisfactory structural validity.

Table 4. AMOS Confirmatory Factor Analysis Results.

Fit Indices	Criteria	Actual Value
χ^2/DF	<3	1.069
RMSEA	<0.05	0.014
SRMR	<0.05	0.031
NFI	>0.9	0.971
RFI	>0.9	0.964
IFI	>0.9	0.998
AGFI	>0.9	0.954
TLI	>0.9	0.998
CFI	>0.9	0.998
GFI	>0.9	0.968
PRATIO	>0.5	0.813
PNFI	>0.5	0.789
PCFI	>0.5	0.812

Note: AGFI = adjusted goodness of fit index; CFI = comparative fit index; GFI = goodness of fit index; IFI = incremental fit index; NFI = standardized fit index; PCFI = contracted comparison index; PGFI = thrifty good index; PNFI = contracted norm fit index; RFI = relative fit index; SRMR = standardized root mean square residual; RMSEA = root of approximation; TLI = Tucker Lewis index [96].

Convergent Validity. The measurement model was validated in this study using AMOS 24.0 to guarantee that the measurement indicators for each construct have good convergent validity. Calculating the AVE (Average Variance Extracted), SFL (Standardized Factor Loadings), and CR (Composite Reliability) allowed for the evaluation of convergent validity. The analysis's findings are shown in Table 5.

The factor loadings of the items related to safety leadership, safety communication and safety performance are all greater than 0.7, indicating that each item is representative

Table 5. The aggregation validity table.

Path Coefficients			Estimate	AVE	CR
SL6	<---	SL	0.778	0.6234	0.9085
SL5	<---	SL	0.773		
SL4	<---	SL	0.787		
SL3	<---	SL	0.795		
SL2	<---	SL	0.804		
SL1	<---	SL	0.8		
SC1	<---	SC	0.804	0.6653	0.8881
SC2	<---	SC	0.803		
SC3	<---	SC	0.782		
SC4	<---	SC	0.871		
SP1	<---	SP	0.825	0.6201	0.8668
SP2	<---	SP	0.836		
SP3	<---	SP	0.768		
SP4	<---	SP	0.715		

of its respective variable. Additionally, the AVE for all variables exceeds 0.5, and the CR is above 0.8, confirming that the convergent validity is acceptable.

3.5 Discriminant Validity

By comparing the square root of the AVE with the correlations between the latent variables, the study used the Fornell-Larcker criterion to evaluate the discriminant validity of the model. Each latent variable's square root of the AVE must be higher than its correlations with other latent variables in order for it to meet the discriminant validity criterion. Table 6 displays the findings of the discriminant validity test.

Table 6. Results of the discriminatory validity tests.

	SC	SP	SL
SC	0.6653		
SP	0.291***	0.6201	
SL	0.301***	0.302***	0.6234
AVE Square Root	0.815659243	0.787464285	0.789556838

Note: N = 366 *** p < 0.01, with the diagonal representing the Average Variance Extracted (AVE).

The absolute correlation coefficients for safety performance, safety communication, and safety leadership are all less than 0.5 and smaller than the respective square roots of the AVE, indicating strong relationships between them ($p < 0.01$). This suggests that the discriminant validity of the scale data is satisfactory since it shows a certain degree of correlation between the various parameters while retaining a sufficient degree of discriminability.

3.6 PLS-SEM Testing of Measurement Model and ValidityPLS-SEM

This study used AMOS 24.0 and PLS-SEM (Partial Least Squares Structural Equation Modeling) in addition to the conventional CB-SEM (covariance-based Structural Equation Modeling) analysis to further improve the model's predictive power and robustness. PLS-SEM provides a more exploratory and predictive perspective for the model, further supporting the feasibility of the hypothesized model in this research. The data collected were analyzed using Smart-PLS 4.0 software for PLS-SEM. Figure 3 and Table 7 and Table 8 present the findings of the measurement model analysis, which show that the structural indicators attained internal consistency, reliability, convergent validity, and discriminant validity.

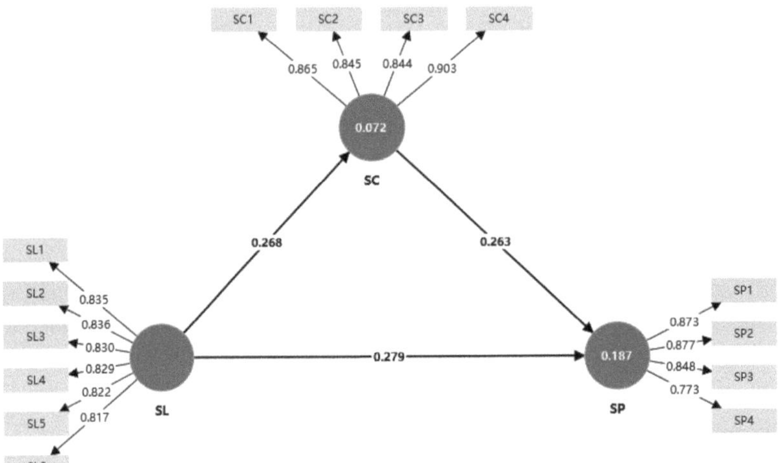

Fig. 3. PLS-SEM Structural Model Analysis.

As can be seen from Fig. 3, all standardized factor loadings for the measurement items (such as SL1, SL2, SC1, SC2, etc.) exceed 0.7, indicating that these items have strong explanatory power for their respective latent variables (safety leadership, safety communication, and safety performance). For instance, the loadings for the safety leadership items (SL1-SL6) are all above 0.8, demonstrating that these items effectively reflect the constructs of safety leadership, while the measurement items for safety performance and safety communication also perform well.

Table 7. Results of Internal Consistency Reliability

	Cronbach's alpha	Average Variance Extracted (AVE)	Composite Reliability
SP	0.866	0.712	0.908
SL	0.908	0.686	0.929
SC	0.888	0.748	0.922

From Table 7, it can be observed that the Cronbach's Alpha values for each dimension are all greater than 0.7, indicating high internal consistency of the constructs. The Average Variance Extracted (AVE) values are all above 0.5, meeting the requirements for convergent validity. Additionally, the composite reliability values exceed 0.7, demonstrating that the measurements for each construct have high reliability.

Table 8. Results of Convergent Validity

Construct, Sub-Construct, and Indicator	Loading	Average Variance Extracted (AVE)	Composite Reliability
SC1	0.865	0.748	0.908
SC2	0.845		
SC3	0.844		
SC4	0.903		
SL1	0.835	0.686	0.929
SL2	0.836		
SL3	0.83		
SL4	0.829		
SL5	0.822		
SL6	0.817		
SP1	0.873	0.712	0.922
SP2	0.877		
SP3	0.848		
SP4	0.773		

From the results in Table 8, it can be observed that the loading values for each construct are all greater than 0.7, indicating a strong correlation between the measurement items and their respective latent variables. This suggests that the model demonstrates good convergent validity.

3.7 Common Method Bias Test

To lessen procedural common technique bias, pilots in this study filled out an anonymous online questionnaire. Table 2 displays the results of the Harman's single-factor test. It shows that three factors with initial eigenvalues greater than one were retrieved by the unrotated exploratory factor analysis. There appears to be no significant common technique bias in the research findings, as indicated by the maximum factor variance explained of 39.265%, which is less than 40%.

Table 9. Main Effects Testing Results

Hypothesis	Path	Estimate	S.E	C.R	P Value	Result
H1	SP <--- SL	0.315	0.064	4.943	***(p < 0.001)	H1 Supported
H2	SC <--- SL	0.307	0.062	4.936	***(p < 0.001)	H2 Supported
H3	SP <--- SC	0.298	0.063	4.751	***(p < 0.001)	H3 Supported

The results in Table 9 indicate that both safety leadership and safety communication exhibit significant positive effects on safety performance. Specifically, the test of Hypothesis 1 (H1) shows that SL positively influences SP, with a standardized path coefficient of 0.315 (p < 0.001), suggesting a strong and statistically significant relationship. Similarly, the results for Hypothesis 2 (H2) demonstrate that SL significantly enhances SC, with a path coefficient of 0.307 (p < 0.001). Finally, Hypothesis 3 (H3) confirms that SC has a positive impact on SP, with a standardized path coefficient of 0.298 (p < 0.001). These findings highlight the critical role that safety leadership and effective communication play in improving overall aviation safety performance. Strengthening pilots' leadership and communication skills will be pivotal in ensuring sustained operational safety.

4 Hypothesis Testing

4.1 Main Effects Testing

Using AMOS 24.0, the study looks at the safety leadership's primary effects on safety performance, the safety communication's effects on safety performance, and the safety communication's mediating effect on safety performance. The structural model is mainly used to evaluate the degree of agreement between the model's empirical findings and theoretical model, particularly determining if the suggested research hypotheses are substantiated by the empirical data. A higher standardized route coefficient in the structural equation model denotes a more robust causal link. Table 9 displays the outcomes of the hypothesis testing.

The results in Table 9 indicate that both safety leadership and safety communication exhibit significant positive effects on safety performance. Specifically, the test of Hypothesis 1 (H1) shows that SL positively influences SP, with a standardized path coefficient of 0.315 (p < 0.001), suggesting a strong and statistically significant relationship.

Similarly, the results for Hypothesis 2 (H2) demonstrate that SL significantly enhances SC, with a path coefficient of 0.307 (p < 0.001). Finally, Hypothesis 3 (H3) confirms that SC has a positive impact on SP, with a standardized path coefficient of 0.298 (p < 0.001). These findings highlight the critical role that safety leadership and effective communication play in improving overall aviation safety performance. Strengthening pilots' leadership and communication skills will be pivotal in ensuring sustained operational safety.

4.2 Mediating Effect Testing

To verify the mediating role of safety communication between safety leadership and safety performance, this study utilized the mediation analysis function in AMOS 24.0. The mediation effect was tested by using the Bootstrap sampling method, with 5,000 resamples taken to estimate the indirect effects and calculate their confidence intervals. Additionally, the Bias-corrected 95% confidence interval was used to assess the significance of the mediation effect.

The mediation effect test results confirmed Hypothesis H4: safety communication serves as a mediator between safety leadership and aviation safety performance, as detailed in Table 10.

Table 10. Results of the Mediation Effect Test.

Parameter	Estimate	Lower	Upper	P	Effect Percentage
Direct Effect	0.302	0.171	0.443	0.001	77.43%
Indirect Effect	0.088	0.042	0.152	0.001	22.57%
Total Effect	0.39	0.254	0.512	0.001	

Table 10 shows that safety communication has a mediating effect of 0.088, or 22.57% of the total effect, between safety leadership and aviation safety performance. The confidence interval excludes 0. This implies that the relationship between safety leadership and safety performance is mediated by safety communication.

PLS-SEM was used to further evaluate the model's hypotheses and the dependability of the findings, building on the hypotheses examined by AMOS. 5,000 resamples were used in a bootstrap process to produce judgments, t-values, standard errors, and beta values. Table 11 displays the outcomes of the hypothesis testing.

The standard deviation for SC → SP is 0.055, with a T value of 4.826 and a P value of 0, indicating that the impact of safety communication on safety performance is significant. For SL → SC, the standard deviation is 0.057, the T value is 4.675, and the P value is 0, also demonstrating a significant effect of safety leadership on safety communication. In the SL → SP path, the standard deviation is 0.057, with a T value of 4.919 and a P value of 0, showing a significant positive effect of safety leadership on safety performance. Last but not least, the SL → SC → SP path's mediation effect has a standard deviation of 0.021, a T statistic of 3.369, and a P value of 0.001, demonstrating the validity of hypothesis H4 and verifying its significance.

Table 11. Results of Structural Model Hypothesis Testing.

Hypothesis	H1	H2	H3	H4
Path	SL -> SC	SL -> SP	SC -> SP	SL -> SC -> SP
Original Sample (O)	0.268	0.279	0.263	0.071
Mean Sample (M)	0.27	0.282	0.264	0.071
Standard Deviation (STDEV)	0.057	0.057	0.055	0.021
Statistic (IO/STDEVI)	4.675	4.919	4.826	3.369
P-value	0	0	0	0.001
Result	Supported	Supported	Supported	Supported

5 Discussion

Flight safety remains a focus for the rapidly recovering global civil aviation industry and its increasingly complex operational environment. It is important to enhance civil aviation pilot's leadership, communication and operational performance so as to improve flight safety. Using a structural equation model (SEM) to validate the hypotheses, this study explores the relationships among safety leadership, safety communication and safety performance in civil aviation pilots. The mediating effect of safety communication between safety leadership (SL) and safety performance (SP) is analyzed.

The study results support Hypothesis H1 that safety leadership has a positive effect on safety communication. This implies positive correlation between the communication efficiency of the other crewmembers and operational personnel to the influence of the key leaders in the civil aviation industry, i.e., pilots. Specifically, the importance lies in the ability of a pilot to make correct decision making or leadership skills needed in crisis management and task coordination. Pilots can relay task requirements, regulations, and emergency procedures in straightforward and timely ways, thereby maintaining safety in flight. Therefore, the safety leadership of a pilot contributes greatly to improving the team's communication potential. This highlights the importance of pilot involvement in team work and communication.

Hypothesis H2 has also been validated, that is, safety leadership is positively associated with safety performance. The decision of a pilot does not only impact the completion of daily flight task execution but also impacts response to emergency measures. This shows that flight operation safety management also lies in good pilot leadership above controlling the flight operations. The result is consistent with previous research on the effect of leadership on high risk industries [18–20], and highlights the need to not only maintain, but enhance pilots' leadership behaviours to ensure flight safety and optimise pilot performance.

Hypothesis H3 supports that safety communication has a major positive effect in safety performance. It is essential to communicate to other personnel in aviation for flight safety. Timely communication of critical information leads to reduction of operational error and unnecessary risks. Regular feedback allows pilots to immediately see where they are going wrong and correct their mistakes, thereby reducing accident rates. The data in this study highlights the importance of good communication on improving pilots' safety performance.

The data support Hypothesis H4, however, that safety communication is used as a mediating variable between safety leadership and safety performance. Results of analysis of path coefficients (e.g., SC <--- SL and SP <--- SC) illustrate a great contribution of safety communication to this mediation pathway. This implies that leaders' performance in improving communication quality enhances safety performance of pilots. This mediating effect underscores the important function of safety communication in verifying or enhancing flight safety and the role of communication as a bridge in high risk worksite communication. Theoretical contribution of this study extends the research on flight safety management, emphasizing the interplay between safety leadership, safety communication, and safety performance. Not only, it empirically validates the impact of leadership on the safety performance but also finds the mediating role of communication, presenting a new theoretical model. This offers fresh insights for future research and a theoretical basis for future work to optimise pilots' performance as well as optimising pilots' leadership and communication training.

The practical implications of this research for flight safety management are substantial. First, the findings emphasize the need for improved training, specifically for pilots, from captains to develop their leadership and communication skills. The leadership communication training of airlines should be strengthened to the extent that every team member is capable of delivering and receiving the right critical safety information. Secondly, this study provides insights for airlines to enhance their safety management system by improving leadership and communication management, which will facilitate a more positive safety culture and consequently minimizes the risks of errors by human players and increase pilots' performance.

6 Conclusion

Structural equation modeling (SEM) is used to study the interrelationship between safety leadership, safety communication and safety performance. The importance of addressing previous research's limitations that have exclusively focused on the impact of individual factors on safety outcomes is confirmed via the finding of the mediating role of safety communication. This research deepens the understanding of the pathways to enhancing safety performance, highlighting the significance of safety communication in the performance of civil aviation pilots and enriching the literature on safety communication in the aviation sector. These findings provide valuable insights for future research.

For airlines, the study emphasizes the importance of strengthening safety leadership and communication to enhance overall safety performance. Particularly in crisis situations, a pilot's leadership and decision-making can significantly improve execution and operational safety through effective communication. Therefore, airlines should enhance leadership training for pilots, especially in areas related to safety communication, to reduce accident risks attributed to human factors. Additionally, ensuring smooth communication channels and transparent information exchange among pilots and crew members contributes to pilots' performance and overall flight safety positively.

7 Limitations

The study has certain limitations. First, the representation of the sample is constrained, as the data is concentrated in a specific country or region, which may not accurately reflect the safety performance of pilots in other cultural contexts. Factors such as civil aviation regulations and the management culture of airlines could influence the expressions of safety leadership and communication. Future research could compare across different cultural and regulatory backgrounds to further validate the applicability and universality of the findings. Secondly, the study utilized a cross-sectional design, collecting data at a single point in time, which limits the ability to observe the long-term effects of safety leadership and communication on pilot safety performance. In future research, it could adopt a longitudinal design, tracking changes in pilot performance across different stages through multiple measurements, thereby gaining deeper insights into the dynamic relationships among these three constructs.

Additionally, this study relied solely on survey data for analysis. Future research might incorporate more actual flight records and accident data for validation.

Acknowledgements. My profound appreciation goes out to each and every pilot who took part in this poll; their enthusiastic participation was crucial to the accomplishment of this study. The funding initiative, which supplied the necessary resources for this investigation, has my sincere gratitude as well. We are very grateful to Mr. Wang Shuaiwei of China Eastern Airlines for his thorough proofreading and insightful comments, which improved the overall caliber of this work.

Declaration of competing interest. The authors declare no known competing financial interests or personal relationships.

Data Availability Statement. The dataset generated and analyzed during this study originates from a questionnaire survey of pilots. Due to privacy concerns, these data are not publicly available but can be obtained from the corresponding author upon reasonable request.

Ethics Statement. The questionnaire survey in this study provided participants with detailed explanations of the research purpose, research process, and potential risks. The study strictly adhered to the Declaration of Helsinki and relevant laws and regulations. During the survey, participants' personal information security was ensured through anonymous submissions, and they were explicitly informed that the collected data would be kept confidential and deleted upon the survey's completion. Additionally, all participants voluntarily clicked on the questionnaire link to participate in the survey. The authors ensured that the questionnaire collection process and data processing complied with relevant legal requirements. Therefore, this study did not require ethics committee approval.

References

1. Iyengar, M.S., Venkatesh, V.R.: Consequences of COVID-19 on aviation industry: a menace to global airlines. Salud Cienc. Tecnol. Ser. Conf. **3**, 687 (2024)
2. Dube, K.: Emerging from the COVID-19 pandemic: aviation recovery, challenges and opportunities. Aerospace **10**(1), 19 (2022). https://www.mdpi.com/2226-4310/10/1/19

3. Basimakopoulou, M., Theologou, K., Tzavaras, P.: Civil aviation approach to safety risk management: a new perspective on a mature process. Int. J. Appl. Res. Manag. Econ. **5**(4), 14–28 (2022). https://dpublication.com/journal/IJARME/article/view/944. Accessed 07 Mar 2023

4. IATA: Competency-Based Training and Assessment (CBTA) Expansion within the Aviation System (White Paper). https://www.iata.org/contentassets/c0f61fc821dc4f62bb6441d7abe db076/cbta-expansion-within-the-aviation-system.pdf. Accessed 15 Mar 2024

5. Stepkin, V.S.: Analysis of the reasons of aviation accidents in educational institutions of civil aviation. Chronos **7**(11(73)), 119–122 (2022)

6. ICAO: Manual of Evidence-Based Training. International Civil Aviation Organization, Montreal (2013)

7. Zhang, Y., Zhao, Y., Liang, A., Xu, H.: Core competency evaluation of pilot based on analytic hierarchy process. J. Mol. Med. **38**, 110–114 (2022). https://www.researchgate.net/ publication/366480192_Core_Competency_Evaluation_of_Pilot_Based_on_Analytic_H ierarchy_Process. Accessed 19 Oct 2024

8. Dinçer, M.S.: Pilots' knowledge-based decision-making process in flight operations in civil aviation. Bilgi Yönetimi (2023). https://www.semanticscholar.org/paper/Pilots%E2%80% 99-Knowledge-Based-Decision-Making-Process-in-Di%CC%87n%C3%A7er/9086f27f8 5a52c56fed31dd305e75bfa0c26e730. Accessed 19 Oct 2024

9. Carroll, M.: Decision making in aviation. In: Elsevier eBooks, pp. 563–588 (2023)

10. Mavin, T.J.: Models for and practice of continuous professional development for airline pilots: what we can learn from one regional airline. In: Professional and Practice-Based Learning, pp. 169–188 (2016)

11. Fernández-Muñiz, B., Montes-Peón, J.M., Vázquez-Ordás, C.J.: Safety leadership, risk management and safety performance in Spanish firms. Saf. Sci. **70**, 295–307 (2014)

12. Salmon, P.M., Walker, G.H., Stanton, N.A.: Pilot error versus sociotechnical systems failure: a distributed situation awareness analysis of air France 447. Theor. Issues Ergon. Sci. **17**(1), 64–79 (2015)

13. Pasha, T., Stokes, P.R.A.: Reflecting on the Germanwings disaster: a systematic review of depression and suicide in commercial airline pilots. Front. Psychiatry **9**, 86 (2018)

14. Slade, D., et al.: The role of communication in safe and effective health care. In: Slade, D., et al. (eds.) Communicating in Hospital Emergency Departments, pp. 1–23. Springer, Heidelberg (2015). https://doi.org/10.1007/978-3-662-46021-4_1. Accessed 02 Nov 2019

15. Crowch, C.T.: Making the healthcare system truly "error tolerant." Clin. Risk **14**(4), 127–129 (2008)

16. Strother, J.B.: Communication failures lead to airline disasters. J. Bus. Commun. **7**, 29–34 (2003)

17. Kaya, M., Ateş, S.S.: The share of communication errors in aircraft accidents and artificial intelligences that can be developed based on communication in aviation. Int. J. Entrep. Manag. Inq. **7**(12), 82–95 (2023). https://dergipark.org.tr/en/pub/ijemi/issue/79373/ 1143651. Accessed 07 Nov 2023

18. Indrayana, D.V., et al.: Safety leadership and performance in Indonesia's construction sector: the role of project owners' maturity. Int. J. Saf. Secur. Eng. **13**(4), 635–646 (2023)

19. Zara, J., Nordin, S.M., Isha, A.N.: Influence of communication determinants on safety commitment in a high-risk workplace: a systematic literature review of four communication dimensions. Front. Public Health **11**, 1225995 (2023). https://www.ncbi.nlm.nih.gov/pmc/ articles/PMC10442955/

20. Naji, G.M.A., et al.: Assessing the mediating role of safety communication between safety culture and employees safety performance. Front. Public Health **10** (2022)

21. Sandora, R., Kurniasih, D., Putri, G.A.: Influence of safety management practices on safety performance with safety knowledge as intervening variable in safety representative. Tibuana **6**(1), 38–43 (2023)

22. Abdul Rahim, N., et al.: Improving safety performance by influence safety management practices and safety culture: a conceptual framework. Int. J. Acad. Res. Bus. Soc. Sci. **13**(10) (2023). https://hrmars.com/papers_submitted/19064/improving-safety-performance-by-influence-safety-management-practices-and-safety-culture-a-conceptual-framework.pdf. Accessed 14 Aug 2024
23. Susanto, Y., et al.: The effect of task complexity, independence and competence on the quality of audit results with auditor integrity as a moderating variable. Int. J. Innov. Creat. Change **12** (2020). https://ijicc.net/images/vol12/iss12/121268_Susanto_2020_E_R.pdf. Accessed 19 Oct 2024
24. Remawi, H., Bates, P., Dix, I.: The relationship between the implementation of a safety management system and the attitudes of employees towards unsafe acts in aviation. Saf. Sci. **49**(5), 625–632 (2011)
25. Widyanty, W., et al.: Human resource management strategy and safety culture as competitive advantages in order to improve construction company performance. Bus. Entrep. Rev. **20**(2), 123 (2020)
26. Chen, M., Ma, S., Zhang, Y., Chen, Y.: Development of a safety performance-based model for assessing the civil aviation organization's risk (2022)
27. Stemn, E., et al.: Examining the relationship between safety culture maturity and safety performance of the mining industry. Saf. Sci. **113**, 345–355 (2019)
28. ICAO: Safety Management Manual (SMM). International Civil Aviation Organization, 3rd edn. (2013). https://www.icao.int/SAM/Documents/2017-SSP-GUY/Doc%209859%20SMM%20Third%20edition%20en.pdf
29. Chen, M., Chen, Y., Ma, S.: Identifying safety performance indicators for risk assessment in civil aviation. IOP Conf. Ser. Mater. Sci. Eng. (2021). https://www.semanticscholar.org/paper/Identifying-Safety-Performance-Indicators-for-Risk-Chen-Chen/41d0653c0fb4e477400374c6ef9646827b5a3064. Accessed 19 Oct 2024
30. Song, K., et al.: The influence of perceived human resource strength on safety performance among high-speed railway drivers: the role of organizational identification and psychological capital. J. Saf. Res. (2023). https://doi.org/10.1016/j.jsr.2023.04.001
31. Fan, P., et al.: High conflict, high performance? A time-lagged study on work-family conflict and family support congruence and safety performance. Saf. Sci. **172**, 106403 (2024)
32. Li, Q., et al.: Revealing the effects of increased workload and distraction on the pilot's situation awareness neurobehavioral activities (2023)
33. Weber, D.E., et al.: Exploring the use of categories in the assessment of airline pilots' performance as a potential source of examiners' disagreement. J. Cogn. Eng. Decis. Mak. **8**(3), 248–264 (2014)
34. Ziakkas, D., Michael, W.S., Pechlivanis, K.: The implementation of competency-based training and assessment (CBTA) framework in aviation manpower planning. Transp. Res. Procedia **66**, 226–239 (2022)
35. Zhang, S., et al.: How does leadership in safety management affect employees' safety performance? A case study from mining enterprises in China. Int. J. Environ. Res. Public Health **19**(10), 6187 (2022)
36. Alidrisi, H.M., Mohamed, S.: Systematic review of safety leadership: a fresh perspective. In: Şahin, S. (ed.) EPPM 2017. LNME, pp. 215–223. Springer, Cham (2018). https://doi.org/10.1007/978-3-319-74123-9_23
37. Jing, T., et al.: Analysis of safety leadership using a science mapping approach. Process. Saf. Environ. Prot. **140**, 244–257 (2020). https://doi.org/10.1016/J.PSEP.2020.04.031
38. Cheung, C.M., et al.: The antecedents of safety leadership: the job demands-resources model. Saf. Sci. **133**, 104979 (2021)
39. Andoko, B.W., et al.: The future of leadership: exploring the relationship between transformational leadership and organizational performance. RGSA **18**(7) (2024)

40. Abbas, N.: Leadership and Performance Beyond Expectations. Academia.edu (1985). https://www.academia.edu/54210339/Leadership_and_performance_beyond_expectations
41. Lyubykh, Z., et al.: A meta-analysis of leadership and workplace safety: examining relative importance, contextual contingencies, and methodological moderators. J. Appl. Psychol. **107**(12) (2022)
42. Willis, S., et al.: Identifying the optimal safety leader: a person-centered approach. J. Manag. Psychol. **36**(3), 226–240 (2021)
43. Fischer, S.A.: Safety-specific transformational leadership. JONA J. Nurs. Adm. **53**(11), 561–562 (2023)
44. Adra, I., et al.: What is safety leadership? A systematic review of definitions. J. Saf. Res. (2024)
45. Mattson Molnar, M., et al.: Leading for safety: a question of leadership focus. Saf. Health Work **10**(2), 180–187 (2019). https://www.sciencedirect.com/science/article/pii/S20937911 16302918?via%3Dihub. Accessed 12 Dec 2019
46. Eva, N., et al.: From competency to conversation: a multi-perspective approach to collective leadership development. Leadersh. Q. **32**(5), 101346 (2019)
47. Blanco-Fernández, D., et al.: Multi-level adaptation of distributed decision-making agents in complex task environments. arXiv preprint (2021)
48. Anderegg, A., et al.: Predicting new risks: crew resource management in a human-machine team. In: AIAA AVIATION 2022 Forum (2022)
49. Klein, K., Kozlowski, S.W.: Leadership: enhancing team adaptability in dynamic settings (2008)
50. Day, D.V., Harrison, M.M.: A multilevel, identity-based approach to leadership development. Hum. Resour. Manag. Rev. **17**(4), 360–373 (2007)
51. Bienefeld, N., Grote, G.: Shared leadership in multiteam systems. Hum. Factors **56**(2), 270–286 (2013)
52. Cooper, D.: Effective safety leadership: understanding types & styles that improve safety performance. Prof. Saf. **60**(2), 49–53 (2015). https://onepetro.org/PS/article-abstract/60/02/ 49/33312/Effective-Safety-Leadership-Understanding-Types?redirectedFrom=fulltext
53. Papasava, A., Njeru, B.B.: Leadership styles as perceived in the changing aviation industry and their effect on pilot commitment: a Kenyan case study. Leadersh. Dev. Soc. **7**(1), 85–108 (2022)
54. Yueh-Ling, H., et al.: Structuring critical success factors of airline safety management system using a hybrid model. Transp. Res. Part E Logist. Transp. Rev. (2010). https://doi.org/10. 1016/J.TRE.2009.08.005
55. Timbang, A., et al.: The perspective of leadership and management commitment in process safety management. Indian Chem. Eng., 1–14 (2023)
56. Santosa, A., et al.: Safety-based dynamic uncertainty reduction to increase safety performance in aviation industry. Uncertain Supply Chain Manag. **11**(3), 1159–1166 (2023)
57. Zhang, X., Li, D., Guo, X.: Antecedents of responsible leadership: proactive and passive responsible leadership behavior. Sustainability **14**(14), 8694 (2022)
58. Schwartz, M.D., Hobbs, W.H.: Teaching aviation crew resource management in a pharmacy curriculum. Am. J. Pharm. Educ. **78**(3), 66 (2014)
59. Mızrak, F.: Strategies for effective human resource management in the aviation industry: a case-based analysis. Beykoz Akad. Derg. (2023)
60. Cigularov, K.P., Chen, P.Y., Rosecrance, J.: The effects of error management climate and safety communication on safety: a multi-level study. Accid. Anal. Prev. **42**(5), 1498–1506 (2010)
61. Liao, P., et al.: A cognitive perspective on the safety communication factors that affect worker behavior. J. Build. Constr. Plan. Res. **2**(3), 183–197 (2014)

62. Yeong, S.S., Shah Rollah, A.W.: The mediating effect of safety culture on safety communication and human factor accident at the workplace. Asian Soc. Sci. **12**(12), 127 (2016)
63. Alcantara, J., et al.: Towards a safety culture in chiropractic: the use of the safety, communication, operational reliability, and engagement (SCORE) questionnaire. Complement. Ther. Clin. Pract. **42**, 101266 (2021)
64. Reader, T.W.: Stakeholder safety communication: patient and family reports on safety risks in hospitals. J. Risk Res. **25**(7), 807–824 (2022)
65. Pandit, B., et al.: Fostering safety communication among construction workers: role of safety climate and crew-level cohesion. Int. J. Environ. Res. Public Health **16**(1), 71 (2018). https://www.ncbi.nlm.nih.gov/pmc/articles/PMC6339066/. Accessed 07 June 2019
66. Gabelica, C., Popov, V.: "One size does not fit all": revisiting team feedback theories from a cultural dimensions perspective. Group Organ. Manag. **45**(2), 105960112091085 (2020)
67. Acheampong, A., et al.: Impact of construction workers informal safety communication (CWISC) on safety performance on construction sites. Eng. Constr. Archit. Manag. (2024)
68. Mavin, T.J., Dall'Alba, G.: A Model for Integrating Technical Skills and NTS in Assessing Pilots' Performance (2017). https://www.semanticscholar.org/paper/A-model-for-integrating-technical-skills-and-NTS-in-Mavin-Dall%E2%80%99Alba/e28be264934574f19e7384d7fb872328a3d144e4. Accessed 19 Oct 2024
69. Communication. Adv. Skin Wound Care **25**(5), 200 (2012)
70. Typeset.io: Modeling a Repertoire of Pilots' Professional Communication Skills for Meeting Flight Safety and Aviation Security Challenges (2022). https://typeset.io/papers/modeling-a-repertoire-of-pilots-professional-communication-14dmflp6
71. Hofmann, D.A., Stetzer, A.: The role of safety climate and communication in accident interpretation: implications for learning from negative events. Acad. Manag. J. **41**(6), 644–657 (1998)
72. Parker, S.K., Axtell, C.M., Turner, N.: Designing a safer workplace: importance of job autonomy, communication quality, and supportive supervisors. J. Occup. Health Psychol. **6**(3), 211–228 (2001). https://pubmed.ncbi.nlm.nih.gov/11482633/
73. Wilson, C., et al.: The role of feedback in emergency ambulance services: a qualitative interview study. BMC Health Serv. Res. **22**(1) (2022). https://bmchealthservres.biomedcentral.com/articles/10.1186/s12913-022-07676-1
74. Walker, K.: Employee Feedback: how to provide feedback and recognition regularly. Strateg. HR Rev. **23**(2) (2024)
75. Kath, L.M., Marks, K.M., Ranney, J.: Safety climate dimensions, leader-member exchange, and organizational support as predictors of upward safety communication in a sample of rail industry workers. Saf. Sci. **48**(5), 643–650 (2010)
76. Vredenburgh, A.G.: Organizational safety. J. Saf. Res. **33**(2), 259–276 (2002)
77. Jakobus, B., Henrique, P., Souza, C.: Feedback. In: Apress eBooks, pp. 103–114 (2022)
78. Hasanspahić, N., et al.: Safety leadership as a means for safe and sustainable shipping. Sustainability **13**(14), 7841 (2021)
79. Atikasari, C.D., et al.: The effect of safety leadership, safety culture, and safety behavior on safety performance after a company merger: a case study. J. Sist. Manaj. Ind. **6**(2), 187–199 (2022)
80. Beveridge, S.D.H., et al.: Command and control. Aviat. Psychol. Appl. Hum. Factors **8**(1), 1–10 (2018)
81. Lyubykh, Z., et al.: Shared transformational leadership and safety behaviours of employees, leaders, and teams: a multilevel investigation. J. Occup. Organ. Psychol. **95**(2) (2022)
82. Burrows-McElwain, J.B., et al.: Ambiguity in leadership communication: a latent hazard in the aviation community? J. Aerosp. Sci. Technol. **2**(1) (2016). https://www.davidpublisher.com/Public/uploads/Contribute/5775d932ed8f6.pdf. Accessed 22 June 2022

83. Rashid, R.A., et al.: Influence of leadership communication in fostering employees' safety commitment in oil and gas industry. KnE Soc. Sci., 312–321 (2023). https://knepublishing.com/index.php/KnE-Social/article/view/14611. Accessed 02 Jan 2024

84. Obraztsov, R.A., Sharov, V.D.: On the use of fuzzy neural networks in the framework of a risk-based approach in control and supervisory activities in civil aviation. Civ. Aviat. High Technol. **26**(1), 58–71 (2023)

85. Virgil, B.A., Iosif, G.: Communication for performance in aerospace. INCAS Bull. **8**(4), 175–182 (2016)

86. Karanikas, N., Kaspers, S.: Frequency and variance of communication characteristics in aviation safety events. Poster Session Presented at: HFES Europe Charter Conference 2017, Rome, Italy (2017)

87. ICAEA: Exploring the Aviation English Training Needs of: Ab-Initio Pilots and Air Traffic Controllers, and Aircraft Maintenance Personnel. ICAEA Workshop 2019 Proceedings (2019). https://commons.erau.edu/icaea-workshop/2019/proceedings/. Accessed 19 Oct 2024

88. Ali, M., Nouban, F.: Analyzing the role of leadership in promoting a positive safety culture in the construction sector. World J. Adv. Res. Rev. **21**(1), 882–887 (2024)

89. Erceylan, N., Atilla, A.G.: Aviation safety and risk management during COVID-19. In: Advances in Hospitality, Tourism and the Services Industry (AHTSI) Book Series, pp. 126–145 (2022)

90. Bleich, M.R.: Leadership roles in standards and policy development. J. Contin. Educ. Nurs. **48**(5), 203–205 (2017)

91. Shively, R.J., Lachter, J., Koteskey, R., Brandt, S.L.: Crew resource management for automated teammates (CRM-A). In: Harris, D. (ed.) EPCE 2018. LNCS, vol. 10906, pp. 215–229. Springer, Cham (2018). https://doi.org/10.1007/978-3-319-91122-9_19

92. Masood, F.I., Jha, B., Magd, H.: Crew resource management development. In: Advances in Logistics, Operations, and Management Science, pp. 98–117 (2022)

93. Kutlu, E.B., Başdemir, M.: Examining the relationship between pilot's leadership styles and crew resource management practices (CRM) in airline operations. Havacılık Uzay Çalışmaları Derg. (2022)

94. Wang, X.Z.: Assessment of pilot core competencies based on an improved GRA-TOPSIS method. J. Xi'an Aeronaut. Univ. **1**, 19–25 (2024). https://doi.org/10.20096/j.xhxb.1008-9233.2024.01.004

95. Neal, A., Griffin, M.A.: A study of the lagged relationships among safety climate, safety motivation, safety behavior, and accidents at the individual and group levels. J. Appl. Psychol. **91**(4), 946–953 (2006). https://zero.sci-hub.tw/2661/e2e47ce173c4c02b82315d1f390a8f07/neal2006.pdf#view=FitH

96. Lin, C., Shunxin, Y.: Research on a post-competency model of civil aviation flight cadets. Int. J. Occup. Saf. Ergon. **29**(4), 1558–1571 (2023)

97. Meng, X., Zhai, H., Chan, A.H.: Development of scales to measure and analyse the relationship of safety consciousness and safety citizenship behaviour of construction workers: an empirical study in China. Int. J. Environ. Res. Public Health **16**(8), 1411 (2019)

98. Karanikas, N.: Critical review of safety performance metrics. Int. J. Bus. Perform. Manag. **17**(3), 266 (2016)

99. Roelen, A., et al.: Effectiveness of risk controls as indicator of safety performance. AUP Adv. **1**(1), 175–189 (2018). https://www.amsterdamuas.com/binaries/content/assets/subsites/aviation/safety-publications/risk-control-effectiveness_icsc-2017.pdf?1525899945883. Accessed 10 Mar 2020

100. Zhang, G., Chen, D., Feng, Y.: Evaluation of airline pilots' safety behaviors based on fuzzy neural network. J. Xi'an Aeronaut. Univ. **13**, 429–432 (2013)

101. Kukharenko, V.N., Shunevych, B.I., Kravtsov, H.M.: Distance learning expert and leader. Educ. Dimens. **8**, 19–40 (2023). https://acnsci.org/journal/index.php/ed/article/view/597

102. Wu, Y., et al.: The Influence of safety-specific transformational leadership on safety behavior among Chinese airline pilots: the role of harmonious safety passion and organizational identification. Saf. Sci. **166**, 106254 (2023)

103. Shirali, G., Shekari, M., Angali, K.A.: Assessing reliability and validity of an instrument for measuring resilience safety culture in sociotechnical systems. Saf. Health Work **9**(3), 296–307 (2018)

104. Todaro, N.M.N., et al.: Safety climate in high safety maturity organisations: development of a multidimensional and multilevel safety climate questionnaire. Saf. Sci. **166**, 106231 (2023)

105. Fala, N.. Data-driven safety feedback as part of debrief for general aviation pilots (2019)

106. IATA: Competency Assessment and Evaluation for Pilots, Instructors and Evaluators Guidance Material (2023). https://www.iata.org/contentassets/c0f61fc821dc4f62bb6441d7 abedb076/competency-assessment-and-evaluation-for-pilots-instructors-and-evaluators-gm.pdf

107. Grote, G.: Diagnosis of safety culture: a replication and extension towards assessing "safe" organizational change processes. Saf. Sci. **46**(3), 450–460 (2008)

108. Chen, Y., McCabe, B., Hyatt, D.: A resilience safety climate model predicting construction safety performance. Saf. Sci. **109**, 434–445 (2018)

109. Clark, D.: Leadership Matrix Survey (2015). http://www.nwlink.com/~donclark/leader/matrix.html

110. Skybrary: HUMAN FACTORS (2022). https://skybrary.aero/sites/default/files/bookshelf/3163.pdf

111. Padfield, G.D., Clark, G.M., Taghizad, A.: How long do pilots look forward? Prospective visual guidance in terrain-hugging flight. Aerosp. Sci. Technol. **52**(2), 134–145 (2007)

112. Weimann, E., Weimann, P.: Be a visionary leader. In: Springer eBooks, pp. 193–207 (2017)

113. Díez, F., et al.: The learning process to become a military leader: born, background and lifelong learning. Front. Educ. **8** (2023)

114. Taşçı, G., Titrek, O.: Evaluation of lifelong learning centers in higher education: a sustainable leadership perspective. Sustainability **12**(1), 22 (2019)

115. García, M.R.: The role of leadership in lifelong learning. Adult Learn. **15**(3–4), 28–29 (2004)

What Does Cabin Crew Need During Inflight Emergencies? A SHELL-Model Analysis

Elizabeth Manikath[1,2]([✉]) [iD], Wen-Chin Li[1] [iD], and Pawel Piotrowski[2] [iD]

[1] Safety and Accident Investigation Centre, Cranfield University, Cranfield, UK
[2] Lufthansa Technik AG, Hamburg, Germany
`elizabeth.manikath@cranfield.ac.uk`

Abstract. Although flight attendants are responsible for the safety of millions of passengers per year, their safety role is publicly often trivialized. Extensive training is provided by the airlines to support cabin crew to handle emergencies, however, is the training sufficient to overcome the challenges flight attendants face? Technological evolutions to minimize errors in the cockpit can be found throughout the past century, however, most of the equipment which cabin crew are using are outdated and do not meet the requirements of today's air travel. **Research question.** Following research questions will be addressed in this study: RQ1: Which challenges do cabin crew face during inflight emergencies? RQ2: How can cabin crew be supported during inflight emergencies? RQ3: How can technological aids, such as illumination, support cabin crew handling emergencies? **Methodology.** A qualitative study was conducted with 15 cabin crew members. Open-ended questions were asked to assess which challenges cabin crew face and how they can be supported during emergencies. The SHELL-model framework was used to analyze and categorize the open-ended questions. **Results and Discussion.** Major concerns were unruly passengers as well as panicking and uncontrollable behaviour. Fire and smoke were another concerns belonging to the Environment- Liveware interface. Improving flight attendant training with regards to duration, content, and frequency were highlighted as an effective measure to increase confidence in cabin crew applying their knowledge and skills. It was mentioned that trainings should be more realistic, such as using actors to mime anxious passengers. **Conclusion.** This study identified flight attendant's challenges using the SHELL model framework. Flight attendants could gain more confidence in handling emergencies by improving the training frequency, duration and content. Technological aids such as smart and/or optimized emergency buttons could further improve discreet communication between flight attendants and cabin crew.

Keywords: Cabin crew emergency processes · Passenger safety · Cabin crew training · SHELL Model Analysis · Inflight emergency

D. Harris et al. (Eds.): HCII 2025, LNCS 16334, pp. 101–115, 2026.
https://doi.org/10.1007/978-3-032-12392-3_6

1   Introduction

Cabin crew are the first responders to inflight emergencies. According to commission regulation (EC) No. 859/2008 [6] every operator should have procedures in place for abnormal situations. In a study conducted by Manikath et al. in 2025 [18] passengers and cabin crew stated commonly medical emergencies and unruly passengers as cases for inflight emergencies. Cabin crew in addition mentioned fire and smoke as emergency scenarios. Passengers considered aircraft damage as emergency scenarios. However, it is unclear whether other situations handled by cabin crew shall be additionally responded to as inflight emergencies. According to EASA Part CC cabin crew are trained in general knowledge in aviation and aviation regulations, communication, human factors and crew resource management, passenger handling and cabin surveillance, inflight medical emergencies and first aid, dangerous goods, general security aspects in aviation, fire and smoke training, as well as survival training [7]. Although, every operator needs to have procedures in place for abnormal and for emergency situations and cabin crew receive extensive training, the question remains whether these are sufficient to ensure effective and efficient task response. Therefore, the following paper assesses following questions:

RQ1: Which challenges do cabin crew face during inflight emergencies?
RQ2: How can cabin crew be supported during inflight emergencies?
RQ3: How can technological aids, such as illumination, support cabin crew handling emergencies?

Cabin crew's safety behaviour is vital for the overall safety performance of an airline [12]. Effective communication is one of the crucial skills indicating a good performance of cabin crew [2]. A literature review was conducted to understand current challenges in communication between cabin crew and passengers. The SHELL-model framework was used to analyse the results.

1.1   The SHELL-Model

The SHEL-model was originally designed by Prof. Elwyn Edwards in 1972 to understand how multiple components affect human performance [23]. Further, it is described in the ICAO Document 9859 Safety Management Manual Chap. 2 "Safety Management Fundamentals" to aid states, product, and service providers to establish a safety management system [11]. The model describes the relations between Software, Hardware, Environment, and Liveware. The concept was further refined in 1987 by adding a second "L" to incorporate interpersonal relationships [9]. The model puts the human (Liveware) in the center and analyses the interfaces between the other components of the system. Since humans are not standardized as the other components of the model, tensions at the interface might arise compromising human performance and contributing to human error [11]. The interfaces are described in the following:

Liveware–Hardware (L–H):
This interface describes the interaction between humans and physical aspects of machines, equipment, and facilities [11]. This is commonly referred to as the human-machine interface [23]. In an aviation context these could be controls and surfaces, displays, seats to fit the human body etc. [23].

Liveware–Software (L–S):
All laws, regulations, orders, conventions, procedures which define how things are usually done are described in the Software category. Software also refers to the computer-based programs.

Liveware–Environment (L–E):
This interface cannot be actively controlled by humans, namely the physical environment [23]. Environmental influences such as radiation, light, noise, temperature, weather are summarized in this category.

Liveware–Liveware (L–L):
The relationship between humans in the workplace is defined in this interface. Prominent examples are organizational culture, however, also staff-management relationships. Aspects, such as communication, interpersonal skills, and group dynamics are important for human performance [11].

1.2   Analysis of Communication Between Passengers and Cabin Crew Using the SHELL-Model

In the conducted literature review following challenges have been identified affecting the communication between passengers and cabin crew. The results are clustered using the SHELL-model.

Liveware–Hardware (L–H):
The main purpose of the existing Passenger Call Button (PCB) is to call cabin crew and shall be used by passengers. However, cabin crew also have their own routine of using the PCB to e. g. notify fellow crew members for help or to indicate a seat row where service is needed. This results in cabin crew not knowing who initiated the call [27]. Another problematic aspect is the lack of urgency indication by the PCB [14]. As identified by Wong and Neustaedter [27] there is "only a light and sound indication". Alarm sensitivity and prolonged response times could be results of the frequent use of the PCB by passengers for service requests [17]. In the air accident investigation report of flight BA762 [1], passengers used the existing PCB to alarm the cabin crew. However, the lead flight attendant was only alerted by the "highly unusual" behaviour of the passengers using the PCB multiple times and during take off [1].

Liveware–Software (L–S):
Company policies emphasizing service duties were found to negatively impact safety performance of cabin crew [5]. Time pressure and failure to meet the safety duties are consequences of the airline specific performance standards for service duties. Thus, flight attendants are constantly fighting the dilemma of safety vs. service tasks. The implications for communication are that passenger calls are often expected to be service related which could lead to prolonged response times or no response and resulting in passenger frustration [16].

Liveware–Environment (L–E):
Noise inside the cabin has been found as a negative work condition for cabin crew which could affect communication with passengers [25]. As identified by previous research the cabin noise makes it difficult to hear information such as audio alerts and adversely affects speech intelligibility [27].

Liveware–Liveware (L–L):
Unruly passengers were identified by Tsaur et al. [25] as negative working conditions for flight attendants. Since 2022, the number of unruly passengers has increased according to IATA [10]. Further, cabin crew are subject to "verbal and physical violence" and sexual harrassment [25] by passengers. Additionally, there are behavioural differences in the different travel classes as reported by Manikath et al. [15]. All these factors have a negative impact on communication between passengers and cabin crew. However, there were also cases where flight attendants did not take information seriously which passengers communicated. As in case of the Air Ontario Dryden accident in 1989 a passenger informed the flight attendant about the ice buildup on the wing [20]. This vital information was not processed further by the flight attendant leading to the fatal crash [20].

To summarize the majority of literature regarding challenges in communication between passengers and cabin crew was found in the Liveware–Software and Liveware–Liveware interface.

2   Methodology

Cabin crew receive extensive initial training in handling inflight emergencies and are obliged to participate in recurrent trainings. This study aims to understand whether the provided trainings are sufficient for cabin crew's task response and whether there are any technical aids which could support the flight attendants in detecting and handling inflight emergencies.

2.1   Participants

15 cabin crew members with a medium age of $M = 46$ ($SD = 10.4$) and an average flying experience of $M = 19.6$ ($SD = 9.8$) years participated in the

online study. Participants were recruited through convenience sampling, were over 18 years old, and were either former or active flight attendants. The survey link was shared with the participants, ensuring their participation remained anonymous. Data was collected between June 2024 and February 2025. Ethics approval (CURES/21010/2023) was granted by the institutional research ethics committee.

2.2 Material

A qualitative online study was conducted with former and active flight attendants to understand what are the major concerns and how technical aids could support cabin crew during inflight emergencies. The questionnaire started with basic demographic questions (such as: gender, age, work experience, working class, etc.) to categorize the participants. Lastly, three open ended questions were asked as follows:

Q1: What is your biggest pain point/fear while dealing with inflight cabin emergencies? What are your major concerns?

Q2: Would it help if the area where the emergency was declared would be illuminated in a special way e. g. coloured flashing light, e. g. red ambient light, dimming or turn on maximum brightness of cabin lights? What would be your suggestions?

Q3: Do you have any suggestions on how to tackle your above mentioned pain points/fears? What could help you handling inflight cabin emergencies?

2.3 Research Design

Qualtrics (www.qualtrics.com) was used to generate and distribute the questionnaire. Firstly, the participants needed to read and sign the consent form containing relevant information about the study before starting the survey. It was possible to exit the study at any time by closing the browser window. All participants needed to firstly answer the basic demographic questions before moving forward to the three open ended questions. It was possible to complete the questionnaire within 10 min. Data was coded using NVivo 14.

3 Results

For the thematic analysis data was coded and categorized into the four elements Software, Hardware, Environment, and Liveware. Regarding the first question biggest pain points and concerns dealing with inflight emergencies most of the codes referred to the Liveware–Liveware interaction (twelve participants, $M_{\mathrm{age}} = 46$ years, $SD = 9.4$). Seven participants mentioned specifically challenges with passengers ($M_{\mathrm{age}} = 48$ years, $SD = 9.7$). Four participants were specifically concerned about panicking or uncontrollable behaviour of passengers (*"Passengers may get panicky"*, *"people as they and their reactions are most unpredictable"*, *"panicking of pax"*, and *"[...] human factors"*). Additionally, three cabin crew ($M_{\text{age}} = 52$ years, $SD = 4.9$, $M_{\text{work experience}} = 24.3$ years, $SD = 3.3$) mentioned either violent (*"Passenger violence"*) or interfering/non-compliant passengers (*"Pax interference. Pax taking pictures and blocking access."*, *"The fact that passengers are oblivious to the dangers surrounding them (disrespecting the fasten seat belt sign)"*).

Another code which falls under the Liveware–Liveware interaction can be summarized as Crew Resource Management. Four participants highlighted issues regarding team performance (*"[...] poor performance"*), stress reactions (*"Stress. You never know how you are going to react in a stressful situation (freeze, flight, fight)."*), and crew coordination (*"Coordination is key. Crew members must work together in a coordinated manner. Roles have to be clear."*). Two flight attendants additionally mentioned that lack of staff could be an issue especially in case of multiple scenarios or a fully occupied flight (*"Multiple smoke spots together with medical emergency and lack of staff."*, *"In case of a large and fully booked aircraft (B777-300) and where half of the crew is resting, your active team is small in case of an emergency. Of course you can wake up the resting crew, but it takes time. Experience shows that passengers can also be assisting."*). Further, lack of assertiveness (*"Lack of assertiveness [...]"*) and miscommunication (*"Miscommunication and escalation of the situation"*) were also described as pain points.

The most often stated code belonging to the Environment–Liveware interface was fire. Fire and smoke were mentioned by six cabin crew ($M_{\text{age}} = 50$ years, $SD = 9.6$) as a major concern. Especially the "uncontrollable" situation (*"uncontrollable size of fire"*), smoke (*"Fire or heavy smoke especially when the source cannot be found."*, *"multiple smoke spots"*) and the required fast reaction times by cabin crew to handle the situation (*"Fire spreads fast (abt 20 min time to get it under control, otherwise plane is most probably lost, esp. over open water"*) were of a major worry. Surprisingly, time was listed only as the second most common subcode mentioned by three participants. Cabin crew were worried about lack of time which emphasizes the time criticality to find a solution during emergencies (*"Time for handling the emergency is spare"*, *"Not having the right amount of time to take necessary actions"*, *"[...] shortness of time [...]"*). One flight attendant named the constricted cabin space to be one potential challenge which is faced during emergencies (*"[...] lack of space, crowding [...]"*). Furthermore, one cabin crew mentioned serious injuries as a concern.

Three codes were identified for the Liveware–Hardware interface, whereas two were referring to Hardware used by passengers. Smartphones were mentioned as one factor which is hindering flight attendants from effective emergency response (*"The biggest problem in my opinion is the introduction of smartphones into the cabin. This forms a major distraction for colleagues, feels quite threatening, and gets in the way generally of being able to handle the emergency."*). Passengers taking pictures and obstructing the already limited space in the cabin are distracting and impeding flight attendants in their duties (*"[...] Pax taking pictures and blocking access."*). Interestingly, one cabin crew member stated that some of the emergency equipment cannot be conveniently used (*"[...] the effectiveness and ease of some of the emergency equipment"*) (Fig. 1).

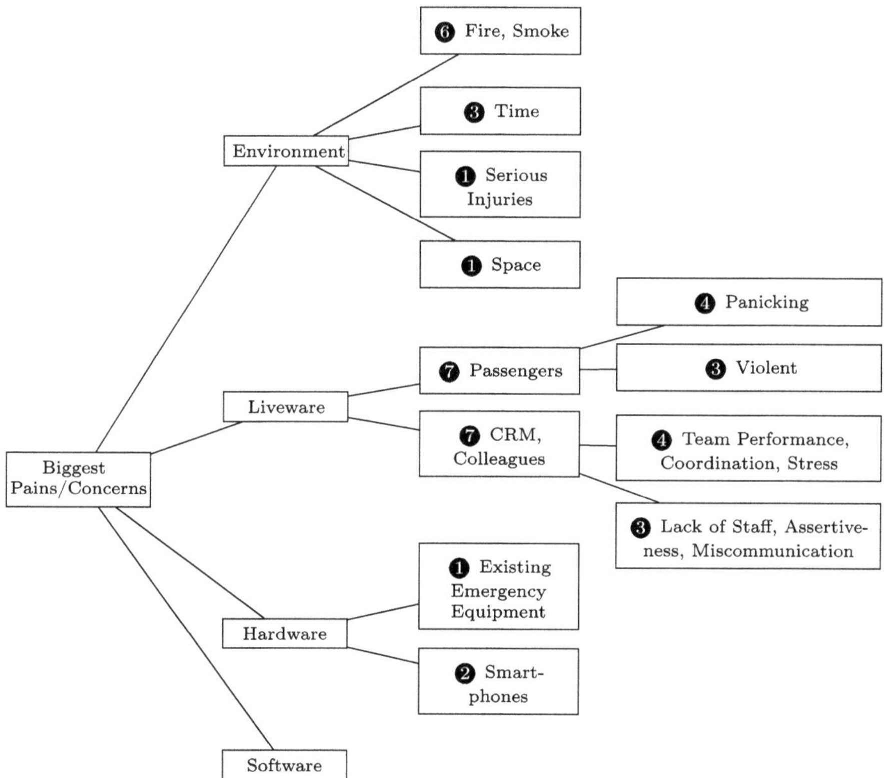

Fig. 1. SHELL-model analysis: biggest pains during inflight emergencies.

The second question was about how to tackle these challenges and what does cabin crew need to handle inflight emergencies. The majority of codes was in the Liveware–Liveware interaction (15 codes), thereof five in the subcode Training. Participants (M_{age} = 45 years, SD = 9.5) either suggested to improve the frequency of the training (*"Practice during yearly training."*, *"more frequent training [...]"*) or the content. One flight attendant mentioned the existing training to not be very realistic (*"[...] Trainings are often not realistic"*). Other cabin crew members suggested improvement of the existing training by e. g. training with actors who mime scared passengers, or to include assertiveness and communication in the training. Familiarity with confined space and simulated events was also stated as a potential training enhancement. In the subcode passengers one flight attendant stated it would be helpful to know where medical personnel are seated. The other participants comments reflected on how to improve the communication between passengers and flight attendants e. g. *"information of pax, and pax keeping calm and pax listening and reacting to instructions of crew"*, *"You have to talk with pax if you want them to cooperate"*. Another suggested approach was to provide another written instruction card to passengers besides the existing ones especially warning about the consequences in case of heavy turbulences to increase passenger's awareness to comply with cabin crew's instructions. Regarding the subcode colleagues *"[...] knowing the procedures and having the experience"* was considered to be useful. One flight attendant and flight safety trainer additionally mentioned a behavioural aspect on how to de stress to be able to improve task response by *"Take a deep breath or recognize the behaviour of a colleague. If you take some time in most situations you can think about the procedures that you have learned."*. Lastly, communication between senior colleagues and the flight deck shall be kept short and precisely (*"When starting abc procedure, (attack, buddy, communicator) communication with senior purser and cockpit should be very short and accurate by interphone. Don't keep the line busy. Mention if abc is medical or fire."*) was another suggestion.

One flight attendant suggested four different technological solutions which could support cabin crew during emergencies (Liveware–Hardware). The first recommendation was to include automatic sensors, e. g. include automated fire extinguishers in waste bins. The second suggestion was to install an emergency button for cabin crew when they are alone in the galley area. Additionally, an emergency button for passengers was also proposed. Further, a messaging option via the IFE system for cabin crew and passengers to send messages between each other was also mentioned (*"[...] Perhaps the option to send a message via the screen that ends up at the main panel of the IFE system. Conversely, crew can send messages to passengers from there (per section and per seat)"*). Automated announcements could also support flight attendants (*"[...] automatic announcement asking everyone to remain in their seats, keep smartphones and tablets away and respect the crew?"*).

Suggestions in the Software–Liveware interface were made predominantly regarding laws, regulations and procedures. One proposal was to punish illegal behaviour more severely (*"[...] Severe punishment of illegal behaviour (DBP) as deterrent."*). Improvement of communication procedures was mentioned twice (*"Getting all the information you need. Get control of the communication"*, *"Enhanced standard communication procedures"*), as well as one flight attendant stated fire handling procedures (Fig. 2).

The last question was specifically about whether and how illumination of the emergency area could support cabin crew. In this study five participants had a positive attitude towards special lighting of the emergency area and two expressed a negative opinion. Subcodes were brightness, coloured light or flash

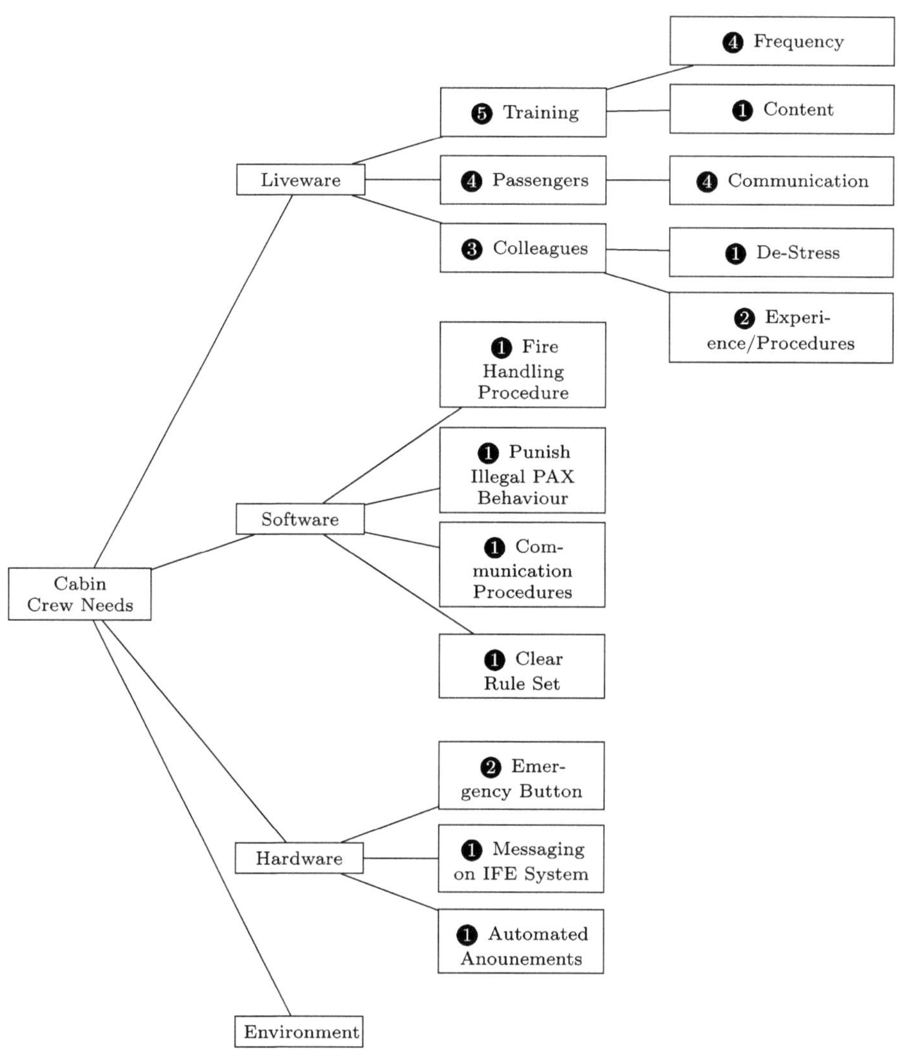

Fig. 2. Cabin crew needs during inflight emergencies

lighting. Brightness was mentioned by five participants to be helpful (*"Bright, steady white/clear lighting may help."*, *"Brightness would be good to find the spot immediately - especially in case of dimmed light during night. [...]"*). However, two flight attendants also mentioned the missing discretion which could also lead to panic and stress of the passengers (*"Potentially to alert the crew, but sometimes a more discrete scenario (i. e. a pax death) you might not want the whole cabin to know, especially on a night flight. In addition, alerting the whole cabin to a warning could cause panic prior to the crew being able to handle the emergency."*). Participants were more negatively inclined towards coloured light

e. g. red light (*"Flashing light or red ambient light = no way"*), whereas flashing light was rated more positively (*"May be the area call light on the ceiling can turn into flashing."*, *"A flashing light in the area of the incident"*).

3.1 Summary of the Main Results

To summarize the results, the majority of codes regarding biggest pains and concerns of flight attendants while dealing with inflight emergencies, belonged to the Liveware–Liveware interface. Challenges dealing with uncontrollable, violent, panicking passenger behaviour was described by seven cabin crew members. Concerns regarding intra-team performance, crew coordination, and stress reactions were also mentioned by seven flight attendants. Fire and Smoke, belonging to the Environment–Liveware was the second most stated concern. The uncontrollable situation and the required fast reaction times seemed to be most worrying to the participants. Regarding the needs and how to tackle the challenges, the majority of codes was again in the Liveware–Liveware interface. Improvement of training frequency, content were frequently mentioned, as well as to improve the communication between passengers and flight attendants. With regard to whether illumination could be of help to increase situation awareness, some of the participants were more positively inclined. However, there were also participants mentioning that either coloured light or flashing light could cause panic and discretion in these cases could be compromised.

4 Discussion

The following qualitative study is the first of its kind to use the SHELL-model framework to identify cabin crew's challenges and needs handling inflight emergencies. The findings of this study are beneficial to support cabin crew during inflight emergencies by e. g. improving trainings and procedures. One of the main findings of this study is that most of the challenges which cabin crew face are in the Liveware–Liveware interface. This is in accordance with the findings of the previously conducted literature review (see 1.2). Passengers which are either panicking, or even violent or incompliant were mentioned as a major concern. This is consistent with the findings in Tsaur et al. [25] where unruly passengers were found to be a negative working condition for cabin crew. Moreover, IATA [10] identified a rising number of unruly passengers since 2022, which can be seen as a worrying development. Further, team performance, stress reactions, and crew coordination were mentioned as an uncertainty in the Liveware–Liveware interaction. Collaboration is important for flight attendant's for delivering on-board safety and customer service duties [27]. Wong et al. [27] compares the collaborative procedures of flight attendants with other team-based professions such as firefighters or medical trauma care. Similarities in the roles are e. g. although flight attendants work in different positions during the flight they know the work procedures of colleagues in other positions. Their tasks and challenges are changing depending on the individual passenger and situation. Therefore, it is important that during emergencies the roles within the team are clearly defined and crew members work together in a coordinated way. A lack in teamwork can be embarrassing and could even lead to incidents or accidents [22].

Miscommunication, lack of staff, and assertiveness were also stated as major concerns. When it comes to communication during emergencies, firefighters for example have a personalized radio which will be used to communicate with each other, however flight attendants collaboration tools are often stationary and they need to rush to the specific position to be able to communicate e. g. via cabin interphone. During emergencies, this can lead to "communication breakdowns", because the existing equipment is not meeting the collaborative needs of flight attendants [27]. In an observational study conducted by Damos et al. [5], it was highlighted that cabin crews were not able to meet all the safety, security, and service tasks within a given time to achieve performance levels set by the airlines. Further, a reduction in staffing to the minimum required amount was seen critically especially during domestic flights by Damos et al. [5]. Participants of this study mentioned as well lack of staff as an issue during emergencies. "Lack of assertiveness" could be linked to either external factors such as the public trivialization of flight attendant's role or lack of training. The flight attendant's main responsibility is to ensure safety and security of the passengers during flight [5,17]. Although cabin crew are responsible for the safety and the security of millions of passengers annually, the public image still remains of the "trolley dolly", "space waitress" (Hochschild, 1983 as cited in [19]) and keeping the cabin "clean and tidy" [3]. Further, often flight attendants are belonging to the younger workforce and, therefore, may not have the experience to dissolve conflict situations [19]. In a study conducted by Rhoden et al. [21] regarding effectiveness of training for unruly passengers, participating cabin crew overall felt they had the abilities and knowledge to handle the situations, however, confidence in applying these skills varied. Further, it was identified that existing training should be either prolonged, more frequent and more realistic to increase confidence in flight attendants.

Fire and smoke were major concern belonging to the Environment–Liveware interface. In a study conducted by Manikath et al. [18] fire and smoke were found to be of most concern with cabin crew since flight attendants are trained in active fire fighting. Fire, as also mentioned by the participants of this study is an uncontrollable situation which is highly time critical. Fire and smoke could also be the result of overheated portable electronic devices (PED). In December 2024 Southwest Airlines Flight 3316 was evacuated in Denver after one passenger's mobile phone battery caught fire [13]. Participants of this study mentioned that passenger's taking pictures and blocking aisles would disturb cabin crew while performing evacuation tasks. This was also the case for the accident of Emirates flight EK521 where passengers who evacuated via the escape slides stayed near the aircraft to take videos and pictures and therefore delayed the passenger flow to the evacuation area [8]. Further, passengers also disobeyed cabin crew's instructions to leave carry-on baggage behind before evacuation. However, the investigation report revealed that several passengers delayed the evacuation process because they took carry-on baggage with them and blocked the aisles.

4.1   Suggestions to Improve Handling of Inflight Emergencies

What are cabin crew's needs and how could they be supported? Particularly, with regards to passenger violence one flight attendant suggested to have more severe punishment of illegal passenger behaviour. According to the Tokyo convention (1963) [4] the aircraft commander has the power to disembark or restrain an offender to ensure safety and security of the passengers and of the aircraft. Although the Tokyo convention is the first international treaty in aviation history which grants immunity and power to the aircraft commander, there are also major weaknesses. As discovered by Sopilko and Shevchuk [24] one of the major weaknesses of the treaty is the weak enforcement system meaning that in certain circumstances offenders could leave without punishment. One of the main aspects which the participants of this study mentioned is to improve either frequency or the content of the trainings. Participants further mentioned that the training is not realistic and should be enhanced by hiring actors which "mime" frightened passengers. This finding is in line with the results in a study conducted by Rhoden et al. [21] where flight attendants claimed that the duration of the training is not sufficient, but also trainings are not realistic. The behavioral consequences are that cabin crew lack confidence in application of knowledge and skills. Improvement of communication and communication procedures was also described frequently by the participants which could help handling inflight emergencies. Collecting all the necessary information and informing passengers was highlighted, as well as, having standardized communication procedures. Informing passengers satisfies two purposes: avoiding panic and involving passengers to cooperate. As already identified by Manikath et al. [14] there are several challenges involved in the communication between passengers and cabin crew. Manikath et al. [14] especially pointed out the missing discretion in case of emergencies and the need for the passenger to discreetly alert cabin crew. It was also identified that the existing equipment is not supporting the communication needs of passengers and cabin crew [17]. Flight attendants of this study suggested interestingly mainly technological aids intended to improve communication between passengers and cabin crew such as automated announcements e. g. to remain seated during turbulences or emergencies. Additionally emergency buttons and the possibility to send messages to passengers IFE screen was also suggested.

4.2   Illumination as a Potential Support?

The opinions of the study participants regarding illumination as a potential aid during emergencies were divided. Whereas, the majority of flight attendants agreed that brightness would be of help to increase situation awareness, there were also concerns regarding missing discretion and causing panic. In case of for example dimmed cabin light during night flights, passengers might be disturbed if suddenly the illumination changes (*"Lighting that part of the cabin at least gives an indication that 'something' is going on. A auto message in the screens near the pax in that area would be useful as an explanation, because during a night flight, passengers are startled when lights come on all at once.[...]"*). Winzen et al. [26] suggested to have different lighting conditions according to the operational tasks. Previous research found out that the targeted application of coloured lights could not only have a benefit on passengers, but also on flight and cabin crew [26]. Participants of this study were more concerned about the use of flashing lights or red light since it could create panic and discomfort for the passengers. In a study conducted by Yao et al. [28] it has been shown that the visual comfort of passengers is linked mainly to the lighting in the aircraft cabin. Flashy lights could therefore be perceived as uncomfortable for the eyes. Colours are also important for visual comfort considering the psychological effects which colours have on behaviour and human perception [28]. Thus, red lights could be perceived as a threat. There is innovative potential for situation-controlled illumination of the cabin area, which could be part of the implementation of an automated smart cabin concept. Based on various flight, time, and cabin scenarios triggering the Emergency Call Button could launch an automated routine that adapts the cabin lighting smoothly to an optimum configuration, thus supporting the crew.

5   Conclusion

Aviation is one of the safest modes of travel. Reasons for this are increased reliability and technological development of aircraft, and extensive training requirements for pilots and cabin crew. Over the past decades a lot of research involved on how to improve flight deck design in order to enable pilots to improve task performance and reduce failures, however, research on cabin crew's safety performance is scarce. This study contributes to highlight pain points from a cabin crew's perspective on how to handle inflight emergencies and what could be done to support task performance. The study participants, namely flight attendants who are responsible for the safety of millions of passengers annually contributed to highlight major concerns but also suggestions on how to handle inflight emergencies in this study. Firstly, this research focuses on the needs of flight attendants during emergencies. One of the main concerns are the interaction and reactions with passengers in stressful situations. Specifically, unruly passengers and the uncontrollable human behaviour under stress were mentioned as a major concern. Moreover, fire and smoke was also a worrying scenario due to the unpredictability of the situation.

So, what do flight attendants need to combat the challenges? Firstly, more frequent and realistic training was mentioned by the majority of participants. For instance, actors who mime panicking passengers could make the training more realistic. Secondly, stricter punishment of violent passengers and improvement of communication procedures could also be of support. The latter one can also be found in the literature, cf. [16,17]. Lighting has a major influence in the visual comfort of passengers and targeted use of lighting could support cabin crew and pilots during operational tasks. However, too bright light and red coloured light should be avoided in order to avoid panic and reduce visual discomfort. The findings of this study are relevant for cabin crew trainers and training providers in order to improve training content and frequencies. Additionally, further research is needed to investigate how situation awareness of flight attendant's during emergencies can be further improved.

References

1. Air Accidents Investigation Branch: Report on the accident to Airbus A319-131, G-EUOE London Heathrow Airport, 24 May 2013 (2015). https://assets. publishing.service.gov.uk/media/55a4bdb940f0b61562000001/AAR_1-2015_G-EUOE.pdf. Accessed 11 Feb 2024
2. Chen, C.F., Chen, S.C.: Investigating the effects of job demands and job resources on cabin crew safety behaviours. Tourism Manag. **41** (2014)
3. Chute, R.D., Wiener, E.L.: Cockpit-cabin communication: I. A tale of two cultures. Int. J. Aviat. Psychol. **5** (1995). https://doi.org/10.1207/s15327108ijap05032
4. Convention, T.: Convention on offences and certain other acts committed on board aircraft, signed at Tokyo, on 14 september 1963 (Tokyo convention) (2023). https:// www.mcgill.ca/iasl/files/iasl/tokyo1963.pdf. Accessed 24 May 2025
5. Damos, D.L., Boyett, K.S., Gibbs, P.: Safety versus passenger service: the flight attendants' dilemma. Int. J. Aviat. Psychol. **23**, 2 (2013). https://doi.org/10.1080/ 10508414.2013.772822
6. European Commission: Commission Regulation (EC) No 859/2008 (2008). https:// eur-lex.europa.eu/eli/reg/2008/859/oj. Accessed 11 Feb 2024
7. European Union: Regulation (EU) No 1178/2011 (2011). https://www. easa.europa.eu/en/document-library/easy-access-rules/easy-access-rules-aircrew-regulation-eu-no-11782011#:~:text=The%20Easy%20Access%20Rules %20%28EAR%29%20for%20Aircrew%20%28Regulation,with%20advanced %20navigation%20features%20through%20links%20and%20bookmarks. Accessed 11 Feb 2025
8. General Civil Aviation Authority: Air accident investigation sector - final report runway impact during attempted go-around (2020). https://www.icao.int/safety/ airnavigation/AIG/Documents/Safety%20Recommendations%20to%20ICAO/ Final%20Reports/UAE_B777_A6-EMW_3Aug2016.pdf. Accessed 24 Mar 2025
9. Hoermann, H.J.: Human Factor, vol. 1. Springer, Berlin, Heidelberg (2015)
10. IATA: Unruly passengers fact sheet (2024). https://www.iata.org/en/iata-repository/pressroom/fact-sheets/fact-sheet---unruly-passengers/. Accessed 11 Feb 2024
11. ICAO: Doc 9859 safety management manual (2013). https://www.icao.int/SAM/ Documents/2017-SSP-GUY/Doc%209859%20SMM%20Third%20edition%20en. pdf. Accessed 09 Mar 2025
12. Kao, L.H., Stewart, M., Lee, K.H.: Using structural equation modeling to predict cabin safety outcomes among Taiwanese airlines. Transp. Res. Part E **45** (2009). https://doi.org/10.1016/j.tre.2008.09.007

13. Limehouse, J.: Cellphone battery catches fire, causes southwest flight in Denver to evacuate; 2 injured (2024). https://eu.usatoday.com/story/travel/flights/2024/11/15/southwest-flight-evacuated-denver-cellphone-battery-fire/76338463007/. Accessed 24 Mar 2024
14. Manikath, E., Li, W.C.: Developing an innovative health monitoring device to improve communication between passengers and cabin attendants during inflight emergencies. Transp. Res. Procedia **66** (2022). https://doi.org/10.1016/j.trpro.2022.12.014
15. Manikath, E., Li, W.C., Braithwaite, G.R., Piotrowksi, P.: A small icon and its effect on user perception - How the design of the Passenger Call Button shapes passengers communication with Cabin Crew, vol. 14693. Springer Cham (2024). https://doi.org/10.1007/978-3-031-60731-8_6
16. Manikath, E., Li, W.C., Piotrowksi, P.: Usability assessment on existing alerting designs for emergency communication between passengers and cabin crews. conference paper DLRK 2023 in Deutsche Gesellschaft für Luft-und Raumfahrt. Lilienthal-Oberth.e.V. (2024). https://doi.org/10.25967/610019
17. Manikath, E., Li, W.C., Piotrowksi, P., Zhang, J.Y.: Usability Evaluation of an Emergency Alerting System to Improve Discreet Communication During Emergencies, vol. 14018. Springer Cham (2023). https://doi.org/10.1007/978-3-031-35389-5_9
18. Manikath, E., Li, W.C., Piotrowski, P.: Emergency = emergency? Usability evaluation of a novel emergency alerting system for cabin emergencies. Transp. Res. Procedia **88** (2025). https://doi.org/10.1016/j.trpro.2025.05.028
19. Morgan, M., Nickson, D.: Uncivil aviation: a review of the air rage phenomenon. Int. J. Tourism Res. **3** (2001). https://doi.org/10.1002/jtr.327
20. Moshansky, V.P.: Commission of inquiry into the Air Ontario Crash at Dryden, Ontario (1992). https://reports.aviation-safety.net/1989/19890310-1_F28_C-FONF.pdf. Accessed 31 Aug 2023
21. Rhoden, S., Ralston, R., Ineson, E.M.: Cabin crew training to control disruptive airline passenger behavior: a cause for tourism concern? Tourism Manag. **29** (2008). https://doi.org/10.1016/j.tourman.2007.06.002
22. Salas, E., Burke, S.C., Bowers, C.A., Wilson, K.A.: Team training in the skies: does crew resource management (CRM) training work? Human Factors **43** (2001). https://doi.org/10.1518/001872001775870386
23. SkyBrary: ICAO shell model. https://skybrary.aero/articles/icao-shell-model. Accessed 09 Mar 2025
24. Sopilko, I., Shevchuk, Y.: Jurisdiction over crimes committed on board aircraft in flight under the Tokyo convention 1963. Proc. Nat. Aviation Univ. **69** (2016). https://doi.org/10.18372/2306-1472.69.11064
25. Tsaur, S.H., Hsu, F.S., Kung, L.H.: Hassles of cabin crew: an exploratory study. J. Air Transp. Manag. **85** (2020). https://doi.org/10.1016/j.jairtraman.2020.101812
26. Winzen, J., Albers, F., Marggraf-Micheel, C.: The influence of coloured light in the aircraft cabin on passenger thermal comfort. Lighting Res. Technol. **46** (2014). https://doi.org/10.1177/1477153513484028
27. Wong, S., Neustaedter, C.: Collaboration and awareness amongst flight attendants. In: Proceedings of the 2017 ACM Conference on Computer Supported Cooperative Work and Social Computing (CSCW '17). Association for Computing Machinery, New York, NY, USA (2017). https://doi.org/10.1145/2998181.2998355
28. Yao, X., Song, Y., Vink, P.: Exploring factors influencing visual comfort in an aircraft cabin. In: 3rd International Comfort Congress 2021 (2021)

Datamining and Modeling Tacit Knowledge of Air Accident Investigators: Research Aimed at Improving Efficiency and Quality of Investigations Through AI

Miwa Nakanishi[✉] and Mako Ono

Keio University, Hiyoshi 3-14-1, Kohoku, Yokohama, Kanagawa 223-8522, Japan
miwa.nakanishi@keio.jp

Abstract. Improving the efficiency and quality of accident investigations is an issue that needs to be addressed more strongly in industries where safety is critical. In this study, we will use artificial intelligence (AI) to establish a method to support the accident investigators' assessment of accidents and decision-making, which are the core of aviation accident investigations. In this paper, we will present the results of data analysis for constructing an AI model that has been trained using the "tacit knowledge" that accident investigators utilize at each stage of the accident investigation, which was extracted through interview surveys for the purpose of this study. As a result, we were able to identify the matters that accident investigators commonly or individually focus on in each phase of the investigation and analysis. Although this knowledge has not been formalized, it is important for conducting accident investigations at a high level, and it is something that should be passed on to accident investigators who are still inexperienced.

Keywords: Accident investigators · text-mining · tacit knowledge

1 Introduction

Even in the modern age, when the science and technology involved and the various systems that govern the people who use it have matured to the point where the probability of accidents in all industrial fields has been reduced to near-zero, it is still essential to take steps to prevent accidents. There is no doubt that the safety we enjoy today is based on the lessons learned from investigating and analyzing the large and small accidents that have occurred in the past. In industries where safety is critical, when an accident or serious incident occurs, a thorough investigation is carried out to determine the cause and prevent a recurrence, and the conclusions of this investigation guide subsequent safety measures. In some fields, such as aviation, investigations are carried out in accordance with international standards, methods and procedures by organizations that specialize in accident investigation.

The procedures for accident investigation differ slightly depending on the field, but the general outline is as follows.

D. Harris et al. (Eds.): HCII 2025, LNCS 16334, pp. 116–126, 2026.
https://doi.org/10.1007/978-3-032-12392-3_7

1. Initial investigation

After an accident occurs, the staff in charge of the accident investigation are assigned immediately, and as a first response, objective data is collected and interviews are conducted with those involved.

2. Analysis

The collected factual information is analyzed using various analytical methods, and the causal relationship between the accident that occurred and the factors that may have been involved is examined in detail.

3. Identification of the cause of the accident and derivation of measures to prevent recurrence

The causes of the accident, which are explained as a chain of contributing factors, and the recurrence prevention measures that are taken against these contributing factors are summarized and published in a report.

While the procedures for this type of investigation are formalized, the probability of a modern accident occurring is extremely low, and no two accidents are the same, so 1) what information should be collected in the initial investigation of the accident in question, 2) what methods are effective for analyzing this information, and 3) what is the essential cause of the accident and what countermeasures are effective for preventing its recurrence? In addition, there are courses and research groups specializing in "accident investigation studies" at some research and educational institutions in Europe and the United States (the most prominent examples being Cranfield University in the UK and the University of Southern California in the United States), and there is ongoing development of human resources and methods specializing in accident investigation, but the academic field of knowledge and technology related to accident investigation has yet to be fully established. This can increase the workload of those in charge of accident investigations, and at times, it can cause disputes over factual information to prolong investigations and lead to an imbalance in the quality of the final accident investigation report. The lengthening of accident investigations delays the implementation of countermeasures to prevent the recurrence of factors that need to be improved, and the quality of accident investigation reports also affects the direction and reliability of safety measures that have a long-term impact, so it can be said that the efficiency and quality of accident investigations are issues that should be recognized and resolved more strongly in industries with a high safety risk.

In this study, we will use artificial intelligence (AI) to establish a method to support the accident investigators' assessment of accidents and decision-making, which are the core of aviation accident investigations. In this paper, we will present the results of data analysis for constructing an AI model that has been trained using the "tacit knowledge" that accident investigators utilize at each stage of the accident investigation, which was extracted through interview surveys for the purpose of this study. The goal of this research is to demonstrate the potential for using artificial intelligence (AI) as a new methodology for improving the efficiency and quality of accident investigations of social technology systems, which require balanced discussions based on multifaceted and in-depth knowledge of people, systems, laws and systems, and the environment.

2 Discussion of Previous Research and the Policy of This Research

2.1 Previous Research

In the field of aviation, for example, the development of each specialized field related to aviation, such as aircraft performance, weather, pilot skills, maintenance and flight management, and air traffic control methods, is said to contribute to modern aviation safety. In recent years in particular, the effective use of artificial intelligence (AI) has accelerated these developments, and related research and development is progressing in each specialized field. Examples include monitoring the flight status of aircraft, predicting fog and turbulence, image inspection of engine blades, and traffic volume and flow prediction. On the other hand, in terms of accident investigation, there has been progress in the use of engineering technology to enhance individual phases such as the analysis and visualization of measurement and recording devices, and in recent years, we have also seen the use of artificial intelligence (AI). However, there has been little progress in the evolution of engineering approaches to the core processes of accident investigation, from the collection of factual information to the identification of causes (factors), and in particular, the development of methodologies, including the use of AI to enhance and streamline human factor analysis, has not progressed sufficiently to the level of practical application. Against this background, research and development is beginning to use natural language processing (NLP) technology, which has seen significant research and development in recent years, to analyze the document data published in aviation accident investigation reports in order to extract the factors and related human factors of accidents and incidents. A typical example is the research on accident type classification by Ziakkas et al. (Ziakkas & Pechlivanis, 2023) [1].

The authors are attempting to build a HFACS (Human Factor Analysis and Classification System) model using GPT (Generative Pre-trained Transformer; pre-trained document generation AI) as the underlying technology [2]. HFACS is a method developed and approved by the US Department of Defense for analyzing aviation accidents caused by human factors, and consists of four levels of "unsafe acts", "preconditions", "supervision/leadership", "organizational influences" and four levels, each of which is made up of categories (nano-codes) [3]. In HFACS, extremely detailed descriptions are given for each nano-code with the aim of conducting objective and rigorous analysis of the causes of all aviation accidents, and it is suggested that by repeatedly analyzing the causes of individual accidents based on this, knowledge relating to accident prevention from a statistical perspective can be obtained. HFACS is a method that is recognized and used worldwide in the field of aviation accident investigation and analysis, and in the past accident investigation experts who are familiar with the nano-codes and their content have been using this method to extract and classify accident factors. On the other hand, one of the difficulties of analyzing using HFACS is that it requires a great deal of time and effort to analyze, as you have to be familiar with over 100 nano-codes and their classification criteria before you can start analyzing. In this study, we trained GPT to perform HFACS, and used the world's aviation accident investigation reports, which are stored as large-scale language data, as the target for analysis. We demonstrated the possibility and challenges of deriving information that contributes to the prevention of future accidents from the analysis of the causes of past aviation accidents.

Although the advent of GPT has raised expectations for the use of AI in the field of accident investigation and analysis, these studies are still in their infancy, and there is not much related research at present because the people who specialize in accident investigation and analysis are not necessarily close to those who specialize in AI construction. As a study that attempted to quantitatively handle HFACS from the perspective of data analysis, there are studies that have attempted to quantitatively analyze past CFIT (Controlled Flight Into Terrain: abnormal approach of an aircraft to the ground) incidents by classifying the factors using HFACS and analyzing them quantitatively using Bayesian networks (Meng et al., 2022) [4] and a study that has classified the factors of 30 past aviation accidents using HFACS and quantitatively analyzed the relationship between nano-codes and accident types using a systems dynamics approach (Wu et al., 2023) [5], in both cases, the factor analysis using HFACS was carried out by humans, and it was limited to the analysis of several dozen accident cases. In addition, there is a study (Ziakkas et al., 2023) [1] that is closer to this study, in which ChatGPT was made to analyze a specific aviation accident using HFACS, and the output responses were compared with the analysis of experts, but it is limited to case studies.

2.2 Discussion of the Research Policy

The above research explored the possibility of AI objectively and rationally performing the process from assessing the accident and identifying the causes (factors) of the accident, based on the factual information collected, on behalf of human accident investigators, but it has the following limitations and issues. First, there is the issue of estimation accuracy. Although the accuracy indicators used differ, all of the previous studies have been able to extract the causes (factors) of the accident with an accuracy of around 75%. On the other hand, it is said that there is a lack of breadth of investigation and depth of insight into background factors compared to the investigation and analysis carried out by human accident investigators. Second, since the investigation of aviation accidents is always an activity that clarifies unknown issues, there is a concern that the inductive role played by AI in the process of identifying the cause of accidents may blunt or even reduce the ability to think and insight of human accident investigators in the medium to long term. In addition, in light of the experience of the principal investigator in investigating aviation accidents to date, even if a model that can accurately identify the cause of an accident from given factual information can be constructed, the quality of the accident investigation will depend greatly on what factual information is collected in the initial investigation immediately after the accident occurs.

The authors have been discussing with accident investigators who have been involved in aviation accident investigations for many years about measures to solve these limitations and issues. Based on this, we have identified the following three requirements for the use of AI in aviation accident investigations, with the main premise being that it contributes to future aviation safety.

1. The role of AI in aviation accident investigations is not to replace accident investigators, but to provide support that enables accident investigators to maximize and strengthen their inherent abilities.
2. In the investigation of aviation accidents, AI should not narrow down and estimate "answers" to lead investigators in a certain direction, but should instead play a role

in expanding the scope of investigators by estimating a wider range of possible alternatives to "answers".

3. Much of the knowledge that affects the quality of accident investigations is in the "tacit knowledge" of investigators, and it is necessary to construct an AI model that learns this.

The research group of the authors proposes the following application as an AI application for aviation accident investigation that satisfies the above three requirements, and aims to construct, implement, and verify an AI model that achieves this.

1) At each step of the accident investigation (from the collection of factual information to the identification of the cause of the accident), the AI reminds human accident investigators of the factual information that should be collected, the analytical methods that can be applied, and the causal relationships that should be considered (preventing omissions in the items that should be collected or considered).

2) It confirms that the logic of the human accident investigator is appropriate for the purpose of the accident investigation, with regard to the causal relationship between the accident and its cause (factor), and the cause (factor) and the countermeasures to prevent its recurrence, while also encouraging the investigation of other possibilities. (It avoids the fixation of viewpoints and encourages the investigation of the true cause.

3) To efficiently improve the hypothetical experience of accident investigators in preparation for the occurrence of unknown accidents, training scenarios are automatically generated. (This helps to effectively improve the skills of accident investigators.

In this paper, for the purposes of 1) and 2), the mission was to extract the tacit knowledge of experienced accident investigators through interviews, and to analyze it by converting it into data.

3   Method

The "tacit knowledge" possessed by accident investigators was extracted through semi-structured interviews (in-depth probing of what they do and why they do it) with accident investigators. The subjects were five accident investigators with more than 10 years of experience at Japan's official aviation accident investigation agency. The interview questions are summarized in Table 1.

The responses to the interviews with the five accident investigators were analyzed using text mining. Specifically, characteristic words for each question item were extracted by calculating TF-IDF.

Table 1. Interview items on tacit knowledge of accident investigators.

	Question	Answers (Please describe freely.)
Q1: What do you think of the investigator's tacit knowledge (hunches, tricks, ingenuity, consideration, etc.) to be utilized in the initial survey?	What do you think about in relation to the aircraft survey?	
	What do you consider in relation to interviewing the parties concerned?	
	What do you think about in relation to interviewing the parties concerned and witnesses?	
	What else do you think about in relation to your own management (injury prevention, logistics, mental health, personal belongings, etc...)?	
Q2: What tacit knowledge of the investigator do you utilize in your analysis (what difficulties do you have and how do you overcome/resolve them)?	What do you consider in relation to the organization of factual information?	
	What do you consider in relation to the scrutiny of causal relationships?	
	What else do you consider in relation to analytical work (cooperation with other members, collection of literature, review of past cases, etc...)?	
Q3: Regarding the investigator's tacit knowledge to be utilized in the preparation of the report (what difficulties exist and how to overcome/resolve them).	What do you consider in relation to identifying the cause of the accident?	
	What do you consider in relation to deriving measures to prevent recurrence?	
	What else do you think about in relation to the report writing process (cooperation with other members, wording, timelines, etc...)?	

4   Results of the Analysis

The characteristic words for each question are shown in the word clouds in Figs. 1, 2, 3, 4, 5, 6, 7, 8, 9 and 10.

4.1   Initial Investigation (Airframe Investigation)

The characteristic words were "destroy", "component" and "missing". In particular, all investigators responded that they would focus on the destroyed components and compare them with the normal state.

Fig. 1. Image of the Instructions given to GPT.

4.2 Initial Investigation (Interview with the Person Concerned)

The characteristic words that were mentioned were "relaxed", "build" and "(not) deny". In particular, all investigators emphasized the importance of having the parties speak in their own words and building a relationship of trust. Many investigators also mentioned the importance of creating a relaxed atmosphere.

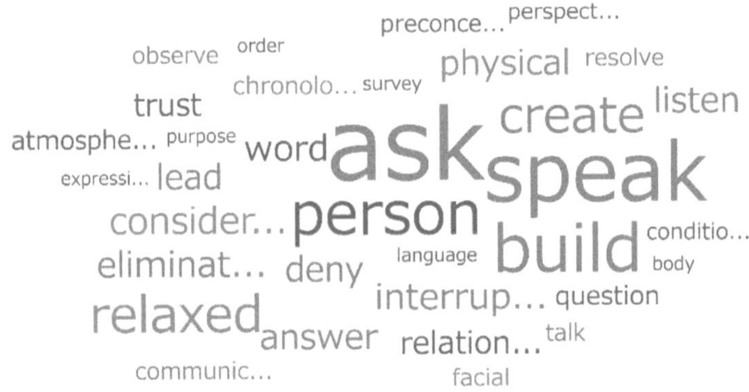

Fig. 2. Image of the Instructions given to GPT.

4.3 Initial Investigation (Interviewing Witnesses and Other Relevant Persons)

The words "specific", "color" and "sound" were mentioned. This is clearly different from the interviews with the parties mentioned in the previous section, and it can be seen that specific facts (sounds, smells, colors, etc.) are emphasized in the interviews with the people involved and witnesses.

Fig. 3. Image of the Instructions given to GPT.

4.4 Initial Investigation (Other)

Some of the characteristic words include "prepare", "transportation", and "equipment". This shows the importance of planning for accommodation and transportation, and preparing the equipment to be used. It also shows that they are careful about their own health, as indicated by the words "rest" and "risk".

Fig. 4. Image of the Instructions given to GPT

4.5 Analysis (Organizing Factual Information)

The characteristic words used were "gather", "evidence" and "source". The attitude of gathering any information that can be gathered was common to experienced investigators. It was also clear that brainstorming was important.

Fig. 5. Image of the Instructions given to GPT

4.6 Analysis (Close Examination of Causal Relationships)

The characteristic words used were "factual", "base" and "method". It was strongly recognized that factual information was the most important thing in analysis. It was also clear that they were conscious of identifying the causes to a certain extent and making effective use of methods.

Fig. 6. Image of the Instructions given to GPT

4.7 Analysis (Other)

The characteristic words were "past", "literature" and "cooperation". It was clear that they placed importance on investigating past cases and related literature when analyzing. Cooperation with other members was also mentioned.

Fig. 7. Image of the Instructions given to GPT

4.8   Report Writing (Identifying the Cause of the Accident)

The characteristic words were "careful" and "individual". There was a strong awareness of the need to avoid placing the blame on individuals. It seems obvious that the cause should be investigated based on the facts and analysis, but this was clearly a concern.

Fig. 8. Image of the Instructions given to GPT

4.9   Report Writing (Deriving Measures to Prevent Recurrence)

The characteristic words were "realistic" and "effective". This was a common response among many investigators, and the emphasis was on whether the report was clear and realistic, who it was aimed at, and whether it was effective.

Fig. 9. Image of the Instructions given to GPT

4.10   Report Writing (Other)

The characteristic words were "cooperation", "opinion", and "member". Not being attached to one's own ideas and cooperating with other members were particularly common. Technical aspects such as creating effective diagrams were also mentioned.

Fig. 10. Image of the Instructions given to GPT.

5   Conclusion

In this paper, we conducted interviews with experienced accident investigators with the aim of establishing a new accident investigation method that makes appropriate use of both AI and accident investigators, and analyzed the data obtained from the interviews. As a result, we were able to identify the matters that accident investigators commonly or individually focus on in each phase of the investigation and analysis. Although this knowledge has not been formalized, it is important for conducting accident investigations at a high level, and it is something that should be passed on to accident investigators who are still inexperienced. In the future, we plan to have AI learn this knowledge, implement it in an application that supports accident investigators in the field of accident investigation, and verify its usefulness.

References

1. Ziakkas, D., Pechlivanis, K.: Artificial intelligence applications in aviation accident classification: a preliminary exploratory study. Decis. Anal. J. **9**, 100358 (2023)
2. Li, W.-C., Nakanishi, M., Wang, T.: Artificial intelligence in aviation: developing generative pre-trained transformer for accident analysis and prevention. ISASI (International Society of Air Safety Investigators), Risbon, October 2024
3. Department of the Air Force Guide HFACS 8.0. https://www.safety.af.mil/Portals/71/docume nts/Human%20Factors/DoD%20HFACS%208.0%20Gu[…]230927%20Corrected%20sm. pdf?ver=UTnHKQ1EvVeA4aSMZTamXQ%3d%3d. Accessed 21 Feb 2025
4. Meng, B., Lu, N.: A hybrid model integrating HFACS and BN for analyzing human factors in CFIT accidents. Aerospace **9**(11), 711 (2022)
5. Wu, Y., Zhang, S., Zhang, X., Lu, Y., Xiong, Z.: Analysis on coupling dynamic effect of human errors in aviation safety. Accid. Anal. Prev. **192**, 107277 (2023)

Correlating Human Operator Risk Profiles and Intel Gain/Loss (IGL) Assessments: An ISR Study

Justin Nelson[1]([✉]), Samuel Johnston[1], Anna Maresca[2], Erica Curtis[2], Justin Morgan[2], Timothy Heggedahl[2], and Jenna Cotter[1]

[1] 711th Human Performance Wing, Airman Systems Directorate, WPAFB, Dayton, OH 45433, USA
`nelson.39@wright.edu`
[2] Parallax Advanced Research, Beavercreek, OH 45431, USA

Abstract. Background: Intelligence, Surveillance, and Reconnaissance (ISR) operations are essential in collecting critical information in an effort to enhance and accelerate continuous mission planning. In particular, ISR collections can provide discernment into our adversary's behavioural patterns, defensive and offensive posture, and regional threats. Nevertheless, the assessment and decision-making process for continuous mission planning remains in the hands of the human operators. Understanding how human operators consider the trade-offs between asset reallocation and continuous mission planning based on real-world collection is an unexplored area within the intelligence community. Therefore, the objective of this study was to determine if human operator risk profiles correlate to intel gain/loss (IGL) assessments. Methods: The study consisted of fifty participants (32 male and 18 female) with an average age of 30.4 (SD = 6.4). During the first phase of the study, participants were provided with 10 geographical maps and requested to select the optimal route based on risk versus reward. Each map had three routes which conveyed distance, number of stops, risk level, and reward factor. In addition, the map was color coded (green, yellow, red) to represent the crime index for a particular region. Green represented a low crime index rate, yellow represented a medium crime index rate, and red represented a high crime index rate. Lastly, each route had an associated probability of success with respect to risk level. The safest rate (low risk) had a probability of success at eighty percent, the moderate route (medium risk) had a probability of success at sixty percent, and the most dangerous route (high risk) had a probability of success at forty percent. Therefore, if the route the participant selected successfully traveled the path, the participant would be rewarded with the monetary value displayed under the map. However, if the route the participant selected was unsuccessful in traveling the route, they would receive no monetary value and their accumulated value would decrease by ten. Participants were unaware of the probability of success but following each of their selections, they were informed if they were successful or unsuccessful in the route they selected. The data from the first phase of the study was categorized with respect to low, medium, and high-risk selection by participant to develop a risk profile. As a result, a sequential ranking of risk was developed which discovered that twenty-three out of fifty participants had a low-medium risk profile

D. Harris et al. (Eds.): HCII 2025, LNCS 16334, pp. 127–136, 2026.
https://doi.org/10.1007/978-3-032-12392-3_8

(i.e., more low and medium risk routes) and twenty-seven out of fifty participants had a medium-high risk profile (i.e., more medium and high-risk routes). Next, participants were provided with an additional 10 geographical maps and requested to select the optimal route based on risk versus reward. However, during this set of maps, each participant traveled the same path and were instructed to make a dynamic decision mid-route between two paths. Again, the map was color coded (green, yellow, red) to represent the crime index for a particular region. The participants were not informed on the success rate for the selected path. The objective in this phase of the task was to assess the risk profile developed from the first phased and determine if a correlation exists between risk profile and dynamic IGL assessments. Results: The findings indicate that there was a statistically significant difference detected with respect to risk profile and dynamic IGL assessment (p < 0.01). One-hundred and fifty-seven out of two-hundred and thirty dynamic IGL routes selected were safer with less reward when participants displayed a low risk profile (68% selected low IGL routes whereas 32% selected high IGL routes). Whereas one-hundred and thirty-nine out of two-hundred and seventy dynamic IGL routes selected were safter with less reward when participants displayed a high-risk profile (51% selected low IGL routes whereas 49% selected high IGL routes). Moreover, it was discovered that as risk profiles increased from low-risk (i.e., risk adverse) to high-risk (i.e., risk-takers), there was a continual decline in safe dynamic IGL selected routes. Conclusion: With human operators supporting mission planning efforts, it's imperative we understand how information is assessed and prioritized. Developing an profile of operators' tendencies towards risk taking can enhance our understanding of their decision-making processes. As a result, strategies can be better informed by understanding risk taking propensity, allowing strategies to be tailored to align with operator's risk profile. For example, a high-risk profile operator may respond better to aggressive strategies with high opportunity while a low-risk operator may prefer prioritizing safety and stability over opportunity gain. In this study, we developed a risk profile across fifty participants based on low, medium, and high-risk path selection. The profile was then correlated to dynamic IGL assessments. Findings provide new evidence that risk profiles could be used as an indicator to assess human operators' decision-making during IGL assessments. Future research should be conducted to determine if the findings can be replicated across other domains.

Keywords: Intelligence · Surveillance · and Reconnaissance (ISR) · Intel Gain/Loss (IGL) · Risk Profile · Continuous Mission Planning · Risk vs Reward

1 Introduction

1.1 Intelligence, Surveillance, and Reconnaissance (ISR) Overview and the Effects on Continuous Mission Planning

With continual advancements in emerging technologies coupled with deceptive tactics, it is becoming more challenging to maintain military superiority across air, ground, and maritime domains over our adversaries (Hutchinson 2006). If strategic, operational, and tactical planners are unable to process, exploit, and disseminate (PED) collected intelligence appropriately within a contested environment, it could significantly hinder future course of actions (COAs). A COA is a developed framework that outlines the actionable plans to accomplish the mission at hand (Boukhtouta et al. 2004). To combat this issue, military operations rely heavily on Intelligence, Surveillance, and Reconnaissance (ISR) collections to support data-driven decisions (Nelson et al. 2023; Deptula & Francisco 2010) (Fig. 1).

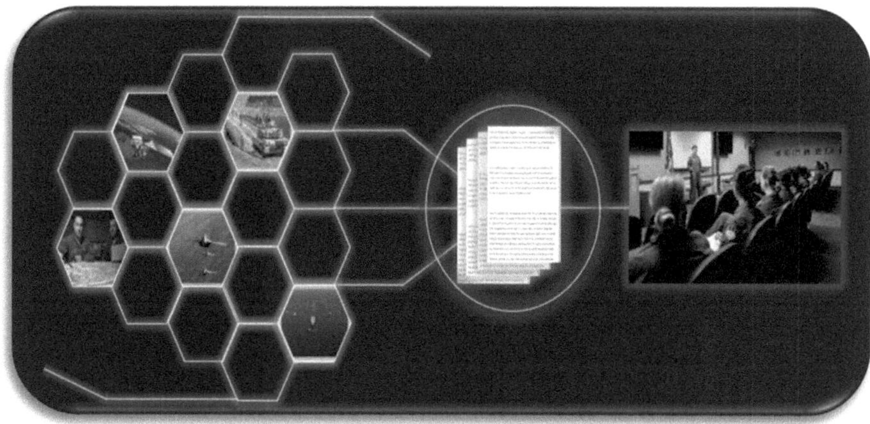

Fig. 1. Processing, Exploitation, and Dissemination (PED) phase of the intelligence cycle to support data-driven decisions (Nelson et al. 2024).

ISR operations is a coordinating process for collecting data on a continual, event-driven, or scheduled basis to enhance situational awareness and support future military direction (Crothers et al. 2009; Haffa & Datla 2014; Nelson et al. 2024). Although there are several methods that can be utilized to collect information within an operational environment, there are five main disciplines that the intelligence community (IC) recognizes which includes human intelligence (HUMINT), signals intelligence (SIGINT), geospatial intelligence (GEOINT), measurement and signatures intelligence (MASINT), and open-source intelligence (OSINT) (Blaxland 2007; Lowenthal & Clark 2015). Independently, each discipline has the ability to enhance battlefield perception within an area of interest. However, when the collected information across multiple disciplines is synchronized, greater transparency will occur leading to better decision-making outcomes. Information collected from ISR operations can then be utilized to augment, in near-real time, continuous mission planning efforts. Yet, understanding how human operators consider the trade-offs between asset reallocation and continuous mission planning based on real-world collection is an unexplored area within the intelligence community.

1.2 Artificial Intelligence and Machine Learning (AI/ML)

Artificial intelligence and machine learning (AI/ML) are transforming mission planning across various industries by improving decision-making, optimizing resource allocation, and boosting efficiency. Within a military setting, AI-powered tools can quickly analyze large datasets, offering real-time insight to support strategic planning, predictive maintenance, and logistics management. These technologies improve risk assessment precision and enhance Joint All-Domain Command and Control (JADC2) coordination in complex environments resulting in enhanced overall mission success. Moreover, machine learning models have the ability to adapt based on incoming data, making mission planning more dynamic and responsive to evolving conditions.

While AI provides valuable data-driven insight, it is critical to understand how human operators consider trade-offs between asset reallocation and continuous mission planning based on ISR collections. Human judgment is essential with regards to ethical, strategic, and situational factors ensuring that technological tools complement rather than replace the critical decision-making roles of operators. Consequently, maintaining human oversight in mission planning remains essential, as it fosters a holistic approach to tackling complex challenges in dynamic environments.

1.3 Human Operator Risk Profiles

As mentioned previously, although the implementation of artificial intelligence and machine learning (AI/ML) algorithms are becoming more applicable in supporting future mission planning efforts, human operators remain as the final decision-makers (Grooms 2019; Kase et al. 2022). Therefore, it is critical to understand how human operators consider trade-offs between asset reallocation and continuous mission planning based on ISR collections (see Fig. 2). The literature has discovered many factors that could significantly influence an operator's ability to prioritize and assess situations involving mission planning and intel gain/loss (IGL) assessments. These include the nature of the task, associated risks and benefits, and personal demographic characteristics (Ozer 2005; Resnik 2017). A study conducted by Lauriola discovered that there was a statistically significant correlation between risk-taking and nature of the task when involving ethical, safety, health, and financial risk (Lauriola & Weller 2018). In addition, a study conducted by Bornovalova discovered that associated risks and benefits significantly influenced decision-making outcomes. As risks and benefits associated with the task increased, participants became more risk-adverse (Bornovalova et al. 2009). Lastly, the correlation between demographic characteristics including age, gender, and education and risk-taking has been extremely diverse in the literature identifying significance at times and not at other time (Byrnes et al. 1999; Nicholson et al. 2005; Thanki & Baser 2019). Yet, little research has been performed with a focus area on developed risk profiles and intel gain/loss (IGL) assessments. The objective of this study was to develop a risk profile and determine if human operator risk profiles directly correlate to IGL assessments.

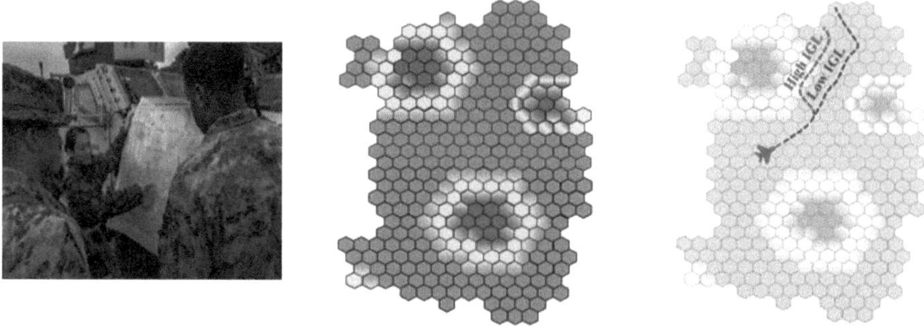

Fig. 2. An Example of Continuous Mission Planning to determine appropriate Course of Actions (COAs) with respect to Intel Gain/Loss (IGL) Assessments.

2   Methods and Materials

2.1   Study Participants

The study protocol was approved by the U.S. Air Force Research Laboratory (AFRL) Institutional Review Board (IRB) on human participants to determine if a correlation exists between human operator risk profiles and IGL decision-making assessments. Fifty participants completed the research study. Participants were excluded from the study if they did not meet the following criteria: must be 18 years old or older, speak fluent English, retain basic computer skills, and be located within the U.S. Participation was completely voluntary and participants were able to complete the task online via the survey platform Qualtrics.

2.2   Task

During the first phase of the study, each participant was provided with 10 geographical maps and requested to select the optimal route based on risk versus reward. Each map had three routes which conveyed distance, number of stops, risk level, and reward factor (see Fig. 3). In addition, the map was color coded to represent the crime index for a particular region. Green hexagons represented a low crime index rate, yellow hexagons represented a medium crime index rate, and red hexagons represented a high crime index rate. Lastly, each route had an associated probability of success with respect to risk level. The safest route (low-risk path) had a probability of success at eighty percent, the moderate route (medium-risk path) had a probability of success at sixty percent, and the most dangerous route (high-risk path) had a probability of success at forty percent. Therefore, if the route the participant selected successfully traveled the entire path, the participant would be rewarded with the monetary value displayed under the map. However, if the route the participant selected was unsuccessful in traveling the entire route, they would receive no monetary value and their accumulated value would decrease by 10. Participants were unaware of the probability of success throughout phase one but following each of their selections, they were informed if they were successful or unsuccessful in the route they selected. The objective of the first phase was to develop a risk profile by participant.

During phase two of the task, each participant was provided with 10 geographical maps and requested to select the optimal route based on risk vs reward. However, in the second phase, each participant traveled the same path and were instructed to make a dynamic decision mid-route between two paths (see Fig. 4). Again, the map was color coded for neighborhood crime index and the participants were shown the distance traveled, number of stops, risk level, and reward factor. However, after the selection of each path, the participants were not informed on the success rate for the path they traveled. The objective in the second phase to assess the risk profile developed from phase one and determine if a correlation exists between risk profile and dynamic IGL assessments in phase two of the study.

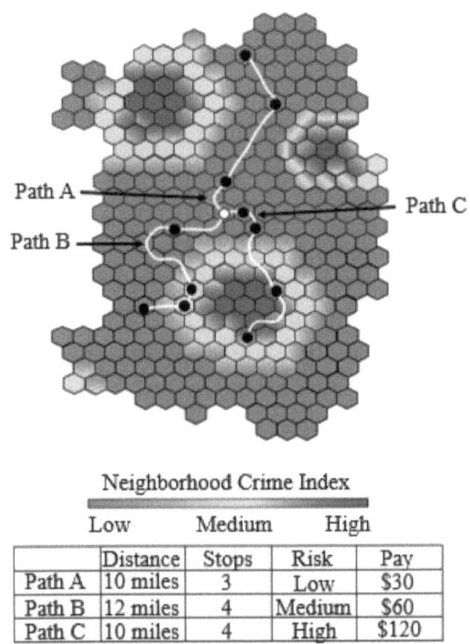

	Distance	Stops	Risk	Pay
Path A	10 miles	3	Low	$30
Path B	12 miles	4	Medium	$60
Path C	10 miles	4	High	$120

Fig. 3. Geographical Representation of the Routes provided to the Participant for Phase One of the Study.

2.3 Hypothesis

Within the literature, it has been discovered that risk (i.e., risk-taking vs risk adverse) have been a contributing factor influencing decision-making assessments, financial assessments, and strategic planning (Broihanne et al. 2014; Coleman, L. 2007; Wiseman & Gomez-Mejia 1998). Therefore, we expect that participants with low-risk profiles will select significantly safer dynamic IGL routes with less reward than participants with a high-risk profile. In addition, we do not expect to discover a correlation with respect to risk profile and demographic characteristics (Anbar & Eker 2010).

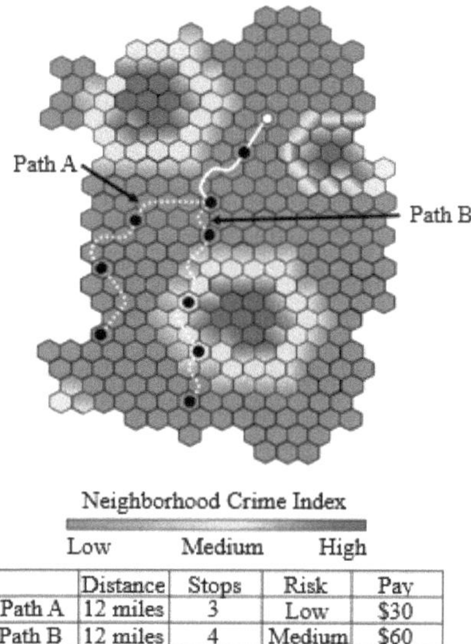

	Distance	Stops	Risk	Pay
Path A	12 miles	3	Low	$30
Path B	12 miles	4	Medium	$60

Fig. 4. Geographical Representation of the Routes provided to the Participant for Phase Two of the Study.

2.4 Data Analysis

Data analysis was performed using R Statistical Analysis Software (R version 4.1.2). R is an open-source programming language with the capability to download library packages from the Comprehensive R Archive Network (CRAN) repository data visualization and data analysis. To test our hypothesis that a correlation exists between participant risk profiles and dynamic IGL assessments, the data from phase one was categorized with respect to low, medium, and high-risk selection by participant. A risk profile was developed and sequentially ranked which discovered that 23 out of 50 participants had a low-med risk profile (i.e., more low and medium risk route selections) and 27 out of 50 participants had a med-high risk profile (i.e., more medium and high-risk route selections). Next, an analysis of variance (ANOVA) was conducting comparing risk profile and dynamic IGL assessments.

3 Results

To begin, we will discuss the results comparing risk profile and dynamic intel/gain loss (IGL) assessments. It was discovered that there was a statistically significant difference detected with respect to risk profile and dynamic intel gain/loss (IGL) assessments ($p < 0.01$) (see Table 1). One-hundred and fifty-seven out of two-hundred and thirty dynamic IGL routes selected were safer with less reward when participants displayed a low risk profile (68% selected low IGL routes whereas 32% selected high IGL routes). Whereas one-hundred and thirty-nine out of two-hundred and seventy dynamic IGL routes selected were safter with less reward when participants displayed a high-risk profile (51% selected low IGL routes whereas 49% selected high IGL routes) (see Fig. 5). Moreover, it was

134   J. Nelson et al.

discovered that as risk profiles increased from low-risk (i.e., risk adverse) to high-risk (i.e., risk-takers), there was a continual decline in safe dynamic IGL selected routes (see Fig. 6).

Table 1. Analysis of Variance (ANOVA) comparing Risk Profile and Dynamic Intel Gain/Loss (IGL) Assessment.

	Source	df	SS	MS	F	p-value
Risk Profile	Between-Conditions	1	3.50	3.50	14.58	< 0.01
	Within-Conditions	498	117.27	0.24		
	Total	499	120.77			

Statistical Significance at alpha level of 0.05

With respect to demographics, there was not a statistically significant correlation with respect to age, gender, and education level and risk profiles/IGL assessments.

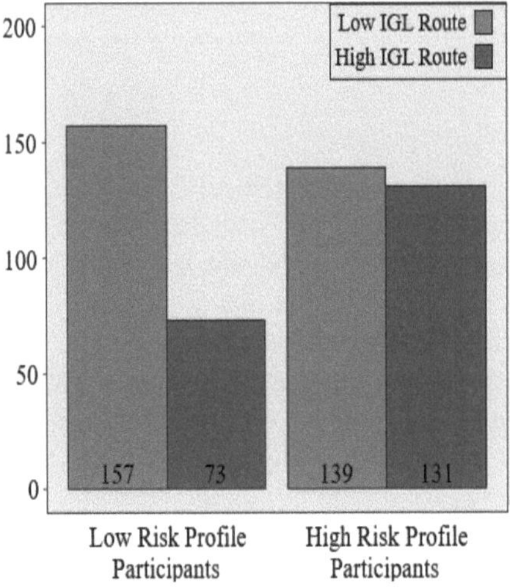

Fig. 5. Risk Profile and IGL Route Selection.

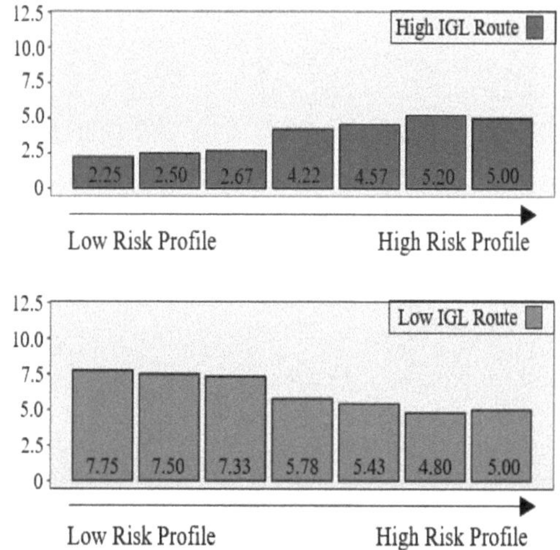

Fig. 6. Risk Profile Spectrum and IGL Route Selection.

4 Conclusion

With human operators supporting mission planning efforts, it is imperative we understand how information is assessed and prioritized when developing course of actions (COAs) for future military direction. Moreover, the research community has been focusing in on personal demographics including age, gender, education, and experience to determine if these factors include decision-making during a risk versus reward task. Yet, little research has been conducted on the development of a human operator risk profile and if the risk profile correlates to intel gain/loss (IGL) assessments. Developing an understanding of operators' tendencies towards risk tasking can enhance our understanding of their decision-making processes. COA development strategies can be better informed by understanding risk taking propensity, allowing strategies to be tailored to align with operator's risk profile. For example, a high-risk profile operator may respond better to aggressive strategies with high opportunity while a low-risk operator may prefer prioritizing safety and stability over opportunity gain. Understanding these differences could ensure that COA strategies are not only data-driven but considering the psychology of the individuals involved in the decisions. In this study, our team developed a risk profile across fifty participants based on low, medium, and high-risk path selection. The profile was then correlated to dynamic IGL assessments. The findings from this study have discovered underlying evidence that a correlation exists between risk profiles and IGL decision-making assessments. This is a promising result and should be replicated to determine if risk profiles are an adequate indicator in support complex, dynamic decision-making scenarios.

Acknowledgment. The views, opinions, and/or findings contained in this paper are those of the author and should not be interpreted as representing the official views or policies, either expressed or implied, of the Air Force, Air Force Research Laboratory or the Department of Defense.

References

Anbar, A., Eker, M.: An empirical investigation for determining of the relation between personal financial risk tolerance and demographic characteristics. Ege Acad. Rev. **10**(2), 503–522 (2010)

Blaxland, J.C.: Harnessing the spectrum: intelligence, surveillance, target acquisition and reconnaissance (ISTAR) for the hardened networked army. Aust. Army J. **4**(2), 77–92 (2007)

Broihanne, M.H., Merli, M., Roger, P.: Overconfidence, risk perception, and the risk-taking behavior of finance professional. Finance Res. Lett. **11**(2), 64–73 (2014)

Bornovalova, M.A., et al.: Risk taking differences on a behavioral task as a function of potential reward/loss magnitude and individual differences in impulsivity and sensation seeking. Pharmacol. Biochem. Behav. **93**(3), 258–262 (2009)

Boukhtouta, A., Bedrouni, A., Berger, J., Bouak, F., Guitouni, A.: A survey of military planning systems. In: 9th International Command and Control Research and Technology Symposium, pp. 5–7 (2004)

Byrnes, J.P., Miller, D.C., Schafer, W.D.: Gender differences in risk taking: a meta-analysis. Psychol. Bull. **125**(3), 367 (1999)

Coleman, L.: Risk and decision making by finance executives: a survey study. Int. J. Manag. Finance **3**(1), 108–114 (2007)

Crothers, B., Lanphear, M.J., Garino, M.B., Konyha, M.P., Byrne, M.E.: US space-based intelligence, surveillance, and reconnaissance. Space Primer (2009)

Deptula, D., Francisco, M.: Air force ISR operations: hunting versus gathering. Air Space Power J. **24**(4), 13–18 (2010)

Grooms, G.: Artificial intelligence applications for automated battle management aids in future military endeavors. Artif. Intell. **6** (2019)

Haffa, R.P., Datla, A.: Joint intelligence, surveillance, and reconnaissance in contested airspace. Air Space Power J. **28**(2) (2014)

Hutchinson, W.: Information warfare and deception. Inf. Sci. **9** (2006)

Kase, S., Hung, C., Krayzman, T., Hare, J., Rinderspacher, B., Su, S.: The future of collaborative human-artificial intelligence decision-making for mission planning. Front. Psychol. **13**, 850628 (2022)

Lauriola, M., Weller, J.: Personality and risk: beyond daredevils – risk taking from a temperament perspective. Psychol. Perspect. Risk Risk Anal. Theory Models Appl., 3–36 (2018)

Lowenthal, M., Clark, R.: The Five Disciplines of Intelligence Collection. Sage (2015)

Nelson, J.M., Heggedahl, T.L., Frame, M.E., Maresca, A.M., Schlessman, B.R.: Building the future of intelligence, surveillance, and reconnaissance (ISR) collections: the development and evaluation of a collaborative ISR tool to support intel analysts. In: IEEE International Conference on Intelligence and Security Informatics (IEEE ISI), pp. 1–6 (2023)

Nelson, J.: Are structured analytic techniques (SATs) the missing component in cognitive warfare? The future of ISR military operations. In: 15th International Conference on Applied Human Factors and Ergonomics (AHFE), Nice, France, 22–27 July. Springer (2024)

Nelson, J., Maresca, A., Schlessman, B.: Can structured analytic techniques enhance intelligence, surveillance, and reconnaissance (ISR) assessments when providing incremental information. In: IEEE Intelligent Human Systems Integration (IEEE IHSI), vol. 69. Springer (2024)

Nicholson, N., Soane, E., Fenton-O'Creevy, M., Willman, P.: Personality and domain-specific risk task. J. Risk Res. **8**(2), 157–176 (2005)

Ozer, M.: Factors which influence decision making in new product evaluation. Eur. J. Oper. Res. **163**(3), 784–801 (2005)

Resnik, D.B.: The role of intuition in risk/benefit decision-making in human subject research. Account. Res. **24**(1), 1–29 (2017)

Thanki, H., Baser, N.: Interactive impact of demographic variables and personality type on risk tolerance. Emerg. Econ. Stud. **5**(1), 42–54 (2019)

Wiseman, R.M., Gomez-Mejia, L.R.: A behavioral agency model of managerial risk taking. Acad. Manag. Rev. **23**(1), 133–153 (1998)

Cognitive and Operational Challenges During Go-Arounds: Insights from Airline Pilots

İbrahim Sarıkaya[1]([⊠]) ⓘ and Fuat Ücrak[2] ⓘ

[1] The Institute for Aviation Psychology Research, Istanbul University, Istanbul, Turkey
isarikaya@thy.com
[2] The Institute of Biomedical Engineering, Boğaziçi University, Istanbul, Turkey

Abstract. Go-arounds are among the most demanding maneuvers in commercial aviation, requiring rapid decision-making, high workload management, and effective coordination under time pressure. This study investigates the cognitive and operational challenges faced by airline pilots during go-arounds, with a comparative focus on First Officers and Captains. Using a cross-sectional survey of 40 commercial pilots across multiple fleets, we explored differences in perceived workload, decision-making strategies, flight path management, use of automation, and training needs. Results showed that while both groups rated go-arounds as high-workload events, first officers reported more frequent task overload and greater difficulty with automation transitions. Captains prioritized manual control and procedural recall, reflecting more internalized strategies shaped by experience. A significant difference was observed in workload mitigation strategies, indicating distinct mental models between the two groups. Both groups expressed strong support for enhanced scenario-based training, particularly involving manual flying and unexpected go-around triggers. These findings underscore the importance of aligning training programs with experience levels and improving procedural design to better support pilot performance during critical flight phases.

Keywords: Go-Around Maneuvers · Pilot Workload · Human Factors · Automation · Decision-Making · Commercial Aviation Safety

1 Introduction

The go-around phase is one of the most critical and high-stakes maneuvers in aviation, requiring pilots to make rapid decisions, manage complex systems, and maintain situation awareness under significant pressure. Despite extensive advances in aviation technology and pilot training, go-arounds remain a persistent area of operational risk. The complexity of modern flight decks and automation interfaces can introduce latent risks, especially when pilots misinterpret flight modes or fail to adequately monitor critical parameters like thrust or air speed during high-automation scenarios [1]. Studies have shown that while the overall number of general aviation accidents has declined, the proportion of fatal accidents occurring during go-arounds has increased over time, particularly under instrument meteorological conditions [2]. Analysis of large-scale trajectory

© The Author(s), under exclusive license to Springer Nature Switzerland AG 2026
D. Harris et al. (Eds.): HCII 2025, LNCS 16334, pp. 137–146, 2026.
https://doi.org/10.1007/978-3-032-12392-3_9

data indicates that go-around rates are often underestimated due to classification challenges, particularly at airports with parallel runways or short climb phases, highlighting the need for improved detection and procedural clarity [3]. Despite clear SOPs, studies show that only 3% of unstable approaches result in a go-around, contributing to over half of runway excursion accidents [4]. This significant noncompliance highlights the gap between policy and practice during the approach phase. Human error studies have shown that failures during go-around execution often stem from delayed actions, incomplete task execution, and confusion between crew members, especially when SOPs are poorly internalized or inadequately trained [5].

Environmental factors, especially wind-related phenomena such as wind shear, gusts, and turbulence, are among the most common reasons for go-arounds. A Go-Around Safety Forum report found that 42% of go-arounds were due to adverse wind conditions, often underestimated by air traffic control systems and more accurately detected by pilots in real-time [6]. Turbulence-induced go-arounds can significantly elevate pilot workload and cause aircraft to exceed performance limits in over 30% of events, highlighting the severity of these operational risks [6].

Moreover, the impact of go-around events extends beyond the individual flight, significantly disrupting arrival sequencing, increasing flight times, and reducing airport operational efficiency [7]. The integration of machine learning techniques to predict go-around events at the airport-runway level has shown promise in optimizing air traffic management, especially when incorporating factors like weather, glide slope deviation, and traffic density [3]. This highlights the urgent need for deeper understanding and targeted interventions aimed at improving go-around execution. Psychological studies indicate that pilots' risk perception and situation awareness play key roles in whether they choose to initiate a go-around [8].

An unstable approach is a common precursor to a go-around, and managing such situations requires pilots to rapidly adapt to dynamic and sometimes conflicting goals under time pressure. Research adopting a systems perspective has emphasized that successful go-around execution depends not only on procedural adherence but also on pilots' ability to reconcile multiple goals such as safety, operational efficiency, and air traffic control compliance[9]. Simulation-based studies revealed frequent failures in task sharing and cockpit automation awareness during go-arounds, leading to degraded crew coordination [10]. Additionally, language-related communication issues, especially in international and student pilot training contexts, remain underreported yet present critical risks during non-standard and emergency scenarios such as go-arounds [11].

Recent studies reveal that traditional crew-centric standard operating procedures (SOPs), which assume linear task sequences and fixed communication points, may not fully accommodate the operational complexities of go-arounds [12]. When pilots are required to interleave or defer tasks based on real-time conditions, SOP rigidity can impair decision-making and increase the likelihood of error. In contrast, process-based SOP designs, focused on adaptive workflows and contextual decision-making, have been shown to reduce workload and improve pilot response flexibility in complex scenarios [12].

Failure to successfully manage these competing demands can lead to unstable or unsafe outcomes, underscoring the complexity of human factors at play during this critical flight phase. Compounding these challenges, overreliance on cockpit automation has been identified as a contributing factor to loss of situation awareness, increasing the risk of Controlled Flight Into Terrain (CFIT) during high-workload phases such as go-arounds [13]. Upsets due to inappropriate thrust-trim combinations and poor cockpit scan during ATC-instructed go-arounds remain a safety concern [14].

Cognitive workload and situation awareness during go-arounds are further challenged by the demands placed on the Pilot Monitoring (PM). Monitoring duties, which include flight path tracking, communication with ATC, and system cross-checking, become vulnerable to breakdown when procedural tasks are not effectively distributed [15]. A lack of shared mental models and attention tunneling under stress can further degrade performance during go-arounds, especially for less experienced crews. Enhancing the PM role through improved training and procedure design is essential for reducing error likelihood in high-stakes scenarios [15].

Recognizing these challenges, recent advancements have explored the application of artificial intelligence (AI) and machine learning techniques to support decision-making during the approach and landing phases. Predictive models have been developed to anticipate go-around events in real-time based on environmental conditions, flight parameters, and pilot behavior [16]. Studies using ensemble imbalance learning frameworks have shown that machine learning models, especially when combined with interpretability tools like SHAP analysis, can accurately predict missed approach events triggered by factors such as low-level wind shear, runway orientation, and situation variables [17]. Beyond prediction, sophisticated approaches have been designed to automatically detect go-around maneuvers using real-time ADS-B data analysis, enabling earlier and more accurate recognition of abnormal flight statuses [18]. Furthermore, unsupervised learning algorithms such as clustering techniques have been employed to distinguish between nominal and anomalous go-arounds, revealing distinct energy profiles and trajectory deviations associated with higher-risk events [19].

Moreover, emerging methods utilizing open-source ADS-B data have demonstrated the feasibility of detecting go-arounds based purely on flight trajectory and velocity changes, offering new avenues for real-time operational monitoring [20]. These developments underscore the transformative potential of data-driven and AI-enhanced approaches in improving situation awareness and supporting timely decision-making in aviation operations. These AI developments, while not applied in the current study, provide a forward-looking context for the human performance challenges explored herein.

This study aims to investigate the specific challenges faced by less experienced and expert pilots during go-around procedures, with a focus on decision-making under pressure, workload management, automation reliance, and adherence to standard operating procedures (SOPs). To achieve a comprehensive understanding of these issues, a mixed-methods approach was employed, incorporating survey data and manual thematic analysis of pilot responses. Although this study did not utilize AI-based methods, it contributes to the growing body of research that may support the development of future AI tools. By identifying key pilot challenges and human factors associated with go-around maneuvers, these findings can inform the refinement of pilot training programs, procedural frameworks, and decision support systems to enhance operational safety in commercial aviation.

2 Methods and Materials

2.1 Study Design

This study utilized a quantitative, cross-sectional design to investigate pilot perceptions and challenges associated with go-around maneuvers. The research aimed to compare responses from two distinct pilot groups, First Officers (less experienced pilots) and Captains (experienced pilots), focusing on differences in workload perception, decision-making, flight path management, and reliance on automation during go-arounds.

In addition to experience differences, the roles of first officers and captains entail distinct operational responsibilities. Captains typically hold command authority and make final decisions during critical phases, while First Officers serve in a supporting and monitoring role, executing assigned tasks and managing communication. These role-based distinctions were considered in interpreting pilot responses.

2.2 Participants

The study sample consisted of 40 commercial airline pilots, including 20 First Officers and 20 Captains. Participants represented a range of fleet types (A320, A330/350, B737, B777/787) and age groups, with career experience ranging from early-stage to senior command roles. The selection aimed to capture a representative distribution of operational experience levels in both real-world and simulator-based go-around scenarios.

2.3 Data Collection

Data was collected through a structured electronic questionnaire designed specifically for this study. The survey consisted of multiple-choice, Likert-scale, and short-response items exploring the following key domains:

- Frequency and type of go-around experiences
- Perceived workload and confidence during go-arounds
- Challenges related to manual control, automation, and decision-making
- Preferences in workload mitigation strategies
- Views on current training and perceived training needs

Pilots completed the survey anonymously, enabling honest disclosure of operational perceptions and difficulties encountered during go-around procedures.

2.4   Statistical Analysis

All statistical analyses were conducted using SPSS Statistical Software v24 (IBM Corp., Armonk, NY, USA). The following techniques were applied:

- Descriptive statistics (mean, standard deviation, median, minimum, maximum) were used to summarize central tendencies and variability in key variables such as workload and confidence ratings.
- Chi-Square Tests of Independence and Fisher's Exact Tests (for small expected cell counts) were used to examine associations between categorical variables, such as role (First Officer vs. Captain) and perceptions of specific go-around challenges.
- Mann-Whitney U Tests were employed to compare group differences in ordinal or non-normally distributed continuous variables, such as self-rated workload and manual flying confidence.

The statistical significance threshold was set at $p < 0.05$. Where results did not meet this criterion, findings were interpreted as not statistically significant.

2.5   Ethical Considerations

All participants were informed about the voluntary and anonymous nature of the study before participation. No personally identifiable information was collected. The study design conformed to ethical research standards and posed minimal risk to participants.

3   Results

This section presents the key findings from the comparative analysis of go-around challenges experienced by First Officers (n = 20) and Captains (n = 20). Data analysis focused on differences in perceived workload, decision-making, flight path management, and training needs. All reported p-values reflect results from Chi-Square, Fisher's Exact, or Mann-Whitney U tests, with significance set at $p < 0.05$.

3.1   Demographics and Operational Context

Captains were significantly older than First Officers ($p < 0.001$), consistent with expected career progression. Fleet distribution varied across roles, with First Officers more frequently flying B737 and Captains more often assigned to wide-body aircraft such as the A330/350. However, fleet type distribution differences were not statistically significant ($p = 0.157$).

3.2   Frequency and Nature of Go-Around Events

Go-arounds were most commonly reported as rare (1–2 per year) across both groups. Captains reported a slightly higher incidence of frequent go-arounds, but the difference was not statistically significant ($p = 0.188$). Most pilots found the decision phase of the go-around more challenging than execution, with no significant role-based differences ($p = 0.500$).

3.3 Workload Perception and Confidence

Both First Officers and Captains rated go-arounds as moderately high workload events (median $= 4$ on a 5-point scale), with no significant differences (p $= 0.904$). Confidence in manual flying during go-arounds was also similar across groups (median $= 4$), with Captains showing slightly higher means, though not statistically significant (p $= 0.221$).

Task overload was reported more frequently by First Officers, though the difference did not reach statistical significance (p $= 0.190$). Transitioning between automation modes emerged as a commonly cited challenge, particularly among First Officers (40%). Captains more often cited pitch control as difficult (45%).

3.4 Use of Automation and Flight Path Management

No significant differences were found in use of automation during go-arounds (p $= 0.726$). Most pilots reported "often" or "always" using automation. Preferences for managing flight path leaned toward starting with manual control and transitioning to automation for both groups (First Officers: 70%, Captains: 65%). Monitoring of flight path during go-arounds was consistently high, with 70% of First Officers and 80% of Captains reporting "always" doing so (p $= 0.716$).

3.5 Decision-Making and Workload Mitigation

A significant difference was observed in workload mitigation strategies (p $= 0.040$). Captains predominantly prioritized manual control of the flight path, whereas First Officers showed more varied strategies, including greater reliance on automation. As shown in Fig. 1, Captains were significantly more likely to prioritize manual flight control during go-arounds, while First Officers employed a broader mix of strategies, including reliance on automation and SOPs.

Decision-making during time-critical go-arounds was guided by standard operating procedures (SOPs) in both groups, with Captains more consistently relying on SOP recall (75% vs. 50%). Both groups identified rapidly changing environmental conditions as the most challenging factor in decision-making during go-arounds (First Officers: 70%, Captains: 50%).

3.6 Perceived Training Needs

Pilots identified multiple areas for training improvement. First Officers emphasized the need for training in manual flying, energy management, and unexpected go-around triggers. Captains expressed a broader interest in scenario-based training, automation management, and procedural adaptability. Despite differences in emphasis, both groups highlighted the importance of incorporating more real-world variability into training scenarios.

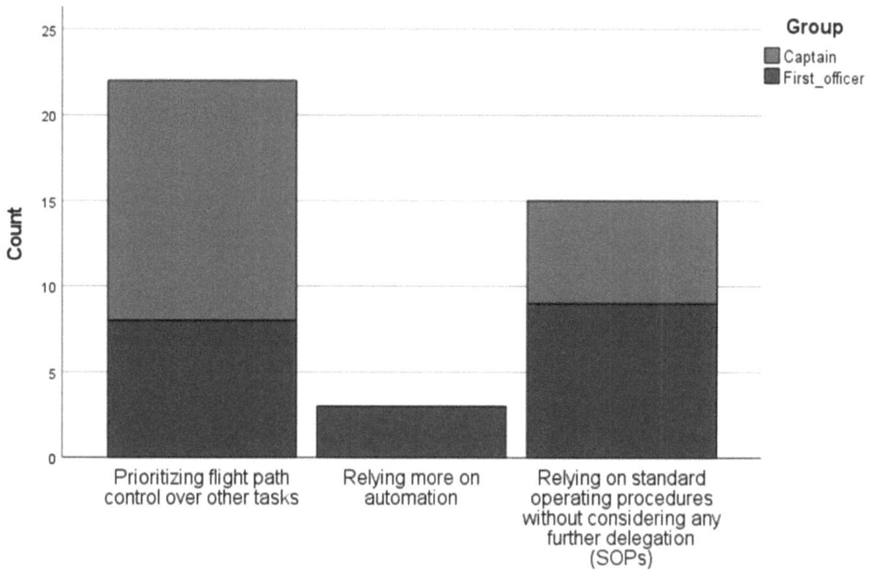

Fig. 1. Workload Mitigation Strategies Used by Captains and First Officers (p = 0.040).

4 Discussion

This study examined the challenges pilots face during go-around procedures by comparing responses from First Officers and Captains. Although many operational patterns were similar across roles, important distinctions emerged in workload perception, task prioritization, and training needs. These findings have significant implications for human-computer interaction in aviation, particularly regarding automation, decision-making, and adaptive training design.

4.1 Workload and Task Management

While both groups rated go-arounds as moderately high workload events, First Officers reported a higher frequency of perceived task overload and cited transitions between automation modes as especially demanding. Captains, on the other hand, expressed more difficulty with pitch control and vertical flight path management, reflecting the nuanced demands of manual flight in complex environments.

The significant difference in workload mitigation strategies, where Captains preferred prioritizing manual flight control, while First Officers showed more reliance on automation, suggests differing mental models and risk management strategies. This aligns with previous literature that highlights experience-based adaptation as a key factor in dynamic decision-making during high-stakes tasks [1, 5, 10, 12].

4.2 Use of Automation and Procedural Interaction

Despite increasing integration of automation in modern flight decks, both groups demonstrated a preference for starting go-arounds manually before engaging automation—a finding consistent with prior studies on automation trust and transitional workload [1, 10, 12]. The shared reliance on SOPs during time-critical go-arounds further reflects the central role of procedural consistency in managing uncertainty [4, 12, 15].

However, the results also indicate potential limitations in SOP design. Both less experienced and expert pilots identified issues such as hesitation, ambiguity, and inadequate task distribution during go-arounds. These findings support the shift advocated by process-based procedure design research, which emphasizes flexible task sequencing and adaptive workflows over rigid checklist adherence [4, 8, 10, 12].

4.3 Decision-Making Under Pressure

The decision phase of go-arounds was perceived as more cognitively demanding than the execution phase, a distinction consistent with prior research linking high time pressure and complexity to impaired decision-making [1, 10, 12]. Rapidly changing parameters like wind shear or ambiguous ATC instructions intensified the challenge, often disrupting otherwise standard workflows [8, 9]. Interestingly, Captains were more likely to rely on procedural recall, while First Officers responded more directly to ATC, reflecting experience-driven procedural internalization versus rule-based execution in less experienced crew [1, 12]. These findings support earlier observations that high situation complexity leads even seasoned pilots to rely on heuristics [9], though rapidly evolving environmental conditions remained the leading barrier to effective go-around decisions among captains [8, 10].

4.4 Training Implications

Both Captains and First Officers voiced a strong preference for more immersive, scenario-based training, particularly scenarios involving unexpected go-around triggers and manual flight under stress. While First Officers emphasized the importance of mastering energy management and automation transitions, Captains pointed to the value of reinforcing procedural adaptability and flight path control. These preferences align with existing literature that promotes training grounded in real-world complexity rather than rote procedural compliance [4, 8, 10, 12, 14]. Furthermore, tailoring training strategies to pilot experience level may enhance both confidence and performance during high-pressure phases like go-arounds [4, 12]. A key limitation of this study is the relatively small sample size (n = 40), which may constrain the generalizability of findings and limit the statistical power to detect subtler effects between groups. Another limitation of this study is that responses combined simulator and real-world go-around experiences. Future research should distinguish between the two to better capture context-specific pilot challenges.

Based on the findings of this study, it is recommended that training programs for go-around procedures be tailored to pilot experience levels, with a particular emphasis on scenario-based simulations that replicate real-world complexity. First Officers would benefit from focused training on manual flying, energy management, and automation transitions, while Captains may require reinforcement in procedural adaptability and flight path control under dynamic conditions. Additionally, standard operating procedures (SOPs) should be revisited to incorporate more flexible, process-based frameworks that support adaptive decision-making and task allocation during high-pressure situations. Enhancing the role of pilot monitoring through targeted training and improved SOP design is also critical for maintaining situation awareness and coordination. These targeted interventions can help bridge the gap between policy and practice, ultimately improving safety and performance during go-around maneuvers.

5 Conclusion

This study provides a nuanced understanding of the operational and cognitive challenges pilots face during go-around maneuvers, comparing the experiences of First Officers and Captains. Despite both groups reporting similar levels of workload and confidence, key differences emerged in task prioritization, automation handling, and decision-making strategies.

Captains tended to prioritize manual control and procedural recall, reflecting greater experience and internalization of standard operating procedures. In contrast, First Officers more frequently relied on automation and reported higher task overload, especially during transitions between automation modes. These differences suggest distinct mental models shaped by experience, which should be considered when designing and tailoring training programs.

Findings also highlight the limitations of traditional SOPs in handling dynamic, high-pressure scenarios like go-arounds. Both groups identified the need for more flexible and adaptive procedures that better accommodate the complexity and time sensitivity of real-world events. The study reinforces previous literature advocating for process-based procedure design and scenario-driven training as effective ways to prepare pilots for unexpected challenges.

Finally, the strong preference among both less experienced and experienced pilots for scenario-based training, particularly involving manual flying and unexpected triggers, signals a clear direction for improving training curricula. Enhancing realism and emphasizing decision-making under stress may better align training with the operational demands of modern aviation. Given the modest sample size, future studies with larger participant pools are needed to validate and extend these findings across broader pilot populations. Continued research into pilot behavior during go-arounds, especially under varying environmental and operational conditions, remains essential for improving safety, refining procedures, and developing more effective training strategies.

References

1. Causse, M., et al.: Impact of automation level on airline pilots' flying performance and visual scanning strategies: a full flight simulator study. Appl. Ergon. **125**, 104456 (2025)
2. de Voogt, A., et al.: Go-around accidents and general aviation safety. J. Safety Res. **82**, 323–328 (2022)

3. Monstein, R., et al.: Large landing trajectory dataset for go-around analysis. Eng. Proc. **28**(1), 2 (2022)
4. Tzvetomir Blajev, W.C.: Go-Around Decision-Making and Execution Project. Flight Safety Foundation (2017)
5. Li, W.-C.: The analysis of human errors in a large commercial aircraft when performing a go-around. J. Aeronaut. Astronaut. Aviat. Ser. A, **42**(1), 21–29 (2010)
6. O' Connor, A., Kearney, D.: Evaluate the effect of turbulence on aircraft during landing and take-off phases. Int. J. Aviat. Aeronaut. Aerosp. (2018)
7. Figuet, B., et al.: Analysing the impact of go-around occurrences at large European airports. J. Open Aviat. Sci. **1**(2) (2023)
8. Garrin Ross, L.T.: Go-around noncompliance during unstabilized approaches and landings in commercial aviation: a human factors analysis. In: 21st International Symposium on Aviation Psychology, pp. 299–302 (2021)
9. Moriarty, D., Jarvis, S.: A systems perspective on the unstable approach in commercial aviation. Reliab. Eng. Syst. Saf. **131**, 197–202 (2014)
10. Fanny Rome, G.A., Condette, J., Dehais, F., Causse, M.: Go-around manoeuver: a simulation study. In: European Association for Aviation Psychology (EAAP), Villasimius, Italy, pp. 1–7, September 2012
11. Baugh, B., Stolzer, A.: Language-related communications challenges in general aviation operations and pilot training. Int. J. Aviat. Aeronaut. Aerosp. (2018)
12. Schmidt, T.A., Kourdali, H.K., Nixon, J.: Evaluating process-based and crew - centred approaches to procedure design in aviation: workload and performance changes in go-around manoeuvres. Appl. Ergon. **90** (2021)
13. FAA, F.A.A.: General Aviation Controlled Flight Into Terrain Awareness (2019). Accessed 28 Apr 2025. https://www.faa.gov/documentLibrary/media/Advisory_Circular/ac61-134.pdf
14. Courville, B.d.: Go-around decision and maneuver: how to make it safer. In: EASS - European Aviation Safety Seminar, Istanbul (2011)
15. (IFALPA), I.F.o.A.L.P.A.: Enhancing pilot monitoring. In: Briefing Leaflet (2024)
16. Dhief, I., et al.: A machine learned go-around prediction model using pilot-in-the-loop simulations. Transp. Res. Part C Emerg. Technol. **140** (2022)
17. Khattak, A., et al.: Missed approach, a safety-critical go-around procedure in aviation: prediction based on machine learning-ensemble imbalance learning. Adv. Meteorol. **2023**, 1–24 (2023)
18. Wang, G., et al.: An automatic flight go-around maneuvers identification method based on action feature analysis. In: 2024 IEEE 6th International Conference on Civil Aviation Safety and Information Technology (ICCASIT), pp. 476–482 (2024)
19. Kumar, S.G., et al.: Classification and analysis of go-arounds in commercial aviation using ADS-B data. Aerospace **8**(10), 291 (2021)
20. Xu, Z., Lu, X., Zhang, Z.: Aircraft go-around detection employing open source ADS-B data. In: 2021 IEEE 3rd International Conference on Civil Aviation Safety and Information Technology (ICCASIT), pp. 259–262 (2021)

Quantitative Study on Fatigue Indicators in Air Traffic Controllers

Lili Wang[(✉)] and Mincong Zhu

Civil Aviation University of China, Jinbei Highway 2898, Tianjin 300300, China
`llwang@cauc.edu.cn`

Abstract. Air traffic controllers (ATC) play critical roles in aviation operations, and their fatigue levels have a direct impact on safety and efficiency in the industry. A multifaceted approach is adopted for the purpose of evaluating fatigue levels, encompassing various indicators such as reaction time, pupil diameter, electroencephalography (EEG), and the Stanford Sleep Scale (SSS). Subsequent to data collection, a series of paired-samples t-tests are conducted for the purpose of data analysis. The results obtained demonstrate a clear increase in all indicators, thus indicating that the fatigue level increases after the shift. In light of these findings, a comprehensive assessment approach for ATC fatigue, termed CAAF, is proposed, which incorporates all relevant indicators. The Pearson related coefficient between CAAF and SSS is remarkably 0.439, attesting to the effectiveness of the proposed approach on ATC fatigue assessment.

Keywords: Air traffic controller · Fatigue · Aviation Safety

1 Introduction

The increasing volume of air traffic represents a significant challenge to both the existing fixed airspace structure and aviation safety. Consequently, there is a necessity to optimize air traffic control services. Air traffic controllers (ATC) play a crucial role in this process, and their fatigue levels have a direct impact on aviation safety. Therefore, the assessment of ATC fatigue levels is vital for the improvement of safety and operation efficiency.

There are two broad categories of approaches to assess ATC fatigue levels [9]. Firstly, there is the subjective approach, in which the Multidimensional Fatigue Inventory (MFI) is applied. This is a multidimensional measure of fatigue and is scored by the subject filling in the relevant form. Examples of this include Multidimensional Fatigue Symptom Inventory-Short Form (MFSI-SF) [11] and MFI-16 [13]. In contrast, objective approaches involve the analysis of various physiological, biochemical, and behavioral parameters, which are recorded by instruments, including Galvanic Skin Response (GSR) [10], electrocardiogram (ECG) [8], electroencephalography (EEG) [10], eye movement [7], to assess fatigue levels.

D. Harris et al. (Eds.): HCII 2025, LNCS 16334, pp. 147–159, 2026.
https://doi.org/10.1007/978-3-032-12392-3_10

Lal [8] and Eoh [5] observed that δ wave and θ wave activities will increase significantly, and the ratio of β, $(\alpha + \beta)/\beta$ would show a significant difference. And the observation of the EEG signal indicates a gradual loss of responsiveness after 70 min of work [3], and Arico et al. [1] established fatigue function based on EEG signal. The sleep deprivation experiment results in a reduction of cognitive and reflex functions in ATC [12].

Qi et al. [6] investigate the variation of eye movement indices under fatigue. By incorporating eye movement, specifically saccadic and gaze behavior, and subjective fatigue score, it shows a significant difference and believes to be effective indices for assessing ATC fatigue level. Cao et al. [2] used tower simulation software and eye tracker to record controllers' eye movement data, which were combined with subjective fatigue values and changes in EEG to jointly assess the degree of fatigue and control ability. Results showed that in the fatigue state, the controllers needed longer time to find the target, expended more energy, and their senses and control ability deteriorated. There is also prototype system for real-time monitoring of controller fatigue status based on machine vision on facial [14] and body movement [4]. Wang et al. [15] employed Grey relational theory to analyze radar control simulation test data, thereby facilitating the exploration of fatigue indicators. The findings of this study indicated that reaction time, control skills, and shift duration were hallmark indicators of fatigue.

In conclusion, the majority of scholars provide ideas and methods of controller fatigue research from a variety of perspectives and aspects. The research focuses primarily on the development of fatigue testing methods and measurement indexes, which play a significant role in the evaluation of controller fatigue. However, there is a lack of quantitative studies on the fatigue indexes of controllers. Therefore, this paper focuses on the quantification of fatigue indicators of controllers. In this study, we first analyzed several indicators related to fatigue in controllers, including eye movement (reaction time, pupil diameter), physiological (electroencephalographic index, galvanic skin index) and subjective fatigue scale data. Then, we conducted a paired-sample t-test on five key fatigue indicators. The results showed that there was a significant difference before and after shift in indicators. Consequently, a model for quantitatively assessing controller fatigue was proposed, and the Pearson correlation test was conducted between the model output and the subjective fatigue scale values. The results showed that the correlation was significant.

2   Data Source

For the purpose of noise shielding, the instruments, light and temperature conditions are maintained at the same level as in a real air traffic control room. As shown in Fig. 1, data are recorded from approach radar control interface, eye movement signal display interface, and pilot simulation interface. The test controllers wear the corresponding physiological signal acquisition equipment. The role of the simulated pilot is assumed by a trainee controller, while the controller instructor is responsible for observing the reaction time and special situation handling of the subject controller, and evaluating the controller's performance.

Fig. 1. A photo of experiment environment, the screens are used for display interfaces and controllers are installed with measurement instruments.

The test group was responsible for the collection of physiological data prior to and following their assigned duties, according to the shift schedule of a control center of a control unit. According to the shift schedule of 24 h of work and 48 h of rest for the aforementioned control center's controllers, the prior shift test was conducted prior to the commencement of the controllers' duties from 08:00 am. to 12:00 p. m. The post-service test was conducted after the controllers had completed their 24-hour shift from 01:00 am. to 05:00 am., with the specific test time being the end of the controllers' work that night. To ensure the objectivity and accuracy of the test, the controller was not aware of the topic setting before the test, while the content of the before and after tests was the same, and the experiments included simulating the control command for 40 min and filling in the Stanford Sleep Scale (SSS) after the test. In order to reduce the influence of additional variables on the test, the subjects were informed of the test procedure and test precautions before the test.

During the experiment, the eye movement data and polysomnographic data of each subject were collected for approximately 30 min, with the Tobii-eye-tracker operating at a sampling rate of 120 Hz, the Mangold-10 EEG signals at 256 Hz, the dermatoglyphic signals at 32 Hz, and the electromyographic signals at 32 Hz. A total of 48 controllers from a control centre participated in the test, serving as the primary release orders. Each of the 48 controllers involved in this test at the control centre is a first-line release order, and collectively, they possess an average of more than 340,000 pieces of data. To ensure the seamless execution of the experiment and the precise collection of data, a substantial amount of time, manpower and energy was dedicated to the study.

3   Quantization of ATC Fatigue

This paper presents a range of indicators with the aim of characterizing fatigue. A fatigue assessment model is obtained through linear summation, and finally a Pearson correlation analysis is conducted between the output values of the model and the difference between the first and last states of the SSS.

3.1   Indicators for ATC Fatigue Assessment

There are various of indicators for ATC fatigue assessment. Reactivity is the average value of the time difference between the entry of all aircraft into their jurisdiction and the controller's recognition of each aircraft throughout the simulated control experiment. As fatigue accumulates, controllers become less responsive [2,15]. Data were collected via eye-tracking device. EEGs are indicative of the transition from a normal state to a state of fatigue. This transition is characterized by a gradual increase in slow-wave signals and a concomitant decrease in fast-wave signals. Consequently, the relative power spectrum of β-waves has been utilized as an EEG indicator to characterize the fatigue state [8]. The data were collected using a Mangold-10 Multi-Conductor Physio meter. As fatigue builds up, the sweat glands secrete more liquid, which in turn increases the flow of electric current, leading to an increase in skin conductivity [10] and a decrease in resistivity. The mean value of skin resistivity was used as a physiological indicator characterizing the fatigue state extracted from the skin electrical signals. The data were collected with a generic Mangold-10 multi conductor physio meter. And the pupil diameter of the human eye becomes larger [7]. The data is collected through an eye-tracker.

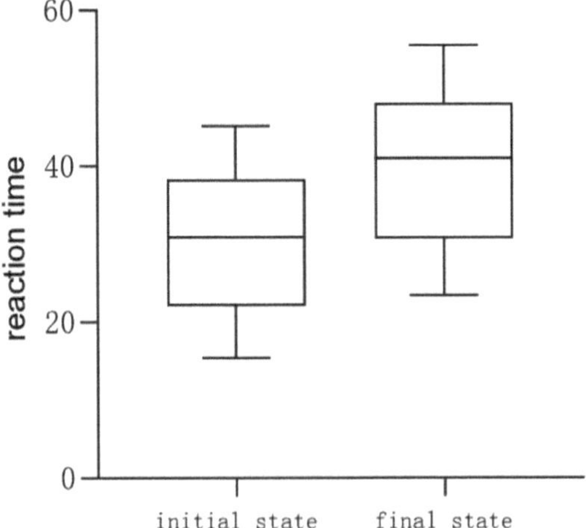

Fig. 2. Reaction time variation before and after shift.

Reactivity. Reactivity is characterized by the average reaction time RE, i.e. the average value of the time interval between the appearance of an aircraft and the first glance of the controller. Formulate as

$$RE = \frac{\sum\limits_{i=1}^{n}(t'_i - t_i)}{n} \tag{1}$$

where n is the number of aircraft, t'_i is the controller's first look for aircraft i, while t_i is the time the radar observed the ith aircraft.

As shown in Fig. 2, controller reaction times in the end state were generally significantly higher than in the initial state, implying fatigue after 24 h of work, resulting in a reduction in controller end-state responsiveness.

Electroencephalography (EEG). As the controller's level of fatigue increases, the power of the α and β waves decreases and the value of the θ wave increases. Since the β wave can reflect a person's mental arousal state and thus indicate the degree of controller fatigue, the relative power spectral value of the β wave is currently used as an EEG index P'_β to assess the change in controller fatigue through the trend of the β wave value. By analyzing the changes in the power value of the EEG β wave of 48 controllers in the initial and final states, it can be seen from Fig. 3 that the EEG index of most controllers in the final state is lower than that of the initial state, and the lower the value of the fatigue index characterized by the value of the EEG β wave, the stronger the fatigue state of the controller.

Galvanic Skin Response (GSR). The mean value of skin resistance is higher in the awake state and decreases significantly in the state of mental fatigue. Analyzing the change in skin resistance index data of 48 control subjects in the baseline and final states, Fig. 4 shows that the mean value of skin resistance in most of the final states was lower than that in the baseline state. Taking the mean value of skin resistivity of the subjects in the baseline and final states respectively, it is found that the skin electrical index of the final state is smaller than that of the baseline state, indicating that the fatigue state has an effect on the skin electrical value.

Pupil Diameter. Established studies have shown that the primary eye of right-handed people tends to be the right eye, so the mean right pupil diameter of the controls was chosen for analysis. As fatigue progresses, there is a tendency for a person's pupil diameter to increase. A comparison of the mean pupil diameter of the right eye of the first and last state controllers was plotted as shown in Fig. 5. It was found that the mean pupil diameter in the final state was larger than that in the initial state for most of the controllers.

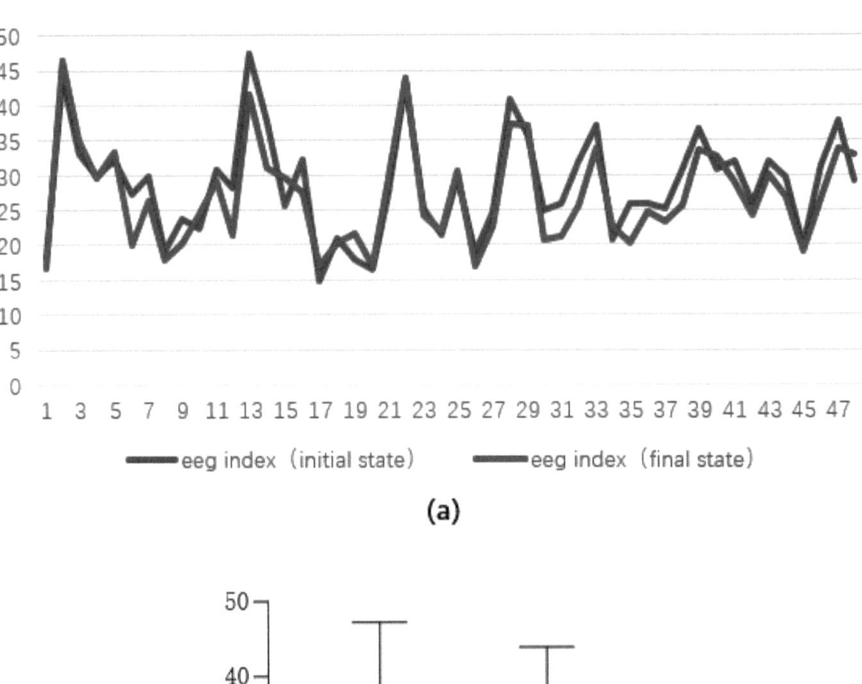

(a)

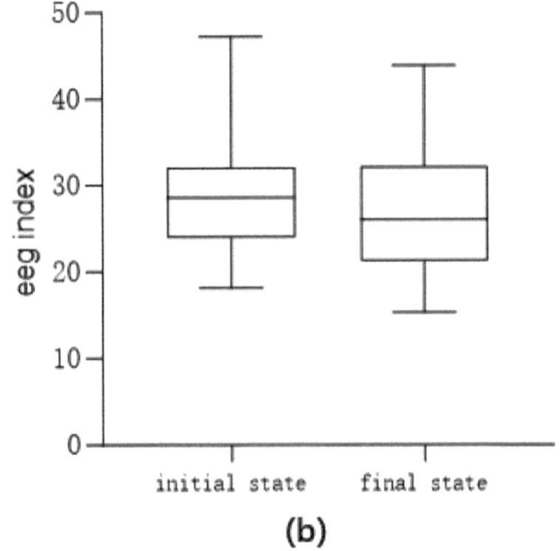

(b)

Fig. 3. Variation of EEG index before and after shift.

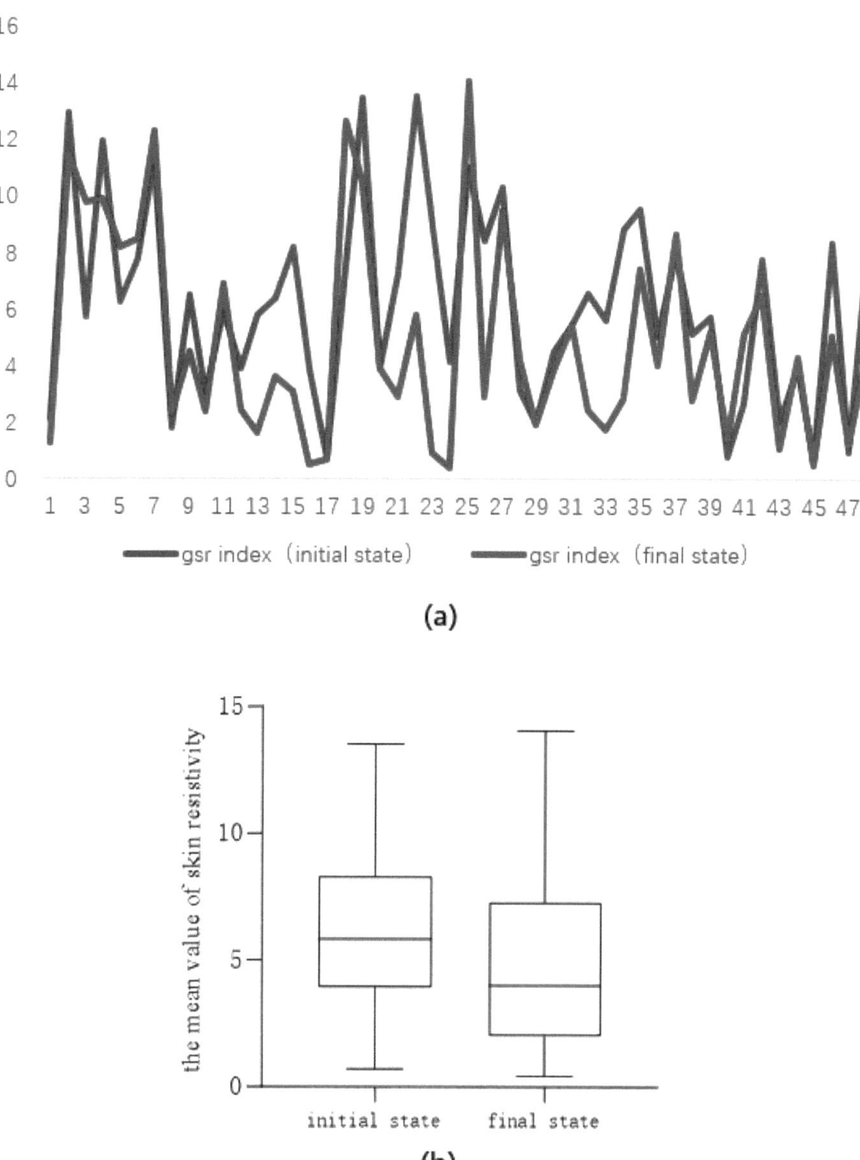

Fig. 4. Variation of GSR index before and after shift.

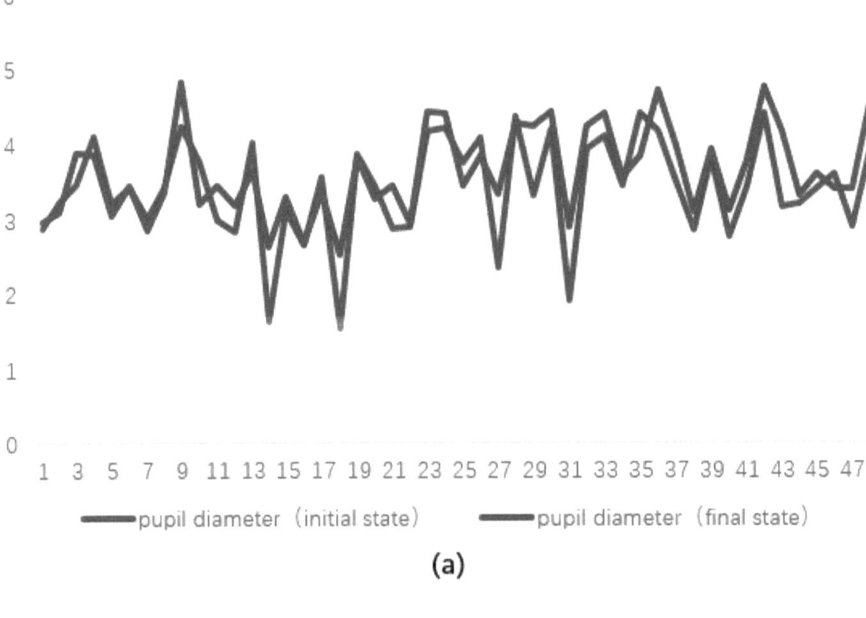

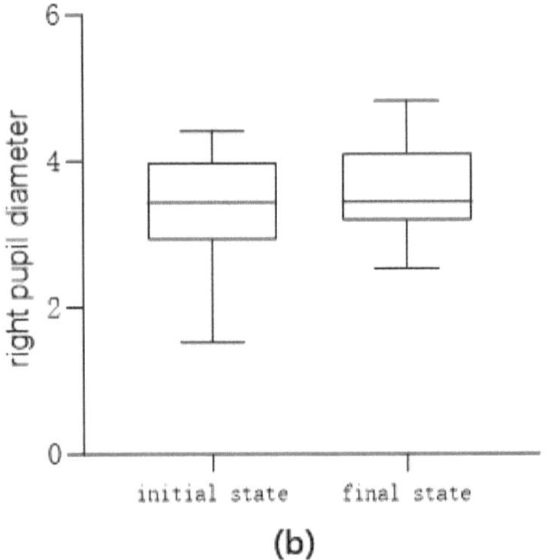

Fig. 5. Variation of pupil diameter before and after shift.

Stanford Sleep Scale (SSS). The subject controllers were asked to complete the Stanford Sleepiness Scale before each test to record the subject's subjective fatigue scores, which were used for comparison with the objective indicator data. The contents of the Stanford Sleepiness Scale are shown in Table 1, and the controllers assessed their current state of fatigue by subjective judgement according to the entries in the table.

Table 1. Stanford Sleep Scale (SSS)

Status statement	Rank
Fully awake: feeling very alert and in a good state of mind.	1
Slightly drowsiness: Feeling a bit tired, but in good condition.	2
Moderate drowsiness: feeling sleepy and needing to be extremely alert.	3
Fairly drowsy: difficulty staying awake, need to concentrate.	4
Very drowsy: difficult to stay awake, requires conscious concentration.	5
Extreme drowsiness: difficulty staying awake, sometimes 'dozing off'.	6
Extremely lethargic: unable to stay awake, always on the verge of dozing off.	7

As illustrated in Fig. 6, the subjective fatigue values in the final state exceeded those in the initial state, with the exception of subjects 12 and 43, who exhibited equivalent levels of drowsiness in the initial final state. This finding suggests that in the final-state test, all the subjective controllers perceived an increase in their own fatigue at a subjective level. The fatigue values in The highest fatigue values were recorded for subjects 06, 09, 10, 19, 20, 21, 27, 30, and 47, where the drowsiness level reached 6. A significant disparity was observed between the fatigue values in the initial state and those in the final state.

The paired samples t-test was conducted on the initial and final state data of the aforementioned four indicators, and the significance of the difference between them was analyzed as shown in Table 2.

Table 2. Significance of the difference between initial and final states, SD stands for standard deviation, CI stands for 95% confidence interval, LB stands for lower bound, UB stands for upper bound, DOF stands for degree of freedom.

Indicators	Mean	SD	Mean(SD)	CI LB	CI UB	t	DOF	Sig
Reaction Time	−14.6297	13.9607	2.0151	−18.6835	−10.5760	−7.620	47	0.001
EEG index	1.5449	3.0653	0.4424	0.6548	2.4350	3.492	47	0.001
GSR index	1.3267	2.7620	0.3987	0.5247	2.1287	3.328	47	0.002
Pupil diameter	−0.2173	0.4128	0.0596	−0.3372	−0.0975	−3.648	47	0.001
SSS	−2.0833	1.1077	0.1599	−2.4050	−1.7617	−13.031	47	0.000

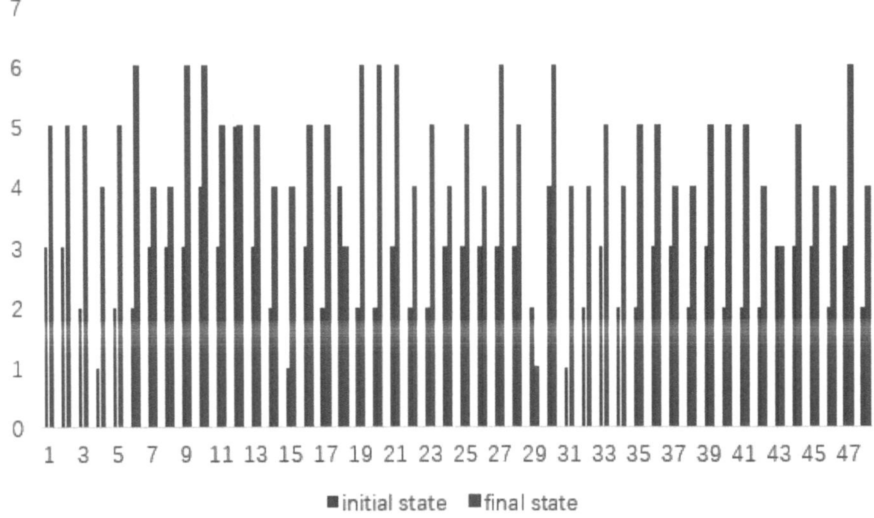

Fig. 6. Stanford Sleepiness Scale values of 48 controllers.

It is evident that there are substantial variances in the data of reaction time, EEG index, GSR index, right eye pupil diameter and SSS values of controllers before and after the shift. Consequently, in this section, the four indexes are employed as the indexes to characterize the controller's fatigue, and further model building and quantitative assessment of fatigue level are conducted. The direct correlation of the fatigue scale with the perceived fatigue levels of the subjects validates the quantitative assessment formula, as evidenced by the utilization of the fatigue scale for verification.

3.2 Comprehensive Assessment Approach for ATC Fatigue (CAAF)

In order to quantitatively assess the fatigue level of the controllers, a fatigue quantitative assessment model (CAAF) was firstly established through the fatigue evaluation index. The quantitative fatigue value of the subjects was then calculated and analysed in relation to the age of the controllers.

It is hypothesized that the controller is not fatigued prior to commencing work under typical conditions; therefore, the fatigue state of the controller evaluated prior to the shift is designated as the initial state, and the fatigue state of the controller evaluated after the shift is designated as the end state. Consequently, the fatigue index FI is delineated as the fatigue value accumulated during the controller's operational period, that is, the difference between the end state and the initial state, thus there is a relation

$$FI = \Delta W + \Delta H + \Delta RE + \Delta PD \tag{2}$$

where

$$\Delta W = W_1 - W_2$$
$$\Delta H = H_1 - H_2$$
$$\Delta RE = RE_2 - RE_1$$
$$\Delta PD = PD_2 - PD_1$$

(3)

where W is EEG index, H is GSR index, RE is mean reaction time and PD is pupil diameter, subscript 1 stands for initial state and 2 stands for end state. It has been established that, in general, the EEG index and cutaneous electrical index decrease with the accumulation of fatigue; that is to say, the amount of index decrease is positively correlated with the level of fatigue. Therefore, the initial state value minus the end-state value is used as the data for this index. Conversely, parameters such as reaction time, pupil diameter, and fatigue self-measurement value typically exhibit an increase with the progression of fatigue, i.e., the amount of index increase is positively correlated with the level of fatigue. Therefore, the end-state value minus the initial state value is employed as the data for these indices. A small number of individuals with negative indicator values after taking the difference were considered to have very low fatigue, and their negative values were retained for Min-Max standardization with other smaller positive values

$$z = \frac{x - x_{min}}{x_{max} - x_{min}}$$

(4)

where x is raw data and z is standardized data. The normalized values are recorded as ZW, ZH, ZRE, ZPD, and the sum of these values is calculated to obtain the fatigue rating value FI. It is important to note that the larger the FI, the greater the fatigue degree.

Pearson correlation analysis was performed after standardizing the output of the model FI with the difference between the controller's fatigue scale at the beginning and end of the state. The correlation matrix is shown in Table 3, from which the results show that there is a correlation with the fatigue scale and FI, thereby proving that the fatigue quantification model is reliable.

Table 3. Pearson value of fatigue model output value and scale value correlation analysis

	FI	SSS
FI Pearson correlation	1	0.439
Sig.		0.000
Case	48	
SSS Pearson correlation		1
Sig.	0.000	
Case	0.439	48

The analysis was conducted in conjunction with the age of the controllers. The fatigue index values of the 48 controllers were then ranked in ascending order according to their length of service, after which a plot of the fatigue index FI of the controllers against their length of service was drawn (see Fig. 7).

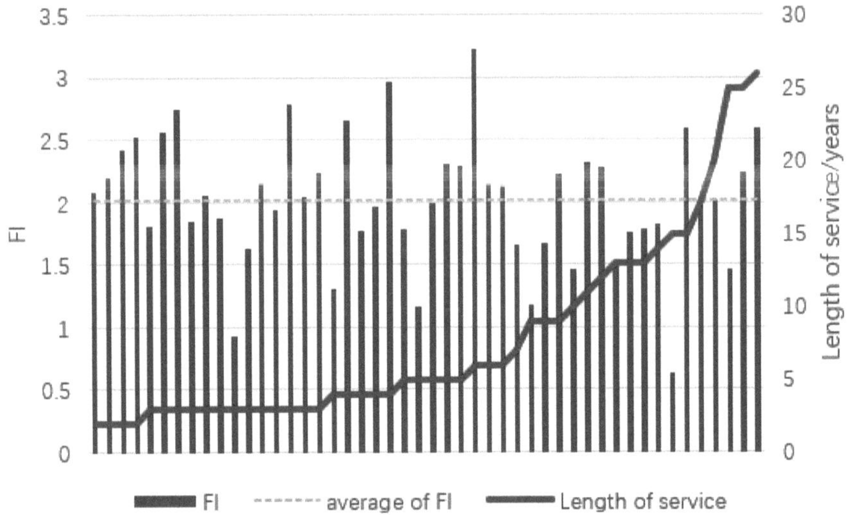

Fig. 7. Controller fatigue index FI versus length of service.

As is evident in the graph, the fatigue index values of the subject controllers can be visualised, with the curve indicating the corresponding length of service of the controllers and the grey dotted line denoting the average value. It is apparent that some controllers exhibit significantly higher fatigue quantitative values than the average. The total number of controllers with a length of service less than or equal to 6 years is 30, of which 20 have a post fatigue index value greater than the overall average fatigue index value (2.0), accounting for 66.67%. The total number of controllers with a length of service greater than or equal to 6 years is 18, of which Of these, 8 have a post fatigue index value greater than the overall average fatigue index value (2.0), accounting for 44.44%. This indicates that the fatigue index value of the controllers with a length of service less than or equal to 6 years is significantly greater than the overall average fatigue index value (2.0). This finding suggests that controllers with less than or equal to 6 years of service are more prone to fatigue than those with more than 6 years of service.

4   Conclusion

The quantitative assessment model of controller fatigue was proposed, and the effect of post-age on fatigue was analyzed; finally, the Pearson correlation test was conducted between the model outputs and the subjective fatigue scale scores, and the results showed that the correlation was significant.

Due to the limited research time, only four fatigue indicators are selected in this paper. A future study would consider more fatigue related indicators.

References

1. Arico, P., et al.: Reliability over time of EEG-based mental workload evaluation during air traffic management (ATM) tasks. In: 2015 37th Annual International Conference of the IEEE Engineering in Medicine and Biology Society (EMBC), pp. 7242–7245. IEEE (2015)
2. Cao, B., Liu, H., Wei, K., Qi, H.: Study on low of gaze transfer before and after fatigue in air traffic controller. Aerosp. Med. Med. Eng. (Chinese) **1**, 25–29 (2019)
3. Dasari, D., Crowe, C., Ling, C., Zhu, M., Ding, L.: EEG pattern analysis for physiological indicators of mental fatigue in simulated air traffic control tasks. In: Proceedings of the Human Factors and Ergonomics Society Annual Meeting. vol. 54, pp. 205–209. SAGE Publications Sage CA: Los Angeles, CA (2010)
4. Deng, W.: Research on Controller Status Detection Based on Deep Learning (Chinese). Master's thesis, Civil Aviation Flight University of China (2020)
5. Eoh, H.J., Chung, M.K., Kim, S.H.: Electroencephalographic study of drowsiness in simulated driving with sleep deprivation. Int. J. Ind. Ergon. **35**(4), 307–320 (2005)
6. Jin, H., Liu, Y.: Performance trace experimental study of the eye movement index and its effect on detecting the fatigue of the air traffic controller. J. Safety Environ. (Chinese) **18**(03), 1004–1007 (2018)
7. Kim, T., Lee, E.C.: Experimental verification of objective visual fatigue measurement based on accurate pupil detection of infrared eye image and multi-feature analysis. Sensors **20**(17), 4814 (2020)
8. Lal, S.K., Craig, A.: Driver fatigue: electroencephalography and psychological assessment. Psychophysiology **39**(3), 313–321 (2002)
9. Li, T., Bai, F., Wu, Q.: Perceived fatigue of air traffic controllers in china: a survey of 927 air traffic controllers. In: 2019 IEEE 1st International Conference on Civil Aviation Safety and Information Technology (ICCASIT), pp. 454–457. IEEE (2019)
10. Mohanavelu, K., Lamshe, R., Poonguzhali, S., Adalarasu, K., Jagannath, M.: Assessment of human fatigue during physical performance using physiological signals: a review. Biomed. Pharmacol. J. **10**(4), 1887–1896 (2017)
11. Mohapatra, S., Sarkar, R., Ghosh, D.: Assessment of fatigue among aviation personnel involved in military flying in India employing multidimensional fatigue symptom inventory-short form (mfsi-sf). Indian J. Aerosp. Med. **64**(2), 68–75 (2020)
12. Rakitin, B.C., Tucker, A.M., Basner, R.C., Stern, Y.: The effects of stimulus degradation after 48 hours of total sleep deprivation. Sleep **35**(1), 113–121 (2012)
13. Sun, R., Ma, G., Yuan, L.: Revision on multidimensional fatigue inventory for controllers and analysis on reliability and validity analysis. Occup. Health (Chinese) **32**(22), 3053–3056 (2016)
14. Wang, L., Sun, R.: Study on face feature recognition-based fatigue monitoring method for air traffic controller. Chin. J. Saf. Sci. (Chinese) **22**(7), 66–71 (2012)
15. Wang, L., Wang, K.: Analysis on mark index of controller fatigue based on grey relational theory. J. Saf. Environ. (Chinese) **22**(02), 810–818 (2022). https://doi.org/10.13637/j.issn.1009-6094.2020.1560

Human-Automation Teaming

HAT-TIME: Human Automation Teaming - Trust Interaction Measurement Environment

James Blundell[1]([⊠]) [iD], Christopher Burns[1] [iD], and Jaume Perello March[2] [iD]

[1] Cranfield University, Bedfordshire, UK
`James.Blundell@cranfield.ac.uk`
[2] Toulouse, France

Abstract. This paper introduces HAT-TIME, a novel test environment for assessing human-automated teaming (HAT) interactions in control tasks such as driving, flying, and human-robot collaboration. By providing a standardized environment, HAT-TIME aims to address cross-study comparison challenges that have interfered with the potential to make comparisons between HAT concepts, and distinguish operator states amid interrelated factors like trust, workload, and fatigue. The paper outlines the HAT-TIME environmental and automation agent parameter manipulations, which are validated through an experiment with 15 participants. Findings highlight a potential automation calibration and surprise protocol, revealing key similarities and differences between subjective workload and automation trust. Future HAT-TIME developments and research will explore its application in examining variations across HAT interaction concepts (e.g., shared vs. traded control) and its role in advancing neuroergonomic studies of automation interaction.

Keywords: Human-Automation-Teaming · Trust · Workload

1 Introduction

A cross-cutting challenge faced by various fields is the development of human automated teaming (HAT) systems that embody efficiency and trustworthiness. However, despite the expanding quantity of targeted research endeavours, it remains unclear how to best measure these properties within HAT concepts.

Trust is defined by Lee and See [1] as *"the attitude that an agent will help achieve an individual's goals in a situation characterized by uncertainty and vulnerability."* Foundational trust research by Parasuraman [2] and Lee and See [1] in the 1990s paved the way for modern investigations into automation trust. The research at this time largely involved the use of "microworlds", simplified versions of real-life operational environments such as managing the automated systems of a flight deck or an assembly line. Critically, the outcomes of this body of work emphasised the need, and challenge, to develop automation that prompted humans to rely upon it *appropriately*. Parasuraman characterized appropriate reliance along the continuum of misuse and disuse; a system that fostered appropriate trust would be one where the human does not over rely (misuse), or under rely (disuse), upon the system's given capabilities. Lee and See's seminal

D. Harris et al. (Eds.): HCII 2025, LNCS 16334, pp. 163–180, 2026.
https://doi.org/10.1007/978-3-032-12392-3_11

work offered insight into how to develop systems that promoted appropriate automation trust based on the perspectives offered from the large body of research describing interpersonal trust dynamics. Notably, they underlined three that factors which encouraged good effective calibration [1]: performance, process, purpose. *Performance* representing the current and historical operation of the automation and includes characteristics such as reliability. *Process* relates to the understandability of an automation underlying algorithms, whilst *Purpose* is being used within the realm of the designer's intent. The first two factors, at least, have received substantial research interest from the human factors community [3]. In addition, these three factors continue to be relevant within more modern models of the automation trust [4].

Another driver for the recent prevalence of HAT trust research is due to increased interest in neuroergonomic approaches to objectively measuring operator state involving electroencephalography (EEG) and functional near infrared spectroscopy (fNIRS) [5–7]. However, it is notable that these same measures have been employed in automation interaction studies as markers of other operator states, including fatigue, workload and situation awareness. Consequently, this raises questions about the specificity of neuroergonomic measures to distinct operator states. Concerning trust, this is problematic because of both its highly latent nature and the for being highly entwined fatigue and workload in determining the behaviour of interest – automation reliance. For example, a case of disuse might occur in a high taskload situation where an operator might decide not to engage the automation because they do not have the cognitive capacity required to make the initial appraisal to rely on the automation or not – regardless of the operator's trust in the automation. Furthermore, many studies have been based on domain specific automation applications (driving, aviation, assembly), involve high fidelity simulation environments. As a result, both aspects mean that cross study comparisons are difficult to make, comparisons which would support the determination of the specific neuroergonomic underpinning of these distinct operator states.

To address this, this paper introduces HAT-TIME (Human Automation Teaming - Trust and Interaction Measurement Environment), a novel tool for objectively comparing interaction qualities within and across different *generalised* HAT concepts. The ambition of HAT-TIME is to also act as a 'test-bench' for comparing different markers of operator state – be that subjective or physiological markers.

This paper is structured in two parts. Part 1 provides an introductory overview of the HAT-TIME tool, including a description of its capabilities. Part 2 includes results from a HAT-TIME validation experiment with 15 participants on a traded control task using subjective measures of trust and workload.

2 Part 1: HAT-TIME

2.1 Design Rationale

The requirement for the HAT-TIME tool is spurred by the increase in multi-disciplinary research focused on how to foster trustworthy interactions with advanced automation, near autonomous, systems within the fields of human factors, cognitive neuroscience and computer science – among others. As this point it is important to acknowledge other generalised tools that share similar properties to HAT-TIME, which have informed its development rationale. Most notably would be the NASA multiple attribute test battery (MAT-B), which represents simplified cockpit system management tasks, used extensively in early automation interaction research. The original MAT-B was developed by Comstock and Arnegard in 1992 [8], but in recent years an open-source version of MAT-B – OpenMATB [9] – has become a prominent testbed for HAT research in various human factors labs. In addition, more domain specific test batteries have emerged in recent years owing to the importance of furthering understanding of HAT within the respective domain specific environments. One example being the defence orientated Interactive Measures of Performance and Assessment of Cognitive Tasks (IMPACT) [10]. Important capabilities of these tools include the high level of task customisation that they provide, both within and across their respective tasks, software extendibility and the higher level of experimental replicability that these tools offer over the majority of simulation-based experiments.

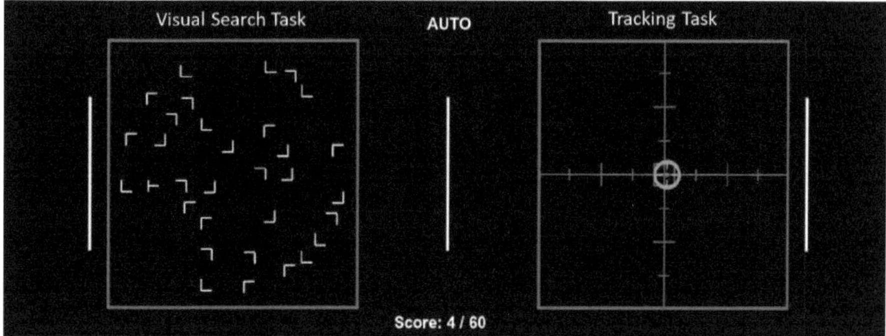

Fig. 1. HAT-TIME presentation. The *Visual* task and the *Tracking* task are presented on the left- and right-hand side of the screen. The "Auto" text communicates the current status of the automation teammate – active if "Auto" present and inactive if absent.

HAT-TIME seeks to also provide these capabilities, yet in a domain agnostic environment with greater emphasis upon task sharing with automation and on the evaluation of trust during those interactions. Furthermore, the ambition of HAT-TIME is to offer a tool to human factor researchers and practitioners that can enhance their ability to (1) systematically evaluate measures of trust – subjective and / or physiological, (2) systematically evaluate and compare different forms of human-automation interaction, and (3) provide both evaluation types across different points of the trust processes (calibration and expectancy violation – i.e., "automation surprise").

The current iteration of HAT-TIME comprises of a dual-visual-task paradigm. Similarly to MAT-B, this includes a primary *Tracking* task - requiring the human and automation to collaborate on an error-cancelling manual control task - and a secondary *Search* task – a visual search task that is completed by the human alone. Figure 1 above shows how the two tasks appear to the human operator, the *Search* and *Tracking* tasks presented on the left- and right-hand side of the screen, respectively. HAT-TIME was developed and is executed using MATLAB based code using Psychophysics OpenGL Toolbox extensions [11].

Critically, within the scope of a HAT context, the human operator's objective is to maximise system performance, in collaboration with the automated agent, by correctly performing the *Search* task whilst not exceeding a prescribed error tolerance on *Tracking* task. To encourage collaboration with the automation a system performance objective is set for the human operator, achievement of which will result in the operator receiving a form of reward (e.g., monetary). This target is determined individually by the human operator's ability to perform the dual task without assistance from an automated agent during a series of preceding trials.

Table 1. HAT-TIME parameter manipulation. Arranged by task environment and automated agent.

Task Environment	Automated Agent
Search Task - Number of distractors - Complexity of target characteristics - Target salience *	*Performance* - Range of tracking performance quality - Consistency of tracking performance *Process* - Control authority interaction scheme - Transparency of current automation state *
Tracking Task - Movement Axis - Predictability of cursor movement - Error Tolerance	*Purpose* - 'Cover story' provided to participant of the intent of the automation's behaviour
Overall - Visual separation of tasks	- Auotmation's real-time adaptive capabilities (e.g., use of machine learning / AI) *

Note: * = Incomplete HAT-TIME implementation

Table 1 below is a list of HAT-TIME parameters which the tool offers researchers control over. HAT-TIME offers high level control over both the complexity of the task environment and, in contrast to existing tools, the characteristics of the automated agent. Automated agent characteristics are organised by the three factors that Lee and See stated influence the trustworthiness of automation – performance, process and purpose.

The next sub-sections offer a detailed description of the implementation of the *Search* task and *Tracking* task (along with the corresponding automated agent). In addition, details of how HAT-TIME was configured for the later validation experiment are outlined.

2.2 Search Task

The secondary *Search* task represents a typical visual search task that has been used extensively within cognitive psychology research to understand human attention processes [12, 13]. Other tasks were considered here, such as the more commonly used visual N-back task [14], however the visual search task was preferred owing to having greater taskload profile control through multi-level manipulation of target and distractor feature parameters. Target parameters (Table 1) include the complexity of target features – ranging from being discernible from surrounding distractors based on a single physical feature (e.g. shape) or multiple (e.g., shape, colour, orientation, size) – and the saliency of the overall search array (e.g., overlaying visual 'noise'). The linear scalability of taskload can be achieved by increasing the number of distractors that are present in the search array at a given point in time.

The presentation format of the current Search task was inspired by a recent visual search task used by Annac et al. [15] within a dual-tasking paradigm. Participants are tasked with identifying whether a specified target stimulus is present or absent using specific response. Doing so correctly will result in the participant receiving a single 'point'. Furthermore, participants are penalised a 'point' if they make an incorrect Search task response (i.e., make a response indicating that a target is present when it not / make a response indicating that a target is absent when it not), or failed to make any Search task response.

Validation Experiment Configuration. Search arrays were configured to include a set of 32 distractor letters 'L' ($0°,90°$, $180°$, and $270°$). One-hundred trials were presented where a target letter 'T' (tilted $90°$ vs. $270°$ relative to the upright orientation) was present in half of trials. This meant that the minimum and maximum number of points a participant could achieve in a trial was -100 (all wrong) and 100 (all correct). The size of each stimulus was $0.6°$ X $0.6°$ and arranged across on four invisible concentric circles with radii of $1.7°$, $3.4°$, $5.1°$, and $6.8°$, respectively. Search stimuli were presented for a 2000 ms duration with a variable interstimulus interval of 1000 ms, 1200 ms or 1500 ms. With 100 Trials, the duration of each trial lasted approximately 5-min. The screen background was black (RGB = 0, 0, 0) and all search stimuli were grey (RGB = 128, 128, 128).

2.3 Tracking Task

The *Tracking* task mirrors those widely used in MAT-B protocols (Cegarra et al., 2020; Comstock Jr & Arnegard, 1992), replicating a continuous error-cancelling compensatory control task, such as in aircraft flight path or automobile lane following. Participants must keep a moving cursor within a rectangular target area at the centre of a graduated scale. Failure to do so invalidates *Search* task responses (correct and incorrect response will be counted as errors that incur a point deduction). This approach serves to set the *Tracking* task as the priority task. The cursor movement follows a function based on summed sinusoidal waves in the X and Y axes, forming a Lissajous curve—seemingly random but identical across participants.

As described in Table 1, HAT-TIME gives researchers control over the following properties of the tracking task: (1) Predictability of the cursor movement – control over the quantity, and individual complexity (phase, frequency), of summed sinusoidal waves; (2) Movement axes – ability to restrict cursor movement to a single axes, and; (3) Error tolerance – the size of the target area.

Validation Experiment Configuration. For configuration for the cursor movement with the validation experiment three sinusoidal waves were summed to produce the resultant cursor movement signal, which was limited to the X axis. The target box area was $1.2°$ x $1.2°$ in size. the screen background was black (RGB = 0, 0, 0) and all search stimuli were grey (RGB = 128, 128, 128).

2.4 Automated Agent

Fundamental to the HAT concept of HAT-TIME, the primary *Tracking* task is shared with an automated agent. A similar capability exists within MAT-B, however the default automation behaviour in MAT-B represents an absolute compensation of tracking error [9]. HAT-TIME, in contrast, offers multiple dimensions in which the processes that control the quality of this behaviour (i.e. the *performance)* can be manipulated. This is achieved through several automation functions within HAT-TIME that models the automation's ability to (1) sense tracking current deviations and past cursor velocity trend during the past 500 ms, (2) compute appropriate planned responses and (3) execute planned responses. Failures can be inserted at any one of these stages to produce distinct automated agent performance decrements.

Another key purpose of HAT-TIME is the ability to understand and compare human automation interaction methodologies in terms of human workload and trust influence. In the context of a manual control task, one possibility is to examine differences in control authority interaction scheme – i.e., how task authority is transferred between the human and the automated agent. HAT-TIME currently offers two control authority interaction schemes that are the subject of ongoing research: conventional traded schemes and shared control schemes. Traded control involves transitioning authority as a lumped whole between the human and automated agent (like how interactions with adaptive cruise control systems occur in automobiles). Shared control represents an interaction where the control inputs of the human and automated agent are continuously combined. In this way the automated agent's control inputs are always present, transforming the human's control strategy to one of automation control augmentation [16]. The comparison of authority interaction schemes within the human factors research literature is limited. With traded control it can be assumed, based on the uncertainty of an automated agent's current state during human control, that a high cognitive 'overhead' would be entailed when deciding the rely on the automation [2]. Such as 'overhead' might be lessened with a shared control scheme. Comparisons of these high-level control authority interaction schemes are possible within the current iteration of HAT-TIM. Planned extensions of the tool will permit more focussed within scheme comparisons, such as changes in authority gradient for a shared control scheme.

Finally, automation state transparency is an aspect of human-automation interaction that HAT-TIME intends to address. Transparency is a pivotal design principle within human factors design [17, 18] positing that the human-machine interface should directly communicate the automation's capabilities and goals to enhance the human operator's mental model of the automation's current state. In this way transparency design principles align with Lee and See's Process factor. In the context of a manual control task, an imminent transparency feature for HAT-TIME is the presence of haptic force feedback to communicate the automation's real-time control input through the operator's physical control device. Like shared control schemes, discussed above, haptic force feedback remains an under explored area of trust research with the human factor's community. Particularly, from the perspective of how the factors of transparency (e.g., force feedback) and control authority interaction scheme (e.g., shared vs traded) interact to influence trust [19–21]. Beyond haptic force feedback, automation transparency depicted through other sensory modalities (visual, auditory, tactile) are futures features intended for HAT-TIME.

Validation Experiment Configuration. In the current validation experiment the performance of the automated agent was manipulated by introducing a failure into its *planning* of executed responses (i.e., sensing of tracking error and control execution were intact). Briefly, when the automation was functioning or not its respective maximum error tolerance was set to 0.3° and 3.5° of the centre. The latter being beyond the 1.2° limit of the target box.

For the current validation experiment, trust in automation was manipulated by pairing participants with two automated agents that exhibited differences in the consistency of their performance. Figure 2 presents the 300 s timeline for trials where participants were paired with either a "good" or "poor" automated agent. A "good" automated agent spent 15% ± 5% of a trial duration in a failure state (equating to 45 ± 15 s), whereas the "poor" automated agent spent 45% ± 5% of a trial duration in a failure state (equating to 135 ± 15 s).

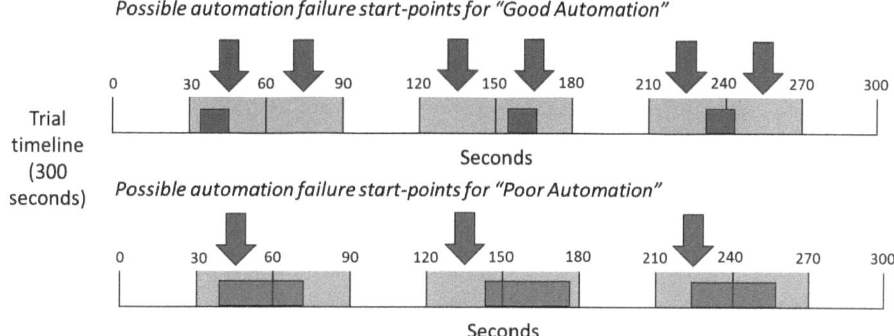

Fig. 2. Timeline of automation failure periods for the "Good" and "Poor" automated agents.

For the control authority interaction scheme in the validation experiment only a traded control scheme is employed. In this case, the participant is responsible for allocating control of the *Tracking* task to either themselves or the automated agent. This is achieved using a toggle button on the physical control device used by the participant. In addition, an "AUTO" message is presented centrally on the HAT-TIME screen whenever the automated agent is engaged.

3   Part 2: HAT-TIME Validation Experiment

Based on the HAT-TIME configuration detailed above, the final part of this paper reports on a 2.5-h HAT-TIME validation experiment where trust and workload of participants is monitored over a 1-h period of automation calibration, with a "good" and "bad" automated agent, that concludes with an automation surprise event.

The aim of the validation experiment was to demonstrate the capability of HAT-TIME to differentiate between trust and workload during different automation interaction phases – calibration and automation surprise.

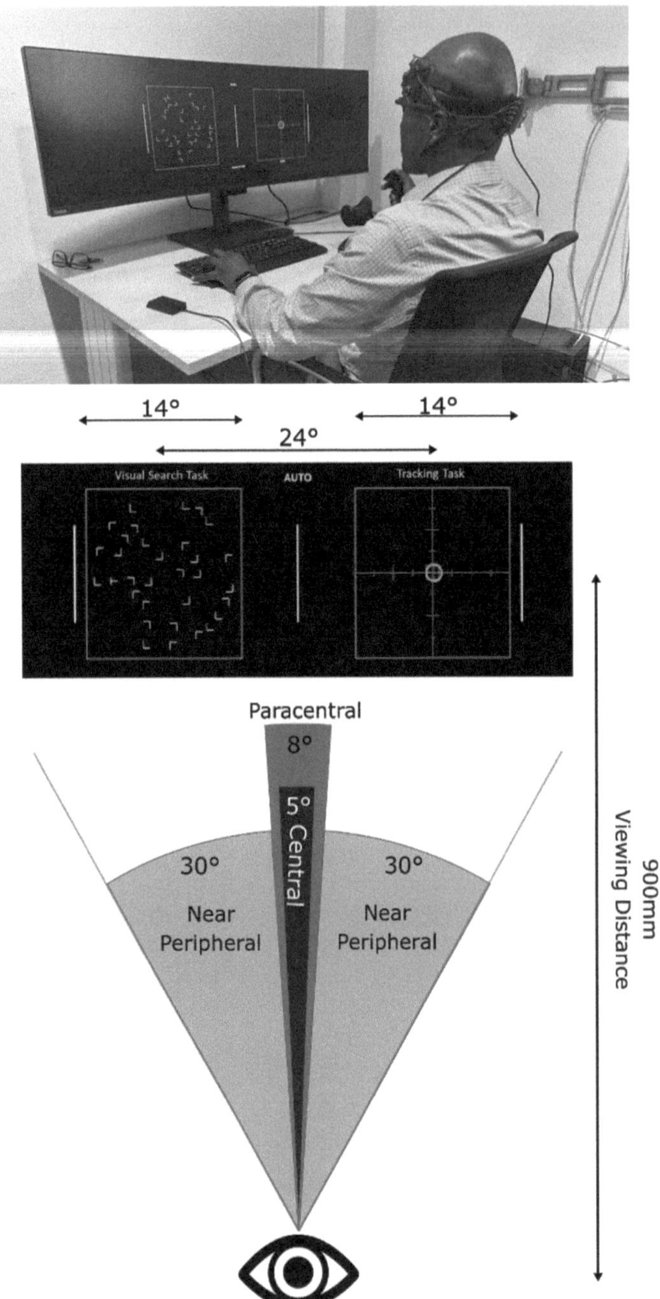

Fig. 3. Top image shows the experimental set up. Bottom image depicts the visual stimuli dimensions mapped onto the visual angle properties of foveal / central and peripheral vision.

3.1   Participants

Fifteen participants took part in the study. This included 6 male and 9 females, with an average age of 32.20 years (SD: 7.59 years). All participants were right-handed and had normal or corrected vision. The research was approved by Cranfield University ethics committee (ID: 26437).

3.2   Apparatus

The experiment was conducted on an Intel computer with a Windows 10 operating system. HAT-TIME was presented on a 1200 mm x 337 mm / 5120 x 1440 pixel monitor (60 Hz refresh rate), positioned at ~ 900 mm distance from the participant, corresponding to a total view area of 76.28° x 21.45° (H x W). Figure 3 shows the experimental setup and the visual distance (visual separation – Table 1) between the *Search* and *Tracking Task*. This configuration ensured that the two tasks could not be viewed with central / foveal vision at the same time to encourage more reliance of divided attention, and thus greater degree of reliance upon the automated agent to perform the *Tracking* task.

Responses to the Search task were recorded using two keyboard keys marked with either a green or red sticker. Using their left-hand, a "green" or "red" key press was used to respectively indicate the detected presence or absence of a target in a search array. Participants used a Trustmaster™ USB joystick to control the Tracking task, with lateral joystick inputs used to manual counteract X-axis cursor tracking error. A joystick button, accessible by participants' thumb, was used to trade control of Tracking task between themselves and the automated agent.

3.3   Procedure

The duration of the study was approximately 2.5 h for each participant. A graphic representation of the procedure is shown in Fig. 4.

In the pre-study details stage participants were briefed that the experiment concerned understanding how humans learn to differentiate, and subsequently collaborate, with a "good" and "poor" automated agent (forming the calibration stage of the experiment). Which automated agents was "good" or "poor" was not divulged, instead participants were informed that the automated agents were named "Alex" and "Sam" (non-gender specific names were chosen to reduce the possibility participant gender biases). Information regarding the final automation surprise stage of the experiment was withheld.

Participants were briefed that a monetary reward of £3.75 would be received each time they completed a trial with an automated agent and achieved over a specified performance criterion (details below). A total of 8 trials with the automated agents were conducted, leading to a total reward of £30 if participants successfully met the performance criterion on every trial. However, regardless of performance, all participants received £30 during the experiment debrief and were informed of the experiments objective to investigate automation surprise as well as calibration.

Following the briefing, participants first provided informed consent and completed demographic information. The demographic information included the revised

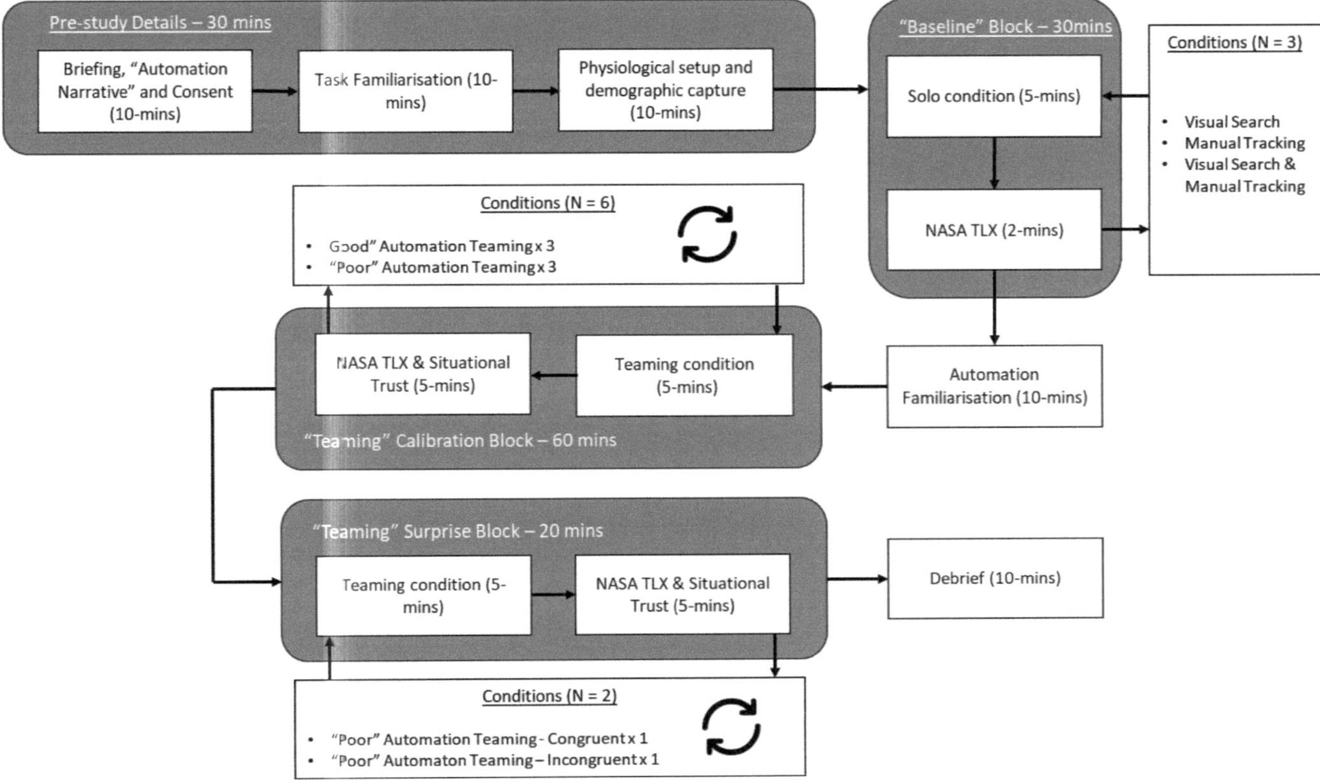

Fig. 4. Procedural sequence for the current study. Including the pre-study, baseline, calibration block, surprise block and debrief.

Automation-Induced Complacency Potential Scale (AICP-R) [22] to capture participant's general disposition to trusting automation. Physiological measures were equipped by participants (including an ear-horn PPG device, eye tracker and fNIRS system) however the data from the devices are not reported here.

The following baseline block provided ~ 30-min for participants to practice the *Tracking* and *Search* tasks both independently and simultaneously. Once participants felt ready, the performance criterion used in the subsequent stages of the experiment, where they would be collaborating with the automated agent, was calculated. This was achieved by having participants repeat the (1) *Search* task and (2) the *Search* and *Tracking* tasks together, taking the performances from these two trials, and using the following formula.

$$Perf\ Criterion = Perf(S) + ((Perf(S) - Perf(ST) * .66)$$

Where *Perf* is a trial's performance score. *S* is the *Search* task only trial and *ST* is the *Search* and *Tracking* task together trial. The intention for using the formula was to produce performance criterions whilst collaborating with the automated agents that were higher than what participants could accomplish on their own whilst doing the dual-task, but not greater than their performance on the *Search* task by itself. Thus, represents a feasible 'goal' for participants that fostered dependency on the automation.

Once the performance criterion was established, participants were given time to become familiar with the automation, including how the traded control interaction worked. This was followed by the calibration block which consisted of 6 trials. Three with each of automated agents in a randomised order. After each trial participants completed the Trust in Automated Systems Scale [23] and the NASA TLX [24].

In the final stage, automation surprise, two trials were completed. Here, both automated agents ("Sam" or "Alex") were both set to "poor". The surprise in this case is that the agent that had been assigned as 'good' in the preceding 6 calibration trials had its failure state prevalence increase from 15% ± 5% to 45% ± 5% of the trial duration.

3.4 Dependent Variables

In this validation experiment four dependent variables are reported from the calibration and automation surprise stages of the experiment.

- Performance Criterion Delta – representing the difference in trial performance with the automated agent against the participant's performance criterion.
- Tracking Task Input – the proportion of time during trials that participants are controlling the *Tracking* task. The inverse representing the degree of automation reliance.
- Subjective Trust – using the Trust in Automated Systems Scale. This scale is comprised of 12 items with a 7-point Likert scale. Items 1 to 5 assess the construct of distrust, and items 6 to 12 assess trust. A total score can also be obtained by reverse scoring those items corresponding to distrust. This is an established scale widely used in research to measure operators' trust in automated systems. [5]
- Subjective Workload – using the NASA TLX. The TLX is a long-established scale designed to capture subjective workload ratings across six workload dimensions:

mental demand, physical demand, temporal demand, performance, effort, and frustration. Each workload dimension is measured on a scale from 0 – 20, where higher ratings represent higher subjective workload. The abridged non-weighted approach was chosen due to the inconclusive evidence that dimension weighting improves the TLX's sensitivity [25].

3.5 Data Analysis

All dependent variables were analyzed with a series of general linear mixed effects models (GLMMs) using the MATLAB Statistical Toolbox. In addition, separate analyses were conducted for the calibration and automation surprise stages.

For the calibration stage GLMMs, a fixed effect for automated agent (2 levels: good, poor) and a fixed effect for time (3 levels: trial 1, 2 3) were fitted. For the automation surprise stage, a fixed effect for automated agent (2 levels: good, poor) and a fixed effect for time (2 levels: pre-surprise, surprise) were fitted. Here, the pre-surprise level was taken from the final calibration stage trial. Random participant intercepts were included in the analysis of fixed effects. Significance of fixed effects (alpha $= 0.05$) were checked using p-values obtained by likelihood ratio tests. Visual inspection of residual plots was used to ensure no obvious deviations from homoscedasticity or normality.

4 Results

4.1 Performance Criterion Delta

A GLMM analysis of the calibration stage data (trial 1 – 3) revealed a main effect of *automated agent*, $\chi2(1) = 23.026$, $p < .001$, and *time*, $\chi2(1) = 21.604$, $p < .01$. An interaction was not observed. Based on Fig. 5, and the corresponding GLMM model estimates, it is surmised that the contribution of the two automation agents improved with each interaction ($\beta = 7.00$, SE: 1.00), and that the contribution of the 'good' agent was greater overall ($\beta = 23.20$, SE: 0.40). Of note is that contribution of 'poor' agent was largely detrimental during early trials (i.e., negative performance criterion delta) and became positive later. During, automation surprise stage, where the failure rate of the 'good' and 'poor' automated agents is symmetrical, the GLMM analysis revealed a main effect or *automated agent*, $\chi2(1) = 12.957$, $p < .001$, and an interaction with *time*, $\chi2(1) = 4.2733$, $p = .038$. Together these effects indicated that a significant difference in performance contribution between automated agents was present at the end of the calibration phase ($\beta = 11.70$, SE: 3.00) and that this difference was abolished by the failure of the *'good'* automated agent ($\beta = -9.10$, SE: 3.00).

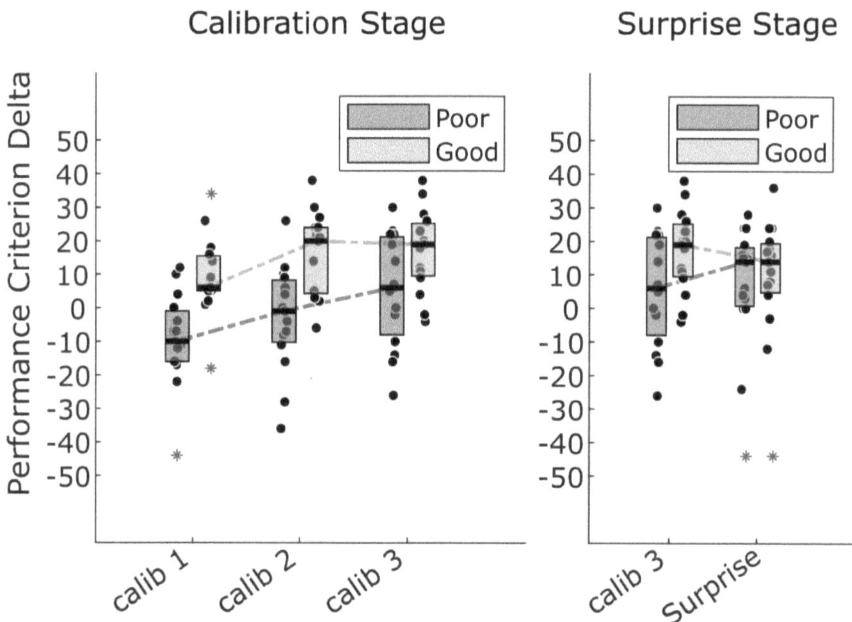

Fig. 5. Performance Criterion Delta boxplot results during 6 trials of the calibration stage (left panel) and the 2 trials of the automation surprise stage (right panel).

4.2 Tracking Task Input

During the calibration phase, clear differences in the proportion of participants' tracking task inputs between the two automated agents was static across trials. This was reflected by a main effect of *automated agent*, $\chi^2(1) = 9.943$, p $<$ .01, with an absence of an interaction or main effect of *time* ($p >$ .05). The model estimated that partnering with the 'good' agent reduced the proportion of tracking input by .233 (SE: .07) (Fig. 6).

In the automation surprise stage an increase in tracking input (decrease in automation reliance) was observed in both automated agents, with a sharper increase in for 'good' agent. The GLMM found significant interaction $\chi^2(1) = 33.333$, $p <$ .001 and main effect of *automated agent* $\chi^2(1) = 52.656$, $p <$ .001, but no main effect of *time* (p $>$ 0.05). Whilst, tracking task input remained lower for the 'good' automated agent, despite having similar failure characteristics to the 'poor' automated agent, the difference was not significantly different ($p =$ .102).

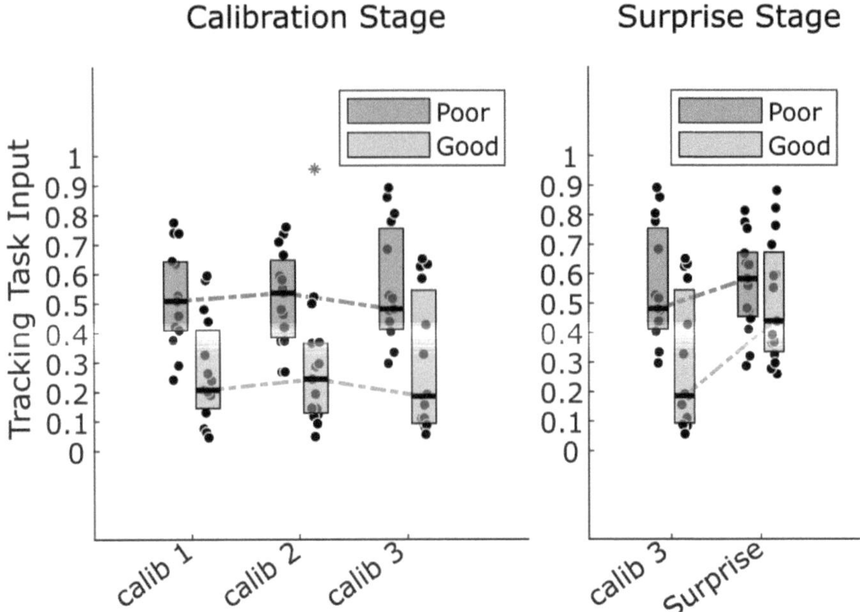

Fig. 6. Boxplot showing participants' portion of manual tracking input during 6 trials of the calibration stage (left panel) and the 2 trials of the automation surprise stage (right panel).

4.3 Subjective Trust

Figure 8 shows the changes in subjective automation trust over the calibration and automation surprise stages. During the calibration stage, a diverging trend was observed where trust in the 'good' and 'poor' automated agents increased and decreased, respectively. However, the GLME only indicated a main effect of *automated agent* - $\chi2(1) =$ 9.038, p < .01 - with trust being higher for the 'good' agent ($\beta = 1.39$, SE: .448) (FIg. 7).

In the automation surprise stage trust decreased for the 'good' agent which exhibited the change in failure prevalence. In contrast, the trust of the 'poor' agent appeared to increase, likely reflective of differences in the consistency of each agents' performance. Interestingly, despite this trend, trust in the 'good' agent remained higher. These observations were supported by the presence of an interaction in the GLMM analysis - $\chi2(1)$ = 4.72, p = .029.

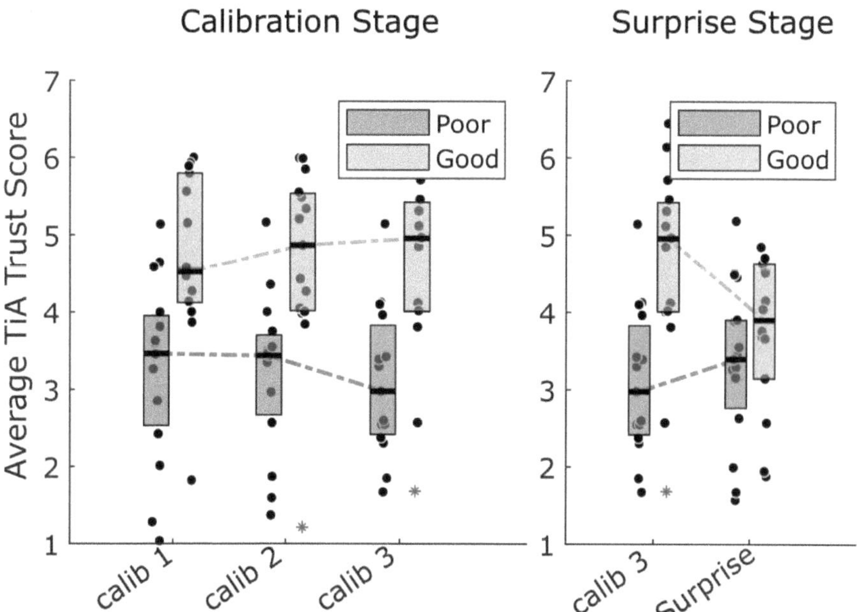

Fig. 7. Boxplot showing participants' self reported trust in the automated agents during 6 trials of the calibration stage (left panel) and the 2 trials of the automation surprise stage (right panel).

4.4 Subjective Workload

Figure 8 shows the changes in overall TLX scores over the calibration and automation surprise trials. During the calibration stage, the GLME included main effects of *automated agent*, $\chi2(1) = 15.453$, $p < .001$, and *time*, $\chi2(1) = 7.3796$, p $< .01$). However, no interaction was observed ($p = .08$), hence, TLX scores were significantly lower for the 'good' agent, and subjective workload decreased with both agents over the course of the calibration trials. The model estimated that partnering with the 'good' agent during calibration reduced TLX scores by 3.48 (SE: .839) and there was a small decrease in TLX of 0.77 (SE: .274) per calibration trial.

In the automation surprise trial, it was found that the difference in TLX scores lessened between agents ($\beta = 1.23$, SE: .543), but this difference remained significantly different between the automated agents, $\chi2(1) = 4.85$, $p = .027$.

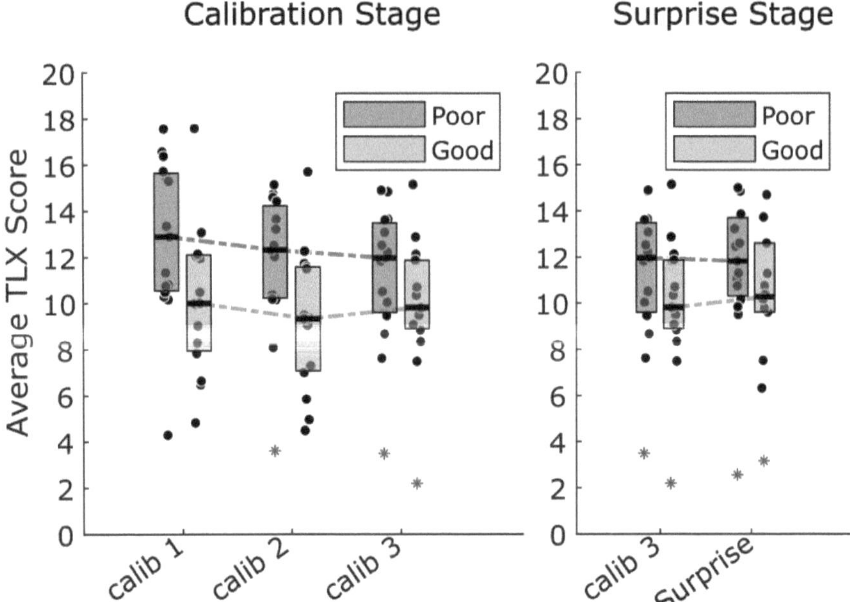

Fig. 8. Boxplot showing participants' subjective workload during 6 trials of the calibration stage (left panel) and the 2 trials of the automation surprise stage (right panel).

5 Discussion and Conclusion

The current paper introduced HAT-TIME, its ambition, its format and a validation experiment detailing how the tool can be used to compare trust and workload between automated agents during different phases of HAT interaction – calibration and surprise.

The validation experiment combined both HAT interaction measures of automation - reliance (Tracking input) and automation system contribution (Performance Criterion Delta) – with subjective measures of automation trust and workload. These validation results revealed that HAT-TIME can be configured to produce significant variations in these measurements by manipulating automation agent reliability and participant expectancy of automation performance. Hence, the aim of the validation experiment for HAT-TIME was achieved.

Interestingly, HAT-TIME was able to depict distinct trends between the different measures used. During the calibration stage, trust increased and decrease with time for the 'good' and 'poor' agents whilst participant reliance behaviours remained static. In fact, the static reliance behaviours where reflective of subjective workload during this phase. In addition, the automation surprise stage effectively abolished differences between each agent's system contribution (as measured by the Performance Criterion Delta). Despite this, participants continued to demonstrate higher reliance, report higher and lower respective trust and workload for the automated agent which had exhibited greater reliability in the preceding trials.

Future developments and research using HAT-TIME will involve the analysis of the physiological data collected in this research. In addition, the current experiment concerned only interactions with high and low reliability automated agents involving a traded control authority scheme. Consequently, the experiment focused solely on comparing automated agents which, according to Lee and See, differed based on *Performance.* Ongoing research with HAT-TIME is exploring the capability of the tool to differentiate between HAT interactions that better encapsulate *Process* characteristics of automation. This will include the comparison of interactions based on different authority schemes, such as shared control. In addition, adjusting levels of transparency in automated agents (presence of haptic force feedback, auditory, tactile, visual feedback) is one other avenue of investigation which HAT-TIME is intended to explore.

Acknowledgments. Dr James Blundell and Dr Christopher Burns are recipients of an EPSRC New Investigator grant (EP/Y00194X/1) used to support their time on this research.

Disclosure of Interests. The authors have no competing interests to declare that are relevant to the content of this article.

References

1. Lee, J.D., See, K.A.: Trust in automation: designing for appropriate reliance. Hum. Factors **46**(1), 50–80 (2004). https://doi.org/10.1518/HFES.46.1.50_30392
2. Parasuraman, R., Riley, V.: Humans and automation: use, misuse, disuse, abuse. Hum. Factors **39**(2), 230–253 (1997). https://doi.org/10.1518/001872097778543886
3. Walker, F., et al.: Trust in automated vehicles: constructs, psychological processes, and assessment. Front. Psychol. **14**, November 2023. https://doi.org/10.3389/fpsyg.2023.1279271
4. Hoffmann, H., Söllner, M.: Incorporating behavioral trust theory into system development for ubiquitous applications. Pers. Ubiquit. Comput. 117–128. Springer, London, January 2014. https://doi.org/10.1007/s00779-012-0631-1
5. Perello-March, J.R., Burns, C.G., Woodman, R., Elliott, M.T., Birrell, S.A.: Using fNIRS to verify trust in highly automated driving. IEEE Trans. Intell. Transp. Syst. 1 (2022). https://doi.org/10.1109/TITS.2022.3211089
6. Perello-March, J.R., Burns, C.G., Birrell, S.A., Woodman, R., Elliott, M.T.: Physiological measures of risk perception in highly automated driving. IEEE Trans. Intell. Transp. Syst. **23**(5), 4811–4822 (2022). https://doi.org/10.1109/TITS.2022.3146793
7. Kohn, S.C., de Visser, E.J., Wiese, E., Lee, Y.C., Shaw, T.H.: Measurement of trust in automation: a narrative review and reference guide. Front. Psychol. **12**, 4138 (2021). https://doi.org/10.3389/FPSYG.2021.604977/BIBTEX
8. Comstock Jr, J.R., Arnegard, R.J.: The multi-attribute task battery for human operator workload and strategic behavior research, Washington (1992)
9. Cegarra, J., Valéry, B., Avril, E., Calmettes, C., Navarro, J.: OpenMATB: a multi-attribute task battery promoting task customization, software extensibility and experiment replicability. Behav. Res. Methods **52**(5), 1980–1990 (2020). https://doi.org/10.3758/s13428-020-01364-w
10. Sabine, G., Thompson, D.J.: Design, development, and validation of a military orientated re-configurable cognitive task battery. In: Proceedings of the Human Factors and Ergonomics Society, pp. 1120–1124. SAGE Publications Inc. (2024). https://doi.org/10.1177/107118132 41278276
11. Brainard, D.H.: The psychophysics toolbox. Spat. Vis. **10**(4), 433–436 (1997). https://doi.org/10.1163/156856897X00357
12. Treisman, A.: Perceptual grouping and attention in visual search for features and for objects. J. Exp. Psychol. Hum. Percept. Perform. **8**(2), 194–214 (1982). https://doi.org/10.1037/0096-1523.8.2.194

13. Treisman, A.M., Gelade, G.: A feature-integration of attention. Cogn. Psychol. **136**, 97–136 (1980)
14. Collins, C., Blundell, J., Huddlestone, J., Harris, D.: A helping hand: benefits of primary task haptic augmentation on secondary visuospatial task performance. In: Kurosu, M., et al. HCI International 2023 – Late Breaking Papers. HCII 2023. Lecture Notes in Computer Science, vol. 14054. Springer, Cham (2023). https://doi.org/10.1007/978-3-031-48038-6_22
15. Annac, E., Zang, X., Müller, H.J., Geyer, T.: A secondary task is not always costly: Context-based guidance of visual search survives interference from a demanding working memory task. Brit. J. Psychol. 381–399, May 2019. https://doi.org/10.1111/bjop.12346.John Wiley and Sons Ltd.
16. (René) van Paassen, M.M., Boink, R.P., Abbink, D.A., Mulder, M., Mulder, M.: Four design choices for haptic shared control. In: Advances in Aviation Psychology, vol. 2, pp. 237–254. Routledge (2019). https://doi.org/10.4324/9781315565712-12
17. Skraaning, G., Jamieson, G.A.: Human performance benefits of the automation transparency design principle: validation and variation. Hum. Factors **63**(3), 379–401 (2021). https://doi.org/10.1177/0018720819887252
18. Endsley, M., Jones, D.: Designing for Situation Awareness: An Approach to User-Centered Design, Second Edn. Taylor & Francis Group, Boca Raton (2012). https://doi.org/10.1080/10686967.2017.11918512
19. Stiger, S., Mulder, M., van Paassen, M.: Design and evaluation of a haptic flight director. J. Guid. Control. Dyn. **30**(October), 2007 (2015). https://doi.org/10.2514/1.20593
20. Van Baelen, D., Van Paassen, M.M., Ellerbroek, J., Abbink, D.A., Mulder, M.: Flying by feeling: communicating flight envelope protection through haptic feedback. Int. J. Hum. Comput. Interact. **00**(00), 1–11 (2021). https://doi.org/10.1080/10447318.2021.1890489
21. Cutlip, S., Wan, Y., Sarter, N., Gillespie, R.B.: The effects of haptic feedback and transition type on transfer of control between drivers and vehicle automation. IEEE Trans. Hum. Mach. Syst. **51**(6), 613–621 (2021). https://doi.org/10.1109/THMS.2021.3107255
22. Merritt, S.M., et al.: Automation-induced complacency potential: development and validation of a new scale. Front Psychol. **10**, February 2019. https://doi.org/10.3389/fpsyg.2019.00225
23. Jian, J.-Y., Bisantz, A.M., Drury, C.G.: Foundations for an empirically determined scale of trust in automated systems. Int. J. Cogn. Ergon. **4**(1), 53–71 (2000). https://doi.org/10.1207/S15327566IJCE0401_04
24. Hart, S.G., Staveland, L.E.: Development of NASA-TLX (Task Load Index): results of empirical and theoretical research Sandra. Adv. Psychol. **52**, 139–183 (1988). Human Mental Workload
25. Hart, S.G.: Nasa-Task load index (NASA-TLX); 20 years later, pp. 904–908 (2006)

Toward a Neurophysiological Approach to Assess Optimal Human-Machine Teaming in the Critical Environment of Air Traffic Control

Christophe Hurter[1,7]([✉]), Alexandre Veyrie[1], Sara Kebir[1], Guillaume Truong[1], Stefano Bonelli[2], Gianluca Borghini[8], Pietro Aricò[8], Fabio Babiloni[8], Marc Baumgartner[6], Juan Alberto Besada[3], Luca Bergesio[3], Almudena Calatrava[3], Jose J. Cañas Delgado[4], Lidia Garcia[9], Raquel Garcia Lasheras[9], Brais Iglesias[3], Martina Jadronova[4], Florencia Lema[9], Alfonso Levantesi[2], Patricia Maria Lopez De Fruto[9], Hossein Mapar[2], Laurie Marsman[5], Job Smeltink[5], Anthony Smoker[6], Maykel van Miltenburg[5], Anna Giulia Vicario[2], Chen Xia[9], and Rolf Zon[5]

[1] Fédération de recherche ONERA–ENAC–ISAE-SUPAERO, Université de Toulouse, Toulouse, France
christophe.hurter@enac.fr
[2] Deep Blue S.r.l., Rome, Italy
[3] Universidad Politécnica de Madrid, Madrid, Spain
[4] Universidad de Granada, Granada, Spain
[5] Royal Netherlands Aerospace Centre (NLR), Amsterdam, The Netherlands
[6] International Federation of Air Traffic Controllers' Associations (IFATCA), Montreal, Canada
[7] EUROCONTROL (European Organisation for the Safety of Air Navigation), Brussels, Belgium
[8] BrainSigns, Spin-off of University of Rome "Sapienza", Rome, Italy
[9] CRIDA A.I.E. (Centro de Referencia de Investigación, Desarrollo e Innovación ATM), Madrid, Spain

Abstract. In Air Traffic Management (ATM), Air Traffic Control (ATC) is becoming increasingly challenging as controllers handle increasing volumes of air traffic while simultaneously adapting to novel technological systems. This surge in complexity places greater cognitive demands on Air Traffic Controllers (ATCOs), making their tasks more mentally demanding. This paper presents some research works coming from Single European Sky ATM Research (SESAR) projects and delivered by a large European Consortium over the past decade. Based on this work, this article seeks to present a neurophysiologically based approach to strengthening HumanMachine Teaming (HMT) in the frame of ATC/ATM by integrating neurophysiological data. By leveraging multimodal signals, including Electroencephalography (EEG), Electrocardiography (ECG), Electrodermal Activity (EDA), Galvanic Skin Response (GSR), and eye-tracking, the framework can be based on the operator's mental states. By targeting specific controller's cognitive and affective states, real-time system adaptations can be used in order to decrease controller's workload, stress and fatigue while enhancing situational awareness, vigilance, and trust. The five projects being discussed here (NINA, MOTO, ARTIMATION, TRUSTY and CODA) collectively demonstrate the growing relevance of the neurophysiology-based approach to developing the new ATC/ATM tools of the years to come.

Keywords: Air Traffic Management · Air Traffic Control · Human-AI Teaming · Neurophysiology · SESAR

1 Introduction

Air Traffic Control (ATC) is one of the most demanding operational domains, requiring constant attention, rapid decision-making, and continuous coordination in high-stakes environments [18,30,34,53]. With the ongoing rise of air traffic density, shrinking airspace margins, and the integration of cutting-edge technologies, the cognitive and operational load on Air Traffic Controllers (ATCOs) is continuously increasing.

Despite the high volume of flights, air transport is currently regarded as the safest mode of transportation and thanks to technological advances, refined expertise, and stringent certification regulations, critical systems in aviation are considered "ultra-safe" [6]. Although critical systems rarely experience failures that compromise safety, the issue of automation was raised early in aviation history [36,55]. Recent investigations have underscored that while automation can augment ATCOs performance, its efficacy is contingent upon the reliability of decision aids; when such aids fail or behave unpredictably, they not only elevate mental workload but also compromise operational safety [45]. These findings underscore the lasting need for human oversight, especially in high-stakes, time-sensitive situations where adaptability and judgment are essential.

Traditional automation has supported ATCOs by assisting with routine or computationally intensive tasks [43]. However, static automation often lacks the contextual adaptability required during dynamic or unexpected events [41] and it has been found that high levels of automation often reduce operator situational awareness, leading to out-of-the-loop problems [29]. Conversely, adaptive automation has led to major technological advances in terms of system adaptability to changing situational contexts [14]. By systematically evaluating how different modes of automation influence situation awareness and workload, [39] highlighted that adaptive automation of perceptual and motor functions, such as information acquisition and action implementation, enhances performance and situation awareness without increasing operator strain. In contrast, automating higher-order cognitive functions, like information analysis and decision-making, can elevate workload due to increased visual demands and interface complexity [41]. These results underscored the importance of aligning automation strategies with operator workload states and task demands [8].

Additionally, it has been observed that facilitating dynamic allocations of system control functions to a human operator or computer over time can moderate operator workload and, at the same time, may facilitate situation awareness, or operator preparedness for unexpected system states, while maintaining some level of operator involvement in control loops [40,46].

As a result and in order to maintain awareness, automation must support user engagement, provide clear feedback, and align with human mental models [29]. Consequently, research is increasingly converging toward a collaborative paradigm centered on Human-Machine Teaming (HMT), wherein human and machine agents operate as adaptive, communicative partners capable of shared decision-making and dynamic role allocation [25,44]. Within this framework, the optimisation of HMT is essential for maintaining safety, enhancing efficiency, and delivering operational resilience in complex, time-critical domains [33,42,52].

To realize this vision, ATC/ATM research projects designed systems that go beyond conventional intelligence by embedding the capacity to dynamically perceive, interpret, and adapt to human operators' cognitive workload, attentional focus, and emotional states–thereby enabling truly symbiotic and resilient humanmachine collaboration in these complex, high-stakes environments [52]. In this context, a framework is proposed that integrates multi-modal neurophysiological signals, including electroencephalography (EEG), electrocardiography (ECG), Galvanic Skin Response (GSR), and eye-tracking, to continuously monitor key cognitive and affective states such as mental workload, sustained attention, emotional arousal, and trust [23,28,42]. These psycho-physiological indicators serve a dual function. First, by enabling retrospective analyses of operator behavior, they support evidence-based system evaluation and iterative refinement of human-machine interface design. Second, by providing real-time input to adaptive algorithms, they facilitate context-aware system modulation aligned with the operator's cognitive state and task complexity. This bi-directional feedback mechanism enables the development of neuroadaptive systems that are not only responsive to fluctuating user states but also capable of enhancing situational awareness, reducing cognitive overload, and improving operational safety and resilience in critical environments such as ATC.

Over the past ten years, European Consortium contributed to several projects aligned with these principles, providing valuable insights into advancing HMT in ATC.

NINA: The project developed a real-time tool grounded on adaptive automation and using neurophysiological data to assess ATCOs' cognitive states and enhance aviation safety and efficiency [4].

MOTO: The project investigated multi-modal technologies in the frame of remote towers to enhance human machine collaboration, by enabling operators to interact with systems through various sensory modalities [3].

ARTIMATION: The project sought to enhance human decision-making by presenting complex data in intuitive ways that align with cognitive processes, particularly for conflict resolution [1].

TRUSTY: The project explores how Explainable Artificial Intelligence (XAI) can help tower ATCOs in managing remote airfields by investigating how neurometrics can be used for adapting the level of operators' trust while using the XAI system [5].

CODA: The project provides a framework for real-time system adaptation addressing cognitive-driven adaptive modules, while being based on user needs and situational demands, ensuring alignment with the operator's cognitive and emotional states [2].

In the following sections, specific contributions of each project will be presented encompassing the experimental protocols, key findings, and their implications. Finally, discussion about insights and future directions on leveraging neurophysiological measures to enhance HMT in ATC will be given.

2   Projects Case Studies

This section provides a detailed overview of the main research projects that have been carried out over the past ten years to improve HMT in ATC. All these projects used neurophysiological data, such as brain activity, heart rate, and eye movements, to help design and test ATC systems that better support ATCOs in their demanding daily tasks.

2.1   NINA

The NINA (Neurometrics Indicators for ATM) project [4] was a research initiative aimed at investigating the feasibility of using neurophysiological measurements to monitor the cognitive state and mental workload of ATCOs [19]. Conducted over 27 months (September 2013 to November 2015) and co-funded by the SESAR Joint Undertaking [17,26], the project successfully demonstrated the potential of neurometrics in the Air Traffic Management (ATM) domain.

The central outcome was the development of a mental state classifier capable of estimating ATCO workload using EEG signals [9,21]. The classifier, designed through collaboration between Deep Blue, Sapienza University of Rome, and ENAC, was validated in ENAC's research facilities with 37 participants (both students and expert controllers) in realistic ATC scenarios (Fig. 1).

Results showed that EEG-based workload estimates closely aligned with established tools such as NASA-TLX [32] and Instantaneous Self-Assessment (ISA) [54], validating its use in ATC operational situation. Beyond workload monitoring, the classifier provided insight into individual expertise levels by analyzing the distribution of brain activity with repeated task exposure, offering a potential objective complement to performance-based training assessments [22].

Additionally, the project explored the application of adaptive automation, where real-time mental state data were used to inform dynamic system behaviors. Besides, the NINA project also introduced and validated four adaptive functionalities intended to support controller situational awareness and reduce cognitive load. These included adjusting Human-Machine Interface (HMI) alerts based on mental state (e.g., reducing or removing alerts), highlighting the calling station using voice recognition, adapting the design of short term conflict alert notifications, and reducing general visual load. The final validation campaign involving ATC students and professionals demonstrated the effectiveness of these adaptive strategies.

Efforts toward the end of the project aimed to enhance the ergonomics and usability of EEG equipment by developing a lightweight, user-friendly cap, potentially enabling deployment in operational environments by non-experts. The long-term vision included commercial exploitation targeting air navigation service providers and training institutions. Collectively, NINA delivered methodological and technological advancements that paved the way for future ATM research on adaptive automation, through contributing 12 advanced adaptive solutions, and reinforced the role of physiological monitoring in optimising both performance and training.

Fig. 1. Experimental setups for the NINA [4] (left) and MOTO [3] (right) projects. Left (NINA): The participant performs ATC tasks while his neurophysiological measurements are monitored in real time. Right (MOTO): The participant operates a remote-tower simulator with eight video screens providing live visual feedback; spatialised audio cues emanate from each screen to help the user detect and localize critical auditory events in the remote airfield environment. The user's brain activity is continuously recorded using an EEG cap.

2.2   MOTO

The MOTO (Embodied Remote Tower) project [3] investigated how multi-modal interaction, through visual, auditory, and haptic channels, can enhance the performance, situational awareness, and sense of presence of ATCOs in remote tower operations [11]. Grounded in the concept of embodied cognition, the project aimed to offload the increasingly saturated visual channel by integrating additional sensory modalities into the human-system interface. A core objective was to identify the key multi-modal stimuli that enhance immersion and presence, ultimately improving operational effectiveness. Sixteen professional ATCOs participated in the experimental validation, which was conducted using a virtual reality platform employing a head-mounted display to simulate a realistic airport control tower environment.

The experimental protocol included continuous monitoring of neurophysiological responses, including EEG, EOG, ECG, and GSR, along with subjective assessments via questionnaires and expert debriefs (Fig. 1). Data analysis showed that the inclusion of spatialized auditory information, particularly in scenarios involving spatial alerts or runway incursions, led to significantly improved response times. When paired with vibro-tactile alerts, performance gains were notable, especially in detecting unauthorized actions or safety breaches. However, the integration of all three modalities simultaneously (visual, auditory, and haptic) often resulted in a perceptible increase in mental workload, suggesting a risk of cognitive overload when too many stimuli are introduced without sufficient selectivity. This effect was more pronounced among controllers less familiar with enriched sensory environments, especially those accustomed to working in sound-proofed towers where audio cues and tactile feedback are typically absent [11].

The MOTO project demonstrated the critical value of neurophysiological monitoring tools in the design and validation of advanced ATM technologies, while also making significant strides in redefining human-machine interaction for remote tower operations. The EEG-based workload index emerged as a sensitive and temporally precise measure of cognitive workload, capturing dynamic fluctuations linked to specific operational events such as runway incursions with sub-minute resolution, far surpassing traditional subjective questionnaires in real-time evaluative capability. Complementing this, GSR measurements provided robust insights into ATCOs' psychophysiological activation, validating their utility as a low-intrusion yet powerful metric for assessing engagement.

These neurophysiological tools enable a more holistic evaluation framework, integrating seamlessly with behavioral and subjective data to enhance operational testing and iterative system design. Moreover, the project underscored the potential of multi-modal augmentation to enhance ATCO performance, provided its implementation is context-aware and accommodates user adaptation. By rigorously confirming the relevance of neurophysiological measures as objective, fine-grained human factors assessment tools in complex ATM environments, MOTO has laid a foundation for future research, though further investigation is essential to extend these findings to multiple remote tower settings and fully evaluate the long-term operational impacts of such augmented systems.

2.3 ARTIMATION

The ARTIMATION (Transparent Artificial Intelligence and Automation To Air Traffic Management Systems) project [1], funded under the SESAR Joint Undertaking within the European Union's Horizon 2020 framework, aimed to address the critical challenge of transparency in automated ATM systems by leveraging XAI techniques [27,38]. The project specifically focused on enhancing human-AI interaction through the development of transparent AI models for two key use cases: Conflict Detection and Resolution (CD&R) and Delay Prediction and Propagation [37].

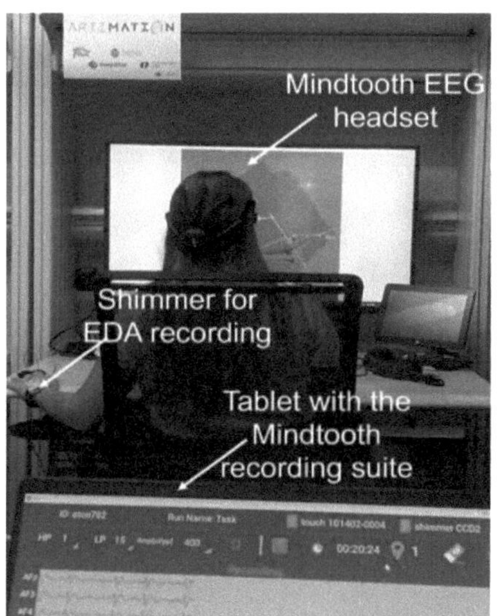

Fig. 2. Experimental setups for the ARTIMATION [1] (left) and CODA [2] (right) projects. Left (ARTIMATION): The participant is interacting with advanced ATC visualization techniques that display AI-generated outcomes for conflict detection and resolution. Right (CODA): The ATCO interacts with a digital assistant to perform shared control and management tasks. In both setups, the user's brain signals are continuously recorded using an EEG cap.

The ARTIMATION project investigated different visualization strategies for AI-generated outputs and assessed their impact on human performance, trust, and acceptance among two distinct groups, expert and students ATCOs. To this end, the project conducted controlled experiments where participants engaged with three visualization techniques representing AI outcomes for conflicts detection and resolution (CD&R) tasks and evaluated trust and usability of three delay prediction algorithms designed to optimize flight operations. Human performance and cognitive-affective responses were comprehensively assessed using a combination of traditional self-report questionnaires (e.g., trust, workload, stress scales), semi-structured interviews, and objective neurophysiological measurements, including EEG and EDA recordings (Fig. 2).

Results demonstrated that ATCOs under operational pressure prefer explanations to be available on demand and integrated directly within their primary work systems, rather than through external interfaces. Moreover, while explainable visualizations enhanced understanding and trust, excessive complexity or poorly-timed information delivery could negatively impact performance. Significant differences emerged between experts and students, suggesting that XAI tools could play a particularly beneficial role in ATC training environments by supporting decision-making reflection.

Overall, the ARTIMATION project provided a foundational proof-of-concept for transparent AI applications in ATM, offering practical guidelines for designing user-centered, adaptive AI systems that enhance controller trust, maintain human agency, and improve operational safety in automated airspaces.

2.4 TRUSTY

The TRUSTY (Trustworthy Intelligent System for Remote Digital Towers) [5] project is an ongoing initiative under the SESAR 3 Joint Undertaking and Horizon Europe, designed to address the pressing need for reliable, transparent, and explainable AI in Remote Digital Tower (RDT) operations. As airports increasingly adopt digital towers, where air traffic services are provided remotely through advanced video and sensor technologies, TRUSTY seeks to ensure that AI systems integrated into these environments are not only efficient and capable but also trusted by human operators [13]. The core objective is to support tower ATCOs in monitoring critical tasks, such as taxiway inspection and runway surveillance, while enhancing overall system resilience, capacity, and safety.

The project combines cutting-edge technologies in artificial intelligence, multi-modal machine learning, and user-centered design. By leveraging interactive data visualization methods, such as visual analytics, data-driven storytelling, and immersive analytics, TRUSTY aims to improve human-machine interaction, making AI decisions more understandable and actionable for controllers. These innovations are especially vital in high-stakes, time-sensitive environments where trust in automation directly influences safety outcomes.

The final validation of the project was recently conducted at the ENAC's ACHIL operational platform in Toulouse (Fig. 3). Seventeen professional ATCOs participated in simulated RDT scenarios involving two distinct airfields: Toulouse-Blagnac Airport (LFBO) and Muret-Lherm Aerodrome (LFBR). At LFBO, controllers communicated with pilots and managed aircraft movements using traditional radio systems, while at LFBR, they relied solely on AI-generated video and audio alerts without direct communication.

The project incorporated advanced bio-metric tools to record real-time data on controller states during operations in order to improve the understanding on the psycho-physiological foundations of trust in AI in the frame of ATC. Electroencephalography (EEG) was recorded via the Mindtooth Touch system, a wearable headset with eight water-based electrodes optimized for usability and data fidelity in operational settings. Electrodermal Activity (EDA) was measured using the Shimmer3 GSR+ device, which detects skin conductance changes tied to emotional arousal and stress. These physiological measurements provided insight into how varying levels of AI transparency and explainability affected cognitive load, stress levels, and trust dynamics.

Fig. 3. Experimental setup for the TRUSTY project [5]: The ATCO is performing control tasks at a physical tower while simultaneously managing a remote digital tower (on the screen to his right). Neurophysiological data are being collected using the Mindtooth Touch EEG headset and the Shimmer3 GSR+ device to evaluate his fluctuations in trust toward the proposed solution for the RDT.

The collected data will be used to refine AI interfaces to better adapt explanations based on user state, enabling real-time, personalized support. This aligns with TRUSTY's broader ambition to develop adaptive systems that dynamically adjust their level of transparency and explanation according to user needs and situational complexity. Through these efforts, TRUSTY not only contributes to the advancement of remote tower technology but also lays the groundwork for future air traffic management systems that are both highly automated and deeply human-centered.

2.5 CODA

The CODA (Controller Adaptive Digital Assistant) project [2] is an ongoing initiative under the SESAR 3 Joint Undertaking and Horizon Europe aiming to transform ATM through advanced human-AI collaboration. The project focuses on reducing the cognitive and emotional strain placed on ATCOs by developing a digital assistant that dynamically supports decision-making in real time.

The assistant leverages AI to predict future traffic scenarios and assess the controller's current mental state, including workload, stress, attention, and fatigue, to determine whether they can handle the anticipated operational demands. Based on this assessment, the system follows an adaptive automation strategy, which may involve increasing automation levels, activating AI-based support tools, or modifying airspace configuration to maintain safety and efficiency.

A central element of CODA's research involved conducting experimental validations using a range of physiological and psychological measurement tools to evaluate mental state indicators (Fig. 2). EEG was the primary neurophysiological method used, capturing electrical brain activity via the Mindtooth headset. These measurements revealed critical cognitive markers: increased frontal midline theta activity indicated higher mental workload, while alpha and beta band variations helped identify stress and fatigue levels. Additionally, eye-tracking systems assessed blink frequency and duration, key indicators of visual attention, fatigue, and cognitive strain. A reduced blink rate was associated with high workload, while increases in blink duration were linked to fatigue.

To complement these objective measures, subjective tools like ISA and pre and post-run questionnaires (SOFI and DSSQ-3) were used. Instantaneous Self-Assessment (ISA) captured perceived workload at regular intervals, while SOFI and DSSQ-3 offered deeper insights into fatigue and stress dimensions such as sleepiness, motivation, task engagement, and distress. This multi-modal approach enabled CODA to build a rich, real-time profile of controller mental states and use that data to refine adaptive support mechanisms.

Results from these experiments demonstrated the potential of CODA's adaptive assistant to enhance decision-making during high-stress moments by dynamically adjusting automation based on mental state feedback. Participants experienced the system's ability to detect and respond to stress and cognitive overload in real time, which not only optimized task allocation but also significantly improved safety margins and performance reliability.

3 Overview of Projects Detailing Benefits and Challenges of Neurophysiological Integration

A chronological overview of the research projects included in this study is provided in Fig. 4. Each project addresses distinct yet interrelated aspects of human factors and technological integration within air traffic management, with a shared objective of enhancing ATC operations through the incorporation of neurophysiological measurements into the validation and refinement of proposed solutions. The progression of the projects illustrates a thematic evolution, starting with investigating the feasibility of using neurophysiological measurements to monitor the cognitive state and mental workload of ATCOs with NINA project. MOTO project explored the potential for enhancing ATCO performance through multi-sensory feedback in remote tower operations. The research trajectory further advanced toward the development of transparent and explainable AI systems with ARTIMATION project, along with emphasizing the importance of fostering trust between ATCOs and AI-based decision support tools in RDTs in TRUSTY project. Finally, the focus shifted in CODA project toward the design and implementation of cognitive-driven adaptive systems aiming at optimizing human-AI teaming.

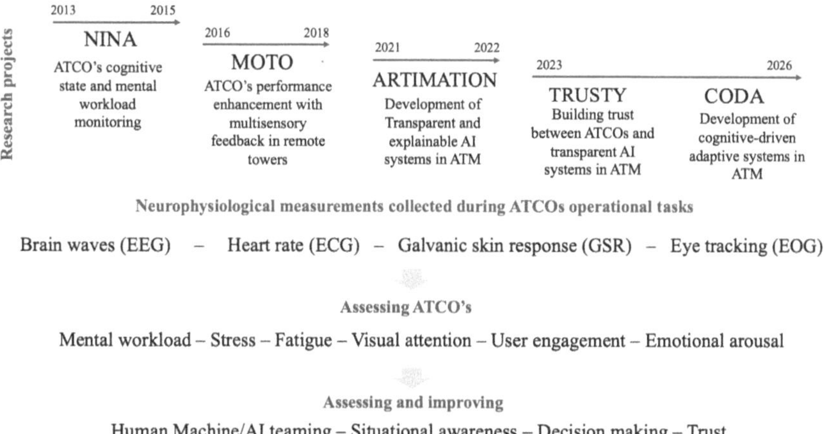

Fig. 4. A global timeline of the evolution of neurophysiological methods for assessing humanmachine teaming in air traffic management. Although not exhaustive, this sequence highlights major projects that have used real-time neurofeedback to enhance operator performance in HMT contexts. It illustrates the rising interest and technological maturity of neuroadaptive approaches, particularly within the ATC/ATM domain.

Across these initiatives, a comprehensive suite of neurophysiological signals was systematically collected during ATCOs' engagement in realistic task environments. These included EEG for capturing electrical brain activity, ECG for monitoring heart rate variability, GSR for assessing autonomic arousal through skin conductance changes, and EOG and other eye-tracking measures to evaluate visual attention and ocular behavior. The multi-modal integration of these bio-signals enabled a robust and fine-grained assessment of a range of cognitive and affective states, including mental workload, stress, fatigue, visual attention, user engagement, and emotional arousal. These psychophysiological metrics were employed both as diagnostic indicators and as real-time feedback sources to inform the development of adaptive interfaces and AI-driven support systems. By mapping neurophysiological responses to specific task demands and environmental conditions, the studies aimed to uncover latent patterns that characterize sub-optimal performance or elevated cognitive strain. Such insights are critical for dynamically adjusting system behavior to maintain operator performance within optimal bounds, particularly in time-sensitive ATM scenarios.

The overarching objective of these investigations is to advance human-centered automation design and optimize human-AI collaboration by leveraging neurophysiological insights to enhance both moment-to-moment operational performance and long-term cognitive sustainability. Real-time EEG and ECG monitoring provide objective, dynamic assessments of operators' cognitive states, enabling adaptive ATC systems to maintain optimal workload levels, mitigate fatigue-related risks, and reinforce trust in AI-assisted decision support tools. These capabilities are critical for sustaining situational awareness, ensuring timely decision-making, and fostering calibrated trust–key requirements for resilient and adaptive ATM systems facing increasing operational complexity. Furthermore, by detecting cognitive strain or discomfort, such systems can proactively adjust task management strategies, improving interaction quality and team coordination. In multi-operator environments, shared neurophysiological monitoring facilitates intelligent task distribution and communication, ultimately boosting performance in high-demand ATC scenarios. This integration of real-time neurocognitive feedback with adaptive automation represents a transformative step toward cognitively supportive and operationally robust airspace management, that is one the most important SESAR's goal in the future to come [52].

Despite these advantages, several critical challenges remain. One key issue is individual variability; physiological responses to stressors or cognitive demands can differ significantly across individuals, necessitating personalized calibration or baseline measures to interpret signals accurately [10,12]. Additionally, neurophysiological signals are highly context-sensitive. For example, elevated workload does not necessarily correlate with impaired performance and may even be indicative of deep engagement in certain scenarios. Another important consideration is the timing of adaptation. In high-demand or safety-critical environments, system interventions must be carefully timed to avoid destabilizing the user's experience or distracting them during peak workload periods. Finally, the risk of over-adaptation, where systems change behavior too frequently in response to fluctuating physiological states, can lead to user confusion, decreased predictability, and reduced system usability. Addressing these challenges requires careful design and validation of adaptive algorithms, as well as a deep understanding of the interplay between physiological markers and cognitive processes.

Overall, these different projects collectively highlight that he integration of neurophysiological monitoring with intelligent systems represents a significant advancement in the development of human-centered technologies for ATC. By capturing real-time indicators of mental workload (e.g., EEG), stress (e.g., ECG), and attention (e.g., eye-tracking), these systems enhance alignment between human and machine agents, promoting trust, adaptability, and accurate decision-making in high-stakes operational contexts. A major focus lies in addressing the asymmetry between human and machine situational models, which often leads to misaligned expectations and degraded team performance. By analyzing the dynamic interplay between human perception and machine logic, the goal is to foster mutual understanding and ensure transparent, context-sensitive decision-making. This interdisciplinary effort rooted in cognitive science, neurophysiology, human factors, and artificial intelligence, enables the design of resilient and scalable HMT systems that are specifically tailored for the operational constraints and cognitive demands of ATC environments.

To validate the effectiveness of these neuroadaptive systems, a dual-assessment methodology is implemented, combining continuous neurometrics with conventional evaluation techniques [8,12,20]. On the one hand, physiological indicators are continuously captured to assess cognitive states such as workload, stress, vigilance, and attentional focus. On the other, self-reported trust, usability or acceptability metrics, and objective performance indicators, such as communication efficiency, conflict resolution time, and error rates, are used to benchmark system impact. This hybrid evaluation framework facilitates a comparative analysis of the diagnostic sensitivity and operational relevance of each metric type, contributing to a more holistic understanding of system performance. However, one of the persistent technical challenges in neurophysiological monitoring is the gap between laboratory-quality data and the realities of field deployment. High-fidelity neurophysiological sensors used in lab settings are often invasive, expensive, and impractical for operational use. In contrast, wearable sensors, absolutely essential for real-world ATC applications, offer greater practicality but at the cost of signal quality and increased artifact susceptibility [8,35]. Extracting reliable, interpretable features from these noisier data streams remains an ongoing research frontier. Ensuring usability without compromising signal integrity is crucial for deploying neuroadaptive technologies in complex, real-time operational environments.

Building on this dual-assessment methodology, recent advancements in human-centered AI research offer complementary insights that can inform the design and evaluation of neuroadaptive systems in operational environments such as ATC. For instance, studies on interactive machine learning [50] and abstraction alignment [16] emphasize the importance of aligning AI behavior with human conceptual models, which is essential when interpreting neurometrics in context and designing adaptive responses. Moreover, the emotional and social dimensions explored in longitudinal studies on AI conversational agents [24] and in the AURA framework [56] highlight the need to consider not only cognitive workload but also emotional resilience and user well-being as part of system validation. These findings reinforce the value of hybrid evaluation approaches that combine physiological monitoring with user-centered measures, particularly in high-stakes domains where trust and transparency are critical. Furthermore, ethical design perspectives articulated by [51] underline the imperative of embedding these systems within responsible, interpretable, and sustainable frameworks. Together, these contributions point toward a broader paradigm in which the technical challenges of wearable sensor fidelity and artifact management are addressed not in isolation, but through integrative design strategies that prioritize explainability, user alignment, and ethical deployment.

Interestingly, recent research on the sense of agency during human-machine interactions further deepens our understanding of the cognitive mechanisms underlying effective HMT. Indeed, experimental studies investigating joint tasks between a human agent and either another human or an artificial co-agent [31,47,48] demonstrate that both the representation of the co-agent's action in one's own cognitive system and the implicit sense of agency are significantly attenuated when interacting with machine partners. Specifically, it has been proposed that individuals are less likely to incorporate machine behavior into their own sensorimotor predictions, central to anticipation and coordination, and consequently, experience difficulties in building a sense of shared control during human-machine interactions [49]. These findings highlight the need for designing neuroadaptive ATC systems that help individuals internalize machine behaviors, enhancing their sense of shared agency, and thereby supporting effective HMT.

4   Discussion and Conclusion

This article highlighted the potential of integrating neurophysiological measurements into the design of ATC systems for optimizing humanmachine teaming. After more than a decade of interdisciplinary research and development across many projects–including NINA, MOTO, ARTIMATION, TRUSTY, and CODA–it has been shown that real-time monitoring of neurophysiological signals such as EEG, ECG, GSR, and eye-tracking provides valuable information about operators' cognitive and emotional states. These signals can be used both for analyzing real-time performance and for enabling adaptive system responses during operations, helping to meet the growing demands of air traffic control environments.

The valuable insights coming from these projects allow us to affirm that neuroadaptive systems enhance operational resilience by dynamically regulating task complexity, fostering transparency, and supporting situational awareness. The integration of these signals facilitates more intuitive, context-aware, and user-aligned automation, addressing core limitations of traditional static systems and supporting more collaborative and efficient decision-making. Moreover, the implementation of iterative prototyping and user feedback loops in our projects underscores the importance of designing with controllers, not just for them. By engaging ATCOs throughout the development process via workshops and high-fidelity simulations, the resulting systems preserve essential collaborative dynamics, operational flexibility, and resilience. These human-centered design principles ensure that novel interfaces not only align with cognitive ergonomics but also enhance coordination, redundancy, and trust in distributed ATC teams. Despite the clear benefits, several important challenges persist. These include individual differences in physiological responses, the balance between how precisely systems adapt and how predictable they remain, and the technical limitations of current wearable sensors. In addition, applying these models in real-world settings will require scalable system designs and strong privacy measures to protect sensitive physiological data.

This work provides a foundation for the next generation of HMT systems in the ATC environment, which will not only react to user needs but also anticipate them. This will allow AI systems to engage proactively and take a more active and helpful role in supporting human operators.

This path has been explored in the CODA project, particularly through the development of the HumanMachine Performance Envelope (HMPE), a dimension that addresses the quality of interaction between AI digital assistants and the human operator. This idea is based on the Human Performance Envelope (HPE), introduced by Bittner in 1985 [15], which is a multidimensional psycho-behavioral model that evaluates an operator's performance based on human factors like mental workload, stress, and attention. These factors determine whether performance remains acceptable or degrades into dangerous levels. Future goals will focus on extending this concept to the HMPE, which captures not only the operator's cognitive state but also the quality of interaction with the systems based on real-time physiological monitoring and enables AI systems to adapt dynamically and support collaborative decision-making.

The integration of neurophysiological measurements into the design of ATC systems for enhancing HMT aligns closely with the principles outlined by [7] in their seminal work on Guidelines for Human-AI Interaction. Their framework emphasizes the importance of designing AI systems that are transparent, context-aware, and responsive to user needs–principles that are directly reflected in the neuroadaptive systems developed in projects like those presented in this paper. The real-time adaptation of automation levels based on physiological states such as mental workload, vigilance, or stress exemplifies how AI systems can be designed not only to respond to user input but also to proactively anticipate user states and support collaboration. Specifically, the HMPE developed in CODA seeks to operationalize several of these guidelines by ensuring the system (1) communicates what it can do and how well it can do it, (2) learns from operator behavior over time, and (3) adapts cautiously in ways that foster trust, situational awareness, and predictability. This evolution from static automation to dynamic, human-aligned interaction design represents a critical step in operationalizing theoretical contributions from [7] within high-stakes environments such as ATC. Additionally, the work provided by Endsley [29] directly complements [7] and ongoing research in neuroadaptive systems for ATC. Whereas [7] offers guidelines for interface and interaction design, [29] focuses more on cognitive integration, especially preserving human awareness in the presence of intelligent agents.

This neurophysiological-monitoring approach (EEG, ECG, EDA, GSR, eye-tracking) to maintain cognitive alignment and dynamically adapt automation levels (e.g., via the HMPE) will operationalize recommendations from [29] and [7], offering a data-driven solution to the situational awareness loss problem described. In this way, future directions should be more oriented toward expanding the HMPE framework to include multimodal, data-driven models capable of capturing higher-order constructs such as shared situational awareness, team cognition, emotional synchrony, reliance, and adaptive trust.

Acknowledgments. This study was supported by the following projects: 1) CODA (Controller Adaptive Digital Assistant), financed by the SESAR JU under the EU's Horizon 2022 Research and Innovation programme (GA: 101114765), 2) TRUSTY (Trustworthy Intelligent System For Remote Digital Tower) project financed by the

SESAR JU under the EU's Horizon 2022 Research and Innovation programme (GA: 101114838), 3) ARTIMATION (Transparent Artificial Intelligence and Automation To Air Traffic Management Systems), financed by the SESAR JU under the EU's Horizon 2020 Research and Innovation programme (GA: 894238), 4) MOTO (Embodied Remote Tower), financed by the SESAR JU under the EU's Horizon 2020 (GA: 699379), 5) NINA (Neurometrics Indicators for ATM) research project supported within SESAR Work Package E.

Disclosure of Interests. The authors declare no conflict of interest.

References

1. ARTIMATION: Transparent artificial intelligence and automation to air traffic management systems. https://www.artimation.eu/. Accessed 15 May 2025
2. CODA: Controller adaptive digital assistant. https://iptc.upm.es/coda. Accessed 15 May 2025
3. MOTO: Embodied remote tower. https://cordis.europa.eu/project/id/699379. Accessed 15 May 2025
4. NINA: Neurometrics indicators for ATM. https://research.dblue.it/nina/. Accessed 15 May 2025
5. TRUSTY: Trustworthy intelligent system for remote digital towers. https://research.dblue.it/trusty/. Accessed 15 May 2025
6. Amalberti, R.: Dysfonctionnements des systèmes et dysfonctionnements de la cognition.-contribution à la compréhension de la sécurité des systèmes ultra-sûrs. Revue générale nucléaire (1), 55–62 (1998)
7. Amershi, S., et al.: Guidelines for human-ai interaction. In: Proceedings of the 2019 Chi Conference on Human Factors in Computing Systems, pp. 1–13 (2019)
8. Aricò, P., et al.: Adaptive automation triggered by EEG-based mental workload index: a passive brain-computer interface application in realistic air traffic control environment. Front. Hum. Neurosci. **10**, 539 (2016). https://doi.org/10.3389/fnhum.2016.00539
9. Aricò, P., et al.: Reliability over time of EEG-based mental workload evaluation during air traffic management (ATM) tasks. In: Proceedings of the 37th Annual International Conference of the IEEE Engineering in Medicine and Biology Society (EMBC), pp. 7242–7245. IEEE (2015). https://doi.org/10.1109/EMBC.2015.7320063
10. Aricò, P., Borghini, G., Di Flumeri, G., Sciaraffa, N., Colosimo, A., Babiloni, F.: Passive BCI in operational environments: insights, recent advances, and future trends. IEEE Trans. Biomed. Eng. **64**(7), 1431–1436 (2017). https://doi.org/10.1109/TBME.2017.2694856
11. Aricò, P., et al.: How neurophysiological measures can be used to enhance the evaluation of remote tower solutions. Front. Hum. Neurosci. **13**, 303 (2019). https://doi.org/10.3389/fnhum.2019.00303
12. Aricò, P., et al.: Human factors and neurophysiological metrics in air traffic control: a critical review. IEEE Rev. Biomed. Eng. **10**, 250–263 (2017)
13. Begum, S., Ahmed, M., Barua, S., Kabir, M., Masud, A.: Research issues and challenges in the computational development of trustworthy AI. In: Proceedings of the 2024 IEEE International Conference on Artificial Intelligence in Engineering

and Technology (IICAIET), pp. 300–305. IEEE (2024). https://doi.org/10.1109/IICAIET62352.2024.10730209
14. Bernabei, M., Costantino, F.: Adaptive automation: status of research and future challenges. Robot. Comput.-Integrated Manuf. **88**, 102724 (2024)
15. Bittner, A., Harbeson, M., Kennedy, R., Lundy, N.: Assessing the human performance envelope: a brief guide. SAE Transact. **94**, 375–385 (1985). http://www.jstor.org/stable/44742942
16. Boggust, A., Bang, H., Strobelt, H., Satyanarayan, A.: Abstraction alignment: comparing model-learned and human-encoded conceptual relationships. In: Proceedings of the 2025 CHI Conference on Human Factors in Computing Systems, pp. 1–20 (2025)
17. Bolić, T., Ravenhill, P.: Sesar: the past, present, and future of European air traffic management research. Engineering **7**(4), 448–451 (2021)
18. Bonaceto, C., Estes, S., Moertl, P., Burns, K.: Naturalistic decision making in the air traffic control tower: combining approaches to support changes in procedures. In: 7th International Conference on Naturalistic Decision Making, Amsterdam, The Netherlands (2005)
19. Borghini, G., Aricò, P., Babiloni, F., Granger, G., Imbert, J., Benhacene, R., et al.: Nina: neurometrics indicators for ATM. In: Proceedings of the 3rd SESAR Innovation Days (SID 2013). SESAR Joint Undertaking, Stockholm, Sweden (2013)
20. Borghini, G., et al.: EEG-based cognitive control behaviour assessment: an ecological study with professional air traffic controllers. Sci. Rep. **7**, 547 (2017). https://doi.org/10.1038/s41598-017-00633-7
21. Borghini, G., et al.: Skill, rule and knowledge-based behaviour detection by means of ATCOS' brain activity. In: Proceedings of the 5th SESAR Innovation Days (SID 2015). SESAR Joint Undertaking, Bologna, Italy (2015). https://hal.archives-ouvertes.fr/hal-01240319v2
22. Borghini, G., Aricò, P., Graziani, I., Salinari, S., Babiloni, F., et al.: Analysis of neurophysiological signals for the training and mental workload assessment of ATCOS. In: Proceedings of the 4th SESAR Innovation Days (SID 2014). SESAR Joint Undertaking, Madrid, Spain (2014)
23. Borghini, G., Astolfi, L., Vecchiato, G., Mattia, D., Babiloni, F.: Measuring neurophysiological signals in aircraft pilots and car drivers for the assessment of mental workload, fatigue and drowsiness. Neurosci. Biobehav. Rev. **44**, 58–75 (2014). https://doi.org/10.1016/j.neubiorev.2012.10.003
24. Chandra, M., et al.: Longitudinal study on social and emotional use of AI conversational agent. arXiv preprint arXiv:2504.14112 (2025)
25. Chen, J., Barnes, M.: Human-agent teaming for multirobot control: a review of human factors issues. IEEE Trans. Hum.-Mach. Syst. **44**(1), 13–29 (2014). https://doi.org/10.1109/THMS.2013.2293535
26. Crespo, D.C., De Leon, P.M.: Achieving the single European sky: goals and challenges, vol. 8. Kluwer Law International BV (2011)
27. Degas, A., et al.: A survey on artificial intelligence (ai) and explainable ai in air traffic management: current trends and development with future research trajectory. Appl. Sci. **12**(3), 1295 (2022). https://doi.org/10.3390/app12031295
28. Di Flumeri, G., et al.: Brain-computer interface-based adaptive automation to prevent out-of-the-loop phenomenon in air traffic controllers dealing with highly automated systems. Front. Hum. Neurosci. **13**, 296 (2019)
29. Endsley, M.R.: Automation and situation awareness. In: Automation and Human Performance, pp. 163–181. CRC Press (2018)

30. Giraudet, L., Imbert, J., Tremblay, S., Causse, M.: High rate of inattentional deafness in simulated air traffic control tasks. Procedia Manuf. **3**, 5169–5175 (2015). https://doi.org/10.1016/J.PROMFG.2015.07.555
31. Grynszpan, O., et al.: The sense of agency in human-human vs human-robot joint action. Conscious. Cogn. **75**, 102820 (2019)
32. Hart, S.G., Staveland, L.E.: Development of NASA-TLX (task load index): results of empirical and theoretical research. In: Advances in Psychology, vol. 52, pp. 139–183. Elsevier (1988)
33. Hedayati, S., Sadeghi-Firoozabadi, V., Bagheri, M., Heidari, M., Sze, N.: Evaluating differences in cognitive functions and personality traits among air traffic controllers with and without error history. Saf. Sci. (2021). https://doi.org/10.1016/J.SSCI.2021.105208
34. Hilburn, B.: Cognitive complexity in air traffic control: a literature review. EEC Note **4**(04), 1–80 (2004)
35. Hogervorst, M., Brouwer, A., van Erp, J.: Combining and comparing EEG, peripheral physiology and eye-related measures for the assessment of mental workload. Front. Neurosci. **8**, 322 (2014). https://doi.org/10.3389/fnins.2014.00322
36. Hopkin, V.D.: The impact of automation on air traffic control systems. In: Automation and Systems Issues in Air Traffic Control, pp. 3–19. Springer (1991)
37. Hurter, C., et al.: Usage of more transparent and explainable conflict resolution algorithm: air traffic controller feedback. Transp. Res. Procedia **66**, 270–278 (2022). https://doi.org/10.1016/j.trpro.2022.12.027
38. Islam, M.R., Ahmed, M.U., Barua, S., Begum, S.: A systematic review of explainable artificial intelligence in terms of different application domains and tasks. Appl. Sci. **12**(3), 1353 (2022)
39. Kaber, D.B., Perry, C.M., Segall, N., McClernon, C.K., Prinzel, L.J., III.: Situation awareness implications of adaptive automation for information processing in an air traffic control-related task. Int. J. Ind. Ergon. **36**(5), 447–462 (2006)
40. Kaber, D.B., Riley, J.M., Tan, K.W., Endsley, M.R.: On the design of adaptive automation for complex systems. Int. J. Cogn. Ergon. **5**(1), 37–57 (2001)
41. Kaber, D., Endsley, M.: The effects of level of automation and adaptive automation on human performance, situation awareness and workload in a dynamic control task. Theor. Issues Ergon. Sci. **5**(2), 113–153 (2004). https://doi.org/10.1080/1463922021000054335
42. Langan-Fox, J., Canty, J.M., Sankey, M.J.: Human-automation teams and adaptable control for future air traffic management. Int. J. Ind. Ergon. **39**(5), 894–903 (2009)
43. McGee, J.P., Parasuraman, R., Mavor, A.S., Wickens, C.D.: The Future of Air Traffic Control: Human Operators and Automation. National Academies Press (1998)
44. McNeese, N., Demir, M., Cooke, N., Myers, C.: Teaming with a synthetic teammate: insights into human-autonomy teaming. Hum. Factors **60**(2), 262–273 (2017). https://doi.org/10.1177/0018720817743223
45. Metzger, U., Parasuraman, R.: Automation in future air traffic management: effects of decision aid reliability on controller performance and mental workload. In: Decision Making in Aviation, pp. 345–360. Routledge (2017)
46. Parasuraman, R.: Designing automation for human use: empirical studies and quantitative models. Ergonomics **43**(7), 931–951 (2000)
47. Sahaï, A., Caspar, E., De Beir, A., Grynszpan, O., Pacherie, E., Berberian, B.: Modulations of one's sense of agency during human-machine interactions: a

behavioural study using a full humanoid robot. Q. J. Exp. Psychol. **76**(3), 606–620 (2023)

48. Sahaï, A., Desantis, A., Grynszpan, O., Pacherie, E., Berberian, B.: Action co-representation and the sense of agency during a joint Simon task: comparing human and machine co-agents. Conscious. Cogn. **67**, 44–55 (2019)

49. Sahaï, A., Pacherie, E., Grynszpan, O., Berberian, B.: Predictive mechanisms are not involved the same way during human-human vs. human-machine interactions: a review. Front. Neurorobot. **11**, 52 (2017)

50. Sanchez, T., Caramiaux, B., Françoise, J., Bevilacqua, F., Mackay, W.E.: How do people train a machine? Strategies and (mis) understandings. Proc. ACM Hum.-Comput. Interact. **5**(CSCW1), 1–26 (2021)

51. Schmidt, A., Giannotti, F., Mackay, W., Shneiderman, B., Väänänen, K.: Artificial intelligence for humankind: a panel on how to create truly interactive and human-centered ai for the benefit of individuals and society. In: IFIP Conference on Human-Computer Interaction, pp. 335–339. Springer (2021)

52. SESAR Joint Undertaking: European atm master plan: 2025 edition, Technical report, SESAR Joint Undertaking, Brussels, Belgium (2024). https://www.sesarju.eu/masterplan

53. Suarez, N., López, P., Puntero, E., Rodriguez, S.: Quantifying air traffic controller mental workload. Fourth SESAR Innovation Days **220** (2014)

54. Tattersall, A.J., Foord, P.S.: An experimental evaluation of instantaneous self-assessment as a measure of workload. Ergonomics **39**(5), 740–748 (1996)

55. Wickens, C.D.: Automation in air traffic control: the human performance issues. In: Automation Technology and Human Performance: Current Research and Trends, pp. 2–10 (1999)

56. Zhang, A.Q., Amores, J., Shen, H., Czerwinski, M., Gray, M.L., Suh, J.: Aura: amplifying understanding, resilience, and awareness for responsible ai content work. Proc. ACM Hum.-Comput. Interact. **9**(2), 1–45 (2025)

Evaluation of a Plan and Goal Recognition System for Inferring the Pilot's Intent in Helicopter Operations

Dominik Künzel[(✉)] and Axel Schulte

Institute of Flight Systems, University of the Bundeswehr Munich, Neubiberg, Germany
{dominik.kuenzel,axel.schulte}@unibw.de

Abstract. In our contribution, we evaluated a plan and goal recognition (PGR) system to enable adaptive pilot assistance in dynamic helicopter missions. In highly dynamic environments, pre-planned mission sequences often become obsolete when the mission environment changes. To provide efficient support, the assistant system requires an understanding of the pilot's current intent. We implemented a PGR system based on hierarchical task networks (HTN) to recognize tactical goals and plans from pilot behavior and situational data. We performed an experimental evaluation in our mission and cockpit simulation environment with 10 professionally trained helicopter pilots. The system successfully inferred the plan and tactical goals, aligning with data labeled by the participants. Recognized intentions can serve as triggers for adaptive interventions, enabling implicit communication and real-time assistance to adaptively support the pilot in executing the mission.

Keywords: Adaptive Pilot Assistance · Plan and Goal Recognition · Intent Recognition · Human-Autonomy-Teaming · Helicopter Operations

1 Introduction

In complex applications like military helicopter missions, the mission objective and pre-mission generated plans are usually used to ensure that the mission is executed efficiently and safely. These plans describe a discrete sequence of activities that must be performed throughout the mission. They provide guidance for the pilot and enable advanced assistance systems to understand the mission objectives as well as the required and expected actions (Miller & Hannen, 1999; Brand & Schulte, 2017). However, this plan often becomes obsolete due to rapid, unpredictable environmental changes. If the pilot adapts to the changed situation and deviates from the predefined plan without initiating re-planning and system reconfiguration, the assistance system may no longer provide effective support and might even act in contradiction to the pilot's actions. To avoid this, assistant systems should be capable of recognizing the pilot's current plan and goal based on observed actions and the current tactical situation. This approach allows to establish a shared understanding and enables adequate support, without requiring

D. Harris et al. (Eds.): HCII 2025, LNCS 16334, pp. 200–212, 2026.
https://doi.org/10.1007/978-3-032-12392-3_13

the pilot to actively communicate the intent in time- or attention-critical moments (c.f. Fig. 1). We developed a PGR system based on hierarchical task networks (HTN) that recognizes the pilot's goal and the underlying tactical plan, based on the current situation and pilot observation in helicopter operations. In contrast to more structured domains, our operational context is characterized by an event-driven and situational progression of mission, requiring recognition-based adaptation rather than plan-based tracking. The long-term goal is to integrate the recognized plan and goal information into a broader adaptive assistance framework that dynamically adjusts its intervention strategies based on the inferred plan and goal.

In this contribution, we present the evaluation of the PGR system in our mission and cockpit simulation environment involving 10 professionally trained helicopter pilots. Our initial concept was presented in Künzel and Schulte (2024). The main contribution lies in demonstrating the applicability of the HTN-based PGR system in this domain and its potential for enabling adaptive support in real-time.

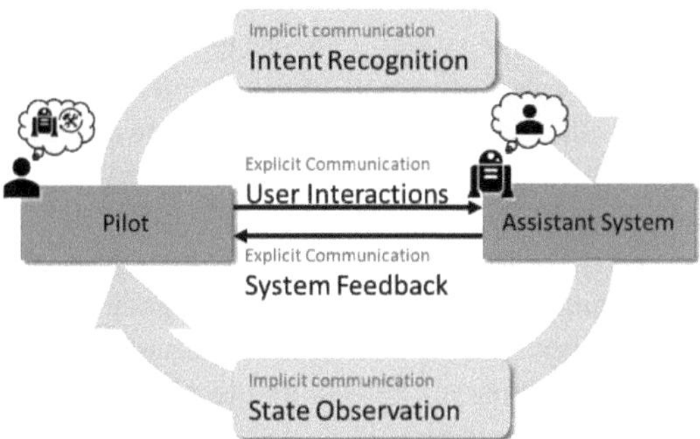

Fig. 1. Explicit and implicit information flow between pilot and assistant system.

2 Background

Advanced pilot assistant systems can be described as cooperative agents with a heterarchical relationship to the pilot, intending to improve the pilot's performance and safety (Schulte et al., 2016; Theissing & Schulte, 2013). To fulfill this role, the assistant system should act as a cooperative crew member, contributing to mission success in a manner aligned with the pilot's goals and actions. This can be taken in various forms, e.g., through the adaptive intervention to balance the pilot's mental workload (Brand & Schulte, 2017) or estimation of the situation awareness (Schwerd & Schulte, 2021). Often, the idea of such systems is to avoid errors or to lead to an optimal solution (e.g., inform the pilot about a missed task or information). To make this possible, both – the pilot and the system – should have knowledge of each other's intentions (Billings, 1991). This knowledge usually comes from prior mission planning or a pre-mission defined plan. However, such approaches fail in dynamic contexts where the pilot deviates from the plan or plans are nonexistent. If we want to support the pilot continuously during a dynamically changing mission, the system needs a shared understanding of the pilot's mental state and their doing as well as the current situation. Through plan and goal recognition (PGR) this knowledge can be obtained, inferring goals and future actions from behavior. Goal Recognition can be defined as "inferring an agent's intention through its actions and their effects on the environment" (Han & Pereira, 2013). Van-Horenbeke and Peer (2021) define plan recognition as the inference of "set of actions that have been or will be performed [...] to reach that goal". PGR can be divided into the domain theory-based approach (also referred to as plan-recognition-as-planning) or the plan library-based approach (Van-Horenbeke & Peer, 2021). Usually, the term intent recognition refers to plan and goal recognition. In more structured domains, e.g. IFR Flight, Pilot Intent and Error Recognition has been used as part of a pilot assistance system to suppress disruptive warnings that relate to intentional deviations from the plan and would otherwise have been classified as errors (Wittig & Onken, 1992; Strohal & Onken, 1998). If intentions are recognized instead, the plan can be adapted accordingly, and support can be continued. Estes et al. (2016) used PGR for supporting during different phases and tasks concerning a current flight plan. Suck and Fortmann (2016) applied a Hidden Markov Model to infer the most probable current intention. Another example is the usage of a Theory-Of-Mind assistant agent for intent-based UAV mission management in a mixed initiative system (Theissing & Schulte, 2013). Using a plan-recognition-as-planning approach allows us to use an off-the-shelf planning algorithm such as HTN planning. Höller et al. (2018) use HTNs for an empirical evaluation of typical planning problems, while Jamakatel et al. (2023) applied this approach to recognize the pilot's intention in general aviation.

To our knowledge, there is currently no research addressing goal and plan recognition systems for adaptive assistance in military helicopter missions, which are highly dynamic due to their dependence on the changing tactical situation and the absence of a pre-defined plan. Our work aims to close this gap by evaluating an HTN-based PGR system in a simulated, event-driven mission context.

3   Method

To recognize the pilot pursued plan and goal, we implemented our PGR system, which is based on HTN planning to generate multiple plan hypotheses describing possible tactical courses of action. Based on observations about the pilot and the changing state related to the actions, the hypotheses are used to perform probabilistic reasoning.

3.1   HTN Planning

In this article, the intent refers to the sub-goal and related actions pursued by the pilot within the overall mission. Three different types of intentions are considered, which can be applied to multiple targets, resulting in a wide variety of possible courses of action. For each intent, we use HTN planning to generate multiple plan hypotheses based on the underlying situation. This approach enables a hierarchical decomposition of tactical approaches, beginning from high-level strategic planning to detailed sequences of low-level actions. An HTN planning problem is described by a tuple $P = (D, s_0, t_{nI})$, where D is the domain, s_0 the initial state, and t_{nI} the initial task network.

The domain D is defined by the tuple (L, C, A, M, δ). L refers to the preconditions and propositional environment facts, which define the state-based part of the problem (Höller et al., 2018). C is the set of compound tasks, corresponding to higher-level activities such as mission phases and subphases (e.g., "Transfer Assets" or "Prepare Asset"). The set of actions A (primitives) defines the lowest level of the hierarchical task network (e.g., "Define Position" or "Classify Target Object"). M is the set of methods used for the decomposition. $\delta = (prec, add, del)$ defines the preconditions (prec), as well as the positive (add) and negative (del) effects, that result from the successful execution of a task. The initial state s_0 is derived as preconditions based on the available information from the simulation environment about the world. This includes e.g., groups of target objects/assets, locations, proximity to other objects and groups, pre-classifications, type and specifications of the available assets, and effectors. Note that this comprises only data that is also available to the pilot (to prevent any advantage over the human operator). Since there is not a firmly defined environment here - as the number of objects to be considered in planning can change - the methods must be able to deal with different numbers of objects. To manage this, all objects that are relevant to a particular plan are combined into a logical group which is decomposed recursively. This allows us to apply the methods across varying logical group sizes.

These sequences of actions (and resp. Tasks) may differ depending on the situation and tactical approach (e.g., tasking of the ownship prior to the UAV), although the objective remains the same. The differences do not have any impact on the overall goal and therefore allow us to define our partial-order planning problem. Since all actions are performed by the pilot (i.e., the pilot using available assets), the planning problem can be modeled as a single-agent problem.

3.2 HTN Planning Pipeline

Figure 2 shows the integrated HTN planning pipeline based on the PANDA-Planning Framework[1]. Various problem definitions are created based on the scenario analysis. The individual problem definitions are parsed and then transferred to the HTN Planner. Using the generated problem definitions and the domain definition, the HTN planner generates HTNs for each defined problem. Here, the domain definition covers all tasks and actions and the corresponding decomposition methods. The specific sequences of actions can then be taken from the created HTNs.

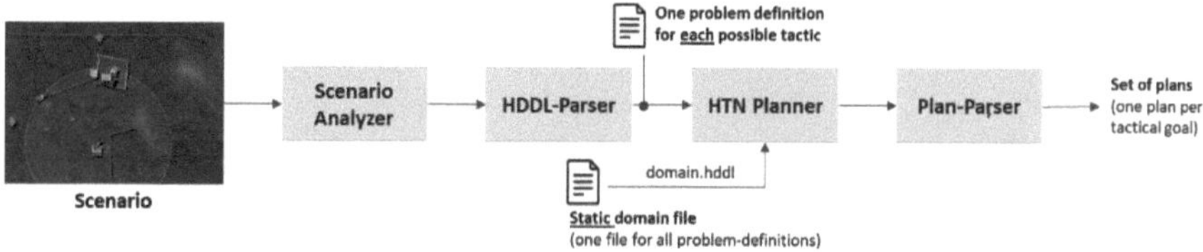

Fig. 2. Integrated HTN-Planning Pipeline.

---

[1] https://github.com/panda-planner-dev.

3.3 Pilot Observation

The result of the planning process is a sequence of actions which describe the tactical course to accomplish the objective, based on the initial state s_0. We continuously observe the pilot and the situation to understand which actions of the plan hypotheses are being carried out. In standard HTN planning for PGR, primitive actions are typically modeled as directly observable activities (cf. Höller et al., 2018). In our context, the activities can often not be observed directly, as they represent sequences of sub-actions within a tactical approach[2]. In addition, we have observations of interactions with the system (e.g. pressing a button on the HOCAS or classifying an object via the control elements on the tactical map) as well as observations of how the system is used. Examples include positioning assets in scenario to perform a specific task or aligning a sensor. To interpret these tactical-situational observations accurately the tactical situation must be considered. An intuitive example is aligning the sensor with the object. For this purpose, it is checked whether different evidences are present together: (1) sensor image is shown in the cockpit; (2) object is within sensor range, (3) sensor is aligned on the object. Those evidences can either take on binary values – true or false – or require a likelihood function to represent their belief state. Aligning the sensor on an object, commanding the autopilot, or changing the classification of an object all result in binary values, because those features can be observed on specific button presses or generated system entries. The likelihood functions are defined based on expert knowledge provided by domain specialists and describe how strongly a feature (like the location of a point) indicates the relevance to an object.

3.4 Reasoning and Heuristic-Based Plan Identification

Based on the observation probabilities of individual pilot actions, we use probabilistic reasoning to infer the likelihoods of higher-level tasks up to the top-level intent. In this initial approach, we apply a simple density function:

$$P(B|A_1, .., A_n) = \frac{1}{n}\sum\nolimits_{i=1}^{n} P(A_i)\beta_i \tag{1}$$

At this stage, we do not assign task-specific weights β to different actions. To prioritize nested plans – those composed of multiple subtasks or plans – we introduce a scoring mechanism. In concrete terms, this means that we use a score to give the nested plans a higher prioritization by nominating the plans by the number of actions.

To finally identify the pursued intent, we apply a heuristic approach to determine which intent is being pursued by analyzing whether the score of one or more intent hypotheses clearly separates from the rest. This separation can occur as (1) a single distinct intent, (2) a group of intents targeting the same object with similar tactics but involving different assets, or (3) no clear distinction. For instance, when a pilot approaches a target with both assets as a group but engages with only one, the system may recognize

---

[2] Example: Defining an observation position for the helicopter is generally an observable action. Since the pilot can define different positions for the various objects, it is necessary to find out which specific action has been carried out based on the situation analysis.

a group of intents. An intent or group is only considered valid if all members refer to the same target and tactical goal. The earliest point at which such separation exceeds a defined threshold is used as the trigger for assistance.

4 Experimental Study

The goal of the study was to validate our first approach of the plan and goal recognition system. The experiment was conducted in our helicopter mission and cockpit simulation environment at the Institute of Flight Systems (University of the Bundeswehr Munich), which is shown in Fig. 3. The single-pilot cockpit is equipped with HOCAS flight controls and three multitouch displays for the interfaces. On the center interface, a tactical map and the simulated electro-optical sensor stream are given. System information and a timeline for tasking the assets are displayed on the side screens. The cockpit is placed inside a 210° horizontal and 75° vertical field of view sphere onto which the outside view is projected. This allows us to simulate MUM-T military scenario missions in a highly immersive cockpit and mission simulation environment.

Fig. 3. Cockpit of the helicopter research mission and cockpit simulator. The center display shows the tactical map. Both side displays are used for planning or system information. The system is equipped with eye-tracking cameras and HOCAS.

4.1 Study Design and Procedure

Each participant first gave their informed consent to participate in the study, then received an introduction to our experiment and filled out a demographic questionnaire and a General Trust in Automation Inventory Questionnaire. All participants have been trained on our system for approximately 10 h (in total). The training included system familiarization and training on different system functionalities and procedures. In between, additional time was available to become comfortable with the capabilities. Finally, a training mission was performed with the possibility to interact with the experimenter. The experiment itself started with a mission-specific briefing in which the participant received the overarching situation and overall mission objective. Each participant performed one experimental mission in which the pilot had to perform different tactical courses of action to fulfill the mission objective. The mission took approximately 0.75 h. After completion of the experiment, participants were asked to label the recorded data. Therefore, each participant had to describe the pursued courses of action (incl. Pointing out relevant/significant situations). This allows us to compare the different inferred tactical approaches with those labeled by the pilot. All simulation and pilot observation data are collected for the post-evaluation.

4.2 Task

The experimental task consists of one MUM-T helicopter mission to secure a designated area, divided into two parts. As described above, we consider three types of intentions, which can be applied to multiple objects, resulting in a wide variety of possible courses of action. These include, e.g., specific engagement with the ownship or a UAV, coordinated actions, or solving an off-nominal situation (with one or both assets). To achieve the mission objective, the pilot must choose between them based on the situation. The scenario was designed in a way that the pilot was required to use their own helicopter and one available unmanned aerial vehicle (UAV). In the first part of the mission, there are seven objects that need to be engaged with. The first four targets are characterized by clear distance from each other and challenging terrain characteristics, which need to be considered (e.g., positions must be chosen carefully to ensure the necessary line-of-sight in a mountainous environment). The remaining three objects are close to each other, which also allows parallel tasking on the different targets. In the second part, the participant had to solve an off-nominal situation. It was necessary to gain situational awareness (SA), update the tactical information in the system, and engage with the objects if necessary. The situation is reported visually via the tactical map and a radio call.

4.3 Participants

We conducted the experiment with 10 professionally trained helicopter pilots. The mean age of the subjects was 40 years (range: 31 to 50 years; SD: 6.67 years). The group had a mean flight experience of 2272.6 h (range: 600 to 4400 h; SD: 1493.2 h) on different helicopter types (scout, utility, and heavy lift) and roles (e.g., air mission commander, experimental test pilots). All subjects stated that they expected automation to improve their performance, productivity, and help to accomplish tasks more quickly. At the same time, they showed a slight tendency to disagree that automation always 'proved to be the advice they needed to make a decision'.

5 Results

We evaluated the experimental results according to the overall achieved score related to the tactical approaches and to what extent those phases can be used to trigger intent-specific assistance based on the recorded simulation and observation data.

5.1   Assessment of the Individual Recognition

Figure 4 summarizes the mean values of the maximum probabilities achieved during the experimental mission for each individual object (S1, V1 to V14) and for each tactical category. A total of 70 different goals and plans were pursued by all participants, categorized into three types: Specific Approaches (SA), Coordinated Approaches (CA), and Direct Support (DS). This includes 50 SA (mean: 0.67, SD: 0.13) 10 CA (mean: 0.83, SD: 0.06), and 10 DS mean: 0.86, SD: 0.14). Among the three categories, SA shows the lowest mean. Therefore, this category was analyzed in more detail, focusing on V4, V5, and V6. The maximum probabilities for these targets range from a mean probability of 0.47 (SD:0.05) for V5 to 0.75 (SD: 0.12) for V4 and 0.75 (SD: 0.08) for V6. Compared to the other values, V5 shows the lowest value, which is also clearly below the SA mean (as will be discussed in Sect. 6.1).

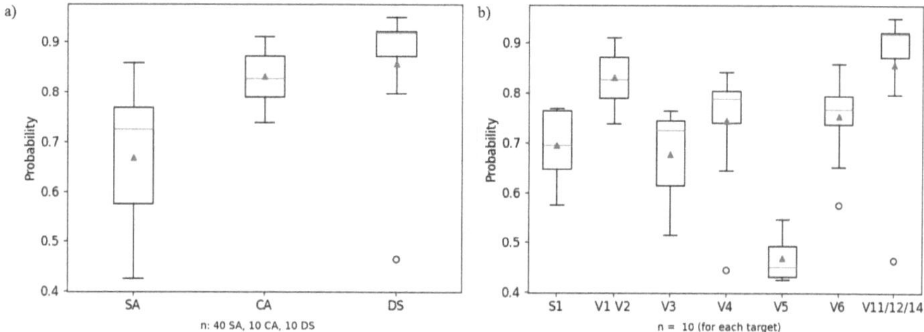

Fig. 4. Overview of the calculated maximum probabilities. Subfigure *(a)* shows the probabilities for each reference object (for all pilots), and *(b)* shows the probabilities reached related to the different types of intentions.

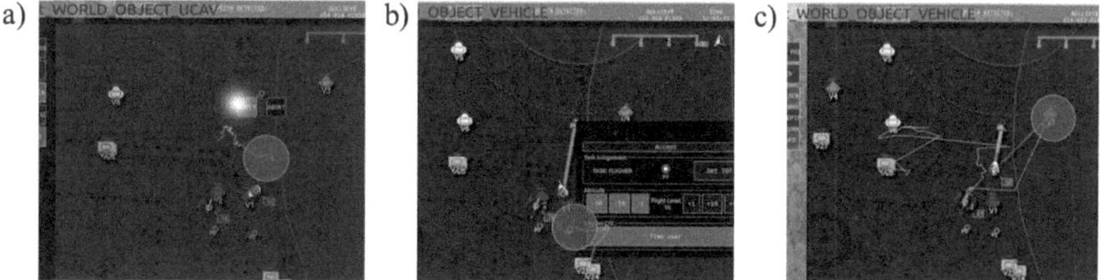

Fig. 5. Observing the task "Transfer UAV" based on the display interaction (white dot indicates touch inputs). The pilot defines *(a)* the destination, the *(b)* task parameters for transferring to the position, and *(c)* observes the system afterwards.

To further illustrate the observation of the pilot's interaction and the reasoning in this context, Fig. 5 provides an example of actions performed to engage V3. The pilot firstly *(a)* defines a target location and *(b)* initiates a transfer task for the UAV. V3 is here the reference object which the pilot intended to engage. Considering the individual probabilities associated with the actions, a combined value of approximately 0.88 for the higher-level task "Transfer one asset" is obtained. This value is derived from the underlying likelihood function, which accounts for the distance between the reference object V3 and the specified point. Together with the probability of each task, this, resulted in a root task probability of 0.43.

5.2 Identification of the Pursued Plans

Since we want to use the recognized plans and goals for triggering assistance, we analyzed the recognition of the different tactical approaches. Figure 6 illustrates a segment of the mission execution in which various plans from the category SA and CA were performed. Within the mission segment, the different plans pursued by the pilot can be identified as distinct phases. Based on a heuristic-based evaluation the figure also visualizes potential trigger points for assistance (cf. 3.4). To assess whether the pursued plans can be recognized by the system, we conducted a qualitative comparison between the labeled data from the pilot and system's output. Additionally, we have evaluated different threshold values for our heuristic-based plan identification approach. The accuracy Acc_p refers to the correct classification compared to all expected classifications (based on the labeling with the pilots). We also calculated the *Precision*, which indicates the proportion of correct classifications among all cases that the system identified as positive. A classification of the heuristic-based identification results is given in Table 1. Overall, the model's accuracies for the different thresholds are $Acc_{p0.05} = 0.9$, $Acc_{p0.10} = 0.77$, and $Acc_{p0.15} = 0.71$.

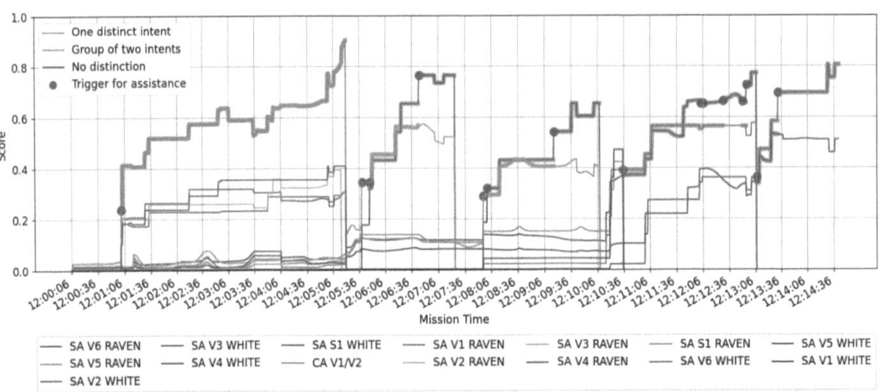

Fig. 6. Heuristic-based approach with a curve separation score threshold of 0.1. A green highlighted curve indicates that one distinct intent was recognized; an orange highlighting indicates that a group of intents is recognized. The red dot indicates the beginning of curve separation.

Table 1. Classification of heuristic-based plan separation analysis.

Threshold	Correct class.	Wrong class.	No class.	Acc_p	*Precision*
0.05	63	2	5	0.9	0.97
0.10	54	3	13	0.77	0.95
0.15	50	2	18	0.71	0.96

6 Discussion

6.1 Reached Scores

An analysis of the results shows that while the different pursued plans are identifiable throughout the mission progress, recognition performances vary across the different tactics and targets. While CA and DS generally yield higher maximum probabilities, the performance of SA varies noticeably between targets, suggesting that some tactics within this category are less effectively identified by the system. Maximum probability is only reached when all planned actions are executed as intended. As pilots often deviate from the optimal plan based on the situation, actual lower scores can be expected. Additionally, one great influence was target V5 (mean probability 0.47%) which was deliberately misclassified by design, causing the system to generate a plan misaligned with the pilot's actual task. The wide distribution within SA tactics suggests further consideration to better understand which specific actions and observations contribute to successful recognition.

6.2 Reasoning

As noted in Sect. 3.4, it is necessary to consider either one distinct intent, a group of intents (with the same target and goal state for the group but different assets), or none for interventions. Recognizing a group of intents creates challenges for asset-specific support. However, since the goal state and plan (e.g., approaching an object) are similar across both intents, it is possible to provide assistance for achieving the goal state. In the direct support scenario, the scores can be grouped into different tactical approaches on the same objects (Fig. 7). The actual pursued plan reached the highest score. There, the participant performed the direct support by using both assets. Slightly lower scores represent similar tactical approaches using only one asset. Subsequent groups reflect different tactical goals, such as coordinated or specific approaches on distinct objects. This suggests that a hierarchical analysis of the scores can point to the overall tactical goal of the performed approach.

We used a heuristic approach and tested it with different thresholds to detect the pursued plan. In post-processing, we found that a threshold between 0.05 to 0.1 reliably distinguishes between plans. However, minor score peaks may also be interpreted as a recognized plan, but not every peak should trigger an intervention to avoid false positives.

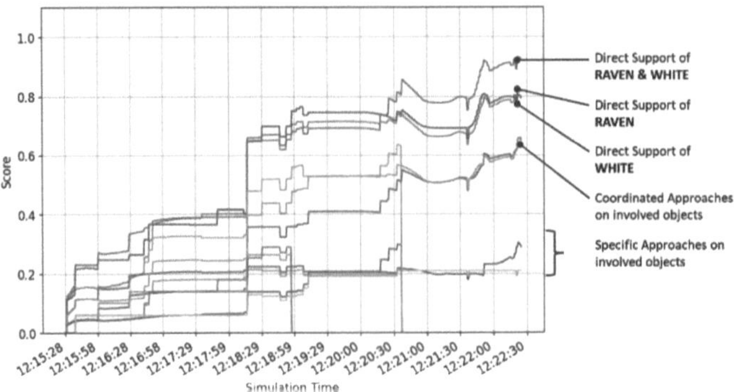

Fig. 7. Score diagram for the direct support scenario.

6.3 Mission Design

The recognition of the plans for V4, V5, and V6 is more ambiguous than for the other objects with higher false-negative results. The demarcation was not clearly given. All scores showed a rapid increase as soon as the participant set one of those as the new target. This is likely due to their close spatial proximity, allowing pilots to easily reach all the targets from a single position. Thus, the defined position is used for each target and has a similar impact on different plans. Additionally, pilots often worked on these targets in parallel or switched rapidly between them, while still pursuing distinct plans. To improve recognition in such cases, integrating gaze data could help to capture the pilot's visual attention and enhance the recognition.

6.4 Post-Mission Analysis and Derivation of Assistance Requirements

Post-mission analysis revealed a clear demand for pilot assistance during mission execution. To address this, we reviewed the missions with a focus on identifying potential support measures to enhance operational effectiveness and reduce cognitive load. Three areas that suggest the demand for support emerged: **support execution**, **optimization**, and **error prevention**. The following support possibilities have been identified:

- **Mission Planning:** Tactical elements could be proposed to the pilot, aiding in the formulation of mission strategies.
- **Future State Prediction:** Generate predictions regarding future states (e.g., positions, resource consumption), to increase SA.
- **Adaptive Information Presentation:** Provide or highlight context-relevant information to reduce the pilot's effort in collecting and processing information.
- **Reactive Behavior:** Offers shortcuts to automate the process of configuring the system or planning sequences of actions.

Our goal is to support the pilot during mission execution, enhancing mission performance and safety. It should be noted that we are not focused on achieving the optimal solution but rather assisting the pilot in their current activity.

7 Conclusion

We were able to recognize the pursued tactical plans and goals using our system, which can be used as a trigger for providing assistance using an HTN-based intent recognition system. The probability trends over time matched the labeled data, allowing us to observe different courses of action in the mission. However, certain elements which are conceptually close could not be clearly separated. In some scenarios, depending on task design and pilot behavior, the recognition performance declined. To address this, additional parameters should be incorporated into the model. This suggests the need for refinement through methods such as cost or penalty functions. Another option is gaze analysis, which can help identify areas receiving high visual attention and thus provide deeper insight into intent. In situations where plan and goal inference were ambiguous, a more sophisticated intent estimation model is required. A follow-up experimental campaign will be conducted, in which the recognized plan and goal will be used to generate adaptive interventions that support the pilot during mission execution.

References

1. Billings, C.E.: Human-centered aircraft automation: a concept and guidelines, vol. 103885. National Aeronautics and Space Administration, Ames Research Center (1991)
2. Brand, Y., Schulte, A.: Model-based prediction of workload for adaptive associate systems. In: IEEE International Conference on Systems, Man, and Cybernetics (SMC) (2017)
3. Estes, S.L., et al.: Digital copilot: cognitive assistance for pilots. In: 2016 AAAI Fall Symposium Series (Cognitive Assistance in Government and Public Sector Applications) (2016)
4. Han, T.A., Pereira, L.M.: State-of-the-art of intention recognition and its use in decision making. AI Commun. **26**, 237–246 (2013). https://doi.org/10.3233/AIC-130559
5. Künzel, D., Schulte, A.: Plan and Goal Recognition System for Adaptive Pilot Assistance in Tactical Helicopter Operations. In: Harris, D., Li, W.-C. (eds.) Engineering Psychology and Cognitive Ergonomics, pp. 201–213. Springer Nature Switzerland (2024)
6. Miller, C.A., Hannen, M.D.: The rotorcraft pilot's associate: design and evaluation of an intelligent user interface for cockpit information management. Knowl.-Based Syst. **12**(8) (1999)
7. Schulte, A., Donath, D., Lange, D.S.: Design patterns for human-cognitive agent teaming. In: Harris, D. (eds.) Engineering Psychology and Cognitive Ergonomics. EPCE 2016. Lecture Notes in Computer Science(), vol. 9736. Springer, Cham (2016). https://doi.org/10.1007/978-3-319-40030-3_24
8. Schwerd, S., Schulte, A.: Operator state estimation to enable adaptive assistance in manned-unmanned-teaming. Cogn. Syst. Res. **67**, 73–83 (2021). https://doi.org/10.1016/j.cogsys.2021.01.002
9. Strohal, M., Onken, R.: Intent and error recognition as part of a knowledge-based cockpit assistant. In: Rogers, S.K., Fogel, D.B., Bezdek, J.C., Bosacchi, B., (Eds.) SPIE Proceedings, Applications and Science of Computational Intelligence, p. 287. SPIE (1998). https://doi.org/10.1117/12.304818
10. Suck, S., Fortmann, F.: Aircraft Pilot Intention Recognition for Advanced Cockpit Assistance Systems. In: Schmorrow, D.D., Fidopiastis, C.M. (eds.) Foundations of Augmented Cognition: Neuroergonomics and Operational Neuroscience, pp. 231–240. Springer International Publishing (2016)

11. Theissing, N., Schulte, A.: Intent-based UAV mission management using an adaptive mixed-initiative operator assistant system. In: Guidance, Navigation, and Control and Co-located Conferences. AIAA Infotech@Aerospace (I@A) Conference, American Institute of Aeronautics and Astronautics (2013). https://doi.org/10.2514/6.2013-4802
12. Van-Horenbeke, F.A., Peer, A.: Activity, plan, and goal recognition: a review. Front. Robot. AI **8**, 1–18 (2021). https://doi.org/10.3389/frobt.2021.643010
13. Wittig, T., Onken, R.: Pilot intent and error recognition as part of a knowledge based cockpit assistant. In: AGARD (Hg.): Combat Automation for Airborne Weapon Systems: Man/Machine Interface Trends and Technologies. AGARD Conference Proceedings 520, vol. 9, p. 2 (1992)

CAAD: A Cognitive-Aware Framework for AI Agent Design in Complex Tasks

Jieyu Luo$^{(\boxtimes)}$ and Xinxiong Liu

Huazhong University of Science and Technology, Wuhan, Hubei, China
`jieyuluo@hust.edu.cn`, `xxliu@mail.hust.edu.cn`

Abstract. Large language model (LLM)-powered agents have demonstrated promising capabilities in assisting data analysis tasks. However, existing designs predominantly emphasize autonomous completion of predefined tasks rather than offering tailored support aligned with user needs. In complex, multi-phase analytical workflows, users frequently encounter diverse cognitive challenges-including vague task definitions, information overload, and decision-making uncertainty-that generic agent designs inadequately address.

This paper presents the CAAD (Cognitive-Aware Agent Design) framework, a structured, stage-based design methodology grounded in cognitive load theory. CAAD decomposes the analytical process into four distinct phases: task definition, analysis, decision-making, and output. It guides the development of targeted agent interventions explicitly designed to reduce cognitive effort and enhance user experience.

We applied the CAAD framework to a real-world case by analyzing task logs, conducting user interviews, and observing actual analytical behavior. Based on identified cognitive challenges, we developed specific support modules-including parameter selection cards, visual analytical aids, Chain-of-Thought (CoT) prompting for prioritization, and structured recommendation tools. Internal evaluation indicated that CAAD-based agent interventions reduced task completion time by 44.13% and significantly increased user confidence, as assessed through structured feedback sessions and surveys.

Our findings underscore the necessity of aligning intelligent agent designs closely with users' cognitive workflows. CAAD provides a generalized, transferable approach for designing explainable, adaptive agents particularly beneficial in high-stakes, cognitively demanding fields such as healthcare, finance, and scientific research.

Keywords: Human-Centered AI Agents · Cognitive-Aware Design · Cognitive Load Theory

1 Introduction

Recent advancements in large language models (LLMs) have significantly expanded the capabilities of intelligent agents in supporting complex data analysis tasks [3, 19, 58]. However, despite their technical promise, most existing agent

D. Harris et al. (Eds.): HCII 2025, LNCS 16334, pp. 213–230, 2026.
https://doi.org/10.1007/978-3-032-12392-3_14

systems are designed around automation and speed, rather than nuanced alignment with human cognitive processes [16,61]. In real-world, multi-phase analytical workflows, users are not passive recipients of outputs, but active participants navigating ambiguity, synthesizing information, and making high-stakes decisions—often under considerable cognitive pressure [6,8,49].

Prior research has identified that many intelligent systems adopt static, one-size-fits-all support strategies, offering little sensitivity to the evolving nature of users' cognitive needs across task stages. Prior studies suggest that current AI-supported systems often lack stage-sensitive collaboration mechanisms, neglect cognitive ergonomics, and fail to fully account for human needs in cognitively demanding settings [14,16,61].

These limitations are compounded by the fragmented nature of existing support mechanisms, such as one-off summaries or isolated recommendations, that fail to integrate into users' broader reasoning workflows. Prior work has highlighted missed opportunities to scaffold and augment users' cognitive processes through system design [22]. In contrast, adaptive and cognitively-aligned agent interventions have been shown to reduce mental workload and improve sense-making and user confidence [36,65].

Despite increasing interest in human-AI collaboration, most existing systems remain limited to shallow forms of support, such as interface hints, one-time recommendations, or generalized summaries, that fail to adapt to users' evolving cognitive states throughout analytical workflows [16,22,61]. These limitations are especially critical in complex, high-stakes environments where users face multi-phase cognitive challenges: from resolving ambiguous goals and interpreting noisy data to synthesizing insights under time pressure [42,58,65]. While some prior work explores cognitive load in interface design or task-specific automation [14, 21], few approaches offer a systematic framework that explicitly aligns agent interventions with distinct phases of human cognition. This lack of structured cognitive alignment not only impairs user performance but also limits the transparency, trustworthiness, and transferability of current intelligent systems [10,16,42,61,65].

Cognitive load theory suggests that when task complexity exceeds cognitive processing capacity, users experience overload and degraded performance, particularly in multi-phase problem-solving contexts [56]. Motivated by cognitive load theory and grounded in empirical user research, this paper addresses the urgent need for intelligent agents that dynamically adapt to users' cognitive workflows. Such agents should not only automate subtasks, but also provide scaffolding for core cognitive activities: clarifying ambiguous goals, filtering and prioritizing information, structuring complex judgments, and presenting results in interpretable formats.

To this end, we introduce the Cognitive-Aware Agent Design (CAAD) framework, which structures analytical workflows into four core cognitive phases: task definition, analysis, decision-making, and output. For each phase, CAAD identifies representative cognitive bottlenecks and guides the development of targeted design strategies and agent modules that directly address phase-specific demands.

Preliminary evaluation conducted in a real-world case demonstrates that CAAD substantially improves analytical performance, reducing task completion time by 44.13% while boosting user confidence and satisfaction. By systematically aligning agent interventions with stage-specific cognitive challenges, CAAD offers a novel and transferable approach to designing explainable and cognitively supportive AI agents. This paradigm holds particular promise in domains such as healthcare, finance, and scientific research, where clarity, trust, and decision quality are critical.

2   Related Work

2.1   AI Agents

The emergence of LLM-powered agents has transformed data analysis workflows by automating tasks such as data querying, report generation, and insight extraction. Recent systems, such as DB-GPT [66], AgentCoder [23], and Data-Copilot [68], demonstrate how multi-agent frameworks can orchestrate subtasks ranging from data ingestion to recommendation generation with minimal human intervention. These advancements have enabled more scalable and rapid analysis pipelines, particularly in domains requiring repetitive or large-volume data handling.

However, the prevailing emphasis in these systems remains on technical automation and architectural optimization, with limited attention to the role of human cognition in collaborative analytical processes. Most systems optimize for performance metrics like latency or task completion rates, yet often disregard how users perceive, interpret, and interact with AI-generated outputs. This results in a mismatch between agent capabilities and user needs, particularly in cognitively intensive scenarios where decision-making involves ambiguity, trade-offs, or contextual reasoning.

Moreover, current agent designs tend to treat users as endpoints of automation pipelines, offering limited interactivity or adaptive support throughout the analysis lifecycle. For instance, generated summaries or dashboards are often static and fail to reflect users' evolving information needs or cognitive states. As noted in recent literature reviews, such shallow interaction models can hinder trust calibration, lead to misinterpretation of system suggestions, and ultimately reduce the effectiveness of human-AI collaboration.

These observations highlight a critical gap: while AI agents have matured in terms of task automation, there is a pressing need to integrate more human-centric principles into their design. Specifically, agents should be equipped to understand and respond to the cognitive dynamics of users engaged in complex analytical reasoning. Addressing this gap requires insights not only from system engineering but also from fields such as human-computer interaction, cognitive science, and educational psychology.

In the following sections, we build on this motivation by reviewing relevant work in human-AI collaboration, task modeling, and cognitive load theory, laying the foundation for the CAAD framework proposed in this paper.

2.2 Human–AI Collaboration

The field of Human-AI Collaboration (HAIC) is undergoing a notable shift-from automation-oriented tool design to a partner-oriented model of collaboration. Increasingly, researchers have moved beyond treating users as passive recipients of AI outputs, and instead conceptualize them as epistemic collaborators, actively interpreting, adapting, and steering the AI system throughout complex cognitive tasks. This shift aligns with the vision of Human-Centered Artificial Intelligence (HCAI) advocated by Shneiderman et al. [50], which emphasizes that AI systems should augment rather than replace human judgment, while ensuring safety, accountability, and cognitive compatibility in high-stakes decision-making.

To support this vision, a growing body of work has introduced mixed-initiative, phase-aware, and interpretable agents. For example, Zheng et al. [70] present a diagnostic agent grounded in data-frame theory that facilitates hypothesis construction with clinicians. Ma et al. [35] propose a deliberative agent powered by LLMs, supporting dimension-level reasoning in policy design and improving trust calibration. He et al. [20] design DeCoDe, which uses concept bottlenecks to enable instance-specific decision deferral. Other work models shared mental states between users and agents [36], or promotes co-adaptive loops to maintain long-term cognitive alignment [15].

Empirical studies across domains further validate these approaches. Ma et al. [35] report that LLM-driven deliberation improves decision quality and user confidence. Zheng et al. [70] demonstrate that phase-aware diagnostic support increases accuracy and interpretability. Tariq et al. [57] observe reduced cognitive workload and faster incident resolution with role-adaptive agents. He et al. [20] show that users better understand and trust concept-driven agents. Okamura and Yamada [38,39] design trust calibration agents that adaptively regulate user reliance based on behavioral cues. Castaneda et al. [7] develop the InDecision agent, which scaffolds users during early-stage decision formulation and helps them retain rationale over time. Collectively, these works reflect growing attention to cognitive alignment in human-AI systems, though most target isolated mental states or limited phases of interaction.

Despite these advances, most current agent systems remain limited in their ability to sense and respond to users' evolving cognitive states. Support strategies are often static, overly generic, or limited to one-time suggestions, failing to adapt to the distinct challenges of different analytical stages. This leads to persistent cognitive misalignment, especially in workflows involving ambiguity, information overload, or high-stakes trade-offs. While some prior work explores adaptive behavior or phase-awareness, few systems offer a unified framework that maps cognitive challenges to agent interventions across task phases.

2.3   Task Modeling in Complex Analytical Workflows

In complex analytical settings, users rarely approach problems in a single linear motion. Instead, decision-making and sensemaking are composed of iterative and cognitively distinct phases, each characterized by different informational needs, reasoning strategies, and degrees of uncertainty.

Several recent systems have implemented phase-based models grounded in cognitive theory. For instance, Fok et al. [13] present DimInd, which segments LLM-assisted literature review workflows into four stages mapped to sensemaking loop [43], dynamically detecting phase shifts to adjust interface behaviors. This approach reduced user effort and improved outcome interpretability. Similarly, Jung et al. [25] propose DeepStress, a dual-mode sensemaking system for personal informatics based on Frame Congruence Theory, which dynamically surfaces causal links at appropriate stages. In the domain of fact-checking, He et al. [21] design MST workflows that decompose verification tasks into multi-step subtasks and apply phase-specific adaptation strategies to improve user reliance and reduce cognitive load.

These systems demonstrate that phase-based decomposition offers concrete design benefits. First, it facilitates adaptive timing of system aid, such as surfacing explanations or prompting user reflection when uncertainty thresholds are crossed [21,43]. Second, it enables phase-aligned interface strategies, such as shifting from evidence gathering to synthesis with corresponding granularity changes in interface feedback. Third, it provides a structured basis for managing user-AI control transitions. For example, Tariq et al. [57] propose the A2C framework, which models three distinct decision stages: automation, selective deferral, and collaborative exploration. Simulation results show that this segmentation improves role alignment and decision accuracy.

Theoretically, these models are rooted in well-established frameworks. Sensemaking loop [43], data-frame theory [28], and recursive decision models such as Bhargava et al.'s three-phase framework [4] offer foundational guidance for identifying cognitively distinct phases and transitions. These cognitive frameworks emphasize that effective support must be tailored not only to task content but also to users' evolving reasoning states and cognitive constraints.

While the benefits are clear, important challenges remain. Rigid phase boundaries can overwhelm users in simpler tasks [21], and current phase detection methods, such as those based on Hidden Markov Models [1], remain under-validated in real-world settings. Furthermore, personalization is limited, most systems do not build longitudinal user profiles or tailor phase support over time.

By aligning support strategies with users' cognitive stages, such models can improve interpretability, decision quality, and HAIC in complex, high-stakes analytical workflows.

2.4   Cognitive Load Theory for Agent Design

Cognitive Load Theory (CLT) provides a foundational framework for understanding the mental demands placed on users during complex tasks. Originally developed in educational psychology, CLT distinguishes between three types of cognitive load: intrinsic, extraneous, and germane load [56]. Intrinsic load arises from the inherent complexity of the material, extraneous load stems from the way information is presented, and germane load refers to the cognitive effort devoted to learning or constructing schemas.

Recent empirical studies have applied CLT's subtypes in AI-enhanced and interactive system contexts across education, training, and digital interfaces. For example, field studies of AI-enriched textbooks [29] and cybersecurity chatbots [69] used multi-item self-report instruments (e.g., Leppink scale) to assess cognitive load and its correlation with feature usage and task outcomes. In educational settings, researchers have measured cognitive load during AR-based science learning [30], VR tutorials [59], and physics instruction [64], often using the Paas or Leppink frameworks to identify where extraneous or intrinsic load can be reduced. Beyond static assessments, several studies explored behavioral proxies and log-based modeling to estimate load. For instance, adaptive LMSs have been proposed using ECL/ICL/GCL log triggers [55], while digital classroom studies [54] and gamified cognitive training platforms [48] link interface features to self-reported load. While these efforts offer valuable insights into how CLT can inform system design, most remain focused on localized or post hoc analyses. Building on this foundation, our work aims to integrate these insights into a structured, phase-aware framework for cognitively aligned agent design.

Motivated by these findings, our work builds on CLT to guide the modular design of agent interventions across distinct stages of analytical reasoning. Rather than treating cognitive load as a static design constraint, the CAAD framework incorporates phase-specific support strategies informed by the expected cognitive challenges at each stage-bridging cognitive theory and agent architecture in a structured and transferable manner.

3   CAAD: The Cognitive-Aware Agent Design Framework

3.1   Framework Overview

While prior work has demonstrated the potential of AI agents to augment human reasoning, most existing systems offer limited support for the diverse and evolving cognitive demands users encounter across different phases of analytical workflows. As discussed in the previous section, users are not passive recipients of AI-generated outputs but active participants engaged in complex, multi-stage tasks, each phase presenting unique challenges. To better accommodate these varying demands, we propose the Cognitive-Aware Agent Design (CAAD) framework, which structures agent interventions in alignment with the cognitive characteristics and support opportunities specific to each phase of analytical work (Fig. 1).

The primary objective of the CAAD framework is to enhance the cognitive compatibility of intelligent agents in complex analytical workflows. Specifically, it seeks to:

(1) provide phase-specific cognitive scaffolding that aligns with users' evolving information processing needs;

Fig. 1. Overview of the CAAD framework. Task-level triggers such as phase and challenge inform the agent's support strategy and implementation modules, aiming to regulate different types of cognitive load based on CLT.

(2) improve the transparency and interpretability of AI interventions by making their role and rationale explicit at each stage of the task.

Through these aims, CAAD offers a design paradigm that bridges technical automation with human-centered reasoning, enabling more explainable and cognitively supportive AI systems.

3.2 Triggers: Task Phase and Associated Cognitive Challenges

In complex analytical tasks, user cognition does not remain static but evolves dynamically as the task progresses. Prior literature has highlighted that such workflows are inherently multi-phase in nature, with each phase characterized by distinct cognitive objectives, information states, and reasoning strategies [13,21,43]. A phase-based structuring enables AI agents to align their support more precisely with users' evolving cognitive needs, facilitating better timing, relevance, and effectiveness of interventions. Without such segmentation, agent responses risk being either too generic or misaligned with users' situational demands, leading to increased extraneous load and reduced decision quality.

We structure the CAAD framework around four phases:

(1)Task Definition. Users clarify goals, formulate questions, and scope their analytical intent.

(2)Analysis. Users explore data, identify patterns, and synthesize relevant information.

(3)Decision-Making. Users evaluate alternatives, prioritize findings, and commit to judgments.

(4)Output. Users organize and present insights, often tailoring them to external stakeholders.

This decomposition is grounded in cognitive task analysis and sensemaking theory, which consistently show that users progress through distinct cognitive modes as their goals, information states, and reasoning strategies evolve. Foundational models such as Pirolli and Card's sensemaking loop and Klein et al.'s DataâĂŞFrame Theory outline similar transitions—from problem framing and information foraging (Task Definition and Analysis), to hypothesis evaluation and judgment (Decision-Making), and finally to the communication of insights

(Output) [11,26,27,43,53,60]. These stages not only reflect conceptual differences but also align with observable shifts in attentional focus and cognitive load.

By adopting this four-phase structure, CAAD enables targeted agent interventions tailored to users' evolving mental states. It provides a principled basis for mapping phase-specific cognitive challenges, such as information overload during analysis, and for designing support modules that respond accordingly [11,45,60].

Each of these phases introduces distinct cognitive challenges that, if not properly addressed, can lead to overload, decision errors, or disengagement. We summarize the key challenges associated with each phase as Table 1.

Mapping typical cognitive challenges to each task phase provides a structured foundation for agent design. CAAD supports designers and developers in anticipating the likely cognitive bottlenecks users may face at each stage. This perspective enables the proactive design of phase-specific support modules that are cognitively aligned and purpose-driven.

3.3   Responses: Support Strategy and Agent Module

Building on the phaseâĂŞchallenge mapping, the CAAD framework introduces a support strategy layer that translates cognitive insights into actionable agent design. Rather than prescribing a one-size-fits-all solution, CAAD emphasizes modular intervention design, where each support module is tailored to a specific task phase and its associated cognitive bottlenecks. These interventions are not intended to fully automate users' workflows, but to scaffold key cognitive activities—such as clarifying ambiguous goals, reducing information overload, supporting trade-off reasoning, or structuring complex outputs. By aligning the form, timing, and purpose of agent support with users' evolving cognitive needs, CAAD fosters more explainable, adaptive, and cognitively ergonomic HAIC.

To bridge the identified cognitive challenges and agent design, CAAD introduces a structured mapping: from cognitive challenges, to corresponding support strategies, to concrete agent modules. Table 2 illustrates selected examples across task phases, showing how cognitively grounded needs can inform modular and targeted intervention design.

Together, these modules illustrate how phase-specific challenges can be systematically translated into modular, cognitively-aligned interventions. Rather than designing agent features in isolation, CAAD supports a layered, workflow-sensitive approach to agent design—helping developers scaffold user cognition at moments where it matters most.

3.4   Effects and Evaluation

The CAAD framework is designed to align agent interventions with users' cognitive needs across task phases, with the intended effect of balancing cognitive load throughout complex analytical workflows. Drawing on CLT, our goal is not

Table 1. Cognitive Challenges across Task Phases.

Phase	Cognitive Challenge	Description
Task	Unclear or ill-defined goals [2,4,17]	Difficulty articulating clear, specific objectives, leading to lack of focus or direction.
	Confirmation bias in framing [26,40]	Tendency to let prior beliefs or salient cues unduly shape problem framing and initial questions.
	Scope creep or overcomplexity [2,17,60]	Taking on overly broad or shifting goals, resulting in being overwhelmed by task complexity.
Analysis	Information overload [2,46,53]	Being swamped by excessive or noisy data, straining cognitive resources and hurting comprehension.
	Data foraging vs. synthesis imbalance [11,60]	Spending disproportionate effort on gathering data at the expense of integrating and making sense.
	Fragmented mental models [27,40]	Struggling to construct or update coherent schemas to integrate disparate or conflicting information.
Decision	Premature closure [26,43]	Settling on an answer or interpretation before adequately exploring alternatives or assessing evidence.
	Trade-off blindness [4,27]	Overlooking, neglecting, or underweighting relevant options or criteria when making evaluations.
	Cognitive overload in judgment [46,60]	Difficulty managing and comparing complex alternatives, leading to decision fatigue or errors.
Output	Structuring coherent arguments [11,60]	Difficulty organizing findings into logical, clear, and persuasive narratives for intended audiences.
	Translation gap to stakeholders [2,45]	Challenges in making technical or complex findings understandable and actionable for non-experts.
	Loss of analytical rationale/provenance [53]	Failure to capture and convey the reasoning or evidence supporting conclusions, impairing transparency.

merely to reduce load, but to optimize its composition—minimizing extraneous burden, managing intrinsic complexity, and fostering germane reasoning. Each module is thus mapped to a specific cognitive load type and phase, forming an integrated support structure.

To systematically evaluate the cognitive effects of CAAD-aligned agent interventions, we reviewed and compiled a set of validated evaluation methods from prior research. These cover subjective, behavioral, and task-level indicators commonly used in HCI and cognitive load studies. Table 3 summarizes representative

Table 2. Support Strategies and Agent Modules for Cognitive Challenges across Task Phases.

Cognitive Challenge	Support Strategy	LLM-based Agent Module
Problem Scoping & Framing Confusion	Goal Framing & Guided Input	Dynamic Prompt Generator (e.g., Guided question-based chat; structured parameter card) [9,34,41]
Information Overload & Fragmentation	Cognitive Decomposition & Automation	Planning Scaffolds & Analysis Tools (e.g., CoT, ReAct, node-link diagrams, multi-level outputs) [12,24,62,63]
Judgment & Prioritization Failures	Multi-Criteria Decision Matrices & Justification prompts	Priority Ranking & Decision Action Recommendations (e.g., Decision support interface; rank options based on selected criteria) [34,41]
Communication & Translation Gaps	Genre-based Scaffolds & Traceable Reasoning	Structured Output Wizards (e.g., summary generation, evidence trace, interactive refinement panels) [67]

metrics across three categories: Cognitive Load, User Behavior, and Perceived Experience.

These metrics provide a multi-dimensional view of how agent modules affect user cognition and experience. In particular, by mapping each agent's intent to expected cognitive load effects (e.g., reducing extraneous load or boosting germane processing), we can assess not only task outcomes, but also the quality of cognitive engagement they enable.

4   Case Study

To evaluate the effectiveness of the CAAD framework, we applied it to design and deploy an intelligent agent within an enterprise internal operations platform, where analysts routinely monitor task metrics, assess operational risks, and generate data-driven insights. This domain involves high cognitive demands, particularly across complex, multi-step reasoning tasks under time constraints.

4.1   Application Context and Design Process

The agent was developed to assist with end-to-end analytical workflows, including task scoping, data exploration, risk triage, and insight summarization. Guided by the CAAD framework, we structured the agent around four core

Table 3. Summary of cognitive, behavioral, and experiential measures used to evaluate the effectiveness of CAAD-aligned agent interventions across task phases.

Category	Metric	What it Measures
Cognitive Load	NASA-TLX (full/aggregate)	Workload (mental, physical, temporal, effort, performance, frustration)[32,37,44,52]
	1–5 "Workload Watch" Scale	Overall subjective workload (composite)[18]
	Pupillometry (pupil dilation/variability)	Physiological cognitive load[18,33,47,52]
	Eye-tracking (gaze, saccades, fixation)	Attention, cognitive load proxies[18,31,32,37]
	HRV, heart rate, ECG	Physiological stress/load state[31,32,44,47,51]
	GSR (Galvanic Skin Response)	Physiological arousal/stress[31,32]
User Behavior	Task accuracy, error rate, time-on-task	Objective task performance[5,33,37,51]
	Secondary-task reaction time	Instantaneous behavioral cognitive load[32]
	Help-request count, dwell time, learning curve	Support-seeking, adaptation/learning [5,33]
	Head pose, skeleton, self-touch, keystroke dynamics	Attention, effort, stress, trust[31,32]
Perceived Experience	NASA-TLX (full/aggregate)	Perceived burden and experience (subscales)[32,37,44,52]
	Usability/acceptance/ trust questionnaires	Trust, usability, collaboration satisfaction[31,47,51,52]
	AutoAAR (After-Action Review)	Self-reported workload (momentary)[44]
	Custom post-task questionnaires	Perceived mental effort, stress, collaboration[31,32]

phases: task definition, analysis, decision-making, and output. For each phase, we implemented a distinct support module targeting the phase-specific cognitive challenges identified through internal research and field study (see Fig. 2).

Our design process was informed by:

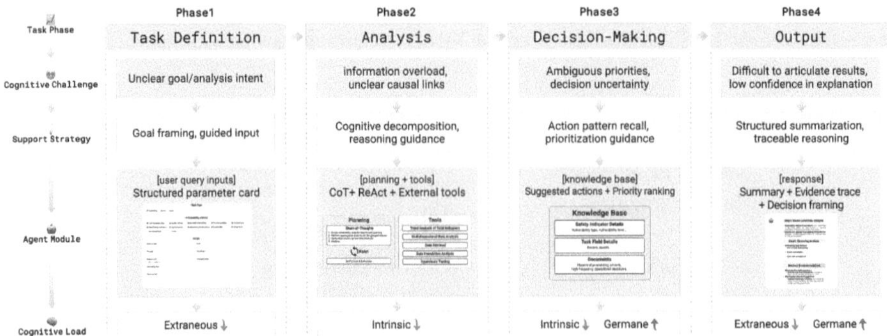

Fig. 2. Application of the CAAD framework, showing how its five-dimensional mapping across task phases guides agent design.

(1)Semi-structured interviews with platform analysts and engineers (n=35), focusing on cognitive bottlenecks and coping strategies;

(2)Internal workflow documentation outlining formal task flows and tool usage patterns;

(3)Log analysis of over 300 historical analytical sessions to extract high-frequency operations and decision behaviors.

These inputs helped us map recurring cognitive challenges such as vague task initiation, information overload, and difficulty articulating decisions. Each support module was designed to mitigate these load points through a combination of interaction design and reasoning scaffolds:

(1)Structured parameter cards for task goal clarification;

(2)Visual and prompt-based scaffolding for analytical decomposition;

(3)Knowledge-guided prioritization modules for decision support;

(4)Structured summary blocks with evidence traces for result explanation and justification.

4.2   Deployment and Evaluation

The CAAD-guided agent was deployed internally to support daily analytical tasks within the enterprise operations platform over a two-week period. A total of 35 participants interacted with the system and participated in the evaluation process.

We collected both quantitative and qualitative data:

(1)Task logs recording completion time, backtracking behavior, and system feature usage;

(2)NASA-TLX questionnaires administered post-task to capture perceived workload;

(3)Structured interviews assessing users' perception of clarity, control, and output usability.

The evaluation yielded both quantitative and qualitative evidence of the CAAD framework's effectiveness. First, deployment of the CAAD-guided agent led to a 44.13% reduction in average task completion time relative to baseline workflows, indicating enhanced task fluency and reduced operational friction. These improvements were observed across all four analytical phases, with particularly strong effects during task definition and decision-making.

Second, subjective workload ratings, collected using the Raw NASA-TLX questionnaire, revealed meaningful reductions in perceived cognitive burden. Participants reported lower scores in mental demand (âĂŞ19.2%), temporal pressure (âĂŞ21.5%), and effort (âĂŞ22.3%), suggesting that CAAD-aligned interventions effectively mitigated both time-sensitive and resource-intensive aspects of analytical work. While individual-level data are not published due to organizational constraints, all reported values reflect aggregate differences between baseline and CAAD-supported sessions across 35 participants.

Third, qualitative feedback obtained through structured interviews highlighted improvements in the clarity, structure, and cognitive alignment of system outputs. Participants emphasized that CAAD-guided agent responses were easy to interpret and directly applicable, especially when outputs included structured reasoning traces. This transparency was seen as critical for supporting internal validation and collaborative decision-making.

Finally, 82.9% of users reported greater confidence in applying the system's recommendations. This increase in trust was attributed to enhanced interpretability and closer alignment between agent behavior and users' reasoning processes.

These results suggest that the CAAD framework is not only feasible to apply in real-world design, but also effective in enhancing usability, supporting cognitive flow, and improving decision confidence. More importantly, it provides a scalable design logic to align intelligent agents with the evolving mental demands of human analysts.

5 Conclusion

This paper introduced CAAD, a cognitively aware framework for AI agent design in complex analytical tasks. By structuring agent interventions according to task phase and cognitive challenge, CAAD promotes a more nuanced form of human-AI collaboration, one that supports users' evolving mental strategies rather than replacing them.

Our deployment study within a real-world enterprise operations platform demonstrated the practical value of the CAAD framework. Agent modules designed according to CAAD principles led to a 44.13% reduction in task completion time, improved subjective workload evaluations, and a marked increase in user confidence. These findings highlight the potential of phase-sensitive cognitive scaffolding to significantly improve both the usability and trustworthiness of intelligent systems in complex, goal-driven environments.

Future research may extend CAAD to domains with different task rhythms or explore adaptive implementations that sense and respond to user state in real time. We hope this work encourages further exploration of cognitive alignment as a foundational principle in the design of next-generation AI systems.

Disclosure of Interests. The authors have no competing interests to declare that are relevant to the content of this article.

References

1. Aboufoul, M., Wesslen, R., Cho, I., Dou, W., Shaikh, S.: Using hidden Markov models to determine cognitive states of visual analytic users (2018). https://doi.org/10.1109/MLUI52768.2018.10075648
2. Albers, M.: Human-information interaction with complex information for decision-making (2015). https://doi.org/10.3390/informatics2020004
3. Ali, T., Kostakos, P.: HuntGPT: integrating machine learning-based anomaly detection and explainable AI with large language models (LLMS). arXiv preprint arXiv:2309.16021 (2023)
4. Bhargava, H., Krishnan, R., Whinston, A.: On integrating collaboration and decision analysis techniques (1994). https://doi.org/10.1080/10919399409540229
5. Buchholz, V., Kopp, S.: Towards an adaptive assistance system for monitoring tasks: assessing mental workload using eye-tracking and performance measures (2020). https://doi.org/10.1109/ICHMS49158.2020.9209435
6. Calvano, M.: Design and evaluation of high-quality symbiotic ai systems through a human-centered approach. In: Proceedings of the 28th International Conference on Evaluation and Assessment in Software Engineering, pp. 488–493 (2024)
7. Castaneda, C., Mindel, J., Page, W., Stec, H., Yu, M., Holstein, K.: Supporting ai-augmented meta-decision making with indecision. arXiv preprint arXiv:2504.12433 (2025)
8. Chen, P., et al.: Coexploreds: framing and advancing collaborative design space exploration between human and AI. In: Proceedings of the 2025 CHI Conference on Human Factors in Computing Systems, pp. 1–20 (2025)
9. Chen, T.J., Mohanty, R.R., Krishnamurthy, V.R.: Queries and cues: textual stimuli for reflective thinking in digital mind-mapping (2021). https://doi.org/10.1115/1.4052297
10. Dalal, N.P., Kasper, G.M.: The design of joint cognitive systems: the effect of cognitive coupling on performance. Int. J. Hum Comput Stud. **40**(4), 677–702 (1994)
11. Davidson, K., Lisle, L., Whitley, K., Bowman, D., North, C.: Exploring the evolution of sensemaking strategies in immersive space to think (2022). https://doi.org/10.1109/TVCG.2022.3207357
12. Dhanoa, V., Wolter, A., Le'on, G.M., Schulz, H.J., Elmqvist, N.: Agentic visualization: extracting agent-based design patterns from visualization systems (2025)
13. Fok, R., et al.: Facets, taxonomies, and syntheses: navigating structured representations in LLM-assisted literature review. arXiv preprint arXiv:2504.18496 (2025)
14. Frejus, M., Lahoual, D., Gras-Gentiletti, M.: Making human-ai interactions sustainable: 7 key questions for an ergonomics perspective on artificial intelligence. Ergonomics Des. **47**(47) (2022)
15. Gebreegziabher, S.A.: Cognition-inspired interactive frameworks for human-AI alignment (2025). https://doi.org/10.1145/3708557.3716147

16. Gomez, C., Cho, S.M., Ke, S., Huang, C.M., Unberath, M.: Human-AI collaboration is not very collaborative yet: a taxonomy of interaction patterns in ai-assisted decision making from a systematic review. Front. Comput. Sci. **6**, 1521066 (2025)
17. Graham, L., et al.: Applying cognitive task analysis to health services research. (2022). https://doi.org/10.1111/1475-6773.14106
18. de Greef, T., Lafeber, H., van Oostendorp, H., Lindenberg, J.: Eye movement as indicators of mental workload to trigger adaptive automation. In: Schmorrow, D.D., Estabrooke, I.V., Grootjen, M. (eds.) FAC 2009. LNCS (LNAI), vol. 5638, pp. 219–228. Springer, Heidelberg (2009). https://doi.org/10.1007/978-3-642-02812-0_26
19. Hassan, M.M., Knipper, A., Santu, S.K.K.: ChatGPT as your personal data scientist. arXiv preprint arXiv:2305.13657 (2023)
20. He, C., Zou, B., Xing, J., Chen, J., Shi, Y., Ma, H.: Decode: defer-and-complement decision-making via decoupled concept bottleneck models (2025)
21. He, G., Hemmer, P., Vossing, M., Schemmer, M., Gadiraju, U.: Fine-grained appropriate reliance: human-AI collaboration with a multi-step transparent decision workflow for complex task decomposition (2025). https://doi.org/10.48550/arXiv.2501.10909
22. Heer, J.: Agency plus automation: designing artificial intelligence into interactive systems. Proc. Natl. Acad. Sci. **116**(6), 1844–1850 (2019)
23. Huang, D., Zhang, J.M., Luck, M., Bu, Q., Qing, Y., Cui, H.: Agentcoder: multi-agent-based code generation with iterative testing and optimisation. arXiv preprint arXiv:2312.13010 (2024)
24. Jiang, P., Rayan, J., Dow, S.W., Xia, H.: Graphologue: exploring large language model responses with interactive diagrams (2023). https://doi.org/10.1145/3586183.3606737
25. Jung, G., Park, S., Lee, U.: Deepstress: supporting stressful context sensemaking in personal informatics systems using a quasi-experimental approach (2024). https://doi.org/10.1145/3613904.3642766
26. Klein, G., Moon, B., Hoffman, R.: Making sense of sensemaking 1: alternative perspectives (2006). https://doi.org/10.1109/MIS.2006.75
27. Klein, G., Moon, B., Hoffman, R.: Making sense of sensemaking 2: a macrocognitive model (2006). https://doi.org/10.1109/MIS.2006.100
28. Klein, G., Phillips, J.K., Rall, E.L., Peluso, D.A.: A data–frame theory of sensemaking. In: Expertise Out of Context, pp. 118–160. Psychology Press (2007)
29. Koć-Januchta, M.M., Schönborn, K.J., Roehrig, C., Chaudhri, V.K., Tibell, L.A.E., Heller, H.C.: Connecting concepts helps put main ideas together: cognitive load and usability in learning biology with an AI-enriched textbook. Int. J. Educ. Technol. High. Educ. **19**(1), 1–22 (2022). https://doi.org/10.1186/s41239-021-00317-3
30. Küçük, S., Turan, Z., Çağla Nur Özkan, Taş, Y.F., Gürsoy, T.: An innovative approach in middle school science courses: effects of collaborative augmented reality activities on motivation, cognitive load, and satisfaction (2024). https://doi.org/10.1080/10494820.2024.2408582
31. Lagomarsino, M., Lorenzini, M., Balatti, P., Momi, E., Ajoudani, A.: Pick the right co-worker: online assessment of cognitive ergonomics in human-robot collaborative assembly (2022). https://doi.org/10.1109/TCDS.2022.3182811
32. Lagomarsino, M., Lorenzini, M., Momi, E., Ajoudani, A.: An online framework for cognitive load assessment in assembly tasks (2021). https://doi.org/10.1016/j.rcim.2022.102380
33. Lini, S., Hannotte, L., Beugniot, M.: Effect of a real-time psychophysiological feedback, its display format and reliability on cognitive workload and performance (2016). https://doi.org/10.5220/0005939500750079

34. Liu, J., Jiang, B.: Scaffolding students' ill-structured problem solving via LLM - multi-armed bandit problem as a case (2024). https://doi.org/10.58459/icce.2024. 4827
35. Ma, S., et al.: Towards human-AI deliberation: Design and evaluation of LLM-empowered deliberative AI for AI-assisted decision-making (2024). https://doi. org/10.1145/3706598.3713423
36. Viros-i Martin, A., Selva, D.: A framework to study human-AI collaborative design space exploration. In: International Design Engineering Technical Conferences and Computers and Information in Engineering Conference, vol. 85420, p. V006T06A052. American Society of Mechanical Engineers (2021)
37. Mingardi, M., Pluchino, P., Bacchin, D., Rossato, C., Gamberini, L.: Assessment of implicit and explicit measures of mental workload in working situations: implications for industry 4 (2020). https://doi.org/10.3390/app10186416
38. Okamura, K., Yamada, S.: Adaptive trust calibration for human-AI collaboration (2020). https://doi.org/10.1371/journal.pone.0229132
39. Okamura, K., Yamada, S.: Empirical evaluations of framework for adaptive trust calibration in human-AI cooperation (2020). https://doi.org/10.1109/ACCESS. 2020.3042556
40. Papautsky, E., Strouse, R.V., Dominguez, C.: Combining cognitive task analysis and participatory design methods to elicit and represent task flows (2020). https:// doi.org/10.1177/1555343420976014
41. Park, S., Subramonyam, H., Kulkarni, C.: Thinking assistants: LLM-based conversational assistants that help users think by asking rather than answering (2023)
42. Peng, Y., et al.: Navigating the unknown: a chat-based collaborative interface for personalized exploratory tasks. In: Proceedings of the 30th International Conference on Intelligent User Interfaces, pp. 1048–1063 (2025)
43. Pirolli, P., Card, S.: The sensemaking process and leverage points for analyst technology as identified through cognitive task analysis. In: Proceedings of International Conference on Intelligence Analysis, vol. 5, pp. 2–4. McLean, VA, USA (2005)
44. Qian, Z., Savko, L.O., Neubauer, C., Gremillion, G., Unhelkar, V.: Measuring variations in workload during human-robot collaboration through automated after-action reviews (2024). https://doi.org/10.1145/3610978.3640677
45. Rahman, S., Kandogan, E.: Characterizing practices, limitations, and opportunities related to text information extraction workflows: a human-in-the-loop perspective (2022). https://doi.org/10.1145/3491102.3502068
46. Sacha, D., Stoffel, A., Stoffel, F., Kwon, B.C., Ellis, G.P., Keim, D.: Knowledge generation model for visual analytics (2014). https://doi.org/10.1109/TVCG.2014. 2346481
47. Savko, L.O., Qian, Z., Gremillion, G., Neubauer, C., Canady, J.D., Unhelkar, V.: Rw4t dataset: data of human-robot behavior and cognitive states in simulated disaster response tasks (2024). https://doi.org/10.1145/3610977.3637481
48. Shaban, A., Pearson, E., Chang, V.: Evaluation of user experience, cognitive load, and training performance of a gamified cognitive training application for children with learning disabilities (2021). https://doi.org/10.3389/fcomp.2021.617056
49. Shergadwala, M.N., Seif El-Nasr, M.: Human-centric design requirements and challenges for enabling human-AI interaction in engineering design: an interview study. In: International Design Engineering Technical Conferences and Computers and Information in Engineering Conference, vol. 85420, p. V006T06A054. American Society of Mechanical Engineers (2021)

50. Shneiderman, B.: Human-centered artificial intelligence: reliable, safe & trustworthy. Int. J. Hum.-Comput. Interact. **36**(6), 495–504 (2020)
51. Souchet, A.D., Amokrane-Ferka, K., Burkhardt, J.M.: AI-assistance to decision-makers: evaluating usability, induced cognitive load, and trust's impact (2024). https://doi.org/10.1145/3673805.3673845
52. St-Onge, D., et al.: Planetary exploration with robot teams: implementing higher autonomy with swarm intelligence (2020). https://doi.org/10.1109/MRA.2019.2940413
53. Stasko, J., Görg, C., Liu, Z.: Jigsaw: supporting investigative analysis through interactive visualization (2007). https://doi.org/10.1057/palgrave.ivs.9500180
54. Surbakti, R., Umboh, S.E., Pong, M., Dara, S.: Cognitive load theory: implications for instructional design in digital classrooms (2024). https://doi.org/10.70177/ijen.v2i6.1659
55. Suryani, M., et al.: An initial user model design for adaptive interface development in learning management system based on cognitive load (2024). https://doi.org/10.1007/s10111-024-00772-8
56. Sweller, J.: Cognitive load during problem solving: effects on learning. Cogn. Sci. **12**(2), 257–285 (1988)
57. Tariq, S., Chhetri, M.B., Nepal, S., Paris, C.: A2C: a modular multi-stage collaborative decision framework for human-AI teams. arXiv preprint arXiv:2401.14432 (2024)
58. Tariq, S., Singh, R., Chhetri, M.B., Nepal, S., Paris, C.: Bridging expertise gaps: the role of LLMS in human-AI collaboration for cybersecurity. arXiv preprint arXiv:2505.03179 (2025)
59. Urech, A., Meier, P., Gut, S., Duchene, P., Christ, O.: Mapping or no mapping: the influence of controller interaction design in an immersive virtual reality tutorial in two different age groups (2024). https://doi.org/10.3390/mti8070059
60. Vuckovic, M., Schmidt, J.: On sense making and the generation of knowledge in visual analytics (2022). https://doi.org/10.3390/analytics1020008
61. Wasi, A.T., Islam, M.R.: CogErgLLM: exploring large language model systems design perspective using cognitive ergonomics. In: Peled-Cohen, L., Calderon, N., Lissak, S., Reichart, R. (eds.) Proceedings of the 1st Workshop on NLP for Science (NLP4Science), pp. 249–258. Association for Computational Linguistics, Miami, FL, USA (2024). https://doi.org/10.18653/v1/2024.nlp4science-1.22
62. Weng, L., Wang, X., Lu, J., Feng, Y., Liu, Y., Chen, W.: Insightlens: discovering and exploring insights from conversational contexts in large-language-model-powered data analysis. arXiv preprint arXiv:2404.01644 (2024)
63. Weng, L., et al.: Insightlens: augmenting LLM-powered data analysis with interactive insight management and navigation (2024). https://doi.org/10.1109/TVCG.2025.3567131
64. Wu, X., Valente, D.C.B.: Adapting differentiated cognitive load measurement in physics classroom (2020). https://doi.org/10.1119/perc.2019.pr.wu
65. Xu, X., Konnova, A., Gao, B., Peng, C., Vo, D., Dow, S.P.: Productive vs. reflective: how different ways of integrating AI into design workflows affect cognition and motivation. In: Proceedings of the 2025 CHI Conference on Human Factors in Computing Systems, pp. 1–15 (2025)
66. Xue, S., et al.: Db-GPT: empowering database interactions with private large language models. arXiv preprint arXiv:2312.17449 (2024)
67. Yang, S., Cheng, Q., Ma, R., Zhao, L., Wu, Z., Yu, G.: The wisdom of agent crowds: a human-AI interaction innovation ignition framework (2025)

68. Zhang, W., Shen, Y., Lu, W., Zhuang, Y.: Data-copilot: bridging billions of data and humans with autonomous workflow. arXiv preprint arXiv:2306.07209 (2023)
69. Zhao, C., et al.: CyberBot: towards reliable cybersecurity education via ontology-grounded retrieval augmented generation (2025). https://doi.org/10.48550/arXiv:2504.00389
70. Zheng, C., Miller, T., Bialkowski, A., Soyer, H.P., Janda, M.: Supporting data-frame dynamics in ai-assisted decision making. arXiv preprint arXiv:2504.15894 (2025)

Decoding Societal Acceptance of Innovative Air Mobility (IAM) via Virtual Reality Simulations

Sofia Samoili[1]([⊠]) [iD], Panagiotis-Eleftherios Eleftherakis[2] [iD], Margarida Lopes[1],
Helena Filipe Almeida[1], James Lindsay Afonso de Brito Mcleod[1,1] [iD],
George Anagnostopoulos[2], Konstantinos Iliakis[2], Sotirios Xydis[2],
and Sofia Kalakou[1] [iD]

[1] Instituto Universitário de Lisboa (ISCTE-IUL) - Business Research Unit (BRU-IUL),
Avenida das Forças Armadas, 1649-026 Lisbon, Portugal
`{sofia.samoili,margarida_rosado,helena_filipe_almeida,`
`james_lindsay_afonso_brito_mcleod,sofia.kalakou}@iscte-iul.pt`
[2] School of Electrical and Computer Engineering (ECE), National Technical University of
Athens, 9 Heroon Polytechneiou, Zographou Campus, Athens, Greece
`{pelef,geoanagn,kiliakis,sxydis}@microlab.ntua.gr`

Abstract. The study investigates societal acceptance of Innovative Air Mobility
(IAM) operations, from a perspective of visual and audiovisual pollution in urban
and rural environments. Participants' perception of drone and eVTOL operations
was examined through Virtual Reality (VR) simulations across diverse scenarios, including various drone types, flight paths, and the presence or not of audio
input, to measure the impact on visual/audiovisual pollution. Two methodologies
are developed to quantify drone acceptance: NLP-based and HCI-based Acceptance Analyses. The NLP approach employed sentence-level sentiment analysis
on verbal input of the participants during simulations, to uncover underlying factors affecting drone operation acceptance and implied acceptance beyond self-
stated numerical ratings. The HCI method analysed participants' interactions by
quantifying non-tolerated audiovisual/visual pollution periods through "clicks"
during the VR simulations. Results showed drone type and environment influence public acceptance. Sensing drones received the highest acceptance, while
lower societal acceptance was indicated for passenger drones through lower sentiment scores. English speakers demonstrated higher readiness to approve drone
operations, potentially due to more frequent drone exposure or linguistic differences, with the reasons requiring further investigation. The strong performance of
the XGBoost model in predicting non-tolerated audiovisual/visual pollution validates the indirect predictive approach using HCI-collected biometric data. These
findings provide a comprehensive understanding of human perception and acceptance levels in human-UAV interactions, surpassing self-reported ratings. The
methods provide substantial guidance to UAV stakeholders, urban planners, and
policymakers to design IAM systems accounting for public comfort and societal
expectations.

Keywords: Natural Language Processing · Sentiment Analysis · XGBoost ·
Machine Learning · Classification · Innovative Air Mobility · Drones · Virtual
Reality Simulations · Societal Acceptance

D. Harris et al. (Eds.): HCII 2025, LNCS 16334, pp. 231–242, 2026.
https://doi.org/10.1007/978-3-032-12392-3_15

1   Introduction

The rapid integration of Innovative Air Mobility operations, particularly drones and eVTOLs, in urban and rural areas presents unique challenges for human-computer interaction (HCI) and emerging technologies. This study examines the critical need to understand citizens' human perception and acceptance of drone operations in our environments, focusing on visual and audiovisual pollution, a key concern in HCI, urban and transport planning. Through Virtual Reality (VR) simulations, societal acceptance of drones is explored across diverse scenarios, allowing the assessment of the impact of audiovisual/visual pollution in controlled, immersive environments. This approach bridges multiple disciplines, including psychology, urban planning, and technology acceptance studies, all within the HCI framework.

Urban and rural VR environments are created, studying drone densities with cargo, passenger and sensing drones, as well as variables related to flight paths and audio input. This results in six distinct combinations, in which participants' responses are analysed to examine how surroundings and audiovisual/visual pollution affect user perception and acceptance thresholds in human-vehicle interaction, which are crucial aspects in HCI.

More specifically, the study assesses quantitatively participant responses, aligning with HCI's emphasis on user-centred design and evaluation. This approach facilitates the examination of how various factors in human-UAV interaction affect user perception and acceptance thresholds. Participants explicitly state their level of comfort regarding audiovisual/visual pollution under varying densities of drones, allowing the sentiment analysis of their experience. This implied acceptance indicator offers a more profound understanding of the acceptance of UAVs within various environments, as it allows the identification of implicit behaviour towards UAVs, extending beyond self-stated numerical ratings.

We developed two methodologies to quantify drone acceptance:

- **NLP-based Acceptance Analysis:** VR simulation participants provide verbal-input regarding audiovisual/visual pollution from Innovative Air Mobility (IAM) operations. A sentence-level sentiment-based approach [1, 2] unveils underlying concerns and highlights unstated areas requiring improvement. A sentiment score is computed as proxy of implied drone acceptance through Natural Language Processing (NLP), specifically sentiment analysis, quantifying implied social acceptance of drones beyond self-stated numerical ratings.

- **HCI-based Acceptance Analysis:** Participants take action through long "clicks" during VR simulations. Clicking (Buttondown) intervals indicate periods of non-tolerated visual pollution. The data are analysed cumulatively, extracting a single acceptance metric per simulation, and in a time series-based manner, characterising each time instance within or outside the user's acceptance threshold. In the former case, multiple accumulation methods are employed for the instances of non-tolerated audiovisual/visual pollution (clicks), leading to different views on the data, as elaborated on in Sect. 2.2.

2 Methodology

2.1 NLP Framework for Bilingual Sentiment-Driven Acceptance Analysis

A sentiment-based approach at sentence-level facilitated the identification of trends, and of underlying concerns, as well as highlighted areas requiring improvement based on qualitative feedback.

The NLP-Based Acceptance Analysis methodology comprises multiple steps. Initially, a custom lexicon is constructed combining multiple sentiment lexicons and the associated scores for each of the participants' language (Portuguese and English) to enhance sentiment intensity representation. For English, AFINN [3] and Loughran-McDonald (LM) [4, 5] are enlisted. For Portuguese, SentiLex-PT02 and OpLexicon V3.0 [6–8] are employed. All lexicons include unigrams and multiword expressions, except from LM that includes only unigrams. The lexicons have different sentiment scales, and the Portuguese lexicons have narrower sentiment ranges than the AFINN lexicon for English, which may reduce the sentiment intensity in Portuguese. Consequently, sentiment scores are normalised to a common scale to ensure cross-lexicon comparability, and to align with the 5-Point Likert scale, which is used to assess social acceptance of audiovisual/visual pollution and surrounding characteristics caused by drones, as part of a broader ongoing study on acceptance of IAM operations. Therefore, the common scale is selected to be from 1 to 5.

The next step is automatic language detection of the participants' document input, using Google's Compact Language Detector v2 [9]. Text pre-processing follows, involving tokenisation and lemmatisation, to reduce words to their base or dictionary form. Sentiment analysis is then conducted using a lexicon-based approach [1, 2]. In the developed algorithm, negations, intensifiers or diminutives valence shifters are considered, accounting for context that modifies sentiment's intensity or polarity (e.g., negators like "not", diminutive like "pouco"). These modifiers enhance the accuracy of sentiment analysis, as they may change the context by reversing sentiment polarity, amplifying sentiment intensity, or reducing sentiment intensity, respectively.

The resulting sentiment score is then analysed by environment setting, drone type, and language.

2.2 HCI – Based Acceptance Analysis and Modelling

For the HCI-Based Acceptance Analysis, we focus on the total normalised duration of "clicks" or Buttondown intervals, defining non-tolerated audiovisual/visual pollution according to the user undergoing the experiment. At each time step, the participant's pupil position is recorded, producing various experiment related metrics such as gaze position, velocity, acceleration, saccade- and fixation- related features. A saccade is a rapid eye movement between different points, while a fixation happens when eyes briefly focus on a single object [10]. Regarding gaze, apart from position, velocity and direction parameters are included. For the Cumulative Experiment View analysis, as illustrated in Fig. 1, each experiment is assigned a separate Acceptance Score which is drawn from the total number of Buttondowns a user provides. In Sect. 3, three different methods are used to display the results obtained, including the total number of Buttondowns, the total duration of Buttondowns and the total duration of Buttondowns normalized to the total experiment duration as described by Eq. 1.

$$acceptance\_proxy = 1 - \frac{\sum_1^{total\_presses} duration(press)}{total\_duration} \tag{1}$$

The aforementioned eye-tracking parameters are treated as features of the experiment and are correlated to the Buttondown intervals, therefore to non-tolerated audiovisual/visual pollution, thus we explore the predictability of user acceptance through ML modelling using collected data, requiring no direct user interaction declaring acceptance. We evaluate the XGBoost, RandomForest and MLP classifiers, with the MLP employing two hidden layers. The Models were tuned for relevant hyperparameters and underwent 5-fold Cross Validation, with XGBoost being optimal. This process is illustrated in Fig. 1.

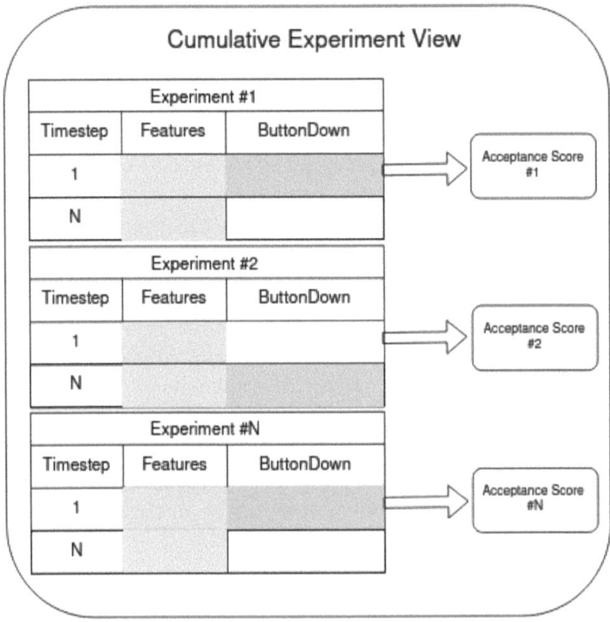

Fig. 1. Cumulative Experiment View, where each experiment is assigned an acceptance score.

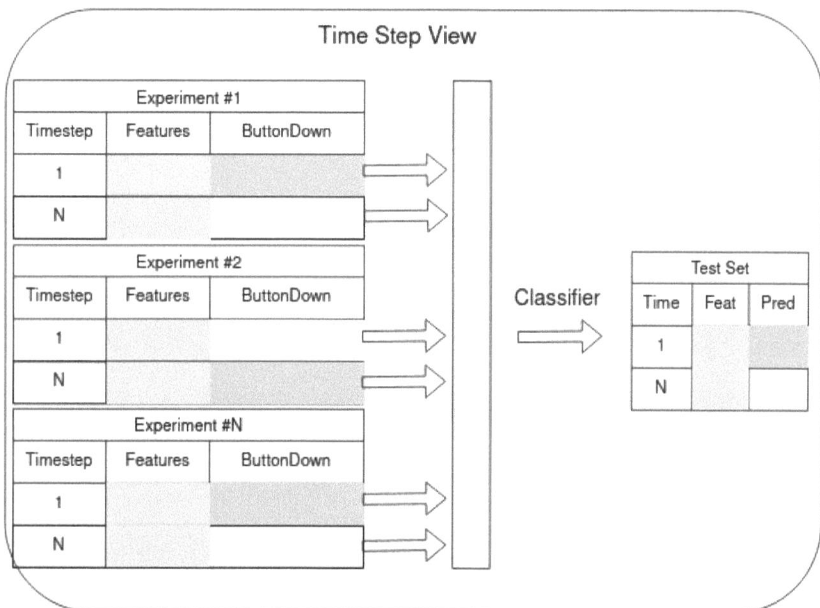

Fig. 2. Time Step View, where each Time Step is treated as a separate sample. A classifier is trained to predict ButtonDown, signifying non-tolerated audiovisual/visual pollution based on the features of the experiment, related to eye-tracking.

3   Results and Discussion

Following the **NLP-based acceptance analysis**, participants' implied acceptance of drones based on environment, drone type and language, is shown in Fig. 2. Overall sentiment scores as proxy of audiovisual/visual pollution acceptance of IAM operations, suggest that IAM is likely accepted.

Highest acceptance is observed for sensing drones in rural settings, particularly among Portuguese-speaking participants. This implies that the relatively smaller size of sensing drones, compared to passenger and cargo drones, may contribute to reduced visual disturbance in less visually congested environments, as opposed to urban areas. This presumably explains also the greater acceptance of drones in urban areas compared to rural areas, among English-speaking participants.

Passenger drones present receiving lower sentiment scores, conveying lower social acceptance, as alternative passenger transport modes remain more affordable and more accessible [11]. Regarding cargo drones, the setting in which are found (urban or rural), affects the extent social approval, as in rural areas with less audiovisual/visual pollution, they might appear more intrusive.

Regarding the language, English speakers seemed readier to approve drones than Portuguese speakers, possibly due to greater exposure to drones. Nevertheless, this observation could stem from linguistic differences. More indirect wording and less exaggerated expressions appear in the Portuguese language than in the English language, and hence narrower sentiment range intensity.

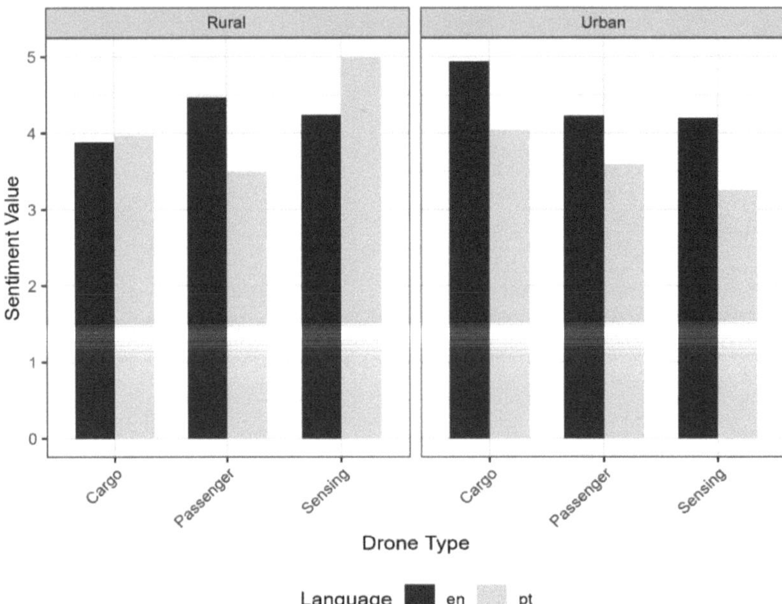

Fig. 3. Sentiment value as proxy of social acceptance of audiovisual/visual pollution due to drone operations per environment, drone type and language.

Regarding the **HCI-based acceptance analysis** and the **Cumulative View on the Data** in specific, results are displayed in Figs. 4, 6 and 5, corresponding to different views on the Buttondown data. The purpose of this study is to be able to predict Acceptance based only on Environment and Drone Type (Experiment Setup).

The **Acceptance Proxy** distribution per-experiment is illustrated in Fig. 6, displaying findings which align with the NLP results showing English-speakers accepting more urban simulations, while cargo drones in rural settings are the least accepted. The acceptance relative order for rural simulations is also consistent with the NLP-based analysis.

As seen in Fig. 4, illustrating the total number of Buttondown intervals, the results are inconsistent in terms both of the relative Acceptance between different drone types as well as the Acceptance comparison between Urban and Rural environments, leading to the conclusion that the total number of Buttondown intervals by itself does not constitute a reliable metric when assessing Acceptance.

Regarding Fig. 5, where the total cumulative duration of the Buttondown intervals is displayed, the higher Acceptance in Urban environments is evident. It is important to note that in Figs. 4 and 5, the Total Buttondown intervals and Total Buttondown duration correspond to non-tolerated audiovisual/visual pollution, therefore the data should be interpreted inversely with respect to the Acceptance Proxy.

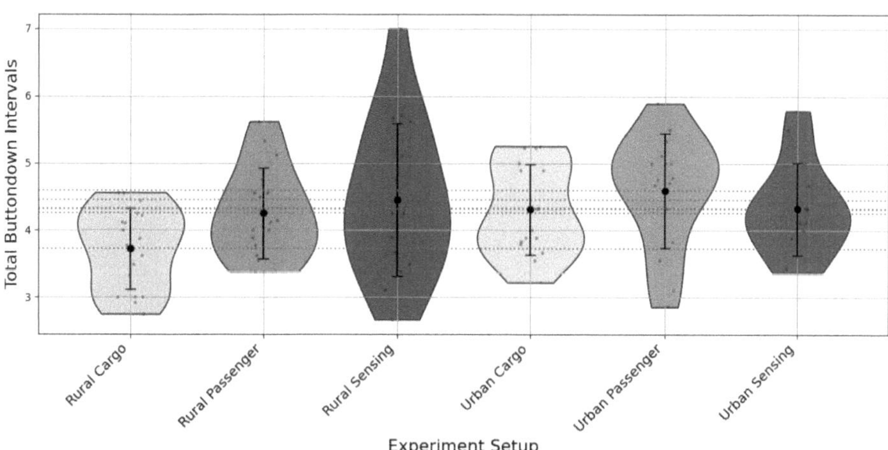

Fig. 4. The total number of Buttondown Intervals corresponding to non-tolerated audiovisual/visual pollution.

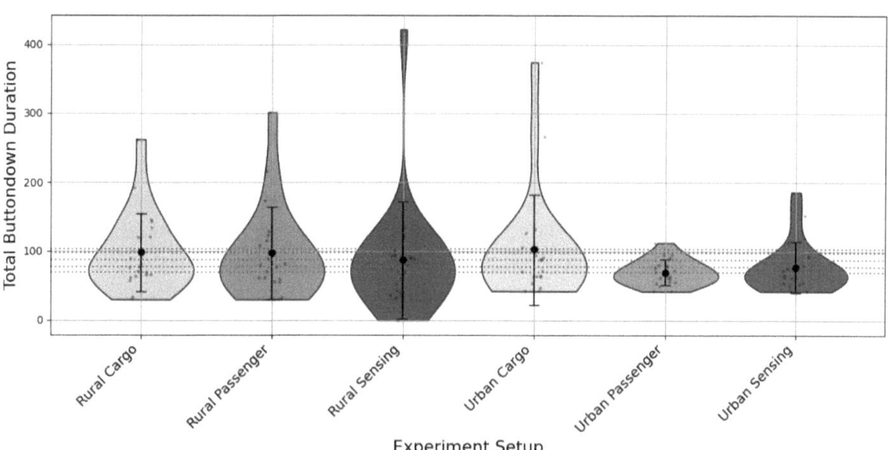

Fig. 5. The total duration of Buttondown Timesteps signifying intervals of non-tolerated audiovisual/visual pollution.

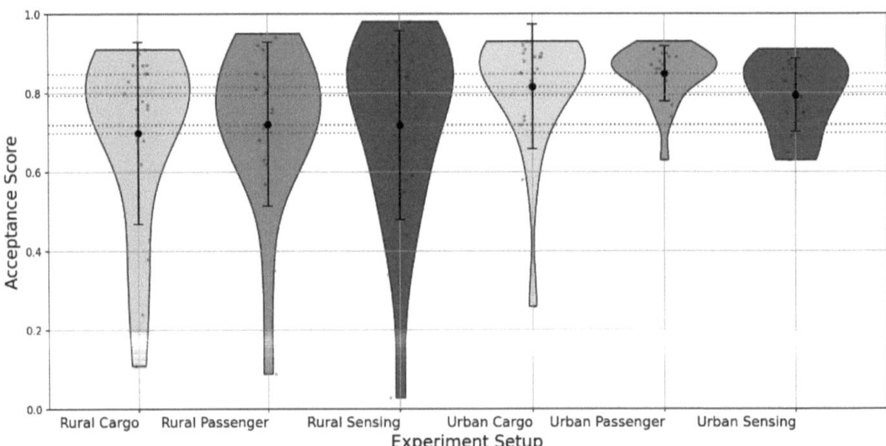

Fig. 6. The *acceptance_proxy* of visual pollution due to drone operations per environment and drone type.

With respect to the **Time-Step View** on the Data of the **HCI-based Acceptance Analysis,** the study aims beyond direct user self- reporting of Acceptance, by predicting acceptance through experiment features mentioned is Subsect. 2.2. To this end, we correlate Experiment Features with binary encoded Buttondown Timesteps signifying user Acceptance or lack thereof. The correlated features are displayed in Fig. 7. For each feature, the distribution of correlation factors of the respective feature with Buttondown intervals is displayed across all the experiments. As observed in Fig. 7, Saccade-related parameters are the most positively correlated features, followed by Fixation parameters. This is expected, as user Fixation on the Drones during VR simulation signifies non-tolerated audiovisual/visual pollution which constitutes the Buttondown intervals. Saccade between different fixation points signifies the existence of multiple drones and induces the concomitant Buttondown intervals from the user. On the other end of the correlation spectrum, we observe the camera and pupil movements to all possible directions, which are the most negatively correlated parameters to Buttondown intervals. This is also expected, as the user's gaze moves in all directions searching for drones during intervals where drones have not yet appeared in the simulation or are sparse enough. During these intervals, the user does not declare non-tolerated audiovisual/visual pollution through Buttondown, hence the negative correlation. Uncorrelated parameters in the middle of the spectrum such as Saccade duration and Saccade amplitude are not relevant to Acceptance.

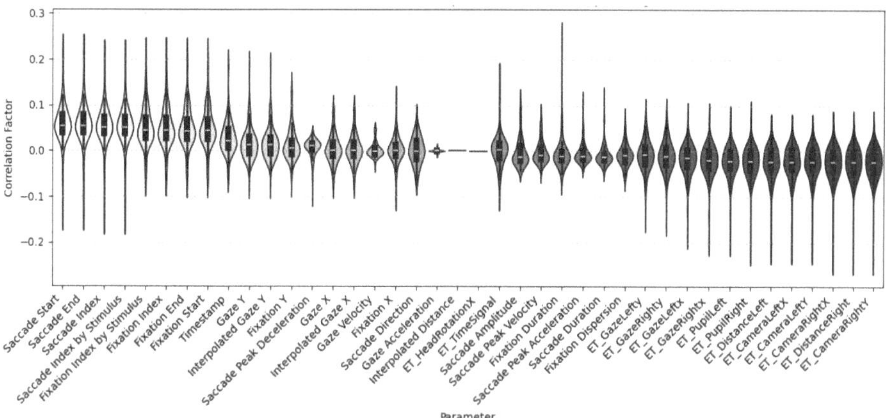

Fig. 7. Sorted Pearson-R correlation coefficients of the Experiment Features with the binary encoded Buttondown intervals.

To develop robust classifiers for identifying user click intervals in sequential input data, we implemented a pipeline that combined data preprocessing, class balancing, model training with hyperparameter optimisation, and comprehensive performance evaluation. The raw CSV files corresponding to the experiments were parsed to extract structured data and annotate intervals corresponding to mouse button events (WM_LBUTTONDOWN and WM_LBUTTONUP). Features were numerically encoded, and missing values imputed. Due to inherent class imbalance, RandomOverSampler was employed to upsample the minority class. Three model types—XGBoost, Random Forest, and a Multi-Layer Perceptron (MLP)—were trained using stratified 5-fold cross-validation and RandomizedSearchCV for hyperparameter tuning. Models were evaluated using precision, recall, F1-score, and area under the precision-recall curve (AUC-PR), with emphasis on recall due to the imbalanced nature of the task. Evaluation on a held-out subset of data files confirmed the models' generalisability. As displayed in Fig. 8, the XGBoost classifier performs optimally, in terms of Area under the Precision-Recall curve. We use this Figure of Merit as a proxy of model accuracy due to the high imbalance of the classes. The assessment of the models seen in Fig. 8 is performed on a subset of the total data amounting to about 1/3 of the CSV files corresponding to the experiments. All experiment setups are treated as one, and the data across all Time Steps are accumulated.

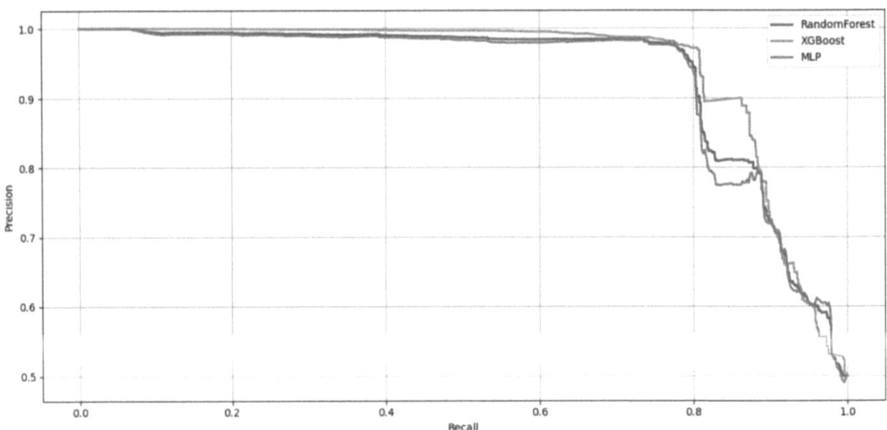

Fig. 8. Precision-Recall curves for the evaluated models. The XGBoost classifier displays optimal accuracy.

Figure 9 depicts the ROC and Precision-Recall curves of the selected XGBoost model. For a Recall of 0.8, Precision exceeds 0.9, rendering this analysis more valuable than accuracy due to class imbalance, with acceptance at 78% of all time steps. Figure 10 illustrates the top 10 features by importance employed by the selected XGBoost classifier. Evidently, the most positively correlated features are included, since they display the greatest absolute correlation as well.

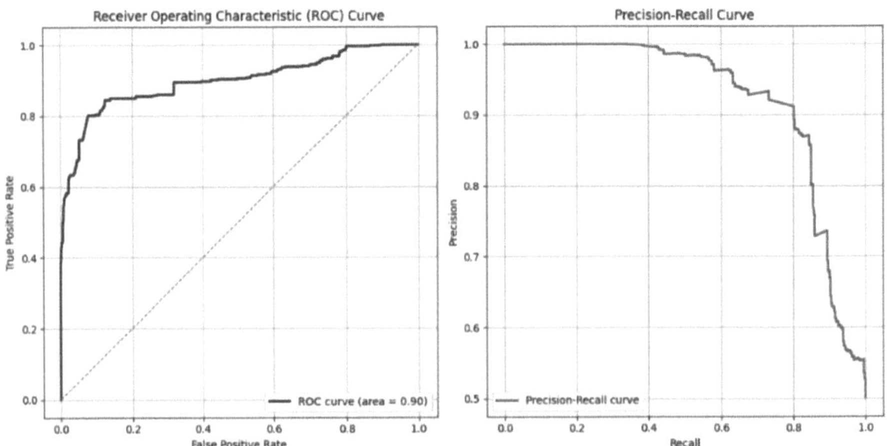

Fig. 9. Receiver Operating Characteristic and Precision-Recall curves of the XGBoost model trained on gaze-related data to predict drone acceptance proxy.

The above findings confirm that the NLP-based analysis can be bypassed, and the Acceptance Scores can be directly determined by eye-tracking data and other features of the VR experiment without direct reporting by the user undergoing the experiment.

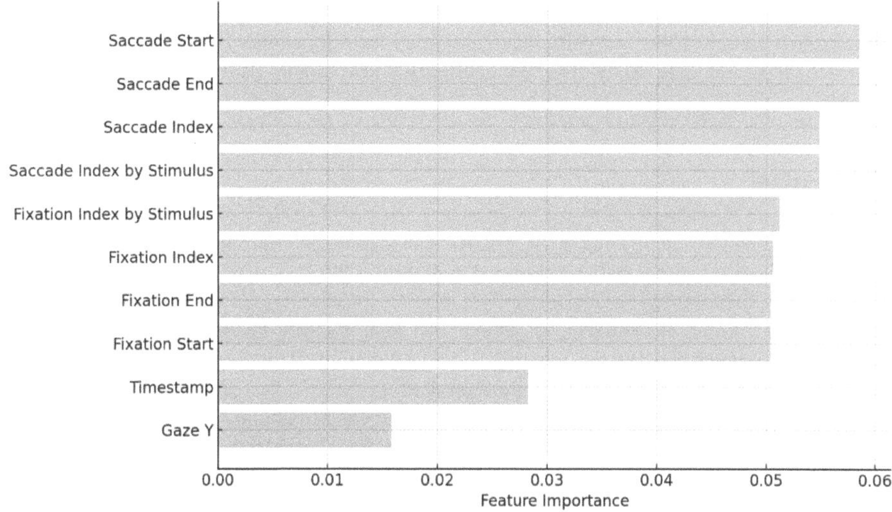

Fig. 10. Top feature importances for the selected XGBoost classifier.

4 Conclusions

This study demonstrates that societal acceptance of Innovative Air Mobility (IAM) operations can be effectively assessed through a dual framework combining bilingual sentiment analysis and HCI-derived biometric data within immersive VR simulations. Environmental context and drone type are consistently identified as key factors influencing public tolerance, with sensing drones receiving the highest levels of acceptance.

HCI-collected biometric data, particularly eye-tracking features such as saccade and fixation patterns, proved reliable predictors of non-tolerated audiovisual/visual pollution, aligning with NLP results. This approach enables implicit inference of acceptance beyond direct user input. The strong performance of the XGBoost model validates this indirect predictive approach.

The research also underscores the importance of accounting for linguistic and cultural nuances in evaluating acceptance, as implied by sentiment discrepancies between English- and Portuguese-speaking participants. These insights provide critical guidance for UAV developers, urban planners, and policymakers, supporting the design of IAM systems that are aligned with public comfort thresholds and societal expectations.

The study proposes further research directions, including comparing self-stated acceptance scores with implied acceptance metrics, to determine whether observed linguistic differences stem from sentiment lexicon limitations or reflect underlying behavioural patterns. Future research will also explore real-world factors, such as UAV regulation, noise levels, and optimised flight path strategies, to enhance public receptivity and ensure the sustainable integration of drone operations into everyday environments, addressing potential challenges in the widespread adoption of IAM operations.

Acknowledgments. The Authors would like to acknowledge the funding provided by the ImA-FUSA project, grant number 101114776. The ISCTE Ethics Committee granted approval for this study to ensure the protection and safeguarding of participants. Upon thorough examination of the informed consent form, the participants provided their signatures and were apprised of the assurances regarding data anonymity, confidentiality, and voluntary participation.

References

1. Ardia, D., Bluteau, K, Borms, S., Boudt, K.: The R package sentometrics to compute, aggregate, and predict with textual sentiment. J. Stat. Softw. **99**(2), 1–40 (2021). https://doi.org/10.18637/jss.v099.i02
2. Borms, S., Ardia, D., Bluteau, K., Boudt, K.: Sentometrics: an integrated framework for textual sentiment time series aggregation and prediction. R package version 1.0.0 (2021). https://CRAN.R-project.org/package=sentometrics
3. Nielsen, F.A.: AFINN. Informatics and Mathematical Modelling, Technical University of Denmark (2011). http://www2.compute.dtu.dk/pubdb/pubs/6010-full.html. Accessed 28 Feb 2025
4. Loughran, T., McDonald, B.: When is a liability not a liability? textual analysis, dictionaries, and 10-Ks. J. Finan. **66**(1), 35–65 (2011). https://doi.org/10.1111/j.1540-6261.2010.01625.xs
5. Bodnaruk, A., Loughran, T., McDonald, B.: Using 10-K text to gauge financial constraints. J. Finan. Quan. Anal. **50**(4), 1–24 (2015)
6. Gonzaga, S.: lexiconPT: Lexicons for Portuguese Text Analysis. R package version 0.1.0 (2017). https://CRAN.R-project.org/package=lexiconPT
7. Souza, M., Vieira, R.: Sentiment analysis on Twitter data for Portuguese language. In: 10th International Conference Computational Processing of the Portuguese Language (2012). https://www.inf.pucrs.br/linatural/wordpress/recursos-e-ferramentas/oplexicon. Accessed 28 Feb 2025
8. Souza, M., Vieira, R., Busetti, D., Chishman, R., Alves, I.M.: Construction of a Portuguese opinion lexicon from multiple resources. In: 8th Brazilian Symposium in Information and Human Language Technology (2011). https://www.inf.pucrs.br/linatural/wordpress/recursos-e-ferramentas/oplexicon. Accessed 28 Feb 2025
9. Ooms, J.: cld2: Google's Compact Language Detector 2, R package version 1.2.5. https://CRAN.R-project.org/package=cld2
10. Klaib, A.F., Alsrehin, N.O., Melhem, W.Y., Bashtawi, H.O., Magableh, A.A.: Eye tracking algorithms, techniques, tools, and applications with an emphasis on machine learning and Internet of Things technologies. Expert Syst. Appl. **166** (2021). https://www.sciencedirect.com/science/article/pii/S0957417420308071. Accessed 28 Feb 2025
11. EASA European Union Aviation Safety Agency: Study on the societal acceptance of Urban Air Mobility in Europe (2021). https://www.easa.europa.eu/sites/default/files/dfu/uam-full-report.pdf. Accessed 15 Jun 2025

The Future Impact of AI on the Human Role in Aviation: A Case Study of Pilots

Veronika Klara Takacs$^{(\boxtimes)}$, Vanessa Arrigoni, Nicola Cavagnetto, and Simone Pozzi

Deep Blue s.r.l, Via Daniele Manin 53, 00185 Roma, RM, Italy
`veronika.takacs@dblue.it`

Abstract. Introducing Artificial Intelligence (AI) into commercial air transport operation is expected to remarkably impact future roles by 2050. This paper introduces the results of the EU Horizon Project HAIKU, where a series of workshops and interviews were conducted with subject matter experts (SMEs) in aviation to explore the key milestones in the evolution of human roles in industry. Furthermore, the paper presents the likely changes required by personality traits, skills and training through the example of commercial airline pilots, as one of the key roles impacted the most by the introduction of artificial intelligence in operation.

Keywords: Artificial intelligence · Human role · Human-AI teaming · Five factor model · Crew resource management · Knowledge management

1 Introduction: The Impact of AI on the Human Role in Future Aviation

As a result of technological advancements, the role of humans in complex socio-technical systems is foreseen to evolve. As a result, the skills and knowledge that are required by the future workforce to accomplish everyday tasks will also change, mostly due to an increase in automation, and Artificial Intelligence (AI). Consequently, anticipating these future skills and knowledge is necessary to strategically design adequate training and educational paths and to ensure the smooth transition of professionals in the field [1], thus maintaining safe and secure operation within aviation. By 2050, AI might gradually become a full-fledged team member in the cockpit, ops rooms and airports. This opens to a set of questions that need to be answered to have a clear view of the future workforce and to ensure the continuity of a seamless and safe operation.

This paper reports the findings of the EU Horizon project HAIKU, where a strand of work was dedicated to the analysis of AI impact on the human role, and definition of recommended training approaches to address this challenge. More specifically, the analysis has focused on three aspects to investigate in relation to the introduction of AI into operations:

- What will be the impact of AI on the current human role in aviation?
- How will the required personality traits, skills and training change as a response to AI introduced in operation?

D. Harris ct al. (Eds.): HCII 2025, LNCS 16334, pp. 243 261, 2026.
https://doi.org/10.1007/978-3-032-12392-3_16

- How can the aviation sector maintain its attractiveness to future generations' workforce?

The recent paper introduces a set of empirical data collection procedures that resulted in the identification of (1) how the human role will likely evolve in aviation as a result of artificial intelligence introduction in operation; (2) how personality traits of commercial airline pilots, as well as hard and soft skills, and the way these skills are trained may shift in the future as a result of introducing AI in operation.

2 Step 1: Investigation of the Evolution of Human Role in Future Aviation

In order to build a comprehensive understanding of the likely evolution of human roles in future aviation, three workshops with Subject Matter Experts (SME) have been organized to discuss and analyze the AI systems' introduction into operations, and identify the likely necessary changes in human roles, skill set and competencies.

2.1 Workshops on the Evolution of the Human Role in Future Aviation

The three workshops took place in Italy, Sweden and Belgium, and involved $n = 30$ subject matter experts from 7 countries, covering all aviation segments, namely 8 SMEs from the ATM segment, 6 SMEs on UTM and UAM; 12 SMEs from airlines; 4 SMEs from airports.

The workshops were based on future scenarios (2050) developed earlier within the HAIKU project [2]. A variety of brainstorming methodologies were used to outline the human role's evolution from the present day to 2050. More specifically, relying on backcasting, forecasting and the lotus blossom methodologies, participants were able to explore and discuss the evolution of human role in a creative, yet systematic way, ensuring that no important aspects have been overlooked. Backcasting is a strategic planning methodology that involves working backward from a desired future scenario to the present, identifying the necessary steps and actions required to reach that future state. It is not focused on predicting the future, but rather on designing a pathway to achieve a specific vision by determining the policies, measures, and interventions needed to realize the desired outcome [3, 4]. Forecasting, on the other hand, is a method of projecting future values by analyzing current trends. It begins with the present as a starting point and extrapolates future trajectories to attain a desired future outcome [5]. In the context of the "Future Workforce Workshop" sessions, forecasting worked in tandem with backcasting, offering a comprehensive insight into both the existing state and potential future advancements. Finally, the lotus blossom method is a brainstorming technique that involves the systematic exploration of ideas around a central idea which can then be broken down into deeper sub-themes [6]. As a complementary research step, interview sessions have been organized with n = 5 subject matter experts to further elaborate on the expected changes of key roles in aviation. In this paper, only the results of the role of commercial airline pilots are presented.

3   Step 2: Exploring Pilots' Future Personality, Skills and Required Training

In Step 2, the role of commercial airline pilots has been chosen as a specific role in aviation to demonstrate the likely change in the future job profile, the variety of tasks to perform along with the technical and soft skills required to perform these tasks successfully, and finally, the way these skills may be trained.

First, desk research has been performed to investigate the state of the art in the current personality profile required by commercial airline pilots, focusing on studies that applied the Five Factor Model or Big 5 (FFM) as a theoretical approach to personality [7]. As an important future challenge closely related to climate change, the frequency and severity of extreme weather events is expected to increase, demanding a stronger focus on situations in which they have a significant impact on the airline operation (e.g. the necessity to quickly re-route due to extreme weather event) or on the state of the pilot (e.g. a startling effect caused by a lightning strike).

Second, two workshops have been organized to understand the necessary skills of pilots in two potentially hazardous situations, where quick reaction to the changing environmental conditions is a key factor in maintaining operational safety, namely: (i) startling/surprising events in the cockpit, (ii) route re-planning. The importance of these skills was also discussed in a possible future, where "single pilot operations" may take place and an AI-based intelligent assistant is foreseen to support the pilot in the aforementioned situations.

Third, based on the comparison between the as-is and future operation, a gap analysis has been performed, highlighting the most relevant changes in the skill set and future personality of pilots that future training programs and selection procedures may take into consideration.

As the last step, a semi-structured interview has been conducted to reason on the necessary changes in future training. By completing these interlinking research steps, a variety of recommendations have been formed on the changing role of pilots in terms of personality in future selection (who to train?), the changing nature of skills to train in the future (what to train?) as well as the ways these skills could be trained in the future (how to train?).

3.1   Desk Research: The Evolution of Personality Traits of Pilots

Personality is defined as a unique set of predispositions for a person to respond in particular ways. Personality permits a prediction of what a person will most likely do in each situation. These trait characteristics, being relatively stable over time, lead people to behave in distinctive and consistent ways across situations. As personality plays a key role in how individuals react to different situations, the personality of an aviator is very likely to have its own impact on how a pilot approaches different scenarios, including more demanding ones [8, 9]. While psychomotor skills and cognitive abilities have long been commonly employed in pilot selection, personality assessment as a means of predicting one's aptitude has gained incremental validity more recently [10]. Although there is an ongoing controversy of whether there is a unique combination of characteristics that make up the "ideal pilot", certain personality traits such as being emotionally stable, conscientious, agreeable, and extroverted have been identified as crucial for training success and later job performance.

One of the most commonly used personality indexes in assessing pilots' personality is the Five-Factor-Model (FFM), consisting in five major personality dimensions, often referred to as the "Big Five" of personality [7].

It includes the following factors: Openness to experience (O); Conscientiousness (C); Extraversion (E); Agreeableness (A); Neuroticism (N) [8, 11]:

- *Openness to experience* is defined as the degree of receptivity to a range of internal/external sources of information and new inputs.
- *Conscientiousness* is defined as the amount of persistence, organization, and motivation in goal-directed behaviors.
- Extroversion refers to the amount of energy someone directs outwards to the external environment.
- *Agreeableness* is considered as the quality of one's interpersonal interactions along a continuum from compassion to hostility.
- *Neuroticism* is defined as the one's propensity to experience negative emotions, such as anxiety or depression.

3.2 Workshops on Future Skills of Pilots

To understand the transformation of current skills in the future, two workshops were conducted aiming at exploring the interactions pilots need to engage in for specific scenarios (startle/surprise; route planning/re-planning), both today (2023) and in 2035. Interaction here was defined as a reciprocal action between on the one hand, the pilot and other hand, other human actors, rules, procedures and regulations, the technical system, and the physical requirement. Following this logic, the SHELL model [12, 13] was used to systematically define all possible interactions between pilots and their environment. In this case, the SHELL model provided a comprehensive approach to understanding pilots' interactions with their environment and based on these interactions, the basis for reasoning on the transformation of required skills. Following the logic of the model, the following areas were investigated as aspects with which pilots interact during task execution:

- *Liveware (L):* e.g. cabin crew, ground crew, management, and administration personnel.
- *Software (S):* laws, rules, regulations, instructions, policies, orders, SOPs, safety procedures.
- *Hardware (H):* physical elements of the system (e.g. controls, surfaces, displays of the aircraft; operator equipment, tools, materials, buildings, vehicles, computers, etc.).
- *Environment (E):* the context in which humans operate the system (e.g. cabin/cockpit temperature, air pressure, humidity, noise, vibration and ambient light levels, weather conditions, visibility, turbulence, etc.). This aspect was defined by the participants of the workshop.

To investigate the changes in interactions, and consequently, the transformation of skills, two workshops for the two potentially critical scenarios (startle effect and route re-planning) have been organized, with $n = 4$ participants involved in each session. Participants were, on the one hand, developers of the AI-based intelligent assistants to support single pilots in the future in cases of startling effect and re-route planning. On the other hand, among the participants there were professional pilots of European commercial airlines. The duration of the workshops was 2.5 hours. To ensure that all the important inputs were registered, each session was managed by two facilitators, and key conversations were audio recorded.

The workshop sessions were built around the following two use cases (UC) of how the AI-based intelligent assistants aim at supporting pilots in the aforementioned situations:

- UC#1: The FOCUS ("Flight Operations Companion for Unexpected Situations") AI-based assistant aims to support pilots during startling and surprising events in the cockpit. These events sometimes provoke "freeze" reactions, delay in response time or inappropriate cockpit inputs and can lead to accidents. Startle refers to a stress response to a sudden intense stimulus, whereas surprise is a cognitive and emotional reaction that results from the mismatch between pilot's expectations and reality. As they have an interactive negative effect on performance, they may seriously impair a pilot's ability of troubleshooting and immediate procedural actions [14]. To tackle this, FOCUS aims at offering real-time assistance to commercial pilots, detecting startle events, helping them regain emotional stability and situation awareness. To facilitate the pilot's recovery from initial surprise, the intelligent assistant initiates a collaborative procedure, guiding them in regaining situational awareness and making the necessary decisions for a safe landing.
- UC#2: The intelligent assistant in this case aims at supporting pilots in route planning/replanning ("Flight deck route planning/replanning"). Replanned routes result from new constraints and different hazards, such as weather changes that prevent pilots from landing at their originally targeted airport. Re-planning a route, although based on previously defined alternative routes, requires pilots to adapt to changing circumstances and make decisions in a timely and effective manner. The intelligent assistant developed in UC#2 supports pilots during the flight by translating pilots' high-level intentions into technical flight parameters. As an example, the case of a flight from Bordeaux to Munich was presented, which was delayed by 2 hours. Upon arrival above Lyon, the snowstorm that was forecast turns out to be more severe than anticipated and all the airports in Northeast Europe begin to close. A new route is needed. Options include continuing to Munich, landing in Zurich but unable to reach Munich, or landing in Lyon with a subsequent flight to Munich. Returning to Bordeaux is also feasible. The intelligent assistant compares options, consults services, and prioritizes based on the pilot's intentions (e.g. which criterion to prioritize among airline profitability, pilot workload, passengers' comfort), ensuring effective decision-making.

Participants were first asked to identify today's elements of interactions, then they were asked to perform the same procedure in the same scenario, but referring to 2035, once the intelligent assistant is in operation. Based on the two SHELL boards, a gap analysis was performed, identifying areas of major changes in interactions in the future. Having these major changes in mind, a set of new skills that would be required by pilots to successfully engage in those future interactions was defined.

3.3 Semi-Structured Interview on Future Training

As the last step, a semi-structured interview with one flight instructor from a commercial airline was conducted to elaborate on the key aspects of the workshop results, as well as to reflect on the required modifications in training content and format, in order to align with the envisaged future changes. The interview session was built around the following main questions:

- Having a vision of how the tasks related to this role will change by 2035, how do you envision key skills and competencies to change accordingly?
- What kind of new skills are likely to emerge?
- What kind of skills are likely to become less relevant?
- How will the existing skills be modified in terms of meaning/content (e.g. communication skills - with human/with AI)?
- How do you think current training should be changed to cover this modified set of skills and competencies?

Finally, combining the results of the interview with the outcomes of the previous steps, recommendations on the targets, the content and the format of future training were formulated.

4 Results

4.1 Commercial Air Transport Human-AI Teaming Roadmap: From Today to 2050

By 2050, AI might gradually become a full-fledged team member in the cockpit, ops rooms and airports. Based on the results of the workshop series conducted with subject matter experts in Step 1, the following overarching trends are envisaged as most probable from today to 2050, forming a high-level roadmap for future human roles in aviation as a response to the introduction of AI into operations.

The steps outlined below are coherent with EASA and SESAR AI Roadmaps [15, 16]. All the participants were familiar with these roadmaps; therefore the main key aspects were considered into the HAIKU roadmap. The major difference lies in the focus, with HAIKU roadmap concentrating uniquely on the human perspective on technological changes, on the impact on human skills and competencies.

Between 2025 and 2030. This timeframe is characterized by increased and heterogeneous air traffic managed in segregated airspaces [2]. AI is expected to start supporting Commercial Air Transport operations by assisting humans in identifying optimal solutions and priorities (e.g. in case of medical emergencies on board the aircraft). Especially in the cockpit, a few initial simple and repetitive tasks (e.g. frequency management and taxiing) may be delegated to AI systems. The human role is not expected to change much from now until 2030. In fact, human operators are expected to still be in charge of the majority of tasks, problem solving and decision making. However, these 5 years are expected to be key to:

- Start building a strong relationship of trust between humans and AI, a critical success factor to allow the aviation industry to be open and welcome AI into commercial air operations.
- Re-design roles and job profiles for the forthcoming years according to the technological evolution in the sector, to ensure having the right people, well-trained and equipped, ready to safely and securely operate in the following years.

In the SESAR Roadmap, this corresponds to automation Level 1, and the same applies for EASA's Roadmap.

Between 2030 and 2035. The timeframe is envisaged to be a critical transitional phase characterized by higher operational complexity (still managed by segregation), increased role of AI systems, and consequent regulatory changes. Humans are expected to be key to successfully leading and achieving this transition phase. Some existing roles may be revised, and new temporary ones could be introduced, with a view to shifting human values and contributions from operational positions to more managerial ones.

During these 5 years, AI is expected to assist humans in workload management and be in charge of performing the majority of repetitive tasks (e.g. voice communication) as well as some initial complex tasks for which a transition by segregation is foreseen (e.g. starting from off-peak and night-time slots). Humans are envisaged to remain responsible for the majority of complex tasks, problem solving and decision making, while starting to team up with AI.

The quality of the human-AI interactions may be a crucial success factor in this time frame. Indeed, this would be one of the key elements enabling the creation of an effective learning loop between humans and AI. Furthermore, when delegating tasks to AI, preventing degradation skills will be a must to maintain high safety standards.

The following 5 years are likely to be characterised by the consolidation of important changes from three areas:

- Technological, with the accomplishment of the digitisation process which opens the door to more and more AI applications;
- Operational, with the activation of the shift from segregated to integrated airspace;
- Human, with important changes in roles and responsibilities, and the introduction of new ones.

In the SESAR Roadmap, this corresponds to automation Levels 2 and 3, while in the EASA Roadmap it is Level 2.

Between 2035 and 2040. Within this timeframe, nominal situations are expected to be managed by technological and AI-based systems which will also alert humans to potential risky situations and hazards. AI would also be in charge of coordinating the integration of airspaces as well as harmonizing and standardizing systems across international actors. Human operators are expected to monitor and intervene in case of non-nominal situations.

Ensuring and sustaining human situational awareness, vigilance and system knowledge is expected to be the key challenge for this time frame.

The envisioned concept reaches Level 4 in SESAR Roadmap, and Level 3 for EASA the EASA Roadmap.

Between 2040 and 2050. A progressive strengthening of the relationship between humans and AI is expected to characterize the 2040–2050 decade. AI may extend its contribution to non-nominal situations, providing advice and directly intervening in case of imminent risks. Humans are expected to mostly intervene, teaming up with AI, in case of non-nominal situations.

Societal trust and acceptance may be the major challenge during the 40s.

Looking at the whole picture, ensuring desirability of the human role and retaining aviation job attractiveness and people's motivation are expected to be the major challenges for the industry. People may be willing and happy to welcome AI in operations and teaming up with it, but only if important benefits are perceived not only from the economical and operational perspectives, but also from the safety and human ones.

Similarly, to the previous time frame, this concept reaches Level 4 in SESAR Roadmap, and Level 3 for EASA the EASA Roadmap.

4.2 The Evolution of Pilots' Role Towards 2050

The 2050 reference scenario for Flight Operations foresees Single Pilot Operations (SPO) for both long-haul commercial and cargo flights, considering single pilots in the cockpit supported by on-board, AI-based and intelligent assistants and automation, which would take care of the majority of the Pilot Flying and Pilot Monitoring tasks in nominal operations [17]. In view of this technological and operational trend, during the 2040s the Pilot Flying is projected to progressively absorb some of the Pilot Monitoring tasks.

The Pilot Flying, when in a Single Pilot setting, is expected to assume a more supervisory role during nominal operations, while his/her contribution and competencies would be key in case of non-nominal and emergency situations. In these cases, s/he is expected to be supported by on-board AI systems as well as by remote human assistants. This new role, named Flight Ops Ground Monitor, can be considered as an example of the evolution of Pilot Monitoring. It is projected to support SPO from the ground, monitoring multiple flights at the same time and providing support when Single Pilots need assistance. In case of Single Pilot incapacitation, on-board autonomous landing systems would intervene.

4.3 Who to Train: A Comparison of Pilots' Personality Traits Today and in the Future

Pilots' Personality Traits Today. When it comes to assessing personality traits in aviation, the majority of studies show that pilots, compared to the general population, score lower on Neuroticism, indicating a profile with more balance and emotional stability. This could be due to the need to be less reactive to stress in an industry which is by nature a high stake/high stress environment. With respect to Extraversion, empirical data suggests that the pilot population has higher levels of extraversion compared to the general population. Sociability is typically an important characteristic in commercial aviation, where pilots perform their tasks in a team context. Apart from communicating over the radio, they need to socialize with their fellow pilots and cabin crew (for passenger aircraft) with whom they can be confined for several hours during operations. Openness to experience is a personality trait that does not seem to differentiate between pilots and general population, as both tend to score equivalent on this scale. A possible explanation lies in the nature of the aviation industry: as the job of pilots is highly procedural, there may be less need for a pilot to be creative, adaptive, and receptive to changes. With respect to Agreeableness, pilots in general tend to be less agreeable than the general population, however, in the case of commercial pilots, results are mixed (compared to military pilots and pilots-in-training). This again might result from their higher need to effectively work in a team context where the ability to build trust quickly in a constantly changing crew is crucial. In the case of Conscientiousness, the pilot population appears to trend somewhat higher than the general population, however, this tends to be less of a pattern in the case of pilots-in-training, presumably due to their age, compared to professional pilots in commercial aviation or in the military [11]. While in comparison with professional pilots, pilots-in-training seemed to score somewhat lower on Conscientiousness, a meta-analysis found this personality trait to be a significant positive predictor of training success, along with low levels of Neuroticism. In other words, student pilots, reporting high levels of conscientiousness and low levels of neuroticism appeared to have slightly better chances of passing their flight training successfully [10].

In summary, today's operational context in aviation may require pilots to be emotionally stable, extroverted, agreeable, and conscientious with less importance given to being open to experience.

Pilots' Personality Traits in the Future. Long-term changes in the aviation industry are envisaged to bring significant changes in pilots' job context in terms of who they will team up with in the cockpit. pilots are foreseen to be gradually accompanied by AI, and this is a change that may redefine the typical personality traits of future pilots. The following results on future personality traits are based on the workshops conducted in Step2, and where needed, they are supported by literature:

One important aspect of this anticipated change is related to the social isolation of future pilots [17]. Pilots are expected to have significantly fewer human interactions, exposing them to potential boredom and loneliness in the cockpit. The reduced number of social interactions may favor those who need less external and social stimulus, feel comfortable working alone and may be more indifferent to their direct social environment. In addition, being isolated in the cockpit may require future pilots to be even more stable emotionally, as direct social support in stress management will be reduced and pilots may need to have an even better ability to self-regulate their own emotions and anxiety. Another important aspect of future change will be pilots' willingness and efficiency to team up with AI. General attitudes towards the use of AI may have a significant impact on the skilling, up-skilling and reskilling of professionals in the aviation industry. Therefore, it may be worthwhile to further investigate whether certain personality traits have the potential to predict these attitudes. As individuals who score high on Openness to experience tend to be more innovative and open to new experiences, pilots with higher scores on this scale may exhibit more positive attitudes and acceptance towards teaming up with AI and switching to new technologies, along with a willingness to enroll in new training that these changes require [18]. Similarly, it might be reasonable to think that a higher level of Agreeableness could be linked to more positive attitudes towards the acceptance of AI. As empirical data shows, individuals who score higher on Agreeableness tend to be less skeptical and more tolerant towards the negative aspects of AI [19].

All in all, envisaged changes in future operational context may require future pilots to possess a slightly different personality profile compared to the traits they tend to have today. In the future, an even higher emotional stability and lower level of Extraversion may be required by pilots to be able to cope with reduced human interactions and social isolation, while a higher level of Openness to experience and Agreeableness may be needed to develop positive attitudes towards the use of AI that might affect success in skilling, up-skilling and reskilling.

Personality assessment will most probably continue to play a vital role when it comes to selecting pilots. Considering the high cost of dropouts and substandard performance, a valid and meticulously designed testing of personality traits that takes major future changes into consideration may be vital.

A Revision of Recruitment Strategy. An inevitable supplemental process to reconsider is the recruitment of future pilots to be trained. The anticipated changes in future aviation will certainly require revision on to whom, through which channels and how the future role of pilots should be promoted in order to ensure a sufficient pool of applicants in terms of both quantity and quality. as the envisaged future work environment might be even more difficult to fully imagine for applicants with no real experience in the cockpit, recruitment processes should consider techniques that offer a comprehensive introduction to this future role, with detailed explanations on the tasks, as well as the pros and cons related to the role. one recruitment technique to recommend based on its potential to provide a 360-degree picture on jobs could be a Realistic Job Preview (RJP). This recruitment technique is often associated with the implicit process of self-selection, as it offers a realistic view on the job, thus reducing the probability of mismatch between applicants' competences & needs and the characteristics of the job. Formats May Include Brochures, Testimonial Videos of Pilots, Interactive Digital Work Stimulations, Videos, Etc. While There is a reasonable motivation to attract top-level candidates for training, offering a realistic (not sugar-coated), tangible picture of what a role will look like would support candidates in developing realistic expectations towards their job and career path [20]. To mitigate potential shortcomings on the number of future applicants, the aviation industry should prepare a proactive strategy to anticipate and understand the needs of future generations related to their job and career path as well as to build an action plan on how these needs can be fulfilled in the envisaged, AI-based work environment. The successful and realistic identification of what the future role of pilots requires and what it has to offer would contribute to a better match of candidates' profile and job requirements, thus keeping potential dropouts at the lowest possible level.

4.4 What to Train: Transformation of Pilots' Skills in the Future

Use Case #1: Flight Deck Startle Response – Changes in Interactions Based on the SHELL Model

Liveware. In the future of reference, a "single pilot operation" (SPO) configuration is envisaged, resulting in the pilot flying being in control of the aircraft. Although less resources would be spent on human coordination and communication, pilots would also lose the monitoring ensured by their co-pilot. Co-pilot's cross checking is an important means to ensure that situational awareness is correctly built, system data and parameters are correctly interpreted, and crew members are on the same page during flights. The anticipated lack of spontaneous communication and the non-verbal communication channel is an important related challenge (although non-verbal communication will partly be replaced by biophysical data registered by the IA). Spontaneous, oral communication is an important means of reducing stress and providing social and emotional support under stress, as well as overcoming a potential startle effect. In addition, social isolation itself is a topic to be addressed when identifying future challenges related to SPO configuration. Pilots reportedly need to be able to talk to someone during flights, for which a Generative pre-trained Transformer (GPT) chatbot might be able to provide an alternative solution in the future. Furthermore, oral communication is found to be an important need of pilots in re-building their situational awareness, after a startle effect has taken place. Trust issues related to accepting the support of an AI-based assistant is another challenge to consider. Trust must be neither too high, to avoid overreliance, nor too low, to avoid an increased workload due to multiple evaluations of the AI outcomes. Related to that, pilots in the future might need to learn additional stress management skills (e.g. biofeedback techniques, breathing and relaxation techniques, mindfulness, etc.) in order to successfully self-regulate their own emotions during flights. Detailed technical knowledge on how the AI-based IA supports pilots during flight might also be important in order to address the issues related to trusting the new system. Finally, communication and coordination skills will most probably need to be modified or extended to include ways of effective collaboration with an AI-based teammate. More specifically, a new framework and systematic procedure is needed to support pilots in deciding when and how to call their AI-based teammate into action, what type of information or message to convey to their AI-based teammate and to their human co-actors (cabin crew, ground operation, etc.) and how to build a shared understanding of the crew as a whole.

Software. As human teammates are envisaged to be absent from the cockpit in the future, pilots' decision making, adherence to procedures and the correct execution of these procedures will not be discussed and cross-checked by a team of humans who share the same physical location. Future single pilots under high stress may develop a so-called tunnel-vision, focusing on a limited number of parameters in the cockpit and/or by looking for parameters which reinforce their line of thinking. therefore, they may need to develop enhanced skills in self-critical thinking and the ability to question themselves before making decision. The envisaged human-AI teaming in the future will also require the modification of the CRM procedures, to describe ways of collaboration with the AI teammate.

Hardware. During surprise and startle events, IA is expected to activate itself by certain biophysical parameters (e.g. gaze behaviour, heart rate, etc.) which indicate that the pilot is under startle. Though this can be controlled manually, the interaction between the two teammates is envisaged to be initiated by the IA, leaving the pilot in a more passive and less spontaneous role within the communication loop. To recover from startle, pilots will be expected to master self-relaxation techniques. To regain situational awareness, pilots will need to look at certain key parameters on the cockpit display, guided by signals. if the pilot is looking at these key parameters long enough, the IA will turn itself off, assuming that the pilot has regained situational awareness. Guiding signals on the display might be an efficient way to focus a pilot's attention in case of startle but may also potentially lead to information overload in a cognitive state in which pilots are already struggling to interpret cues from the environment. Furthermore, the application of auditory inputs (voice instructions) besides visual cues might decrease the chance of information overload, by dividing information across modalities. In addition, staring at the displays for an extended period of time does not guarantee enhanced situational awareness if these pieces of information are not actively elaborated ("look but not see" effect). Future knowledge of procedures and checklists to actively assess one's level of situational awareness may be an important additional support in regaining situation awareness during stressful events.

Use Case #2: Flight Deck Route Replanning – Changes in Interactions Based on the SHELL Model

Liveware. In the future of reference, a "single pilot in cruise" (SPIC) configuration is envisaged: one pilot in command during the cruising phase while the second can rest and then take over, but both pilots are present for the preparation, taxiing, take-off, descent and landing phases [21]. Pilots flying will have an advanced support system in making their decision about alternative airports. The intelligent assistant is anticipated to integrate key technical parameters, preferences of different actors and suggest solutions accordingly. While pilots today are trained to integrate parameters from multiple sources and decide based on them, decisions on alternative routes in the future are expected to be based on one single source of information: the intelligent assistant. Therefore, more critical thinking, the ability to question the system and advanced theoretical knowledge about human decision making may be needed in the future. Relying on AI in decision making will also require the ability to understand and trust the system. In addition, pilots in this future context will be required to self-assess their own cognitive comfort, including how comfortable they are with the suggestion of the intelligent assistant. The introduction of AI is also anticipated to impact on the team dynamics of the two pilots. As the intelligent assistant is expected to assist the pilot flying in the decision making, a challenging question will be when to call the other pilot into action, and how to brief them. The introduction of AI may result in a difference in how pilots resting rely on information coming from the pilot flying versus the information coming from the intelligent assistant.

Software & Hardware. In the anticipated future of reference, the intelligent assistant is expected to assist in prioritizing intentions and taking over the procedure of performance calculation. Pilots, as a result, will be required to learn new procedures involving intelligent assistant. As decision making is supposed to be based on one source of information, trust or overreliance in the system will be an important factor to consider. Even if suggestions are proposed by the intelligent assistant, pilots need to remain part of the process. This way, they will be able to actively and critically evaluate these alternatives as well as to maintain situational awareness, anticipate future steps ("being one step ahead of their aircraft") and take over control from the intelligent assistant on the procedure of performance calculation, whenever necessary.

A New Training Perspective: The AI-CRM. Traditional Crew Resource Management (CRM) has revolutionised cockpit safety by emphasising communication, teamwork, and decision-making skills. Integrating AI assistants as full-fledged "teammates" within an AI-CRM framework might present a promising next step in this evolution. Future changes in the crew composition, more specifically the envisaged future human-AI teams [2], will require an update of existing CRM, which should also be captured in the pilots' competency model. Indeed, the model should evolve according, considering the impact on the teamwork area and perhaps accommodating this new type of collaboration as a new competency.

Combining these assumptions with the findings presented above, we argue that the most appropriate training pathway to follow towards 2035 could be a CRM update, considering AI as an effective operative member of the aircrew. By treating AI assistants as teammates, not merely as decision aids, this framework fosters a deeper collaboration, which is continuously leveraging on AI's strengths in data analysis and risk assessment while ensuring that human judgement and skills remain central.

Therefore, considering the CRM Training Table of the EASA Regulation 1178/2011, we defined the following areas as the backbones of a potential future AI-based crew resource management:

- *Stress & Workload Management:* while AI could take on tedious tasks, thus reducing overall workload, managing trust dynamics and potential over-reliance on automation would become crucial. CRM training would need to address concerns about automation bias and equip pilots to effectively delegate and monitor AI performance, potentially mitigating new sources of stress. Integrating AI adds another layer of complexity to the cockpit environment. Pilots might experience stress by managing the AI system, understanding its outputs, and ensuring its proper functioning, while feeling overwhelmed when facing critical situations. In particular, for SPOs, future trainings should provide advanced skills of emotion regulation techniques, a deeper and more detailed understanding of both psychological and physiological aspects of stress, such as the impact on situational awareness (i.e., startle effect; tunnel-vision, losing chance to anticipate future steps), and how to act on them both with short- and long-term strategies, and with an advanced skill-set to assess one's cognitive, physiological and emotional state during flight.
- *Situational Awareness:* if pilots become overly reliant on AI for information processing and decision support, they might lose critical situational awareness skills developed through traditional CRM training failing in perceiving all the necessary aspects of the surrounding environment (breakdown in step 1 – perception), without exploring them actively, failing in understanding them (step 2 – comprehension), or failing in projecting them into the future (step 3) [22], bringing to agreeing with incorrect recommendations [23], changing their mind to match AI recommendations [24], or weighting too much the AI recommendation [25]. The CRM of the future should therefore cope with this challenge by training pilots on how to collaborate

with AI on data processing to significantly enhance situational awareness by providing comprehensive analysis and real-time updates. Regarding situational awareness, CRM of the future should address the skill of gaining and re-gaining control and information quickly in nominal operations, after sleeping and in startle events. From a technical perspective, the interaction with explainable AI-based IAs will be a key factor in enabling pilots to recover from a mismatch between what is expected and what is experienced (Situational Awareness first level - Perception) and to anticipate future steps (Situational Awareness third level - Projection to future) [22].

- *Communication & Teamwork*: clear and concise communication would remain fundamental, but the focus might shift towards effectively conveying human intent and goals to the AI teammate, and vice versa. Sperber & Wilson [26], following the studies of Grice [27], define communication as the expression and recognition of intentions. While AI can process and generate information efficiently, its lack of human-like expressiveness can hinder communication flow. Therefore, differences in communication styles and information processing between humans and AI could lead to misunderstandings. Pilots and crew might misinterpret AI outputs or struggle to convey their intent and goals effectively, potentially hindering teamwork and decision-making. CRM training would need to address potential communication barriers and communication hazards due to differing processing styles and ensure that all team members (human and AI) have a shared mental model. Therefore, communication with AI could be addressed by deepening the concepts of on-demand communication (i.e., non-spontaneous), without clues usually used by humans to increase consistency in communications (i.e., absence of non-verbal modalities).

- *Leadership & Control over automation*: excessive trust in AI recommendations could lead to complacency and reduce the pilot's ability to make independent decisions, thus potentially creating dangerous situations when manual intervention is needed. Moreover, managing a crew with humans (e.g. cabin crew, ground operation) and AI-based actors, adjusting communication practices, content and style to the needs of the different actors may be challenging. The CRM should therefore address these challenges, aiming to develop a leadership model that encompasses the management of human-AI teams, fosters trust, and ensures clear communication and delegation of tasks and considers both a human communication model and a data-driven approach. To foster effective control over automation, deep knowledge of both generic motoric skills to prevent skill loss (e.g. eye-hand coordination), transversally applicable and technical skills to understand AI behavior will be required. Training these skills will increase the human ability to take control whenever needed.

- *Problem Solving & Decision Making*: implementing AI as a teammate in an air crew may be helpful to pilots in various aspects: first, it provides support in analyzing vast amounts of data and presents pilots with insights and recommendations on how to enhance human capabilities. It also allows pilots to free up cognitive resources by taking over tedious tasks. Finally, it could play a key role in overcoming human biases such as overconfidence and anchoring, by presenting different perspectives. At the same time, blind reliance on AI recommendations can lead to automation bias, where pilots neglect crucial information, and if AI decision-making lacks transparency or explanation. This overreliance may result in a "black box" effect, hindering trust and making it difficult for pilots to critically evaluate recommendations and potentially leading to flawed decisions. Finally, complex ethical issues may arise in flight decision making. Pilots need frameworks and support to navigate these situations with responsible and transparent decision-making, even when they are influenced by AI. A specific recurrent training aiming to enhance basic digital literacy of pilots could also support the development of a decision-making process which considers the different AI communication and processing style, limiting biases such as data misinterpretation or failures in coordination between humans and AI. To foster an effective future decision-making, other skills such as critical thinking will need to be enhanced to mitigate false positive and false negative solutions provided by the AI-based assistant, having the right situational awareness to correctly question the received support.

4.5 How to Train: Recommendations for Future Training and Knowledge Sharing

In addition to the anticipated changes in what skills and knowledge will be crucial to address during training, another important question will be how to teach them in the future. The format of training may have a key impact on whether and how effectively these new skills are acquired and applied in real-life situations. Continuous technological developments in the aviation sector require an increasing number of new technical skills, resulting in an education path for pilots that is mostly based on formal training. On the other hand, the subjective experiences, know-how, perceptions, and attitudes of professional pilots represent an important and valuable form of knowledge. As required technical skills and procedures might slightly differ among airlines, the related know-how and experiences of pilots also represent a collection of tacit knowledge being unique to each airline. If collected and shared effectively, this knowledge could be an important additional asset in training future pilots as well as overcoming the initial difficulties of teaming up with AI.

Nonaka and Takeuchi's "SECI" model [28] of knowledge management represents a practical approach to how knowledge within a company is created and re-created, as different forms of explicit and tacit knowledge are continuously transforming into one another. According to the model, the four forms of knowledge creation are:

- *Socialization* (tacit to tacit): a form of knowledge sharing that is based on physical proximity. During socialization, knowledge is shared and captured by direct observation, imitation and/or practice through apprenticeship.
- *Externalization* (tacit to explicit): the other form of knowledge sharing, during which tacit knowledge becomes explicit, crystallized, and shared with others, thus becoming the basis of new knowledge. This way, personal tacit knowledge becomes useful for others in an explicit, understandable, and interpretable form (e.g. concepts, documents, images).
- *Combination* (explicit to explicit): it involves the organization and integration of knowledge, whereby different forms of explicit knowledge are merged, and finally a new form of explicit knowledge is created. Examples of combinations involve writing a report or building a prototype.

- *Internalization* (explicit to tacit): the receiving and application of explicit knowledge by an individual. Explicit knowledge becomes part of an individual's knowledge base, typically by the act of learning-by-doing.

As was highlighted during the semi-structured interview, pilots-in-training today acquire knowledge mostly through the process of internalization and socialization. By acquiring theoretical knowledge on aviation and by practicing technical and non-technical skills on a simulator (learning-by-doing) they internalize explicit knowledge that is required to become a pilot. This internalized knowledge is then expanded and fine-grained by observing the other pilot during flights, in other words, a form of socialization takes place. Externalization as a knowledge sharing form, however, is often present in a less formal and therefore ad-hoc form, resulting in valuable subjective experiences and best practices remaining unshared.

On the other hand, unexpected events or other stressful, high workload situations often provoke intensive subjective feelings and emotions, like frustration, insecurity, lack of control or even fear. These subjective experiences may activate very diverse individual reactions, from which some prove to be successful, thus turning into a recurrent coping skill, in other words, the best practice of the individual. These subjective feelings and related coping mechanisms are, however, prone to remain unshared, even though they could be important knowledge accumulated and shared within the company. This is mostly due to the prevailing masculine organizational culture within aviation [29] where - as pinpointed during the semi-structured interview - talking openly about emotions and personal weaknesses is still a challenging area. A potential mitigation strategy could be the application of formally organized focus group sessions, facilitated by psychologists. These sessions would provide an opportunity to share individual best practices and make them explicit. Based on that, the collection, organization and sharing of this knowledge would ensure that it becomes part of the knowledge management spiral, and thus, part of the organization's collective knowledge. The presence of a facilitator, on the other hand, would give a guarantee that a psychologically safe atmosphere is provided for pilots to talk about their subjective experiences openly and freely.

Anticipated changes in the future related to AI will also result in a major transformation of airlines' existing knowledge base. A considerable amount of explicit and tacit knowledge will likely become outdated and irrelevant, as technology and the related procedures, regulations and policies will transform radically. On the other hand, new forms of explicit knowledge will be required, and along with that, a remarkable amount of new know-how will be accumulated in the form of tacit knowledge. This knowledge, if shared and organized efficiently, could be channeled into the future training of pilots, thus accelerating successful human-AI teaming. Organizations in the aviation sector are therefore highly encouraged to build a proactive strategy on how to consciously manage organizational knowledge in the future, when AI will become an important actor in the cockpit. One challenging aspect of this transformation would be to discover how an AI teammate could be involved in the organization's knowledge management spiral. A potential area in which AI could play a key role in the future is the process of Combination, during which AI-teammates would create new forms of explicit knowledge by merging different sources of already existing explicit knowledge. AI will most likely also be crucial in the storage, organization and provision of explicit knowledge when needed in the cockpit.

Changes in the future do not only call for new forms of training among pilots: flight instructors are also expected to be up-skilled to develop new knowledge and a detailed understanding of the systems on which they train their students, as well as the related technical and non-technical skills. In addition, flight instructors in the future will likely face the challenge of the different training requirements related to the skilling and reskilling of pilots. In other words, a detailed understanding will be needed on what and how to train students with no previous knowledge in aviation and professional pilots who need to overwrite already existing knowledge. Moreover, some instructors may be expected to experience difficulties in training due to potential negative attitudes or initial resistance towards learning and re-learning a system where AI acts as full-fledged teammate in the cockpit. Therefore, it could be important that flight instructors receive regular feedback and supervision from several different professionals (flight instructors, psychologists, pedagogues) on the way they train in forms of "train the trainer" sessions. This guided feedback would support them in the future to maximize the effectiveness of training, as well as enable them to provide personalized forms of education to students, be they new cadets or re-skilled professional pilots.

5 Conclusions

Undoubtedly, new technologies and, more specifically, AI are powerful means to support aviation operators, allowing the industry to safely and effectively face the envisaged rise in traffic complexity, due to increased demand and heterogeneity in traffic. However, technological evolution is expected to significantly change the human role. AI may gradually absorb human tasks, probably leading to a significant change in the workforce landscape in the next 30 years. In fact, some roles are expected to change. others to become obsolete and new roles may be introduced.

AI, as a promising future direction in aviation, is undoubtedly expected to require a novel approach in how humans operate successfully within this industry. In addition to being a supporting tool for pilots in finding optimal solutions or priorities, future IAs are also envisaged as full-fledged, active, and key actors in the cockpit. Therefore, to anticipate the requirements and prepare for a potential future where humans team up with AI is crucial.

This process should start with systematically revising recruitment strategies and the key principles based on which future pilots are selected for training. The radical change in the working environment may result in current recruitment trends becoming outdated. As new generations will gradually enter the aviation industry, understanding their career needs and matching them with what the envisaged future work environment has to offer will become a priority in human resource management.

Similarly, personal characteristics that are likely to predict a high job performance today may change consistently, as future pilots will most likely require a personality profile with more openness and trust to collaborate with new technologies and less need for social stimulation and human interactions. A potential revision of the personality profile of future pilots could save important resources for companies in terms of time and costs, as the successful selection of pilots may minimize the risk of dropouts and attrition in later career stages.

The required technical and non-technical skills to become a pilot will need to be modified and extended by the aspects of collaboration with an AI-based teammate. By developing a detailed understanding of future skills and by breaking them down into tangible behavioral indicators would not only support smooth human-machine interaction, but they would also serve as new anchors of selection and performance appraisal thus ensuring a valid process of aptitude testing.

Finally, the way this modified skill set will be trained seems to be another interesting area to revolutionize in the future. As the transformation of the work environment, the ways of working as well as the requirements on technical and non-technical skills will necessarily result in the accumulation of new explicit knowledge and implicit know-how, defining effective ways of knowledge management and training formats in which these new knowledge and know-how can be successfully acquired will be a key in maintaining human performance and aviation safety.

Acknowledgments. This publication is based on work performed in the HAIKU Project (Human AI teaming Knowledge and Understanding for aviation safety) which has received funding from the European Union's Horizon Europe research and innovation program, under Grant Agreement n.101075332. Any dissemination reflects the authors' view only and the European Commission is not responsible for any use that may be made of information it contains.

Disclosure of Interests. The authors have no competing interests to declare that are relevant to the content of this article.

References

1. Cavagnetto, N., Golfetti, A., Napoletano, L., Tomasello, P., Drogoul, F.: To innovate is clever, to anticipate is smart: towards new skills in Air Transport. In: 34th Conference of the European Association for Aviation Psychology. Transportation research Procedia, vol. 66, pp. 156–166 (2022)
2. HAIKU D2.1: Vision and Scenarios (2023)
3. Robinson, J.: Future subjunctive: backcasting as social learning. Futures **35**, 839–856 (2003). https://doi.org/10.1016/S0016-3287(03)00039-9
4. Holmberg, J., Robèrt, K.-H.: Backcasting - a framework for strategic planning. Int J Sust Dev World **7**, 291–308 (2000). https://doi.org/10.1080/13504500009470049
5. Armstrong, J.S. (ed.): Principles of Forecasting: A Handbook for Researchers and Practitioners. Springer, US (2001)
6. Lotus Blossom in Mitre Ideation Toolkit. https://itk.mitre.org/toolkit-tools/lotus-blossom/
7. McCrae, R.R.: The five-factor model of personality traits: consensus and controversy. In: Corr, P.J., Matthews, G. (Eds.) The Cambridge Handbook of Personality Psychology, pp. 148–161. University Press, Cambridge (2009). https://doi.org/10.1017/CBO9780511596544.012
8. Fitzgibbons, A., Davis, D., Schutte, P.C.: Pilot personality profile using the NEO-PI-R (No. NASA/TM-2004-213237) (2024)
9. Ganesh, A., Joseph, C.: Personality studies in aircrew: an overview. Ind. J. Aerosp. Med. **49**(1), 54–62 (2005)

10. Breuer, S., Ortner, T.M., Gruber, F.M., Hofstetter, D., Scherndl, T.: Aviation and personality: Do measures of personality predict pilot training success? updated meta-analyses. Personal. Ind. Diff. **202**, Article 111918 (2023) https://doi.org/10.1016/j.paid.2022.111918
11. Chaparro, M., Carroll, M.B., Malmquist, S.: Personality trends in the pilot population. Coll. Aviat. Rev. Int. **38**(2) (2020). https://doi.org/10.22488/OKSTATE.20.100219
12. Edwards, E.: Man and machine: systems for safety. In: Proceedings of British Airline Pilots Association, London, pp. 21–36 (1972)
13. Hawkins, F.H., Orlady, H.W.: Human Factors in Flight, Second ED. Aldershot, UK (1993)
14. Piras, M., Landman, A., Van Paassen, M.M., Stroosma, O.: Easy as ABC: a mnemonic procedure for managing startle and surprise. In: 22nd International Symposium on Aviation Psychology. Rochester (NY) (2023)
15. SESAR Master Plan (2025)
16. EASA Artificial Intelligence Roadmap 2.0 (2023)
17. HAIKU D8.1. Human Role in Future Aviation (2023)
18. Sindermann, C., et al.: Acceptance and fear of artificial intelligence: associations with personality in a german and a chinese sample. Discov. Psychol. **2**(8) (2022). https://doi.org/10.1007/s44202-022-00020-y
19. Kaya, F., Aydin, F., Schepman, A., Rodway, P., Yetişensoy, O., Kaya, M.D.: The roles of personality traits, AI anxiety, and demographic factors in attitudes toward artificial intelligence. Int. J. Hum.–Comput. Interact. **40**(2), 497–514 (2024). https://doi.org/10.1080/10447318.2022.2151730
20. Morgan, K.: Let's Get Real: The Value of Realistic Job Previews in Recruitment Strategy. CONCEPT **46** (2023)
21. HAIKU D3.1: Human-AI Teaming Framework and Design Document (2023)
22. Endsley, M.R.: Toward a theory of situation awareness in dynamic systems. Hum. Fact. **37**(1), 32–64 (1995). https://doi.org/10.1518/001872095779049543
23. Buçinca, Z., Malaya, M.B., Gajos, K.Z.: To trust or to think: cognitive forcing functions can reduce overreliance on AI in AI-assisted Decision-making. In: Proceedings of the ACM on Human-Computer Interaction, 5(CSCW1), pp. 188:1–188:21 (2021). https://doi.org/10.1145/3449287
24. Kim, A., Yang, M., Zhang, J.: When algorithms err: differential impact of early vs. late errors on users' reliance on algorithms (SSRN Scholarly Paper ID 3691575). Social Science Research Network (2020). https://doi.org/10.2139/ssrn.3691575
25. Logg, J.M., Minson, J.A., Moore, D.A.: Algorithm appreciation: people prefer algorithmic to human judgment. Organ. Behav. Hum. Decis. Process. **151**, 90–103 (2019). https://doi.org/10.1016/j.obhdp.2018.12.005
26. Sperber, D., Wilson, D.: Relevance: Communication and Cognition. Harvard University Press (1995)
27. Grice, H.P.: Logic and conversation. In: Studies in the Way of Words. Harvard University Press (1957)
28. Nonaka, I., Takeuchi, H.: The knowledge creating company: how Japanese companies create the dynamics of innovation. Oxford University Press, New York (1995). ISBN 978-0-19-509269-1
29. Gorlin, I., Bridges, D.: Aviation culture: a 'glass sky' for women pilots - literature review. Int. J. Aviat. Aeronaut. Aerosp. **8**(2) (2021). https://doi.org/10.15394/ijaaa.2021.1587

Agent Transparency and Human Performance in the Context of Autonomous Collision Avoidance

Koen van de Merwe[1,2]([⊠]) [iD], Salman Nazir[2] [iD], Steven Mallam[2,3] [iD],
and Øystein Engelhardtsen[1]

[1] DNV, Høvik, 1363 Oslo, Norway
koen.van.de.merwe@dnv.com
[2] University of South-Eastern Norway, 3184 Borre, Norway
[3] Memorial University of Newfoundland, St. John's 1C 5S7, Canada

Abstract. Transparency is a design principle that aims to enhance the understandability and predictability of autonomous systems by depicting their decisions, planned actions, and reasoning to end-users. With transparency, it is anticipated that the availability of this information, directly perceivable on an interface, expedites the information processing for the user and improves situation awareness. However, there is limited research regarding the applicability of transparency in the maritime domain. To address this, a project was initiated to investigate its effects on key human performance variables in the context of autonomous collision avoidance. The project's main results indicate that improvements in situation awareness can be expected when applying transparency principles, without increasing mental workload. However, future work should investigate transparency's applicability to time critical applications due to heightened information processing requirements with depicting the system's analytical processes. Still, the results from this research project showed that transparency is an important prerequisite for supervisory control towards safe and effective autonomous shipping.

Keywords: Transparency · Situation Awareness · Task Performance · Mental Workload · Autonomous Shipping

1 Introduction

In future maritime transport, Artificial Intelligence (AI)-enabled systems may allow ships to sail without direct human involvement [1, 2]. Considering the safety-critical nature of maritime navigation, this means that these systems need to demonstrate a high degree of reliability and robustness across a wide range of situations. However, given the limitations of such systems to operate in novel and complex situations, careful design, implementation, and operation is required when deploying these in real-world environments [3, 4]. Therefore, proposed autonomous ship concepts typically employ human operators to monitor, supervise, and potentially intervene to ensure required performance and safety levels are achieved [5, 6].

© The Author(s), under exclusive license to Springer Nature Switzerland AG 2026
D. Harris et al. (Eds.): HCII 2025, LNCS 16334, pp. 262–274, 2026.
https://doi.org/10.1007/978-3-032-12392-3_17

Decades of research have demonstrated that there are significant human performance challenges associated with assigning humans a supervisory role of highly automated systems [7, 8]. Since operators are tasked with supervising systems that make their own decisions and actions, they are typically removed from much of the system's information- and decision-making loop [9]. For AI-enabled systems, these concerns are exacerbated given their opaqueness, especially for systems using machine learning algorithms and neural networks [4, 10, 11]. Consequently, operators may find it challenging to evaluate, understand, and predict system behavior. In addition, passive information processing may lead to complacency [12, 13], biases in decision making [14], a reduced ability to detect critical information [7], an over- or underreliance on the system [15], and high workload when switching from supervised- to manual control [16]. As a result, their capability to intervene is affected [17].

In sum, these issues culminate to the "automation conundrum", which states that "the more automation is added to a system, and the more reliable and robust that automation is, the less likely that human operators overseeing the automation will be aware of critical information and able to take over manual control when needed" [7, p. 8]. This conundrum is primarily the result of the supervisor's reduced ability to build and maintain adequate Situation Awareness (SA). SA is defined here has "the perception of the elements in the environment within a volume of time and space, the comprehension of their meaning, and the projection of their status in the near future" [18]. Because supervisors are less involved in the system's information processing loop, they are reduced in their ability to understand "what is going on" and therefore may find it difficult to make decisions regarding the system's performance and when to potentially intervene [9]. However, recent research has suggested that by disclosing the system's decisions, planned actions, and internal reasoning to the operator, i.e., by making the system "transparent", SA of the system may be supported and some of these challenges may be alleviated [19, 20].

In this context, "transparency" implies making apparent what "an intelligent agent" [21], or "the automation" [22], is currently doing, but also why it is doing it, and what it will do next [7]. This way, the agent's understandability and predictability can be enhanced for its supervisor. However, considering the novelty of the application of AI-enabled systems in safety-critical domains, there is limited experience with the effect of transparency in these settings. In other words, few studies have addressed transparency in safety-critical settings such as the maritime domain. Considering the developments towards autonomy in this domain, a research project was initiated to explore the application of transparency and address how agent transparency can support human performance in supervisory control. As such, this paper aims to provide a summary of the research activities as documented in [23], including an outlook for further work.

2 Methods

This project applied a mix of quantitative and qualitative methods. First, a Systematic Literature Review (SLR) was performed, applying the Preferred Reporting items for Systematic review and Meta-Analysis method (PRISMA) [24]. 17 peer-reviewed articles were analyzed addressing the relationship between transparency and key human factors variables: SA, mental workload, and task performance [25]. Second, a Goal-Directed Task Analysis (GDTA) [26] was performed with input from in-situ observations, -interviews onboard passenger ferries with 11 licensed navigators, and a detailed study of the collision regulations (COLREGs) [27, 28]. Third, a model for human information processing, as developed by Parasuraman, Sheridan, and Wickens [22], provided the basis for a transparency model [29]. Fourth, realistic traffic situations and Human Machine Interfaces were developed based on an iterative design process and workshops with 5 navigators [30]. Finally, a controlled experiment was performed with 34 licensed navigators, assessing the effects of levels of transparency on SA, mental workload, and task performance [31, 32].

3 Results

3.1 Systematic Literature Review

Out of a sample of 1714 potential records, 17 studied were found eligible for detailed analysis. The SLR found that experimental studies on transparency typically employed three human-automation interaction types: responding to agent-generated proposals, supervisory control of agents, and monitoring only [25]. Overall, there was a trend in the data pointing towards a beneficial effect of transparency. Specifically, there was a promising effect of transparency on SA and task performance, without affecting mental workload, for studies where participants were responding to proposals or supervising automation. There were limited findings for our variables when humans were monitoring automation only. The study suggested that strategies to improve human performance, when interacting with intelligent agents, should focus on allowing humans to see into its information processing stages, considering the integration of information in existing Human Machine Interface (HMI) solutions (Fig. 1).

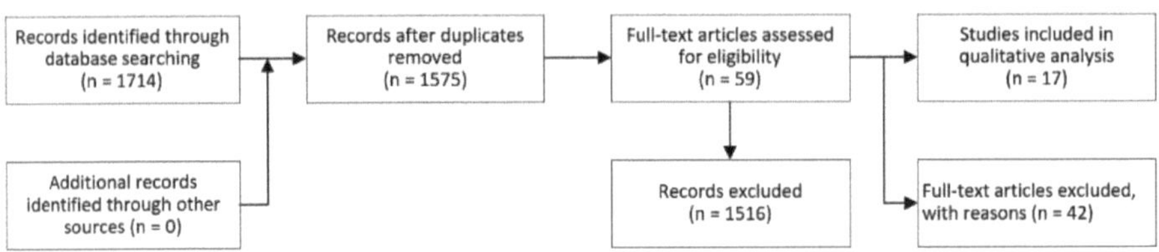

Fig. 1. Data reduction and selection for the SLR, adopted from [25].

3.2 Goal-Directed Task Analysis

The GDTA mapped and analyzed the goals, decisions, and cognitive tasks associated with conventional- and supervised collision and grounding avoidance [27] (see Fig. 2 for an example). The results provided a detailed analysis of the change in information requirements from conventional- to supervised collision avoidance. Specifically, the study identified specific requirements to make agents, capable of collision and grounding avoidance, transparent to their users. The results further indicated the shift in cognitive activities when the navigator's task changes from *performing collision avoidance* to *supervising a system performing collision avoidance*. To support operators in this change, explicit information requirements were identified that should allow for insight into the agent's decisions, planned actions, and underlying reasoning.

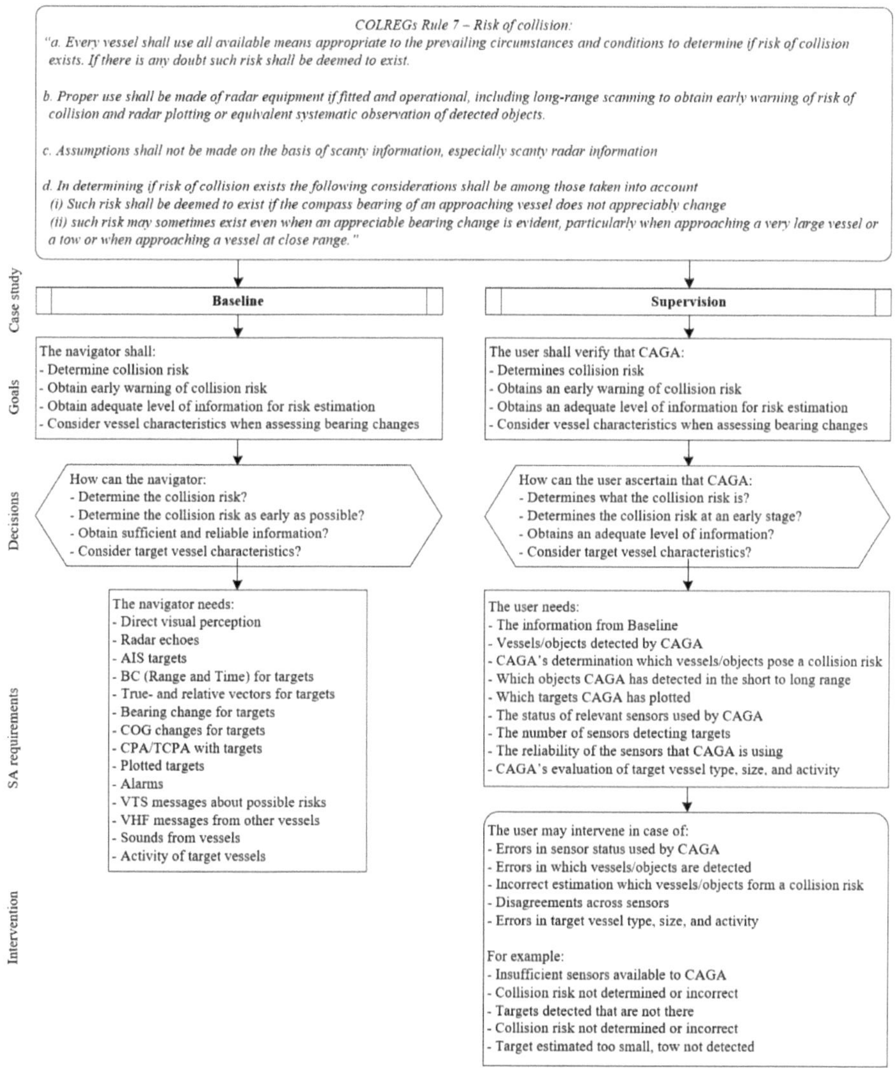

Fig. 2. Example of the results for the GDTA for COLREG rule 7 – Risk of collision (adopted from [27]).

3.3 A Model for Transparency

A model of information processing was used to structure the data from the GDTA and generate layers of transparency for a hypothetical Collision and Grounding Avoidance (CAGA) system [29] (see Table 1 for example information requirements). The model by Parasuraman, Sheridan, and Wickens (PSW) [22] was contextualized to the maritime collision avoidance setting such that the information from the GDTA could be structured into unique and distinct layers. It was suggested that this model may serve as a framework for transparent design as the steps in the model could represent the agent's input parameters, analysis, decisions, and planned actions. Using the model in this way, a minimum set of information requirements was made, organized in layers per processing step, resulting in a model for transparency.

Table 1. Structuring the results from the GDTA using the PSW model, adopted from [29].

Information processing stage	Information requirements (excerpts)
1. Condition detection: CAGA performs object detection, basic classification, object tracking, and status	- Detected objects short & long range - Identified target ship - Target object type and size - Identified target object as OT/HO/CR - Uncertainties in the radar/ sensor data - Status of sensors
2. Condition analysis: CAGA performs object classification, tracking, situation analysis, and risk estimation	- Objects that pose risk - Plotted objects - Risk object type and size - Risk object priority - Risk object course and speed - Risk object intended trajectory - Risk object conflict type - Safe speed parameters
3. Action planning: CAGA decides on collision avoidance manoeuvring and determines an updated passage plan	- Own ship priority (GW/SO) - Target vessel priority (GW/SO) - Own ship intended track and speed
4. Action control: CAGA executes the plan	N/A: only action implementation

3.4 HMI Development

To support human supervision of autonomous collision avoidance systems, HMI concepts were created to provide transparency for supervisors using a Human-Centered Design (HCD) process [30, 33]. Realistic traffic scenarios were developed by a navy-certified navigator, with symbology based on maritime equipment standards [34]. This symbology was integrated into the radar display, applying the PSW model to establish different levels of transparency.

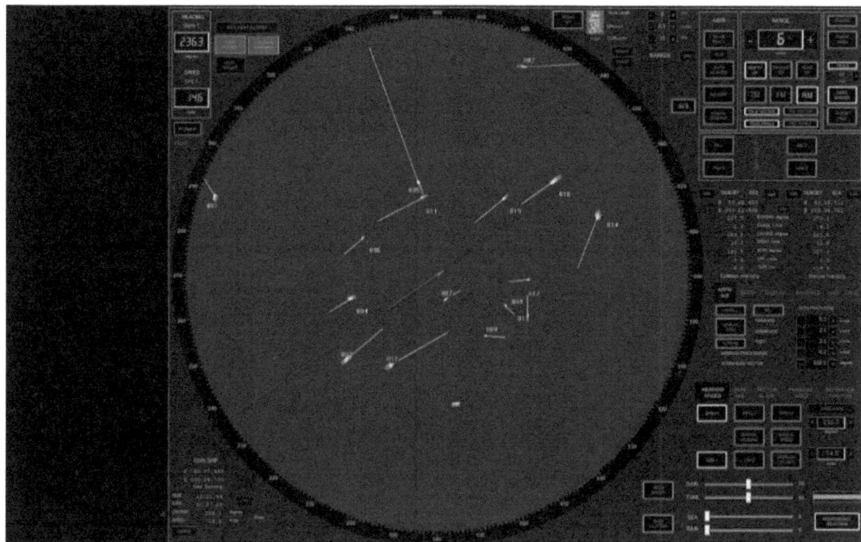

Fig. 3. Traffic situation without transparency information, adopted from [23].

Figure 3 shows a radar view with ownship at the center and several vessels within a 6nm range. Ownship is in a head-on situation with ship "003". According to COLREG rule 14, both ships should turn starboard to pass on each other's port side. However, ship "004" obstructs free maneuvering, requiring caution to avoid causing another collision. For larger HMIs, see the supplemental material to [31].

In the *low transparency* variation (see Fig. 4 for the application of this transparency level to an alternative traffic situation), own ship shows its planned avoidance maneuver by displaying its intended track for the next three steps, with each step representing six minutes. The system also indicates "GW" next to the own ship symbol to show it intends to "give way" to the target vessel.

In the *medium (A) transparency variation* (see Fig. 5 for the application of this transparency level to an alternative traffic situation), the red target indicates the highest risk. Symbols next to the targets show conflict type and vessel. A risk circle shows where the ship can maneuver within one vector length. Factors affecting the vessel's safe speed are listed in the table on the left.

In the *medium (B) transparency variation* (see Fig. 6 for the application of this transparency level to an alternative traffic situation), all layers are shown except for the "information analysis" layer. In this scenario, the system reveals its decisions, actions, and the information it has gathered. However, it does not disclose how it analyzes this information, such as the risks it has identified. This transparency level was included to provide an alternative to the cumulative approach mentioned earlier and to allow for a systematic comparison between transparency levels in an experimental setting.

In the *high transparency variation* (see Fig. 7 for the application of this transparency level to an alternative traffic situation), all transparency information identified with the task analysis is presented on the HMI. Each target is assigned an identifier (green circles)

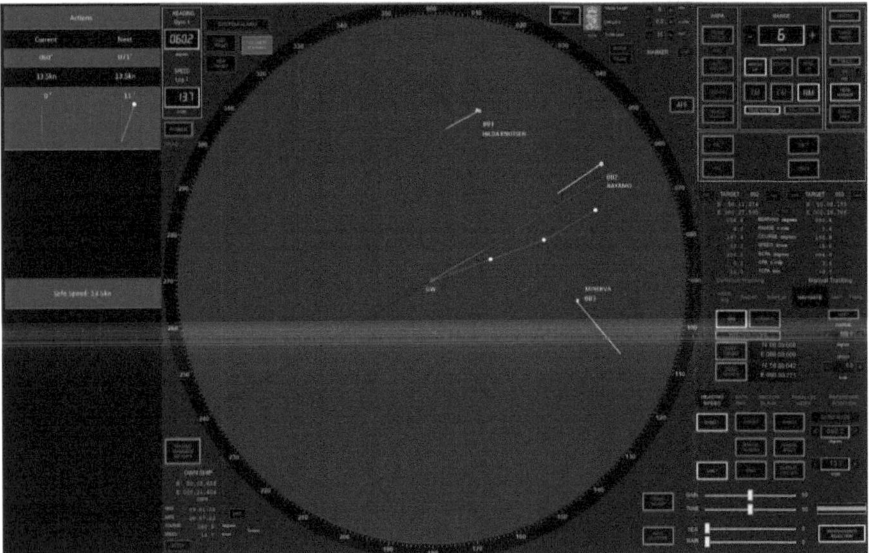

Fig. 4. Traffic situation with low transparency, adopted from [23].

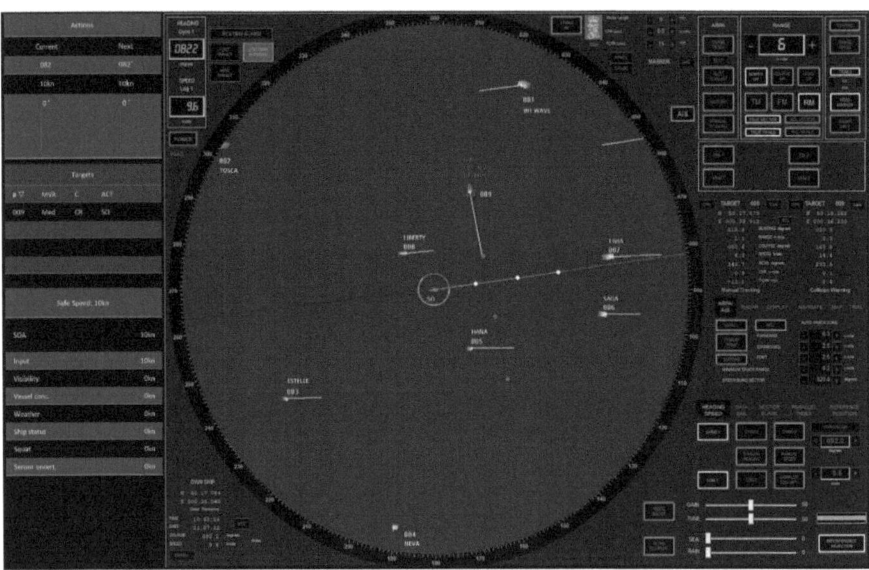

Fig. 5. Traffic situation with medium (A) transparency, adopted from [23].

and an initial classification, indicating ship types and relevant conflict type indicators. Additionally, the status of the system's sensors is displayed in the tables to the left of the radar screen.

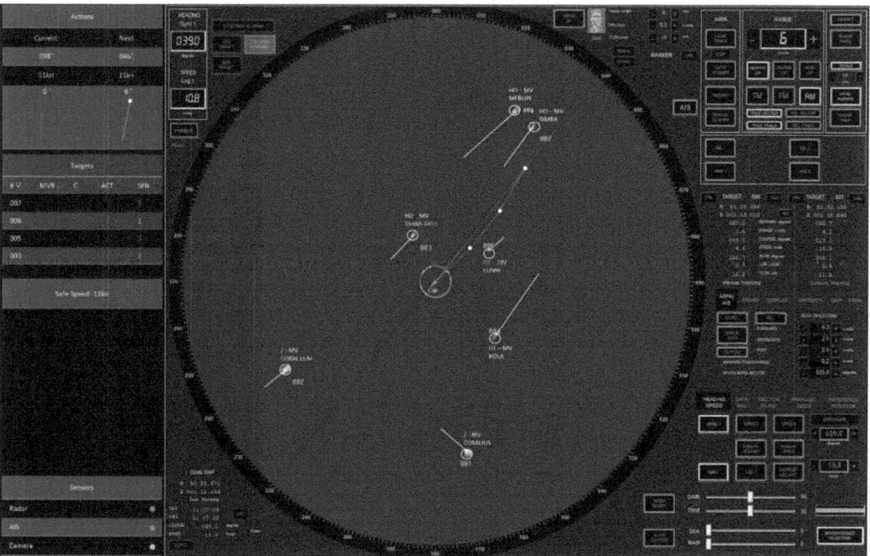

Fig. 6. Traffic situation with medium (B) transparency, adopted from [23].

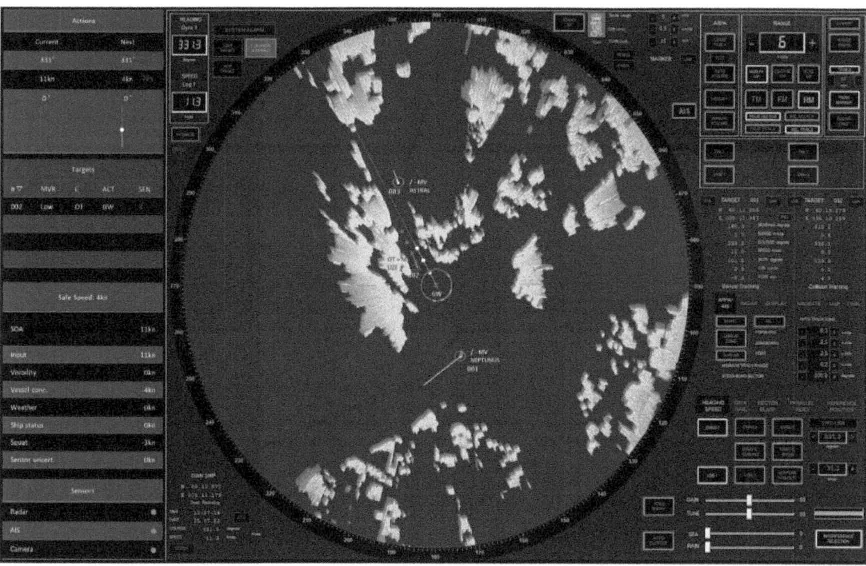

Fig. 7. Traffic situation with high transparency, adopted from [23].

This activity provided the groundwork for the experimental evaluation of agent transparency in a maritime collision avoidance context. In addition, the results demonstrated the value of the PSW model as a design framework for creating levels of transparency for autonomous agents.

3.5 Experimental Evaluation

The effect of transparency on SA, mental workload, and task performance was evaluated using a controlled experiment. Based on the PSW model and the abovementioned traffic situations, four levels of transparency and two levels of traffic complexity were varied in an experiment with 34 navigators. The results demonstrated a positive effect of transparency on SA without affecting mental workload. However, the time to comprehend the provided information increased with higher levels of transparency. These findings suggest that applying transparency principles to autonomous collision avoidance systems can enhance SA, but care should be taken in time-critical conditions where additional transparency information might impact timely decision-making.

Additionally, participants preferred levels of transparency where the system's risk analysis was depicted. A thematic analysis of the interview data showed that navigators were most interested in understanding how the CAGA system evaluated the traffic situation's risk picture. Considering the safety-critical nature of collision avoidance maneuvering, and the supervisor's role in ensuring the system performs according to its standards, this highlights the need for disclosure of the system's inner reasoning to support supervisor SA. Furthermore, given the absence of the effect of transparency on mental workload, these results also indicate the importance of proper HMI design through a structured and systematic human-centered design process (Fig. 8).

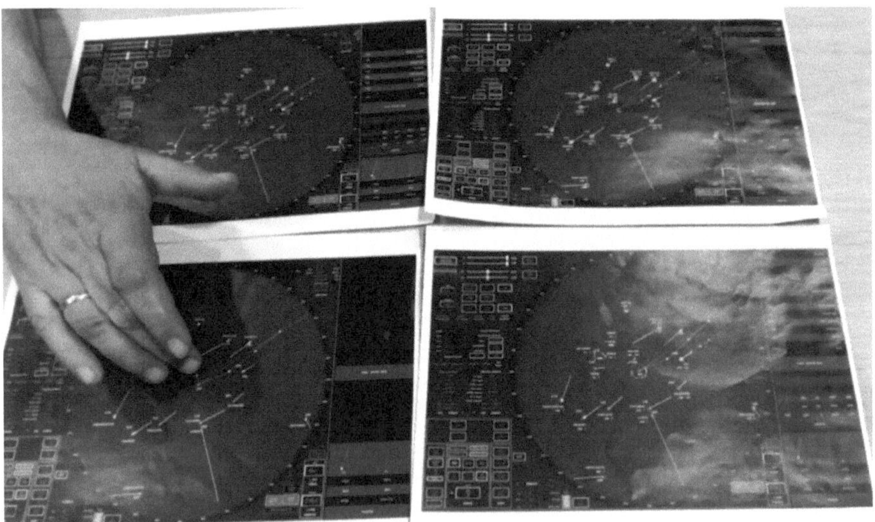

Fig. 8. Screenshot from the interviews from one of the participants, adopted from [32].

4 Discussion

This research project investigated the role of agent transparency in supervisory control and contributed with knowledge, methods, and tools regarding transparency in general and its application to the maritime domain specifically. As humans are foreseen to play a critical role in overseeing the functioning of AI-enabled systems [35], the operator's ability to understand, predict, and evaluate agent behavior becomes a critical aspect of the human's supervisory task repertoire [20]. Consequently, it is essential that humans are informed and supported in making accurate decisions to enable timely and appropriate control when needed. Therefore, the aim of this research project was to generate and advance the knowledge on how supervisory control can be supported through agent transparency.

Considering the potential changes in tasks, roles, and responsibilities for humans within the domain of ship autonomy, it is important to ensure that novel concepts adhere to principles of equivalent safety [36]. This means that relevant authorities should set clear expectations and acceptance criteria concerning the need for supporting humans in their (new) supervisory role. This means that when developers of autonomous ships seek approval from relevant authorities and classification societies, they typically are required to demonstrate that "the combined human/machine capabilities [...] should be the same or better than the conventional capabilities. This is in order to achieve an equivalent or better level of safety" [37, p. 51]. Specifically, "special attention should be placed on [...] the ability of the human to establish sufficient situational awareness so that correct actions can be taken within reasonable time" [37, p. 27]. This means that developers of autonomous ship solutions should develop HMIs that convey the essential information needed for effective supervision. Furthermore, in cases where human intervention is required due to "system-limitations or failures, [...] ample time [should be allowed] for the human to get the required situational awareness in order to be able to make good decisions" [37, p. 41].

This research suggests that understanding intelligent agents' reasoning processes, given their advanced sensory, information processing, decision-making, and action capabilities, is crucial in developing SA of the system under supervision. Therefore, to ensure equivalent safety in concepts where autonomous functions take over tasks previously performed by humans, developers should emphasize supporting the cognitive processes necessary for effective human supervisory control. Based on the findings of this research project, this implies offering insights into the system's decisions, planned actions, and reasoning. For collision avoidance systems specifically, this could include illustrations of the ship's intended avoidance maneuver and its timing, assessment of priority (give-way or stand-on), anticipated actions of the target ship, detected objects and their types, as well as any restrictions on maneuverability. Additionally, the system should convey its interpretation of collision risk and the rationale behind its actions, such as critical (Time to) Closest Point of Approach (CPA, TCPA), or other risk indicators such as available sea room. Moreover, it should specify which COLREG situation is applicable – whether it be head-on, overtaking, or crossing – and identify the relevant target ship. However, considering the effect of transparency on the time needed to process the information, future research should explore the application of transparency in time-sensitive environments and examine the impact of adjustable forms of transparency that can be tailored to specific circumstances [38, 39].

As demonstrated throughout this project, research on the utility of transparency as a design principle is ongoing and continuously evolving [25]. Therefore, further research to consolidate definitions, models, and design processes for transparency is needed.

Nonetheless, this research project demonstrated that the well-established HCD process is an effective method for developing transparent systems, as it enables multidisciplinary design teams to develop systems that support the needs of end-users [33]. This implies that developers, tasked with creating transparent systems, have a well-known process available to design systems that support the understandability and predictability needed to perform supervisory control of autonomous ships. Consequently, this research proposes the application of transparency principles, applied in a HCD process, to derive design solutions supportive of effective supervisory control in safety-critical domain.

5 Conclusion

This research project has highlighted the importance of transparency to support human performance in safety-critical domains. It has examined the impact of autonomy on cognitive tasks performed by operators, developed a model for transparency, applied this model to maritime navigation, and evaluated its effects in a controlled experimental setting. Additionally, this research has clarified the role-changes that may occur with the introduction of autonomous systems. Based on these findings, this research emphasizes the importance of providing human operators with an understanding of the reasoning behind autonomous systems and identifies transparency as a crucial factor for achieving safe and effective human-supervisory control. With these insights, it is possible to create meaningful human work where the combined capabilities of human-agent teams can be optimized.

Acknowledgments. The authors would like to express their gratitude to the navigators for their participation in the research activities. Also, we would like to express our sincere gratitude to Koen Houweling for his contribution in developing the traffic situations and the transparency illustrations. This research is sponsored by the Research Council of Norway, project nr. 311365 and 327903.

Disclosure of Interests. The author(s) declared no potential conflicts of interest with respect to the research, authorship, and/or publication of this article.

References

1. Royce, R.: Rolls-Royce unveils a vision of the future of remote and autonomous shipping. https://www.rolls-royce.com/media/press-releases/2016/pr-12-04-2016-rr-unveils-a-vision-of-future-of-remote-and-autonomus-shipping.aspx. Accessed 16 May 2022
2. Kongsberg: Kongsberg maritime and Massterly to equip and operate two zero-emission autonomous vessels for ASKO. https://www.kongsberg.com/maritime/about-us/news-and-media/news-archive/2020/zero-emission-autonomous-vessels/. Accessed 18 Nov 2020
3. Endsley, M.R.: Ironies of artificial intelligence. Ergonomics, 1–13 (2023). https://doi.org/10.1080/00140139.2023.2243404

4. Littman, M., et al.: Gathering Strength, Gathering Storms: The One Hundred Year Study on Artificial Intelligence (AI100) 2021 Study Panel Report. Stanford University, Stanford (2021). http://ai100.stanford.edu/2021-report
5. Alsos, O., et al.: NTNU Shore Control Lab: designing shore control centres in the age of autonomous ships. J. Phys. Conf. Ser. **2311**, 012030 (2022). https://doi.org/10.1088/1742-6596/2311/1/012030
6. Porathe, T., Fjortoft, K., Bratbergsengen, I.L.: Human factors, autonomous ships and constrained coastal navigation. IOP Conf. Ser. Mater. Sci. Eng. **929**(1), 012007 (2020). https://doi.org/10.1088/1757-899X/929/1/012007
7. Endsley, M.R.: From here to autonomy: lessons learned from human-automation research. Hum. Factors **59**(1), 5–27 (2017). https://doi.org/10.1177/0018720816681350
8. Bainbridge, L.: Ironies of automation. Automatica **19**(6), 775–779 (1983). https://doi.org/10.1016/0005-1098(83)90046-8
9. Endsley, M.R., Kiris, E.O.: The out-of-the-loop performance problem and level of control in automation. Hum. Factors **37**(2), 381–394 (1995). https://doi.org/10.1518/001872095779064555
10. Doshi-Velez, F., Kim, B.: Towards a rigorous science of interpretable machine learning. arXiv:1702.08608 [cs, stat], March 2017. http://arxiv.org/abs/1702.08608. Accessed 20 Apr 2021
11. Lipton, Z.C.: The mythos of model interpretability. arXiv:1606.03490 [cs, stat], March 2017. http://arxiv.org/abs/1606.03490. Accessed 3 Dec 2020
12. Parasuraman, R., Manzey, D.H.: Complacency and bias in human use of automation: an attentional integration. Hum. Factors **52**(3), 381–410 (2010). https://doi.org/10.1177/0018720810376055
13. Wickens, C.D., Clegg, B.A., Vieane, A.Z., Sebok, A.L.: Complacency and automation bias in the use of imperfect automation. Hum. Factors **57**(5), 728–739 (2015). https://doi.org/10.1177/0018720815581940
14. Mosier, K., Skitka, L.: Human decision makers and automated decision aids: made for each other?. In: Parasuraman, R., Mouloua, M. (eds.) Automation and human performance: theory and applications, vol. 40, pp. 201–220. Lawrence Erlbaum Associates, Inc. (1996)
15. Parasuraman, R., Riley, V.: Humans and automation: use, misuse, disuse, abuse. Hum. Factors **39**(2), 230–253 (1997). https://doi.org/10.1518/001872097778543886
16. Onnasch, L., Wickens, C.D., Li, H., Manzey, D.: Human performance consequences of stages and levels of automation: an integrated meta-analysis. Hum. Factors **56**(3), 476–488 (2014). https://doi.org/10.1177/0018720813501549
17. Metzger, U., Parasuraman, R.: The role of the air traffic controller in future air traffic management: an empirical study of active control versus passive monitoring. Hum. Factors **43**(4), 519–528 (2001). https://doi.org/10.1518/001872001775870421
18. Endsley, M.R.: Toward a theory of situation awareness in dynamic systems. Hum. Factors **37**(1), 217–249 (1995). https://doi.org/10.4324/9781315092898-13
19. Chen, J.Y.C., Procci, K., Boyce, M., Wright, J., Garcia, A., Barnes, M.J.: Situation awareness-based agent transparency. U.S. Army Research Laboratory, Aberdeen Proving Ground, ARL-TR-6905, April 2014. https://doi.org/10.21236/ADA600351
20. Endsley, M.R.: Supporting human-AI Teams: transparency, explainability, and situation awareness. Comput. Hum. Behav. **140**, 107574 (2023). https://doi.org/10.1016/j.chb.2022.107574
21. Russell, S.J., Norvig, P.: Artificial intelligence: a modern approach. In: Pearson Series in Artificial Intelligence, 4th edn. Global edition. Pearson, Harlow (2022)
22. Parasuraman, R., Sheridan, T.B., Wickens, C.D.: A model for types and levels of human interaction with automation. IEEE Trans. Syst. Man Cybern. **30**(3), 286–297 (2000). https://doi.org/10.1109/3468.844354

23. van de Merwe, K.: Agent transparency and human performance in supervisory control. Doctoral thesis, University of South-Eastern Norway (2024). https://openarchive.usn.no/usn-xmlui/handle/11250/3145497. Accessed 12 Aug 2024

24. Moher, D., et al.: Preferred reporting items for systematic review and meta-analysis protocols (PRISMA-P) 2015 statement. Syst. Rev. **4**(1), 1 (2015). https://doi.org/10.1186/2046-405 3-4-1

25. van de Merwe, K., Mallam, S., Nazir, S.: Agent transparency, situation awareness, mental workload, and operator performance: a systematic literature review. Hum. Factors **66**(1), 180–208 (2024). https://doi.org/10.1177/00187208221077804

26. Endsley, M.R., Bolté, B., Jones, D.G.: Designing for Situation Awareness: An Approach to User-Centered Design. Taylor & Francis, London, New York (2003)

27. van de Merwe, K., Mallam, S., Nazir, S., Engelhardtsen, Ø.: Supporting human supervision in autonomous collision avoidance through agent transparency. Saf. Sci. **169**, 13 (2024). https://doi.org/10.1016/j.ssci.2023.106329

28. IMO: Convention of the International Regulations for Preventing Collisions at Sea (COLREGS). International Maritime Organisation, Montreal, Canada, July 1977

29. van de Merwe, K., Mallam, S., Engelhardtsen, Ø., Nazir, S.: Towards an approach to define transparency requirements for maritime collision avoidance. Proc. Hum. Factors Ergon. Soc. Annu. Meet. **67**(1), 483–488 (2023). https://doi.org/10.1177/21695067231192862

30. van de Merwe, K., Mallam, S., Engelhardtsen, Ø., Nazir, S.: Operationalising automation transparency for maritime collision avoidance. TransNav. Int. J. Mar. Navig. Saf. Sea Transp. **17**(2), June 2023. https://doi.org/10.12716/1001.17.02.09

31. van de Merwe, K., Mallam, S., Nazir, S., Engelhardtsen, Ø.: The influence of agent transparency and complexity on situation awareness, mental workload, and task performance. J. Cogn. Eng. Decis. Mak. **18**(2), 156–184 (2024). https://doi.org/10.1177/15553434241240553

32. van de Merwe, K., Mallam, S., Nazir, S., Engelhardtsen, Ø.: Navigators' perspective on information requirements for supervisory control of autonomous ships. In: Proceedings of the Human Factors and Ergonomics Society Annual Meeting, p. 10711813241261686, August 2024. https://doi.org/10.1177/10711813241261686

33. ISO: ISO 9241–210:2019 Ergonomics of human-system interaction - Part 210: Human-centred design for interactive systems (2019)

34. IEC: NEK IEC 60945:2002 Maritime navigation and radiocommunication equipment and systems - General requirements - methods of testing and required test results (2002)

35. European Commission: Regulation (EU) 2024/1689 of the European Parliament and of the Council of 13 June 2024 laying down harmonised rules on artificial intelligence and amending Regulations (EC) No 300/2008, (EU) No 167/2013, (EU) No 168/2013, (EU) 2018/858, (EU) 2018/1139 and (EU) 2019/2144 and Directives 2014/90/EU, (EU) 2016/797 and (EU) 2020/1828 (Artificial Intelligence Act), June 2024. http://data.europa.eu/eli/reg/2024/1689/oj/eng. Accessed 16 Aug 2024

36. IMO: Guidelines for the approval of alternatives and equivalents as provided for in various IMO instruments. International Maritime Organisation, Montreal, Canada, MSC.1/Circ.1455, June 2013

37. DNV: Autonomous and remotely operated ships. DNV, Høvik, Norway, DNV-CG-0264 (2024). https://www.dnv.com/maritime/autonomous-remotely-operated-ships/class-guideline

38. Tatasciore, M., Loft, S.: Can increased automation transparency mitigate the effects of time pressure on automation use? Appl. Ergon. **114**, 104142 (2024). https://doi.org/10.1016/j.apergo.2023.104142

39. Vered, M., Howe, P., Miller, T., Sonenberg, L., Velloso, E.: Demand-driven transparency for monitoring intelligent agents. IEEE Trans. Hum. Mach. Syst. **50**(3), 264–275 (2020). https://doi.org/10.1109/THMS.2020.2988859

Eye Tracking, Cognition, and Situation Awareness

Comparative Analysis of the Effects of Age on Cognitive Performance in European and Asian Populations

Mickaël Causse[1]($\boxtimes$) , Ami Ogawa[2] , Damien Mouratille[1] , Pauline Eder[1], and Jean-Paul Imbert[1]

[1] Fédération Enac Isae-Supaero Onera, Université De Toulouse, Toulouse, France
Mickael.Causse@isae-supaero.fr
[2] Department of System Design Engineering, Faculty of Science and Technology, Keio University, Yokohama, Japan

Abstract. We aimed to quantify the cognitive effects of aging in European and Asian populations. A first objective was to determine whether early signs of cognitive aging could be detected in a moderately aged population still within the working-age range. Another objective was to examine whether European and Asian participants exhibited different cognitive performances, potentially influenced by genetic, cultural, or lifestyle factors. We administered a comprehensive battery of cognitive tests to 30 participants, with a primary focus on executive functions. The participants were divided into four groups according to age and ethnic background: younger Europeans, younger Asians, older Europeans, and older Asians. We collected indirect measures of brain activity via heart rate all along the test performance to examine the compatibility of our results with the CRUNCH model. Body mass index (BMI) and several fitness measurements were also taken at rest to examine their correlation with cognitive performance. The results of this preliminary study show a decline in cognitive performance with age across multiple cognitive domains, including vigilance, mental flexibility, inhibition, short-term memory, working memory, attention, and reasoning. Additionally, European participants demonstrated higher performance in short-term and working memory, whereas Asian participants exhibited faster reaction times in the attention test. BMI was lower in Asians than Europeans but had no influence on cognitive performance. A better understanding of the specific cognitive functions that may be affected by aging will assist in decision-making regarding the retirement age and offer insights into aspects of the occupation that could be adjusted for senior individuals.

Keywords: Cognitive Aging · Executive Functions · Workforce · Cross-Cultural Study · Body Mass Index (BMI)

1   Introduction

1.1   Aging Effects on Cognition

The current aging of the workforce in both Western and Eastern countries is a natural consequence of the demographic evolution. Managing this shift presents a significant challenge for society and raises questions about extending the retirement age. Beyond economic considerations, it is crucial to explore strategies for maintaining performance and safety at work for older individuals. This concern applies not only to physically demanding jobs but also to critical and cognitively demanding occupations that require rapid decision-making, such as piloting (van Drongelen et al. 2017) and air traffic control (Heslegrave 1998).

Understanding how we can adapt working conditions to older people would benefit from a deeper understanding of how time alters cognitive performance. It is well established that several cognitive functions are affected during normal aging, including working memory (Salthouse 1994), spatial abilities (Techentin et al. 2014), or visual search (Hommel et al. 2004). Fluid intelligence is more impacted by aging than crystallized intelligence, with a more pronounced effect on executive functions and working memory. A study by Fisk and Sharp (2004) suggests that aging affects three major executive functions (Miyake et al. 2000): mental set shifting ("Shifting"), information updating and monitoring ("Updating"), and inhibition of prepotent responses ("Inhibition").

Working memory and short-term memory gradually decline throughout the adult life span (Craik 1994) as well as spatial working memory, another form of working memory, with a decline in accuracy and response times (Nagel et al. 2009). Other abilities such as verbal fluency or reasoning are considered more preserved by some authors (Treitz et al. 2007). A decline in memory can have serious consequences in fast-paced occupations that require processing large amounts of information (Baumgartner et al. 2024). Functional neuroimaging has highlighted anatomical and physiological changes that affect the brain during this period (Cabeza et al. 2002). Reuter-Lorenz et al. (2008) proposed that, due to reduced neural efficiency, older individuals engage brain regions more intensively when performing tasks of moderate difficulty, as if the challenge were artificially greater for them. At intermediate to high levels of cognitive load, they exceed their processing capacity, leading to lower brain activity compared to younger individuals. At this stage, performance may decline. This model is known as Compensation-Related Utilization of Neural Circuits Hypothesis, or CRUNCH (Reuter-Lorenz & Lustig 2005).

1.2   Cross-Cultural Studies of Cognitive Performance

Introducing a cross-cultural dimension to the study of cognitive neuroscience and aging (Park 2002) may help identify factors that mitigate the effects of aging on cognition. There is evidence suggesting that East Asians tend to process information in a holistic and contextual manner, whereas Westerners are more inclined toward an analytical, feature-based approach. According to Park et al. (1999), these cultural differences in information-processing styles are so pervasive that they influence cognitive functions at fundamental levels, including the underlying mechanisms of cognition. Several factors, including genetics, education, and lifestyle, may contribute to these differences.

A study compared the executive performance of 20 South Asian and 20 White adults (Kallambettu et al. 2017) and found no significant difference in performance on the Behavioral Assessment of the Dysexecutive Syndrome (BADS; Wilson et al. 1996). However, on the Functional Assessment of Verbal Reasoning and Executive Strategies (FAVRES; MacDonald & Johnson 2005), white participants scored significantly higher on accuracy in two out of four subtests and on rationale in three subtests. Shadlen et al. (2001) examined the influence of ethnicity on cognitive performance in older adults while considering education as a factor. Their findings indicated that African Americans scored lower than Japanese Americans and Caucasians on the Cognitive Abilities Screening Instrument. However, higher education levels helped reduce the ethnic gap, suggesting that disparities in cognitive test scores among lower-education groups may reflect differences in educational quality.

1.3 Aging Effects and Cultural Differences

The relationship between cultural background and cognition raises an important question: does aging amplify the influence of cultural origin on cognitive processes? One hypothesis is that prolonged immersion in a specific cultural and lifestyle environment throughout one's lifetime could intensify these effects. However, Park et al. (1999) proposed a more nuanced perspective. They suggest that while cultural influences on cognition may strengthen with age in some cases, they may also diminish in others. For example, although young adults exhibit significant cultural differences in cognitive tasks, these differences may fade over time due to universal neurobiological decline. As cognitive function deteriorates with age, individuals across cultures may rely on similar cognitive strategies, leading to greater cross-cultural convergence in late adulthood. These findings highlight the complex interplay between culture, cognition, and aging. While cultural influences shape cognitive processing styles, the aging process itself may act as a universal equalizer, reducing some of these differences over time.

A study (Hedden et al. 2002) explored these dynamics by comparing 32 younger and 32 older adults from China and the United States on numerically and spatially based measures of processing speed and working memory. Younger Chinese participants outperformed their American counterparts on numerically based tasks. However, as task complexity increased and participants aged, this cultural advantage diminished, aligning with the framework proposed by Park et al. (1999). Interestingly, no significant cross-cultural differences were observed in visuospatial measures of working memory or processing speed for either age group. Few studies in aviation have attempted to investigate the aging effect in a cross-cultural fashion. However, a study compared 100 Asian and Western pilots over the age of 60 (Nawaz & Modatheeri 2024), and found that Western pilots outperformed their Asian counterparts in deductive reasoning. No significant differences were observed in motor speed.

1.4 Objectives

Several studies have examined differences in academic achievement and cognitive abilities across countries and ethnic backgrounds. However, few have systematically assessed a broad range of cognitive skills in both Asian and Western European populations while considering the effects of aging. In this study, European and Asian participants underwent an extensive battery of cognitive tests. The first objective was to determine whether early signs of aging could be detected before the age of 65. The second objective was to investigate whether European and Asian populations exhibit differences in cognitive performance, also taking age into account. The third objective was to evaluate whether the results align with the CRUNCH (Compensation-Related Utilization of Neural Circuits Hypothesis) model (Reuter-Lorenz & Cappell 2008), which posits that older adults recruit additional cognitive effort and brain regions compared to younger adults when performing the same task, as a compensatory mechanism for age-related neural decline. Rather than using direct brain measurements typically employed to validate the CRUNCH model, we collected indirect indicators of brain activity through heart rate monitoring throughout task performance. Finally, several fitness measures—including resting blood pressure, resting blood oxygen levels, and body mass index (BMI)—were collected to explore their possible correlations with cognitive performance.

1.5 General Hypotheses

We hypothesized that cognitive performance would decline in the older group and that cognitive differences might exist between European and Asian participants. Additionally, we proposed that Asian individuals might be less affected by aging due to differences in lifestyle, education, culture, or nutrition. We also expected findings consistent with the CRUNCH model. Finally, we anticipated that fitness measures could predict cognitive performance; for instance, a higher BMI might be negatively correlated with executive function performance.

2 Method

2.1 Cognitive Tests

Participants underwent a series of cognitive tests (mainly from the PEBL battery, available at http://pebl.sf.net/battery.html) evaluating vigilance, cognitive flexibility, inhibition, short-term memory, working memory, attention, and fluid reasoning. To minimize order effects, the sequence of cognitive tests was randomized for each participant. Before each test, a training session was performed to ensure the participant understood the instructions. The entire experiment lasted around two hours.

Vigilance. To assess vigilance, we used the PEBL version of the Mackworth Clock Test (Mackworth 1948). The total task duration was 5 min, with 300 trials (i.e., 300 dot movements). The performance indicator was the percentage of correct responses.

Cognitive Flexibility. We used the PEBL version of the Wisconsin Card Sorting Test (Berg 1948) to measure cognitive flexibility, the ability to adapt to changing environments or rules. The total task duration was about 5 min with 115 trials, with the rule changing every 10 correct trials. Performance indicators included accuracy and perseverative errors.

Inhibition. We used the PEBL version of the numerical Stroop test (Hernández et al. 2010). Task duration was about 4.5 min with 192 trials. Performance measures were the percentage of correct responses and reaction times in different conditions (average of congruent and incongruent trials).

Short-Term Memory. Two tests were used to assess short-term memory. We programmed a forward digit span memory test with PEBL language. The test started with 4 digits presented one per second, and then the participant must reproduce them in the correct order using the keyboard. The number of digits increased by 1 after each success. After 3 failures, the test stopped, thus the number of trials depended on the performance of the participant. Average test duration was about 4 min. The second test was the Corsi test, evaluating spatial short-term memory (Piccardi et al. 2008). After 3 failures, the test stopped, thus the number of trials also depended on the performance of the participant. Test duration was about 4 min. In both tests, the performance indicator was the maximum size of correctly recalled items.

Working Memory. Two tests were used to assess working memory. We programmed a backward digit span memory test with PEBL language. It is identical to forward digit span memory test except that the participant must reproduce items in reverse order. Performance indicator was the maximum size of correctly recalled items. Average test duration was about 4 min. We also used the Toulouse N-back Task (Mandrick et al., 2016), reproduced in PEBL language. It is a classic n-back task combined with arithmetic operations. 72 trials were administered, with 24 trials for each 3 levels of difficulty. Performance indicator was the percentage of correct responses. Test duration was about 8 min.

Attention. We used the Attention Network Test (ANT) from the PEBL battery to assess three attentional networks: alerting, orienting, and executive control (for details, see Fan et al. 2002). The total task duration was about 4 min, with 3 experimental blocks of 20 trials each. Performance metrics included accuracy and reaction times (for both measures, we calculated average results of the three attentional networks).

Fluid Reasoning. We used the abbreviated nine-item version of the Raven's Standard Progressive Matrices test (Bilker et al. 2012) that we programmed with PEBL. This abbreviated version significantly reduces administration time compared to the full version. In each trial, the participant must identify the missing element that completes a pattern. Total duration was about 4 min depending on participants' response time. Performance indicator was the percentage of correct responses.

2.2 Cardiovascular Measures

We measured heart rate continuously during the cognitive test to estimate mental effort during the TNT test. It allowed us to estimate the effect of task difficulty (Causse et al. 2010; Henelius et al. 2009) and explore whether older participants exert more mental effort compared to their younger counterparts, in intermediate and higher levels of difficulty, as predicted by the CRUNCH model. Additionally, we examined the impact of task difficulty on heart rate. A Bitalino PPG with a sampling rate of 500 Hz was used. An electrode was placed on the ear of the participant. Signals were visually inspected, and occasional artifacts were replaced with the values of adjacent intervals (Peltola 2012).

2.3 Fitness Measures

Several physiological measurements were taken at rest before the experiment to assess their potential relationship with task performance. We also examined possible differences based on ethnicity.

Blood Pressure. A Beurer BM 28 was placed on the forearm to measure diastolic and systolic blood pressure (single measurement) before the experiment.

Blood Oxygenation. An Oxy-one Plus PC-60F oximeter was placed on the fingertip to measure blood oxygenation level (SpO2 level, single measurement) before the experiment.

Body Mass Index. Body mass index was calculated for each participant as followed: $\mathrm{BMI} = \frac{Weight\ in\ kg}{(Height\ in\ meters)^2}$.

2.4 Participants

We recruited 30 participants, comprising 15 Western Europeans (all Caucasians) and 15 Asians (13 Japanese, 1 Vietnamese, 1 Indonesian), divided into four groups based on age and population origin: younger Europeans (25–45 years old, average age $= 29.2$; n $= 10$), younger Asians (25–45 years old, average age $= 27.3$; n $= 10$), older Europeans (45–60 years old, average age $= 56.18$; n $= 5$), and older Asians (45–60 years old, average age $= 56.4$; n $= 5$). The study complied with the Declaration of Helsinki for human experimentation and was approved by an ethical committee from Keio university. All participants provided written informed consent prior to the experiment.

2.5 Statistical Analysis

All statistical analyses were carried out using R (R Core Team 2013). Normality was first checked for the parameter value distributions by means of the Shapiro-Wilk test. Then, non-parametric analyses of variance (permutation tests, Frossard & Renaud 2021) were performed including two between-subject factors: age (2 levels of age: Younger and Older) $\times$ ethnicity (2 levels of ethnicity: Europeans and Asians). To determine the presence of a statistically significant difference between conditions, a significance threshold of $\alpha = 0.05$ was selected. Post hoc analyses were conducted using Tukey's Honest Significant Difference (HSD) test. For the CRUNCH aspect, we analyzed the interaction between age and difficulty on accuracy and heart rate during the TNT test. Thus, permutations tests for ANOVA were computed including two between-subject factors and one within-subject factor: age (2 levels of age: Younger and Older) $\times$ ethnicity (2 levels of ethnicity: Europeans and Asians) $\times$ difficulty (3 levels of difficulty: easy, medium, difficult).

3 Results

3.1 Cognitive Tests

Vigilance. For the vigilance test, a main effect of age was observed on the accuracy ($F(1,28) = 7.42$, $p = .01$, η2 $= .22$, see Fig. 1): younger participants ($M = 96.85$, $SD = 3.49$) were better than older participants ($M = 91.58$, $SD = 6.75$). More precisely, younger participants ($M = 0.62$, $SD = 0.47$) made fewer false alarms ($F(1,28) = 9.21$, $p < .01$, η2 $= .06$) than older participants ($M = 2.53$, $SD = 2.83$). No main effect of ethnicity and no interaction was observed.

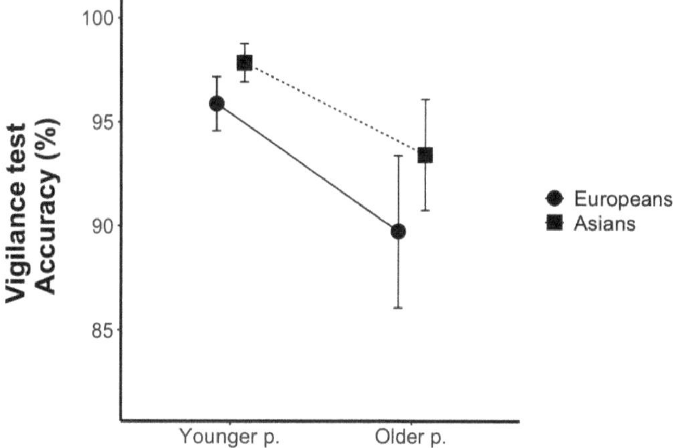

Fig. 1. Accuracy on the vigilance test according to Age and Ethnicity.

Cognitive Flexibility. We found an effect of age on accuracy ($F(1,28) = 9.98$, $p < .01$, η2 $= .29$, see Fig. 2) of the cognitive flexibility test: younger participants ($M = 83.24$, $SD = 3.90$) were better than older participants ($M = 76.29$, $SD = 7.36$). More precisely, younger participants ($M = 11.34$, $SD = 2.50$) made fewer perseverative errors ($F(1,28) = 8.05$, $p = .01$, η2 $= .25$) than older participants ($M = 15.16$, $SD = 4.61$). No main effect of ethnicity and no interaction was observed.

Inhibition. On the inhibition part, accuracy was not different between age groups, but a main effect of age was found on the reaction times ($F(1,28) = 9.37$, $p = .01$, η2 $= .27$, see Fig. 3) with faster responses for the younger participants ($M = 552.53$, $SD = 96.90$) compared to the older participants ($M = 663.74$, $SD = 69.56$). Neither main effect of ethnicity nor interaction was measured.

Short-term Memory. For the short-term memory part, a main effect of ethnicity was observed for the forward digit span test ($F(1,28) = 4.25$, $p = .05$, η2 $= .18$, see Fig. 4). Europeans ($M = 9.15$, $SD = 1.48$) had higher memory span than Asians ($M = 7.45$, $SD = 2.10$). No main effect of age or interaction was observed. For the spatial memory test, a main effect of age was observed ($F(1,29) = 5.84$, $p = .02$, η2 $= .17$), younger

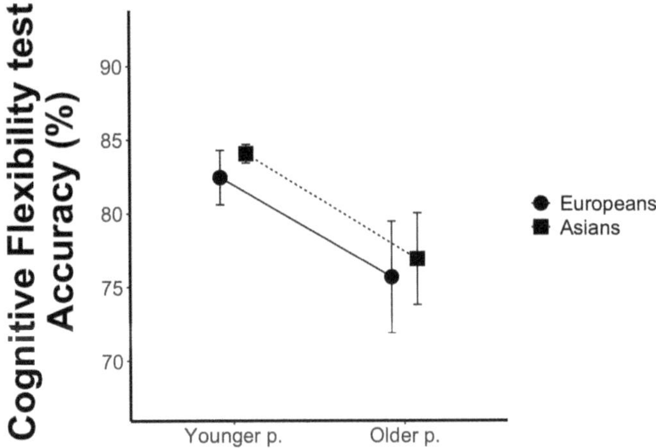

Fig. 2. Accuracy on the cognitive flexibility test according to Age and Ethnicity.

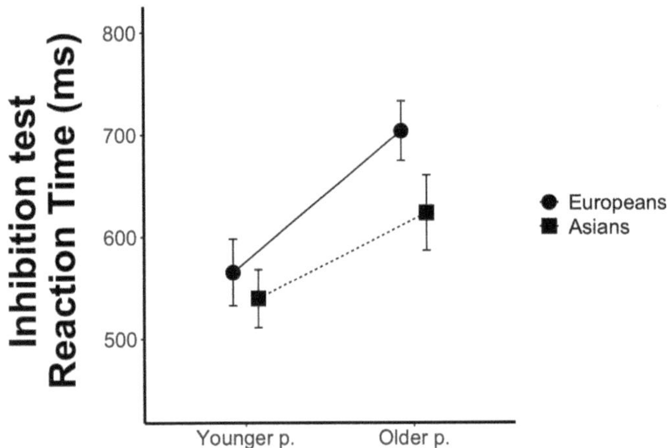

Fig. 3. Reaction Time on the inhibition test according to Age and Ethnicity.

participants exhibited a higher memory span ($M = 6.18$, $SD = 0.90$) compared to older participants ($M = 5.27$, $SD = 0.97$). No main effect of ethnicity or interaction was found.

Working Memory. With the working memory (backward digit span memory test), a main effect of age was observed ($F(1,29) = 7.87$, $p < .01$, $\eta2 = .18$, see Fig. 5) with better performance in younger ($M = 8.05$, $SD = 1.70$) vs older participants ($M = 6.10$, $SD = 1.18$). A main effect of ethnicity was also measured ($F(1,28) = 9.57$, $p < .01$, $\eta2 = .23$) with higher performance in Europeans ($M = 8.15$, $SD = 1.94$) than Asians ($M = 6.00$, $SD = 1.20$).

Moreover, a main effect of age was observed on the Toulouse N-back Task accuracy ($F(1,28) = 14.92$, $p < .01$, $\eta2 = .12$, see Fig. 6). Younger participants ($M = 87.57$, $SD = 7.72$) had a superior accuracy than older participants ($M = 75.56$, $SD = 7.38$). In

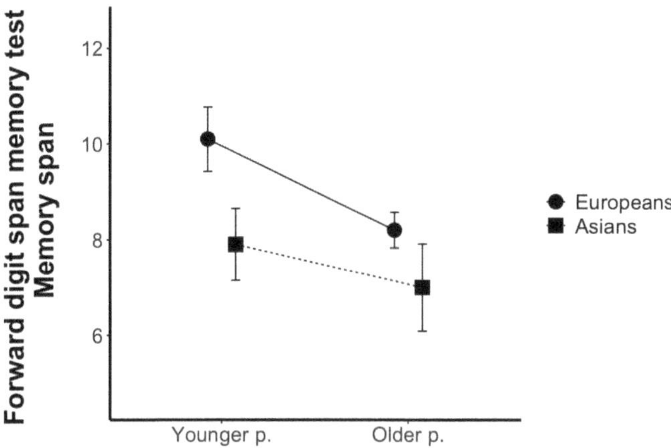

Fig. 4. Memory span on the forward digit span memory test according to Age and Ethnicity.

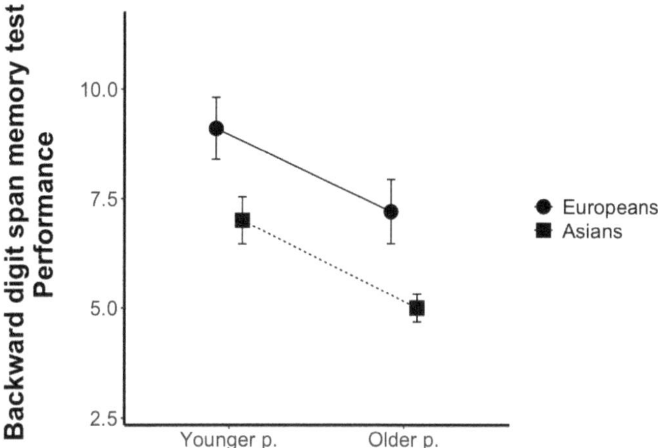

Fig. 5. Performance on the backward digit span memory test according to Age and Ethnicity.

addition, a main effect of the difficulty (F(2,56) = 36.74, p < .001, η2 = .35) and, as predicted by the CRUNCH model, an interaction between age and difficulty (F(2,56) = 5.13, p = .01, η2 = .05) were found. Older participants had a better performance during the easy condition (M = 93.27, SD = 5.66) than during the medium (M = 66.48, SD = 15.24, p < .001) and difficult conditions (M = 66.94, SD = 11.17, p < .001). During the medium condition, younger participants (M = 88.42, SD = 10.92) were better than older participants (M = 66.97, SD = 11.11). No main effect of ethnicity nor other interactions was found.

Attention. We also found an effect of age ($F(1,28) = 26.89, p < .001, η2 = .49$, see Fig. 7) and ethnicity ($F(1,28) = 4.93, p = .04, η2 = .05$) on the response time during the attention test: older participants ($M = 711.19, SD = 114.55$) were slower than younger participants ($M = 542.51, SD = 63.45$), and Europeans ($M = 662.98, SD = 83.80$)

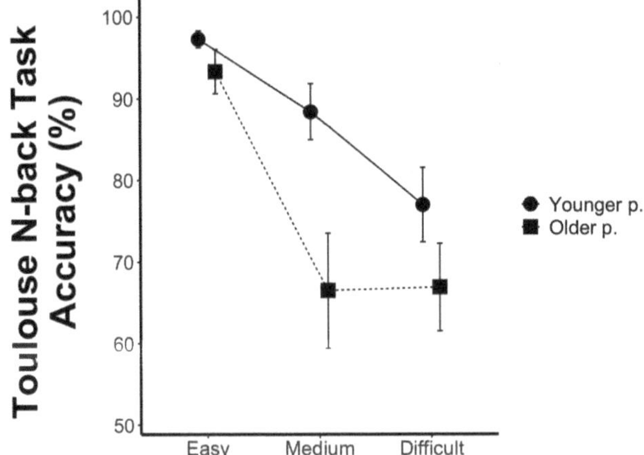

Fig. 6. Accuracy on the Toulouse N-back Task according to Age and Task Difficulty.

were slower than Asians ($M = 590.72$, $SD = 94.20$). Nevertheless, no effect of age was observed on the accuracy during the attention test.

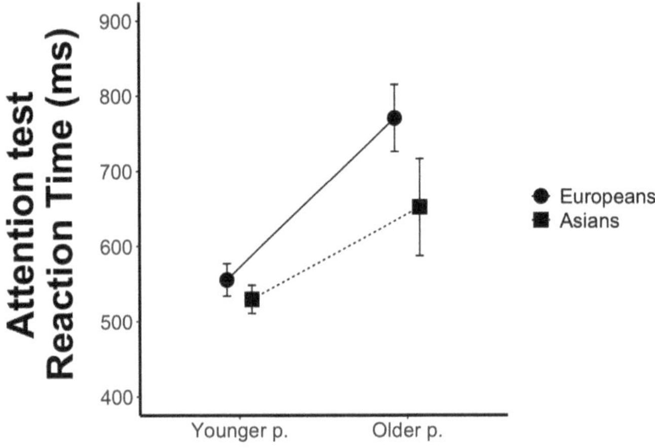

Fig. 7. Reaction time on the attention test according to Age and Ethnicity.

Fluid Reasoning. With the fluid reasoning test, a main effect of age was observed on the accuracy ($F(1,29) = 16.21$, $p < .001$, $\eta2 = .37$, see Fig. 8) with a better accuracy for the younger participants ($M = 57.72$, $SD = 14.11$) compared to the older participants ($M = 37.27$, $SD = 14.49$). No main effect of ethnicity nor interaction was found.

3.2 Cardiovascular Results

A main effect of difficulty was measured for the heart rate variable during the Toulouse N-back Task ($F(2,56) = 8.19$, $p < .01$, $\eta2 = .04$). Heart rate was higher in the Difficult

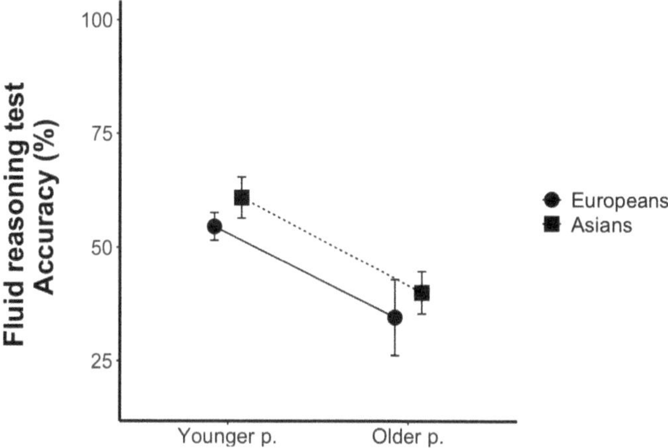

Fig. 8. Reaction time on the fluid reasoning test according to Age and Ethnicity.

condition ($M = 84.09$, $SD = 11.56$) compared to the Medium ($M = 78.91$, $SD = 13.96$, $p < .001$) and Easy ($M = 77.85$, $SD = 12.80$, $p < .001$) conditions. However, contrary to CRUNCH predictions, we found no interaction between Age and Ethnicity ($p > .05$, see Fig. 9).

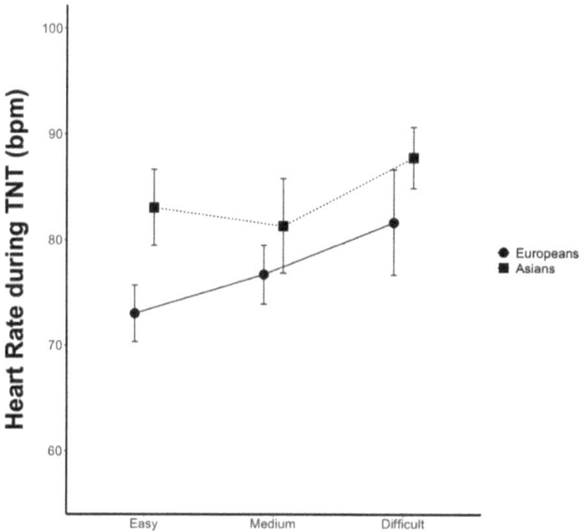

Fig. 9. Heart rate during the Toulouse N-back Task according to Difficulty and Ethnicity.

3.3 Fitness Results

A main effect of Ethnicity was measured for the BMI ($F(1,28) = 10.80$, $p < .01$, $\eta2 = .21$, see Fig. 10), Europeans ($M = 23.96$, $SD = 3.63$) had a higher BMI than Asians ($M = 20.16$, $SD = 1.95$). An interaction was also measured between age and ethnicity variables ($F(1,28) = 5.51, p = .03, \eta2 = .14$) with higher BMI for Older Europeans ($M = 26.44, SD = 3.65$) compared to Younger Europeans ($M = 21.49, SD = 3.62, p = .03$), Younger Asians ($M = 20.40, SD = 2.40, p < .01$) and Older Asians ($M = 19.92, SD = 1.49, p = .01$). No main effect of the Age variable was observed. For blood pressure and SP02 variables, no significant difference was measured between groups (all $ps > .05$).

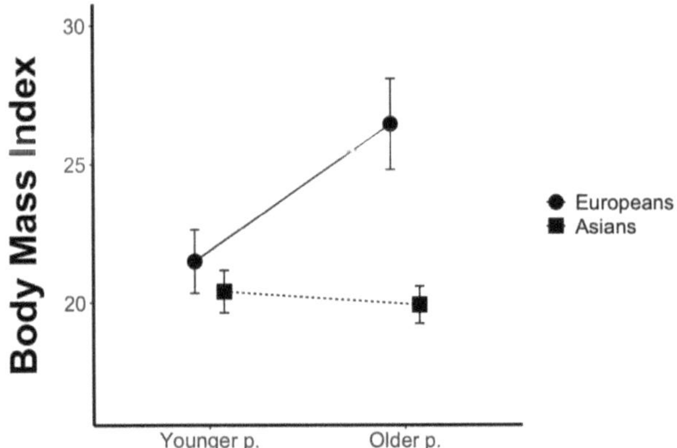

Fig. 10. Body Mass Index according to Age and Ethnicity.

No significant correlation was found between cognitive results and fitness variables (all $ps > .05$, see Fig. 11 for an example).

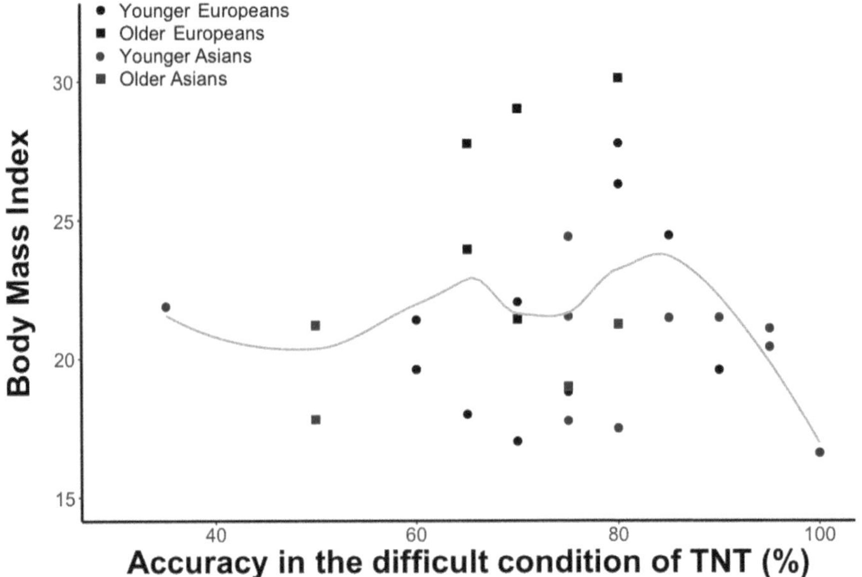

Fig. 11. Non-significant association between BMI and performance during the TNT test (difficult condition). Note that BMI was lower in Asians.

4 Discussion

The results of this preliminary study showed a decline in cognitive performance among moderately aged individuals (average of approximately 56 years old) who are still of working age, across a wide range of abilities, including attention, vigilance, mental flexibility, short-term memory, working memory, inhibition, and reasoning.

The current study is original in that it examines the effects of aging in a relatively "young" population. Typically, age-related effects are studied in older populations, for example, with an average age of about 71 years for the older group (Schneider-Garces et al. 2010). Fortunately, this cognitive decline can be somehow compensated by professional experience (Hertzog & Jopp 2010), but this aspect must be carefully considered in professions with high-paced environments and high workloads, such as piloting or air traffic control (Causse et al. 2025). A better understanding of the specific cognitive functions that may be affected by aging helps in assisting decision-making regarding the retirement age and offers insights into aspects of the job that could be adjusted for senior individuals. Managing the effects of aging, for example through individualized cognitive evaluations, could be beneficial beyond a certain age (Baumgartner et al. 2024).

We also identified differences between Western Europeans and Asian populations: European participants exhibited higher performance in short-term memory and working memory and conversely, Asian participants had faster reaction time for attention ability. Compatible with these difference in reaction times, a recent study found cognitive differences between Japanese and US participants, with Japanese showing better performances in processing speed (Fujii et al. 2024), however differential educational attainment between the two countries largely explained the difference. In our current sample, education was controlled between age groups to limit this kind of effect, so it cannot be clearly attributable to this factor. Beyond education, cognitive differences between Western and Asian and Cultures are also considered to be the reflection of genetic, neurobiological, and sociocultural influences (Zaroff et al. 2013).

We also observed an effect compatible with the CRUNCH model during the TNT test (working memory), where older participants showed more pronounced performance degradation at medium (but not higher) levels of difficulty. This was not supported by heart rate results since we did not find higher heart rate in older participants for the medium and high level of difficulty. We found also an increase in heart rate with increasing task difficulty during the TNT test, confirming that heart rate is a reliable index of mental effort.

We finally found interesting results with fitness data, with a BMI markedly lower in older Asian vs older Europeans. But BMI did not correlate with cognitive performance, contrary to some previous results from the literature (Gunstad et al. 2007) that found that elevated BMI is negatively correlated with executive performances.

Some limitations to this study must be acknowledged. While our results revealed interesting differences based on ethnicity, those related to age should be taken with caution due to the small sample sizes in the older age groups of each population. Collection of more data will be performed in the future. Also, in the Asian group, while we targeted mainly Japanese people, 2 out of 15 were living in Japan but were from other origins (1 from Vietnam in the younger group, 1 from Indonesia in the older group). This may have slightly influenced the results as some cognitive differences have found between

Asian regions. In a cross-cultural comparison of neurobehavioral performance in Asian workers, a study found that the far East Asian group outperform other Asian groups in adjusted test scores, with significant differences observed in both genders for Symbol Digit and Finger Tapping Speed (Katsanos et al. 2023). The influence of cultural background on Symbol Digit was found to be comparable to the effect of approximately 10 years of education.

5 Conclusion

This preliminary study suggests that the effects of aging on cognitive performance can emerge at a relatively moderate age and impact a broad range of cognitive functions. We also identified cross-cultural differences, particularly in short-term and working memory, where European participants outperformed their Asian counterparts, independent of education level. Conversely, Asian participants exhibited faster reaction times in the attention test. Our findings partially align with the CRUNCH model in the working memory task (TNT), as older participants performed similarly to younger ones on easy tasks but showed a marked decline when task difficulty increased to a moderate level. However, heart rate data did not support this result, not showing higher mental effort in older individual. We observed the expected increase in heart rate with rising difficulty during the TNT test, confirming that heart rate is a reliable indicator of mental effort. Future research incorporating cross-cultural perspectives may provide deeper insights into strategies for preserving cognitive functions in aging populations.

References

Baumgartner, M., Cabon, P., Drogoul, F., Causse, M., Imbert, J.-P., Mouratille, D.: Scientific evaluation of the impact of an increase in the retirement age on the cognitive functions and well-being of air traffic controllers (ATCOs). Adv. Hum. Factors Transport. (2024)

Berg, E.A.: A simple objective technique for measuring flexibility in thinking. J. Gen. Psychol. **39**(1), 15–22 (1948)

Bilker, W.B., Hansen, J.A., Brensinger, C.M., Richard, J., Gur, R.E., Gur, R.C.: Development of abbreviated nine-item forms of the raven's standard progressive matrices test. Assessment **19**(3), 354–369 (2012). https://doi.org/10.1177/1073191112446655

Cabeza, R., Anderson, N.D., Locantore, J.K., McIntosh, A.R.: Aging gracefully: compensatory brain activity in high-performing older adults. Neuroimage **17**(3), 1394–1402 (2002)

Causse, M., Mouratille, D., Baumgartner, M., Imbert, J.-P. : The Impact of Age on Cognitive Performance at Work: A Focus on Pilots and Air Traffic Controllers. In Handbook of Aviation Neuropsychology A Practical Guide for the Clinician, pp. 499–512. Hogrefe Publishing Corp (2025)

Causse, M., Sénard, J.-M., Démonet, J.F., Pastor, J.: Monitoring cognitive and emotional processes through pupil and cardiac response during dynamic versus logical task. Appl. Psychophysiol. Biofeedback **35**, 115–123 (2010)

Craik, F.I.: Memory changes in normal aging. Curr. Dir. Psychol. Sci. **3**(5), 155–158 (1994)

Fan, J., McCandliss, B.D., Sommer, T., Raz, A., Posner, M.I.: Testing the efficiency and independence of attentional networks. J. Cogn. Neurosci. **14**(3), 340–347 (2002)

Fisk, J.E., Sharp, C.A.: Age-related impairment in executive functioning: updating, inhibition, shifting, and access. J. Clin. Exp. Neuropsychol. **26**(7), 874–890 (2004)

Frossard, J., Renaud, O.: Permutation tests for regression, ANOVA, and comparison of signals: the permuco package. J. Stat. Softw. **99**, 1–32 (2021)

Fujii, D.E., Kaseda, E.T., Sakamoto-Pomeroy, M.: Japanese performance profile on the WAIS-IV and purported cultural influences. Arch. Clin. Neuropsychol. **39**(8), 1321–1331 (2024)

Gunstad, J., Paul, R.H., Cohen, R.A., Tate, D.F., Spitznagel, M.B., Gordon, E.: Elevated body mass index is associated with executive dysfunction in otherwise healthy adults. Compr. Psychiatry **48**(1), 57–61 (2007)

Hedden, T., Park, D.C., Nisbett, R., Ji, L.-J., Jing, Q., Jiao, S.: Cultural variation in verbal versus spatial neuropsychological function across the life span. Neuropsychology **16**(1), 65 (2002)

Henelius, A., Hirvonen, K., Holm, A., Korpela, J., Muller, K.: Mental workload classification using heart rate metrics, pp. 1836–1839 (2009)

Hernández, M., Costa, A., Fuentes, L.J., Vivas, A.B., Sebastián-Gallés, N.: The impact of bilingualism on the executive control and orienting networks of attention. Bilingual.: Lang. Cogn. **13**(3), 315–325 (2010)

Hertzog, C., Jopp, D.S.: Resilience in the face of cognitive aging: experience, adaptation, and compensation. New Frontiers in Resilient Aging: Life-Strengths and Well-Being in Late Life, pp. 130–161 (2010)

Heslegrave, R.: Fatigue: Performance impairment, sleep and ageing in shiftwork operations. Managing Fatigue in Transportation. In: Proceedings of the 3rd Fatigue in Transportation Conference (1998)

Hommel, B., Li, K.Z.H., Li, S.-C.: Visual search across the life span. Dev. Psychol. **40**(4), 545–558 (2004). https://doi.org/10.1037/0012-1649.40.4.545

Kallambettu, V., Burda, A.N., Wakeman, N.: South Asian adults' performance on executive function tests. Am. J. Speech Lang. Pathol. **26**(4), 1254–1261 (2017)

Katsanos, A.H., et al.: World-wide variations in tests of cognition and activities of daily living in participants of six international randomized controlled trials. Cerebral Circul.-Cogn. Behav. **5**, 100176 (2023)

MacDonald, S., Johnson, C.: Assessment of subtle cognitive-communication deficits following acquired brain injury: a normative study of the Functional Assessment of Verbal Reasoning and Executive Strategies (FAVRES). Brain Inj. **19**(11), 895–902 (2005)

Mackworth, N.H.: The breakdown of vigilance during prolonged visual search. Quar. J. Exper. Psychol. **1**(1), 6–21 (1948)

Miyake, A., Friedman, N.P., Emerson, M.J., Witzki, A.H., Howerter, A., Wager, T.D.: The unity and diversity of executive functions and their contributions to complex "frontal lobe" tasks: a latent variable analysis. Cogn. Psychol. **41**(1), 49–100 (2000)

Nagel, I.E., et al.: Performance level modulates adult age differences in brain activation during spatial working memory. Proc. Natl. Acad. Sci. **106**(52), 22552–22557 (2009)

Nawaz, S., Modatheeri, J.: Comparative cognitive performance of 60-year-old asian and western pilots on the cogscreen test: a cross-sectional study. Int. J. Innovat. Sci. Res. Technol. **9**(5) (2024). https://doi.org/10.38124/ijisrt/IJISRT24MAY1488

Park, D.C.: Aging, cognition, and culture: a neuroscientific perspective. Neurosci. Biobehav. Rev. **26**(7), 859–867 (2002)

Park, D.C., Nisbett, R., Hedden, T.: Aging, Culture, and Cognition. The Journals of Gerontology: Series B **54B**(2), P75–P84 (1999). https://doi.org/10.1093/geronb/54B.2.P75

Peltola, M.A.: Role of editing of R-R intervals in the analysis of heart rate variability. Front. Physiol. **3**, 148 (2012)

Piccardi, L., Iaria, G., Ricci, M., Bianchini, F., Zompanti, L., Guariglia, C.: Walking in the Corsi test: which type of memory do you need? Neurosci. Lett. **432**(2), 127–131 (2008)

R Core Team. R: A language and environment for statistical computing. Foundation for Statistical Computing, Vienna, Austria (2013)

Reuter-Lorenz, P.A., Cappell, K.A.: Neurocognitive aging and the compensation hypothesis. Curr. Dir. Psychol. Sci. **17**(3), 177–182 (2008). https://doi.org/10.1111/j.1467-8721.2008.00570.x

Reuter-Lorenz, P.A., Lustig, C.: Brain aging: reorganizing discoveries about the aging mind. Curr. Opin. Neurobiol. **15**(2), 245–251 (2005)

Salthouse, T.A.: The aging of working memory. Neuropsychology **8**(4), 535 (1994)

Schneider-Garces, N.J., et al.: Span, CRUNCH, and beyond: working memory capacity and the aging brain. J. Cogn. Neurosci. **22**(4), 655–669 (2010). https://doi.org/10.1162/jocn.2009.21230

Shadlen, M., et al.: Ethnicity and cognitive performance among older African Americans, Japanese Americans, and Caucasians: the role of education. J. Am. Geriatr. Soc. **49**(10), 1371–1378 (2001)

Techentin, C., Voyer, D., Voyer, S.D.: Spatial abilities and aging: a meta-analysis. Exp. Aging Res. **40**(4), 395–425 (2014). https://doi.org/10.1080/0361073X.2014.926773

Treitz, F.H., Heyder, K., Daum, I.: Differential course of executive control changes during normal aging. Aging Neuropsychol. Cogn. **14**(4), 370–393 (2007). https://doi.org/10.1080/13825580600678442

van Drongelen, A., Boot, C.R., Hlobil, H., Smid, T., van der Beek, A.J.: Risk factors for fatigue among airline pilots. Int. Arch. Occup. Environ. Health **90**, 39–47 (2017)

Wilson, B.A., Alderman, N., Burgess, P.W., Emslie, H., Evans, J.J.: BADS: behavioural assessment of the dysexecutive syndrome. Pearson London (1996)

Zaroff, C., D'Amato, R.C., Bender, H.A.: Understanding differences in cognition across the lifespan: Comparing eastern and western cultures. In: Davis, J., D'Amato, R. (eds.) Neuropsychology of Asians and Asian-Americans. Issues of Diversity in Clinical Neuropsychology. Springer, New York, NY (2013). https://doi.org/10.1007/978-1-4614-8075-4_6

Do Our Eyes Behave Differently When Automation Increases? The Influence of Automation on the Eye-Tracking Strategies During Ground Movement Management

Maik Friedrich[(✉)], Meilin Schaper, Lennard Nöhren, Lukas Tyburzy, Kathleen Muth, Florian Rudolph, Olga Gluchshenko, and Lisa Liepe

Deutsches Zentrum für Luft- und Raumfahrt, Lilienthalplatz 7, 38108 Braunschweig, Deutschland
Maik.Friedrich@dlr.de

Abstract. The area of air traffic control provides an excellent task environment to analyse the influence of automation systems. This is not only because EURO-CONTROL estimated a lack of 700 qualified air traffic controllers but also because the task has high workload demands and is restricted to defined procedures. An increase in automation has influence on the interaction between operator and system. In this paper we focus on the influence of increased automation on the eye movement in the task environment of an air traffic controller for ground movement management. An existing surface management system was extended to simulate the stages of support or automation in combination with a notification option. Ten air traffic control officers participated in the validation and tested the feasibility of the overall approach. Their eye movement was captured and analysed for different patterns during four conditions. The results show that higher automation leads to an increase in overall monitoring. The paper then discusses this implication on the task itself and the future design of automation systems.

Keywords: ground movement management · automation · eye-tracking · strategy shift

1 Introduction

The rapid advances of systems that increase automation have introduced transformative changes across industries. Additionally, the application of increased automation is a growing influence on modern day society. The opportunities fuelled by artificial intelligence seem endless, especially in the area of developing automated system based on excessive amounts of previously collected data. Due to the nature of air traffic control, a well-defined task in a restricted environment, the methods of increased automation can be applied particularly well. A first use case is the optimisation of air traffic ground trajectories to ensure a smooth and environmentally friendly traffic, e.g. by reducing the time the engines are running. Advanced assistant systems that can either support the Air Traffic Control Officers (ATCO) by reducing their workload while additionally satisfying more constraints or automate e.g., the planning of taxi times completely. The general aspect of this process is the transition from support to automation that is still under discussion in different domains, e.g. marketing [1], driving [2, 3], or aviation [4].

As an extension of this general discussion in the aviation domain, for this paper we are focusing on the influences of automation. Due to automation increase the impact for ATCOs can have two directions, leading to either increase in boredom or additional tasks. When automation efficiently handles repetitive and routine processes, operators may find themselves with fewer engaging tasks, resulting in boredom. Conversely, automation can also create additional workload for ATCOs. Operators might need to monitor and evaluate each automation decision to ensure safety and reliability. This shift can demand higher technical skills and continuous learning, transforming the role of the ATCO into one that is more dynamic and multifaceted. In either way, the goal of increased automation should be to make the processes more efficient, reliable, and personalized, while also ensuring that ATCOs feel supported and engaged.

To achieve the goals of increased automation a user-centered design approach is needed. This process includes the automation and the ATCO at the same time. For the automation the key operator tasks, that are repetitive, time-consuming, or prone to human error, have to be identified. For the ATCO side the needs and preferences of the interaction with an automated system, and the changes in behavior have to be thoroughly analyzed. This minimizes the margin for error in this safety driven environment. Of course, the process itself has to ensure that automation aligns with ethical standards, data security, fairness and respects user privacy.

The analysis of the goals of increased automation can be performed in multiple ways. Following the flow of information by a user-centered design approach the operator gathers information from the environment by listening and observing. [5] describes applied features to support the operator in gathering information. In a previous paper [6] we published the validation setup as well as interview and questioning results showing influence of automation on a subjective level by the operators. In this paper, because the transition process also influences the observation pattern of the ATCOs we focus on eye movements.

There are several publications on the influence of increased automation to the eye movement behavior [7, 8]. In general, automation has influence on attention [9, 10] of each user that results in a change of an eye movement pattern. This shift of focus could go in any direction, but if supported with a user-centered design, can lead to a transition of today's e.g. manual process tasks to tasks related to strategic decision making. This can increase the situation awareness of the overall system but comes at the cost of reduced focus on manual process tasks.

As support for the user-centered design approach, we need to identify and define the expected influence of increased automations on eye movement. In the future, this knowledge helps to decide if and how the design needs to change to ensure users have all the information when needed. In the driving domain, authors [11, 12] provide evidence that operators spend more dwell time on the overall situation rather than focus on supervision of the automation. This transition of dwell times could also indicate a shift in gaze pattern [13], as it is also the case in the driving domain. As for other domains, this information can be used to support the user-centered design approach and decide if the driver has to monitor critical automated systems in case of error.

In the air traffic control (ATC) environment the ATCOs' gaze patterns play a crucial role in maintaining safety and preventing accidents. Changes in gaze patterns can significantly impact situation awareness, decision-making, and overall performance in conflict situations. Therefore, the evaluation of changes must go beyond assessing their impact on gaze pattern. While gaze pattern can be important for productivity and resource management, prioritizing safety is the highest goal, as it directly affects human well-being.

The evaluation of changes to the gaze pattern is in general based on the measurement of eye movement and can be done with various methods. It often involves analysing eye-tracking data to measure parameters like fixation duration, saccade amplitude, and areas of interest (AOI) transitions. These metrics can reveal shifts in how individuals process visual information, such as transitioning from broad scanning to focused attention. Techniques like statistical analysis, event detection algorithms, and experimental tasks are commonly used to assess these changes [14].

2 Research Questions

As we can see, even with the rapid advances the automation research field remains relatively nascent. As a result, the full implication of increased automation is still not fully understood. This uncertainty underscores the importance of an explorative research approach. Exploratory research is invaluable for capturing the nuances increased automation influence on workforce dynamics and procedures during safe ATC. With the focus on the influence of automation in the area of ATC and with the specialization on eye-tracking we identified following three research questions (RQ).

The first question has the focus on the general eye movement behaviour during increased automation. **RQ1: How is the ATCOs' eye-tracking behaviour in general influenced by the automated system?** Based on RQ1 we further analyse the influence on a strategy level. This also might provide inside for user-interface designers that have to know the strategies normally used for an interface. **RQ2: Are there any changes to the eye-tracking strategies on a behaviour level?** The last RQ concerns the ATCOs ability to regain situational awareness of manual task if the increased automation fails and how is this connected to the eye movement. If ATCOs realize that the increased automation failed could they be able to perform a system input in response. **RQ3: How long is the average response time in eye tracking and acknowledgment if the automated system fails?**

3 Validation

Increased automation, characterized by its ability to support or completely perform system functions in response to changing conditions, is best examined in a human-in-the-loop (HITL) validation. This approach integrates ATCOs into the automation loop, allowing their behaviors, decisions, and interactions to directly influence the system and vice versa. This ensures most realistic eye behavior in a safe environment. The automation and experimental setup are already published in [5, 6]. In order to provide the reader with the necessary information we provide a brief description of the experimental set-up and focus on the data gathering of the eye-tracking to support the formulated RQ.

3.1 Participants

The study sample comprised 10 ground and apron controllers (including one female) working at German airports located in Leipzig, Berlin, Munich, Hannover, and Sylt. Participants ranged in age from 23 to 57 years (M = 34.20, SD = 10.66) and had an average of 10.25 years (SD = 8.61) of professional experience as active controllers.[6] None of the participants had work experience at the work environment airport selected for the validation.

3.2 Set-Up

The NARSIM [15] was used in the Airport Tower Simulator (ATS360) at the institute of Flight Guidance from the German Aerospace Center (DLR). It is a 360-degree view real-time simulator to generate a realistic environment. The simulator allows for HITL simulation with specific configurations for the controller working position (CWPs). A work environment based on Hamburg airport (EDDH) was selected, because of its complex apron routing structure. Runway 33 was active for the departures and runway 23 for the arrivals. This configuration was fixed during all validation runs. The ATS360 was equipped with a ground CWP, responsible for all aprons and taxiways, and a tower CWP. The increased automation was implemented with the Traffic Management Intrusion and Compliance System (TraMICS). The TraMICS is a surface manager system (see Fi. 1, the AOIs are explained in detail in 3.4), developed by the DLR to increase security and efficiency for the ground controller workplace [6]. TraMICS can identify security threats with a precise conformance monitoring [16]. Only the TraMICS automation and therefore the ground CWP was the subject of our investigation [6]. The tower CWP only simulated the normal handover procedures between ground and tower controller to increase external validity.

We used a within-subject design with 2x2 conditions (Assistance; Notification) in a combination with a 5th explorative automation failure run [6]. This combination allowed the evaluation of all three RQ. The level of assistance was "support" and "automation". In the "support" condition the TraMICS would provide recommendations when and how to act for the ATCO. In the "automation" condition the TraMICS would initiate the recommendation via datalink directly to the simulation pilots and inform the ATCO about realized actions. The level of notification was "alerts" and "no alerts". The alerts were used to inform the ATCO about specific situations that were detected by the TraMICS. If "no alerts" were provided the ATCO had done identify specific situations on his/her own. Three types of specific situations were used: A flight moves without appropriate clearance, a flight deviates from its cleared taxi route and a flight is cleared for movement but does not start movement within a certain time. Table 1 shows a summary of all the 2×2 conditions in combination with each other and with the increase in automation.

A training scenario and five simulation scenarios, comparable in complexity but different on order of aircrafts, were used to reduce training effects. Four scenarios were

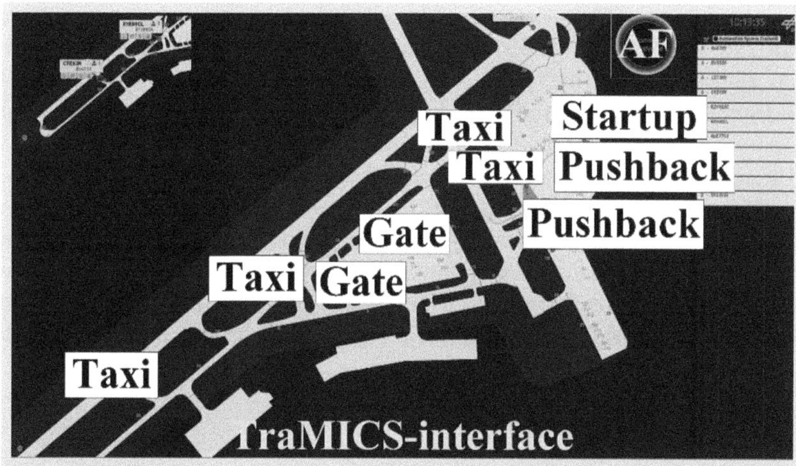

Fig. 1. TraMICS interface for the apron of Hamburg airport with static AOIs (yellow, AF - automation failure button and the complete TraMICS-interface) and dynamic AOIs of the aircrafts in different situations (in white, Taxi, Gate, Pushback, or Startup) (Color figure online)

Table 1. The 2 × 2 design with an expected stepwise increased automation for each condition in brackets.

		Assistance	
		support	automation
Notifications	no alerts	support-no-alerts (low)	automation-no-alerts (medium-high)
	alerts	support-alerts (medium-low)	automation-alerts (high)

randomized with the 2 × 2 conditions for each participant. Only the 5th scenario was equal for all participants because it always contained the automation failure situation. During this scenario Notification provided "alerts" and Assistance was on "automation" but both systems failed after 20 min and without the knowledge of the participants. At the same moment the AF button started to flash red (see Fig. 1). If the participants did not acknowledge the flashing AF button, they were instructed by the observers to do so. The scenario one to four had a duration of 45 min, and scenario five had a duration of 39 min, because the measurements for their reaction times was after 20 min. For details on the traffic mixture see [6].

3.3 Procedure

Participants, after given informed consent, were briefed on their task, the CWP and the experimental schedule. They were instructed to follow system recommendation in the "support" and "automation" condition and received a training run on the features and functionalities of the CWP. They were also briefed on reporting the specific situations described above as well as any comments, remarks or questions which may occur during the runs. Before each run, the eye-tracking glasses were calibrated. As mentioned above, each participant performed each of the four main conditions support-no-alerts, support-alerts, automation-no-alerts, and automation-alerts in a random order, each in dedicated run. The fifth run was always the scheduled failure of the automated system. Thereby the participants had to identify the failure and regain full situation awareness to control the traffic by themselves again. If they did not do it intuitively, the experiment observers encouraged them to press the flashing button to acknowledge the failure of the automated system, after a maximum of 3 min. Each participant was debriefed at the end. A complete run with instructions, training, 5 runs and debriefing took around one and a half day.

3.4 Measurements

Experimenters observed the participants during the runs and collected general feedback. We also used questionnaires and debriefings after each run. Eye-tracking was used to record the individual gaze behaviour during each run. The eye movement was captured with a pupil labs "I can see clearly now" package that had a custom-made frame for the head tracking [17]. The raw 50Hz eye data was captured with the simulations time stamp and analysed with the DLR software EyeTrackingAnalyser [18]. For the identification of fixations a velocity based algorithm with an individual speed threshold of 5% fastest transitions and a minimum fixation duration of 30ms was used [19]. The AOI are divided into static (TraMICs-interface, AF, Outside) and dynamic (Gate, Pushback, Startup and Taxi). The static AOIs were always at the same position of the screens. The dynamic AOIs depend on the individual aircraft label positions and operational states. The AOI Gate became active 120 s before planed push back. Then the AOI Pushback, Startup and Taxi became active depending on the participants decision making or Assistance "automation". The eye data of run #1 to #4 was connected to the dynamic AOIs (see Fig. 1). All dynamic AOIs were on top of the static TraMICS-interface AOI. The static Outside AOI represents the view into the 360° panoramic view of the airport. The run #5 was connected to the response times of eye tracking and acknowledgement after the failure of the increased automation.

During each run the Instantaneous Self-Assessment [20] was used to evaluate the workload. After each run the situation awareness for SHAPE, Assessing the Impact of Automation on Mental Workload in the short version and SHAPE Automation Trust Index, and the System Usability Scale were used to support the validation process of the increased automation, because this is not the focus of this paper, see analysis in [6].

4 Results

The results section provides a detailed analysis for each RQ. For each participant five sets of eye movement data (for each of the runs) was collected. Only one set of data had to be removed from the analysis because the recording of the eye movement stopped unnoticed after 1 min. The remaining 49 data sets had on average 95.2% (sd = 2.76, min = 86.8, max = 98.5) of valid data.

For RQ1 (general eye-tracking influence of the automated system) we analyzed the general eye distribution throughout the different conditions and AOIs, either dynamic or static. The first step in the analysis was the adjustment of eye data and the dynamic AOIs Gate, Pushback, Startup, Taxi. The influence of level of automation and alerts was tested for each AOI individually. The descriptive results are summarized in Fig. 2.

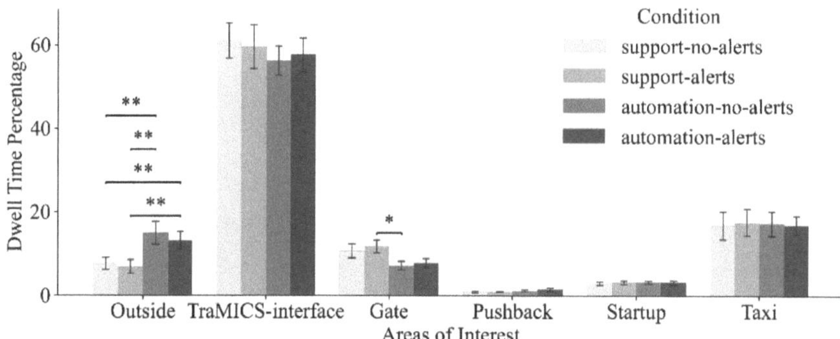

Fig. 2. Comparison of average dwell percentages per AOI in the experimental conditions. Significance stars: * p < 0.05, ** p < 0.01, *** p < 0.001. Differences were determined using a t-test.

Six 2x2 repeated measures ANOVA were conducted to examine the effects of Assistance and Notifications. For the AOI Outside the main effect of level of Assistance was significant, $F(1, 8) = 32.245, p < .002$, partial $\eta^2 = .233$. The main effect of Notifications was not significant, $F(1, 8) = 1.686, p = .23$, partial $\eta^2 = .006$ and so was the interaction between both factors $F(1, 8) = 1.376, p = .275$, partial $\eta^2 = .004$. The post-hoc pairwise comparisons showed both Assistance conditions (automation-no-alerts versus support-no-alerts $t(8) = 4.404$, $p_{holm} = .0008$, automation-no-alerts versus support-alerts $t(8) = 4.516$ $p_{holm} = .0008$, automation-alerts versus support-no-alerts $t(8) = 5.306$, $p_{holm} = .0002$ and automation-alerts versus support-alerts $t(8) = 6.101$, $p_{holm} = .0003$) are significantly higher than their counterparts in the Notification condition. For the AOI Gate only the main effect for Assistance was significant, $F(1, 8) = 12.683, p < .007$, partial $\eta^2 = .180$. The post-hoc test showed a significant difference between automation-no-alerts and support-alerts $t(8) = -4.106, p_{holm} = .02$. As for the AOI Gate, for the AOI Pushback only the main effect for Assistance $F(1, 8) = 6.141, p = .038$ was significant, but none of the post-hoc test was significant.

The analysis for RQ2 (changes to eye-tracking strategies) focuses on transitions probabilities. A single transition represents the change from one AOI to another AOI or itself if the velocity of the eye movement is high enough to reach the velocity threshold. In a first step the transitions for all AOIs were counted and their probability in relation to all other AOIs was calculated. Figure 3 shows the transitions probability between the AOIs separated by the four conditions. The probabilities in each metrics represent an eye movement behavior pattern depending on the conditions. The differences in transition probabilities between the conditions are minimal. The correlation coefficient between the conditions is almost $r = 1$ for all combination, with a minimum correlation of r

300   M. Friedrich et al.

= 0.9907 between automation-no-alerts and support-alerts. The transition probability indicates the eye movement on this general level is equal.

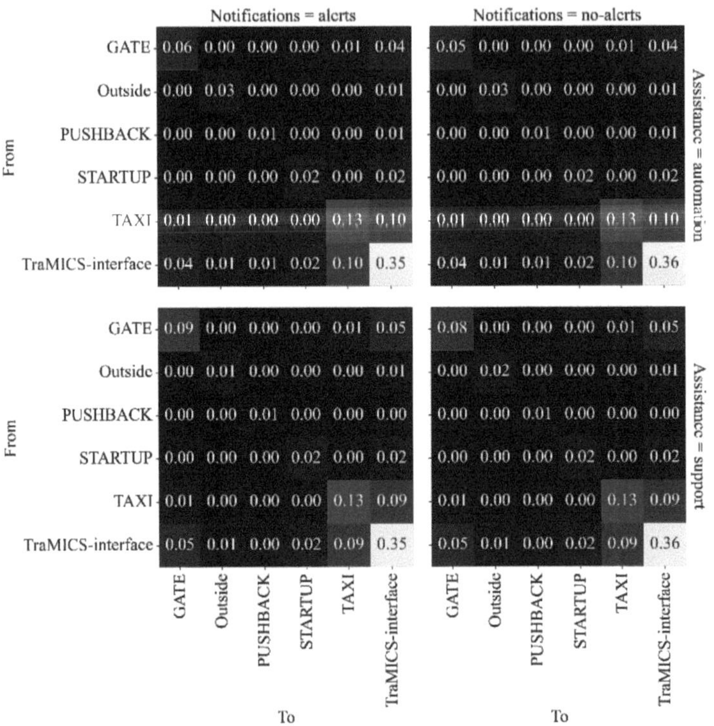

Fig. 3. Visualization of transition probability from each AOI to each AOI: Each heatmap represents the transitions probability for each of the four conditions. Darker colors indicate lower values, while lighter shades represent higher values.

Based on the results of RQ1 (significant difference for AOI Gate) and Fig. 3 (no difference in the general AOI transitions), we focus for the second step for RQ2 on the AOI Gate. The smallest transition for a strategy patter is a triple transition between AOIs. Figure 4 shows the seven main AOI triplet transition for each condition containing the AOI Gate. The largest difference is between the assistance conditions, especially with no-alerts. The triplet with the largest difference is Gate-Gate-Gate that refers to the total amount of AOI changes within the AOI Gate.

For RQ3 (reaction time at system failure) we compare two reactions times. First, we measured the time between the failure and the next fixation on the AOI AF (automation failure see Fig. 1) as a visual reaction time. Second, the time between the failure and the push of the automation failure button was calculated as physical response time, to identify when the participants were able to acknowledge the automation failure. The results of the response times are presented in Fig. 5. The physical response times are on average 32.1 s longer than the visual reaction times. The linear correlation between both times is $r^2 = .06$. An independent one-tailed t-test was conducted to examine whether the visual

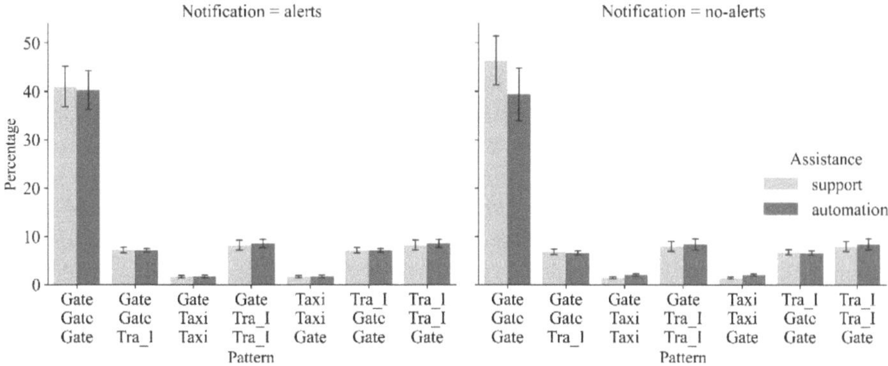

Fig. 4. The 7 main transition including the AOI Gate for each level of Assistance and Notification (TraMICs-interface was shortened to Tra_I to increase readability).

reaction times demonstrated significantly lower times compared to the physical reaction times. The results indicated that visual reaction times ($\mu = 5.17$s, $sd = 8.27$) exhibited significantly lesser values than physical response times ($\mu = 37.3$s, $sd = 48.11$), t(17) $=$ -1.971, p $= 0.032$ (one-tailed). The responses were also part of the debriefing after the failure run and the results showed a large variety of answers. From angry participants due to the - intentionally not briefed - surprise situation to participants admitting that they did not understand the consequences of the system failure.

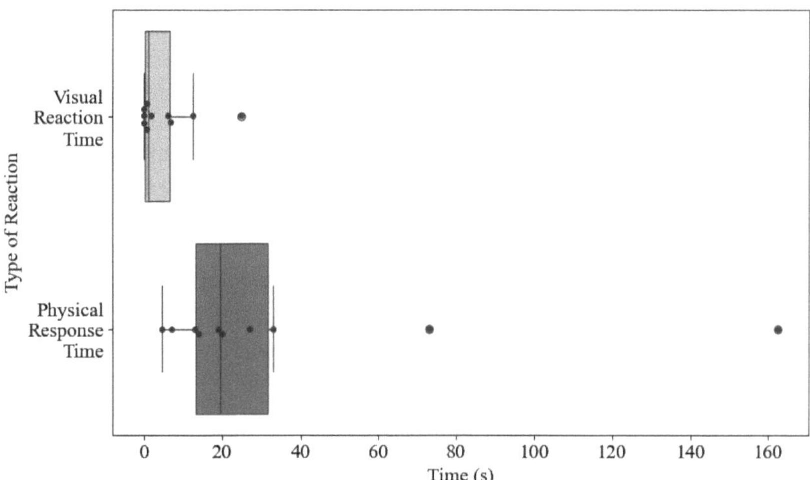

Fig. 5. Comparison of visual reaction times and physical response times, with clear outlier detection. The dots represent each measured timing.

5 Discussion

The data used in this study demonstrates high-quality characteristics across multiple dimensions. Completeness is ensured, with only one missing data set due to technical issues with the recording. The accuracy of the data was maintained through careful measurement protocols, minimizing potential errors. The data set is highly relevant and contains the necessary variables linked to three RQs, without extraneous or redundant data. The distribution of the data was assessed, revealing a normal distribution with minor outliers that were analyzed and retained to ensure validity. Regarding validity, the data was collected with only ATCOs as participants, making them representative of the population of interest. Consistency checks confirmed that no contradictions exist within the data set. The data collection process is fully documented, providing reproducibility under the same conditions and is in context with ethical and data safety regulations.

While this study provides valuable insights, several limitations should be acknowledged before the RQs are discussed. First, the sample size is relatively small that limits the generalizability of the findings to a larger group of ATCOs. Additionally, the data was collected within a HITL simulation that of course is realistic but not the reality. Although efforts were made to ensure the validity of the measurements, e.g., potential biases in data collection cannot be entirely ruled out, especially for the failure run that was not varied with the other runs.

RQ1 was concentrated on the general influence on the eye movement in relation to the conditions Assistance and Notifications of automation. The results show that Assistance influences the amount of time that participants spend on AOIs, but not equally for all AOIs. The Assistance has no effect on the monitoring of the AOIs Startup, Pushback, or Taxi but the AOI Outside and Gate. The transition of the ATCOs dwell time percentages within the AOI Outside is as we would expect in a system with increased automation. Dwell time is spent more on the Outside because the increased automation manages on the TraMICS-interface. At the same time, the AOI Gate decreased in relevance with increased automation and even significantly more if there are no additional notification, that draw attention. We can derive that, that the decrease in dwell time percentage on the AOIs Gate and TraMICS-interface is transferred to the AOI Outside that provides an alternative view on the task relevant areas.

Due to the general influence of automation identified for RQ1, RQ2 should provide insights into how the eye-tracking strategy changes. The correlation between the AOI transition for each experimental condition was almost equal indicating that no changes between the AOIs transitions occur. However, the change in dwell time percentage was significant and therefore change in eye movement behaviour occurred. The triplet transition analysis showed the difference especially for repeating AOI fixation. In the context of the ATC this indicates that increased automation would not lead to the neglection of less task relevant AOIs but a reduction of dwell time. The RQ2 analysis does not show where the fixations increase. Of course, in general they increase on the AOI Outside, but there is no detailed data where exactly. As mentioned above, the outside view contains task relevant information, e.g., aircraft positions but in a different representation than on the TraMICS-interface. Do the ATCOs look at the aircraft at the gates or do they monitor safety critical situation, do they just relax by looking outside to the real aircraft instead of aircraft icons on the display, or enjoying the traffic controlled by the automation? Based on our analysis we cannot definitively answer this new research question.

RQ3 has the lowest explanatory power because the experimental design in this case was the weakest, due to the fact that each participant could only be surprised once with the system failure. Also, the meaningfulness of reaction versus response times to click the flashing button is low, as the participants were not briefed to do that action and it was only a tool of acknowledgment of the new situations. Nonetheless, the reaction times show a fast reaction to visual stimuli that indicated that the salience of the button itself is high enough to inform the ATCO. The delay between visual reaction and physical response indicates a duration of adaptation to the changed situation is needed.

6 Summary and Outlook

The increase in automation will change workplaces and the work itself. We have to figure out how this change will happen and how we can support the process benefiting everyone. This study provides valuable insight into changes in eye movement pattern with increased automation for the ATC ground workplace. This helps to understand the transition for future ATCOs that transit from an active position into a monitoring task. Three RQs were used to identify the critical points during the transition.

With RQ1 we have the certainty that automation supporting the ATCO influences the dwell time. Even though this might not be a big surprise, on the one hand it has to be acknowledged first to justify the additional effort when designing future system and on the other it is important to know where change is to be expected. Then, these changes were the focus of RQ2. The analysis showed that the change is not at the expense of the overview pattern, but at the expense of the dwell times on AOIs which are less task-relevant (see the GATE AOI). Sadly, that analysis did not allow insights whether the fixations move to another task relevant information on the AOI Outside. RQ3 shows that the visual hint in form of the flashing button, that the automation failed influences the eyes of the participant quickly, so the hint is clearly visible. The results allow no clear picture about the reaction during system failure but indicate that reaction time can be longer than the visual reaction to salient buttons. Even though the results in this study were not 100 percent conclusive, the authors are convinced that a good share of work between ATCO and automation increases safety by supporting the ATCOs with repetitive and easy tasks and therefore creating buffers for the acknowledgement of critical situation.

Future research should address mentioned limitations by expanding the sample size and employing alternative methodologies to strengthen the validity and reliability of the results. Additionally, a detailed analysis of gaze patterns will be required to better understand how and where participants' visual attention shifts during the tasks and with increased automation.

References

1. Bucklin, R., Lehmann, D., Little, J.: From decision support to decision automation: a 2020 vision. Mark. Lett. **9**(3), 235–246 (1998). https://doi.org/10.1023/A:1008047504898

2. Bosetti, P., Lio, M.D., Saroldi, A.: On curve negotiation: from driver support to automation. IEEE Trans. Intell. Transp. Syst. **16**(4), 2082–2093 (2015). https://doi.org/10.1109/TITS.2015.2395819

3. Aguilera, V., Glaser, S., Arnim, A.V.: An advanced driver speed assistance in curves: risk function, cooperation modes, system architecture and experimental validation. In: Editor (Ed.)^(Eds.) Book An Advanced Driver Speed Assistance in Curves: Risk Function, Cooperation Modes, System Architecture and Experimental Validation, pp. 807–812 (2005), https://doi.org/10.1109/IVS.2005.1505204

4. Cummings, M.L.: Automation bias in intelligent time critical decision support systems: decision making in aviation, 1st Edition edn., pp. 289–294. Routledge (2017)

5. Nöhren, L., Schaper, M., Tyburzy, L.: Towards full ATC automation for aircraft ground movement: a first step. In: Proceedings of the 43rd Digital Avionics Systems Conference. San Diego, USA (2024). https://elib.dlr.de/209427/

6. Schaper, M., et al.: Validation of an automated ground movement management system. CEAS Aeronaut. J. (in press)

7. Hasse, C., Bruder, C.: Eye-tracking measurements and their link to a normative model of monitoring behaviour. Ergonomics **58**(3), 355–367 (2015). https://doi.org/10.1080/00140139.2014.967310

8. Fidopiastis, C.M., et al.: Impact of automation and task load on unmanned system operator's eye movement patterns. In: Editor (Ed.)^(Eds.) Book Impact of Automation and Task Load on unmAnned System Operator's Eye Movement Patterns, pp. 229–238. Springer (20090)

9. Baer, M., and Plattfaut, R.: Human friendly automation: a literature review on the role of the human factor in AI-driven business process automation. In: Editor (Ed.) ^(Eds.) Book Human Friendly Automation: A Literature Review on the Role of the Human Factor in AI-Driven Business Process Automation, pp. 287–301. Springer Nature Switzerland (2024)

10. Yaqot, M., Menezes, B., Mohammed, A., Moloney, K.: A state-of-the-art review and framework for human-centric automation in industry 5.0. In: Editor (Ed.)^(Eds.) Book A State-of-the-Art Review and Framework for Human-Centric Automation in Industry .0, pp. 385–400. Springer Nature Switzerland (2024)

11. Liang, N., et al.: Using eye-tracking to investigate the effects of pre-takeover visual engagement on situation awareness during automated driving. Accident Anal. Prevent. **157**, 106143, (2021). https://doi.org/10.1016/j.aap.2021.106143

12. Ulahannan, A., Jennings, P., Oliveira, L., Birrell, S.: Designing an adaptive interface: using eye tracking to classify how information usage changes over time in partially automated vehicles. IEEE Access **8**, 16865–16875 (2020). https://doi.org/10.1109/ACCESS.2020.2966928

13. Hergeth, S., Lorenz, L., Vilimek, R., Krems, J.F.: Keep your scanners peeled: gaze behavior as a measure of automation trust during highly automated driving. Hum. Factors **58**(3), 509–519 (2016). https://doi.org/10.1177/0018720815625744

14. Holmqvist, K., Nyström, M., Andersson, R., Dewhurst, R., Jarodzka, H., Van de Weijer, J.: Eye tracking: a comprehensive guide to methods and measures. OUP Oxford (2011)

15. Ten Have, J.: The development of the NLR ATC Research Simulator (Narsim): design philosophy and potential for ATM research. Simul. Pract. Theory **1**(1), 31–39 (1993)

16. Schaper, M., Gluchshenko, O., Muth, K., Tyburzy, L., Rusko, M., Trnka, M.: 'The traffic management intrusion and compliance system as security situation assessment system at an air traffic controller's working position. In: Editor (Ed.)^(Eds.) Book The Traffic Management Intrusion and Compliance System as Security Situation Assessment System at an Air Traffic Controller's Working Position, pp. 2825–2831 (2021). https://doi.org/10.3850/978-981-18-2016-8_550-cd

17. https://pupil-labs.com/products/neon/specs

18. Friedrich, M., Rußwinkel, N., Möhlenbrink, C.: 'A guideline for integrating dynamic areas of interests in existing set-up for capturing eye movement: looking at moving aircraft. Behav. Res. Meth. **49**(3) (2016). https://doi.org/10.3758/s13428-016-0745-x
19. Salvucci, D.D., Goldberg, J.H.: Identifying fixations and saccades in eye-tracking protocols. In: Editor (Ed.) ^(Eds.) Book Identifying Fixations and Saccades in Eye-Tracking Protocols, pp. 71–78. ACM Press (2000)
20. Tattersall, A.J., Foord, P.S.: An experimental evaluation of instantaneous self-assessment as a measure of workload. Ergonomics **39**, 740–748 (1996)

A Study of Eye Movement Behavioral Differences Among Air Traffic Controllers

Qiuli Gu[✉] and Lili Wang

Civil Aviation University of China, Tianjin 300300, China
`qlgu@cauc.edu.cn`

Abstract. The present study explores the relationship between eye movement behaviour and control ability in the context of cognitive workload. The role of eye movement behaviour of radar controllers in the control process was analysed in the light of the actual work of the controllers. It is posited that controllers primarily utilise eye gaze and scanning behaviours to obtain flight information and monitor the flight operation situation in the sector, thereby ensuring the safety of the aircraft. The thesis thus undertakes a comparative and analytical investigation of the gaze and scanning behaviours exhibited by level 3, 4 and 5 controllers, with a view to ascertaining the disparities in their control abilities. Additionally, it explores the influence of accumulated workload on controllers' control ability, by comparing the gaze and scanning behaviours of controllers of the same level before and after posting.

Keywords: air traffic controllers · gaze behavior · scanning behavior · difference analysis

1 Introduction

The primary responsibility of air traffic controllers is to ensure the safe, orderly and efficient operation of aircraft. In the context of the continuous updating and iteration of the ATC automation system, the intelligent operation system has been demonstrated to reduce the operation load of radar controllers in the human-computer interaction system [1, 2], whilst concomitantly increasing the cognitive load generated by a greater number of visual behaviours. Radar controllers obtain flight information and monitor the flight operation situation in the sector primarily through vision during the control process, combining this with their own control experience to predict the possible risks of flights and make decisions. The eye movement behaviour of these operators is closely related to their control ability and cognitive workload [3]. Therefore, the study of the differences in eye movement behaviour is essential to improve their control ability and ensure the safety of aviation operations.

A synthesis of the extant research conducted by scholars from both domestic and international backgrounds on the subject of eye movement behaviour in controllers principally encompasses the following two aspects. Firstly, the relationship between eye movement behaviour and different work tasks is to be studied. Ahlstrom [4] et al. found

D. Harris et al. (Eds.): HCII 2025, LNCS 16334, pp. 306–317, 2026.
https://doi.org/10.1007/978-3-032-12392-3_20

that with an increase in the number of flights, the controller's workload increased linearly, and the blink duration and the average sweep distance decreased with an increase in the number of flights. The study by Stasi et al. [5] involved the establishment of three tasks with varying levels of complexity (low, medium, and high) and investigated the relationship between subjective cognitive load and sweep speed in 23 subjects. Mauro Marchitto [6] et al. analysed the effect of complex traffic situations on eye movement behaviour and showed that when the geometric complexity of the traffic situation becomes greater, the effect on large magnitude of sweeping behaviour is more pronounced, with smaller peak sweeping velocities and larger sweeping durations. The results showed that as cognitive load increased, reaction time increased and peak sweep speed decreased. Imants et al. [7] found significant differences in sweep time and gaze duration between nine subjects when completing different tasks by setting up three specified control tasks. H. J. Wee et al. [8] found that as flight traffic increased, controllers had longer average gaze durations and a larger percentage of gaze time. The second approach involves the analysis of variations in eye movement behaviours exhibited by controllers with varying degrees of experience in control. Wang Yanqing [9] et al. investigated the alterations in eye movement behaviours of 22 controllers in control simulation scenarios with three traffic levels (large, medium, and small). Their findings revealed significant disparities in eye movement behaviours between novice and experienced controllers. Moreover, the study demonstrated that experienced controllers exhibited superior situational awareness and robust information searching capabilities. In the study by Wang Chao [10] and his colleagues, 20 controllers were selected for analysis of the cognitive situation in skilled and unskilled controllers during the deployment of flight conflicts. The study found that skilled controllers require multiple consecutive and repetitive gazes to obtain sufficient information, whereas unskilled controllers demonstrate an inefficient allocation of attention, with insufficient focus on flight information and an inability to accurately identify the location of the conflict point. This results in a lower control efficiency. Wang Yanjun et al. [11, 12] statistically analysed the eye movement behaviour data of 25 controllers with varying levels of control experience. Their findings indicated that control experience exerts a significant influence on gaze and scanning behaviours. Furthermore, the study concluded that controllers with greater control experience demonstrate superior information searching capabilities.

A review of the extant literature reveals a strong relationship between a controller's cognitive workload and eye movement behaviour, and that control experience exerts a significant effect on a controller's eye movement behaviour. Previous studies have primarily concentrated on the disparities in eye movement behaviour between licensed mature controllers and control trainees. However, no scholars have examined the disparities in eye movement behaviour between controllers with different licence levels. The present study has therefore been designed to address this research gap by conducting an experiment to study the differences in eye movement behaviours among controllers with license levels III, IV and V, as well as the changes in eye movement behaviours of controllers of the same level before and after work. The results of the study can provide a reference for improving the competence of controllers.

2 Introduction to the Experimental Design Program

The control process can be described using Boyd's OODA decision cycle, i.e. the controller observes, locates, decides and takes action in a reciprocal cycle. The controller first observes the flight operational situation in the sector he is responsible for, locates the specific flight, obtains the flight information including flight number, flight position, altitude, speed, etc.; combined with his own control experience and based on the flight information, investigates and evaluates the flight operational situation in the sector as well as the possible risks, and makes a decision whether it is necessary to adjust altitude, change course, change speed, etc., and sends control instructions to the pilots. The controller issues control instructions to the pilots and then continuously monitors and observes the operational situation of the aircraft. Throughout the control process, the controller constantly switches between scanning and gaze behaviour to monitor the flight operation status in the sector and ensure the safety of flight operations, so it is crucial to study the controller's eye movement behaviour.

2.1 Introduction to the Programme

In order to study the differences in eye movement behaviour of controllers with different licence levels and the effects of cumulative load on controllers' post-duty eye movement behaviour, the experimental group designed a pre-duty and post-duty eye movement behaviour test for controllers according to the shift time of a control centre of a control unit, and in order to reduce the interference of experimental equipment on controllers, the on-screen eye tracking device was used to collect controllers' pre-duty and post-duty eye movement behaviour data in the simulated control test. According to the 48-h rest regulation for the 24-h work of controllers at the control centre, the pre-service test is conducted before the controllers go on duty from 08:00 to 12:00, and the post-service test is conducted after the controllers finish the 24-h work from 01:00 to 05:00, with the specific time of the test being the end of the controllers' work that night.

The content of the pre and posttest is the same, with 40 min of simulated air traffic control. The airspace is a moderately complex sector airspace, the traffic flow increases from medium to very large (10 to 30 flights), during which 3–4 special situations occur. The types of situations included: emergency descent, engine failure, low fuel operation, etc. The test controller did not know in advance the time and nature of the conditions. In order to minimise the impact of additional variables on the test, the subjects were informed of the test procedures and precautions to be taken prior to the test and to ensure that the participating controllers were in good health on the day of the test.

2.2 Test Subjects

The test group recruited 41 controllers from the Control Centre's first regional release order to participate in the test, including 23 level 5 controllers, 9 level 4 controllers (including 1 female controller) and 9 level 3 controllers (including 1 female controller). There were 39 males and 2 females, all right-handed. Their ages ranged from 25 to 48 years, with a mean age of 29.88 years; their posting ages ranged from 3 to 26 years, with a mean posting age of 7.06 years, as shown in Fig. 1.

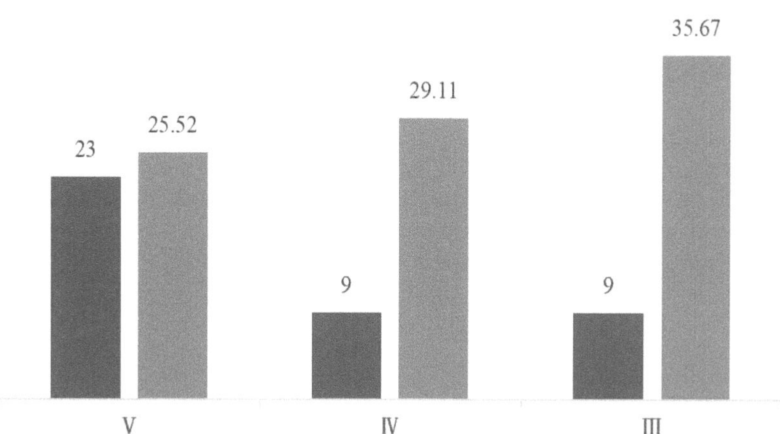

Fig. 1. Distribution of controllers by age and license level.

2.3 Test Platforms

The test location is the control centre retraining simulation control room, and the equipment is an air traffic control simulator and a Tobii on-screen eye-tracking device. The on-screen eye-tracking device is a non-contact eye-tracking device that can reduce the interference of instrumentation on the controller, as shown in Fig. 2. The on-screen eye tracker is used to collect the controller's eye movement data during the control simulation, including scanning time and gaze time.

Fig. 2. Simulation control site.

2.4 Calculation of Eye Movement Behavior Indicators

Combined with the actual work of radar controllers, the controller searches for target flights by scanning behaviour and obtains key information of the flights by watching behaviour in order to locate the operational status of the flights and provide information for decision-making. The whole process of monitoring and controlling the operational status of flights by continuously switching between scanning and watching behaviour.

The controller's scanning behaviour can be quantified by Saccade Duration (SD), which refers to the time from the end of one gaze movement to the beginning of the next gaze movement, i.e. the controller's search time for the target, and a short scanning time indicates a strong search ability. The controller's gaze behaviour can be quantified by the Total Fixation Duration (TFD), which refers to the time interval between the controller's gaze on the aircraft to extract key information and search and judge the operational status of the aircraft to make a decision, and the short gaze time (usually more than 100 ms) indicates the information extraction ability, which can effectively assess the controller's information extraction ability. The specific calculation formula is as follows.

The formula for calculating the mean value of scanning time:

$$\overline{SD} = \frac{1}{M} \sum_j z_j \tag{1}$$

Where, $\overline{SD}$ represents the mean value of sweep time, ms; Z_j represents the time of the first j sweep movement, ms; M $= 1,2,\ldots,$j represents the number of sweeps.

The formula for calculating the mean value of gaze time:

$$\overline{TFD} = \frac{1}{N} \sum_i y_i \tag{2}$$

Where, $\overline{TFD}$ represents the mean value of total gaze time, ms; y_i represents the total time to gaze at the i th aircraft, ms; N $= 1,2,\ldots,$i represents the number of aircraft sorties.

3 Differential Analysis of Controller Visual Behavior

3.1 Pre-service Eye Movement Behavior Analysis

Comparative Analysis of Scanning Time. According to the calculation, the average scanning time of level 5 controllers is 45.35 ms, the average scanning time of level 4 controllers is 50.89 ms, and the average scanning time of level 3 controllers is 53.39 ms in the simulation control test. The scanning time of level 5 controllers is more than that of level 3 controllers by 8.04 ms, and more than that of level 4 controllers by 2.50 ms. The scanning time of the level 3 controllers is the shortest, the scanning time of the level 4 controllers is the next shortest, and the scanning time of the level 5 controllers is the longest, as shown in Fig. 3. And the level V controllers had the longest sweep time, as shown in Fig. 3. The normality test was performed on the scanning time of the group of controllers with licence classes III, IV and V. All three groups of data satisfy the normal distribution. The independent samples t-test was conducted in pairs, and there was no significant difference in scanning time between the groups of level 3 and level 4 controllers and between the groups of level 4 and level 5 controllers. The group of level 3 and level 5 controllers, which satisfies the chi-square (F $= 0.383$, p > 0.05) and the p-value is less than 0.05 by independent samples t-test (t $= 30$, p $= 0.01$), suggests that the ability to search for target flights of level 5 controllers is significantly different from that of level 3 controllers, as shown in Table 1.

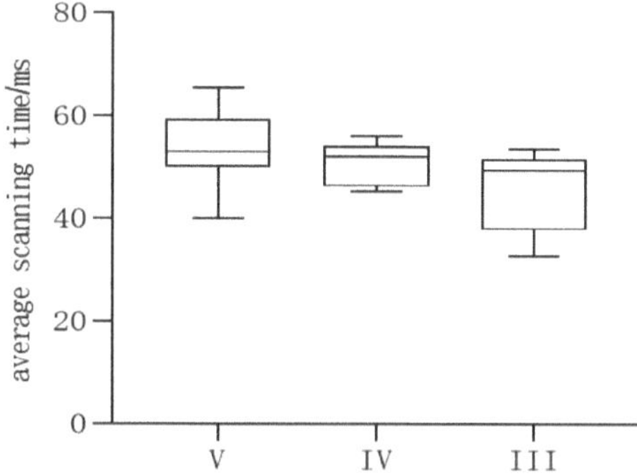

Fig. 3. Comparison of pre-post sweep time for level 3, 4 and 5 controllers.

Table 1. Independent samples t-test results for sweep and gaze time for controllers of different licence levels.

visual behaviour		licence level	No.	mean	standard error margin	Levine's test of variance equivalence		Mean equivalence t-test	
						F-value	P-value	t-value	P-value
pre-post	Sweep time	III	9	53.39	2.91856	.383	.541	−2.753	.010
		V	23	45.35	3.00408				
	Gaze time	III	9	521.44	37.89233	9.896	.006	2.485	.029
		IV	9	427.26	37.89233				
Post-post	Sweep time	III	9	49.03	3.00026	3.973	.055	−2.533	0.017
		V	23	56.30	2.31036				
	Gaze time	III	9	580.53	28.41419	1.175	.295	4.844	.000
		IV	9	422.90	28.41419				
		III	9	580.53	43.82864	8.000	.008	3.154	.004
		V	23	463.52	30.76019				

Comparative Analysis of Gaze Time. According to the calculation, the mean gaze time of the level 5 controllers in the simulation control test is 434.50 ms, the mean gaze time of the level 4 controllers is 427.26 ms and the mean gaze time of the level 3 controllers is 521.44 ms. The level 5 controllers have 86.93 ms more than the level 3 controllers and 7.24 ms more than the level 4 controllers. Level III controllers had the longest look time, as shown in Fig. 4. The normality test was performed on the gaze data of the controllers with licence levels three, four and five, and all three groups of data met the normality distribution. The independent samples t-test was performed on two pairs and there was no significant difference in gaze time between the group of level 3 and level 5 controllers and between the group of level 4 and level 5 controllers. The group gaze time of level 3 and level 4 controllers, which did not satisfy the chi-square (F = 0.9986, p < 0.05), was tested by an independent samples t-test (t = 2.485, p = 0.029), and the p-value was less than 0.05, indicating that level 3 controllers had a significant difference in their gaze time from level 4 controllers, as shown in Table 1.

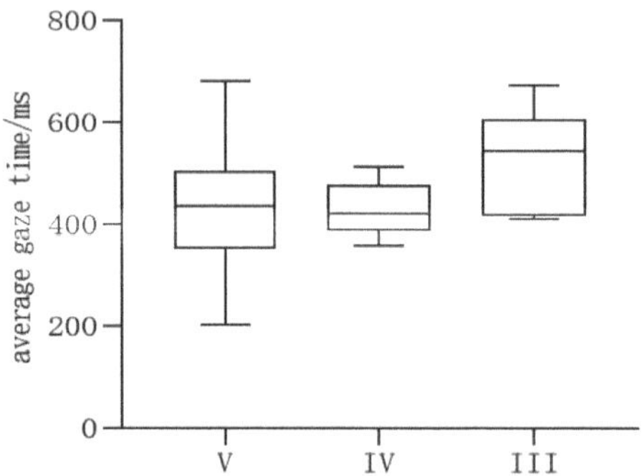

Fig. 4. Comparison of pre-post gaze time for level 3, 4 and 5 controllers.

3.2 Post-Post Visual Behavior Difference Analysis

Comparative Analysis of Sweep Time. According to the calculation, the average scanning time of the post-Service level 5 controllers is 56.30 ms, the average scanning time of the level 4 controllers is 52.40 ms, and the average scanning time of the level 3 controllers is 49.03 ms.The scanning time of the level 5 controllers is 7.27 ms more than that of the level 3 controllers and 3. The scanning time of the level 4 controllers is 90 ms more than that of the level 3 controllers, which is the same as the pre-calculation, and the scanning time of the level 3 controllers is the shortest and the scanning time of the level 5 controllers is the longest, as shown in Fig. 5. Was the shortest and the level 5 controllers had the longest scanning time, as shown in Fig. 6. The normality test was performed on the sweep times of controllers with licence levels three, four and five, and all three groups of data satisfied the normal distribution. Two pairs of independent samples t-tests were performed and there was no significant difference between the sweep time of the group of level III and IV controllers and the group of level IV and V controllers. The group of level 3 and level 5 controllers, satisfy the Chi-square (F = 3.973, p > 0.05), by independent sample t-test (t = -2.533, p = 0.017), the p-value is less than 0. 05, which indicates that there is a significant difference between the sweep time of level 3 and level 5 controllers, and that level 3 controllers have the shortest post-post sweep time and the strongest ability to search for the target, which is consistent with the results of the pre-posttest, as shown in Table 1.

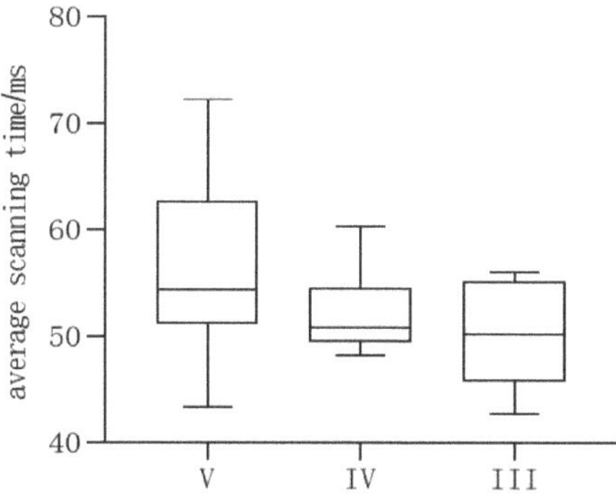

Fig. 5. Comparison of post-post sweep time for level 3, 4 and 5 controllers.

Comparative Analysis of Gaze Time. After calculation, the mean gaze time of level 5 controllers was 463.52 ms, the mean gaze time of level 4 controllers was 422.90 ms, and the mean gaze time of level 3 controllers was 580.53 ms. Level 5 controllers had 117.01 ms less scan time than level 3 controllers and 40.62 ms more than level 4 controllers, as shown in Fig. 6. Level IV controllers had the shortest looking time and level III controllers had the longest looking time. The normality test was performed on the gaze data of level three, four and five controllers, respectively, and all three sets of data satisfied the normal distribution.

Level 3 and Level 4 controllers' gaze time satisfied ANOVA chi-square (F = 1.175, p > 0.05),by independent samples t-test (t = 4.844, p = 0.000),p-value is less than 0.05,which indicates that there is a significant difference between Level 3 and Level 4 controllers' gaze time. Level 3 and Level 5 controllers did not satisfy the variance chi-square (F = 8.000, p < 0.05), by independent samples t-test (t = 3.154, p = 0.04), p-value is less than 0.05, which indicates that there is a significant difference in gaze time between Level 3 and Level 5 controllers. There was no significant difference in gaze time between level 4 and level 5 controllers. After service, level 3 controllers had the longest gaze behaviour and were significantly different from both level 4 and level 5 controllers, while before service was only significantly different from the gaze time of level 4 controllers, as shown in Table 1.

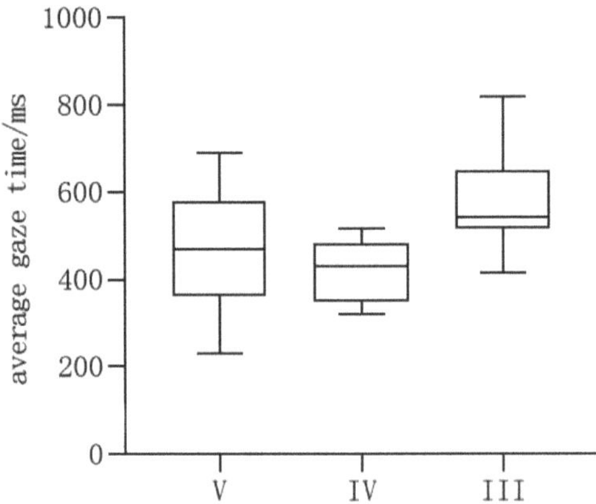

Fig. 6. Comparison of post-post gaze time for level 3, 4 and 5 controllers.

3.3   Comparative Analysis of Pre- and Post-service Visual Behavior of Controllers of the Same Rank

1. Comparative analysis of pre-service and post-service scanning time of controllers of the same rank. In order to verify the effect of fatigue on the controllers generated by the increase in individual load after the post-post, the paired sample t-test of pre-post and post-post sweeping time was conducted for three groups of controllers of the same level, and the sweeping time of the three groups satisfied the normal distribution, and there was a significant difference between pre-post and post-post for level 5 controllers and level 3 controllers after the paired test, as shown in Table 2. This indicates that after one cycle of work, the post-post generates a greater increase in individual load-generating fatigue, which affects the post-post sweeping behaviour, and the search ability is weakened. There is no significant difference between level 4 controllers, which indicates that level 4 controllers have a smaller increase in individual load after post and the increase in scanning time is 1.51 ms, but it does not have much effect on scanning ability, as shown in Fig. 7.

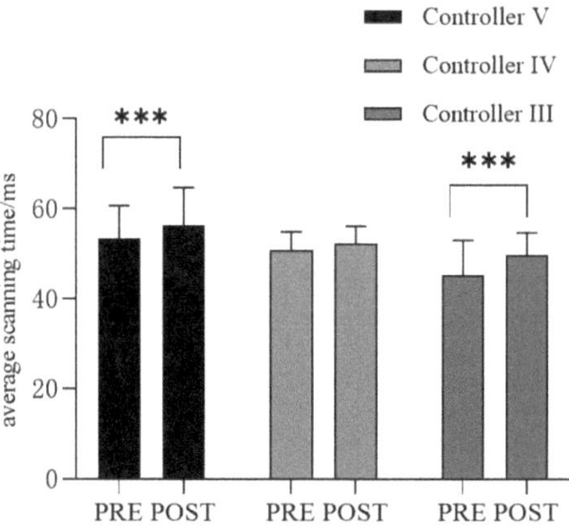

Fig. 7. Comparison of pre-post and post-post scanning time.

Table 2. Paired samples t-test results for pre-post visual data for same-rank controllers

	(math.) pairing difference					t	degrees of freedom	Sig. (Two-Tailed)
	average value	(an official) standard misalignment	Standard Error Mean	Difference 95% confidence interval				
				lower limit	limit			
Pre-post Controller V	-2.90783	4.24492	.88513	-4.74347	1.07219	−3.285	22	.003
Pre-post Controller III	−4.45556	3.58365	1.19455	−7.21020	−1.70092	−3.730	8	.006
Post-post Controller V	−29.01261	60.46761	12.60837	−55.16077	−2.86445	−2.301	22	.031

2. Comparative analysis of pre-service and post-service gaze time for same-level controllers. The paired sample t-test of pre-service and post-service gaze time was conducted for three groups of controllers of the same rank, and all three groups of gaze time satisfy the normal distribution, there is no significant difference between pre-service and post-service for level 3 and 4 controllers, and p = 0.031 is less than 0.05 for level 5 controllers, and there is a significant difference between pre-service and post-service gaze time, as shown in Table 2. This means that after one cycle of work, the ability of level 5 controllers to extract key information ability was significantly weakened, as shown in Fig. 8.

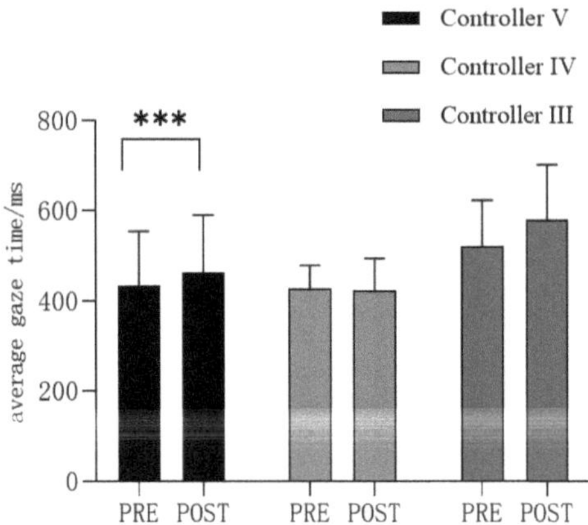

Fig. 8. Comparison of pre-post and post-post gaze time.

4 Conclusion

1. The comparison of the scanning behaviour data of controllers with different licence levels shows that the scanning time under normal and fatigue conditions is shortest for level 3 controllers and longest for level 5 controllers, from which it can be concluded that control experience has a greater impact on the controller's ability to search for the target. Level 3 controllers are experienced and have a clear understanding of the control area they are responsible for and the flight path information, so they are able to find the target flights in a shorter time and have the strongest search ability. Level 5 controllers have less control experience and are not able to locate the target flight quickly and accurately, so it is recommended that they increase their control experience through more simulation training to improve their search ability.

2. Comparison of the gaze behaviour data of controllers with different licence levels shows that level 4 controllers have the shortest gaze time under normal and fatigue conditions, while level 3 controllers have the longest gaze time, and the fatigue condition has a greater effect on level 3 controllers after posting, It can be speculated that the ability to acquire information is weakened by the age of the individual and the age of posting, and that there is a need to be more cautious in the working posture due to the influence of experience and the need to look several times to acquire flight information to ensure that the information is accurate. Further research is needed to obtain flight information and ensure the accuracy of the information.

3. By comparing and analysing the gaze and scanning behaviour of controllers of different licence levels before and after posting, it is found that Grade 3 controllers have the strongest searching ability, Grade 4 controllers have the strongest ability to acquire key information, and Grade 5 controllers need to improve their control skills through more training and experience, and it is also found that Grade 3 controllers have the strongest ability to acquire key information, and it is found that Grade 4 controllers have the strongest ability to acquire key information, and it is found that Grade 5 controllers need to improve their control skills through more training and experience.

4. In this paper, only two indicators, namely gaze and scanning time, were selected to analyse the differences between controllers of different licence levels, and fewer indicators were used. In the future, more eye movement indicators will be selected to analyse in depth the differences between controllers' eye movement behaviour, in order to provide a reference for improving controllers' skills.

References

1. Shihai, D.: Progress and challenges of human-computer interaction. J. Comput. Aided Des. Graph. **1**, 1–13 (2004)
2. Wang, J., Zhong, B., Hou, H.: Air traffic control safety performance prediction based on system dynamics. J. Safety Environ. **21**(1), 257–262 (2021)
3. Wickens, C.D., McCarley, J.S.: Applied attention theory. Taylor & Francis (2007)
4. Ahlstrom, U., Friedman-Berg, F.J.: Using eye movement activity as a correlate of cognitive workload. Int. J. Indust. Ergon. **36**(7), 623–636 (2006)
5. Stasi, L.L.D., Marchitto, M., Adoracíon, A., et al.: Approximation of on-li-ne mental workload index in ATC simulated multitasks. J. Air Transp. Manage. **16**(6), 330–333 (2021)
6. Marchitto, M., Stasi, L.L.D., Cañas, J.J.: Ocular movements under taskload manipulations: influence of geometry on saccades in air traffic control simulated tasks. Human Factors and
7. Imants, P., De Greef, T.: [ACM Press the 2014 European Conference-Vienna, Austria (2014.09.01–2014.09.03)] Proceedings of the 2014 European Conference on Cognitive Ergonomics-ECCE \"14-Eye Metrics for Task-Dependent Automation, pp. 1–4 (2014)
8. Wee, H.J., Lye, S.W.: Real Time Eye Tracking Interface for visual monitoring of radar controllers, vol(2), pp. 9–13 (2017)
9. Wang, Y., Wang, J., Hui, J.: Characterization of radar controllers' eye-movement characteristics under heavy traffic control scenarios. Chin. J. Safety Sci. **26**(6), 1–6 (2016)
10. Wang, C., Yu, C., Wang, M.: Research on the cognitive process of controller deployment flight conflict based on attention allocation. J. Safety Environ. **16**(4), 205–209 (2021)
11. Wang, Y., Hu, M., Vu, D.: Air traffic controller behavioral dynamics. Beijing University of Aeronautics and Astronautics Press (2019)
12. Wang, Y., Wang, L., Lin, S., Cong, W., Xue, J., Ochieng, W.: Effect of working experience on air traffic controller eye movement. Engineer-ing (7), 488–494 (2021)

Analysis of Air Traffic Controllers' Situation Awareness Based on Eye Movement Characteristics

Yanqing Wang[1], Xiaolei Zhang[1(✉)], Siyu Wu[1], and Jingrui Ren[2]

[1] College of Safety Science and Engineering, Civil Aviation University of China, Tianjin 300300, China
`wyqcauc@163.com`
[2] College of Flight Technology, Civil Aviation University of China, Tianjin 300300, China

Abstract. The situation awareness level of air traffic controllers is crucial for aviation safety. With the continuous growth of civil aviation traffic, the working scenarios faced by air traffic controllers are becoming increasingly complex. This study analyzes the situation awareness of controllers based on eye movement characteristics, aiming to improve the quality of controller training, optimize the control work process, and enhance the safety of air transportation. In the experiment, 24 male air traffic control students were recruited. They completed the simulation control experiment wearing an eye - tracker under three different simulated control situations (simple, medium, and complex). The research found that these important eye movement indices can serve as effective bases for evaluating the situation awareness of controllers. Follow - up research can optimize the selection and training processes of controllers based on these indices, or apply them to the development of air traffic control work assistance systems, providing more support for ensuring aviation safety.

Keyword: Air Traffic Controllers · Situation awareness · Eye movement

1 Introduction

In modern aviation systems, the situation awareness of air traffic controllers (hereinafter referred to as controllers) is of great significance for ensuring flight safety and improving operational efficiency. Situation awareness (SA) refers to an individual's ability to perceive key elements in the environment, understand them, and predict future events. However, the complex air traffic environment and high - intensity work tasks pose numerous challenges to controllers' situation awareness. In recent years, with the continuous development of eye - tracking technology, its applications in the fields of cognitive science and human factors engineering have become increasingly widespread. As an external manifestation of the cognitive process, eye movement characteristics can provide a new perspective for studying controllers' situation awareness. This study aims to deeply explore the situation awareness performance of controllers in different task phases through the analysis of eye movement characteristics, and reveal the internal relationship between eye movement characteristics and situation awareness.

D. Harris et al. (Eds.): HCII 2025, LNCS 16334, pp. 318–330, 2026.
https://doi.org/10.1007/978-3-032-12392-3_21

2   Literature Review

Situation awareness was first proposed by Endsley [1], and is defined as an individual's ability to perceive key elements in the environment, understand them, and predict future events. Endsley's model [2] divides situation awareness into three levels: perception (Level 1), comprehension (Level 2), and projection (Level 3). The perception stage involves the extraction of key information from the environment. The comprehension stage requires the individual to integrate the perceived information and construct a situation model. The projection stage is about inferring future developments based on the current situation. This model provides a theoretical framework for the study of situation awareness and is widely applied in various fields such as aviation, military, and healthcare.

In the aviation field, situation awareness is regarded as a crucial factor for the efficient work of controllers. Endsley's research shows that the level of situation awareness of controllers directly affects their decision - making quality and task performance [3]. When the level of situation awareness is high, controllers can more accurately identify potential conflicts and take timely measures to ensure flight safety. In addition, situation awareness is closely related to workload. When the workload is too high, controllers may not be able to effectively process all the information, resulting in a decline in situation awareness [4].

In the 1980s, domestic and foreign scholars began to conduct relevant research on the SA of key personnel in civil aviation, such as pilots and controllers. Based on the "three - level model" proposed by Endsley and the formation process of pilots' situation awareness proposed by Yi Bo et al. [5], this paper summarizes the formation process of controllers' situation awareness, as shown in Fig. 1.

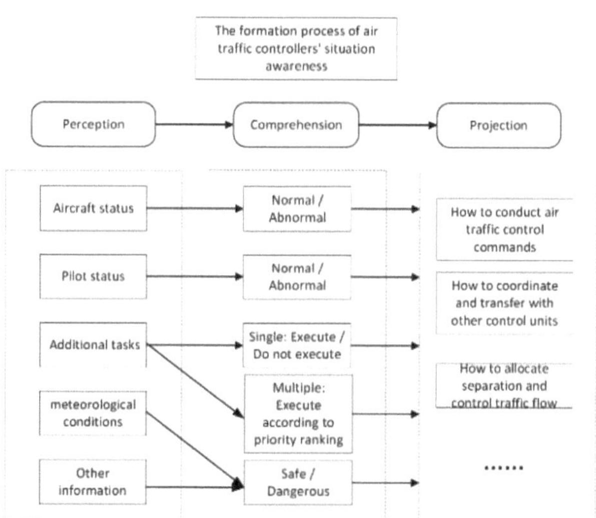

Fig. 1. The formation process of controllers' situation awareness.

In recent years, the application of eye - tracking technology in the field of air traffic control has gradually increased, the research on controllers' situation awareness has also become more multi - dimensional. Rajamanickam Yuvaraj et al. [6] collected and analyzed the electroencephalogram (EEG) and eye movement data of controllers, explored the characteristics of their attention performance, and analyzed the relationship with the SA level of controllers to ensure that controllers can maintain a good SA level to monitor air traffic tasks. Jin Huibin et al. [7] utilized eye movement data and the three dimensional Situation Awareness Rating Technique to analyze the relationship between controllers' SA levels and the allocation of attention resources in different scenarios. The study found that the better the controllers' attention - allocation and decision - making abilities, the higher their SA levels. Liu Yawei et al. [8] employed a remote virtual tower experiment system and an eye tracker to study the impact of audio - visual dual channels on the situation awareness level of air traffic controllers. It was found that compared with the visual single - channel condition, the situation awareness scores of air traffic controllers increased significantly in the audio - visual dual - channel condition. Jin Huibin et al. [9] used the k - Nearest Neighbor algorithm and eye - movement data to analyze the eye - fixation characteristics of air traffic controllers, and divided them into an aggregation group and a dispersion group. It was concluded that the participants with a dispersed fixation pattern had a higher SA level and better operational performance. Bongo Miriam et al. [10] examined the relationships among air traffic controllers' fatigue levels, situation awareness (SA), and control strategies based on the SPAM, SASHA, Samn-Perelli fatigue scale, and visual attention self-report measures. They found that fatigue and workload were inversely related, and both had a significant impact on SA. Álvaro Fernández-Rodríguez et al. [11] monitored the cognitive states of air traffic controllers in a situation - aware environment based on ERP - BCI technology. The experiment revealed that the size of the appearance surface of the target stimulus had a significant impact on the participants' situation awareness. Jianping Zhang et al. [12], in order to measure the safety capabilities of airport controllers when applying digital control towers, established a comprehensive index system from the perspective of situation awareness. This system measured three aspects: the areas of interest that controllers focused on, physiological characteristics, and alertness. The research shows that the safety capabilities of airport controllers based on digital control towers are not lower than those when working in actual control towers. In addition, eye movement characteristics can also be used to evaluate the training effects of controllers. By comparing the eye movement patterns of novice and experienced controllers, researchers found that experienced controllers showed more efficient eye movement strategies during task execution, such as shorter fixation durations and more reasonable saccade paths [13]. However, most of the existing research focuses on the relationship between eye movement characteristics and task performance, and there is relatively little research on the direct connection between eye movement characteristics and situation awareness. This study will fill this gap and deeply explore the situation awareness performance of controllers through the analysis of eye movement characteristics.

3   Design and Implementation of the Simulated Control Experiment

3.1   Experimental Design

This study adopts an experimental research method, collecting the eye movement data of controllers through eye - tracking technology and analyzing it in combination with situation awareness assessment tools. The experimental design is a within - participant design. Each participant is required to complete simulated air traffic control tasks in three different simulated control scenarios (simple scenario, medium - level scenario, and complex scenario).

3.2   Participants

A total of 24 male air traffic control trainees were recruited as participants for the experiment. All participants have mastered the use of radar control simulators, completed relevant courses in air traffic control, and possess basic control capabilities. The age range of the participants is 20–25 years old, with an average age of 22.5 years old. There is no significant difference in the vision of the left and right eyes of all participants, and their vision is normal or corrected to normal.

3.3   Experimental Equipment and Materials

The experimental equipment includes a radar control simulator, and a situation awareness measurement questionnaire (3D - SAGAT). During the experiment, the participants wore aSee Glasses eyeglass - type eye - tracker to record their eye movement data during the simulated air traffic control tasks.

Radar Control Simulator.   The radar control simulator can truly reproduce the scenes in actual air traffic control work. It adopts virtual reality, system simulation, human - computer interaction, database, and network communication technologies to highly simulate the real radar control operating environment, including airspace environment, airway routes, flight dynamics, aircraft performance, etc., with the help of nearly real - life control positions, human - machine interfaces, and communication systems.

The system composition of the radar control simulator includes the simulated air traffic controller position, the simulated pilot position, the data preparation position, and the system control position.

The radar control simulator creates a virtual control airspace and sets up different approach control exercises. When control trainees conduct control simulation training, they carry out experimental plans such as radar identification, radar vectoring, detection and resolution of flight conflicts, and sequencing of approaching aircraft through radio communication with the captain's seat.

3D - SART Situation Awareness Scale.   In this experiment, the 3 - Dimensional Situation Awareness Rating Technique (3D-SART) developed by Taylor [14] in 1990 was used. This scale assesses the operator's situation awareness from three aspects: the demand for attention resources, the supply of attention resources, and situation comprehension. In this experiment, the demand for attention resources includes the likelihood of changes in the control situation, the number of elements that need attention in the control task, and the complexity of the control task situation. The supply of attention resources includes the level of the controller's arousal, the ability to engage in other tasks besides the current control task, the degree of attention focused on the current task situation, and the quality of self - attention allocation. Situation comprehension includes the amount of control information that can be received and understood, the difficulty of extracting task - situation information, and the degree of familiarity with the situation.

After completing the test, participants are required to rate the questionnaire from these three dimensions, and then calculate the total score (Total score = Situation Comprehension score - (Attention Resource Demand score - Attention Resource Supply score)).

aSee Glasses Eyewear - type Eye Tracker. The aSee Glasses eyewear - type eye tracker can record eye movement data while shooting videos through the front - view camera. This eye tracker has a wide tracking range, low latency, and an accuracy of up to $0.5°$, enabling the precise collection of the eye movement data desired in the experiment. The analysis software equipped with the eye tracker can provide more than twenty types of raw data such as pupil diameter, fixation point data, saccade data, and blink data. It can also provide analysis tools such as visual heat maps, gaze trajectory maps, and perspective views.

Fig. 2. aSee Glasses eyewear - type eye tracker.

3.4 Experimental Scenario Setup

The independent variable in the experiment is air traffic complexity, which is set to three simulated control scenarios with different levels of complexity, namely the simple scenario, the medium scenario, and the complex scenario. The dependent variable is the level of situation awareness. The situation awareness levels of the participants are analyzed through the physiological data and questionnaire data obtained from the experiment. The independent variable, air traffic complexity, is divided into three scenarios:

1. Simple scenario: There are eight aircraft (six inbound and two outbound);
2. Medium scenario: There are twelve aircraft (eight inbound and four outbound); and
3. Complex scenario: There are sixteen aircraft (ten inbound and six outbound).

As the number of aircraft increases, the conflicts among them will also increase. Therefore, changes in air traffic complexity will, to a certain extent, affect the controllers' situation awareness (Fig. 2).

In addition, different flight plans are formulated according to the three air - traffic - complexity scenarios. The flight plans include information such as aircraft call signs, departure airports, destination airports, altitudes, and hand - over times. The relatively standardized experimental scenarios facilitate the analysis and comparison of the situation awareness levels of different participants and control the interference of other irrelevant variables on the experiment (Fig. 3).

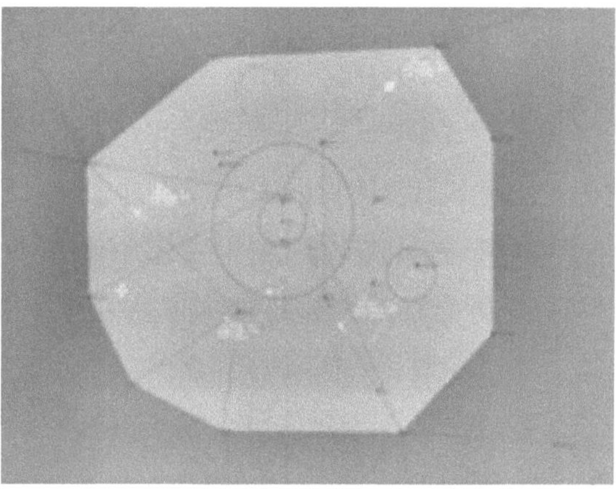

Fig. 3. The control interface under the demonstration of the simple scenario.

3.5 Data Processing and Analysis

After the experiment, the collected eye movement data are pre - processed through the eye movement analysis software (Tobii Pro Lab), including removing noise data and calibrating data. Then, based on the participants' situation awareness scores (3D-SAGAT), the participants are divided into a high situation awareness group (high SA group) and a low situation awareness group (low SA group). The statistical analysis software SPSS 26 is used to analyze the eye movement feature data and questionnaire data to explore the relationship between eye movement features and the level of situation awareness.

4   Experimental Results

4.1   Rating of Situation Awareness Levels

After the simulated control experiments in different scenarios, the 3D - SART scale was used to measure the SA levels of the participants. The participants were divided into the high - SA group and the low - SA group based on the average SA scores of the participants in different scenarios. This way of grading by the average value can effectively reduce the subjective bias of the SART method. The rating and grouping are shown in Table 1 below. Therefore, there were significant differences in SA scores between the high SA group and the low SA group.

Table 1. Descriptive statistics of different SA groups.

Scenario	SA group	SA average score	SA standard deviation	t	sig.
Simple Scenario	Low	13.692	2.097	8.163	<0.01
	High	21.091	2.343		
Medium Scenario	Low	13.462	1.450	6.995	<0.01
	High	18.818	2.272		
Complex Scenario	Low	14.167	2.250	6.704	<0.01
	High	21.091	2.700		

4.2 Analysis of Eye Movement Data

Pre - processing of Eye Movement Data. In the complex scenario of the simulated control experiment, one participant made excessive movements during the experiment, making it impossible to effectively identify the left pupil and obtain accurate and valid eye movement data. Therefore, the eye movement data of this participant in the scenario were deleted. After screening and removing invalid data, the eye movement data of 23 participants were selected as the initial processing data for the simple, medium and complex scenarios.

Calculation of Feature Importance Using the LightGBM Algorithm. Gradient Boosting Decision Tree (GBDT) is a common classification model in machine learning. Its main idea is to use weak classifiers (decision trees) for iterative training to obtain the optimal model. It has advantages such as good training results and being less prone to overfitting. It is generally used for problems such as multi-class classification, click-through rate prediction, and search ranking.Light Gradient Boosting Machine (LightGBM) optimizes and improves the GBDT algorithm. It was initially developed by researchers from Microsoft and Peking University. It supports highly efficient parallel training. Compared with XGBoost (eXtreme Gradient Boosting), it has advantages such as faster training speed, lower space consumption, better accuracy, support for distributed processing, the ability to quickly handle massive data, and prevention of overfitting. The uniqueness of this algorithm lies in its adoption of one - sided gradient sampling, mutually exclusive feature bundling, and a leaf - node - based generation approach with depth constraints[15–17]. Therefore, this paper selects the LightGBM algorithm to calculate feature importance.

1. Building Iterative Trees. The LightGBM algorithm performs gradient boosting through multiple rounds of iteration on the training dataset. In each iteration, gradient information is used to fit a new tree, and the best split is adopted for each split node at each level of the tree. That is, a greedy approach is used when building the model.

2. Feature Importance Index. According to the research by Guyon et al. [18], the heuristic information of iterative trees can serve as an important measure for features. In each iteration, the variables of different features are split. Through multiple iterations, the total number of splits T-split of different features is finally selected as the basis for measuring important feature variables. The definition of T-split is as follows:

$$T\_Split = \sum_{t=1}^{k} Split_t.$$

3. In machine learning, applying different combinations of hyperparameters can lead to significant differences in the generalization ability of the model. The LightGBM model has many hyperparameters. Therefore, it is very important to search for the combination of hyperparameters that enables the model to have the best generalization ability. The main hyperparameters of the LightGBM model in this study are shown in Table 2.

Table 2. Main Hyperparameters of LightGBM.

Name	Meaning
Max-depth	Maximum depth of the tree
Num-leaves	Number of leaves of the tree
Learning-rate	Learning rate
Bagging-fraction	Data sampling ratio in each iteration
Feature-fraction	Feature sampling ratio in each iteration
n-estimators	Number of decision trees

Results of Feature Importance Ranking. The eye movement data, including pupil diameter, number of fixations, fixation duration, and number of saccades, were collected using the eyewear - type eye tracker. Based on the literature and the actual situation of the simulated control experiment, the following eye movement indicators were selected for subsequent data processing: Gaze Velocity (GV), Pupil Diameter (PD), Saccade Velocity Average (SVA), Fixation Duration Proportion (FDP), Mean Fixation Time (MFT), Average Saccade Time (AST), Average Saccade Ratio (ASR), and Track Distract (TD). The LightGBM algorithm was used to calculate the importance ranking of these eye movement indicators. The results are shown in Table 3.

Table 3. Importance Ranking of Eye Movement Indicators.

Eye movement indicators	Importance ranking
GV	2597
PD	2542
SVA	1828
MFT	1568
FDP	1300
AST	1159
ASR	631
TD	42

Based on the importance ranking results of eye movement indicators for SA, among the eye movement indicators, GV, PD, SVA, and MFT are relatively important for the controller's SA level and AB performance. Therefore, the above - mentioned eye movement indicators should be analyzed emphatically.

4.3 Correlation Analysis Between Eye Movement Features and Situation Awareness

The GV, PD, SVA, and MFT data under different scenarios were statistically analyzed according to the high - and low - SA groups. The specific analysis is as follows:

1. Gaze Velocity (GV)

For the high - SA group, the GV data showed an inverted "U" shape as the air traffic complexity increased. The moving speed of the fixation point was the fastest in the medium scenario, and the GV in the complex scenario was lower than that in the simple scenario. For the low - SA group, the GV data increased as the air traffic complexity increased. It can be seen that in the simple scenario, the moving speed of the fixation point of the low - SA group was lower than that of the high - SA group, while the opposite was true in the complex scenario (Fig. 4).

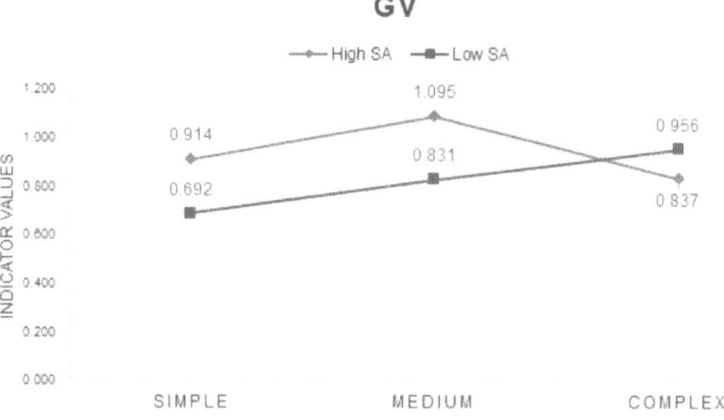

Fig. 4. Gaze Velocity

2. Pupil Diameter (PD)

The PD data of the high - SA group showed an upward trend as the air traffic complexity increased, while the PD data of the low - SA group showed a downward trend. However, the pupil diameter of the high - SA group under different scenarios was smaller than that of the low - SA group (Fig. 5).

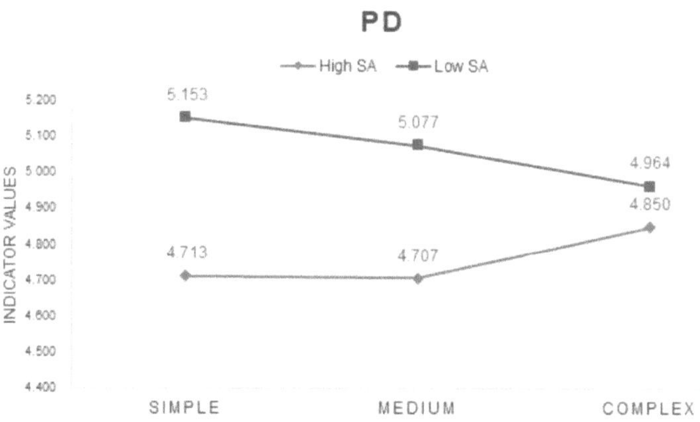

Fig. 5. Pupil Diameter

3. Saccade Velocity Average (SVA)

For the high - SA group, the SVA data showed an inverted "U" shape as the air traffic complexity increased, and the average saccade velocity was the highest in the medium scenario. For the low - SA group, the SVA data also showed an inverted "U" shape as the air traffic complexity increased. Overall, the average saccade velocity of the high - SA group was higher than that of the low - SA group in the simple and complex scenarios (Fig. 6).

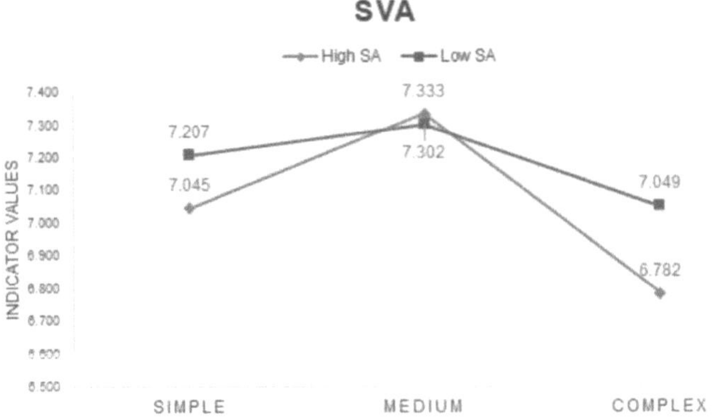

Fig. 6. Saccade Velocity Average

4. Mean Fixation Time (MFT)

For the high - SA group, the MFT data showed an inverted "U" shape as the air traffic complexity increased, and the average saccade velocity was the highest in the medium scenario. For the low - SA group, the SVA data showed a regular "U" shape as the air traffic complexity increased. In the complex scenario, due to the increase in the number of aircraft and conflict points, the average fixation time of all groups was significantly lower than that in the simple scenario (Fig. 7).

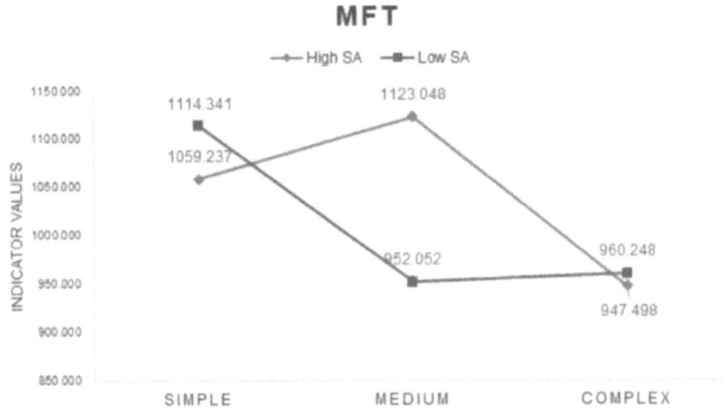

Fig. 7. Mean Fixation Time

In this study, through the analysis of eye movement features, the situation awareness performance of controllers under different complexity scenarios was explored. In the field of air traffic control, there is a close and inherent relationship between eye movement features and controllers' situation awareness. Through the analysis of the four eye movement indicators of GV, PD, SVA, and MFT, significant differences were found between the high - and low - SA groups. In the medium - complexity scenario, the GV data of the high - SA group showed that the fixation point moved the fastest, presenting an inverted "U" shape; the PD data increased with the increase in complexity, indicating that they could effectively mobilize attention resources; the SVA and MFT data showed the highest average saccade velocity in the medium scenario, also presenting an inverted "U" shape, reflecting the high efficiency of the high - SA group in information acquisition, analysis, and processing.

On the contrary, for the low - SA group, the GV data increased with the increase in complexity, and the fixation point moved slower than that of the high - SA group in the simple scenario; the PD data decreased with the increase in complexity; although the SVA also presented an inverted "U" shape, the average saccade velocity in the simple and complex scenarios was lower than that of the high - SA group, and the MFT presented a regular "U" shape, with a short average fixation time in the complex scenario. These features indicate that the low - SA group has deficiencies in information perception, attention allocation, and information - processing ability. These results suggest that eye movement features can serve as potential indicators for evaluating controllers' situation awareness levels, providing a key basis for in - depth research and optimization of air traffic control work.

5 Conclusion

In this study, the eye - tracking technology was used to deeply explore the situation awareness performance of controllers under different complexity scenarios. The results show that there is a significant correlation between eye movement features and the level of situation awareness. The high - SA group showed a more efficient eye movement strategy in the medium scenario, and in the complex scenario, they could maintain a relatively high level of situation awareness by increasing the fixation duration on key information. In contrast, the low - SA group showed excessive information search in the complex scenario but failed to effectively integrate information to form accurate situation awareness. The results of this study provide a scientific basis for training and practice in the field of air traffic control and also offer new directions for future research.

Acknowledgment. This work was supported by Humanities and Social Science Project of the Ministry of Education (No.23YJA190010).

References

1. Endsley, M.R.: Design and evaluation for situation awareness enhancement. In: Proceedings of the Human Factors and Ergonomics Society Annual Meeting, vol. 32, no. 5, pp. 97–101. SAGE Publications (1998)
2. Endsley, M. R., Wise, J., Hopkin, V., et al.: Situation awareness in aviation systems. Handbook of Aviation Human Factors, Second Edition, pp. 257–276 (2009)
3. Endsley, M.R., Jones, D.G.: Situation awareness: a critical but ill - defined phenomenon. Int. J. Aviat. Psychol. **7**(1), 35–51 (1997)
4. Salvucci, D.D., Goldberg, J.H.: Identifying fixations and saccades in eye - tracking protocols. In: Proceedings of the 2000 Symposium on Eye Tracking Research & Applications, pp. 71–78. ACM (2000)

5. Yi, B., et al.: Research on multimodal car interaction design based on situation awareness. Internal Combustion Engine & Parts, no. 05, pp. 82–84 (2023)
6. Yuvaraj, R., Sun, W.L., Wee, H.J.: A real time neurophysiological framework for general monitoring awareness of air traffic controllers. In: 2020 IEEE Asia - Pacific Conference on Computer Science and Data Engineering, pp. 1–6 (2020)
7. Jin, H., Liu, W., Chen, J.: Influence of situation awareness and gaze transfer patterns on tower control conflicts. China Safety Sci. J. **26**(04), 72–77 (2016)
8. Liu, Y., et al.: Research on the influence of audio - visual dual - channel salience on the situation awareness of remote virtual tower controllers. J. Civil Aviat. **5**(03), 45–50 (2021)
9. Jin, H., Liu, Y., Zhu, G.: Measurement of controllers' situation awareness based on eye movement and performance analysis. China Safety Sci. J. **27**(07), 65–70 (2017)
10. Bongo, M., Seva, R.: Effect of fatigue in air traffic controllers' workload, situation awareness, and control strategy. Int. J. Aerospace Psychol. **32**(1), 1–23 (2022)
11. Fernández - Rodríguez, Á., Ron - Angevin, R., Velasco - Álvarez, F., Diaz - Pineda, J., Letouzé, T., André, J.-M.: Evaluation of single - trial classification to control a visual ERP - BCI under a situation awareness scenario. Brain Sci. **13**, 886–903 (2023)
12. Zhang, J., Tian, X., Pan, J., Chen, Z., Zou, X.: A field study on safety performance of apron controllers at a large - scale airport based on digital tower. Int. J. Environ. Res. Public Health **19**, 1623–1636 (2022)
13. Jarodzka, H., van Gog, T., Dorr, M., Scheiter, K.: How eye tracking can inform instructional design. In: Khine, M.P. (ed.) Eye - Tracking Research for Pedagogical Innovation, pp. 13–34. Springer (2010)
14. Taylor, R.M.: Situation Awareness Rating Technique (SART): the development of a tool for the assessment of situation awareness. AGARD Conference Proceedings, vol. 478 (1990)
15. Lv, Z., Gao, X., Xiao, H., et al.: Resistance spot welding defect detection based on vectorized dynamic resistance signal and LightGBM classifier. Meas. Sci. Technol. **35**(8), 086113 (2024)
16. Ke, G., et al.: Lightgbm: a highly efficient gradient boosting decision tree. Adv. Neural Inform. Process. Syst. **30**, 3146–3154 (2017)
17. Mishra, S., Mallick, R.K., Gadanayak, D.A., et al.: Real time intelligent detection of PQ disturbances with variational mode energy features and hybrid optimized LightGBM classifier. IEEE Xplore Digital Library, 25 Mar. 2024. https://ieeexplore.ieee.org/document/10478893
18. Boser, B.E., Guyon, I.E., Vapnik, V.N.: A training algorithm for optimal margin classifiers. In: *COLT '92: Proceedings of the fifth annual workshop on Computational learning theory*, pp. 144–152. Association for Computing Machinery (1992)

A Transformer-Enabled Method for Identifying Air Traffic Controllers' Situation Awareness Using Eye Tracking

Xiaoqing Yu[1,2]($\boxtimes$), Xing Yao[1], Hu Li[1], and Chun-Hsien Chen[1]

[1] School of Mechanical and Aerospace Engineering, Nanyang Technological University, Singapore 639798, Singapore
`xiaoqing.yu@ntu.edu.sg`
[2] Air Traffic Management Research Institute, Nanyang Technological University, Singapore 637460, Singapore

Abstract. Air Traffic Controllers (ATCOs) play a vital role in maintaining the safety and efficient functioning of air traffic control (ATC) systems. To execute their responsibilities effectively and uphold the safety and efficiency of air traffic management, ATCOs must sustain a high degree of situational awareness (SA). A decline in SA can result in operational errors, posing significant risks to aviation safety. Therefore, the purpose of this paper is to propose a real-time Transformer-enabled SA recognition method based on eye-tracking technology, effectively learning temporal information for ATCOs' accurate SA monitoring. To validate the proposed method called ConFormer, an in-lab simulation experiment was conducted with 26 participants involved. The eye movements of participants during each trial were recorded using the eye tracker. Extensive evaluation was performed to validate the effectiveness and reliability of the proposed Transformer-enabled SA estimator. The results demonstrate that the proposed method achieved superior performance, with a recognition accuracy of 98.0%, precision of 97.9%, F1 score of 97.7%, and recall of 97.5%, significantly outperforming baseline models such as LSTM (Long Short-Term Memory). The proposed SA recognition method can significantly enhance human-AI collaboration and aviation safety. This capability allows adaptive automation systems to dynamically adjust support during periods of high cognitive workload, for example, prioritizing alerts when SA declines, while maintaining ATCOs' supervisory roles.

Keywords: Air traffic management · Human-automation interaction · Human factors · Eye-tracking · Human-AI teaming

1 Introduction

Air Traffic Controllers (ATCOs) are essential for ensuring safety and operational efficiency within air traffic control (ATC) systems [18,21]. The effectiveness of

D. Harris et al. (Eds.): HCII 2025, LNCS 16334, pp. 331–341, 2026.
https://doi.org/10.1007/978-3-032-12392-3_22

ATC operations largely depends on human operators, who monitor airspace, manage traffic patterns, and maintain safe separation between aircraft [23]. To successfully carry out these duties and preserve safe and efficient air traffic management, ATCOs must maintain a high level of situational awareness (SA) [15]. Reduced SA can lead to operational errors, significantly endangering aviation safety [12]. While automation enhances efficiency, operators must remain prepared to swiftly take control during emergencies, system failures, or automation errors. This seamless transition of responsibility depends on their ability to rapidly interpret dynamic scenarios, assess risks, and make decisions, which is robust SA. Therefore, it is critical to monitor ATCOs' SA in a timely and accurate manner.

SA of an ATCO involves the capability to accurately perceive the present airspace situation, comprehend key aspects such as aircraft positions and speeds, and predict upcoming events, thereby ensuring safe and effective air traffic management [25]. SA is commonly structured into three hierarchical stages [2]. Level 1 SA, perception, refers to the accurate identification and recognition of key environmental information, including aircraft positions, speeds, and altitudes. Level 2 SA, comprehension, involves interpreting and understanding the meaning and implications of these identified elements, allowing air traffic controllers to clearly grasp the current airspace conditions. Level 3 SA, projection, represents the most advanced stage, encompassing the ability to forecast future airspace scenarios, anticipate possible conflicts or events, and proactively plan suitable interventions. Traditional approaches for assessing SA include the SA Global Assessment Technique (SAGAT) and the SA Rating Technique (SART) [11,14]. Nevertheless, these techniques have notable limitations, particularly when employed beyond controlled experimental conditions. SAGAT involves interrupting the ongoing task for SA evaluation, making it impractical in operational settings. SART, on the other hand, depends on subjective self-ratings collected post-task, which are susceptible to personal biases and might not accurately reflect actual SA.

Alternative objective measures based on behavioral metrics have been developed. These approaches utilize observable behavioral indicators, such as response times, decision accuracy, operational errors, and interaction patterns, to continuously infer SA levels [22]. By capturing objective performance data unobtrusively during tasks, behavioral metrics offer a practical solution for more objective SA assessment. However, behavioral metric-based approaches also present certain drawbacks. These methods typically require statistical analysis conducted after task completion, limiting their capacity to provide immediate, real-time SA feedback [24]. Additionally, the reliance on aggregate behavioral data makes it challenging to promptly detect sudden fluctuations in SA during dynamic operations, potentially reducing their effectiveness for real-time intervention or adaptive support systems [9].

To address the limitations of behavioral metrics, eye-tracking methods have been increasingly applied in monitoring the mental states of human operators, including SA. As a non-invasive technique, eye tracking allows for real-time observation of visual attention and cognitive processing without interfering with task execution [7,19]. Due to its unobtrusive nature and high temporal resolution, eye tracking is particularly well-suited for dynamic and safety-critical environments, offering valuable insights into the operator's cognitive state [8]. Moore & Gugerty (2010) found a positive relationship between ATCOs' SA levels and the amount of time they fixated on specific aircraft, indicating that fixation duration is a key factor in evaluating SA in aviation contexts [10]. Supporting this, Van De Merwe et al. (2012) conducted a flight simulation study and showed that both fixation frequency and dwell time are reliable indicators of SA [16]. Wu et al. (2024) utilized eye-tracking metrics such as time to first fixation, dwell duration, and revisit intervals to continuously estimate workers' SA throughout task execution, demonstrating the effectiveness of this approach across different operational settings [17]. In a similar way, Bhavsar et al. (2017) introduced an innovative technique based on eye gaze patterns to detect operators' SA under abnormal conditions, showing that their method can accurately infer SA levels. These studies underscore the flexibility and accuracy of eye-tracking technologies in complex and dynamic environments [1].

With the advancement of AI, learning-based methodologies have been increasingly adopted to monitor the mental states of human operators [20]. Typical models, such as Support Vector Machines (SVM) and eXtreme Gradient Boosting (XGBoost), have been used to assess operators' SA using physiological signals and eye movement data [5,26]. However, manual feature extraction is required before the data can be input into the machine learning model. More advanced deep learning models are proposed to solve this limitation. For instance, Fu et al. (2024) proposed a CNN-based architecture incorporating an adaptive spatial-channel attention mechanism [4], while Li et al. (2022) developed a cross-subject framework that also leveraged CNNs to achieve state-of-the-art performance [6]. Moreover, Recurrent Neural Networks (RNNs) and their variant, Long Short-Term Memory (LSTM), have been widely used to process temporal eye-tracking data. For example, Singh and Mahmoud (2019) proposed an LSTM-based approach for non-intrusive monitoring of operators' situational awareness (SA) using eye-tracking signals [13]. Additionally, Yu et al. (2024) integrated both Convolutional Neural Networks (CNN) and LSTM models to recognize air traffic controllers' (ATCO) SA in real time. Their results indicated that the combined approach outperformed the individual models [25]. While RNNs and LSTMs based methods are effective in modeling temporal dependencies in sequential data, they often suffer from limitations such as vanishing gradients and difficulty in capturing long-range dependencies.

Therefore, this study proposes a novel approach that integrates CNN with Transformer-based architectures for real-time SA recognition of ATCOs using eye-tracking data. In this framework, CNNs are employed to extract local spatial and semantic features from raw gaze signals, while the Transformer module captures long-range temporal dependencies and dynamic interactions across time steps through self-attention mechanisms. This combination enables the model to learn both local and temporal information, leading to more accurate and robust SA recognition.

2 SA Recognition Model

This section presents the proposed deep learning model for recognizing ATCOs' SA. We begin by framing the SA recognition task, followed by a detailed description of the model architecture and its implementation.

2.1 Problem Formulation

The task of recognizing ATCOs' SA levels is treated as a binary classification problem, where the labels represent either low or high SA. The model takes sequential eye-tracking data as input, defined as:

$$\mathcal{D} : \{\mathcal{X}_i, y_i\}_{i=1}^{N} \tag{1}$$

where $\mathcal{X}_i$ denotes a temporal segment of eye-tracking data with a fixed length l, and $y_i \in 0, 1$ is the corresponding SA label, 1 indicating low SA and 0 indicating high SA. The dataset contains N labeled samples.

Each input $\mathcal{X}_i$ comprises five feature channels:

$$\mathcal{X}_i = [\boldsymbol{s}_x, \boldsymbol{s}_y, \boldsymbol{v}_x, \boldsymbol{v}_y, \boldsymbol{d}_e] \in \mathbb{R}^{l \times 5} \tag{2}$$

where $\boldsymbol{s}_x$ and $\boldsymbol{s}_y$ represent the gaze coordinates, $\boldsymbol{v}_x$ and $\boldsymbol{v}_y$ refer to the gaze velocity in the horizontal and vertical directions, and $\boldsymbol{d}_e$ is the averaged pupil diameter.

The objective is to predict the SA level based on the temporal pattern in the input sequence:

$$\hat{y}_i = \arg\max p(y_i \mid \mathcal{X}_i) \tag{3}$$

2.2 Model Architecture and Training Details

We propose a hybrid deep learning architecture that combines 1D CNN layers with Transformer layers. The CNN layers act as local feature extractors, capturing short-term dependencies and enhancing the input representation. These refined features are then passed to a Transformer module, which models long-range temporal dependencies and captures the global context within the sequence. The overall architecture is summarized in Table 1, where convolutional layers process the raw sequential signals, and the Transformer encoder applies self-attention-based reasoning across time steps. This design leverages the strengths of CNNs for feature abstraction and Transformers for sequential attention modeling.

The hyperparameters listed in Table 1 were tuned to optimize the model's performance. To address class imbalance in the dataset, class weights for the two categories ("Low SA" and "High SA") were calculated and applied during training. Binary cross-entropy was used as the loss function, and the Adam optimizer was employed to update the model parameters. The learning rate and gradient clipping value were set to 0.001 and 0.5, respectively. The model was trained for 100 epochs with a batch size of 64. All experiments were conducted in Python using PyTorch.

Table 1. Structure of the CNN-Transformer Model

Layer	Configuration
Conv1D	Filters = 64, Kernel size = 6, Activation = ReLU
Conv1D	Filters = 64, Kernel size = 3, Activation = ReLU
Conv1D	Filters = 64, Kernel size = 3, Activation = ReLU
Dropout	Rate = 0.6
Transformer Encoder	Heads = 4, FF Dimension = 128, Layers = 2
Dense	Units = 64, Activation = ReLU
Dropout	Rate = 0.6
Dense	Units = 32, Activation = ReLU
Output Layer	Units = 2, Activation = Sigmoid

Note: Transformer Encoder includes multi-head attention and feed-forward layers.

3 SA-Probe Experiment Design

3.1 Participants

Data were collected and analyzed from 26 participants (21 males, 5 females; M = 24.7, SD = 3.08). All participants had normal or corrected-to-normal vision, ensuring they could adequately perceive the visual stimuli. They were enrolled in the Department of Mechanical and Aerospace Engineering and had foundational knowledge and skills relevant to air traffic control operations. Participant recruitment and study procedures were approved by the Institutional Review Board of Nanyang Technological University (Reference No. IRB-2023-776).

3.2 SA-Probe Task Design

Each trial concluded with an SA task immediately following the 10-second radar scenario (shown in Fig. 1). Two types of SA-probe tasks were implemented: (1) a position perception task, requiring participants to identify the last known position of a specified aircraft, and (2) a direction perception task, asking them to select the flight direction of a specific aircraft. These tasks were designed in alignment with Endsley's three-level SA model [3]. A correct response indicated high SA, while an incorrect response was labeled as low SA.

3.3 Experimental Procedure

Before beginning the formal experiment, participants received a briefing and completed an informed consent form. They were then instructed on how to interpret the radar screen, monitor aircraft movements, and respond to SA tasks. A familiarization phase was included to ensure participants were comfortable with the procedures. Calibration of the Tobii eye tracker was then completed, after which the data recording began. Participants watched each radar scenario on

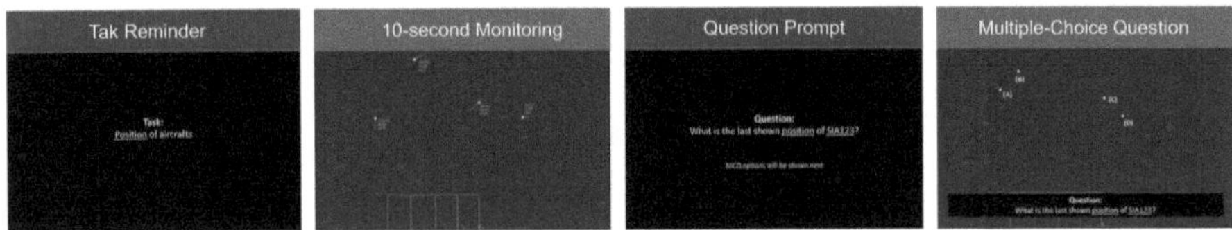

Fig. 1. The SA-probe task design.

the monitor and responded to the SA question verbally, with answers recorded by the experimenter. Each task type was repeated across four trials, resulting in a total of eight trials per participant. Eye movements were recorded throughout each trial.

3.4 Data Preprocessing

Eye-tracking data collected during the experiment were preprocessed before being input into the SA recognition models. Five features were extracted: horizontal gaze coordinate (s_x), vertical gaze coordinate (s_y), horizontal gaze velocity (v_x), vertical gaze velocity (v_y), and average pupil diameter (d_e). Gaze velocities were computed using the temporal and spatial data of gaze points, while the remaining features were derived from Tobii Pro Lab. The data were then downsampled to 10 Hz and standardized using Z-score normalization. A sliding 2-second window was applied, resulting in time series samples of length 20. Each sample was labeled based on the participant's SA performance (1 = Low SA; 0 = High SA). Finally, a stratified 5-fold cross-validation procedure was employed to partition the dataset for training and model evaluation.

4   Results Analysis and Discussion

4.1 Evaluation Metrics and Baselines

The effectiveness of the proposed method is assessed using four evaluation metrics: average accuracy, macro-averaged precision, macro-averaged recall, and macro-averaged F1 score. The following formulas are used to calculate these metrics:

$$\text{Accuracy} = \frac{TP + TN}{TP + TN + TP + TN} \tag{4}$$

$$\text{Macro Precision (MP)} = \frac{1}{2}\left(\frac{TP}{TP + FP} + \frac{TN}{TN + FN}\right) \tag{5}$$

$$\text{Macro Recall (MR)} = \frac{1}{2}\left(\frac{TP}{TP + FN} + \frac{TN}{TN + FP}\right) \tag{6}$$

$$\text{Macro F1 Score} = \frac{2 \cdot \text{MP} \cdot \text{MR}}{\text{MP} + \text{MR}} \tag{7}$$

Here, TP, TN, FP, and FN represent true positives, true negatives, false positives, and false negatives, respectively. Macro-averaged metrics were selected to provide a more balanced evaluation of the model's performance across all classes, with particular attention to the minority class ("Low SA").

We selected several classical machine learning algorithms and deep learning models as the baselines to evaluate the performance of the proposed method.

(1) **SVM-R**. The SVM-R model employs a support vector machine with a radial basis function kernel to classify eye-tracking data. This method is widely used for its robustness in handling non-linear classification tasks and serves as a strong classical baseline.

(2) **XGBoost**. XGBoost is a powerful ensemble learning algorithm based on gradient boosting decision trees. It is known for its scalability and performance in structured data classification tasks, making it a suitable baseline for comparison.

(3) **Random forest**. Random Forest is an ensemble method that constructs multiple decision trees during training and outputs the mode of their predictions. It is effective for handling high-dimensional data and capturing feature interactions.

(4) **LSTM**. The Long Short-Term Memory (LSTM) network is an advanced variant of recurrent neural networks (RNNs) designed to model sequential dependencies in time-series data. Due to its strength in capturing temporal patterns, it is particularly well-suited for processing eye-tracking signals [13]. In this study, LSTM is employed as a baseline model to capture the temporal evolution of operators' visual attention, which reflects their level of SA.

(5) **CNN-LSTM**. The CNN-LSTM architecture combines convolutional neural networks (CNNs) with LSTM units in a unified deep learning model. The CNN layers are used to extract meaningful structural features from the input data, while the LSTM layers learn temporal patterns over time. This hybrid model has been applied in prior research for recognizing SA in ATCOs [25].

(6) **ConFormer** (our method). ConFormer represents our proposed hybrid model, which integrates three convolutional layers with two Transformer layers to process eye-tracking data. The CNN layers extract localized structural features, while the Transformer components model long-range temporal relationships. This combination allows ConFormer to learn rich, dynamic representations of visual attention patterns, making it well-suited for downstream SA recognition tasks.

4.2   Overall Performance Comparison

Table 2 presents the average performance of various models based on 5-fold cross-validation. Among the traditional machine learning models, SVM-R and XGBoost show relatively modest performance, with accuracies of 61.5% and 75.3%, respectively. Random Forest performs significantly better, achieving an accuracy of 89.9%, making it the strongest among classical methods. In terms of deep learning models, LSTM and CNN-LSTM achieve accuracies of 90.9% and 94.5%, respectively, demonstrating strong capabilities in modeling sequential eye-tracking data. Notably, CNN-LSTM outperforms LSTM, indicating that integrating convolutional layers for local feature extraction enhances temporal modeling performance. Among all models compared, ConFormer achieves the highest overall performance. With its hybrid architecture combining CNN and Transformer layers, it records the best results across all evaluation metrics: accuracy (98.0%), precision (97.9%), F1 score (95.9%), and recall (97.5%). These results confirm the effectiveness of leveraging both convolutional operations and self-attention mechanisms for capturing temporal and spectral patterns in eye-tracking signals. In summary, ConFormer demonstrates superior performance, significantly outperforming all traditional machine learning and other deep learning baseline models. This highlights its strong capability in modeling the dynamic visual attention patterns of operators.

Table 2. Performance comparison of ConFormer with other models on SA recognition.

Model	Accuracy	Precision	F1 Score	Recall
SVM-R	0.615 ± 0.008	0.611 ± 0.019	0.597 ± 0.016	0.583 ± 0.012
XGBoost	0.753 ± 0.018	0.687 ± 0.025	0.692 ± 0.011	0.698 ± 0.017
Random forest	0.899 ± 0.007	0.854 ± 0.010	0.856 ± 0.021	0.859 ± 0.012
LSTM	0.909 ± 0.015	0.861 ± 0.012	0.871 ± 0.016	0.881 ± 0.008
CNN-LSTM	0.945 ± 0.006	0.927 ± 0.012	0.927 ± 0.018	0.928 ± 0.013
ConFormer	**0.980 ± 0.002**	**0.979 ± 0.010**	**0.977 ± 0.009**	**0.975 ± 0.003**

Note: Metrics are reported as mean ± standard deviation across validation folds.

4.3 Ablation Study

To evaluate the contributions of different components in ConFormer, we conducted an ablation study by individually removing the CNN module and the Transformer module. As shown in Table 3, ConFormer consistently outperforms both the CNN and Transformer baselines across all metrics. Specifically, ConFormer achieves the highest accuracy of 0.980 ± 0.002, surpassing CNN (0.958 ± 0.012) and Transformer (0.930 ± 0.018). Similar trends are observed for precision (0.979 ± 0.010), F1 score (0.977 ± 0.009), and recall (0.975 ± 0.003), highlighting the effectiveness of combining convolutional and self-attention mechanisms.

Table 3. Ablation study of important components in the ConFormer for SA recognition.

Model	Accuracy	Precision	F1 Score	Recall
CNN	0.958 ± 0.012	0.954 ± 0.017	0.946 ± 0.014	0.938 ± 0.010
Transformer	0.930 ± 0.018	0.929 ± 0.016	0.920 ± 0.022	0.912 ± 0.013
ConFormer	**0.980 ± 0.002**	**0.979 ± 0.010**	**0.977 ± 0.009**	**0.975 ± 0.003**

Note: Metrics are reported as mean ± standard deviation across validation folds.

These results confirm that integrating both local and global feature extraction is critical for achieving superior performance in ConFormer.

5   Conclusion

This study proposed a real-time Transformer-enabled SA recognition framework based on eye-tracking data to monitor the cognitive states of ATCOs. By leveraging the strengths of both convolutional and self-attention mechanisms, the proposed ConFormer model combines CNN and Transformer layers to capture both local feature patterns and long-range temporal dependencies in eye movement sequences. Specifically, the CNN layers efficiently extract fine-grained, short-term visual attention cues, while the Transformer layers model broader temporal dynamics and contextual relationships across time. The model was evaluated through controlled laboratory experiments involving 26 participants and achieved an accuracy of 98.0%, precision of 97.9%, F1 score of 97.7%, and recall of 97.5%, significantly outperforming conventional deep learning models such as CNN, LSTM, and CNN-LSTM. These results confirm the effectiveness and robustness of the hybrid CNN-Transformer architecture in recognizing subtle cognitive variations from eye-tracking signals. The proposed method holds strong potential for enhancing human-automation collaboration by enabling adaptive support systems that respond in real time to fluctuations in operators' cognitive states, ultimately contributing to safer and more resilient air traffic management systems.

Acknowledgments. This research is supported by the National Research Foundation, Singapore, and the Civil Aviation Authority of Singapore, under the Aviation Transformation Programme. The grant number is REQ0532039_FAA_Vertical C. Any opinions, findings, conclusions, or recommendations expressed in this material are those of the authors and do not reflect the views of the National Research Foundation, Singapore and the Civil Aviation Authority of Singapore.

Disclosure of Interests. The authors declare no conflicts of interest relevant to this manuscript.

References

1. Bhavsar, P., Srinivasan, B., Srinivasan, R.: Quantifying situation awareness of control room operators using eye-gaze behavior. Comput. Chem. Eng. **106**, 191–201 (2017)
2. Chi, Y., Nie, J., Zhong, L., Wang, Y., Delahaye, D.: A review of situational awareness in air traffic control. IEEE Access **11**, 134040–134057 (2023)
3. Endsley, M.R.: Situation awareness. In: Handbook of Human Factors and Ergonomics, pp. 553–568 (2012)
4. Fu, R., Hou, Q., Wang, S., Wang, L., Chen, J., Wen, G.: Effectiveness of adaptive attention-based network for situation awareness recognition. IEEE Sensors Journal (2024)

5. Li, Q., Ng, K.K., Simon, C., Yiu, C.Y., Lyu, M.: Recognising situation awareness associated with different workloads using EEG and eye-tracking features in air traffic control tasks. Knowl. Based Syst. **260**, 110179 (2023)
6. Li, R., Wang, L., Sourina, O.: Subject matching for cross-subject EEG-based recognition of driver states related to situation awareness. Methods **202**, 136–143 (2022)
7. Liu, B., Lye, S.W., Yeo, K.X., Chen, C.H.: A human-centric model for task demand assessment based on unsupervised learning-assisted eye movement measure. Adv. Eng. Inform. **65**, 103259 (2025)
8. Liu, B., Lye, S.W., Zakaria, Z.B.: An integrated framework for eye tracking-assisted task capability recognition of air traffic controllers with machine learning. Adv. Eng. Inform. **62**, 102784 (2024)
9. Lyu, M., Li, F., Xu, G., Han, S.: Leveraging eye-tracking technologies to promote aviation safety-a review of key aspects, challenges, and future perspectives. Saf. Sci. **168**, 106295 (2023)
10. Moore, K., Gugerty, L.: Development of a novel measure of situation awareness: the case for eye movement analysis. In: Proceedings of the human factors and ergonomics society annual meeting, vol. 54, pp. 1650–1654. Sage Publications Sage CA: Los Angeles, CA (2010)
11. Salmon, P.M., et al.: Measuring situation awareness in complex systems: comparison of measures study. Int. J. Ind. Ergon. **39**(3), 490–500 (2009)
12. Sethumadhavan, A.: Effects of first automation failure on situation awareness and performance in an air traffic control task. In: Proceedings of the Human Factors and Ergonomics Society Annual Meeting, vol. 55, pp. 350–354. Sage Publications Sage CA: Los Angeles, CA (2011)
13. Singh, H.V., Mahmoud, Q.: LSTM-based approach to monitor operator situation awareness via HMI state prediction. In: 2019 IEEE International Conference on Industrial Internet (ICII), pp. 328–337. IEEE (2019)
14. Taylor, R.M.: Situational Awareness Rating Technique (SART): the development of a tool for aircrew systems design. In: Situational awareness, pp. 111–128. Routledge (2017)
15. Timotic, D., Netjasov, F.: Automation in air traffic control: trust, teamwork, resilience, safety. Transport. Res. Procedia **65**, 13–23 (2022)
16. Van De Merwe, K., Van Dijk, H., Zon, R.: Eye movements as an indicator of situation awareness in a flight simulator experiment. Int. J. Aviat. Psychol. **22**(1), 78–95 (2012)
17. Wu, S., Chen, H., Hou, L., Zhang, G.K., Li, C.Q.: Using eye-tracking to measure worker situation awareness in augmented reality. Autom. Constr. **165**, 105582 (2024)
18. Xia, Z., et al.: A systematic review on human-ai hybrid systems and human factors in air traffic management. J. Eng. Des., 1–49 (2025)
19. Yang, H., Wu, J., Hu, Z., Lv, C.: Real-time driver cognitive workload recognition: attention-enabled learning with multimodal information fusion. IEEE Trans. Industr. Electron. **71**(5), 4999–5009 (2023)
20. Yang, H., Zhou, Y., Wu, J., Liu, H., Yang, L., Lv, C.: Human-guided continual learning for personalized decision-making of autonomous driving. IEEE Trans. Intell. Transport. Syst. **26**, 5435–5447 (2025)
21. Yu, X., Chen, C.H.: A robust operators' cognitive workload recognition method based on denoising masked autoencoder. Knowl.-Based Syst. **301**, 112370 (2024)
22. Yu, X., Chen, C.H., Yang, H.: Air traffic controllers' mental fatigue recognition: A multi-sensor information fusion-based deep learning approach. Adv. Eng. Inform. **57**, 102123 (2023)

23. Yu, X., Chen, C.H., Yang, H.: Cognitive workload quantification for air traffic controllers: an ensemble semi-supervised learning approach. Adv. Eng. Inform. **64**, 103065 (2025)
24. Yu, X., Yang, H., Chen, C.H.: Human operators' cognitive workload recognition with a dual attention-enabled multimodal fusion framework. Expert Syst. Appl. **280**, 127418 (2025)
25. Yu, X., Yao, X., Chen, C.H.: A novel approach to assessing air traffic controllers' situation awareness with deep learning and eye tracking. In: 2024 International Conference on Cyberworlds (CW), pp. 175–178. IEEE (2024)
26. Zhou, F., Yang, X.J., De Winter, J.C.: Using eye-tracking data to predict situation awareness in real time during takeover transitions in conditionally automated driving. IEEE Trans. Intell. Transp. Syst. **23**(3), 2284–2295 (2021)

Innovations in Adaptive and Responsive Environments

Ear Haptics: A Preliminary Suitability Study of a Novel Auricular Haptic Human-Machine Interface

Chris Bodsworth[1]([✉]), James Blundell[2], Stewart Birrell[1], and William Payre[1]

[1] Centre of Future Transport and Cities, Coventry University, West Midlands, UK
bodswor2@uni.coventry.ac.uk
[2] Safety and Accident Investigation Centre, Cranfield University, Bedfordshire, UK

Abstract. Objective: Following both software and hardware development, this study presents the development of the EarPi system – a new haptic human-machine interface (HMI) that produces vibrotactile feedback at four ear locations of the auricle. This paper details the development of all system components and presents key findings from a preliminary semi-structured interview, providing insight into both user attitudes towards ear-based haptics and initial impressions of the experimental prototype.

Method: The HMI has been designed using Fusion 360 and 3D printed using an UltiMaker Method X. This paper outlines the development from concept design and 3D modelling to manufacturing, software development, and electronic component integration. All software, hardware, and methods employed are presented to provide insight for future research and development. The study involved 26 participants answering two sets of semi-structured interview questions separated by a familiarisation task. Interview answers were synthesised and coded to find key themes. A theme was included as a significant result if the frequency among participants was at least 10%. As there were 26 participants, a frequency of 3 was selected to be counted as a key theme.

Results: Familiarity with haptics, openness to the technology, perceived usefulness, and excitement for future development was high among participants. Participants were divided on the comfort level and texture of the earpiece but did not see the weight and aesthetics as a problem. Work must be done to improve the design of the earpiece clip and centre column. Various other improvements, such as adding rubber, smoothing out the surface, making the sizing adjustable and improving the way it attaches to the ear emerged as primary problem points.

Conclusions: A fully functioning HMI prototype has been successfully developed following an iterative design process. Preliminary interviews show a high level of acceptance towards the use of ear-based haptic HMIs, while highlighting the importance of developing bespoke devices tailored to the specific needs and physiology of each individual. Clear design improvements emerged and will be taken forth into future design iterations.

Keywords: Haptics · tactile · ear-haptics · transport communication · accessibility · device development

© The Author(s), under exclusive license to Springer Nature Switzerland AG 2026
D. Harris et al. (Eds.): HCII 2025, LNCS 16334, pp. 345–363, 2026.
https://doi.org/10.1007/978-3-032-12392-3_23

1 Introduction

The ever-presence of computer systems in day-to-day life has highlighted the importance of designing effective Human-Machine Interfaces (HMIs) to interact with them and receive information from them. In transport, both with public means of commuting, such as trains and buses, and with private transportation, such as cars, communication between user and system is primarily facilitated via visual screens and auditory sounds. As these methods of communication are not suited for all users in all situations, researchers have turned towards alternatives such as haptics to bridge what the Motability foundation call the "Accessibility Gap" (Motability 2022). This study presents and evaluates a new device aimed at providing a solution to this HMI inequality.

1.1 The Need for More Accessible Transport Communication

Reducing inequality is the United Nations' 10th goal in the 2030 Agenda for Sustainable Development (United Nations 2025). This goal includes targets for both inequality within and among countries, with a key target (10.2) being increased social, economic, and political inclusion of all people, irrespective of their status or condition. This goal echoes targets from the 11th goal, concerned with making "cities and human settlements inclusive, safe, resilient and sustainable" (United Nations 2025). A key target that exemplifies this need for inclusivity is the target (11.2) to "provide access to safe, affordable, accessible and sustainable transport systems for all, improving road safety, notably by expanding public transport, with special attention to the needs of those in vulnerable situations, women, children, persons with disabilities and older persons". Motability highlight information retrieval as a major transport barrier for those with disabilities (Motability 2022), and the UITP (Union Internationale des Transports Publics), the international association of public transport, highlight the importance of "communicating information on a station's services in several formats" and developing an accessible transport system "that everybody can use, regardless of their age, size, ability or disability" (UITP 2022). As society progresses towards a more accessible world suited to the needs of all passengers, innovations in transport information communication could bridge the divide between those of varying levels of ability.

1.2 The Haptic Research Gap

To tackle this need for more accessible HMIs, the use of haptic devices – defined as devices that "allow the user to feel and interact indirectly with an external environment through physical manipulation of the device." (Escorcia Hernández et al. 2023) – has been extensively explored in academic research, as seen in a recent literature review of haptic devices for Hearing-Impaired People (Flores Ramones et al. 2023). As the human brain is able to, according to Eagleman and Perrota (2023), "dynamically reconfigure itself to absorb and interact with data", haptics provides a method of communication to substitute impaired or unavailable audiovisual resources. Though studies have emerged that involve both the development and evaluation of haptic HMIs, the majority of academic research present the value of haptic feedback at the hands and fingers (Pacchierotti et al. 2017), which is not suitable for all users – especially for those with disabilities – and could be detrimental in certain situations, like when driving. Though recent studies such as EarVR (Mirzaei et al. 2020) and ActivEarring (Lee et al. 2019) have started exploring the ear as an interface for haptic feedback, the present study follows a user-centred approach to evaluate the design of a more compact, self-contained, and user-friendly haptic wearable.

1.3 The Current Study

Both software and hardware development is followed to develop the "EarPi" system – a haptic HMI that produces vibrotactile feedback at four ear locations of the auricle. Hardware and software used, as well as design concepts, are presented to inform future research and provide insight into the development journey. Through device development and a preliminary semi-structured interview of 26 participants, this paper provides insight on user attitudes towards ear-based haptics and initial impressions of the prototype. This research will aim to provide an answer to the question: "Can the auricle be used as an interface for haptic feedback, and if so, what are some design guidelines that are to be considered following user feedback?". This paper will have the following structure: related works in the fields of accessible transport HMI and ear-based haptic feedback will be briefly explored; designed system and development journey will be presented; interview design and process will be explained; themes and design guidelines emerging from user feedback will be presented; and possible design improvements will be discussed, before finishing on an overall conclusion and discussion.

2 Definition of Terms

- Human-Machine Interface (HMI): HMI are defined as software or hardware that allows users to interact with computer systems (National Institute of Standards and Technology 2025).
- Haptic Feedback/Vibrotactile Feedback: Haptic Feedback involves both feedbacks communicated by the sense of touch (Escorcia Hernández et al. 2023) – such as with vibrotactile, thermal, pressure, and electro muscle stimulation – or the sense of proprioception. For the context and scope of this paper, the term Haptic Feedback will be used to describe Vibrotactile Feedback, this being feedback communicated to the cutaneous receptors of the skin via vibrations produced by a computer system.
- Accessibility: The term Accessibility is widely used to refer to the ease-of-use of systems for those experiencing disabilities (Duggin 2016). Expanding on this, Accessibility more generally explores the relationship between a person's capacity and the demands of an environment (Iwarsson & Ståhl 2003). For the context of this paper, the term Accessibility is used to refer to design that allows for HMIs to be used as easily as possible to the same level of functionality for both non-disabled and disabled users.

3 Related Works

3.1 HMI for Transport Accessibility: Anchored and Portable

With the importance of transport information communication, academic research has explored the use of unimodal and multimodal HMI, both anchored – i.e., physically tied to an area (signs and displays) – and portable – i.e., worn or carried on a person (phones, smartwatches). Hörold et al. (Hörold et al. 2015) discuss challenges and solutions for interactive public display design, anchored HMI with specific design challenges, as they communicate information to a wide array of transport users while being anchored to the transport terminal. Four categories of challenges that must be addressed are suggested: *Visibility* (the importance of interfaces being visible from a distance while clearly indicating their purpose); *Positioning* (the importance of size and location of the display, for both the intended space and intended users); *Content* (the importance of displaying content that is necessary and suited to its intended purpose); and *Functionality* (the importance of functions being coherent with user and company goals while being usable by different user groups and reducing usage times).

In a review of portable multimodal systems for users with visual impairments, Kuriakose et al. (2020) discuss the following: 13 papers on Multimodal Navigation Systems, including smartphones, smartwatches, bone conduction headsets, sensors, and custom software; 3 papers on Interfaces, primarily consisting of mobile applications; 8 papers on Maps, consisting of aural and tactile navigation maps; and 6 papers on Virtual Learning Environments. The value of using multiple modalities when communicating information is highlighted, and eight design recommendations are suggested: Multimodality (audio feedback is always expected, and other modalities should be available); Customisability (users should be able to customise the experience); Extendibility (systems should be designed to allow for future expansion and modality addition); Portability (systems should be completely portable without extra burden on the user); Simplicity (addition of extra modalities should not add unnecessary complexity); Dynamic mode selection (multimodal systems should allow users to change the mode of interaction); Adaptability (systems can use machine learning to adjust to their environment); and Privacy and Security of the user should be considered. In the current research, the guidelines of simplicity, portability, and extendibility inspire the development of a unimodal portable HMI, and the above research will inspire future development, such as incorporating multimodality via the addition of speakers and interaction with existing anchored HMI for information retrieval.

3.2 Haptics HMIs: Multimodality, Sensory Substitution and Types

Though most interfaces use auditory or visual channels to communicate information to users, haptic feedback provides an alternative when these channels are either overloaded or unavailable, by either supplementing audiovisual senses with multimodality or replacing audiovisual senses through sensory substitution.

Exploring the use of haptics in multimodality through a meta-analysis of vibrotactile research, Chai et al. (2022) found the following about the nature of tactile displays: they are better than visual unimodal displays for alert information but not significantly different compared to unimodal auditory displays; they are beneficial when added to visual displays for alert and spatial information, or when there was no concurrent task or a visual concurrent task; they are beneficial when added to auditory display for alert information; and they are beneficial when added to audiovisual displays for alert information, or when there was a visual concurrent task. Exploring haptic feedback as a replacement for audiovisual senses, Flores Ramones et al. (2023) conducted a literature review on haptic devices for hearing-impaired individuals. Key findings from the literature show that haptic devices can be defined as being either portable or anchored, passive touch or active touch, and direct contact or indirect contact. The review characterises devices by their type of tactile interaction as being vibration, contact, pressure, temperature, geometry, texture, softness or hardness, electricity or friction.

Methods for haptic feedback include the following: *Pressure* haptics using pneumatics, such as in an immersion jacket using pneumatically actuated airbags (Delazio et al. 2018); *Thermal* haptics using Peltier elements, such as in an ear-based wearable that delivers hot and cold feedback on the auricle (Nasser et al. 2021); *Mid-Air* haptics using ultrasounds discussed in a recent survey (Rakkolainen et al. 2021); *Passive* haptics using manipulation of real-world objects, such as the use of everyday objects in Augmented Reality (Hettiarachchi et al. 2016); and vibrotactile feedback – used in the current study – involving vibrations stimulating the skin with either Eccentric Rotating Mass (ERM) motors (such as in a vibrotactile boot for obstacle avoidance (Gibson et al. 2018)), Linear Resonant Actuator (LRA) motors (such as in the Neosensory Buzz wristband (Perrotta et al. 2021)) or Piezoelectric (Piezo) motors (such as in a piezoelectric coating to replace buttons in automotive interfaces (Nguyen et al. 2023)).

3.3 Vibrotactile Ear-Based Wearables

Emerging research has evaluated the suitability of the auricle – or outer ear – as an interface for haptic feedback, with research including the following: a prototype that connects to a Virtual Reality headset and provides vibrotactile feedback in both ears for sound localisation (Mirzaei et al. 2020); an evaluation of sequential and simultaneous pattern recognition across three locations on the auricle (Lee et al. 2019); an experimental device aimed at translating vibrations to phonemes (Pavlidou et al. 2021); and a wayfinding system using a smartphone, smartwatch, and bone conduction headset for visually impaired navigation assistance (Bie et al. 2019). Findings in literature suggest a high accuracy in correctly identifying vibrations at different locations across the ear (ActivEarring 94.8% location recognition accuracy at 15 Hz) (Lee et al. 2019), a high potential for sequential stimuli recognition, and a general acceptance of the technology. Though existing ear-based haptic research explores experimental prototypes and quantitative performance data, the current study presents the development of a more cohesive wearable with user-centred evaluation and future development guidelines.

4   Methods

4.1   System Overview

To evaluate the suitability of the ear as an interface for haptic feedback, a wearable has been developed to produce vibrations at four locations on the auricle. This system, named the "EarPi", is composed of three elements to provide and control haptic feedback:

- Haptic Hearing Aid: An earpiece providing vibrotactile feedback.
- Pi Housing: A Raspberry Pi Zero microcontroller running a server for device control.
- EarPi Controller: A mobile application to communicate with the server.

The prototype allows for simultaneous and sequential actuation of 4 LRA (Precision Microdrives 2025) coin motors producing various effects from the DRV2605L library.

The full pipeline showcasing how a request is communicated from the EarPi Controller app to the Haptic Hearing Aid via the Pi Housing is illustrated in the following diagram (Fig. 1).

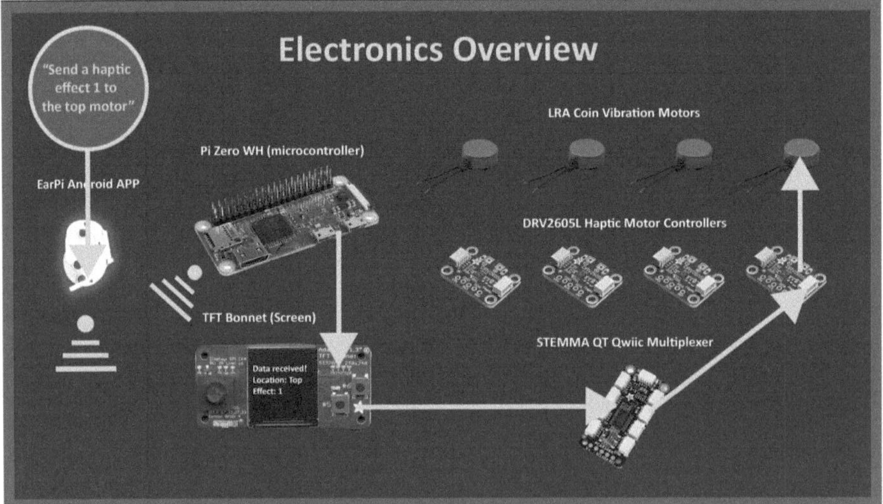

Fig. 1. EarPi System Breakdown.

4.2   System Feature Details

Both computer-generated renders and a photo of the finished prototype are included below. This section of the paper will go through each component of EarPi sequentially, explaining the function of each component and the hardware and software that has been used for its development (Figs. 2 and 3).

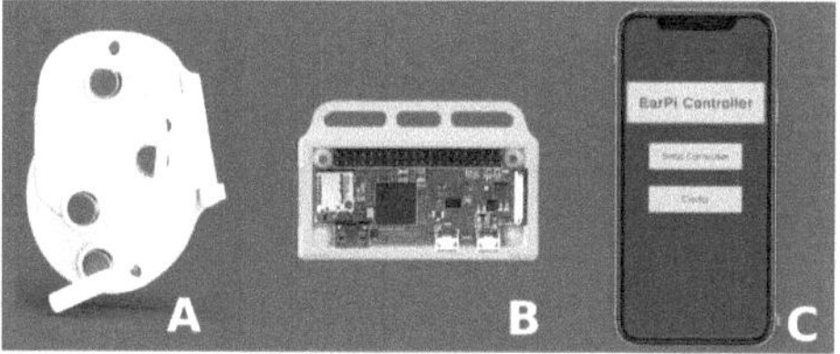

Fig. 2. Renders of the EarPi system (A: Haptic Hearing Aid, B: Pi Housing, C: EarPi Controller).

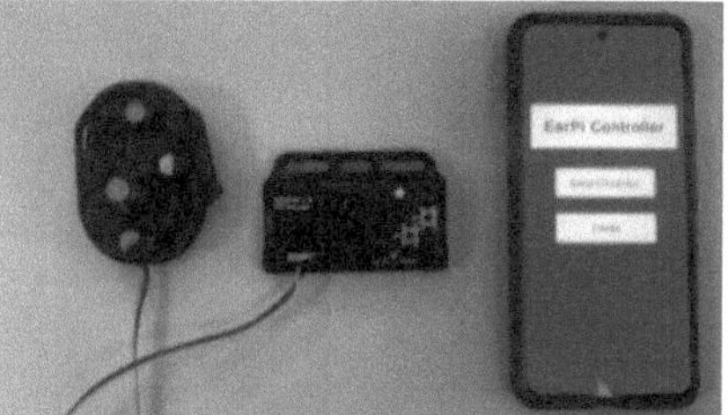

Fig. 3. Photo of the finished EarPi system.

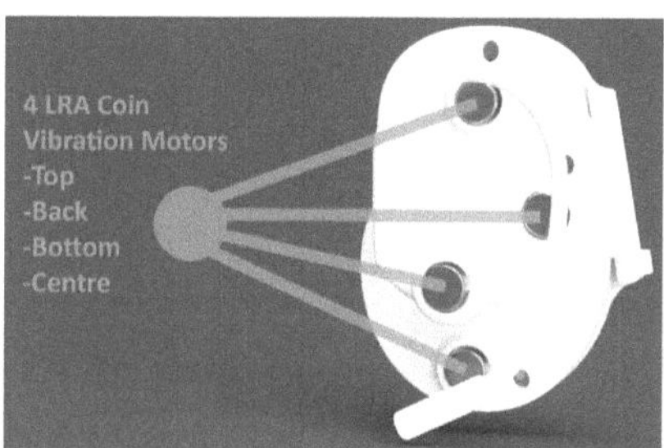

Fig. 4. Render of the Haptic Hearing Aid.

Haptic Hearing Aid

The earpiece, which is worn on the user's ear and provides haptic feedback directly on the auricle, was 3D printed using Acrylonitrile Styrene Acrylate (ASA) filament and printed in three parts (clip, top, bottom) using the UltiMaker Method X 3D printer. To provide various sequences of vibrations across ear locations, four motors are used to target four areas of the auricle that are innervated by different nerves, as seen in Al-Qahtani et al.'s "Textbook of Clinical Otolaryngology" (Al-Qahtani et al. 2021) (Figs. 4 and 5).

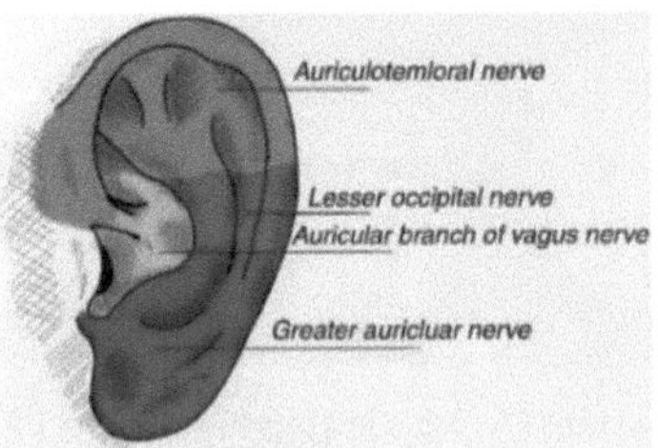

Fig. 5. Schematic drawing of the auricle with sensory nerve supply (Al-Qahtani et al. 2021).

The earpiece opens on a hinge and houses electronic components inside the casing. Each motor is controlled individually by a Adafruit DRV2605L Haptic Motor Controller (Adafruit 2025a), which allows for one of 123 different haptic effects to be used (Texas Instruments 2025). The controllers are then connected via STEMMA QT/Qwiic cables to an Adafruit PCA9548 8-Channel STEMMA QT/Qwiic I2C Multiplexer (Adafruit 2025b). The multiplexer allows for simultaneous and sequential actuation of up to 8 boards on a single I2C bus (Fig. 6).

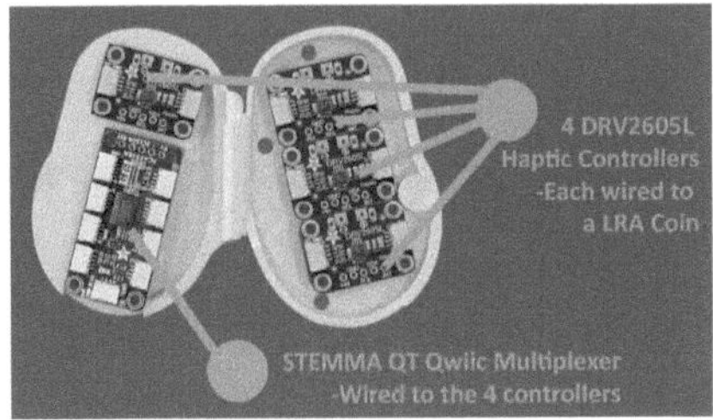

Fig. 6. Render of the inside components of the Haptic Hearing Aid.

Pi Housing

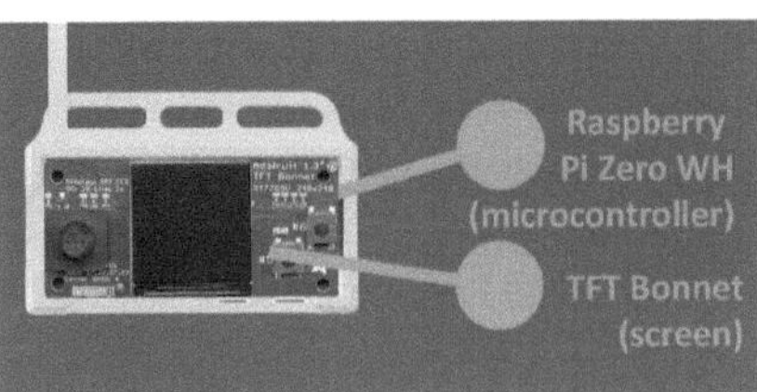

Fig. 7. Render of the Pi Housing.

As housing all components in the earpiece was impractical due to space and weight limitations, a separate casing was designed to be worn as a lanyard. The Pi Housing consists of a 3D-printed case that holds a Raspberry Pi Zero WH (Adafruit 2025c) with an Adafruit 1.3" Colour TFT Bonnet (Adafruit 2025d) connected directly to the Pi's GPIO pins for display, button input, and STEMMA QT output. Power is provided to the EarPi system via the Pi's Micro USB input (Fig. 7).

Two scripts, written in Circuit Python, run on the Pi to control the EarPi system. The first script initialises drivers for the Multiplexer and the DRV2605L boards, and it runs a User Datagram Protocol (UDP) server. The second script manages button input, which controls server shutdown and startup procedures, and display output. The server receives commands from the mobile app, interprets them, and actuates the motors. Scripts are set to boot automatically once the Pi is powered.

EarPi Controller. A mobile app – developed using the Unity Game Engine (version: 2021.3.25f1) – connects to the Pi and sends UDP packages. The "Sandbox" scene is used in the current research to familiarise participants with receiving vibrations at different locations of the auricle. The user is able to select which of the motors will be actuated and with which driver effect. The command is sent to the Pi server, and the haptic pulse is produced.

4.3   The Development Journey: From Concept to Prototype

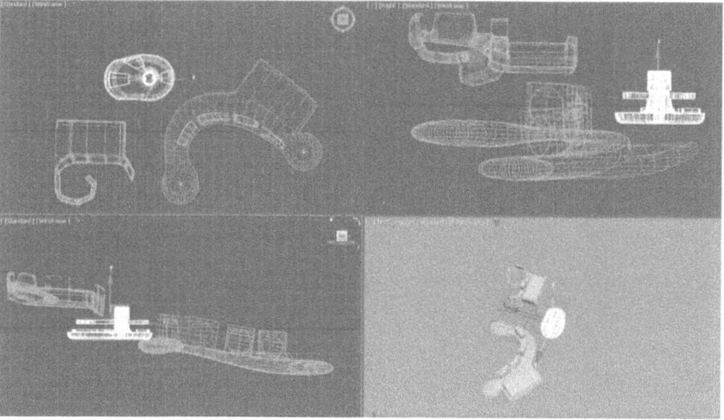

Fig. 8. Screenshot of Autodesk 3ds Max.

– Development started with a concept phase based on four main design goals:

- Multiple Haptic Locations: The device must be able to produce individually controlled haptic pulses at multiple different locations of the ear.
- Self-Contained: The device must have as many of the necessary components as possible contained within the earpiece while still being easy to manufacture within available resources.
- Small Form-Factor: The device must have a small form-factor and be easily attached to and detached from the ear.

- <u>Finished Product:</u> The device must feel as close as possible to a finished commercial product (not an experimental setup).

With these design goals in mind, early design concepts were produced in Autodesk 3ds Max (Autodesk 2025a). Below are the three main iterations produced in this phase (Figs. 8, 9, 10 and 11).

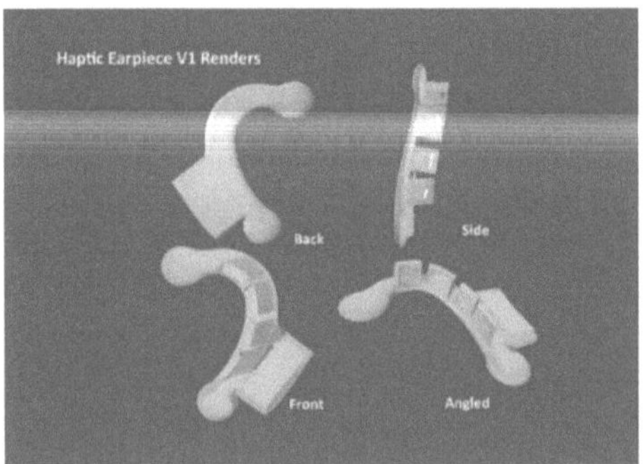

Fig. 9. Haptic Earpiece V1 Renders: Rough design with four haptic motors behind the ear on a hook-shaped device. Good idea but needs refining.

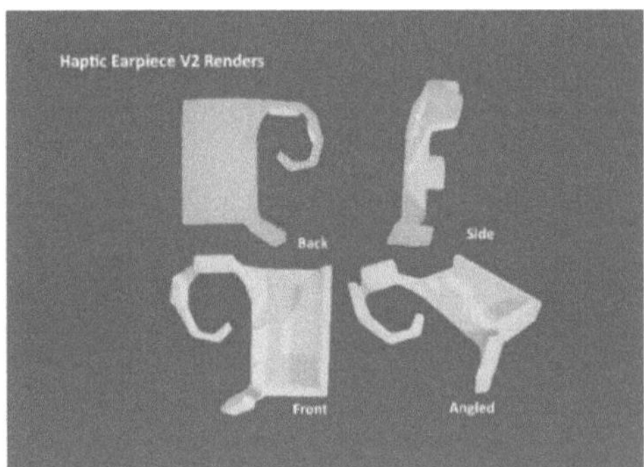

Fig. 10. Haptic Earpiece V2 Renders: More angular shape with larger casing behind the ear to hold electronics. A better iteration over V1 but very angular and bulky design.

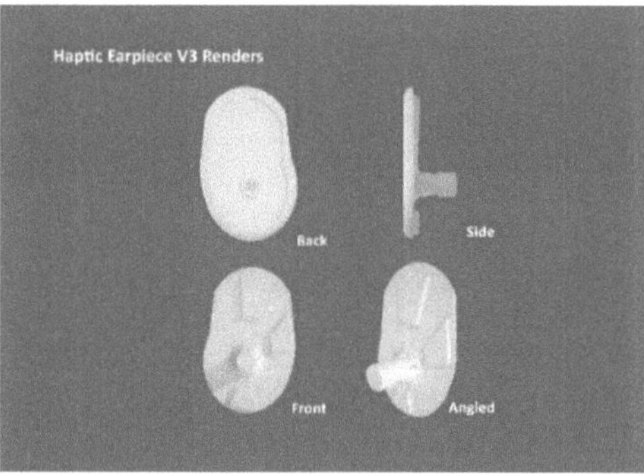

Fig. 11. Haptic Earpiece V3 Renders: An ear-shaped device that sits on the auricle and targets the four enervated zones. A deviation over V2, better vibration locations and more natural shape.

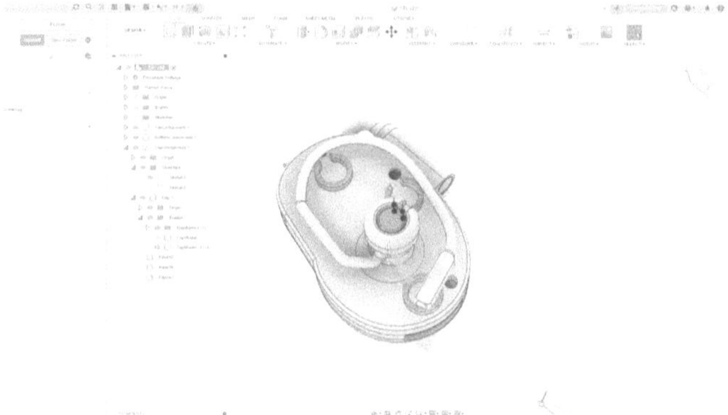

Fig. 12. Screenshot of Autodesk Fusion 360

After doing test prints of each model, V3 was selected as the base design to be improved and carried through to the next development phase (Fig. 12).

Using Autodesk Fusion 360 (Autodesk 2025b), a parametric model of the earpiece was designed for accurate 3D printing and for deciding where and how each electronic component needed to be fitted.

The final design was based on the V3 concept, featuring a detachable clip, motors targeting the top, back, bottom, and centre of the ear, and a hinge to split the casing into two separate pieces and house the multiplexer and driver boards inside the earpiece (Fig. 13).

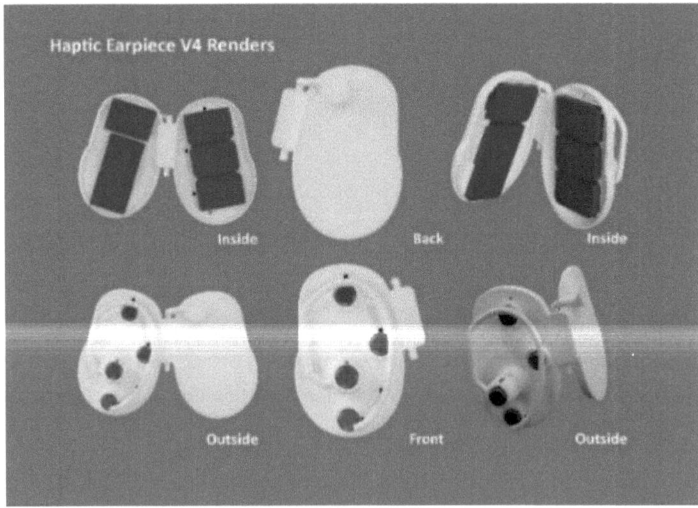

Fig. 13. Haptic Earpiece V4 Renders: A parametric version of the model with a hinge and detachable clip. A magnet and simpler hinge were added later.

The earpiece was printed in 3 parts, with a layer height of 1mm using an Ulti-Maker Method X, ASA filament and dissolvable supports. Electronic components were acquired, soldered, and installed into the prototype. Software was developed for both the mobile application using Unity and the Raspberry Pi server using Circuit Python (Figs. 14 and 15).

Fig. 14. Photo of UltiMaker Method X 3D Printer

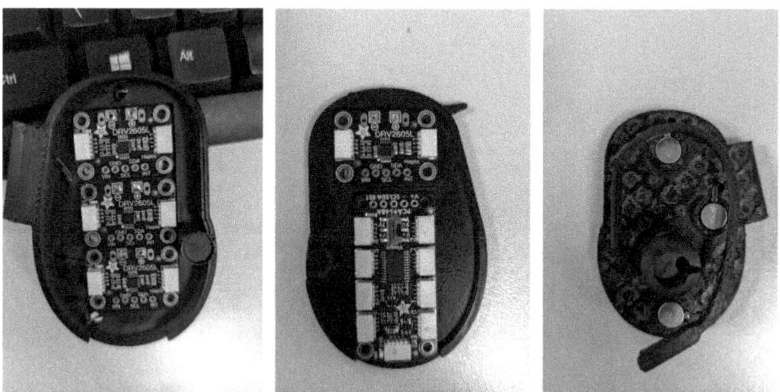

Fig. 15. Photos of the First Assembled Prototype

4.4   Experiment Design and Procedure

A semi-structured interview was conducted to gather user feedback on the EarPi and the suitability of ear-based haptics for information communication. The study involved 26 participants with a 62.5%/37.5% male/female split and ages ranging from 22 to 63. All participants signed consents forms stating that they were happy for results to be included in publication, had no adverse health conditions, and had no problem with any equipment used. Participants performed 30-min familiarisation tasks between interviews outside of the scope of this paper, reported in future publications. For the context of this paper, only qualitative interview answers are reported. Interviews were split into one block about ear haptics in general and one block about device impressions. Interviews involved both unique questions and repeated questions. A flowchart of the interview procedure and the questions asked is included below (Fig. 16).

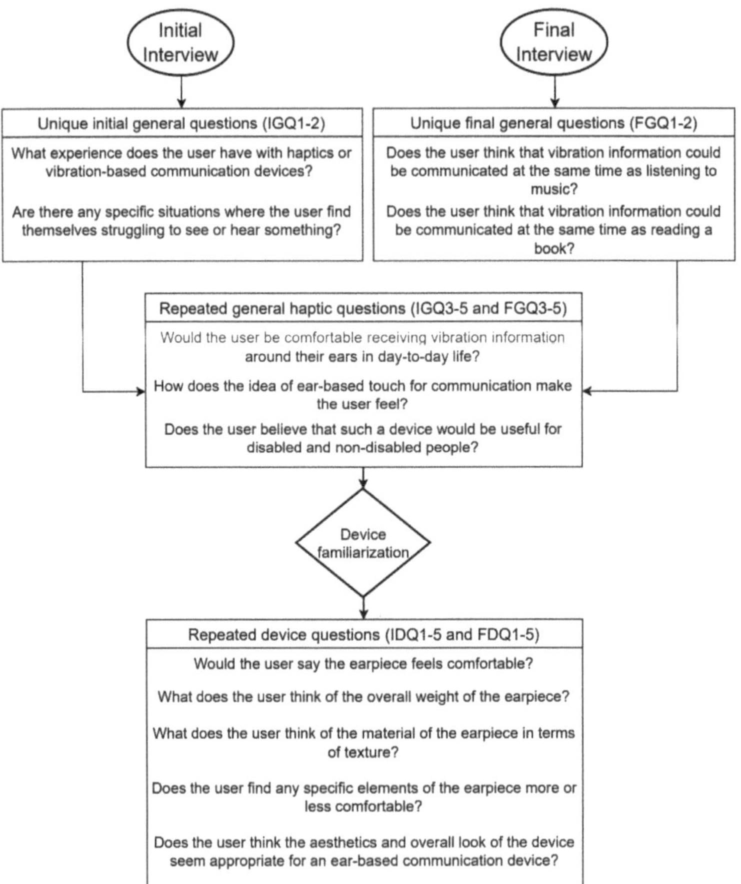

Fig. 16. Flowchart of semi-structured interview question.

5   Results and Discussion

Interview answers were synthesised and coded to find key themes. Themes were included in the following result tables if the frequency was at least 10%. As there were 26 participants, this means that a frequency of 3 was selected to be counted as a key theme. Key themes for each interview question are presented in the following three tables (Tables 1, 2 and 3).

Table 1. Key themes from user's existing haptic experience and audiovisual tasks.

Question	Key themes (at least frequency of 3 out of 26)
IGQ1: Experience with haptics	Phone (23), Game controllers (16), Smartwatches (9), Headphones (3), VR (3)
IGQ2: Audiovisual challenges	Loud public spaces (8), In conversations (4), In public transport (4), While driving (3), For alarms/alerts (3)
FDQ1: Auditory concurrent task (music listening)	Yes (12), No (7), Not sure (4), Depends on audio volume (3)
FDQ2: Visual concurrent task (book reading)	Yes (23)

Table 2. Key themes from user comfort, vibration perception, and usefulness.

Question	Key themes (at least frequency of 3 out of 26) (initial)	Key themes (at least frequency of 3 out of 26) (final)
IGQ3/FGQ3: Comfortable with ear vibrations in day-to-day life	Yes (10), Undecided (6), Needs getting used to it (4), if like earbuds (3), open to it (3)	Yes (20), Maybe (3), If more comfortable (3)
IGQ4/FGQ4: Feelings towards ear vibrations	Interested (6), Curious (5), Good (3)	Good (7), Excited (3)
IGQ5/FGQ5: Disabled/non-disabled usefulness	Yes, for both (23), non-disabled extra information (4), Disabled more benefits (3), Disabled sensory replacement (3)	Yes, for both (23), Use-case/application specific (4), Disabled more useful (3)

Table 3. Key themes from device user experience.

Question	Key themes (at least frequency of 3 out of 26) (initial)	Key themes (at least frequency of 3 out of 26) (final)
IDQ1/FDQ1: Comfort impression	Yes (8), No (8), Not secure enough (4), Both yes and no (3), Column too big (3)	Yes (10), No (10), More uncomfortable over time (3), Too hard (3)
IDQ2/FDQ2:Weight impression	Not heavy (6), Could get worse over time (5), Not an issue (4), Could get used to it (3), Fine (3), Light (3)	Fine (12), Good (3), Possible problem if worn all day (3)
IDQ3/FDQ3:Texture impression	Fine (6), Rough (6), Nice (3)	Fine (6), Ok (4), Hard (4), Needs padding/rubber (3)
IDQ4/FDQ4:Problematic elements	Clip (15), Column (4), Clip needs to be harder/stronger (3)	Column (18), Not really (4), Device needs to be adjustable (3), Clip (3), Size (3)
IDQ5/FDQ5:Aesthetics impression	Yes (5), Ok (5), Like that it looks like an ear (4), Extra work required (3),Prefer smaller (3), Bulky (3)	Yes (8), Good (6), Fine (5), Prefer smaller (3), Ok (3)

5.1 Summary of Results

Looking at the key themes present in the data, participants were familiar with at least one form of haptic feedback, were open to the idea of ear-based haptics, and saw clear uses for both disabled and non-disabled people. Participants saw haptics as a valid form of communication, both when there is an auditory and visual concurrent task (though more variable for auditory), were comfortable with receiving vibrations on their ears and were excited for future developments in the technology.

Participants were divided on the comfort level and texture of the earpiece but did not see the weight as a problem. The clip needs to be reinforced, and the centre column was particularly disliked. The look of the device was positively received, and participants particularly liked that it looked like an ear. Other improvements include adding rubber, smoothening out the surface, making the sizing adjustable, and improving the way it attaches to the ear.

5.2 Emerging Design Guidelines

Using the data collected throughout the user experience interviews, below are six suggested design guidelines for future ear-based haptic wearable design.

1. Padding: Contact points between an ear-worn haptic wearable and the ear must have padding/soft materials to ensure user comfort.
2. Form-factor: Ear-worn haptic wearables need to be as small as possible and conform to the shape of the ear.
3. Safety: Ear-worn haptic wearable must feel secure on the ear and should not make users feel like it may fall off.
4. Adaptable: As the size of the ear fluctuates greatly between individuals, any ear-worn haptic wearable must be adjustable to the size of the individual's ear.
5. Outer-ear: Users are uncomfortable with receiving vibrations too close to the ear canal, vibrations should be primarily aimed at stimulating the auricle only.
6. Similarity: Where possible, ear-worn haptic wearables must be similar in form to ear-based devices that users are already used to using, such as headphones or earbuds.

5.3 Improved Device Mock-Up

Following each guideline, a new version of the EarPi hearing aid should be slimmer, adaptable to different ear sizes, padded, better attached to the ear, similar to an earbud, and without a straight column going into the ear canal. Below is a new mock-up 3D model followed by design decision explanations (Fig. 17).

The new earpiece is designed to only house cables and motors; this reduces size and weight (Guideline 2). The driver boards and multiplexer will be housed in a new version of the Pi Casing. To accommodate different ear sizes (Guideline 4), the earpiece will be printed in three parts with differently sized top and bottom sections that can be swapped out as needed. These three sections will be attached magnetically. The column has been reworked to more closely resemble a conventional earbud (Guideline 6) and is compatible with standard silicone earbud tips (Guideline 1).

As users were uncomfortable with receiving vibration in the ear canal (Guideline 5), the centre motor will now be housed inside the earpiece without direct contact to the skin. Users reported being unable to locate the centre motor when stimulated, so now the centre column will instead make the entire earpiece vibrate. This will allow for the same number of possible patterns and vibrations to be produced, the centre vibration is now replaced with a whole earpiece vibration.

Fig. 17. Haptic Earpiece V5 Renders (Left: Front, Middle: Back, Right: Centre piece only).

The much lighter and slimmer form factor – coupled with the ability to use standard earbud tips – removes the need for a separate clip attachment. The earpiece is now designed to be worn and held in place like a wireless earbud (Guideline 3).

6   Conclusions, Limitations and Future Work

In summary, it was found that participants responded positively to the use of the ear as an interface for haptic feedback and were excited to see how this technology might progress further. It was, however, found that various improvements must be made to ensure user comfort and that the inter-individual variability of the auricle presents challenges for security and adjustability. The importance of developing bespoke ear-based wearables adapted to the unique needs and physiology of each user has been highlighted, and user-centred design must be followed for ear-based wearable development.

Throughout this research project, a fully functioning ear-based haptic HMI has been developed to produce vibration at four locations across the auricle at varying frequencies and amplitudes. A series of semi-structured interviews has validated the prototype, and valuable information on HMI design and attitudes towards ear-based haptics has been collected. Key problem points have been reported, and guidelines of Padding, Form-factor, Safety, Adaptability, Outer-ear, and Similarity have been suggested. These findings are in line with previously found design recommendations for portable HMI design (Kuriakose et al. 2020) and lay the groundwork for future EarPi design iterations.

Various limitations exist within the current study, including limited resources for development (leading to a less polished end product), discomfort caused by sounds produced by the vibrotactile motors, and limited time spent in device familiarisation tasks. More development time and resources – leading to custom designed PCBs and bespoke components – would be beneficial to reduce device size and weight. Motors that produce less sound, or other forms of haptics such as thermal or pneumatic actuators, could lead to greater user comfort. A longer study with multiple weeks of familiarisation may lead to more detailed and accurate user feedback.

Using an improved HMI design that follows guidelines presented in this study, future work will include evaluation of participants' ability to differentiate ear locations and recognise various simultaneous and sequential haptic patterns across the auricle. Other possible avenues of future research could include the following:

- Comparing other forms of haptics (e.g., thermal, pressure, mid-air, passive) on the auricle in unimodal and multimodal haptic HMI.
- Evaluating the use of ear-based haptics in simulation tasks for information communication.
- Exploring differences between left and right ear haptic perception.
- Evaluating the use of both ears for haptic feedback with two earpieces.
- Comparing reaction times between haptics, visual, and auditory alerts in situations with no concurrent tasks, visual concurrent tasks and auditory concurrent task to see if ear-based haptic multimodality is congruent with previous findings in literature (Chai et al. 2022).

References

Adafruit. Adafruit DRV2605L Haptic Motor Controller—STEMMA QT/Qwiic (2025a). https://www.adafruit.com/product/2305

Adafruit. Adafruit PCA9548 8-Channel STEMMA QT / Qwiic I2C Multiplexer - TCA9548A Compatible (2025b). https://www.adafruit.com/product/5626

Adafruit. Raspberry Pi Zero WH (Zero W with Headers) (2025c). https://www.adafruit.com/product/3708

Adafruit. Adafruit 1.3" Color TFT Bonnet for Raspberry Pi - 240x240 TFT + Joystick Add-on (2025d). https://www.adafruit.com/product/4506

Al-Qahtani, A., Haidar, H., Larem, A.: Textbook of clinical otolaryngology. Springer Cham (2021). https://doi.org/10.1007/978-3-030-54088-3

Autodesk. Autodesk 3ds Max: Create immersive worlds and high-quality designs (2025a). https://www.autodesk.com/uk/products/3ds-max/overview

Autodesk. Autodesk Fusion: More than CAD, it's the future of design and manufacturing (2025b). https://www.autodesk.com/uk/products/fusion-360/overview

van der Bie, J., Allouch, S.B., Jaschinski, C.: Communicating multimodal wayfinding messages for visually impaired people via wearables. MobileHCI 10(1145/3338286), 3344419 (2019)

Chai, C., Shi, J., Wu, C., Zhou, Y., Zhang, W., Liao, J.: When to use vibrotactile displays? A meta-analysis for the role of vibrotactile displays in human–computer interaction(2022). https://doi.org/10.1016/J.APERGO.2022.103802

Delazio, A., Nakagaki, K., Klatzky, R.L., Hudson, S.E., Lehman, J.F., Sample, A.P.: Force jacket: pneumatically-actuated jacket for embodied haptic experiences. In: Proceedings of the 2018 CHI Conference on Human Factors in Computing Systems, 1–12 (2018)https://doi.org/10.1145/3173574.3173894

Duggin, A.: What we mean when we talk about accessibility. Accessibility in government (2016). https://accessibility.blog.gov.uk/2016/05/16/what-we-mean-when-we-talk-about-accessibility-2/

Eagleman, D.M., Perrotta, M.V.: The future of sensory substitution, addition, and expansion via haptic devices. Front. Hum. Neurosci. 16, 1055546 (2023). https://doi.org/10.3389/fnhum.2022.1055546

Escorcia Hernández, J. M., Chemori, A., Aguilar Sierra, H. : Chapter 1—Introduction. In: Escorcia Hernández, J.M., Chemori, A., Aguilar Sierra, H. (eds.), Modeling and Nonlinear Robust Control of Delta-Like Parallel Kinematic Manipulators, pp. 1–19. Academic Press (2023). https://doi.org/10.1016/B978-0-32-396101-1.00008-X

Flores Ramones, A., del-Rio-Guerra, M.S.: Recent developments in haptic devices designed for hearing-impaired people: a literature review. Sensors 23(6), Article 6 (2023). https://doi.org/10.3390/s23062968

Gibson, A., Webb, A.K., Stirling, L.: Evaluation of a visual-tactile multimodal display for surface obstacle avoidance during walking. IEEE Trans. Hum.-Mach. Syst. (2018). https://doi.org/10.1109/THMS.2018.2849018

Hettiarachchi, A., Wigdor, D.: Annexing reality: enabling opportunistic use of everyday objects as tangible proxies in augmented reality. In: Proceedings of the 2016 CHI Conference on Human Factors in Computing Systems, pp. 1957–1967 (2016). https://doi.org/10.1145/2858036.2858134

Hörold, S., Mayas, C., Krömker, H.: Interactive displays in public transport – challenges and expectations. Procedia Manufac. 3, 2808–2815 (2015). https://doi.org/10.1016/j.promfg.2015.07.932

Iwarsson, S., Ståhl, A.: Accessibility, usability and universal design—positioning and definition of concepts describing person-environment relationships. Disabil. Rehabil. 25(2), 57–66 (2003). https://doi.org/10.1080/dre.25.2.57.66

Kuriakose, B., Shrestha, R., Sandnes, F.E.: Multimodal navigation systems for users with visual impairments—a review and analysis. Multimodal Technol. Interact. 4(4), Article 4 (2020). https://doi.org/10.3390/mti4040073

Lee, M., Je, S., Lee, W., Ashbrook, D., Bianchi, A.: ActivEarring: spatiotemporal haptic cues on the ears. IEEE Trans. Haptics (2019). https://doi.org/10.1109/TOH.2019.2925799

Mirzaei, M., Kán, P., Kaufmann, H.: EarVR: using ear haptics in virtual reality for deaf and hard-of-hearing people. IEEE Trans. Visual Comput. Graphics (2020). https://doi.org/10.1109/TVCG.2020.2973441

Motability. The Transport Accessibility Gap (2022). https://www.motabilityfoundation.org.uk/media/iwaidhxk/motability_transport-accessibility-gap-report_march-2022_final.pdf

Nasser, A., Zheng, K., Zhu, K.: ThermEarhook: investigating spatial thermal haptic feedback on the auricular skin area. International Conference on Multimodal Interaction 10(1145/3462244), 3479922 (2021)

National Institute of Standards and Technology. human-machine interface. Computer Security Resource Center (2024). https://csrc.nist.gov/glossary/term/human_machine_interface

Nguyen, V.-C., et al.: Haptic feedback device using 3D-printed flexible, multilayered piezoelectric coating for in-car touchscreen interface. Micromachines (2023). https://doi.org/10.3390/MI14081553

Pacchierotti, C., Sinclair, S., Solazzi, M., Frisoli, A., Hayward, V., Prattichizzo, D.: Wearable haptic systems for the fingertip and the hand: taxonomy, review, and perspectives. IEEE Trans. Haptics (2017). https://doi.org/10.1109/TOH.2017.2689006

Pavlidou, A., Lo, B.: Artificial ear—a wearable device for the hearing impaired (2021). https://doi.org/10.1109/BSN51625.2021.9507021

Perrotta, M.V., Asgeirsdottir, T., Eagleman, D.M.: Deciphering sounds through patterns of vibration on the skin. Neuroscience (2021). https://doi.org/10.1016/J.NEUROSCIENCE.2021.01.008

Precision Microdrives. Linear Resonant Actuators – LRAs (2025). https://www.precisionmicrodrives.com/linear-resonant-actuators-lras

Rakkolainen, I., Freeman, E., Sand, A., Raisamo, R., Brewster, S.: A survey of mid-air ultrasound haptics and its applications. IEEE Trans. Haptics (2021). https://doi.org/10.1109/TOH.2020.3018754

Texas Instruments. DRV2605L data sheet, product information and support (2025). https://www.ti.com/product/DRV2605L

UITP. (2022). When is public transport really accessible? http://uitp.org/news/when-is-public-transport-really-accessible/

United Nations. The 17 Goals (2025). https://sdgs.un.org/goals

Exploring Family Engagements with Smart Home Devices: A Multi-case Study from a Distributed Cognition Perspective

Zixiang Feng(✉)

Royal College of Art, Howie Street, London SW11 4AS, UK
`fzxqwq@gmail.com`

Abstract. The predominant literature examined smart home technologies from an individual perspective. However, it remains less explored how multiple family members interact with smart home devices (e.g., their coordination, synchronization, and task allocation) within social and cultural contexts. This study aims to explore obstacles and opportunities in designing smart home systems involving family-member interactions. We present a multi-case study involving 11 case families using smart home devices, conducting 20 in-depth interviews with their members. Drawing on a distributed cognition perspective, our thematic analysis identified three main obstacles in family interactions: insufficient experiential learning, inefficient synchronization of information, and user-unfriendly collaboration mechanisms. The findings highlight the need for design opportunities, including differentiated learning approaches, improved information flow, and better collaboration mechanisms for smart home systems to enhance user experience and efficiency. This study provides deeper insights into socio-cultural dynamics within smart home systems, contributing to smart home scholarship.

Keywords: Distributed cognition · Smart home · Family interactions · Information synchronization · Case study

1 Introduction

Smart home have gained continued scholarly interest in Human-Computer Interaction research. Since its initial exploration by Demiris in 2004 in Human-Computer Interaction field [8], scholars have investigated various aspects of smart home systems. While early research focused on individual interactions with smart home systems [31], studies like Cabitza et al. in 2016 highlighted the importance of goal-oriented interfaces in enhancing user capabilities [6]. Meanwhile, research in the smart home domain has paid significant attention to energy optimization. For example, Gupta and coauthors 2020 proposed a multi-objective reinforcement learning framework that aims to minimize energy consumption while maximizing user satisfaction [12]. Additionally, Verma coauthors 2019 proposed a method to optimize smart home energy consumption by taking user behavior into account[39]. More recently, researchers explored IoT-based smart home security and automation through algorithm optimization, device ranking, and the design of security frameworks [2, 26, 36].

© The Author(s), under exclusive license to Springer Nature Switzerland AG 2026
D. Harris et al. (Eds.): HCII 2025, LNCS 16334, pp. 364–382, 2026.
https://doi.org/10.1007/978-3-032-12392-3_24

Predominant research approached smart homes from an individual perspective, analyzing personal use and engagement with smart home systems. For example, Fu and coauthors proposed a demand-oriented approach to meet users' needs [11], and Zhao and Zhang emphasized optimizing user experience [45]. Goal-oriented, adaptive smart home systems were further advanced by researchers, focusing on intelligent user interaction [27, 38]. Most studies have explored the use of smart home devices from an individual perspective, focusing on user interactions, needs, smart home energy design, security mechanisms, and design strategies.

The home is an important usage scenario for a smart home, where the use of multiple smart home devices can be shared and synchronized between family members through collaboration and interaction. However, less attention has been given to how interactions between family members are embedded within Smart home systems. Significant challenges exist in the collaborative use of Smart home devices among family members. For instance, influenced by sociocultural factors, individuals with varying levels of expertise face numerous obstacles when cooperating in the use of Smart home devices. The obstacles and design opportunities underlying family interactions with smart homes remain unclear.

This study aims to explore the following research questions:

(1) What are the obstacles to changing the use of smart home devices by family members during ongoing interactions?
(2) What design opportunities exist in designing smart homes that inherently involve family member interactions?

We explore these research questions through the theoretical lens of Distributed Cognition (DC). It challenges the traditional view in cognitive science that confines cognition to the individual mind and brain. Instead, it emphasizes that cognitive processes are distributed across interactions between individuals, between individuals and objects, and between individuals and their environment [16]. Such a lens posits that cognitive processes are not limited to individuals but are instead distributed across people, tools, and the environment. Therefore, DC offers a more comprehensive and systematic view, extending the focus beyond the individual user of smart home devices to the entire process, including interactions with other family members, the home environment, smart home devices, and other related information flow tools and systems.

The contribution of this study is twofold. First, we unpack underappreciated dynamics related to family interactions in using smart homes, including their coordination task allocation, conflict resolution, and information synchronization. It introduces the perspective of family interaction into the human-computer interaction of smart homes. Second, it provides deeper insights into the socio-cultural cognitive dynamics within smart home systems, extending our understanding of smart home systems from a distributed perspective.

2 Theoretical Framing and Related Works

2.1 Family Member Interactions in Smart Home

The term Smart Home was first coined by Richard Harper in 1984 at the American Association of House Builders [9]. Since its inception, the concept has been understood in various ways. Early definitions of smart homes, such as Lutolf, describe them as the integration of various services within a home using a common communication system[22]. More recently, Satpathy redefined the concept, emphasizing that a smart home assists inhabitants to live independently and comfortably through a network of interconnected mechanical and digital devices, creating an interactive space[32].

In the field of smart home research, researchers have identified and analyzed a variety of factors that influence user engagement with smart home systems [21, 34, 35] while also focusing on control methods within these systems [25, 40]. Regarding smart home frameworks, Muddasser Alam and coauthors have proposed a new framework that simplifies the modeling, prototyping, and simulation of smart infrastructures, facilitating the construction of smart home models and the application of AI technologies [1]. Additionally, Shushan Hua and her team introduced an innovative system framework that reduces system load and optimizes response times [15]. Further studies have focused on applying smart home systems in energy optimization [23, 30]. Overall, the essence of smart homes lies not just in individual devices but in the interconnectedness and communication within the entire system.

Research has been somewhat limited in family interactions in smart homes, primarily focusing on the elderly and children as key user groups [3, 14, 37]. Notably, [14] developed a Remote Collaboration Smart Home System (RCSSH) based on Digital Twin and Mixed Reality technologies. This system facilitates collaboration between remote users (i. e. the younger generation within families) and in-home users (i. e. the elderly). Another study [43] described a smart home system composed of a smart porch and home portal that supports ubiquitous collaboration among family members. Scenario-based experimental results confirmed that this system enhances the service quality in family collaborations. Additionally, there have been scholarly explorations concerning privacy issues in smart home collaborations [18, 41].

However, current research on smart homes focuses more on the individual user experience, while relatively little attention has been paid to research on interactions involving the entire family unit, which leads to unique challenges posed by smart home devices. For instance, in contemporary family member interactions, family members are still required to synchronize each individual's progress constantly. What is more, they sometimes involve collaboration across different zones and in different usage scenarios, which poses more complex and contextually relevant challenges for the design of smart furniture systems.

2.2 Theoretical Framework: Distributed Cognition

The theory of Distributed Cognition (DC) was introduced by Edwin Hutchins in 1995 [16]. DC seeks to understand cognitive systems not just within individuals but as a broader phenomenon encompassing interactions among people, tools, and the environment. This theory challenges the traditional view of cognitive science, which confines cognition to the individual brain, and instead emphasizes that cognitive processes are distributed across interactions between individuals, objects, and the environment. Liu and coauthors discuss the framework of DC in information visualization, arguing that cognition emerges from interaction with the environment rather than being confined to the individual brain [44]. They further emphasize that cognition should not be studied in isolation but in collaboration with tools and the environment.

In the field of human-computer interaction, Hollan, Hutchins, and Kirsh 2000 proposed that DC offers a new foundation for understanding the interaction between humans and technology, especially in the design and support of human-computer interaction systems. They also introduced two key principles of DC to guide the design of more effective user interfaces and collaborative systems, optimizing the user experience by understanding human-technology interactions [13]. Schrire explored interaction and cognition in asynchronous computer conferencing, emphasizing how DC can help define higher-order thought processes in online environments [33]. Blandford and Furniss introduced Distributed Cognition for Teamwork, a methodology that applies DC to the design of systems for teamwork, highlighting its use in large-scale ambulance control centers [4].

Building on these works, Kirsh introduced the principles of embedding and the interactivity of distributed cognition, providing metrics and evaluation criteria for human-computer interaction design [19]. In DC and the task of science, Magnus suggests that the DC framework can be applied to scientific research, particularly in describing the cognitive processes of scientific projects [24].

Edmondson and Beale, in 2008, extended the DC framework with the concept of "Projected Cognition," suggesting that human behavioral intentions can be projected onto artifacts, enhancing the understanding of complex human-computer interaction [10]. Additionally, Jia, Zhao, and Kong proposed design principles for optimizing mobile human-computer interaction based on DC, focusing on analyzing users' cognitive resources and device contexts to improve user experience [17].

DC theory has also been applied in the smart home domain, aiming to optimize the home environment by understanding interactions between humans and technology. Rajkomar, Mayer, and Blandford applied the DC framework to medical devices in the home, analyzing system activities, information flow, social structures, physical layouts, and artifacts to propose design recommendations that improve patient experiences[29]. D'Angelo and Rampone, in 2018, further developed a cognitive distribution architecture for smart home and pervasive computing, where advanced cognitive systems emerge through interactions between humans and non-human agents [7]. DC embraces several key assumptions:

1. Cognition is distributed: Cognitive processes extend beyond the individual brain, spanning across people, objects, and environments, shaped by interactions with the social and physical context.
2. Tools as cognitive extensions: Objects and tools act as external extensions of cognition, aiding in information processing and problem-solving through interaction with individuals.

3. Goal interactions affect cognition: The interplay between multiple goals in a cognitive system impacts the system's efficiency and effectiveness.
4. Resolving goal conflicts: In multi-goal systems, conflicts between goals must be managed through optimization strategies, with goal coordination improved by supportive designs.
5. Goal prioritization influences cognition: Prioritizing goals based on changing needs influences how resources are allocated, and decisions are made within the system.
6. Adaptability in dynamic environments: Real-time adjustments and redefinitions of goals enhance the flexibility and responsiveness of the cognitive system in dynamic settings.
7. Tool design impacts cognition: The design and functionality of tools significantly shape the processes of information handling and problem-solving in distributed systems.
8. Social interaction enhances cognition: Communication and collaboration between individuals in a distributed cognition system greatly improve overall cognitive capacity.

Utilizing the perspective of DC to study family-member interactions in smart homes offers two main strengths. First, this comprehensive and systematic approach expands the focus beyond individual user experiences with smart home devices to encompass the entire process, including interactions with other family members, the home environment, smart home devices, and other related information flow tools and systems. Second, under the DC framework, we can better understand the relationship between the socio-cultural context and family members' use of smart home devices as a research factor. This helps analyze the events of collaboration between different family members in using smart home devices, identifying potential opportunities and barriers.

3 Methods

We conducted an inductive, exploratory qualitative study to examine family interactions in smart home environments through the lens of DC. We employed a case study methodology, which is particularly effective for empirical inquiry that investigates contemporary phenomena within real-life contexts, particularly when the boundaries between the phenomenon and the context are not clearly evident [42].

We aim to gain an in-depth understanding of the meanings and complexities underlying the phenomenon of smart home interactions. By adopting this methodology, we sought to provide detailed descriptions and insights that could help researchers comprehend broader social phenomena, individual experiences, and cultural differences, thus offering a nuanced interpretation of these dynamics.

3.1 Research Setting

We recruited 11 families within China. These families were selected based on their extensive use of smart home devices and the presence of multiple family members (see Table A1 in APPENDICES). This setting provided an ideal context for exploring our research questions, as it allowed for an in-depth examination of family interactions within environments where smart home technology is seamlessly integrated into daily life.

3.2 Sampling Strategy

We employed purposive sampling, a non-probability sampling technique in which participants are selected based on specific characteristics or criteria that are most relevant to the research question. Unlike random selection of participants, purposive sampling focuses on individuals who are perceived to have the necessary knowledge or experience to provide valuable insights [28]. In this study, we sampled 20 smart home users from different families across China. The participants represented different family roles, and these participants varied in terms of gender, age, family composition, family structure, level of use of smart home devices, and degree of system integration of smart home technologies (see Table A2 in APPENDICES). They were recruited online and participated in semi-structured interviews lasting around 30–50 min, all of which were conducted in Mandarin. This was done to maximize diversity for a wide range of experiences and interactions.

3.3 Data Collection

Our primary data source is semi-structured interviews; each participant is interviewed for approximately 30 to 35 min. This included 15 face-to-face interviews and 9 online interviews conducted via Zoom. We provided all participants with informed consent before conducting interviews.

The interview questions were structured into five main sections. The first section gathered basic demographic information, such as the number of family members, the types and quantity of smart home devices used, the duration of device usage, and the participants' attitudes towards smart home technology. The second section focused on the routine use of smart home devices, where participants described a typical day of using these technologies in their families. The third section asked participants to describe a typical example of family members collaboratively using smart home devices, encouraging them to provide as much detail as possible. The fourth section delved deeper into a specific case involving family member interactions around smart home technology, using prompted questions to explore challenges and opportunities in these interactions.

The offline participants were recruited using a snowball sampling technique, while online participants were recruited through web-based channels. Each participant was scheduled for a semi-structured interview lasting approximately 30 min.

3.4 Data Analysis

This study employed thematic analysis. It involves the identification, analysis, and reporting of patterns (themes) within the data. Rather than merely summarizing the data, thematic analysis provides rich, detailed descriptions and interpretations [5]. In our study, we conducted thematic analysis in an inductive, bottom-up, and exploratory manner, where the theoretical framework was gradually introduced based on the analysis of empirical data.

We began by transcribing the interview data into text, resulting in 192,071 words across 362 data pages. The first step in our analysis was to code events where family members interacted with smart home devices. Here, an event is defined as a scenario or process in which two or more family members use one or more smart home devices together. From the data, we identified 20 distinct events of family interaction with smart home technology.

Each coded event included a detailed description of the interaction process, along with participants' feelings, interpretations, intentions, concerns, and future expectations. Guided by the framework of distributed cognition, we specifically coded for dynamics that aligned with its assumptions, such as how sociocultural factors influence cognition.

Focusing on these dynamics, we examined the barriers to family interaction with smart home technology, as well as the design opportunities to enhance these interactions, addressing our first and second research questions, respectively. This process was iterative, involving repeated refinement in a bottom-up, inductive manner, ultimately leading to stable findings.

4 Findings

Our analysis reveals three major obstacles to family members' use of smart home devices: (1) Learning flow: lack of support for experiential learning; (2) Information flow: insufficient multi-channel information synchronization; and (3) Cooperation flow: the collaboration mechanism (task distribution and integration) is not user-friendly. Below, we elaborate on each of these themes.

4.1 Learning Flow: Lack of Support for Experiential Learning

We have identified shortcomings in smart home devices when it comes to supporting experiential learning for certain family members. Experiential learning refers to a process of learning through direct experience and participation, emphasizing learning from practice and reflecting on these experiences to acquire knowledge and skills [20]. The current learning approaches provided by smart home devices primarily focus on instructional learning or self-directed learning, both of which rely on a basic level of device knowledge and prior experience with smart devices. These approaches are more suitable for learners who can independently solve problems. Our data indicate that in family interactions, older family members especially tend to rely on experiential learning.

In the context of using smart kitchen devices, older adults may not adopt a direct instructional learning method but instead rely on others to operate the devices remotely, following a one-on-one imitation learning process. For example, interviewee P4 mentioned the challenges she faced when directly instructing her elderly family members on using smart home devices:

> "When my parents first started using the smart oven I bought for them, they had difficulties with the basic functions. Whenever they tried using more complex functions for the first time, they encountered issues. They would call me via video chat to help them. The first time they tried roasting chicken thighs; I guided them

via video on how to set the time and temperature on the app. Initially, they were unfamiliar with the technology, but after several such interactions, they became proficient in using multiple functions of the oven."

This phenomenon is also evident in C2, where during an interview with participant P3, we found that older adults, when learning to use smart speakers, tend to observe how other family members use smart home devices to learn these methods. "At first, my grandmother didn't know how to use the new smart devices and was even resistant to them, especially the smart lock and voice control system. She was reluctant to try them at first, but over time, by observing how we used some of the smart products—like voice control—she started mimicking us and eventually began using the devices herself." In another interview with P5, he mentioned that when the elderly at home tried to teach children how to use smart home devices, they encountered many obstacles. However, they were unwilling to learn by reading manuals or searching online. Instead, they relied on family members who knew how to use the devices to provide face-to-face instruction. This indicates that they can only better learn and understand new technology with direct and personal assistance.

In some families, certain members prioritize experiential learning more highly, as reflected in our interview with P12. She mentioned that her mother developed a limited understanding of smart home devices after an incident involving non-smart activation of the smart curtains, which led to a mistaken belief that this was the normal activation method. As a result, every time she used the smart curtains, she would forcefully pull them by hand, thinking this would trigger the smart closing mechanism.

4.2 Information Flow: Ineffective Multi-Channel Information Synchronization

Our analysis shows that there is a general lack of effective multi-channel information synchronization among family members. Here, multi-channel information refers not to sensory channels but to the various inputs generated when multiple family members use the same device, as well as how the device conveys different types of information to the family members. This information disruption occurs between smart home devices and family members or among family members themselves, hindering effective use of the devices, impairing information flow, and reducing their ability to recognize hierarchical information.

In CASE 3's smart lock collaboration scenario, this issue is reflected in the lack of smooth communication between smart home devices and family members. Due to the elderly's fingerprint recognition problems, which often require multiple attempts, the smart lock triggers an alarm after five failed fingerprint attempts, necessitating remote assistance to unlock the door. However, these notifications are combined with regular door lock open/close alerts, leading users to ignore important warnings related to the elderly's difficulties with the smart lock, which often incurs high communication costs. For example, our interviewee P8 mentioned:

> "The smart lock at home has caused my parents a lot of trouble. Their fingerprints and vein recognition are not very sensitive, so they often have to try several times to unlock the door. After five failed attempts, it triggers an alarm, and I have to

unlock it remotely. Although the smart lock notifies me of the door's open/close status via my phone, the notifications are so frequent that I sometimes overlook the important warning that my parents can't enter the house."

Additionally, in the context of using smart cameras to detect elderly falls, the collaboration mode involves machine learning-based predictions followed by phone call alerts to coordinate with other family members. However, due to delayed notifications and inaccurate predictions, redundant phone alerts are often sent. The uniform notification method, without distinguishing between prediction accuracy levels, creates trust issues. The same phone alert is used for both actual falls and predicted falls, making it difficult for family members to assess the severity of the situation in real time. This results in communication breakdowns and incurs significant phone costs. For example, in C4, our interviewee P1 said:

"When using a smart camera to monitor elderly falls, the machine learning predictions were often inaccurate, and the delayed notifications led to frequent false alarms. The warning methods didn't differentiate between the urgency of situations, making it hard for us to quickly assess the seriousness of the fall. I thought that perhaps differentiating between day and night modes or using app notifications instead of phone calls might reduce disruptions."

Finally, miscommunication among family members due to conflicting smart home commands can also lead to a breakdown in device usage synchronization. In CASE5, insufficient information sharing among family members disrupted the preset tasks for the smart kettle. Interviewee P6 noted: "I would always preset the water temperature before heading home to make it easier to prepare baby formula, but during this process, if my mother wanted to make tea, she would override my settings, ruining the temperature suitable for formula. As a result, we ended up buying two kettles, one specifically for making baby formula."

4.3 Cooperation Flow: Collaboration Mechanisms Are not User-Friendly

In our investigation, the collaboration mechanisms supported by smart homes among family members are not particularly user-friendly. The allocation and integration of tasks often lack coherence and organic synergy. Task distribution and integration in a smart home setting involve multiple family members utilizing smart home technologies to make the process of achieving collaborative goals more efficient and harmonious. This integration involves not only technical configurations but also a clear division of rights and responsibilities among family members regarding the use of smart home devices. However, our investigation found that the mechanisms supporting this collaboration are not sufficiently friendly.

For example, in the usage scenario of smart pet care devices, the collaboration between pet owners and other family members tends to lag and is conditionally restricted. This hindrance can lead to uneven task distribution, where the main controller bears more responsibilities—from obtaining information about the smart home devices, understanding and reviewing it, to pass it on to other family members. This method of integration and collaboration is neither friendly nor organic. In Case 6, where the pet owner is away at school, and there is a pet at home, some smart pet care devices last for about five days before requiring manual intervention for food, water, or pet waste disposal, such as replenishing cat litter. Even though these tasks are integrated into the smart home system, manual coordination is still required, where the main controller sends signals to other family members to collaborate in replacing pet consumables. However, this kind of collaboration, which relies on the pet owner's signals to other family members, is often restricted by physical conditions. For instance, when other family members are not at home, they cannot properly participate in collaborative tasks.

Interviewee P3 mentioned, "These smart devices are a series of different products, but they are not part of a unified system. My family doesn't quite understand the specific settings and operational details related to my pets, and they're not willing to download or learn about them. Instead, they rely heavily on me to communicate what needs to be done." A similar issue was found in P7's case with the collaborative use of a smart vacuum robot (Case 10).

Interviewee P7 shared, "We preset the settings for the vacuum robot, such as how long it should clean, the cleaning range, and the mode. If an elderly family member finishes cooking or feels that the floor is dirty, they only need to press a button on the vacuum robot. But if they want to clean a specific area, they'll call me to describe the area, and I control it remotely."

In this case, we observed that family members and the elderly jointly created a collaborative usage scenario for smart cleaning. In this scenario, the elderly person plays an important role, but due to physical limitations, their understanding of complex systems is limited. While they can operate the device using simple buttons when it comes to tasks outside the preset scope, the elderly person must communicate with the remote controller, and this communication is often limited in effectiveness.

For example, interviewee P7 expressed frustration when collaborating with his mother to use the smart vacuum cleaner: "Sometimes, when the elderly family member is trying to describe the area that needs to be cleaned, it's hard to understand, and the outcome isn't always great—the entire area doesn't get cleaned properly." This indicates that the integration of this collaboration is not particularly friendly, and the role of family member collaborators is especially important.

In the context of smart kitchen devices, there are issues related to task duplication due to problems in the collaboration mechanisms, which further highlight that the task distribution and integration among family members are not particularly user-friendly. In P8's interview, he noted, "When family members work together in the kitchen to complete a cooking task, insufficient communication or unclear task distribution sometimes results in smart kitchen devices not providing status notifications. This leads to multiple people performing the same task, such as two people preparing the same ingredient. This overlap not only wastes resources but also increases the complexity and confusion of kitchen activities."

5   Discussion

Our case study extends smart home scholarship in two ways. First, it introduces a distributed cognition theoretical perspective, offering a broader and more comprehensive framework. This perspective shifts the focus from individual interactions with smart home technologies to a holistic understanding of family dynamics, encompassing task coordination, information synchronization, and conflict resolution among family members. By adopting this lens, we uncover previously underexplored cognitive dynamics within the family context that directly affect the usability and efficiency of smart home devices. Second, we integrate a family interaction perspective, highlighting how socio-cultural factors influence the ways in which family members interact with smart home technologies. This approach emphasizes the impact of varying levels of expertise and socio-cultural backgrounds on collaborative use within families, offering valuable design insights for creating more inclusive and effective smart home systems that cater to the diverse needs of different family units.

5.1   Implications for Design Practice

Based on the challenges identified in smart home usage, our data highlighted several design opportunities. First, the learning flow involves providing varied methods in learning design to enhance user interaction. Second, we emphasize offering differentiated levels in information transmission design to improve clarity and user comprehension in the information flow. Lastly, the cooperation flow underlines the importance of involving device collaborators in the system design process to foster better integration and functionality.

Learning Flow: Providing Differentiated Methods in Learning Design. Designing the learning approach refers to the planning and implementation of education and training processes for users during the initialization phase of smart home systems. Differentiated methods refer to creating distinct experiential approaches based on varying social and cultural backgrounds or information reception abilities. In Case 2, interviewee P10 mentioned that his mother didn't master the use of the smart oven through the learning methods provided by the smart home system but rather through video calls with her daughter. This indicates that the current learning models designed for smart homes are not suitable for all family members.

For example, when designing learning methods for smart homes, it is essential to provide learning approaches tailored to family members from different social and cultural backgrounds. For those with stronger comprehension and practical experience, text and image-based learning methods should be offered, while for family members with weaker abilities, video-based or interactive learning platforms should be provided. An interactive app or online platform could be created where users can learn the system's functions by exchanging information in groups or forums. Through these platforms, users can gain practical feedback through Q&A sessions and case studies.

Information Flow: Differentiating Levels in Information Transmission Design. Information transmission refers to the methods used to enable the flow of information and commands between home devices, as well as between users and devices, through various technical means and system designs. In this process, "leveling" refers to two aspects. On the one hand, it relates to the path through which smart home devices transmit information to family members. Differentiating these levels allows family members to understand the importance or complexity of the information they receive from smart home devices through different transmission methods. On the other hand, when family members transmit information to the smart home system, differentiating levels refer to how the system manages multiple tasks from various family members, organizing and prioritizing these tasks based on their complexity. This helps streamline the usage of smart home devices across multiple tasks.

In terms of how smart home devices transmit information to family members, interviewee P1 in Case 4 raised the point: "Shouldn't the elderly fall detection alerts from the smart camera be differentiated based on the time of day, like having different alarm modes for day and night?" This suggests that when designing information transmission methods, smart home devices should differentiate the levels of information and use distinct methods to transmit information to family members according to its importance. For instance, when designing smart door locks, there should be a layered transmission system that distinguishes important information, such as the device's health status, from the more routine daily entry and exit data, with different transmission methods to notify family members accordingly.

When family members transmit information to the smart home system, designers should prioritize and layer the multiple goals of different users within the system and set up communication methods between family members to make the whole system more cohesive. For instance, when designing smart cleaning systems, designers should manage the various cleaning tasks assigned to different family members by layering routine cleaning and special cleaning tasks. This allows the tasks to be managed more smoothly, ensuring a more efficient cleaning process.

Cooperation Flow: Emphasizing the Participation of Device Collaborators in System Design. In smart home systems, system design refers to the control mechanisms behind smart homes built on IoT technologies, where information flows between smart home devices and users through remote devices. Each device acts as both an information sender and receiver, with data transmitted wirelessly to the cloud or interacting directly with other devices or users. This concept encompasses the design of how family members control smart home devices. Typically, the management of a smart home system is undertaken by the most technologically savvy member of the family, referred to as the primary user of smart home devices. This person is described as the "super user." Device collaborators in a smart home refer to family members who, due to physical constraints, assist the main controller in completing smart home tasks.

In Case 11, P14 offered suggestions regarding the oversight of collaborators in control systems, stating: "Why can't there be a simplified version of the app that allows me to quickly check who is at the door through the front door camera?" This shows that current smart home control systems focus mainly on the completeness and fluidity of the control system, yet this is predominantly centered around the main controller. The systems supporting collaborators are not fully developed, and research in this area remains relatively limited. Therefore, the participation of device collaborators should be emphasized in system design.

For instance, when establishing a smart pet care system, designers should not only refine the control system for the primary caregiver but also consider the collaboration system for other family members. After perfecting the detailed settings for the main controller, designers should provide a simplified status monitoring system for collaborators, making it easier to coordinate with the main controller of the smart pet care system and achieve the shared goal of caring for the pet.

5.2 Limitations and Future Research

This study is subject to several limitations. The first limitation lies in its focus on families with culturally specific characteristics, particularly those within Eastern context. We encourage future research to adopt a more diverse range of families from different cultural backgrounds, considering their varying cultural practices and usage patterns.

The second limitation is the lack of validation for the proposed design strategies. Given that this study is exploratory in nature, prioritizing an in-depth investigation into existing family interaction patterns and challenges, less attention was devoted to the validation phase. Future research could develop prototypes based on the proposed strategies and conduct systematic evaluations of their effectiveness.

Finally, future studies could incorporate quantitative methods to provide descriptive analyses of family collaboration in the use of smart home technologies. This would complement the qualitative data from this research, offering a more comprehensive interpretation of family interactions in smart homes.

A Appendices

A.1 Sampled Cases (see Table A1)

A.2 Demographics of the participants (see Table A2).

Table 1. Sampled Cases

	Event	Family members in event	Smart Home Devices
C1	Elderly family members accompany children to build Lego	An elderly, a child	Smart TV, Mobile phones
C2	Younger people remotely help older people with oven function settings	Two elderlies, a daughter	Smart Oven, Mobile Phone
C3	Remotely help the elderly who can't open the fingerprint door lock at home to open the door remotely	An elderly, a daughter	Smart Door Lock, Mobile Phone
C4	Using smart cameras to help inspect elderly falls	An elderly, a daughter, a son	Smart Camera, Mobile Phone
C5	Stay-at-home mum uses kettle to heat and keep warm remotely on a timer	Mother, father, elderly family members, one child	Smart Kettle, Mobile Phone
C6	Remote feeding devices necessitate family collaboration when members are on business trips	Mother, a son, a cat	Smart feeder, Smart Water feeder, Camera, Mobile Phone
C7	Elderly man, father learning smart audio to control smart devices at home	An elderly, father, mother, a child	Smart audio, Door locks, Smart lights, Smart curtains
C8	The morning light setup activates before the elderly typically wake up, ensuring their safety	An elderly, a mother, a child	Smart Lights, Mobile Phone
C9	Use a smart air conditioner's remote to adjust pet temperatures in extreme weather	Dogs, pet owners	Smart Air Conditioner, Mobile Phone, Camera
C10	Elderly people are using the sweeping robot in their homes in a collaborative scenario	An elderly, a daughter	Smart Sweeper, Mobile Phone
C11	Daughter ensures family safety by having them check the door camera via their phones	Father, mother, a daughter	Smart Camera, Mobile Phone

* C = Case

Table 2. Demographics of the participants

	Age	Gender	Composition of family members	Technology acceptance level	Living conditions	Complexity of smart home technology	The level of systematic integration of smart home technologies
P1	21	Female	Boy friend, mother	High	Long-term residence	High	Low
P2	22	Male	Mother, father	Low	Long-term residence	Low	Extremely low
P3	24	Male	Mother, a cat	Medium	Long-term residence	High	High
P4	30	Female	Mother, father Boy friend	High	Long-term residence	High	Medium
P5	20	Male	Mother, father Grandfather, Grandmother	Medium	Long-term residence	Low	Low
P6	45	Male	Wife, mother Father, one child	High	Long-term residence	Medium	Low
P7	47	Female	Husband, two cats	High	long-term travel	High	High
P8	35	Female	Husband, one child	High	Long-term residence	Medium	Medium
P9	32	Male	Wife, mother Father, one child	High	Long-term residence	High	High
P10	21	Female	Mother, father, Grandma, a dog	High	Long-term residence	High	Low
P11	21	Female	Mother, father, Grandma	Medium	long-term travel	Extremely High	Medium
P12	30	Female	Mother	Medium	long-term travel	High	Low
P13	17	Male	Mother, father Grandma, brother	Medium	Long-term residence	Medium	Low
P14	16	Female	Mother, father, aunt Niece, brother, sister	Medium	Long-term residence	High	Low
P15	20	Male	Mother, father Grandfather, grandmother	Medium	Long-term residence	Low	Low

(continued)

Table 2. (*continued*)

	Age	Gender	Composition of family members	Technology acceptance level	Living conditions	Complexity of smart home technology	The level of systematic integration of smart home technologies
P16	24	Female	Mother, father, Little brother, daughter,	High	Long-term residence	High	Medium
P17	22	Female	Niece, sister, brother	Medium	Short-term residence	Low	Low
P18	23	Female	Mother, father	High	Long-term residence	High	High
P19	22	Female	Mother, father, niece	High	Long-term residence	Medium	Medium
P20	24	Female	Aunt, uncle, niece	Medium	Long-term residence	Medium	Low

* P = Participant

References

1. Alam, m., Alan, A.T., Rogers, A., Ramchurn, S.D.: Poster abstract: towards a smart home framework
2. Allifah, N.M., Zualkernan, I.A.: Ranking security of IoT-based smart home consumer devices. IEEE Access **10**, 18352–18369 (2022). https://doi.org/10.1109/ACCESS.2022.3148140
3. Bal, M., Shen, W., Hao, Q., Xue, H.: Collaborative Smart Home technologies for senior independent living: a review. In: Proceedings of the 2011 15th International Conference on Computer Supported Cooperative Work in Design (CSCWD), pp. 481–488 (2011). https://doi.org/10.1109/CSCWD.2011.5960116
4. Blandford, A., Furniss, D.: DiCoT: a methodology for applying distributed cognition to the design of teamworking systems. In: Gilroy, S.W., Harrison, M.D. (eds.) Interactive Systems. Design, Specification, and Verification. DSV-IS 2005. LNCS, vol. 3941. Springer, Berlin, Heidelberg (2006). https://doi.org/10.1007/11752707_3
5. Braun, V., Clarke, V.: Using thematic analysis in psychology. Qual. Res. Psychol. **3**(2), 77–101 (2006). https://doi.org/10.1191/1478088706qp063oa
6. Cabitza, F., Fogli, D., Lanzilotti, R., Piccinno, A.: Rule-based tools for the configuration of ambient intelligence systems: a comparative user study. Multimedia Tools Appl. **76**(4), 5221–5241 (2017). https://doi.org/10.1007/s11042-016-3511-2
7. D'Angelo, G., Rampone, S.: Cognitive distributed application area networks. In: Security and Resilience in Intelligent Data-Centric Systems and Communication Networks, pp. 193–214. Elsevier (2018). https://doi.org/10.1016/B978-0-12-811373-8.00009-4
8. Demiris, G., et al.: Older adults' attitudes towards and perceptions of "smart home" technologies: a pilot study. Med. Inform. Internet Med. **29**(2), 87–94 (2004). https://doi.org/10.1080/14639230410001684387
9. Dingli, A., Seychell, D.: 2015. Smart homes. In: Dingli, A., Seychell, D. (eds.) The new digital natives: cutting the chord, pp. 85–101. Springer, Berlin, Heidelberg. https://doi.org/10.1007/978-3-662-46590-5_7

10. Edmondson, W.H., Beale, R.: Projected Cognition - extending Distributed Cognition for the study of human interaction with computers. Interact. Comput. **20**(1), 128–140 (2008). https://doi.org/10.1016/j.intcom.2007.10.005

11. Fu, J., Jiang, B., Yang, X.: Design and management methods of Smart Home human-computer relationship. In: 2016 2nd International Conference on Cloud Computing and Internet of Things (CCIOT), pp. 148–151 (2016). https://doi.org/10.1109/CCIOT.2016.7868322

12. Gupta, S., Bhambri, S., Dhingra, K., Buduru, A.B., Kumaraguru, P.: Multi-objective Reinforcement Learning based approach for User-Centric Power Optimization in Smart Home Environments (2020). https://doi.org/10.48550/arXiv.2009.13854

13. Hollan, J., Hutchins, E., Kirsh, D.: Distributed cognition: toward a new foundation for human-computer interaction research. ACM Trans. Comput.-Hum. Interact. **7**(2), 174–196 (2000). https://doi.org/10.1145/353485.353487

14. Hu, G., Wang, Y., Mao, M., Zhao, Y.: Remote care and collaboration for empty nest family: smart home, digital twin and mixed reality. In: 2022 8th International Conference on Virtual Reality (ICVR), pp. 126–134 (2022). https://doi.org/10.1109/ICVR55215.2022.9847779

15. Hu, S., Tang, C., Liu, F., Wang, X.: A distributed and efficient system architecture for smart home. Int. J. Sensor Networks (2016). Retrieved January 20, 2025 from https://www.inderscienceonline.com/doi/https://doi.org/10.1504/IJSNET.2016.074701

16. Edwin, H.: Cognition in the wild. The MIT Press (1995). https://doi.org/10.7551/mitpress/1881.001.0001

17. Jia, H., Kong, F., Zhao, F.: To optimize mobile HCI information from distributed cognition theory and context-awareness technology (2013). https://doi.org/10.1049/cp.2013.2425

18. Kilic, D., Crabtree, A., McGarry, G., Goulden, M.: The cardboard box study: understanding collaborative data management in the connected home. Pers. Ubiquit. Comput. **26**(1), 155–176 (2022). https://doi.org/10.1007/s00779-021-01655-9

19. Kirsh, D.: Distributed cognition: a methodological note. Pragmat. Cogn. **14**(2), 249–262 (2006). https://doi.org/10.1075/pc.14.2.06kir

20. Kolb, D.: Experiential learning: experience as the source of learning and development (1984)

21. Li, J., et al.: It's up to the consumer to be smart": understanding the security and privacy attitudes of smart home users on reddit. In: 2023 IEEE Symposium on Security and Privacy (SP), pp. 2850–2866 (2023). https://doi.org/10.1109/SP46215.2023.10179344

22. Lutolf, R.: Smart Home concept and the integration of energy meters into a home based system. In: Seventh International Conference on Metering Apparatus and Tariffs for Electricity Supply 1992, pp. 277–278 (1992). Retrieved January 20, 2025 https://ieeexplore.ieee.org/document/187310

23. Machorro-Cano, I., Alor-Hernández, G., Paredes-Valverde, M.A., Rodríguez-Mazahua, L., Sánchez-Cervantes, J.L., Olmedo-Aguirre, J.O.: HEMS-IoT: a big data and machine learning-based smart home system for energy saving. Energies **13**(5), 1097 (2020). https://doi.org/10.3390/en13051097

24. Magnus, P.D.: Distributed cognition and the task of science. Soc. Stud. Sci. **37**(2), 297–310 (2007). https://doi.org/10.1177/0306312706072177

25. Neßelrath, R., Lu, C., Schulz, C., Frey, J., Alexandersson, J.: A gesture based system for context-sensitive interaction with smart homes (2011). https://doi.org/10.1007/978-3-642-18167-2_15

26. Netinant, P., Utsanok, T., Rukhiran, M., Klongdee, S.: Development and assessment of internet of things-driven smart home security and automation with voice commands. IoT **5**(1), 79–99 (2024). https://doi.org/10.3390/iot5010005

27. Palanca, J., del Val, E., Garcia-Fornes, A., Billhardt, H., Corchado, J.M., Julián, V.: Designing a goal-oriented smart-home environment. Inf. Syst. Front. **20**(1), 125–142 (2018)

28. Palinkas, L.A., Horwitz, S.M., Green, C.A., Wisdom, J.P., Duan, N., Hoagwood, K.: Purposeful sampling for qualitative data collection and analysis in mixed method implementation research. Adm. Policy Ment. Health **42**(5), 533–544 (2015). https://doi.org/10.1007/s10488-013-0528-y

29. Rajkomar, A., Mayer, A., Blandford, A.: Understanding safety–critical interactions with a home medical device through Distributed Cognition. J. Biomed. Inform. **56**, 179–194 (2015). https://doi.org/10.1016/j.jbi.2015.06.002

30. Reinisch, C., Kofler, MarioJ., Iglesias, F., Kastner, W.: ThinkHome energy efficiency in future smart homes. EURASIP J. Embed. Syst. **2011**(1), 104617 (2011). https://doi.org/10.1155/2011/104617

31. Rocha, A.P., Ketsmur, M., Almeida, N., Teixeira, A.: An accessible smart home based on integrated multimodal interaction. Sensors **21**(16), 5464 (2021). https://doi.org/10.3390/s21165464

32. Satpathy, L.: Smart housing: technology to aid aging in place - new opportunities and challenges. theses and dissertations (2006). Retrieved from https://scholarsjunction.msstate.edu/td/3967

33. Schrire, S.: Interaction and cognition in asynchronous computer conferencing. Instr. Sci. **32**(6), 475–502 (2004). https://doi.org/10.1007/s11251-004-2518-7

34. Shuhaiber, A., Mashal, I.: Understanding users' acceptance of smart homes. Technol. Soc. **58**, 101110 (2019). https://doi.org/10.1016/j.techsoc.2019.01.003

35. Singh, D., Psychoula, I., Kropf, J., Hanke, S., Holzinger, A.: Users' perceptions and attitudes towards smart home technologies. In: Mokhtari, M., Abdulrazak, B., Aloulou, H. (eds.) Smart Homes and Health Telematics, Designing a Better Future: Urban Assisted Living. ICOST 2018. LNCS, vol 10898. Springer, Cham ((2018)). https://doi.org/10.1007/978-3-319-94523-1_18

36. Sotoudeh, S., Hashemi, S., Garakani, H.G.: Security framework of IoT-based smart home. In: 2020 10th International Symposium onTelecommunications (IST), pp. 251–256 (2020). https://doi.org/10.1109/IST50524.2020.9345886

37. Sun, K.: A Smart Home for 'Us': Understanding and designing a parent-child engagement mechanism for child access and participation in the smart home. In: Proceedings of the 22nd Annual ACM Interaction Design and Children Conference, pp. 773–776 (2023). https://doi.org/10.1145/3585088.3593927

38. Vega-Barbas, M., Pau, I., Martín-Ruiz, M.L., Seoane, F.: Adaptive software architecture based on confident HCI for the deployment of sensitive services in Smart Homes. Sensors (Basel, Switzerland) **15**(4), 7294–7322 (2015). https://doi.org/10.3390/s150407294

39. Verma, M., Bhambri, S., Gupta, S., Buduru, A.B.: Making smart homes smarter: optimizing energy consumption with human in the loop (2020). https://doi.org/10.48550/arXiv.1912.03298

40. Vogiatzidakis, P., Koutsabasis, P.: Frame-based elicitation of mid-air gestures for a smart home device ecosystem. Informatics **6**(2), 23 (2019). https://doi.org/10.3390/informatics6020023

41. Windl, M., Mayer, S.: The skewed privacy concerns of bystanders in smart environments. In: Proceedings of the ACM on Human-Computer Interaction 6, MHCI: pp. 1–21 (2022). https://doi.org/10.1145/3546719

42. Yin, R.K.: Case study research: design and methods. SAGE (2003)

43. Yu, Y.-C., You, S., Tsai, D.-R.: Smart door: a ubiquitous collaboration system for home activities in the smart home. J. Inf. Sci. Eng. **29**, 1227–1248 (2013)

44. Liu, Z., Nersessian, N., Stasko, J.: Distributed cognition as a theoretical framework for information visualization. IEEE Trans. Visual. Comput. Graph. **14**, 6, 1173–1180 (2008). https://doi.org/10.1109/TVCG.2008.121
45. Human-computer interaction and user experience in smart home research: a critical analysis. Issues In Information Systems (2016). https://doi.org/10.48009/3_iis_2016_11-19

Designing Metaverse Environments to Enhance Creativity in Discussion: The Impact of Avatar Gender Swapping on Male-Female Discussions

Atsushi Hiyama[1,5(✉)], Katsuomi Kobayashi[1], Yuki Abe[2], Yuta Yoshino[2], Feby Juana Candra[3], Haruki Kitagawa[3], Yingting Chen[3], Yohsuke Ohtsubo[4], and Taro Kanno[3]

[1] Research Center for Advanced Science and Technology, The University of Tokyo, 4-6-1, Komaba, Meguro-ku 153-8904, Tokyo, Japan
`hiyama@star.rcast.u-tokyo.ac.jp`
[2] Advanced Technology R&D Division, Ricoh Company, Ltd., 2-7-1, Izumi, Ebina-shi 243-0460, Kanagawa, Japan
[3] Graduate School of Engineering, The University of Tokyo, 7-3-1, Hongo, Bunkyo-ku 113-8656, Tokyo, Japan
[4] Graduate School of Humanities and Sociology, The University of Tokyo, 7-3-1, Hongo, Bunkyo-ku 113-0033, Tokyo, Japan
[5] Graduate School of Social Data Science, Hitotsubashi University, 2-1, Naka, Kunitachi 186-8601, Tokyo, Japan

Abstract. Advancements in virtual reality (VR) technology have enabled us to engage in embodied communication within metaverse environments as part of our daily interactions. This evolution has spurred research into the "Proteus Effect," a phenomenon where individuals' self-perception and perception of others are influenced by their avatars, leading to behavioral changes. In this study, we explored how metaverse platforms can facilitate creative communication in workplace settings by enabling diverse individuals to share opinions more openly. Focusing on gender bias, we examined the impact of using avatars of a different gender during male-female interactions on speech and receptivity. Our findings indicate that gender-swapped avatars can influence communication dynamics, potentially enhancing openness.

Keywords: Metaverse · Avatar · Proteus Effect

1 Introduction

Since COVID-19, online conferencing has become widely used in business settings as a means of everyday communication. However, videoconferencing is said to lack nonverbal communication information and is not well suited for creative discussions. VR technology is expected to compensate for the lack of non-verbal communication information in videoconferencing.

In recent years, inexpensive, high-quality Head Mounted Displays (HMD) have appeared on the market, and smartphones, which we use daily, can also be utilized as HMDs, with inexpensive lens attachments also available on the market. The emergence of 360-degree cameras has also made shooting VR videos more accessible to the public. In addition, social media now support 360-degree videos, and VR has become a part of our daily lives more than ever before.

Communication through avatars has the potential to exhibit creativity beyond face-to-face communication in the future by utilizing the psychological effect known as the Proteus effect [1]. In this study, we discuss the design of a metaverse space to induce highly creative discussions by utilizing a metaverse space with VR technology. Specifically, we categorize design elements into environmental elements and avatar elements as elements that can be extended and make it possible to freely set parameters according to the user and environment.

Regarding the environmental elements, it is possible to configure any space that is comfortable for users to show their creativity. The augmentable avatar elements can be divided into static appearance elements and dynamic interaction elements. The interaction element can be further extended with non-verbal body movement information and verbal voice information. The non-verbal body movement information can also be augmented with biofeedback as an internal element of the body.

Below are specifics for each of the avatar elements.

As elements related to static appearance, it is known that selecting height, age, gender, race, etc. like or different from that of the person operating the avatar has effects on the sense of body ownership over the avatar and in building relationships with others with whom one communicates. In addition, changing the avatar's appearance into an entity that is completely different from a human being may induce a physical sensation that cannot be obtained with a real human being, and may remove a barrier in communication with others.

The elements involved in dynamic body movements include nonverbal postures, movements, facial expressions, etc. It is also known that intervention in those variables within the metaverse space can act on the avatar operator's sense of one's own body and the flow in communication. Nodding, eye contact, interpersonal proximity, etc. are related to the characteristics of individual communication and may greatly influence the impression in communication. Intervention in tone and volume of voice as verbal information can also have an impact on the impression and presence that creates the flow of communication. In addition to pitch and formant as speech parameters, the development of AI-based voice transformation technology may expand the range of intervention in verbal information.

In addition, ethical considerations must also be discussed for the use of such systems that augment various elements in the metaverse space.

If we can correctly utilize the metaverse environment, we can wipe out various communication biases, including gender bias, which inhibit our daily communication, and facilitate creative discussions in which everyone can frankly and equally exchange opinions and share diverse viewpoints.

The basic system consists of the following equipment.

First, an HMD that presents visual information which immerses the user in the metaverse environment. A voice transformation module to convert the audio information of the participants engaged in the discussion in the metaverse environment. A PC to control the audiovisual information, and a network that synchronizes these basic systems in a remote space to establish real time online communication.

In this paper, we provide a literature review of research on VR technologies related to the above and discuss the design theory of platforms that enhance the creativity of discussions within the metaverse environment.

2 Static Avatar Element

There are number of studies that examine the Proteus effect using the static appearance of avatars as a parameter.

Regarding the modification of parameters related to body appearance, it has been reported that an avatar of higher height will offer conditions favorable to him in negotiations in dialogues in the metaverse space, while a shorter height will lead to acceptance of unfavorable conditions [1].

In a study using body weight as a parameter, a study conducted on females in a tennis game reported that when an obese avatar was manipulated, there was a decrease in physical activity compared to when a non-obese avatar was manipulated [2]. A similar trend was observed when the same experiment was conducted on males, but the trend was stronger for females [3]. It has been shown that when women use an avatar with a larger body shape, their dissatisfaction with body image increases, but when they use a relatively small avatar after using a thick avatar, their dissatisfaction with the body image is smaller than when they used the avatar before experiencing larger avatar [4].

A study using age as a parameter reported a decrease in implicit cognitive bias toward the elderly before and after the experience of performing the Tower of London test using an avatar of Einstein as the avatar of the elderly [5]. Another study reported that after an income allocation task using an avatar with one's own face versus an avatar with an aged face of one's own, the group using the avatar with the aged face was allocated more money to prepare for retirement [6]. Conversely, it has been studied that experience with a child's avatar has been found to exhibit a tendency to estimate the size of objects larger than the actual size when compared to experience with an adult avatar of the same scale, and changes in associating oneself with child-like attributes as a result of the IAT also have been found [7]. There is also technology that enables to experience the real world on as a child's scale with research and devices that present a child's point of view and a sensation of hand size in the world of augmented reality [8].

In a study for which gender was used as a parameter, the researchers evaluated the difference in performance of female participants in a test that measures working memory under conditions in which they use either a male or female avatar, with and without exposure to the stereotype that test results are known to be gender dependent. Results showed that under conditions of stereotype exposure, working memory was impaired when the female avatar was used, but that the working memory impairment was lifted when the avatar was changed to a male avatar. Conversely, in conditions of no exposure to stereotypes, the use of a male avatar worked in the direction of working memory impairment [9]. In an experiment in which male and female avatars were used to perform an arithmetic test task, both male and female participants who used a male avatar to compete against a female avatar reported the highest performance results [10]. In another study on math tests and gender stereotypes, a male avatar with an intimidating attitude toward women teaching math versus a male avatar who was not intimidating resulted in lower learning effects when either male or female avatars were used, and under these conditions, the Proteus effect was reported to be not significant [11]. In a study of working environments, a female avatar experiencing a negative scenario in a meeting simulation in a metaverse space, where her opinions were not listened to, she was not invited to other meetings, and her work was not valued or promoted, reported a significant reduction in implicit gender bias compared with the pre-experience condition [12]. A study that simulated a job interview in a metaverse environment explored the anonymizing effect of using an avatar that differed from the participant's actual gender, reducing anxiety during the interview [13].

Based on the above studies, it is possible that the Proteus effect can be achieved by using avatars that look different from their actual appearance. However, the effect is likely to be reduced if people are unable to recognize as themselves avatars that look different from their own appearance. To be able to recognize an avatar as oneself, one must consider using attributes that are similar to oneself. For example, when the avatar's ethnicity and gender were changed, matching ethnicity was shown to improve all Embodiment of appearance, response, and sense of body ownership, regardless of gender. In addition, gender matching has been reported to significantly increase body ownership [14]. In order to maximize the Proteus effect, it is important to prepare avatars with attributes as close as possible to those of the participants, except for the elements for which the intervention effect is expected, and to allow sufficient time for the participants to become used to the avatar manipulation.

3 Dynamic Avatar Element

Other than appearance, the intervention elements for avatars include voice, a verbal element closely related to communication, and non-verbal elements such as facial expressions, eye contact, gestures, and interpersonal distance. In addition, interaction scenarios experienced through avatars have been examined for their effectiveness in inducing behavioral change.

In a study that examined the effect of voice transformation on the verbal element, the speaker's voice was transformed into that of an older adult using real-time voice transformation technology and feedback was provided through bone- conducting headphones, and the implicit cognitive bias toward the older adult was reduced while the speaker's voice was being transformed into that of the older adult. On the one hand, this reduces the implicit cognitive bias toward the older adults while their own voice is being converted into the voice of the older adults. On the other hand, ownership of the voice is significantly reduced, but the transformed voice of the elderly person is significantly perceived as his or her own voice being transformed, as reported in [15].

As for the nonverbal element, when visual feedback is provided by adding prediction or delay to one's own motion captured avatar in real time, adding prediction within a certain time range makes the body feel lighter and in better condition, while adding delay within a certain time range makes the body feel heavier and more exhausted. It has also been reported that the sense of body ownership decreases when the range of predictions or delays exceeds a certain duration [16].

The effect of designing experience elements other than the avatar element in the metaverse space to transform people's mindset has also been studied: when participants were given the experience of flying around a VR urban space as either a helicopter or a superhero to rescue a child, the latter experience was reported to have significantly more likely to help the experimenter in picking up a pens after the experiment [17].

In a study that encourages paper recycling, it was also noted that the experience of cutting down trees in a VR environment had the effect of reducing the amount of paper napkins for 20% for cleanup when the experimenter spilled water after the experiment [18]. It has been reported that having the task of perspective-taking of a homeless person in a VR environment significantly increases the signing of petitions in support of the homeless, although empathy is still increased when the person is given a video or simply given the information [19]. Thus, it is expected that perspective-taking of others through VR experiences may increase empathy for different demographics with specific point of view.

4   Enhancing Creativity in Metaverse

As people develop empathy and an understanding of different viewpoints, they can consider various aspects of an issue. This leads to increased creativity. Group discussions that incorporate diverse perspectives and approaches are said to be key to improving overall creativity [20]. One study examined the impact of avatar appearance on discussion flow. Communication using avatars that aligned with sociodemographic attributes (age and gender) was compared to communication using avatars that did not align with these attributes. The removal of these attributes led to a significant increase in both objective and subjective communication balance [21].

Based on the above, we believe that creating a situation that facilitates the exchange of diverse opinions and promotes understanding of others' points of view in discussions will lay the groundwork for creativity. Generally, there is a gender stereotype that men are more active, and women are more passive [22]. In this study, we examined whether using gender-swapped avatars in one-on-one male-female dialogues in the metaverse would balance speech by making men more reserved and women more active, compared to using avatars of the same gender. Furthermore, we decided to verify whether this effect would persist when dialogue was conducted with avatars of the actual gender after the gender swap.

5   System Design

The basic system consists of the following equipment. First, an HMD to present visual information that immerses the participants in the metaverse environment; a module to transform the voice of a participant in a discussion in the metaverse environment; a PC to control the audiovisual information; and a network to synchronize the basic system in a separate room and to establish communication.

5.1 System Configuration

The Sword-16-HX-B14VFKG-5001JP (MSI) was used to generate the metaverse experience, and the PICO 4 Ultra (PICO) was used as the VR headset. A VT-4 Voice Transformer (Roland) was used to anonymize the voice. The ATH-GL3 (Audio-Technica) was used for audio. Two sets of these items were prepared for the experiment, which was designed for pairs of two participants. One Sword-16-HX-B14VFKG-5001JP (MSI) was used as the terminal to facilitate the metaverse environment. The overall system configuration is shown in the Fig. 1. Each terminal is connected via Wi-Fi, and the position and posture information of the controllers held in both hands and a headset are reflected in the avatar's body movements. These movements are shared in real time, together with the speech data. Speech utterances of the participants are recorded by an IC recorder.

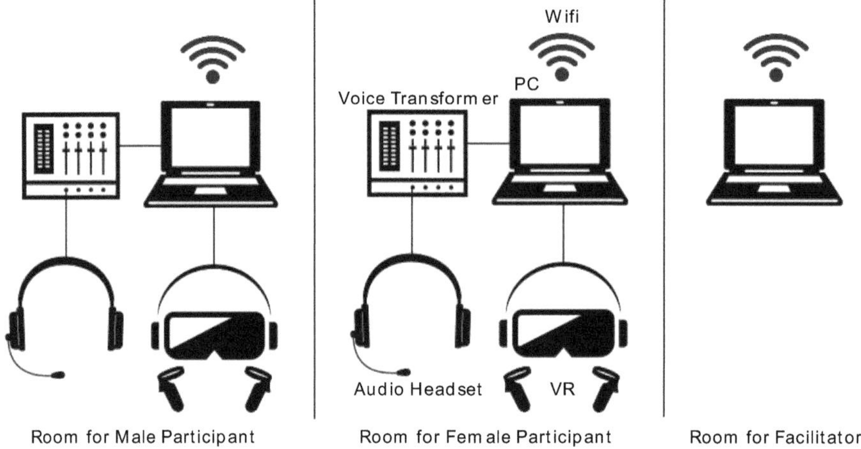

Fig. 1. System configuration.

5.2 Metaverse Environment

The metaverse environment is designed to resemble an office room constructed using Unity, with one wall featuring a life-sized mirror (see Fig. 2). By looking into this full-length mirror, participants can visually confirm that their avatars move in sync with their own physical movements. The mirror incorporates functionality akin to a smart mirror, displaying participants' spoken words as text notes (see Fig. 3). This setup is intended to simulate a scenario where individuals stand before a whiteboard in an office space to engage in discussions. By viewing the discussion notes, participants naturally see both their own and their partner's avatars reflected in the mirror, thereby enhancing the sense of embodiment within their avatars. A facilitator, located in a separate room, inputs the discussion notes as a scribe for each pair of participants. The facilitator's terminal provides an overhead view of the metaverse space, allowing them to participate solely through voice without possessing an avatar.

Fig. 2. Developed metaverse environment.

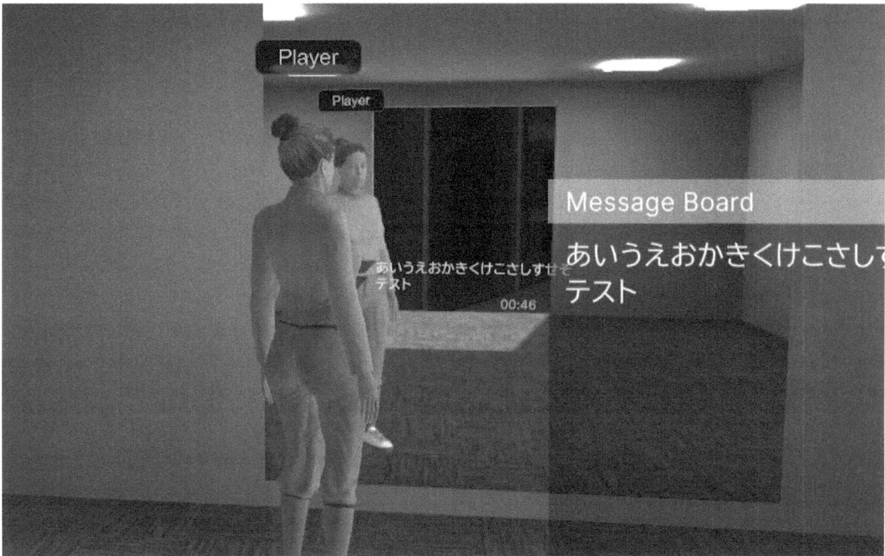

Fig. 3. Discussion memo displayed on the virtual smart mirror.

5.3 Avatars

Avatars representing both male and female participants across age groups from their 20 to 60 were prepared for the experiment (see Fig. 4). The avatars' head and arm movements are synchronized with the user's VR headset and controllers, and their mouths move in response to speech input. However, functionalities such as eye gaze, blinking, and facial expression recognition are not implemented.

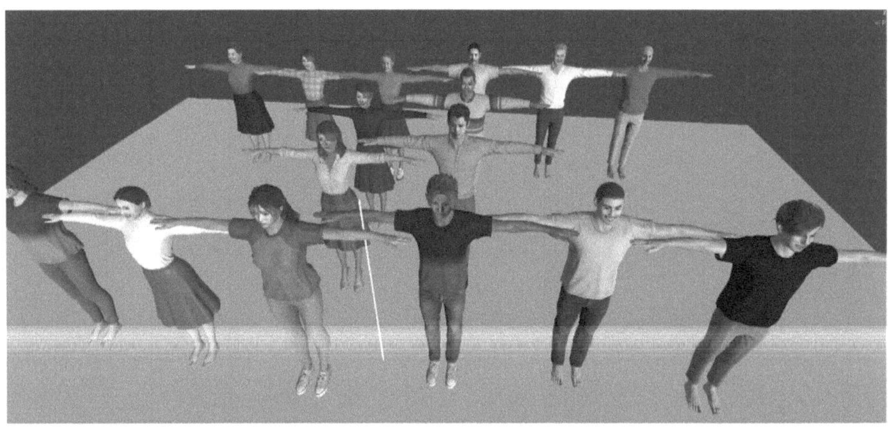

Fig. 4. Avatars used in the experiment.

6 Experimental Design

6.1 Participants

A total of 19 male-female pairs participated in the experiment, with participants recruited through a marketing company. Each participant received a compensation of 5,000 yen. To identify individuals with high levels of implicit gender bias, the marketing company surveyed a pool of 1,034 male and female subjects. Participants were asked to consent to the experiment and complete an Implicit Association Test (IAT) related to gender and occupation. Candidates who scored 0.65 or higher on the IAT—indicating a strong implicit bias—were selected for the study [23]. These candidates also answered 90 questions assessing their preferences across various fields, allowing researchers to identify topics on which they held strong opinions. A subset of these questions is presented in the following Table 1. Participant pairs were matched based on being in the same age group and holding opposing views on at least three of the assessed topics.

Table 1. A subset of the pre-survey question set to assess whether participants hold strong opinions. Participants are asked to choose either opinion A or B. Responses were recorded using a 5-point Likert scale (1: Strongly agree to A – 5: Strongly agree to B).

Opinion A	Opinion B
The Japanese content with the most international competitiveness is film.	The Japanese content with the most international competitiveness is music.
To deepen one's education, it is more effective to learn deeply about one country.	To deepen one's education, it is more effective to learn broadly about many countries.
In creative activities, group work is more suitable for producing good outcomes.	In creative activities, individual work is more suitable for producing good outcomes.
The beverage that contributes more to health is coffee.	The beverage that contributes more to health is tea.

(continued)

Table 1. (*continued*)

Opinion A	Opinion B
As a hobby, outdoor activities are more suitable for stress relief.	As a hobby, indoor activities are more suitable for stress relief.
For Japanese people to become global citizens, it is more important to study Japanese history.	For Japanese people to become global citizens, it is more important to study world history.
The more economical pet to own is a dog.	The more economical pet to own is a cat.
The type of movie that should be shown to children later is action movies.	The type of movie that should be shown to children later is romance movies.
If taxes are to be increased further, it should be on alcohol.	If taxes are to be increased further, it should be on tobacco.
As a future hobby, it is better to invest in collecting physical items.	As a future hobby, it is better to invest in experiential activities.

6.2 Experimental Procedure

The experiment proceeded as follows: Each male-female participant pair was scheduled to arrive at separate locations within the facility to ensure they did not meet prior to the experiment. Upon arrival, they were guided to individual experimental rooms where they donned VR equipment to participate. After confirming the functionality of their avatars, the experiment commenced.

A facilitator, located in a separate room, initiated the session with a verbal greeting and led a warm-up exercise to familiarize participants with avatar operations. Participants received verbal instructions to perform a series of avatar movements, including moving forward and backward, changing body orientation, and facing each other to simulate a handshake.

Subsequently, participants engaged in three five-minute debates on topics where their pre-survey responses indicated opposing viewpoints. After each debate, participants completed a questionnaire displayed within the metaverse environment using their controllers. The experiment was conducted with approval from the Ethics Committee of the University of Tokyo (approval number: 24–415).

Participants were divided into two groups: In one group, consisting of 10 pairs (female participants aged 39–61, average age 54.4; male participants aged 39–67, average age 54.3), avatars' genders were swapped in the second session. In the other group, comprising 9 pairs (female participants aged 32–68, average age 57.0; male participants aged 37–68, average age 57.3), participants consistently used avatars matching their actual gender.

To maintain anonymity and align voice characteristics with avatar gender, participants' voices were modified in pitch and formant during interactions, regardless of whether they used same-gender or opposite-gender avatars. After the experiment, participants were dismissed separately to prevent any face-to-face encounters. An experimental scene is shown in Fig. 5.

Fig. 5. An experimental scene.

6.3 Evaluation Through a Questionnaire

Participants' subjective experiences were evaluated after each debate session. To assess perceived psychological closeness toward their discussion partners, the Inclusion of Other in the Self (IOS) scale was employed [24]. This scale presents seven pairs of circles with varying degrees of overlap, representing the relationship between "self" and "other." Participants selected the pair that best described their perceived closeness to their discussion partner.

Additionally, participants responded to a series of statements regarding their impressions of their avatars and their discussion partners. Responses were recorded using a 5-point Likert scale (1: Strongly disagree – 5: Strongly agree). The statements were as follows:

1. I felt as if the avatar was myself.
2. I felt as if I were playing a different version of myself.
3. It was easy to express my own opinions.
4. I was able to understand the other person's opinions.
5. I incorporated the other person's opinions.
6. I felt that the other person was expressing their true feelings.
7. I was satisfied with the outcome of the discussion.

These measures aimed to capture participants' sense of embodiment within their avatars and the quality of their interpersonal interactions during the virtual reality sessions.

6.4 Evaluation Through Conversation Analysis

As an objective evaluation of the participants' performance, dialogue text analysis was conducted. Transcribed dialogues were processed using a large language model (LLM) to label each utterance, thereby classifying and evaluating the speech categories [25].

7 Results

As a result of the experiment, analysis was conducted on 17 pairs of participants—excluding 2 pairs where dialogue did not occur—comprising 9 pairs in the gender-swapped group and 8 pairs in the non-swapped group.

The analysis of subjective evaluations focused on assessing the impact of the second discussion session. This was achieved by comparing the differences between the first and third sessions—both conducted with avatars matching the participants' actual gender—using paired t-tests. Regarding the Inclusion of Other in the Self (IOS) scale, no significant effects were observed in either the gender-swapped or non-swapped groups when comparing the first and third sessions. For the seven questionnaire items, significant differences between the first and third sessions were identified as follows:

Female Participants:

- Gender-Swapped Group: Participants reported finding it easier to express their own opinions ($p = 0.03$).
- Non-Swapped Group: Participants felt a stronger sense of identification with their avatars ($p = 0.01$).

Male Participants:

- Gender-Swapped Group: Participants experienced an increased sense of identification with their avatars ($p = 0.01$) and perceived their partners as expressing genuine thoughts ($p = 0.03$).

Additionally, items showing a trend toward significance included:
Female Participants:

- Gender-Swapped Group: Participants felt a greater understanding of their partner's opinions ($p = 0.07$).

Male Participants:

- Both Groups: Participants found it easier to express their own opinions (Gender-Swapped Group: $p = 0.08$, Non-Swapped Group: $p = 0.07$).

These findings suggest that experiencing discussions through gender-swapped avatars can influence participants' perceptions of self-expression and understanding in metaverse.

The analysis of transcribed dialogues involved comparing differences between the first and third sessions to evaluate the impact of gender swapping in the second session. This evaluation was conducted using Welch's t-test, which does not assume equal variances between samples. Findings are as follows.
Male Participants:

- In the group without gender swapping, there was a significant increase in negative expressions (excluding nouns) compared to the group with gender swapping ($p = 0.04$).
- There was also a trend toward a significant increase in the number of utterances in the non-swapped group ($p = 0.08$).

Female Participants:

- No significant changes were observed.

In the second session, analysis of gender ratios within each group revealed:

- In the gender-swapped group, female participants produced more characters in their utterances (p = 0.09).
- The gender-swapped group had a near-equal male-to-female speaking time ratio of 1.01, whereas the non-swapped group exhibited a male-dominant ratio of 1.70 (p = 0.07).

Further analysis for female participants, considering prior research indicating that female participants are more susceptible to the influence of avatar appearance, additional analyses were conducted using paired t-tests:

Between Sessions 1 and 2:

- Operating male avatars led to a significant decrease in the number of speaking turns (p = 0.04).
- There was a trend toward decreased number of utterances and total characters spoken (p = 0.05).

Between Sessions 2 and 3:

- Returning to female avatars resulted in significant increases in the number of utterances (p = 0.01), total characters spoken (p = 0.01), and responses to partner opinions (p = 0.03). There was also a trend toward increased speaking time (p = 0.06).

Experiencing discussions through gender-swapped avatars can influence communication behaviors, particularly among female participants, highlighting the importance of avatar embodiment.

8 Conclusion and Future Work

As a benefits of avatar gender swapping, the experiment confirmed that avatar gender swapping made it easier for female participants to express their opinions. Additionally, male participants began to perceive that women were speaking more candidly. This suggests that women may become more proactive during gender-swapped interactions.

As a drawbacks of avatar gender swapping, it was observed that female participants experienced a strong sense of discomfort when embodying male avatars. This indicates the need to consider women's sensitivity to avatar gender when determining how to implement such practices.

For the future study, it will be important to examine whether avatar gender swapping for women enhances assertiveness, receptivity, and a sense of agreement. Based on the findings of this experiment, it is necessary to allocate sufficient time for participants to become accustomed to male avatars before conducting debates, in order to enhance embodiment for women using male avatars.

Acknowledgments. This study was funded by a Social Cooperation Program, Ricoh Company, Ltd.

References

1. Yee, N., Bailenson, J.: The proteus effect: the effect of transformed self-representation on behavior. Hum. Commun. Res. **33**, 271–290 (2007). https://doi.org/10.1111/j.1468-2958.2007.00299.x
2. Pe√/±a, J., Kim, E.: Increasing exergame physical activity through self and opponent avatar appearance. Comput. Hum. Behav. **41**, 262–267, ISSN 0747-5632 (2014). https://doi.org/10.1016/j.chb.2014.09.038
3. Pe√/±a, J., Khan, S., Alexopoulos, C.: I am what i see: how avatar and opponent agent body size affects physical activity among men playing exergames. J. Comput.-Mediat. Commun. **21**(3), 195–209 (2016). https://doi.org/10.1111/jcc4.12151
4. Ferrer-Garc√/≠a, M., Porras Garcia, B., Moreno, M., Bertomeu, P., Gutirrez-Maldonado, J.: Embodiment in different size virtual bodies produces changes in women's body image distortion and dissatisfaction. In: Annual Review of CyberTherapy and Telemedicine, pp. 111–117(2018)
5. Banakou, D., Kishore, S., Slater, M.: Virtually being einstein results in an improvement in cognitive task performance and a decrease in age bias. Front. Psychol. **9**, 917 (2018). https://doi.org/10.3389/fpsyg.2018.00917
6. Hershfield, H.E., et al.: Increasing saving behavior through age-progressed renderings of the future Self JMR. J. Market. Res. **48**, S23–S37 (2011). https://doi.org/10.1509/jmkr.48.SPL.S23
7. Banakou, D., Groten, R., Slater, M.: Illusory ownership of a virtual child body causes overestimation of object sizes and implicit attitude changes. Proc. Natl. Acad. Sci. USA **110**(31), 12846–12851 (2013). https://doi.org/10.1073/pnas.1306779110
8. Nishida, J., Takatori, H., Sato, K., Suzuki, K.: CHILDHOOD: wearable suit for augmented child experience. In: Proceedings of the 2015 Virtual Reality International Conference (VRIC 2015). Association for Computing Machinery, New York, NY, USA, Article 22, 1–4 (2015). https://doi.org/10.1145/2806173.2806190
9. Peck, T.C., Doan, M., Bourne, K.A., Good, J.J.: The effect of gender body-swap illusions on working memory and stereotype threat. IEEE Trans. Visual Comput. Graph. **24**(4), 1604–1612 (2018). https://doi.org/10.1109/TVCG.2018.2793598
10. Lee, J.E., Nass, C.I., Bailenson, J.N.: Does the mask govern the mind?: effects of arbitrary gender representation on quantitative task performance in avatar-represented virtual groups. Cyberpsychol. Behav. Soc. Netw. **17**(4), 248–254 (2014). https://doi.org/10.1089/cyber.2013.0358
11. Chang, F., Luo, M., Walton, G., Aguilar, L., Bailenson, J.: Stereotype threat in virtual learning environments: effects of avatar gender and sexist behavior on women's math learning outcomes. Cyberpsychol. Behav. Soc. Netw. **22**(10), 634–640 (2019). https://doi.org/10.1089/cyber.2019.0106
12. Beltran, K., et al.: Reducing implicit gender bias using a virtual workplace environment. In: Extended Abstracts of the 2021 CHI Conference on Human Factors in Computing Systems (CHI EA '21). Association for Computing Machinery, New York, NY, USA, Article 277, 1–7 (2021). https://doi.org/10.1145/3411763.3451739
13. Kim, J., Sandhaus, H., Fussell, S.R.: VR Job Interview Using a Gender-Swapped Avatar. In Companion Publication of the 2023 Conference on Computer Supported Cooperative Work and Social Computing (CSCW '23 Companion), pp. 154–159. Association for Computing Machinery, New York, NY, USA (2023). https://doi.org/10.1145/3584931.3606976
14. Do, T.D., Protko, C.I., McMahan, R.P.: Stepping into the right shoes: the effects of user-matched avatar ethnicity and gender on sense of embodiment in virtual reality. IEEE Trans. Visual Comput. Graphics **30**(05), 2434–2443 (2024). https://doi.org/10.1109/TVCG.2024.3372067

15. Arakawa, R., Kashino, Z., Takamichi, S., Verhulst, A., Inami, M.: Digital speech makeup: voice conversion based altered auditory feedback for transforming self-representation. In: Proceedings of the 2021 International Conference on Multimodal Interaction (ICMI '21), pp. 159–167. Association for Computing Machinery, New York, NY, USA (2021). https://doi.org/10.1145/3462244.3479934

16. Kasahara, S., et al.: Malleable embodiment: changing sense of embodiment by spatial-temporal deformation of virtual human body. In Proceedings of the 2017 CHI Conference on Human Factors in Computing Systems (CHI '17), pp. 6438–6448. Association for Computing Machinery, New York, NY, USA. https://doi.org/10.1145/3025453.3025962

17. Rosenberg, R.S., Baughman, S.L., Bailenson, J.N.: Virtual superheroes: using superpowers in virtual reality to encourage prosocial behavior. PLoS ONE 8(1), e55003 (2013). https://doi.org/10.1371/journal.pone.0055003

18. Ahn, S.J., Bailenson, J.N., Park, D.: Short- and long-term effects of embodied experiences in immersive virtual environments on environmental locus of control and behavior. Comput. Hum. Behav. 39, 235–245 (2014), ISSN 0747–5632, https://doi.org/10.1016/j.chb.2014.07.025

19. Herrera, F., Bailenson, J., Weisz, E., Ogle, E., Zaki, J.: Building long-term empathy: a large-scale comparison of traditional and virtual reality perspective-taking. PLoS ONE 13(10), e0204494 (2018). https://doi.org/10.1371/journal.pone.0204494

20. Hoever, I.J., van Knippenberg, D., van Ginkel, W.P., Barkema, H.G.: Fostering team creativity: Perspective taking as key to unlocking diversity's potential. J. Appl. Psychol. 97(5), 982–996 (2012). https://doi.org/10.1037/a0029159

21. Ide, M., Ichino, J., Yokoyama, H., Asano, H., Miyachi, H., Okabe, D.: Mitigating impacts of appearance-based social cues to facilitate balanced participation in virtual environments across age and gender. In: 2023 IEEE International Symposium on Mixed and Augmented Reality Adjunct (ISMAR-Adjunct), pp. 364–368. Sydney, Australia (2023). https://doi.org/10.1109/ISMAR-Adjunct60411.2023.00078

22. Broverman, I.K., Vogel, S.R., Broverman, D.M., Clarkson, F.E., Rosenkrantz, P.S.: Sex-role stereotypes: a current appraisal. J. Soc. Issues 28(2), 59–78 (1972). https://doi.org/10.1111/j.1540-4560.1972.tb00018.x

23. https://angle.changewave.co.jp/article/anglereport202208

24. Aron, A., Aron, E.N., Smollan, D.: Inclusion of Other in the Self Scale and the structure of interpersonal closeness. J. Pers. Soc. Psychol. 63(4), 596–612 (1992). https://doi.org/10.1037/0022-3514.63.4.596

25. Kitagawa, H., Kanno, T., Chen, Y., Yoshino, Y., Watanabe, S.: Utilizing Large Language Models (LLM) for the analysis of meeting utterance data. In: The 39th Annual Conference of the Japanese Society for Artificial Intelligence (2025). (In Japanese)

CalmaStep: Designing Playful Interaction for Managing Collective Stress

Yunyin Lou$^{(\boxtimes)}$ and Jun Hu

Eindhoven University of Technology, Eindhoven, Netherlands
`y.lou@student.tue.nl` , `j.hu@tue.nl`

Abstract. This study introduces CalmaStep, a system designed to physicalize collective stress with an integrated notification feature. The prototype anonymously displays individual stress levels in a modular format, encouraging playful interactions and the exchange of subtle messages within an office setting while accommodating preferences for emotional privacy. Quantitative methods have been used to measure changes of stress levels following notifications, while qualitative methods have been used to investigate participants' interpretations of the notifications and the resulting social dynamics. The quantitative analysis did not show a significant reduction in stress levels, while qualitative findings demonstrated CalmaStep's potential to promote discussions on common topics and enhance social dynamics.

Keywords: Collective stress · Stress physicalization · Social dynamics office environment · Employee wellness · Industrial design · Flexible interactive interface

1   Introduction

In the context of social activities, stress is a prevalent phenomenon. It originates from the mismatch between resources and needs [24] and can manifest itself in physical and psychological ways [14]. People under stress can have an increase in heart rate and blood pressure, and can be perceived with changes in heart rate variability(HRV), which is the most commonly used parameter to identify stress states [8].

When considering specifically the office environment, the term "collective stress" refers to collective coping responses to stressors [11]. Different from the stress mentioned in daily life, collective stress focuses more on the level of the working group and is also analyzed from a collective perspective. The stressors in this context can be competition among colleagues, impending work deadlines, etc. These will lead to the emergence of collective stress and have an impact on collective work efficiency, team atmosphere, and interpersonal communication [6]. A significant proportion of related research currently focuses on the visualization of collective stress data and the subsequent feedback from the

D. Harris et al. (Eds.): HCII 2025, LNCS 16334, pp. 397–412, 2026.
https://doi.org/10.1007/978-3-032-12392-3_26

tested groups, to study the impact of a more comprehensive understanding of collective stress. One innovative approach to addressing collective stress is through physicalization, which involves creating tangible representations of data to facilitate understanding and interaction. Physicalization offers unique opportunities to apply traditional individual stress relief techniques at the group level. For example, Ren et al. [20] developed a physical artifact that visualizes collective stress through changing light patterns, which encourages fitness and relaxation exercises. The rationale for choosing physicalization lies in its ability to make abstract feelings more concrete and tangible, thereby fostering collective engagement and reflection. Research has shown that tangibility helps problem solvers perform better, achieve higher learning gains, collaborate better, explore more alternative designs, and perceive problem solving as more playful [23].

This research aims to explore how a collective stress physicalization that invites people to interact impacts on stress feelings and social dynamics in the office environment. By physicalizing people's stress levels anonymously in a modular way, the installation designed in this study, called CalmaStep, ideally can be embedded in the ground near the entrance of the office. When people step on its flexible surface to relieve stress, a notification will be sent to the person associated with the bubble. This builds a stress-relieving connection among people working in or visiting this office and tries to make the message flow between communities in a relatively safe and interesting way. A total of 24 participants were recruited into the experiment to complete two separate studies. The results of the research indicated that the effect of the system on stress was not statistically significant. On the other hand, the system had a positive effect on increasing participants' social interest, drawing attention to collective stress, and helping to inspire discussions around common topics.

2   Related Work

2.1   Interventions for Collective Stress in Work Environments

Workplace stress is an important issue that needs to be addressed to improve the mental health and overall well-being of employees across various industries and countries [13]. An effective strategy to reduce workplace stress involves using relaxation rooms equipped with auditory and visual stimuli, which have been shown to promote recovery after acute stress [4].

In recent years, there has been a growing interest in visualizing collective stress and studying its meaning and impact on the community. Many studies primarily focus on how to present and feed data back into the work environment, enabling employees to recognize and manage their stress levels more effectively. For instance, a shared display of individual stress-related physiological data, such as heart-rate variability, through collective visualization significantly increases awareness and understanding of both personal and organizational stress [28]. Another practical application of visualization is the BallBounce system, a workplace biofeedback tool that anonymously visualizes collective stress data from office workers. This system aims to decrease physiological stress and inspire ideas for stress-relieving measures [16]. Studies also show that engaging office workers in co-constructing stories around their stress experiences has revealed six clusters of benefits for collective stress visualization, enhancing well-being and productivity in their daily routines [26].

In the design of interventions related to physical interaction, PopStress effectively reduces collective office stress by turning it into energy for a popcorn machine, encouraging natural and entertaining social stress-relieving behaviors among office workers [1]. Another design named LightSit comprises a sensor mat that can be embedded in an office chair to measure the posture of the user sitting and the variability of the heart rate and a lighting display that is integrated into a monitor stand to present information unobtrusively, facilitating fitness and relaxation exercises during micro-breaks [20].

Other emerging directions in workplace stress management include the use of virtual reality (VR) interventions. A scoping review of the available evidence has shown that VR might reduce workplace stress levels, although more quality research is needed to fully understand its unique contributions to stress management [15]. An example of such an intervention is Stressjam, a VR game using biofeedback, which shows potential in improving people's stress mindset [12].

2.2   Designs for Relieving Stress

Designs for relieving stress encompass a wide range of approaches, emphasizing the importance of both emotional expression and physical activities. Simply expressing emotions and receiving empathy can provide comfort, which is a key factor in stress reduction [17].

Physical activities such as yoga and meditation are well-documented stress relievers. Yoga reduces stress through positive affect, self-compassion, inhibition of the posterior hypothalamus, and salivary cortisol [21]. Similarly, meditation practices lead to decreased physiological stress markers across diverse populations [18]. Mindfulness meditation apps such as Calm have been shown to effectively reduce stress and improve mindfulness and self-compassion in stressed individuals [9].

One of the areas of interest in the field of physical intervention is the act of squeezing objects. This action helps individuals feel less stressed by reducing the perceived loss of control over their environment [19]. It can also activate the stress response system, involving neurochemical mediators like monoamines and cytokines, and engaging regions of the brain associated with emotion regulation [7]. Interactive prototypes such as Squeeze-it, Marmoro, and Wigo provide tactile feedback to support stress reduction. These devices recognize stress-related behaviors and offer relaxation feedback, demonstrating the potential of tactile interaction in stress management [3].

2.3   Opportunities

To sum up, current research on collective stress focuses on using visual methods to present data to arouse people's reflection. Intervention methods for collective stress, therefore, also rely more on the formation of reflection than on the design of a more physical interactive experience, which is often the case when intervening on individual stress. In addition, current intervention methods for stress tend to be narrowly focused on regulating individual physiological states. However, it is rarely considered from the perspective of inducing social interaction, which is an important factor in understanding the causes and effects of stress.

The exploration of the potential benefits of physical interaction in alleviating collective stress raises questions about its impact on emotional responses and social dynamics of the office environment, taking into account factors including reflection on collective stress, social dynamics, and the diverse office environment. This design research thus aims to propose a system based on the physicalization of collective stress to establish a bridge for information transmission in the office environment. This exploration seeks to provide guidance and reference for subsequent design interventions that address collective stress.

3   Design and Implementation

3.1   The Ethical Concerns About Intervention for Collective Stress

Expressing emotions and receiving empathy reduce stress, but the comfort of having shared a message is a key factor in reducing stress [17]. When exploring potential interventions, it is crucial to ensure the privacy of emotional information. This implies allowing individuals to self-identity disclosure in a subgroup because people have different preferences for sharing their stress [27]. This is particularly important given that dealing with collective stress inevitably involves social relationships.

3.2   The Way to Physicalize and Assess the Collective Stress

The primary method of analyzing collective stress is to collate individual stress data. Existing research on the assessment of collective stress is relatively limited in scope. There is a method proposed for frequently measuring group stress levels by generating estimation models based on body motion data [25], of which the effectiveness remains to be verified. Consequently, the present study employs a physicalization approach, in which the emotions of each individual are anonymously physicalized and collectively displayed. In subsequent experimental evaluations, attention is paid to changes in individual stress.

3.3   Physicalization and System Design

The prototype developed for this research is named CalmaStep. It anonymously physicalizes people's stress levels in a modular format (see Fig. 2), with each module corresponding to an individual in the office without revealing their identity. When people feel stressed, the flexible interfaces on these modules inflate like bubbles. This process can be achieved by the PPG sensor detecting HRV and sending a signal. This design ensures the privacy of employees' emotional states. The prototype is designed to be embedded in the ground near the office entrance, with the number of modules matching the number of people working in the office. When entering or exiting the office, individuals can step on stress bubbles to relieve stress, equivalent to the act of squeezing plastic bubble wrap. Upon interaction, a notification is sent to the person associated with the bubble and is displayed on the computer (see Fig. 1). This notification consists of two parts: visually, the computer screen of the associated person will display a popping bubble effect, and aurally, individuals will hear a popping sound through their earphones. In the current prototype stage, flexible interfaces are made using balloons and air pumps. For future iterations, the design could be improved by using silicone molds to create more durable and aesthetically pleasing modules.

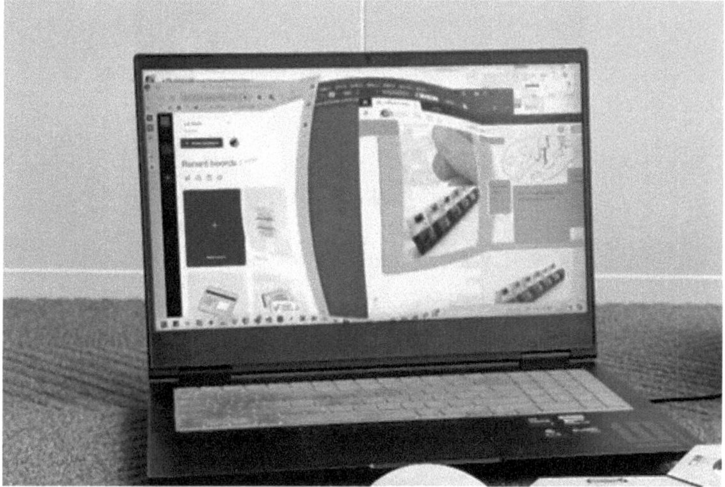

Fig. 1. The notification will temporarily affect the working interface.

4   Experiments

The entire research consists of two experiments. The objective of Study 1 is to examine the influence of the designed system on the social patterns among those at work and their interpretation of the messages they receive, and the social decisions they may make. Study 2 will examine how individuals who interact with the prototype interpret the notifications being conveyed to those who are working, and their expectations of the response from the working groups.

Although divided into two studies and conducted separately in time, Study 1 and Study 2 can be considered as events that occur concurrently within the same scenario. Participants, in this scenario, respectively assume the roles of individuals engaged in workplace tasks in Study 1 and those interacting with devices in Study 2.

Fig. 2. The functioning prototype in context.

4.1 Participants

A total of 24 participants were recruited for the experiment, all of whom are from
Eindhoven University and between the ages of 20 and 30, including 9 males and
15 females.

In Study 1, 20 participants were recruited. In Study 2, 6 participants were
included, of whom two had previously participated in Study 1, while the remaining four had not. All participants have experience of working in an open space
environment, with no heart or psychological diseases. Before the study, a consent
form was provided to them.

4.2 Apparatus

To investigate the effects on two distinct groups of individuals âĂŞ those experiencing stress in the workplace and those engaging in device interaction âĂŞ
within the same context, the environmental setups for Study 1 and Study 2 were
designed to be similar.

For this study a meeting room with a capacity of 4 persons was arranged (see
Fig. 4 and Fig. 5). Outside of the meeting rooms, the prototype would be placed
on the ground, adjacent to the room with a power connection. The prototype in
the experiment consists of 4 modules, corresponding to the number of people in
the meeting room. The flexible interfaces of the two modules will be intermit-
tently inflated during specific study phases (see Fig. 3), aligning with assumed

Fig. 3. The prototype at work in the experiment

increases in stress rather than real-time physical data collection. The transparent glass walls of the meeting room allow participants to see the prototype, while those outside can also observe the activities inside.

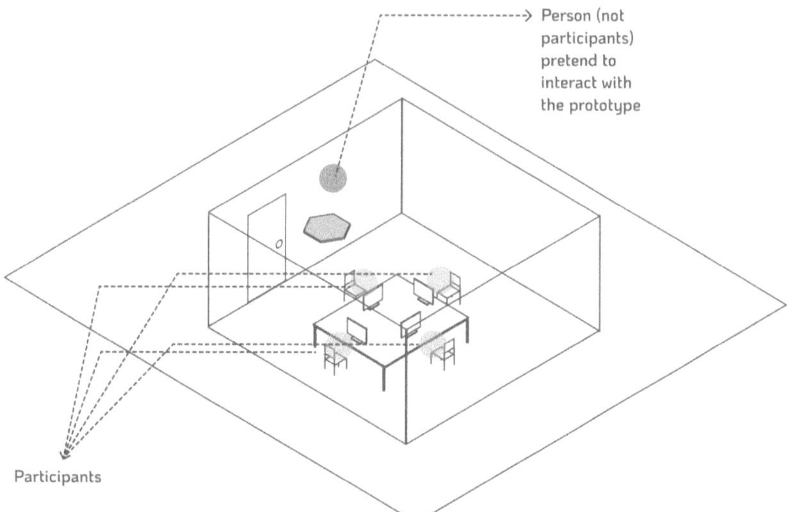

Fig. 4. Settings graph for Study 1.

4.3   Study 1 Procedure

In Study 1, 4 participants who were acquainted with each other were assembled in a group setting to simulate the dynamics of an office environment. Upon the presentation of scenario information to participants, it was made clear to them

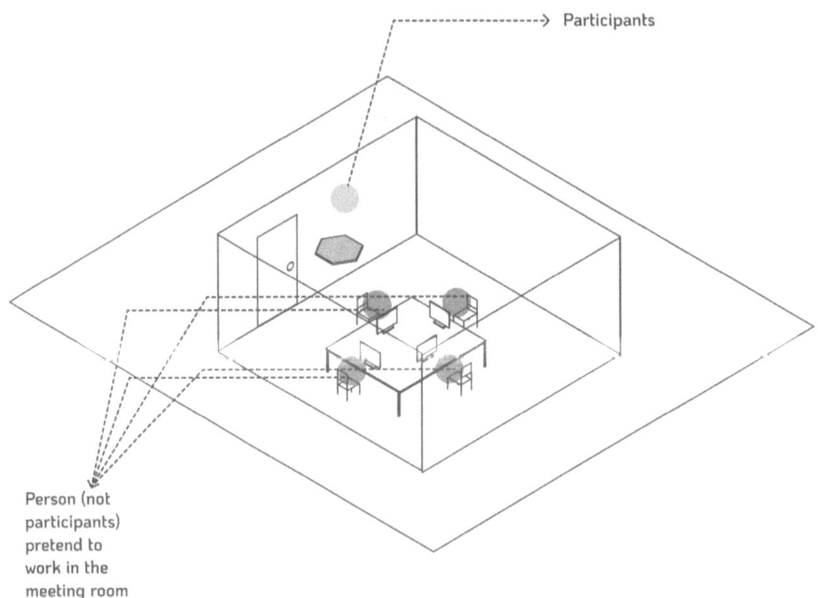

Fig. 5. Settings graph for Study 2.

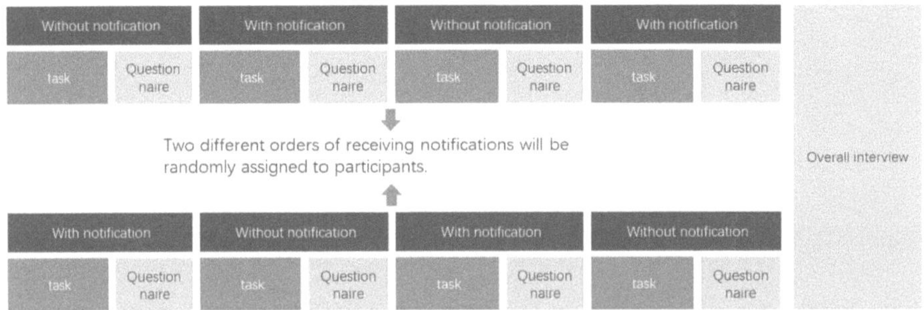

Fig. 6. Procedures for Study 1.

that the prototype situated outside the room was linked to them. Participants were informed that they could discuss or exchange information throughout the entire process. Each participant is required to bring their computer, mouse and headphones.

In the experiment, participants will be randomly assigned two different PowerPoint documents. The number of participants assigned to each file is equivalent. Each document contains two math question videos with notification effects and two static math question pages without notification effects. The difference between the two documents lies in the order of the videos with notification effects (see Fig. 6). The static pages and videos present the same sixty math problems, involving single digit addition, subtraction, multiplication, and division, designed to induce a certain level of stress [5]. The participants used the pen tool within the PowerPoint document to write their answers on a full-screen canvas. This setup ensured that the notification effects were displayed without interruption during the test while preventing the video playback bar from appearing. This is designed to prevent direct control over participants' computers while ensuring that visual and sound effects of notifications can still be achieved on their computers, also enhancing participants' immersion in the experimental scenario.

Corresponding to the design of the document, participants were required to complete four rounds of testing. The main purpose of conducting four rounds of tests is to reduce participants' expectations and predictions about whether they will receive notifications in the subsequent round. In each round of the tests, participants will have 3 min to complete the 60 math equations.

Following each round of tests, participants will be required to fill in the stress self-report form. The participants are able to take a break while filling in the forms and to refresh themselves for the next test. After completing the four rounds of tests, participants will have an overall interview.

Study 1 lasts about one hour (Fig. 7).

Fig. 7. In Study 1, the task is being completed by the participants, who are working on their own computers.

4.4   Study 2 Procedure

In Study 2, four individuals were situated in the meeting room, simulating the working scenario for the participants (see Fig. 5), who were instructed to act as though they were engaged in personal work.

The participants were presented with a scenario introduction, which provided a brief overview of the research and explained how the prototype functions. Following this, the participants chose whether to interact with the prototype.

After the interaction was finished, they were interviewed. Each participant was tested individually in this study, which lasted approximately 20 min.

4.5   Data Collection Methods

Stress Self-report. State-Trait Anxiety Inventory (STAI) [2] is used in Study 1 for participants to fill in after each round of tests.

Observation. In Study 1, observations focused on how many bubbles participants interacted with, as well as any other notable reactions. In Study 2, the observations included whether participants looked outside the meeting room after receiving the notification, talked with each other, made eye contact, or showed other notable reactions.

Interview. The interview for Study 1 aimed to understand participants' interpretations of the notification, their perception of individual and collective stress, and the social dynamics triggered by the intervention. Questions also explored factors influencing social interest during the session, perceived differences compared to non-notification scenarios, and participants' general coping strategies for collective stress in office environments. For Study 2, interview questions explored the factors that inspire social interests, participants' interpretation of the notification, and their perception of collective stress, as well as the social dynamics that would arise in this context.

5   Results

5.1   Quantitative Analysis

In Study 1, 40 sets of data were obtained from 20 participants. It was assumed that the data were independent of each other. In order to ensure the reliability of the quantitative results, the analysis was performed on the original data (Notif, NoNotif) and on the data averaged from the same participants under the same experimental conditions (Notif-Avg, NoNotif-Avg).

To facilitate the subsequent analysis and discussions, the following abbreviations will be used.

Notif: Original data of experimental group with notifications.

NoNotif: Original data of control group without notifications.

NoNotif-Avg: Average of the data from the control group without notifications.

Notif-Avg: Average of the data from the experimental group with notifications.

Before conducting the comparative analysis, the normality of the data contributions for both conditions (original data and averaged data) was assessed using the Shapiro-Wilk test since the sample size of the research data is less than

50 [10]. The NoNotif and NoNotif-Avg groups do not exhibit normality characteristics, while the Notif and Notif-Avg groups demonstrate normal distribution
properties. Given the non-normal distribution of at least one of the groups, it
was deemed appropriate to employ a non-parametric test to facilitate a comparison between the Notifi(-Avg) group and NoNotif(-Avg) group. The Wilcoxon
signed-rank test was chosen as it does not require the assumption of normality
and is suitable for within-subject study designs [22].

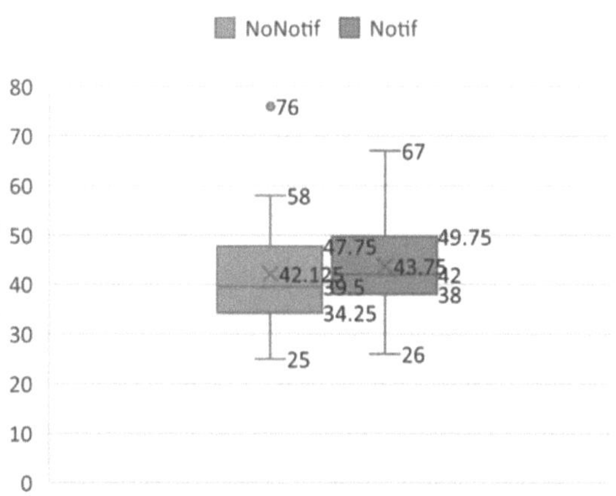

Fig. 8. STAI results for original data.

The data presented in the box plots (see Fig. 8 and Fig. 9) illustrates a slight
increase in median and average values for the Notifi(-Avg) group compared with
NoNotifi(-Avg) group, suggesting that the notification received during the experiment tends to increase the stress levels of participants.

However, the results of the Wilcoxon signed rank test do not indicate statistically significant differences between the two paired data sets (p>0.05).

5.2   Qualitative Analysis

The Interpretation of the Notification. In Study 1, the participants at
work provided a notable divergence in their interpretation of the underlying
meaning conveyed by the notifications they received. Eleven participants stated
that they perceived the notification as a positive message that prompt them to
pay attention to their stress and seek solutions. With the anonymity of the link
between individuals and designed modules had been introduced, P7 remarked,
"My first reaction was that this was someone I knew interacting with the device,
trying to help me stop being anxious and go out for a walk and chat." P9
commented, "I think It's like someone is joking with us." P20 noted, "The person
interacting with the prototype may want to help us relieve stress."

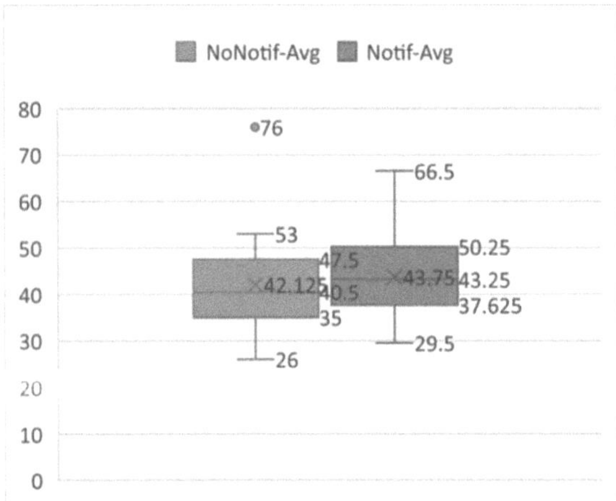

Fig. 9. STAI results for the data averaged from the same participants under the same experimental conditions.

On the other hand, seven participants said that they did not think too much about other people's intentions when receiving notifications, and simply regarded it as a reminder. P1 said, "I was startled and thought there was not enough time." P3 noted, "I know this may be friendly, but I was stunned for two seconds and started to think about whether I was stressed just now."

In Study 2, all six participants unanimously stated that they chose to interact with the prototype because they wanted to convey kindness and care. P4 expressed, "I don't want to disturb them directly, but I think I should do something to help them."

The Awareness and Reflection of the Stress Level. In Study 1, most participants said that the notifications they received increased the awareness of their stress state. Regarding collective stress, or concern for the stress of others, five participants reported becoming more curious about the emotional states of others. P7 stated, "I pay attention to others because I don't want to be the only one feeling anxious", and both p11 and p12 said "I looked at the prototype outside to see what was going on about people's stress."

In Study 2, all participants confidently distinguished whether stressed individuals constituted the majority based on the device's output.

The Impact of Factors that Inspire Social Interests. Among the elements of sound, visual effects, and timing of notification appearances, 6 out of 20 participants highlighted the influence of the timing of notifications on their inclination towards socializing. For example, P3 remarked, "Because there is no great pressure, I want to take this opportunity to chat. But if it is very stressful, I will ignore it." 10 participants mentioned that visual effects could disrupt their focus on work. P14 said, "I feel a little annoyed, and even fell like to go out and complain to person." Additionally, 14 participants found soft sound effects enjoyable and conducive to relaxation.

The Social Decision Has Been Made. Among the five groups in Study 1, three groups briefly discussed topics related to this notification. Among them, some participants in the G2 and G4 groups took the initiative to mention that they had received the notifications, while the topic in the G4 group started with a tactful inquiry, "What happened?" The G2 group displayed particularly active social engagement, seamlessly transitioning from notification discussions to more general topics. During interviews, P9 said, "Actually, I also want to say hi to the people outside there." This sentiment was also shared by seven other participants. Moreover, ten participants indicated their intention to leave their seats, anticipating potential social opportunities.

In Study 2, following an understanding of the experimental context, all the participants chose to interact with the stress bubble that had been inflated on the prototype. Two out of the six participants attempted repeated interactions while observing the reactions of the people present in the meeting room. When asked about their expectations for social events, four participants expressed a desire for simple forms of communication with people in the meeting room, such as eye contact, waving, etc.

6   Discussion and Limitations

6.1   Design Considerations About the Prototype and Notifications

In study 1, some suggestions on notification were collected and considered. Six participants noted that the current notification's bubble-bursting effect on the screen was distracting, and thus hindering the workflow. P14 said "It would be better if it could be shrunk to the corners of the screen."

In the design section, the anonymity of module-person associations was mentioned but lacked elaboration. For future iterations, randomly assigning individuals to different modules daily could enhance anonymity. Mutable associations can prevent participants from gradually discerning their link to the prototype, thus preserving identity transparency over time.

6.2   The Impact of Multiple Factors on Social Dynamics

Firstly, while lab experiments provide valuable insights, real-world dynamics still can be different. Students accustomed to public spaces may not grasp the full extent of workplace collective stress. To enhance accuracy, future experiments could be conducted in authentic office settings, employing actual employees as participants.

Secondly, during the interviews, participants frequently speculated that their social decisions might vary if the task were less serious than math problems. This indicates the considerable influence of task nature on social dynamics. Concurrently, the observation of social interactions within Study 1 groups, which comprised familiar individuals, revealed substantial differences in social dynamics. These variations could be attributed to diverse group norms or underlying factors such as cultural backgrounds.

Research shows that collective stress and coping mechanisms vary across cultures, with many coping mechanisms being collective, learned, uniform responses to remove stressors or change interpretations of situations [11].

6.3 The Balance Between Emotional Information Protection and Intervention Methods

The unexpected outcome of the experiment was that no one mentioned the discomfort of being exposed to a certain degree of their own emotions. Furthermore, some participants took the initiative to communicate with others about their stress status after receiving the notification. When queried about their interpretation of notifications, the divergences observed in Study 1 were found to be closely related to the participants' preferences for processing emotions. All participants who perceived the notifications as a social invitation reported that they usually expressed their emotions to a greater or lesser extent to relieve stress. Some participants who are inclined to be reserved in expressing emotions perceived notifications as "reminders" rather than as "social invitations." This appears to create a buffer zone for the degree of disclosure of stressful emotions. When the design leaves room for user interpretation, people subconsciously interpret ambiguous information in a way that suits their preferences, thus achieving a certain degree of balance.

7 Conclusions

In this research, a physicalization of collective stress with a notification system is designed. The prototype, which anonymously physicalizes people's stress levels in a modular way, aims to provide the affordance for interaction and attempts to implicitly convey information among people in an office environment in a playful way, which also leaves more room for interpretation of the notification, while at the same time raising the awareness of the stress.

In the experiment, quantitative methods are used to measure the changes in stress in participants at work after receiving the notification, and qualitative methods are used to explore how people interpret the notification they receive or send, as well as what kind of social activities might arise after raising the awareness of stress. Although the effect on stress levels is not significant in quantitative analysis, the qualitative results highlight the benefits of CalmaStep in fostering discussions around common topics and social interests.

Acknowledgments. We are grateful to all the professionals and participants who kindly shared their feedback and insights during the process.

References

1. Bao, Y., Xue, M., Gohumpu, J., Cao, Y., Hu, J.: PopStress: designing organizational stress intervention for office workers. Frontiers Comput. Sci. **5** (2023). https://doi.org/10.3389/fcomp.2023.1265399
2. Barnes, L.L.B., Harp, D., Jung, W.: Reliability generalization of scores on the Spiel-Berger state-trait anxiety inventory. Educ. Psychol. Measur. **62**, 603–618 (2002). https://doi.org/10.1177/0013164402062004005
3. Bruns Alonso, M., Varkevisser, M., Keyson, D.V.: Expressive stress relievers. In: Proceedings of the 7th Nordic Conference on Human-Computer Interaction: Making Sense Through Design, pp. 761–764. NordiCHI 2012, Association for Computing Machinery, New York, NY, USA (2012). https://doi.org/10.1145/2399016.2399134
4. Byun, K., et al.: Investigating how auditory and visual stimuli promote recovery after stress with potential applications for workplace stress and burnout: protocol for a randomized trial. Front. Psychol. **13** (2022). https://doi.org/10.3389/fpsyg.2022.897241
5. Caviola, S., Carey, E., Mammarella, I.C., Szucs, D.: Stress, time pressure, strategy selection and math anxiety in mathematics: a review of the literature. Front. Psychol **8** (2017). https://doi.org/10.3389/fpsyg.2017.01488, https://www.frontiersin.org/journals/psychology/articles/10.3389/fpsyg.2017.01488
6. Festinger, L.: A theory of social comparison processes. Hum. Relations **7**(2), 117–140 (1954)
7. Gold, P.: The organization of the stress system and its dysregulation in depressive illness. Mol. Psychiatry **20**, 32–47 (2014). https://doi.org/10.1038/mp.2014.163
8. Hernando, A., et al.: Inclusion of respiratory frequency information in heart rate variability analysis for stress assessment. IEEE J. Biomed. Health Inf. **20**, 1016–1025 (2016). https://doi.org/10.1109/JBHI.2016.2553578
9. Huberty, J., Green, J., Glissmann, C., Larkey, L., Puzia, M., Lee, C.: Efficacy of the mindfulness meditation mobile app "calm" to reduce stress among college students: randomized controlled trial. JMIR mHealth and uHealth 7 (2019). https://doi.org/10.2196/14273
10. Kline, R.B.: Principles and Practice of Structural Equation Modeling. Guilford publications (2023)
11. Lansisalmi, H., Peiro, J.M., Kivimaki, M., IV.: Collective stress and coping in the context of organizational culture. Eur. J. Work Organ. Psy. **9**(4), 527–559 (2000)
12. Maarsingh, B.M., Bos, J., Van Tuijn, C.F., Renard, S.B.: Changing stress mindset through StressJAM: a virtual reality game using biofeedback. Games Health J. **8**(5), 326–331 (2019)
13. Maulik, P.K.: Workplace stress: a neglected aspect of mental health wellbeing (2017)
14. Michie, S.: Causes and management of stress at work. Occup. Environ. Med. **59**(1), 67–72 (2002)
15. Naylor, M., Ridout, B., Campbell, A.: A scoping review identifying the need for quality research on the use of virtual reality in workplace settings for stress management. Cyberpsychol. Behav. Soc. Netw. **23**(8), 506–518 (2020)
16. Nkem, D., Xue, M.: BallBounce: designing collective stress-related visualizations for office workers using galvanic skin response sensor. In: Proceedings of the 2023 ACM Symposium on Spatial User Interaction, pp. 1–5 (2023)

17. Ono, M., Fujita, M., Yamada, S.: Physiological and psychological responses to expressions of emotion and empathy in post-stress communication. J. Physiol. Anthropol. **28**(1), 29–35 (2009)
18. Pascoe, M.C., Thompson, D.R., Jenkins, Z.M., Ski, C.F.: Mindfulness mediates the physiological markers of stress: systematic review and meta-analysis. J. Psychiatr. Res. **95**, 156–178 (2017)
19. Pickering, T.G.: Mental stress as a causal factor in the development of hypertension and cardiovascular disease. Curr. Hypertens. Rep. **3**(3), 249–254 (2001)
20. Ren, X., Yu, B., Lu, Y., Zhang, B., Hu, J., Brombacher, A.: LightSit: an unobtrusive health-promoting system for relaxation and fitness microbreaks at work. Sensors **19**(9), 2162 (2019)
21. Riley, K.E., Park, C.L.: How does yoga reduce stress? A systematic review of mechanisms of change and guide to future inquiry. Health Psychol. Rev. **9**(3), 379–396 (2015)
22. Rosner, B., Glynn, R.J., Ting Lee, M.L.: Incorporation of clustering effects for the Wilcoxon rank sum test: a large-sample approach. Biometrics **59**(4), 1089–1098 (2003)
23. Schneider, B., Jermann, P., Zufferey, G., Dillenbourg, P.: Benefits of a tangible interface for collaborative learning and interaction. IEEE Trans. Learn. Technol. **4**(3), 222–232 (2010)
24. Selye, H.: What is stress. Metabolism **5**(5), 525–530 (1956)
25. Tsuji, S., Sato, N., Ara, K., Yano, K.: Estimating group stress level by measuring body motion. Front. Psychol. **12**, 634722 (2021)
26. Xue, M., et al.: Co-constructing stories based on users lived experiences to investigate visualization design for collective stress management. In: Proceedings of the 2023 ACM Designing Interactive Systems Conference, pp. 652–663 (2023)
27. Xue, M., Liang, R.H., Hu, J., Yu, B., Feijs, L.: Understanding how group workers reflect on organizational stress with a shared, anonymous heart rate variability data visualization. In: CHI Conference on Human Factors in Computing Systems Extended Abstracts, pp. 1–7 (2022)
28. Xue, M., Liang, R.H., Yu, B., Funk, M., Hu, J., Feijs, L.: AffectiveWall: designing collective stress-related physiological data visualization for reflection. IEEE Access **7**, 131289–131303 (2019)

A Survey on Data Interoperability: Progress and Future Directions

JunJie Su, GuoChao Peng[(✉)], WeiZhen Lin, Xiao Cheng, and Yue Zhao

School of Information Management, Sun Yat-sen University, Guangzhou 510006, China
penggch@mail.sysu.edu.cn

Abstract. Data Interoperability focuses on enabling effective communication and collaboration among heterogeneous data sources, systems, or applications. It represents a core challenge for achieving cross-system and cross-domain data sharing and integration, as well as a critical technical foundation for maximizing the value of data assets. This paper systematically reviews the research motivations, technical frameworks, and practical applications of data interoperability, summarizes the main limitations of current research and looks forward to future research directions.

Keywords: Data Interoperability · Scenario-driven Design · Data Lineage

1 Introduction

The circulation and sharing of data are not only essential for driving the high-quality development of the digital economy but also crucial for unlocking the potential of data and fostering its deep integration with technology and application scenarios. Data generation involves multiple stakeholders and is utilized by various organizations and their hierarchical levels at different stages to achieve the data value chain [1–3]. However, due to disparities in the digitalization levels of organizations, as well as the diverse governance frameworks, development entities, and methodologies underlying different business systems, there exists significant heterogeneity in the semantics and structures of data across industries and systems. In the face of an increasingly complex and diverse data environment, merely aggregating vast amounts of data generated under different scenarios, systems, and standards does not guarantee effective data integration and sharing. The question of "how to enhance the interoperability of data from diverse sources, scenarios, systems, and standards" has emerged as one of the critical challenges requiring urgent resolution in the advancement of the digital economy.

In this paper, we examine the current landscape of the field of data integration and interoperability and discuss the limitations of existing studies as well as future research directions. We begin by providing a concise overview of five relevant aspects from the perspective of information resource management researchers:

- Studies on data elements
- The development of data management frameworks

- Practical applications of data interoperability
- Business needs and scenario-specific characteristics
- The role and implications of data lineage

2 Overview of Data Element Research

In prior research, scholars have primarily investigated the circulation, asset transformation, governance, value realization, and market dynamics of data elements from economic and information science perspectives.

Studies on the circulation of data elements primarily investigate the circulation mechanisms, overall frameworks, and implementation strategies for cross-domain data element circulation. Zhao et al. have utilized the division of labor theory to conduct in-depth research on the origins, market mechanisms, and challenges associated with data element circulation. They not only uncovered the underlying logic of data element circulation but also explored in depth its market operational pathways, further elucidating the patterns and development trajectories of data element circulation [4].

Studies on the monetization of data elements primarily focus on rights confirmation and pricing mechanisms for data elements. Wen et al. have conducted comprehensive research on regional legislative approaches for data rights confirmation in China using the grounded theory method, drawing several significant conclusions. They highlighted that China's regional legislative strategies for data rights confirmation exhibit a distinct trend toward data rights confirmation. Additionally, the concept of data rights is extensively incorporated in regional legislation. Furthermore, researchers found that these legislative strategies generally adopt a dual-directional rights confirmation approach to facilitate data circulation and utilization. Lastly, the boundaries of rights exercise are clearly delineated in regional legislation [5]. Huang et al. have investigated the pricing strategies of data products, based on the fundamental principles of data price formation, and explored the pricing mechanisms of data products [6].

In studies on the governance of data elements, Xia conducted comprehensive research on the cultivation of China's data element market by examining the relationship between the market-driven allocation of data elements and the reform of government data governance approaches. She highlighted that China demonstrates significant advantages in data aggregation, complemented by a robust governmental mobilization capability, and thus, the development of the data element market should be advanced through the establishment of a government data governance framework [7]. Zheng et al. developed relevant governance approaches and system frameworks for industrial data security governance in complex information environments. They specifically highlighted the importance of administrative measures in industrial data security governance, utilizing technical architectures and administrative measures as primary tools to establish a holistic industrial data security governance framework that encompasses the entire process of data supply, circulation, and use. This framework aims to ensure data security and compliance while fostering the sustainable development of industries [8]. Grounded in information ecology theory, Shen et al. undertook comprehensive analyses of the current dilemmas in data element governance and explored relevant preventive measures. They examined the issues and challenges in data element governance and suggested effective strategies from multiple perspectives to promote the sustainable and orderly growth of the data element market [9].

Ma et al. have undertaken comprehensive research on the value realization of data elements. Building on a comprehensive examination of concepts related to data rights confirmation, they explored approaches to establishing a data property rights system to facilitate data rights confirmation. They precisely delineated specific methods for data classification and grading and further analyzed the impact of these methods on various stages of data value realization [10]. Additionally, they methodically categorized the storage methods and characteristics of data elements, uncovering the underlying mechanisms for realizing the value of data elements. Leveraging the value chain theory, they strategically developed implementation frameworks, encompassing basic business activities, supportive activities, and value creation, thereby establishing a robust theoretical basis for promoting the structured development of the data element market [11].

Regarding research on the data factor market, Ma et al. have conducted an in-depth analysis of key issues such as data ownership verification, category classification, ensuring privacy, and resource allocation and sharing, providing a comprehensive assessment of the challenges faced by the current data factor trading market. They have thoroughly reviewed the operational mechanisms and regulatory frameworks of the data factor trading market, delved into various issues, and proposed a series of theoretical foundations and practical solutions to address these challenges [12]. Wang has extensively studied multiple critical aspects of the marketization of data factors, including the centrality of data resources, resource allocation, well-defined property rights, valuation, price determination in the market, supply chain management, demand generation, as well as regulatory governance and regulated development of the market [13]. Guan et al., based on theories related to the market economy and data value chain, have explored the ecosystem of the data factor market and its participants from both broad and specific perspectives. They elaborated in detail on the networked structure among entities participating at various levels of the data market and examined the challenges these entities face during their growth. Furthermore, it compares the models, supply methods, regulatory systems, and cultivation strategies of representative countries with China, which was under the guidance of imparting "value and security" to data market participants, along with their respective advantages and disadvantages. Finally, they put forward several policy proposals [14]. Driessend et al. have detailed the primary application areas of the data market and, in light of advancements in digital technology, proposed design frameworks for the operation of the data market. They focused on the operational and technical aspects of the data market to ensure efficient, secure, and regulation-compliant data flow [15]. Additionally, Gonzal et al. have conducted in-depth research on data privacy preservation in the Internet of Things (IoT) domain, exploring how to facilitate the optimal utilization of IoT data and the growth of associated industries while safeguarding data privacy [16]. Meanwhile, Andrej and other scholars have extensively analyzed the application of big data and machine learning technologies in the marketing industry, demonstrating how these technologies can help enterprises better understand customer needs, refine marketing strategies, and improve customer experience and value proposition [17]. These studies have explored the technical challenges and practical applications in data market development from multiple perspectives, offering insightful references and inspiration for the healthy growth of the data factor market.

In summary, scholars in the field of information resource management have undertaken a substantial body of research and preliminary explorations on topics related to data factors. However, there is currently insufficient attention to the challenges of data interoperability within the discipline. Consequently, the distinctive strengths of the information resource management discipline have not been leveraged to conduct more thorough and holistic research on data interoperability, integrating perspectives such as scenarios, requirements, technology, and data.

3 The Origin and Evolution of Data Management Frameworks

The origins of data management frameworks date back to the 1960s, developed by the American computer scientist Charles Bachman. In 1969, Bachman introduced a data management system known as "Integrated Data Store (IDS)", which represented one of the earliest efforts to integrate data models and management methodologies [18]. Internationally, in recent years, a multitude of theoretical models and knowledge frameworks pertaining to data management have emerged:

- The CMMI Data Management Maturity Model is a holistic assessment framework that provides comprehensive evaluation standards for areas such as strategies for data management, governance of data, quality of data, platforms and architectural frameworks, interoperability of data, and supporting processes [19]. These standards are designed to assist organizations in identifying their strengths and areas for enhancement in data management, thereby improving the maturity and operational efficiency of data management. In addition to these core areas, the model also incorporates supporting processes, such as the management of stakeholder requirements and the management of the relationship between business processes and data quality.
- The DCAM (Data Management Capability Assessment Model) is a holistic framework aimed at assessing an organization's capabilities and maturity in data management [20]. DCAM categorizes data management into eight functional domains, including strategies for data management, business cases for data management, data management processes, governance of data, architectural frameworks for data, technical architectural frameworks, quality of data, and interoperability of data. It outlines 37 capabilities and 115 sub-capabilities associated with the development of sustainable data management initiatives. These capabilities offer organizations concrete action guidelines to strengthen their performance across various dimensions of data management.
- IBM's data governance efficiency evaluation plan was created by a consulting group consisting of 55 experts, following steps such as planning, conception, implementation, and inspection. It conducts in-depth analysis on the business, technical, procedural aspects of data management, and improvement measures, summarizing a complete set of complexity measurement standards [21]. IBM categorizes data management into 11 key domains: data risk and compliance management, value enhancement, organizational structure and awareness, strategy and policies, operational strategies, data quality oversight, data lifecycle management, data confidentiality and privacy

protection, data interoperability and sharing architecture, metadata governance, and audit reporting and logging.

- In 1980, volunteers in the fields of international data management and business established a non-profit global network—DAMA International, dedicated to advancing the study and expanding the application of data management as a discipline. Since its inception, DAMA has established chapters in over 50 regions worldwide, attracting thousands of data professionals. The organization has published the DAMA Dictionary of Data Management and the DAMA Data Management Body of Knowledge (DAMA-DMBOK1.0 and DAMA-DMBOK2.0), which have garnered widespread acclaim in the industry. These publications encapsulate the insights and practical contributions of numerous industry leaders, serving as foundational standards for the data management field. The data management framework proposed by DAMA-DMBOK comprises three visual representations: the DAMA Wheel, the Environmental Factors Hexagon, and the Knowledge Area Context Diagram [22]. The DAMA Wheel delineates 12 key data management knowledge areas, including data governance, data architecture, data modeling and design, data storage and operations, data security, data integration and interoperability, document and content management, reference and master data management, data warehousing and business intelligence, metadata management, and data quality management. The Environmental Factors Hexagon depicts the interrelationships among people, processes, and technology, with core elements encompassing goals and principles, organizational culture, tools, activities, roles and responsibilities, deliverables, and technology. The Knowledge Area Context Diagram provides a detailed breakdown of each knowledge area, highlighting their connections to people, processes, and technology.

Data interoperability serves as a pivotal component in data management, functioning as a bridge between upstream and downstream processes: upstream, it depends on the enterprise's foundational efforts in data governance, data architecture design, data security management, and metadata management; downstream, it is a prerequisite for subsequent activities such as constructing data warehouses, performing data analysis, advancing business intelligence, and facilitating data sharing, circulation, and transactions. Given its critical role, we argue that the issue of data interoperability warrants greater attention from the academic community, particularly scholars specializing in information resource management and data management.

4　The Application and Deepening of Data Interoperability in Multiple Fields

The concept of interoperability originated in the field of computer science in the 1990s and has since been extensively applied and developed across various domains, including military, healthcare, transportation, industry, construction, and cultural tourism. With the emergence of related concepts, the connotation and scope of interoperability research have continued to expand. Interoperability encompasses multiple dimensions, such as business interoperability, process interoperability, service interoperability, and data interoperability. Business interoperability refers to the interaction and collaboration of business processes across different organizations or systems, while process interoperability focuses on the integration and automation of workflows across disparate systems or components. Service interoperability emphasizes the composition, coordination, and invocation of services, whereas data interoperability, the central focus of this study, emphasizes the processes of data exchange, sharing, and utilization [2, 23, 24]). The term "data interoperability" is widely utilized in the fields of computer science and information systems. According to the ISO/IEC 20944-1 standard, it is defined as the ability of different functional units to communicate, execute programs, or transfer data. This definition underscores the interaction capabilities among diverse systems, components, or functional units, highlighting their interoperability in terms of information exchange and collaborative functionality [25, 26]. When applied to the domain of data, data interoperability extends beyond mere data sharing and exchange; it encompasses the entire lifecycle of data, from generation to utilization. Data interoperability focuses on enabling the creation, interpretation, computation, utilization, transmission, and exchange of data across heterogeneous systems, platforms, or formats, thereby ensuring data interoperability and usability. Data interoperability represents a result-oriented capability that aims to facilitate the exchange, comprehension, and application of data across different systems or components. Specifically, it addresses the interaction between two or more systems or components to enable seamless data exchange, mutual understanding, and collaborative use across systems. This capability necessitates not only the transmission or sharing of data but also the assurance of data readability, consistency, and interpretability across different systems.

In this paper, data interoperability is defined as the capability to establish seamless connections between data platforms, facilitating secure data flow and efficient exchange, while fulfilling the demands of collaborative business operations and operational convenience. The central challenge addressed by data interoperability research lies in the heterogeneity of data originating from diverse sources, including different storage systems, organizations, or even distinct scenarios and domains. To more precisely assess the presence of heterogeneity, existing studies on interoperability frequently analyze and identify the contextual semantic relationships inherent in the data. The contextual semantics of data encapsulate the underlying knowledge, encompassing scenario-specific characteristics, business logic, and user requirements. The semantics pertinent to this paper can be broadly categorized into two types.

Storage-level Semantics. The primary source of data contextual semantics is derived from the directly associated storage-level semantics. Databases utilized for data storage can be categorized into two main types: relational databases and non-relational databases. Prominent examples of relational databases include Oracle, SQLServer, DB2, and MySQL, whose schemas are composed of databases, tables, and fields. Specifically, a database encompasses tables, a table encompasses fields, and the "foreign key" attribute of a field signifies the relationships between tables [27]. In contrast, non-relational databases encompass various forms, such as document stores, key-value stores, wide-column stores, and graph stores. With the ongoing advancements in artificial intelligence, the adoption of graph databases has seen significant growth [28]. Notable graph databases include Neo4j, GraphDB, and InfiniteGraph. The schema of a graph database comprises nodes, relationships, and properties, where relationships serve to connect nodes, and both nodes and relationships may possess properties.

Multimodal Semantics. Information originates from diverse sources and manifests in various forms, each of which is termed a modality. Multimodal semantics involves the transformation of different forms of information (e.g., text, images, audio) into a shared semantic representation, facilitating mutual understanding and interaction among these diverse information forms [29]. The objective is to enable seamless integration across different media, ensuring that information retains consistent meaning and semantic interpretation regardless of its form of expression. Constructing such a unified semantic representation necessitates the convergence of multiple disciplines, including natural language processing, computer vision, and audio processing. The core challenge in understanding multimodal data semantics lies in the effective fusion of data from different modalities to derive more comprehensive and accurate insights. This requires leveraging advanced machine learning algorithms and deep learning techniques, such as Convolutional Neural Networks (CNN), Recurrent Neural Networks (RNN), and Transformers.

Building on this foundation, existing research has proposed diverse perspectives on the classification of data heterogeneity. For instance, Batini primarily categorizes data heterogeneity issues into name conflicts and structural conflicts [27]; Sheth emphasizes structural heterogeneity and semantic heterogeneity [30]; Kahng's classification includes data model heterogeneity and semantic heterogeneity [31]; Sujansky offers a more granular classification, encompassing structural heterogeneity, naming heterogeneity, semantic heterogeneity, and content heterogeneity [32]; while Zhang Ying classifies data heterogeneity into structured heterogeneity and unstructured heterogeneity based on its origins [33]. By synthesizing existing research and classifications from both domestic and international sources, we believe that two types of heterogeneity issues are particularly salient in the current context of data sharing, circulation, and exchange: semantic heterogeneity and structural heterogeneity.

Semantic heterogeneity refers to the presence of diverse semantic representation methods within datasets or information systems. These varying representation methods may encompass different semantic models, conceptual expressions, and domain-specific knowledge, among other factors. Such heterogeneity can result in semantic mismatches between distinct systems or data sources, ultimately compromising data accuracy and consistency. Consequently, addressing semantic heterogeneity constitutes a critical task for enabling multimodal semantic understanding and facilitating data integration.

- Cross-domain semantic heterogeneity: Across different domains, the representation of identical concepts may differ, and the specialized terminology employed may also vary. For instance, the terminology used to describe the same biological process in the medical and biological fields may diverge, resulting in cross-domain semantic heterogeneity.
- Semantic differences in knowledge graphs: Within knowledge graphs, various data sources may employ distinct ontologies or semantic models to represent entities and their relationships. The integration of such heterogeneous knowledge graphs often necessitates addressing semantic mapping challenges between differing ontologies.
- Visual semantic heterogeneity in image recognition: In the context of image recognition tasks, diverse visual feature extraction models may produce varying visual semantic representations. These discrepancies often necessitate effective semantic fusion in multimodal scenarios.

- Relationships between categories: When two objects from distinct information sources represent identical or similar real-world entities, their categories may exhibit equivalence, sub-concept/super-concept relationships, or partial overlaps.
- Structural differences: Two objects that belong to compatible categories may exhibit structural discrepancies. For instance, an object in one system might include a specific attribute, whereas an object in another system might not incorporate this attribute.
- Units: Even when two objects belong to compatible categories and share identical structures, they may employ different units.

Structural heterogeneity refers to the presence of diverse structures or types within a dataset. Such variations may encompass differences in data representation, attribute types, distribution patterns, and the occurrence of missing or anomalous values.

- Mixed data types: A dataset may comprise various data types, including numerical, textual, categorical, and temporal data. For instance, an e-commerce dataset might encompass product sales (numerical), product descriptions (textual), and product categories (categorical), along with other data types.
- Multimodal data: A dataset may encompass data from various modalities, such as images, text, and audio. For instance, a multimodal social media dataset could comprise user profile images, textual posts, and voice-based comments.
- Heterogeneous database integration: In scenarios involving database integration or fusion, data from disparate database systems may be incorporated, each potentially utilizing distinct structures and schemas.

Research on data interoperability began in the 20th century, and to date, significant progress has been made in related foundational technical studies. According to the category of heterogeneous problems to be solved, the contextual semantics extracted from heterogeneous data, and the varying research emphases, this field is categorized into two main areas: data interoperability research focused on semantic heterogeneity issues and data interoperability research focused on structural heterogeneity issues.

Research on Data Interoperability for Semantic Heterogeneity Issues. Guo et al. put forward a framework of concept-related near-synonyms or synonyms with the same concept to eliminate ambiguity [34]. Zhu et al. integrated the structural features of semantic networks (e.g., path length and depth) with the semantic information content of concepts to develop a method for measuring semantic similarity between concepts in graph databases (e.g., WordNet and DBpedia) [35]. Fareh et al. employed ontology alignment or collaborative techniques to acquire and collaborate on the semantics of different categories of data, specifically: they transformed resources at the data layer, metadata layer, and knowledge layer into ontologies, and then through multi-layer ontology collaboration, generated a fused ontology as a unified data & metadata & knowledge storage model [36].

Research on Data Interoperability for Structural Heterogeneity Issues. Haslhofer et al. established levels of data interoperability to address structural heterogeneity issues hierarchically, categorizing data interoperability based on metadata building blocks [37]. Specifically, these levels are: M0 - metadata layer (instance layer), M1 - metadata schema layer (model layer), M2 - schema definition language layer (meta-model layer), and M3 - general modeling language (meta-meta-model layer) [38, 39]. Among these, M3 defines meta-models, offering foundational models to rapidly assemble meta-model packages, including the definition of domains, classes, attributes, relationships, and other elements necessary for meta-models. M2 represents the meta-model, an instantiation of M3, which serves as a model specification by describing the components of models and their interrelationships, such as the Common Warehouse Metamodel [40], Unified Modeling Language (UML) metamodel, and business metamodel [41]. M1 constitutes the model layer, which comprises data used to describe other data, such as databases, tables, and fields corresponding to the Common Warehouse Metamodel; objects and interfaces corresponding to the UML metamodel; and businesses and services corresponding to the business metamodel.

In recent years, the introduction of new data-sharing paradigms, such as data lakes and data-sharing spaces, has underscored the importance of sharing at the metadata level. For instance, Jagodnik et al. introduced a digital object-sharing framework that leverages metadata to enable automatic indexing of digital objects and utilizes JSON for the exchange of digital objects [42]. Furthermore, regarding unstructured data, Diamantini et al. emphasized the need to extract sufficient semantic information from unstructured data sources to enhance the secondary utilization of data resources within shared environments. They proposed a method for extracting topic-oriented views from heterogeneous and unstructured data sources and quantitatively assessed this approach using structural cohesion metrics commonly applied in network analysis (e.g., clustering coefficient and density). The findings demonstrate that the method yields higher clustering coefficients and average density, thereby offering users enhanced and comprehensive data semantic information [43].

In summary, existing research on interoperability predominantly concentrates on addressing single data heterogeneity issues. However, in practical scenarios, big data across various industries and domains frequently exhibit both semantic and structural heterogeneity simultaneously. Empirical evidence indicates that methods and tools designed to tackle single heterogeneity issues often fall short in effectively resolving the complexities inherent in contemporary multi-dimensional data integration and circulation processes.

5 Scenarios-Driven Data Interoperability: Meeting Business Needs

The aforementioned extensive research on data interoperability has sought to resolve heterogeneity issues from the supply and technical perspectives. However, Pang have highlighted that these efforts frequently neglect the significance of users and contextual scenarios. Consequently, Pang introduced the concept of scenario-based data interoperability [44].

Indeed, business requirements and scenario characteristics hold significant importance in data interoperability research. Within the framework of collaborative data governance, user groups originate from diverse professional domains, data generation involves multiple stakeholders, and data are utilized across various business processes. Concurrently, These data are used by various organizations and individuals at different levels for different stages of the data value chain. Traditional data processing approaches are generally limited to specific, narrowly defined business contexts. However, when data must be shared and utilized across boundaries, users often lack a comprehensive grasp of heterogeneous professional knowledge. Although user needs may seem similar, the datasets they reference in practical applications can vary due to differences in organizational roles, operational goals, and the semantics of business terminology. Consequently, it is imperative in data interoperability research to thoroughly account for business requirements and scenario characteristics. This ensures data accuracy and consistency, thereby improving the efficacy and efficiency of collaborative data governance.

To tackle the challenge of implicit knowledge reasoning in intelligent responses to user needs, foster a user-centric approach, and mitigate interoperability barriers between users and data resources, it is essential to extract and model the differentiated expertise. By constructing relational connections with data, user needs can be more effectively understood, enabling the delivery of more precise and tailored services. Establishing such relational connections aids in removing barriers between users and data, thereby enhancing the efficiency and value of data utilization. Furthermore, by extracting and modeling differentiated expertise, the management and utilization of data resources can be further refined, offering users more intelligent and efficient data services.

Existing data interoperability methods predominantly integrate heterogeneous data sources from a technical standpoint, focusing on aspects such as the type of storage database, table or field names, field types, and statistical characteristics of data values at the foundational information level. However, these technical approaches are insufficient to fully address heterogeneity issues arising from business complexity and uncertainty. Within traditional information systems, the business knowledge underlying data achieves consensus within a confined scope. Yet, when data resources are detached from their original systems and shared or applied more broadly, this business knowledge is not adequately preserved. Consequently, data sources lack sufficient supplementary semantic information during interoperability, complicating the identification of meaningful semantic distinctions between similar data. When data is disassociated from its original information system, the related semantic descriptive knowledge is not effectively transferred. This manifests primarily in two ways: first, the absence of contextual information regarding complex business data sources, which hinders the identification and association of heterogeneous data entities; second, the model heterogeneity of data sources resulting from uncertain business practices. These unmigrated semantic descriptive knowledge are vital for data interoperability and integration, as they facilitate an understanding of the actual meaning and context of data, thereby enhancing data integration and application. To tackle these challenges, it is imperative to conduct thorough research on the effective extraction, modeling, and utilization of these unmigrated semantic descriptive knowledge. This entails a profound comprehension and analysis of the business domain, alongside the appropriate representation and application of semantic descriptive knowledge.

From a data utilization standpoint, current data interoperability methods primarily aim to resolve the heterogeneity issues among data sources [45], yet they largely neglect the expanding user base in industrial interconnection and the growing significance of heterogeneous professional knowledge among users. Additionally, the diversity, complexity, and dynamic nature of user data usage scenarios have not been adequately examined [46]. These challenges present new obstacles for the exploration of the mutual influence between user needs and data resources. Specifically, due to differences in professional understanding among users and environmental changes, the intuitive user goals we derive when interpreting user needs often diverge from their actual intentions, which is mainly reflected in two aspects: the ambiguity and imprecision of user needs, and the uncertainty and dynamic nature of user intentions. These issues make it more difficult to accurately understand and meet user needs, thus necessitating further research and refinement of data interoperability methods to better address these challenges.

In the context of the current complex environment, data sharing should transition from the traditional model to an advanced model. This transformation entails a shift from simply facilitating data auditing, inheritance, and reporting to addressing the data interoperability requirements in diverse practical scenarios. To achieve this goal, it is essential to proactively identify user needs, intelligently align user needs with data resources, and assist users in obtaining the required information. Implementing this strategy enables the efficient and seamless delivery of target information to users. This proactive approach to data services will substantially enhance the efficiency of data sharing, address the current issue of 'data tombs' in data sharing, and facilitate cross-domain, cross-organizational, and cross-disciplinary data resource sharing and utilization.

Traditional data interoperability is commonly seen in the exchange and communication of data between pairs of information systems. In recent years, with the emergence of concepts and applications such as data lakes, data sharing spaces, and data asset platforms, data is shared on a larger scale in a manner independent of the original information systems, and the challenges related to heterogeneity have become more pronounced.

Research on different scenarios of data interoperability primarily encompasses industrial manufacturing, transportation, e-commerce, healthcare, construction engineering, cultural tourism, library and literature, digital archives, military industry, urban areas, and disaster emergency scenarios. Reviewing existing research globally, it has been observed that current scenario-based data interoperability research is predominantly concentrated on single scenarios or domains, with a lack of exploration and validation of data interoperability technologies and methods across industries, fields, and scenarios. For China, to fully realize the value of data elements, it is necessary to achieve cross-industry, cross-scenario, and cross-disciplinary data circulation. To realize data sharing, it is required to adaptively integrate the heterogeneous data sources provided by various parties in the industry interconnection. However, existing data interoperability methods encounter substantial challenges in identifying and associating cross-scenario heterogeneous data owing to the absence of contextual information in data sources.

6 Analyzing Data Lineage

From the initial creation and processing of data to its transmission and exchange, a natural connection is formed as data progresses through its lifecycle, which we refer to as data lineage. As one of the components of metadata, data lineage serves to track the flow path of data tables and fields from the source to the target table [47], thereby assessing the potential impacts that changes in the original data may have on downstream data. Simultaneously, when downstream data is modified, it enables the tracing back to identify potential issues in upstream data [48].

Data lineage is invaluable for the development of data integration and interoperability solutions [22]. When dealing with large-scale and complex datasets, understanding the origin, flow trajectory, and ultimate destination of data is crucial. It not only enables developers to gain a deeper understanding of the relationships between data but also mitigates issues such as data conflicts and redundancies. For data consumers, data lineage offers substantial benefits. When they need to use data, they can efficiently identify the required data sources, understand the processing and changes of the data, and thus enhance their understanding and utilization of the data. As data integration between organizations becomes more prevalent, the importance of data lineage grows in significance. To ensure the accuracy and consistency of data, effective governance is imperative. Among these, recording the origin and trajectory of data movement is a key step. This helps ensure the traceability and transparency of data, thereby ensuring the provision of reliable information to data consumers. Additionally, data sharing agreements may impose various constraints and stipulations for data usage. To ensure compliance, organizations need to have a clear understanding of where data is moved, stored, and retained. This requires relying on data lineage information to ensure that the trajectory and state of data align with the agreements. Some emerging compliance standards, such as the Solvency II regulations in Europe, establish more stringent requirements on data traceability [22]. Organizations must be able to provide a detailed account of the origin of their data and its changes across different systems. This requires the adoption of data lineage technology to build a comprehensive, end-to-end data lineage tracking system [49]. When making changes to data flows, data lineage information is critical [50]. Any changes to data structures, data flows, or data processing methods could potentially affect the entire data ecosystem. Therefore, performing forward and backward lineage analysis can help organizations evaluate the implications of changes and ensure the integrity and accuracy of data [51]. Furthermore, to effectively manage data lineage information, it is essential to integrate it as a key component of metadata solutions. This can help organizations gain a deeper understanding of their data assets, enhance data processing workflows, and ensure data compliance and traceability [49]. As data volumes expand and complexity increases, data lineage will assume a more significant role in future data processing and analysis.

Given the strong correlation between data lineage and business scenarios, we believe that when conducting scenario-based data interoperability research, relying solely on textual content and context to understand semantics is insufficient in terms of depth and comprehensiveness. Understanding the origin, flow trajectory, and ultimate destination of data, as well as comprehending the lineage relationships of data at different stages such as collection, storage, usage, and management, is critical for addressing the issue of data semantic heterogeneity. However, through a comprehensive review of the literature, it has been observed that existing data interoperability research largely overlooks the importance of data lineage.

7 Conclusion

In the digital era, data interoperability has become a critical factor in achieving data sharing and maximizing the value of data. Through a systematic and comprehensive review of relevant research, three limitations in existing studies on data interoperability have been identified:

- Existing data interoperability methods primarily address data heterogeneity issues from the perspective of the data supply side, mainly focusing on addressing structural and semantic heterogeneity problems caused by inconsistent data models from different data sources. However, these methods are limited in their ability to comprehensively address the heterogeneity challenges arising from business complexity and uncertainty. Furthermore, existing approaches tend to focus on solving a single type of data heterogeneity issue, thus failing to effectively address the practical challenges of data circulation in real-world scenarios.
- Current data interoperability methods primarily concentrate on investigating approaches for single scenarios, often overlooking the heterogeneity of professional knowledge among users and the dynamic nature of scenarios. This limitation impedes the realization of cross-domain and cross-scenario data circulation and sharing. When data assets are decoupled from their original information systems and utilized in broader contexts, the absence of cross-scenario data interoperability methods significantly hampers the effective utilization and value maximization of data. Therefore, in promoting the cross-system and cross-domain sharing and application of data assets, it is crucial to emphasize the completeness and accuracy of data source scenario information to ensure the correct identification and association of heterogeneous data entities.
- Data lineage, which records the entire lifecycle of data from generation to usage, is critical for ensuring data accuracy and reliability. In scenario-based data interoperability, integrating data lineage enhances data comprehension and analytical capabilities, enabling researchers to more effectively trace the origin, transformation, and flow of data. This facilitates more efficient data integration, cleaning, and analysis. By leveraging data lineage information, it becomes possible to precisely identify heterogeneous data entities, establish meaningful associations between data, and detect potential data quality issues. However, existing research on data interoperability methods has largely overlooked the integration of data lineage.

Data interoperability plays a critical role in fostering data sharing and innovation, as well as driving economic development and social progress. However, existing research on data interoperability has not adequately addressed the development needs of the current data factor market, and the information resource management discipline requires greater emphasis on interoperability issues. Recently, artificial intelligence has been advancing into domains traditionally reserved for human experts, offering novel tools for data interoperability. Simultaneously, data interoperability provides new insights for general artificial intelligence in the construction of datasets. Wang et al. have addressed the challenge of heterogeneity in robotic data. In their study, data from diverse sources were aligned to a shared representation, allowing the model to interpret these data effectively [52]. In summary, adopting novel perspectives and methodologies to investigate cross-domain heterogeneous data interoperability models holds significant academic and theoretical value, while also addressing the practical demands of contemporary development.

Acknowledgments. This research was supported by a grant funded by the National Natural Science Foundation of China (No.: 72474236).

References

1. Camarinha-Matos, L.M., Fornasiero, R., Ramezani, J., et al.: Collaborative networks: a pillar of digital transformation. Appl. Sci. **9**(24), 5431 (2019)
2. Chen, D., Doumeingts, G., Vernadat, F.: Architectures for enterprise integration and interoperability: past, present and future. Comput. Ind. **59**(7), 647–659 (2008)
3. Yang, C., Huang, Q., Li, Z., et al.: Big data and cloud computing: innovation opportunities and challenges. Int. J. Dig. Earth **10**(1), 13–53 (2017)
4. Zhao, X.Y., Ji, X.F., Hou, X.L., et al.: He germinal logic, connotation, market path and practical dilemma of data element circulation from the perspective of division of labor theory. Inform. Stud.: Theory Appl. **46**(9), 37–46 (2023)
5. Wen, Y.H., Fu, Z.Y.: Local legislation strategy and adjustment on the right confirmation of data elements in china based on grounded theory. Lib. Inform. Serv. **67**(7), 53–66 (2023)
6. Huang, Q.Q., Wang, J.D., Chen, D., et al.: Research on the data pricing mechanism under an ultra-large-scale data element market system. E-Government **2**, 21–30 (2022)
7. Xia, Y.K.: Market-oriented allocation of data elements and reform of government data governance methods. Lib. Inform. **3**, 14–16 (2020)
8. Zheng, R., Gao, Z.H., Wang, X.Y., et al.: Industrial data security governance in a complex information environment: concept definition, governance system, and scenario practice. Inform. Document. Serv. (2023)
9. Shen, X.L., Qian, Q.W.: Data element governance dilemma and prevention mechanisms—a perspective of value and risk integration. J. Inform. Resources Manage. **13**(6), 17–28 (2023)
10. Ma, F.C., Xiong, S.Y., Sun, Y.J., et al.: Impact of data classified and graded rights confirmation on the realization of the value of data elements. J. Inform. Resources Manage. **14**(1), 4–12 (2024)
11. Ma, F.C., Wu, Y.S., Lu, H.Z.: Research on the path to realize the value of data elements. J. Inform. Resources Manage. **13**(2), 4–11 (2023)
12. Ma, F.C., Lu, H.Z., Wu, Y.S.: The development and operation of data production factors market. J. Inform. Resources Manage. **12**(5), 4–13 (2022)
13. Wang, F.: Ten questions on the market-oriented allocation of data elements. Lib. Inform. **3**, 9–13 (2020)
14. Guan, Q., Xia, Y.K.: The practical dilemma, international experience and enlightenment of data factor market entity cultivate. Lib. Inform. **2**, 23–33 (2023)
15. Driessen, S.W., Monsieur, G., Van Den Heuvel, W.: Data market design: a systematic literature review. IEEE Access **10**, 33123–33153 (2022)
16. Garrido, G.M., Sedlmeir, J., Uludağ, Ö., et al.: Revealing the landscape of privacy-enhancing technologies in the context of data markets for the IoT: a systematic literature review. J. Netw. Comput. Appl. **207**, 103465 (2022)
17. Miklosik, A., Evans, N.: Impact of big data and machine learning on digital transformation in marketing: a literature review. IEEE Access **8**, 101284–101292 (2020)

18. Bachman, C.W.: The origin of the integrated data store (IDS): the first direct-access DBMS. IEEE Ann. Hist. Comput. **31**(4), 42–54 (2009)
19. Ye, L.: The comparative research and reference on capability maturity models for data management library and information service **64**(13), 51–57 (2020). https://doi.org/10.13266/j.issn.0252-3116.2020.13.008
20. Li, B., Bin, J.Z.: Data management capability maturity model. Big Data Res. **3**(4), 29–36 (2017)
21. Li, Q., Wang, Y.: Balancing technical and business aspects in data governance: a case study of IBM's approach. J. Enterp. Inf. Manag. **34**(2), 567–582 (2021)
22. Hu, B.L.: New book order announcement for "DAMA Data Management Body of Knowledge (2nd Edition)". Project Manage. Technol. **18**(8), 143 (2020)
23. Gürdür, D., Asplund, F.: A systematic review to merge discourses: Interoperability, integration and cyber-physical systems. J. Indust. Inform. Integrat. **9**, 14–23 (2018)
24. Weichhart, G., Panetto, H., Molina, A.: Interoperability in the cyber-physical manufacturing enterprise. Ann. Rev. Control **51**, 346–356 (2021)
25. Schindler, S., Marvin, S.: Constructing a universal logic of urban control? International standards for city data, management, and interoperability. City **22**(2), 298–307 (2018)
26. Furner, J.: Definitions of "metadata": a brief survey of international standards. J. Am. Soc. Inf. Sci. **71**(6), E33–E42 (2020)
27. Batini, C., Lenzerini, M., Navathe, S.B.: A comparative analysis of methodologies for database schema integration. ACM Comput. Surv. **18**(4), 323–364 (1986)
28. Angles, R., Gutierrez, C.: Survey of graph database models. ACM Comput. Surv. **40**(1), 1–39 (2008)
29. Han, P., Chen, W.Q.: Review of multimodal named entity recognition studies. Data Analysis and Knowledge Discovery (2023)
30. Sheth, A.P.: Changing focus on interoperability in information systems: From system, syntax, structure to semantics. In: Interoperating Geographic Information Systems, pp. 5–29. Springer (1999)
31. Kahng, J., McLeod, D.: Dynamic classification ontologies. In: Computing the Brain, pp. 241–254. Elsevier (2001)
32. Sujansky, W.: Heterogeneous database integration in biomedicine. J. Biomed. Inform. **34**(4), 285–298 (2001)
33. Zhang, Y.: Research on highway traffic accident prediction considering data heterogeneity. Master's thesis, Chang'an University, Xi'an, China (2018)
34. Guo, J., Da Xu, L., Xiao, G., et al.: Improving multilingual semantic interoperation in cross-organizational enterprise systems through concept disambiguation. IEEE Trans. Industr. Inf. **8**(3), 647–658 (2012)
35. Zhu, G., Iglesias, C.A.: Computing semantic similarity of concepts in knowledge graphs. IEEE Trans. Knowl. Data Eng. **29**(1), 72–85 (2016)
36. Fareh, M., Boussaid, O., Chalal, R.: Reconciliation model of heterogeneous information in decisional information systems. Int. J. Metadata, Semant. Ontol. (2015)
37. Haslhofer, B., Klas, W.: A survey of techniques for achieving metadata interoperability. ACM Comput. Surv. **42**(2), 1–37 (2010)
38. Muller, P.-A., Fleurey, F., Jézéquel, J.-M.: Weaving executability into object-oriented metalanguages. In: Proceedings of the Conference, LNCS, vol. 3713, pp. 264–278. Springer, Heidelberg (2005)
39. Boronat, A., Meseguer, J.: An algebraic semantics for MOF. In: Proceedings of the Conference, LNCS. Lecture Notes in Computer Science, pp. 377–391. Springer (2008)
40. Poole, J., Chang, D., Tolbert, D., et al.: Common warehouse metamodel. Wiley (2002)

41. Ben Hassen, M., Turki, M., Gargouri, F.: A business process meta-model for knowledge identification based on a core ontology. In: Lecture Notes in Business Information Processing, pp. 37–61. Springer (2016)
42. Paten, B., Schurer, S., Dumontier, M., et al.: Developing a framework for digital objects in the Big Data to Knowledge (BD2K) commons: report from the Commons Framework Pilots workshop. J. Biomed. Inform. **71**, 49–57 (2017)
43. Diamantini, C., Lo Giudice, P., Potena, D., et al.: An approach to extracting topic-guided views from the sources of a data lake. Inf. Syst. Front. **23**, 243–262 (2021)
44. Pang, B.: Research on scenario-based data interoperability for industrial interconnection. Ph.D. thesis, Beijing Jiaotong University (2022)
45. Kush, R.D., Warzel, D., Kush, M.A., et al.: FAIR data sharing: The roles of common data elements and harmonization. J. Biomed. Inform. **107**, 103421 (2020)
46. Burke, B., Cearley, D., Jones, N., et al.: Gartner top 10 strategic technology trends for 2020. Smarter with Gartner. https://www.gartner.com/smarterwithgartner/. Retrieved from on November 2, 2019
47. Yang, Y., Liao, H., Fan, J., et al.: Design of data asset map system based on key business indicators. Inform. Technol. Standard. **2021**(09), 35–40 (2021)
48. Wu, L., Guo, J., Shan, R., et al.: Design and application of network data asset catalog based on metadata. J. Hunan Inst. Sci. Technol. (Nat. Sci.) **36**(04), 30–34 (2023)
49. Zhu, J., Fu, X.: Data governance methods integrating data standard management and data lineage construction. Shanghai Qual. **2023**(11), 49–55 (2023)
50. Suo, C., Pai, Y.: Content, methods and strategies of data architecture for library digital transformation. information studies: theory & application, pp. 1–12 (2024)
51. Ma, C.: Data should not only "move" but also be "used." Enterprise Manage. **2020**(12), 100–103 (2020)
52. Wang, L., Chen, X., Zhao, J., He, K.: Scaling proprioceptive-visual learning with heterogeneous pre-trained transformers. ArXiv abs/2409.20537 (2024)

Dream Immersive Interactive Image Visualisation Based on Multimodal Emotion Recognition - An Example from the Design of Dream

Yuxiao Yi[✉] and Yiqi Liu

Beijing Jiaotong University, Beijing, China
2421894679@qq.com

Abstract. Immersive art focuses on deep audience engagement and experience, enabling immersion in the created environment through multiple inputs from the audience's behaviour, body and mind. The design of immersive space requires the use of new media technology and various types of sensors and other equipment, of which XR (Extended Reality) technology in VR, AR, MR virtual and reality fusion of technology and multimodal emotion recognition for immersive art to provide a technical basis for the experience of self-perception and physiological data projection into the scene of the work to form an interactive, rich in the forms of immersive art and enhance the accuracy of emotion recognition. The immersive works constructed by XR technology, compared with traditional creative media and interactive devices, not only pursues narrative and audience's physical interaction as the goal, but also explores the interactivity of perception. In this essay, we will use the immersive interactive artwork 'Dream' as a case study to analyse the artistic expression of immersive interactive video installation, explore how to use multimodal emotion recognition technology to improve the accuracy of emotion recognition and analyse the relationship between sleeping posture, dream and emotion, the narrative design of the dream content image, as well as the interactive behaviour and immersive experience, to explore more dimensions of human-computer interaction under the multimodal emotion recognition, and discuss the future research direction of artistic expression combined with XR technology.

Keywords: Multimodal · Emotion Recognition · Immersive · Interactive Imaging Devices · XR

1 Introduction

Marshall McLuhan in Understanding Media argues that the development of media has the function of extending the human senses, and that such an extension is an amplification of human organs and senses [6]. While traditional art is characterised as visual, sequential and achieved through the medium of the printed word, art forms in the digital age are more electronically mediated, adding more emotional perceptual re-conceptualisation to

D. Harris et al. (Eds.): HCII 2025, LNCS 16334, pp. 429–444, 2026.
https://doi.org/10.1007/978-3-032-12392-3_28

the visualised symbolic form [8]. The researches show that in the process of information reception, the more sensory channels are involved, the more significant the individual's cognitive depth of the information is, the image construction of the thing is closer to the real state, and the memory retention effect is more desirable [7, 15]. The traditional single visual communication mode relies on the visual as a single sensory channel to deliver information in the design and communication mode, and its gradually transformed to a multi-sensory and interactive form of communication. Among them, the immersive interactive image tries to integrate more possibilities of digital technology into the artistic expression and form of the work, which not only changes the way the audience obtains information, but also provides a brand-new form of interaction, and the application of new media technology and sensor devices to the art work brings the audience a more multi-sensory fusion experience. In a digitally-centred era, the integration of emotions into computer systems has become a basic necessity [3]. Interactive art forms integrate the audience's real feelings about the real world with the constructed immersive space by converting the real physical interaction into the image feedback of the immersive space and mobilising more senses of the audience during the interaction. Artworks based on multimodal interaction combine multiple senses of interaction to enhance the audience's sense of novelty and experience, and to obtain multi-dimensional spiritual needs through the innovative forms of digitalisation, multi-media and physiological signal feedback.

This essay will focus on the interactive artwork Dream, which explores human dreams and psychological conflicts through interactive art, visualising dreams and emotions in the immersive space, making the audience feel as if they are walking into the world of their own dreams, and arousing the participating audience to rethink the relationship between the subconscious mind and the dream world. The essay will firstly describe the theory of immersive art, the concept of multimodal interaction and multimodal emotion recognition, and the theory of dream psychology. Secondly, the design concept and technical realisation of Dream will be elaborated, including the narrative design of the video content of the work, the interaction logic of the work, the design of wearable devices and the technical method of generating virtual dream scenes. After that, the key issues of improving the accuracy of emotion recognition, interaction behaviour and immersion experience will be discussed, and finally the value of the work and the application of multimodal interaction to artistic creation will be summarized and future prospects.

2   Theories

2.1   Reviews of Multimodaln Emotion Recognition

Concepts of Multimodal Interaction and Multimodal Emotion Recognition. The concept of multimodality was first proposed from the field of cognitive linguistics, in which it has been explored more in the systemic functional linguistics founded by Michael Halliday [13]. With the further research of scholars, it is believed that in the process of communication not only will convey information through a single language, in addition to language is also accompanied by facial expressions, body movements, voice, and more kinds of physiological data and other non-verbal modalities, these different modalities in the same context to integrate language and more expressions to achieve the role of the joint conveyance of information, which formed the multimodal concept [18]. Multimodality lies in the integration of information through different multi-sensory modalities. Unlike single modality information acquisition, multimodality emphasises multiple perspectives in drawing and analysing data, providing people with more ideas and accuracy in perceiving the environmental space. People construct new linguistic environments through multi-sensory modes of vision, touch, hearing, body movement and internal physiological data, as a basis for more effective and rich information exchange. The concept of multimodality revolves around how to use more perceptual channels to construct environments and interact with them, which constitutes a multimodal interaction for exchanging information.

Emotion recognition, as a core component of multimodal interaction, has become a key driver to change the user experience and is an indispensable aspect of human-computer interaction [7]. By collecting data on facial expressions, voice details and more intrinsic physiological signals and performing multimodal data sentiment analysis and interpretation, the user's emotional state can be captured more accurately and the accuracy of judging people's emotional state at the moment can be improved. The development of multimodal emotion recognition enables a better understanding of the user's needs as well as the implicit needs expressed by the body as reflected in the intrinsic physiological data, which transcends the traditional human-computer interaction, and forms a cross-discipline by cross-discipline integration of disciplines such as computer science, medical science, and psychology, providing more personalised services and data support for more fields.

Research on the Relationship between Physiological Signals and Emotion States. In the progress of emotion recognition research, the addition of more biotechnology has given rise to a variety of emotion recognition schemes. Physiological signals serve as the key research data support for emotion analysis, in which multimodal data such as electrocardiographic information (ECG), brain waves (EEG), respiratory pattern monitoring, electrocorticographic activity (EDA), electromyography (EMG), blood volume pulse (BVP) electromyography (EMG), body temperature, pulse signals, heart rate variability (HRV), and other multimodal data are collected in multimodal data collection for emotion analysis. Different types of physiological signals represent different emotional analysis information. These data amplify and analyse the body's internal biological information to obtain a visualisation of charts or data, which reflects the body's internal physiological information and analyses the emotional state in a multi-dimensional way.

The electrocardiogram (ECG) is mainly used to analyse heart rate variability and heart rate irregularities, for example heart rate changes during anxiety and relaxation states. Electrical Dermal Activity (EDA), on the other hand, is a test that usually represents emotional states of tension or excitement because when emotional excitement leads to sweating, which alters the electrical conductivity of the skin, and therefore the electrical conductivity of the skin area is used to estimate the electrical conductivity of the skin. Electroencephalography (EEG) is a technique used to record the electrical activity of the brain by placing electrodes on the scalp to capture the electrical signals generated by the neurons and convert them into visual waveforms. EEG's visual waveform maps can represent rapid and detailed mood changes and brain activity patterns during testing. Electromyography (EMG) in mood analysis is more about analysing the activities of facial muscles, for example, through EMG to analyse human facial expressions such as smiling, frowning, crying, etc., and to explore micro-expressions through specific tiny changes in the specialised facial muscle groups, and then to infer changes in mood. Breathing pattern monitoring mainly records changes in respiratory rate and respiratory depth through respiratory sensors, and evaluates changes in the current mood through the depth of breathing, for example, slow deep breaths and shallow fast breaths correspond to relaxation and tension, respectively. In the collection and analysis of pulse signals, heart rate variability (HRV) is also measured to assess pressure values [9].

Using the audience's own physiological signal data for interactive experience can visualise the hidden emotions inherent in the body in real time, with different types of physiological signals conveying different bodily information, and different degrees of physiological information corresponding to different emotional states, with the personal physiological information collected by the input sensors, corresponding to the corresponding interactive feedback points through the amplification, processing and analysis of the data, and based on the real-time physiological information is finally transformed into a corresponding immersive space. This use of objective physiological data as an interaction mechanism can bring a unique sense of immersion to the audience, allowing them to better understand their own body information and emotional state.

2.2 Immersive Art Interactive Installation and XR Technology

The core of the traditional interactive installation is to create a unique experience through the interaction between the physical objects in the physical space and the audience, in which the traditional interactive installation is mainly realised through simple mechanical movement and programming of electronic components, and the interaction is relatively single, for example, the common form of touch, move and so on to carry out physical interaction to trigger the interaction mechanism to get feedback [2]. Traditional interactive installations mainly rely on the set physical form and interactive mode, the audience's interaction has a low degree of freedom, and can not be real-time based on complex user behaviour for immediate feedback, so compared with digital art lack of audience personalisation and sense of uniqueness. The development of the information age, based on the concept of interactivity inherent in the digital medium, interactive installations integrate advanced technology and more possibilities between interdisciplinary, compared to the traditional interactive installations of a single message conveyed, immersive art interactive installations around the audience's behaviour, the body and spirit to create a multi-media construction of the immersive space, to explore the interactivity of more dimensions [8, 20].

The book Universal principles of design suggests that the concept of 'immersion' can be understood as a state that leads an individual to be fully engaged in a particular situation, where the individual is so focused on the current situation that he or she forgets about the real world [10]. Based on this understanding, immersive new media installation art, as a cutting-edge art form, aims to create a spatial context that integrates the virtual and the real through the support of new media technology and other innovative means, in order to stimulate the audience's sense of presence and participation. The interactive immersive space takes the audience as an important element of the work, and the audience's participatory behaviour and interactivity become the key point for the expression of the meaning of the work. The audience's interactive behaviour is fed back to the digital space through XR technology, and eventually the audience, audience behaviour, behavioural feedback and the constructed immersive space become a complete whole. This art form not only emphasises the existence of physical space, but also pays more attention to the construction of a multi-level, multi-dimensional hybrid environment, in which the real material and digital virtual elements are intertwined with each other, and together they play a role in the viewer's physical perception and spiritual experience, as well as the viewer's reconstruction of the perception of the real world, conventional space, and the expression of their inner emotions. XR (Extended Reality) refers to the use of computer technology and other generative construction of an environment that supports human-computer interaction combined with real and virtual scenes [16]. XR technology as a way to extend the audience's perceptual ability, interaction and immersion, provide more dimensions of perception, and improve more possibilities for the creation of works of art.

The construction of 'space' immersion as a significant feature of the immersive art interactive installation and XR, unlike traditional art forms, it is not limited to the dimension of space, but rather the integration of the real physical world with the virtual digital space, which not only expands the real world, but also expands the depth of perception of the audience. The audience in this space not only as a viewer, but its behaviour triggered by the work of the feedback with the artist to create a complete immersive art interactive installation.

2.3 Psychological Theories of Dreams

In the evolution of understanding of dreams from classical psychoanalysis to modern cognitive psychiatric disciplines, Freud's The Interpretation of Dreams sees dreams as reflections of the subconscious mind and expressions of inner desires and conflicts. Jungian psychology views dreams and visions as subconscious associations and introspection. Vivid dreams usually occur during rapid eye movement sleep and these are the ones people are most likely to recall. Sleep Stages Normal sleep is divided into two stages, rapid eye movement (REM) and non-rapid eye movement (NREM), of which NREM is divided into four stages. This sleep stage is characterised by very rapid eye movements, similar to wakefulness patterns, but with greatly reduced muscle activity. It usually represents dreaming activity, especially vivid dreams. This part of sleep is associated with maximum breathing and cardiac instability [19]. REM sleep is distinguished from stage 1 by two basic features. The EEG shows sawtooth waves and a jagged appearance most pronounced at the vertex. During strong REM sleep (no eye movements) there is parasympathetic enhancement and increased sympathetic tone. Increased sympathetic nerve activity is observed during stage REM (eye movements), which is explosive. During REM sleep your brain is highly active and brain waves become more variable the cardiovascular system is dominated by parasympathetic activity. During non-REM sleep, breathing is regular and largely metabolically controlled, whereas during REM sleep, breathing becomes irregular and dependent on behavioural factors. REM has specific effects on respiration, with changes in breathing patterns and thoracic depression being most common during stages of REM [4, 11].

Hong Kong Shue Yan University has done a study on dreaming. They conducted a related questionnaire survey on 670 male and female university students, which included the frequency of dreaming, the theme of the dream, the intensity of the dream, and the memory of the dream after waking up [22]. Dreams include images, thoughts and emotions experienced during sleep. Dreams can range from very intense or emotional to very vague, fleeting, confusing, or even boring. Therefore, there are other possible influences in the subject around dreams under the image of subjective personal factors. For example, during this time it may be more of a biological factor or even due to sleep position. For example, when sleeping with your arms on your chest, when stress causes the lungs to breathe and the heart to beat faster, circuits in the brain feed this back into the dream creating a narrative that fits common sense, such as tense exciting chases and nightmares. Among other things, neuroscientists believe that external stimuli and somatic activity during sleep affect physiological data, subconscious layers and sympathetic activity during sleep [1]. At this time the brain in the sleep state is not completely detached from the external environment and stimuli, and it transforms external stimuli into specific images in the brain.

The theoretical compilation of immersive art interaction devices, XR technology and multimodal emotion recognition provides a theoretical foundation for art creation. XR technology, as a technical means to expand the audience's perception ability, interaction mode and immersion, enhances the audience's sense of immersion by integrating visual, auditory, tactile and other multi-sensory modes to create a multi-level and multi-dimensional hybrid environment. Secondly, combining the research of dream psychology theory ensures the rationality and scientificity of the interaction logic of 'Dream', which uses the multimodal emotion recognition theory to capture the user's emotional state more accurately by analysing the data of various physiological signals. Secondly, combining the research of dream psychology theory ensures the rationality and scientificity of the interaction logic of 'Dream', which uses the multimodal emotion recognition theory to capture the user's emotional state more accurately by analysing the data of various physiological signals.

3   Overview of the 'Dream' Project

3.1   Design Concept

Psychologists such as Freud and Jung believed that symbols in dreams can reveal an individual's psychological conflicts, desires, and inner motivations. With the growing concern for mental health, more and more people are paying attention to and taking a keen interest in their dreams, and in popular culture, analysing dream symbols and assigning meaning to them has become a source of entertainment and self-reflection. The symbolic meaning of dreams is a combination of different factors. The chaotic face in dreams is in a sense a variegated mask worn by people in different groups and situations, and according to Jung, personality masks may appear in dreams and in different forms. When the mask of personality conflicts with the collective unconscious, inner tensions and contradictions may appear in another dimension - in dream compilations that reveal the primitive, impulsive and emotional aspects of society, with their corresponding symbolic meanings. The project explores the relationship between dreams and emotions by combining it with a multimodal emotion analysis device. This project, in the form of an interactive installation of visual to show the connection between the body and the dream content under the mask of personality, and to experience the correlation between the brain's circuitry, the body's sleep pattern and the dream symbols during REM sleep. Through the wearable interactive vest capturing the sleeping postures and EEG responses, the private dream experience is transformed into an immersive artistic expression. Simulating the different sleeping postures in the REM sleep stage, different dream contents are formed by different sleeping patterns, capturing and visualising the correlation between brain circuits, body postures, sleeping patterns and dream symbols, visualising their behaviours by using images, and providing real-time feedback by changing sleeping postures to correspond to the corresponding dream contents. Thinking about personality masks and true selves in different dimensions, as a way to dialectically think about and confront social and unconscious desires, thoughts and motives (Figs. 1 and 2).

Fig. 1. Dream's construction site plan.

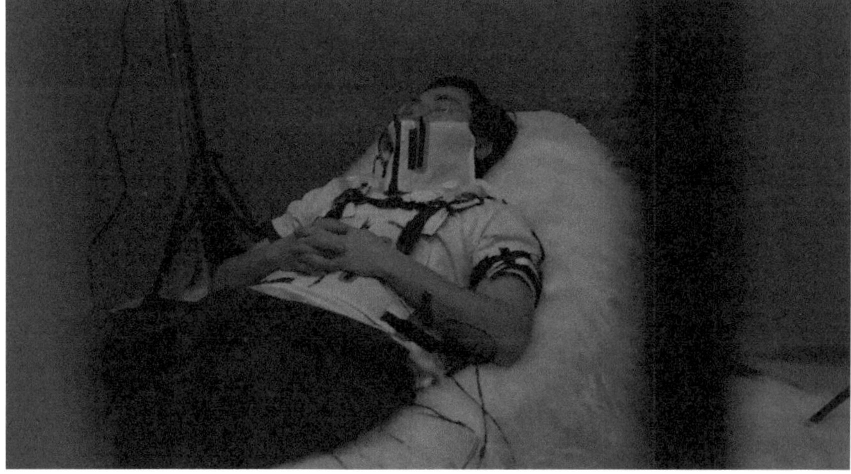

Fig. 2. The Live Audience Experience of 'Dream.

3.2 Technical Realisation

Pressure Sensor Point Design for Wearable Devices. The diversity of interaction behaviours and interactive immersion requires knowledge support from multiple professional fields, including 'vivid dreams', which mostly occur during REM sleep, and the use of sensor devices to capture and extract the audience's body language or physiological data for analysis to correspond to the existence of a variety of interactive possibilities for the programme. The audience is centred on the individual to integrate into the immersive interactive space, in the process of interacting with them, entering, interacting, interacting with the feedback, and transforming it into a visual effect, providing unlimited possibilities for the internal and external perception of the audience and the operation of the work's expression under the diversity of interactive behaviours. Among them, biofeedback is used to collect interactive data, and the interactive experience driven by audience biofeedback collects and amplifies the information of specific internal tissues and organs of the human body, perceives the internal body data in a visual form, collects physiological data by using specific sensors, and analyses and designs them in the interactive scheme of the work. In 'Dream', different body activities trigger the corresponding dream content as the interaction principle, and the pressure sensor points of the wearable device are designed at the neck and cervical vertebrae, the mouth and nose, the left arm, the right arm, the heart, the left lung, the right lung, and the corresponding sensors are triggered by the different sleeping postures and body activities to provide feedbacks on the corresponding dream content of the experiencer (Fig. 3).

In order to ensure the reasonableness of the point design, in the point design, the designer firstly sorted out the common sleeping postures through research and consulting the information, which include right-side sleeping postures, left-side sleeping postures, tilted sleeping postures, prone sleeping, tilted sleeping, as well as the limb activities of the hands and feet, and the state of the mouth and nose at the point. Among them, the left side sleeping position due to the body's gravity pressure on the heart, resulting in accelerated heart rate, limiting the natural breathing pattern, variable breathing pattern, affecting the cardiopulmonary function, and often restlessness and anxiety nightmares. In prone sleeping the body's gravity presses on the heart, leading to an accelerated heart rate and limiting natural breathing patterns, the brain's oxygen supply may be somewhat limited, reducing the work of the prefrontal cortex and causing the brain to think or imagine more in an unconscious state. Blood flow causes the genitals to become more sensitive during rapid eye movement sleep and sleeping on the back puts pressure on the genitals, which in combination with this unconscious thought activity of the physiological brain may increase the probability of sex dreams and nightmares [22, 23]. Sleeping on the back is in the relaxation phase with natural breathing patterns, no tension in the brain, and quiet dreams or no dreams. Different changes in physiological data in different sleeping positions are corresponded into corresponding emotions and possible dream contents (Fig. 4).

Thus the relationship between the sensors corresponding to the sleeping position interaction is that the supine sleeping state triggers the sensor at the neck cervical vertebrae, the right side sleeping state touches the sensor at the right arm, the arm change during sleep randomly triggers the sensors at the heart, the left lung, and the right lung,

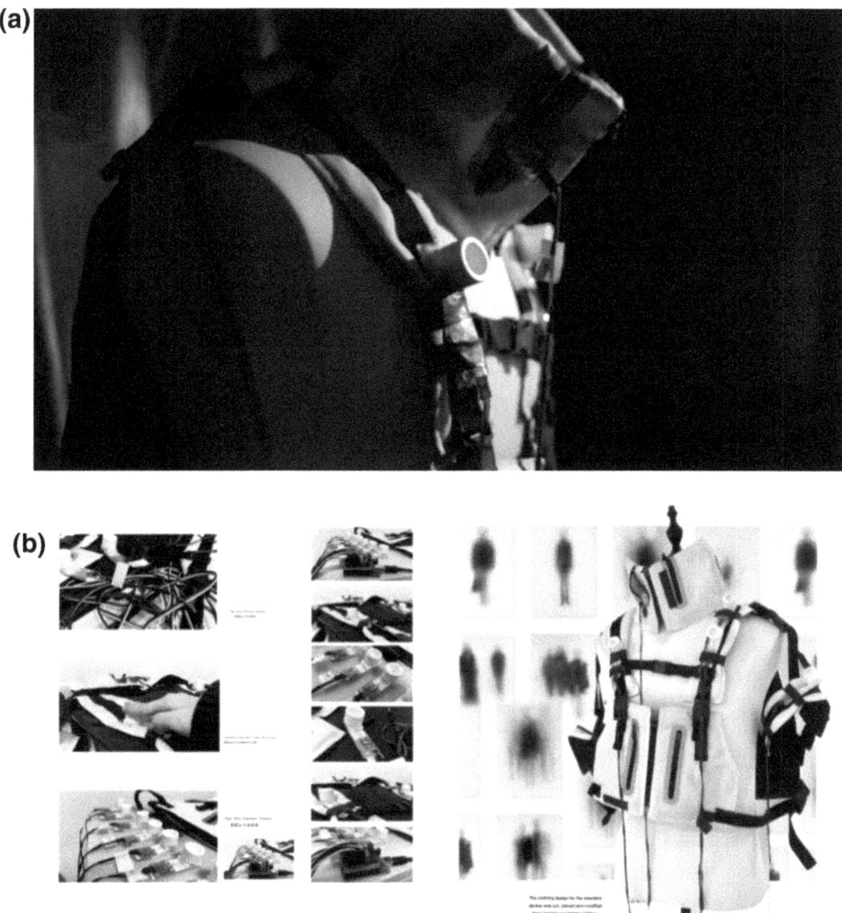

Fig. 3. a) A photo of the wearable device 'Dream; b) Pressure Sensor Point Design Flow for Wearable Devices.

the left side sleeping state triggers the sensor at the left arm, the prone sleeping state corresponds to the sensors at the heart, the left lung, the right lung, and the sensors that affect the sensors at the mouth and nose that affect breathing during sleep.

According to a user-independent method proposed by researchers showed an 85.3% accuracy in recognising three emotions using electrocardiogram (ECG), electrodermal activity (EDA), body temperature and respiration [15]. In the future version of Dream 2.0, the designers will add more physiological data references and design a head-mounted wearable device to collect physiological data of brain waves and body temperature, which will be combined with the sleeping interaction and heart rate collection in the current version of Dream, so that more physiological data of the users will be collected during the real-time interaction of the audience for the multi-dimensional analysis of emotions, and to improve the accuracy of the recognition of multi-modal emotions In

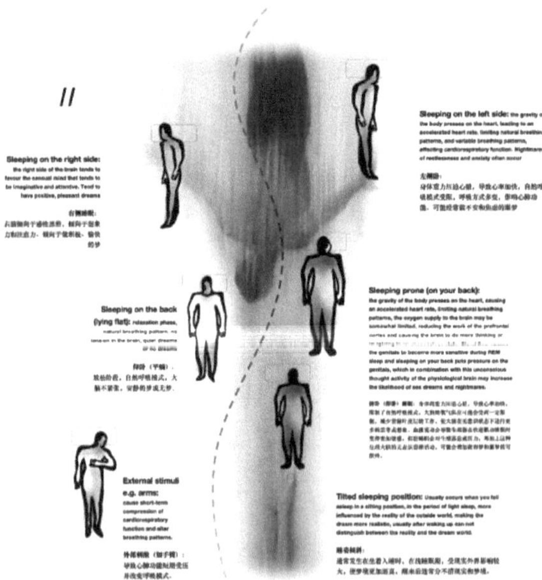

Fig. 4. Correspondence chart between common sleeping positions and current body condition.

order to capture the user's emotional state more accurately, the interactive feedback of 'Dream' can be improved to match the user's real experience of dreaming.

Generate Virtual Dream Scenes. Dream uses biofeedback to collect interactive data and Arduino programming to link with Touchdesigner to generate virtual dream images. The dream scenes are roughly divided into six parts using different emotional states: tranquillity, vitality, tension, anxiety, indulgence, and conflict, where each part is a combination of multiple randomly played dream scenes. On top of the figurative content of the image itself, Touchdesigner is used to respond to and feedback the degree of interaction through sound, colour, and abstract shapes to realise the dreams corresponding to different sleeping positions, unfolding as personality masks, and through the keywords of endless 'disembarkation', and the mentality of the herd when it comes to following the crowd, The content is designed through the keywords of endless 'disembarkation', the psychology of following the crowd, the life of 'conformity', and the serenity of letting go. The contrast between the original image and the particle effect image highlights the unspecificity of the dream, the size and density of the particles, the different coloured lines in the components of the image and the curved wave effect that varies with the size of the sensor data (Fig. 5).

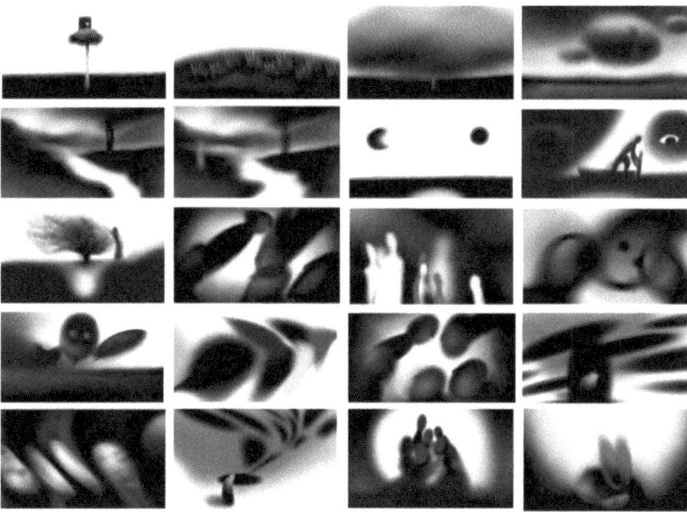

Fig. 5. Dream scenes drawn in the Dream project.

4 Exploration of Key Issues

4.1 Improved Accuracy of Emotion Recognition

In the interactive experience of immersive video installation, the audience's access to information not only requires the communication of the work, but also requires the audience's instinctive senses to actively perceive the information. Emotions as a complex interweaving of physiological and psychological states, in a specific external environment, the audience's instinctive multi-organ participation, in which the first organ to perceive will stimulate the participation of other organs, so as to get more biofeedback and physiological signal changes, the mobilisation and participation of this multi-sensory can be enriched by the interactions between them, the process of extracting information is more enriched, and the data and information of each data argue with each other to get more accurate emotion recognition information. The process of extracting information can be enriched, and the data and information can be argued with each other to obtain more accurate information for emotion recognition. In addition to intuitive changes in body expression, emotional changes are accompanied by changes in body physiological signals and internal subjective psychological factors [7, 8, 18]. Accurate emotion recognition may require the fusion and argumentative analysis of information from multiple modalities, each of which carries unique cues about the underlying emotional state. When the collection of single data is incomplete during data analysis, other modal data are required for corroboration, e.g., when emotions cannot be identified because the audience does not make a sound, heart rate changes and facial expression changes can be analysed for recognition. In the multimodal interactive experience, the rationality of interaction and the audience's experience should also be considered, which needs to pay attention to the relationship between the various modal data, should be based on the design objectives of the design programme for the design of the rationality of the design of the corresponding characteristics of each modality for the design of the target.

4.2 The Relationship Between Figurative Dream Images and Abstract Emotions

The fundamental purpose of the interactive experience under multimodal interaction is to enhance the audience's intuitive understanding of the work and the resonance of emotional perception, which includes the enjoyment of visual effects, inner potential desire feelings, changes in objective body physiological signals, and higher level spiritual needs, in the process of conveying information from the outside to the inside, how to trigger changes in the audience's abstract emotions through the figurative dream images, and how to use physiological data to conduct multimodal emotional analysis and correspond to the corresponding emotions of the figurative dream images are the key issues that 'Dream' needs to pay attention to.

In the process of conveying information from the outside in, how to trigger changes in the abstract emotions of the audience through figurative dream images, and how to use physiological data to analyse multimodal emotions and then correspond to the figurative dream images of corresponding emotions are the key issues to be concerned with in Dream. Among the effects of visual content presentation of dreams obtained through primary and secondary research prior to the project, among the common dream images, researchers found that the seven most common dreams involved being attacked or chased, being late, death of a loved one, falling, flying, going to school, and sex [11]. Scientists have studied psychological need experiences by linking them to everyday and recurring dreams. For example, dreams of falling, says Russell Grant, author of The Illustrated Dictionary of Dreams, 'are a symbol of real-life fears falling often indicates a need to let go more and enjoy life more.' Dream interpreters have studied dreams which include The Zhou Gong Dream Interpreter, The Illustrated Dictionary of Dreams, The Dream Dictionary, The Hidden Meanings of Dreams, and The Dream Dictionary for Dummies, which record common figurative dream images. How brain activity represents specific visual dream content is unclear. Findings suggest that the visual content of dreams is represented by the same neural substrates as those observed during waking perception [19]. So, symbols and memories in dreams are encoding and storing and abstracting reality, and dreams contribute to some extent to the consolidation of information for memory processing.

Therefore, during the audience's experience, seeing common dream images can give them a sense of identity and thus create empathy. The expression of abstract emotions in 'Dream' is expressed through the construction of a complete storyline, in the process of multi-sensory experience of the audience by analysing the real-time physiological data and changes in the sleeping position to correspond to the corresponding dream content, in the enrichment of the experience at the same time will be the combination of sensory perception and the audience's associations. According to the theory of colour psychology, colour can influence the current psychological state of people through visual stimulation, and the colour changes of dream images can also be associated with different abstract emotions, the lines of different colours in the dream images mentioned in the third part of the article will change with the size of the sensor data, for example, the red spectrum is longer, which is prone to excitement, nervousness and agitation, so as to express the corresponding emotional state [12].

4.3 Variety of Interaction Behaviours and Immersive Experiences

In the process of multimodal interactive experience, firstly, multisensory will receive the environmental information for the first time, secondly, the audience will further understand and analyse according to the information obtained, make behavioural interaction, and finally, under the joint effect of the audience's self-feeling and the environmental works, through the interactive feedback of the works, the use of multimodal multisensory fusion will produce a unique perceptual experience to achieve a sense of immersion. When discussing the meaning of dreams, because the interpretation of dreams is both personal and subjective, there is also the universal and scientific presence of the symbolic meaning of dreams. This dual nature reflects the complexity of human mental activity, with aspects of individual differences as well as common psychological structures and symbolic meanings. This provides a theoretical basis for understanding user psychology in multimodal interactions. The diversity of interaction behaviours is designed on the reflection of universality and individuality, so in consideration of the uniqueness of dreaming, the interaction form of AI dialogue will be added in future iterations of Dream to enrich the individual dream experience. Among the multiple interaction mechanisms in Dream, the rationality of the interaction behaviour is particularly important. Research has shown that the way a virtual environment is presented affects the overall perception and immersion of the audience. In the ideal multimodal interactive experience, the audience's psychophysiology and even deeper spiritual pursuits should be taken into account to achieve a deep level of perceptual experience, so as to get a sense of immersion. Based on the diversity of interaction behaviours, the work designs clever interaction mechanisms to weaken the audience's physical interaction, so that the audience can focus on the current situation (Fig. 6).

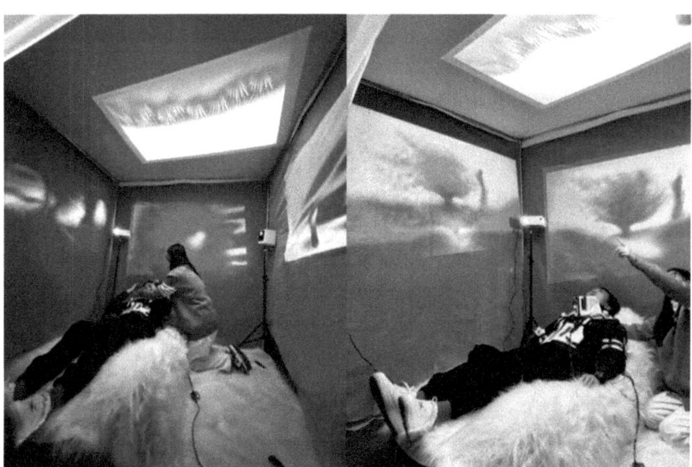

Fig. 6. Visitors experience interactive behaviours live.

In the current designer's 'Dream 2.0' work, the idea of adding AI narrative is proposed to enrich more interactive possibilities based on the dream scene of the original version of 'Dream'. Through the form of AI dialogue, the objectively collected physiological data information and the subjective viewer's self-thought jointly construct a dream scene with the viewer reflecting his/her inner world. In the generation of the virtual dream scene in version 2.0, the viewer's own dream symbols mentioned through the AI dialogue will be presented in the screen to enhance each viewer's experience and sense of uniqueness. Secondly, in the colour and storytelling of the screen, the degree of freedom and randomness will be enhanced, highlighting the sense of random compilation of the subconscious layer of the dreaming brain, and enhancing the diversity of interactive behaviours of the work and the immersive experience of the work's rich dream scenes.

5 Conclusion

With the development of new media technology, immersive interactive installation art has gradually become an important part of pioneering and experimental art. Immersive interaction emphasises the common sense of participation between the audience and the author, co-creation in terms of the degree of completion and connotation of the work, and the construction of interconnections and immersion between the artist himself, the audience, the society and the environment [18, 21]. Sensor devices capture and extract the audience's body language or physiological data for analysis corresponds to the existence of a variety of interactive possibilities in the programme, the audience to the individual as the centre to integrate into the immersive interactive space, in its interaction, access, interaction, interactive feedback, transformed into a visual effect of the process of the diversity of interactive behaviours will be the viewer's internal and external perceptions with the operation of the work of the form of expression to provide unlimited possibilities. Immersive art, as a multi-sensory and interactive way of presenting art, can more effectively mobilise people's subjective emotions, provide a more appropriate aesthetic distance, and break the sense of distance in the presence of the participants to obtain a profound physical and mental experience. At the same time, interdisciplinary cooperation and collaborative innovation is the key to promote the development of XR technology, through the integration of knowledge and resources from various fields such as computer science, psychology, art design, etc., to jointly promote the innovative development of XR technology. Although the theory of multimodal interaction provides more possibilities for the creation and presentation of immersive interactive art, the rationality of its interactive behaviour and the significance of the work cannot be ignored by pursuing the technology alone; it should go deeper into the cognitive, spiritual and cultural dimensions to bring deeper metaphorical meanings of the work and personal spiritual explorations to the work, establish a connection with immersion, and at the same time bring infinite possibilities for artistic creation.

References

1. Agargun, M.Y., Boysan, M., Hanoglu, L.: Sleeping position, dream emotions, and subjective sleep quality. Sleep Hypn. **6**, 8–13 (2004). https://psycnet.apa.org/record/2004-14976-002

2. Ahmed, S.U.: Interaction and interactivity: in the context of digital interactive art installation. In: Kurosu, M. (eds.) Human-Computer Interaction. Interaction in Context. HCI 2018. LNCS, vol. 10902. Springer, Cham (2018). https://doi.org/10.1007/978-3-319-91244-8_20
3. Al-Saadawi, H.F.T., Das, B., Das, R.: A systematic review of trimodal affective computing approaches: text, audio, and visual integration in emotion recognition and sentiment analysis. Expert Syst. Appl. 124852 (2024)
4. Choudhary, S.S., Choudhary, S.R.: Sleep effects on breathing and respiratory diseases. Lung India: official organ of Indian Chest Society **26**(4), 117–122 (2009). https://doi.org/10.4103/0970-2113.56345
5. Edmonds, E.: The art of interaction: what HCI can learn from interactive art. Morgan & Claypool Publishers (2018)
6. Fen, S.N.: Marshall McLuhan's" Understanding Media". J. Educ. Thought (JET)/Revue de La Pensée Éducative **3**(3), 161–180 (1969)
7. Gandhi, A., Adhvaryu, K., Poria, S., Cambria, E., Hussain, A.: Multimodal sentiment analysis: a systematic review of history, datasets, multimodal fusion methods, applications, challenges and future directions. Inform. Fusion **91**, 424–444 (2023)
8. Jieyi, X., Tao, X.: Research on interactive digital art based on multimodal sensory theory. Indust. Des. (2018). https://doi.org/CNKI:SUN:GYSH.0.2018-03-042
9. Katada, S., Okada, S., Komatani, K.: Effects of physiological signals in different types of multimodal sentiment estimation. IEEE Trans. Affect. Comput. **14**(3), 2443–2457 (2022)
10. Lidwell, W., Holden, K., Butler, J.: Universal principles of design, revised and updated: 125 ways to enhance usability, influence perception, increase appeal, make better design decisions, and teach through design. 134.Rockport Pub (2010)
11. Lorrain, D., Koninck, J.D.: Sleep position and sleep stages: evidence of their independence. Sleep **21**(4), 335–340 (1998)
12. Mehrabian, A.: Effects of color on emotions. J. Exp. Psychol. Gen. **123**(4), 394–409 (1994)
13. O'Halloran, K.L.: Multimodal discourse analysis. The Bloomsbury handbook of discourse analysis, pp. 249–282 (2011)
14. Pantic, M., Sebe, N., Cohn, J.F., Huang, T.: Affective multimodal human-computer interaction. In: Proceedings of the 13th Annual ACM International Conference on Multimedia, pp. 669–676 (2005)
15. Pinto, J., Fred, A., da Silva, H.P.: Biosignal-based multimodal emotion recognition in a valence-arousal affective framework applied to immersive video visualization. In: 2019 41st Annual International Conference of the IEEE Engineering in Medicine and Biology Society (EMBC), pp. 3577–3583. IEEE (2019)
16. Rauschnabel, P.A., Felix, R., Hinsch, C., Shahab, H., Alt, F.: What is XR? Towards a framework for augmented and virtual reality. Comput. Hum. Behav. **133**, 107289 (2022)
17. Shuo, Y., Zixiao, L., Wensi, D., et al.: A review of immersive media interaction and collaborative perception based on XR. Pack. Eng. **45**(20), 32–42 (2024)
18. Soleymani, M., Garcia, D., Jou, B., Schuller, B., Chang, S.F., Pantic, M.: A survey of multimodal sentiment analysis. Image Vis. Comput. **65**, 3–14 (2017)
19. Voldsbekk, I., et al.: Evidence for widespread alterations in cortical microstructure after 32 h of sleep deprivation. Transl. Psych. **12**(1), 161 (2022)
20. Yaqi, G., Sheng, L.: Form, dimension, context: on the "Space" recreation of immersive new media installation art. Decoration (2020)

21. Yichan, L., Yongchang, L.: Research on interactive experience design in museums from a multimodal perspective. Design (2024)
22. Yu, C.K.-C.: The effect of sleep position on dream experiences. Dreaming **22**(3), 212–221 (2012). https://doi.org/10.1037/a0029255
23. Yu, C.K.-C., Fu, W.: Sex dreams, wet dreams, and nocturnal emissions. Dreaming **21**(3), 197–212 (2011). https://doi.org/10.1037/a0024085

Research on Immersive and Interactive Prototype Design for Farming and Weaving Pictures in Ancient China in Virtual Reality Environment

Ruiqi Zhang⬤, Zhenyu Zhan⬤, Wei Li⬤, and Ning Zhang^(✉)⬤

Beijing Normal University at Zhuhai, Zhuhai 519087, China
ningzhang@bnu.edu.cn

Abstract. Chinese farming and weaving pictures (FWPs) face challenges in comprehension, presentation limitations, and underutilization of digitization. This study seeks to address these issues by leveraging Virtual Reality (VR) technology to enhance the promotion of traditional Chinese culture depicted in these artworks. Through a literature review, it examines the characteristics of FWPs and the advantages of VR in painting display. A multi-case study of 17 VR-enabled applications related to famous paintings is conducted, with a focus on the representative Pictures as a case for an immersive, interactive prototype design. The proposed VR prototype features five key functions: painting display, environmental navigation, farming tool interaction, basic mode, and advanced mode. This research offers theoretical insights into the design of VR-enhanced painting displays, innovating the presentation of FWPs and facilitating the widespread dissemination of ancient Chinese farming culture.

Keywords: Virtual Reality · Farming and Weaving Pictures · Cultural Heritage · Chinese Ancient Farming Culture

1 Introduction

The McKinsey Technology Trends Outlook 2024 identifies immersive virtual technology as one of 15 key trends, highlighting its expanding applications [1]. Virtual Reality (VR) has been widely used in cultural heritage [2], offering new opportunities for revitalizing Farming and Weaving Pictures (FWPs) and promoting Chinese agricultural culture. FWPs, which depict traditional farming and silk or cotton weaving [3], constitute an important aspect of China's cultural heritage. Over 1,100 such paintings have been systematically cataloged, including 416 specific works [4]. Geng Zhi Tu (耕织图) by Lou Chou of the Southern Song Dynasty is considered the world's first work on agricultural popularization [5]. These paintings embody the artistic and cultural essence of human civilization.

However, the display and dissemination of FWPs face three primary challenges. First, FWPs are difficult for general audiences to interpret due to their implicit spatial-temporal

D. Harris et al. (Eds.): HCII 2025, LNCS 16334, pp. 445–457, 2026.
https://doi.org/10.1007/978-3-032-12392-3_29

rhythms and symbolic depth [6]. Understanding them requires extensive knowledge of ancient agriculture, historical literacy, and artistic appreciation. Second, FWPs lack engagement and interactivity due to static museum displays that rely on physical objects and captions. This object-oriented approach limits their educational impact. To enhance public engagement, museums should adopt a people-centered approach, leveraging digital tools to foster interaction and deepen appreciation of both the paintings and Chinese agricultural culture. Third, the digitization of FWPs remains underdeveloped. While digital technologies enhance cultural heritage preservation and dissemination, VR and AR are still underutilized for FWP displays. This study, therefore, proposes a VR-based prototype framework to enhance the activation and utilization of FWPs.

In recent years, VR has played a crucial role in presenting and disseminating paintings by offering an immersive, interactive, and imaginative experience [7]. It transcends temporal and spatial constraints, allowing users to explore paintings comprehensively and enhancing their engagement [8, 9]. VR environments integrate artistic elements and virtual imagery, fostering deeper cognitive and emotional connections, stimulating abstract thinking, and enhancing the viewing experience [10]. Particularly for Chinese paintings, VR's ability to replicate intricate brushstrokes and color details enhances appreciation and optimizes display methods [11]. While VR has been successfully applied to Western paintings, Chinese landscape paintings, and murals, no dedicated VR framework for FWPs has been developed.

This research proposes a VR-based prototype design for FWPs, leveraging VR's advantages in cultural heritage dissemination. The framework aims to address key challenges, including audience comprehension barriers, limitations of traditional display methods, and the lack of digital applications.

2 Literature Review

2.1 Research on FWPs

Chinese scholars have conducted extensive historical research on the fundamental elements, characteristics, and symbolic depth of Farming and Weaving Pictures (FWPs). This study applies Irving Panofsky's iconographic analysis to synthesize existing research, providing a content foundation for the VR-based FWP prototype framework. Iconographic analysis consists of three levels: pre-iconographic description, iconographic analysis, and iconographic interpretation [12].

The pre-iconographic description involves identifying basic image elements. Scholars have examined the version system [13], farming tools, and depicted figures, which serve as essential components for designing the VR-based FWP prototype.

Iconographic analysis focuses on the narratives embedded within the images. Research indicates that FWPs convey temporal rhythms in agricultural activities [14], reflecting China's traditional agrarian economy and societal structure. Artistically, *Pictures of Farming and Weaving Made Under Imperial Orders* (PFWMUIO) employs Western perspective to create an expansive, fluid pictorial space [15], a feature well-suited for VR environments. Additionally, these paintings exhibit technological illusions, wherein certain tools and agricultural sequences deviate from historical accuracy [16]. Such findings inform the prototype's narrative logic and design principles.

Iconographic interpretation examines cultural and symbolic meanings. The depictions of rice cultivation and silk weaving in PFWMUIO not only illustrate social and psychological structures but also serve as ideological tools reinforcing authority [17]. Designed to educate and persuade farmers, these paintings convey multi-layered symbolism [18]. Experiencing these rich visual narratives immersively enhances comprehension of FWPs. However, research on digitizing FWPs remains limitations [19]. It is meaningful to develop a VR-based prototype for FWPs display and education.

2.2 The Advantages of VR in the Display of Ancient Paintings

International scholars have explored the advantages of VR technology in the display and dissemination of paintings from three primary perspectives. VR enriches painting exhibitions by allowing participants to closely examine details and styles, overcoming the limitations of physical display restrictions. Unlike traditional exhibitions, where direct interaction with artworks is prohibited, VR offers a more immersive aesthetic experience [20]. For intricate Chinese paintings, VR accurately presents the painter's brush strokes, pigment gradients, and ink variations, enhancing viewers' appreciation. In essence, VR overcomes traditional display limitations, bringing the audience closer to the artwork.

VR enhances the viewer's experience by providing a multisensory interaction—engaging sight, sound, and touch [9], which positively impacts aesthetic appreciation [21]. Research by Filip Škola highlights that VR significantly boosts audience presence, engagement, and immersion [22]. From a cognitive perspective, VR fosters a deeper affinity with the medium, enriching the aesthetic experience. Emotionally, the augmented narrative immersion enhances enjoyment, particularly for those with strong hedonic motivation [23].

VR also promotes art education and cultural heritage dissemination. Yang has shown that viewers can tailor information based on their aesthetic preferences, maintaining heightened attention during art appreciation [24]. VR enhances the perceived quality of the information [25] and increases the motivation to engage with the artwork [26]. It also allows for the symbolic reconstruction of the original context in which paintings were created, deepening users' understanding of their purpose and meaning [27]. It fosters two-way interaction between the viewer and the environment, stimulating engagement and enhancing emotional involvement, which in turn improves the intuitive grasp of abstract content [28]. VR technology can enhance learning efficiency and motivation, deepening viewers' understanding of Chinese painting styles and their cultural significance [29].

Academic research demonstrates that VR technology offers innovative display methods, enhances the viewing experience, and improves art education and cultural dissemination, providing a theoretical foundation for the application of VR in the exhibition of paintings.

2.3 Excellent Multi-case Study

The application of VR in the display and dissemination of paintings primarily manifests in two approaches. Firstly, transforming two-dimensional paintings into 3D models provides users with an immersive viewing experience. For instance, *The Night Cafe* [30] converts flat images into 3D spaces that users can explore, allowing them to fully appreciate *Café at Night* and experience the spatial tension conveyed through Van Gogh's brushwork. Secondly, by integrating game elements into paintings, VR enables users to engage with the artwork's unique features through interactive tasks. *1,2,3 Bruegel* [31], an immersive VR game inspired by Pieter Bruegel the Elder's *Children's Games*, allows players to explore Renaissance childhood while searching for hidden children in the virtual depiction of the painting. The second approach, combining art with gameplay, offers more engagement and creativity than the first.

A comprehensive analysis of 17 international VR-enabled applications related to famous paintings identifies three key aspects of design experiences. In terms of visual content, most applications offer high-resolution, complete representations of paintings, emphasizing both the artwork's intricate details and the unique artistic techniques employed. For example, in *Last Supper Interactive*, the Alberti Theorem Virtual Tool (ATVT) enables users to experience the linear perspective employed by Leonardo da Vinci, enhancing appreciation of its geometric principles and visual effects. Additionally, some applications provide insights into the creative background and emotional expression of the paintings through the reenactment of historical scenes [32], virtual character explanations [33], and dialogues with the virtual creator [32].

Core functions of these VR applications include display, navigation, interaction, and content management. The display function predominantly offers three-dimensional renditions of paintings, providing users with immersive perspectives that allow for detailed viewing from multiple angles. For example, in *VR Nine Dragons Diagram* (九龙图) [34], the task system adds an interactive layer to the experience, where users engage with content from the *Nine Dragons Diagram* and *Shan Hai Jing* (山海经) by performing tasks such as dispersing foreign beasts or collecting spiritual fire.

In terms of product features, common characteristics of VR painting applications include immersive experiences and the integration of culture and technology. The inclusion of characters or storytellers within the VR space further enhances immersion [35]. AI technology has also been employed to "resurrect" historical figures, such as Gu Mazhong in the VR *Han Xizai Night Banquet* (韩熙载夜宴图), allowing users to interact with the AI representation through dialogues and Q&A, deepening their understanding of the painting's cultural significance [36].

These existing VR applications provide valuable insights for the design framework of this research, particularly in terms of content presentation and functional modules. While VR prototypes for *Farming and Weaving Pictures* (FWPs) are currently lacking, combining virtual environments with FWPs is theoretically feasible. The proposed VR prototype for FWPs is both necessary and substantiated, offering significant potential for the activation and widespread dissemination of farming culture and cultural heritage.

3   Research Design

3.1   Research Aims and Questions

This research aims to propose a prototype design for FWPs in VR environment to overcome or weaken the current problems in the appreciation of FWPs for the general audience.

The key research question is how to design a prototype for FWPs in ancient China in VR environment.

3.2   Research Processes

The research process is illustrated in Fig. 1. Specifically, it began with a comprehensive literature review on the characteristics of FWPs and the advantages of VR in the display of paintings. Data were collected from the database of Web of Science (WoS) and Chinese National Knowledge Infrastructure (CNKI), resulting in the selection of 428 relevant English articles and 261 Chinese articles for in-depth review.

Subsequently, an online investigation into VR-enabled applications and the current state of FWP display provided practical insights for the design of the VR prototype. The *Pictures of Farming and Weaving Made Under Imperial Orders* (PFWMUIO), created in 1696, is preserved in The Palace Museum of Beijing. The museum employs a static display combining physical objects and captions to showcase the painting. Although the museum database includes an entry for the PFWMUIO, it lacks complete images and 3D models, resulting in a generally limited interactive experience. The current presentation of FWPs suffers from outdated methods, limited engagement, and insufficient digital integration. This online research informed the design of the VR framework for this study, emphasizing the need for such a framework in the presentation of FWPs.

The research then explored the feasibility of integrating FWPs with VR technology through a multi-case analysis of FWPs and a single-case analysis of the PFWMUIO. FWPs encompass all paintings depicting agricultural production and date back to the Warring States period (475–221 B.C.), with the earliest example being an engraved bronze pot depicting mulberry leaf-picking [5]. Early FWPs were often single-panel works, with the *Geng Zhi Tu* created by Lou Chou in the Southern Song Dynasty serving as a model for subsequent works. Since then, FWPs have largely followed Lou Chou's original, with minimal changes to size or content. The PFWMUIO, created in the Qing Dynasty, is the most important and representative FWP of that period. It is a direct imitation of *Geng Zhi Tu* and consists of 46 panels—23 depicting farming and 23 depicting weaving [37]. The painting integrates both Chinese and Western techniques, adopting Western perspective to enhance texture and three-dimensionality, which supports the subsequent construction of virtual environments. The accompanying poem by the Kangxi Emperor reflects his philosophy of promoting agriculture and farming [5]. The PFWMUIO serves as an ideal foundation for the VR FWP prototype, offering a universal and representative model.

This research proposed a well-grounded prototype design for FWPs in a VR environment, which is based on the content, artistic features, and emotional expression of the PFWMUIO, in conjunction with VR system design principles. The significance and limitations of this prototype design were also discussed.

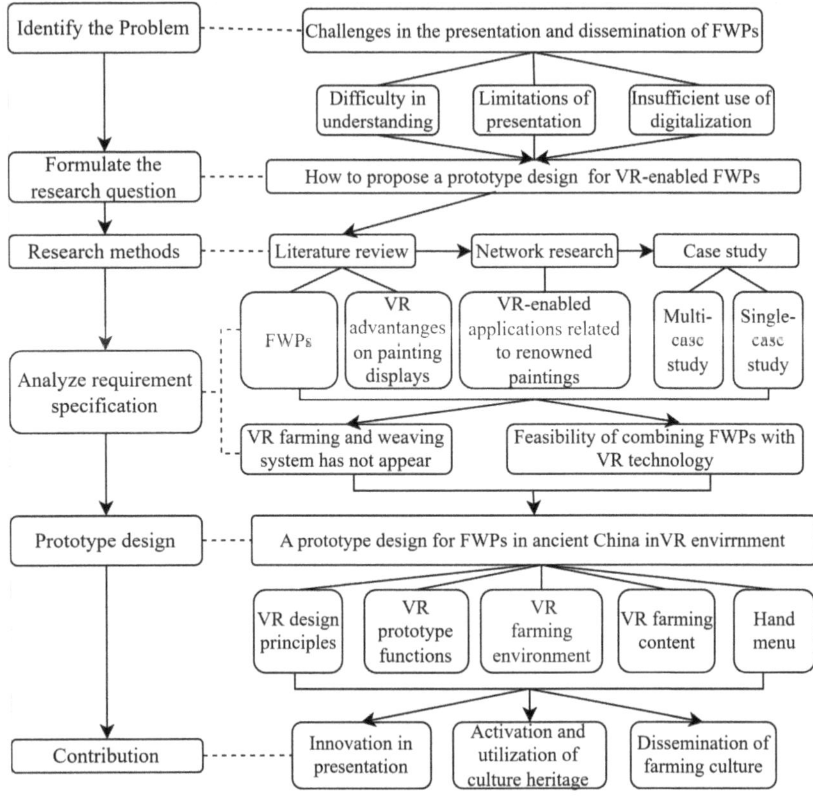

Fig. 1. Research Processes.

4   The Prototype Design for FWPs in VR Environment

4.1   User Requirements

This prototype is primarily designed for agricultural museums and targets kinesthetic learners with limited or no farming experience. The VARK model, proposed by Neil Fleming in 1987, classifies learners into Visual, Auditory, Read/Write, and Kinesthetic categories, with kinesthetic learners requiring hands-on opportunities and practical environments to facilitate learning [38]. VR environments cater to these needs, promoting cognitive development [39]. Kinesthetic learners often prefer gamified designs over static graphics. Research indicates that gamification enhances learning efficacy and optimizes the educational potential of museums [40]. This prototype addresses the needs of kinesthetic and gamified learning approaches.

4.2   Prototype Design

This design employs VR technology to accurately reproduce the scenes, characters, animals, and artifacts depicted in the *Pictures of Farming and Weaving Made Under*

Imperial Orders (PFWMUIO), creating a highly realistic visual experience. It also digitizes Qing Dynasty farming tools and integrates techniques from agricultural texts, including *Agricultural Book by Wang Zhen*(王祯农书) and *Bian Min Tu Zuan* (便民图纂). The immersive, multi-sensory, and persistent characteristics of VR contribute to the revitalization of historical farms and the development of the VR FWPs prototype as show in Fig. 2.

This prototype consists of two main components: the VR farming and weaving environment, and VR farming content. The VR farming and weaving environment recreates both indoor living spaces and outdoor farming activities in the Qing Dynasty. Based on the paddy farming life in southeastern China, the indoor spaces feature thatched roof houses typical of the region, including a room for farming tools, a granary, and a weaving area. The outdoor environment includes the characteristic landscape with paddy fields, rice crops, willow trees, mulberry trees, and wooden bridges. Studies indicate that multi-sensory experiences enhance engagement and immersion, thus improving learning outcomes [42]. To further enrich the VR environment, live animals such as cows, chickens, and sparrows are incorporated, enhancing the idyllic atmosphere and increasing the dynamic, multi-sensory nature of the scene.

Research indicates that incorporating avatars to explain concepts in virtual space significantly enhances the VR experience [35]. This design intends to create a virtual farmer avatar, assign actions to it, and develop an animated guide to demonstrate proper farming techniques. The design of farming tools and cultivation processes, as described above, contributes to the materialization of VR farming environments. Additionally, the inclusion of intangible cultural elements enriches the understanding of agricultural traditions. This approach integrates agricultural practices and customs with farming processes while also curating and producing relevant audio and video content to enhance the VR farming and weaving environment. The four-dimensional historical farms are realized through the development of a VR farming and weaving environment, combining VR farming content with diverse multimedia resources to create an immersive, multi-sensory FWPs prototype.

The FWPs prototype includes five primary functionalities: painting display, environment roaming, farming tool use, basic mode, and advanced mode. In painting display mode, users can view high-resolution paintings up close, zooming in to explore intricate details. Users can also roam freely within the VR environment and interact with objects, allowing them to become familiar with the farming setting. Farming tools are available for use, and users can engage in the farming process in basic mode. Interactions during this mode include recognizing the three-dimensional models of farming tools, exploring the VR scene, listening to audio, watching videos, and answering questions. Additionally, users can browse and share results, participate in two advanced modes—individual or group farming challenges—and access free-farming mode. The interactive prototype enhances human-computer interaction, enriching the user experience. The user interface (UI) is a critical component of VR applications, ensuring intuitive and seamless interactions [2].

The task flows of basic mode are shown in Fig. 3. Specifically, it consists of three tasks: identifying farming tools, acquiring plowing skills, and completing Q&A tests, designed to impart fundamental farming knowledge and provide initial user experience.

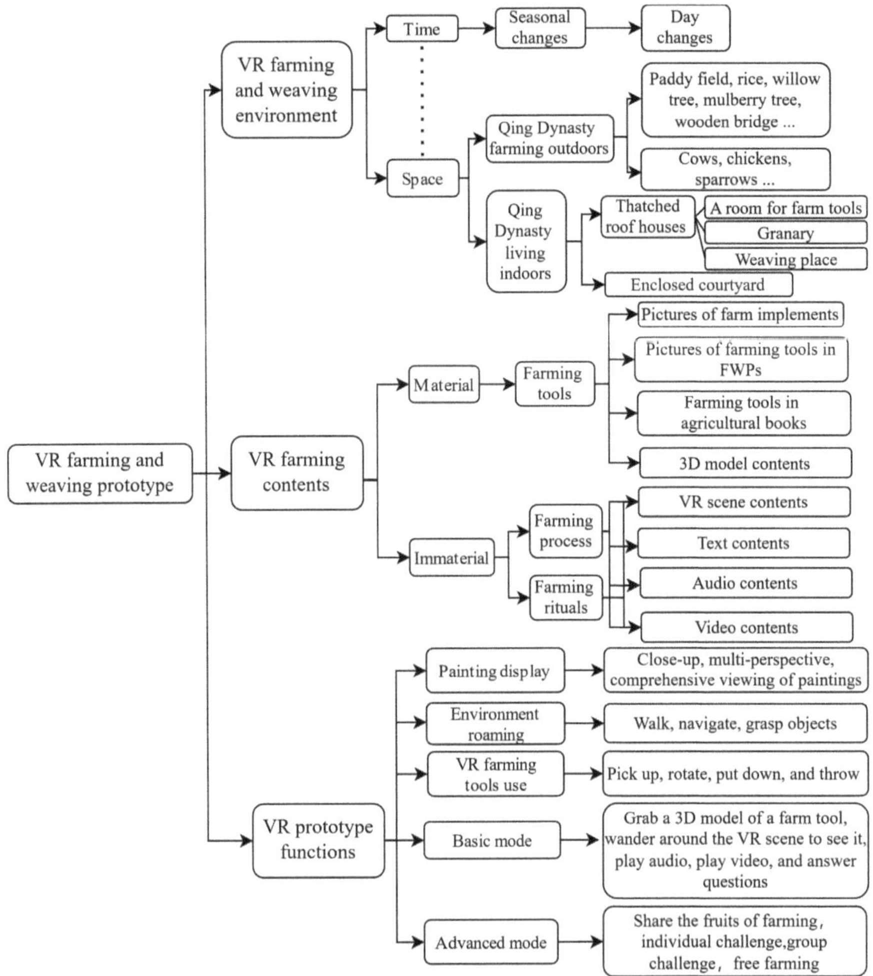

Fig. 2. The prototype design of FWPs in VR environment.

To begin, users select the basic mode option from the menu. Upon entering the scene, voice instructions are triggered, and users can observe animations depicting farming rituals and customs, establishing an atmosphere reminiscent of ancient farming practices. Users are then guided to pick up the designated farming tools in the farming tool room. If the user does not retrieve the tools within one minute, the prototype will rebroadcast the voice instructions. Once the user successfully retrieves the tool, the prototype provides a voice introduction of the tool. Users are then instructed to move from the tool room to the outdoor area. At the designated location, the virtual farmer avatar will guide the user through the farming actions, with the user executing the task as instructed. If the user does not respond correctly within a three-minute timeframe, the virtual farmer will repeat the demonstration. The prototype will continue providing audio explanations of the farming steps until the task is completed. Finally, users answer questions to assess their learning outcomes. Incorrect responses prompt the display of a knowledge card to assist the user in reviewing the material. Correct responses unlock new farming tools and award points, which can be used to purchase seeds for use in free mode. If the user chooses to proceed to the next level, the prototype will display the logo loading page in preparation. Otherwise, the game will conclude. The inclusion of multiple social interactions helps reduce the sense of isolation in the VR experience and fosters greater social engagement [43].

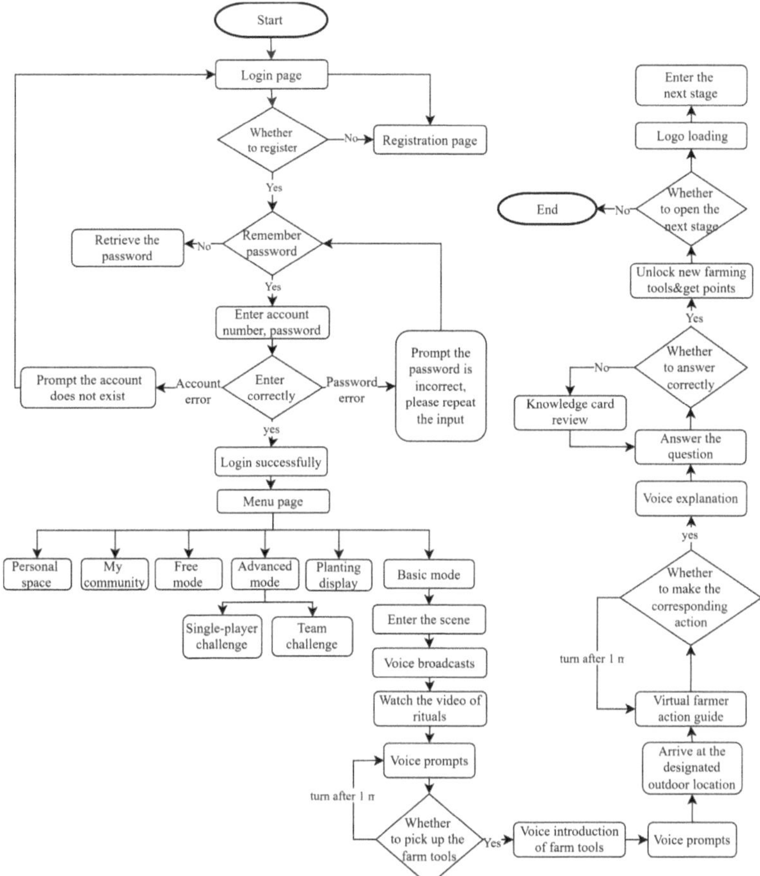

Fig. 3. Task flow of basic mode.

5 Discussion

The functional design of this prototype is grounded in cognitive load theory [44]. From this perspective, general audiences may struggle with recognizing basic elements such as farming tools and agricultural activities, understanding the characteristics of the paintings, and interpreting the deeper meanings conveyed through FWPs. The primary contribution of this VR prototype is to reduce the cognitive load associated with engaging with FWPs, thereby enhancing the viewer's interest and comprehension. Empirical studies have proposed design principles for VR prototypes that effectively address reading challenges. These principles include integrating multimedia resources, providing annotations, decomposing reading tasks, creating embodied reading environments, and offering autonomous interactive controls [45]. In line with these principles, this research incorporates multimedia resources—such as images of weaving maps, three-dimensional models of farming tools, videos, text, audio, and other media—into the VR FWPs prototype. The design organizes game stages based on the sequential decomposition of agricultural practices. This transformation converts two-dimensional paintings into an immersive three-dimensional experience, featuring five interactive functions: painting display, environment roaming, farming tool use, basic mode, and advanced mode.

In basic mode, the design follows the principle of story reconstruction. Story reconstruction refers to the digital retelling of stories based on images and their graphic representations. Story reproduction, which is a key aspect of this process, has four characteristics: explanatory, inspirational, guiding, and participatory [46]. This design extracts elements for story reconstruction by recognizing farming steps and deconstructing the components presented in the paintings, including farming tools, the environment, and characters. These elements are then modeled in 3D. Additionally, multi-sensory components, such as touch and sound, bring static images to life, creating a dynamic and immersive scene. The design also explores the inherent narrative of the farming process depicted in the paintings, supplemented by ancient agricultural texts and research works. The farming steps are broken down into a task flow, allowing users to enter the VR farming and weaving environment, engage with the farming interactions of the characters in the painting, and experience the farming process firsthand.

In conclusion, this research proposes an immersive and interactive prototype design for VR-enabled FWPs, which aids in the dissemination of farming culture. The construction of this design is theoretically grounded, based on a literature review and case analysis. The academic contributions of this research are threefold: innovation in display methods, promotion of farming culture, and the integration of traditional paintings with digitization. First, this design addresses the issue of inadequate display methods for FWPs. As an important cultural symbol of China's traditional farming civilization, FWPs encapsulate the wisdom and aesthetics of ancient agricultural production through poetic and pictorial forms. However, the exhibition methods for these works remain outdated. By leveraging VR technology to display FWPs and enhance interaction between the paintings and viewers, the dissemination efficiency of these artworks is improved, and new channels for displaying cultural content are opened.

Furthermore, the VR FWPs prototype facilitates the dissemination of farming culture and strengthens cultural identity. This framework offers the public an immersive virtual farming experience, deepening their understanding of ancient agricultural technologies and practices while promoting the spread of farming culture. Additionally, the framework allows the public to appreciate the aesthetic value of the paintings and the ingenuity of ancient peoples within a virtual space, fostering a stronger sense of cultural pride and confidence.

Finally, this research innovatively proposes the construction of a VR FWPs prototype framework, providing a theoretical reference for the fusion of traditional paintings and digital technology. Using the PFWMUIO as an example, this study explores the feasibility and value of presenting such paintings through VR, considering their content and cultural characteristics. By employing VR technology, it achieves a seamless integration of art and technology.

6 Conclusion

This research aims to address the challenges associated with the display and dissemination of FWPs by proposing an innovative immersive and interactive prototype design for VR-enabled FWPs. The PFWMUIO, with its rich variety and similarity to FWPs, serves as a representative example for this generalized prototype design. This framework provides a theoretical foundation for the integrated application of VR-enabled painting displays, aiming to revolutionize the dissemination methods of FWPs and promote the widespread propagation of Chinese ancient farming culture.

However, due to time and resource constraints, the study only presents a framework for VR-enabled FWPs, which has yet to be fully developed or tested in real-world scenarios. Further research is needed to assess the practical user experience and the effectiveness of integrating VR technology with FWPs in terms of cultural dissemination.

7 Disclosure of Interests.

It is now specifically state that the authors have no competing interests.

Acknowledgments. This study was supported by the Fundamental Research Funds for the Central Universities entitled "Theoretical Research and Online Platform Development of VR-based Ancient Texts for the Dissemination and Education of Excellent Traditional Chinese Culture" (Project No. 1243300007). It also was funded by Guangdong Province Philosophy and Social Sciences Planning Discipline Development Project entitled "Research on the Pathways of Empowering Classic Readings through Metaverse for Revitalization, Showcase, and Dissemination — with a Focus on Guangdong Province" (Project No. GD23XTS01) and The 2024 Beijing Normal University Teaching Reform Project on "Research and Practice of Design Innovation for the Revitalization of Literary Heritage in Virtual Reality Technology Environments" (Project No. JX2024047).

References

1. McKinsey Technology Trends Outlook 2024. https://www.mckinsey.com/capabilities/mckinsey-digital/our-insights/the-top-trends-in-tech. Accessed 25 Jan 2025
2. Okanovic, V., Ivkovic-Kihic, I., Boskovic, D., et al.: Interaction in extended reality applications for cultural heritage. Appl. Sci. **12**(3), 1241 (2022)
3. Wang, J.H.: The relationship between image and text and the expression of meaning in ancient Chinese images of farming and weaving. Natl. Arts **4**, 141–152 (2022)
4. Wang, H.Y.: The paintings on farming and weaving in ancient China. Red Flag Publishing House, Beijing (2009)

5. Wang, C.S.: A survey of farming and weaving pictures in ancient China. Huashan Literature and Art Publishing House, Shijiazhuang (2023)
6. Wang, J.H.: Manifest and hidden: the spatial and temporal expression of ancient Chinese farming and weaving pictures. Natl. Arts **4**, 119–127 (2016)
7. Burdea, G., Coiffet, P.: Virtual reality technology, 2nd edn. Wiley, New York (2003)
8. Soto-Martin, O., Fuentes-Porto, A., Martin-Gutierrez, J.: A digital reconstruction of a historical building and virtual reintegration of mural paintings to create an interactive and immersive experience in virtual reality. Appl. Sci. (10), 597(2020)
9. Mu, M., Dohan, M., Goodyear, A., et al.: User attention and behavior in virtual reality art encounter. Multimedia Tools Appl. **83**, 46595–46624 (2024)
10. Lin, C.L., Chen, S.J., Lin, R.: Efficacy of virtual reality in painting art exhibitions appreciation. Appl. Sci. **10**(9), 3012 (2020)
11. Cheng, Y., Huang, M., Yang, J., Sun, W.: Enhancing the immersive experience of the Yijing in Claborate-Style painting through virtual reality. In: 2024 IEEE Conference on Virtual Reality and 3D User Interfaces Abstracts and Workshops (VRW), pp. 967–968. Orlando, FL, USA (2024)
12. Erwin, P., Gerda S.: Panofsky. Studies in Iconology: humanistic themes in the art of Renaissance. Westview Press, Boulder (1972)
13. Wang, L.: Exploration on edition and compiling of imperial farming and weaving pictures in qing dynasty. Publish. Res. **13**(2), 142–148 (2013)
14. Wang, J.H.: Explicit and implicit: the spatial and temporal expression of farming and weaving pictures in ancient China. Natl. Arts **4**, 119–127 (2016)
15. Xie, D.: The qing imperial house version of "farming and weaving" research. doctoral Thesis, Xi'an Academy of Fine Arts (2015)
16. Wang, J.H.: The "illusion" of technological dissemination: re-examining the functions of ancient Chinese farming and weaving pictures. J. Chin. Soc. Econ. Hist. **2**, 10–17 (2016)
17. Chen, M.Q.: The interpretation of the social psychology on Kangxi Album of illustrations of agriculture and sericulture. Folklore Stud. (1), 146–155, 159 (2023)
18. Wang, J.H.: Who is the orthodoxy? exploring the political symbolism of ancient Chinese pictures of tilling and weaving. Folklore Stud. (1), 57–71, 154 (2018)
19. Xie, W., Yang, J.Y.: Research on farming and weaving images-oriented knowledge graph design and application. J. Acad. Lib. **42**(1), 83–92 (2024)
20. Chen, J.: Application and challenges of virtual reality (VR) in art exhibition planning. Appl. Math. Nonlinear Sci. **9**(1), 1–23 (2024)
21. Marto, A., Gonçalves, A., Melo, M., et al.: A survey of multisensory VR and AR applications for cultural heritage. Comput. Graph **102**, 426–440 (2021)
22. Škola, F., Rizvić, S., Cozza, M., et al.: Virtual reality with 360-video storytelling in cultural heritage: study of presence, engagement, and immersion. Sensors **20**(20), 5851 (2020)
23. Lee, H., Youn, N.J.: Immersed in art: the impact of affinity for technology interaction and hedonic motivation on aesthetic experiences in virtual reality. Empirical Studies of the Arts (2024)
24. Yang, X., Cheng, P.Y., Liu, X., et al.: The impact of immersive virtual reality on art education: a study of flow state, cognitive load, brain state, and motivation. Educ. Inf. Technol. **29**, 6087–6106 (2024)
25. Li, J., Yu, N.: Key technology of virtual roaming system in the museum of ancient high-imitative calligraphy and paintings. IEEE Access **8**, 151072–151086, IEEE (2020)
26. Kuo, Y.T., Garcia Bravo, E., Whittinghill, D.M., et al.: Walking into a modern painting: the impacts of using virtual reality on student learning performance and experiences in art appreciation. Int. J. Hum. Comput. Interact. **40**, 1–22 (2023)
27. Pagano, A., Palombini, A., Bozzelli, G., et al.: Vision VR game: user experience research between real and virtual Paestum. Appl. Sci. **10**(9), 3182 (2020)

28. Jin, S., Fan, M., Kadir, A.: Immersive spring morning in the Han palace: learning traditional Chinese art via virtual reality and multi-touch tabletop. Int. J. Hum.-Comput. Interact. **38**(3), 213–226 (2022)
29. Cheng, Y., Huang, M., Yang, J., et al.: Enhancing the immersive experience of the Yijing in claborate-style painting through virtual reality. In: 2024 IEEE Conference on Virtual Reality and 3D User Interfaces Abstracts and Workshops (VRW), pp. 967–968. Orlando, FL, USA (2024)
30. The Night Café. https://store.steampowered.com/app/482390/The_Night_Cafe_A_VR_Tribute_to_Vincent_Van_Gogh/. Accessed 25 Jan 2025
31. , 2, 3... Bruegel! https://store.steampowered.com/app/1071310/1_2_3_Bruegel/. Accessed 25 Jan 2025
32. The Scream. https://store.steampowered.com/app/1097120/The_Scream/. Accessed 25 Jan 2025
33. Maria Blanchard Virtual Gallery. https://store.steampowered.com/app/2026860/Maria_Blanchard_Virtual_Gallery/. Accessed 25 Jan 2025
34. Nine Dragons Taking to the Air. https://www.di-award.org/collections/detail/1588.html. Accessed 25 Jan 2025
35. Karuzaki, E., Partarakis, N., Patsiouras, N., et al.: Realistic virtual humans for cultural heritage applications. Heritage **4**, 4148–4171 (2021)
36. "Han Xizai Night Banquet" AI immersive experience exhibition. https://mp.weixin.qq.com/s/igYdA2JsPbbgA_FOkeSBLw. Accessed 25 Jan 2025
37. Li, S.S., Sun, M.H.: Study on the compilation and communication of the "imperially-made farming and weaving pictures" under the concept of emphasizing and persuading agriculture (2), Publishing Research (2024)
38. Qiao, X.M., Yang, J.: The classification and adaptive strategies of learning style-based user models. Mod. Educ. Technol. **29**(1), 101 (2019)
39. Hua, Z.X.: Research on learners' kinesthetic learning mechanism based on the virtual reality technology. China Educ. Technol. (12), 21 (2019)
40. Meng, R., Xin, G., Chen, Y., et al.: Museum visiting experience design under the perspective of gamification–taking shanghai planetarium experience design as an example. Public Commun. Sci. Technol. **11**(7), 185 (2019)
41. Huang, Y., Wang, S.M.: Living history farm: effective approaches to the protection and utilization of agricultural cultural heritage. Agric. Hist. China **32**(1), 100 (2013)
42. Clini, P., Nespeca, R., Ruggeri, L.: Virtual in real. Interactive solutions for learning and communication in the national archaeological museum of Marche. The International Archives of the Photogrammetry, Remote Sensing and Spatial Information Sciences, vol. 42, pp. 647–654. Göttingen University Press, Göttingen State (2017)
43. Shi, Y., Lu, Y., Liu, L., Liu, E.: Virtual reality painting: a structured review of a decade of innovation. Metaverse **5**(1), 1–18 (2024)
44. Sweler, J.: Cognitive load during problem solving: effects on learning. Cogn. Sci. **12**(2), 257–285 (1988)
45. Zhang, N., Miguel, B. N., Li, J.Y., et al.: Designing a virtual reality Chinese ancient book system for reading and culture promotion: a theoretical model development and implementation. Lib. Inform. Serv. **65**(13), 12–24 (2021)
46. Chen, X.H.: Digital design of silk painting of "a dream of red mansions" by sun wen based on VR technology. Dissertation, Jiangnan University (2021)

Author Index

A
Abe, Yuki   383
Almeida, Helena Filipe   231
Anagnostopoulos, George   231
Aricò, Pietro   181
Arrigoni, Vanessa   243

B
Babiloni, Fabio   181
Baumgartner, Marc   181
Bejarano, Carmen   54
Bergesio, Luca   181
Besada, Juan Alberto   181
Birrell, Stewart   345
Blundell, James   3, 163, 345
Bodsworth, Chris   345
Bonelli, Stefano   181
Borghini, Gianluca   181
Burns, Christopher   163

C
Calatrava, Almudena   181
Candra, Feby Juana   383
Cañas Delgado, Jose J.   181
Causse, Mickaël   277
Cavagnetto, Nicola   243
Chen, Chun-Hsien   331
Chen, Yingting   383
Cheng, Xiao   413
Clayton, George   3
Cordero, Jose Manuel   54
Cotter, Jenna   126
Curtis, Erica   126

D
Davis, Ryker   14
De, Raj   35
Di, Xie   73

E
Eder, Pauline   277
Eleftherakis, Panagiotis-Eleftherios   231
Engelhardtsen, Øystein   262

F
Fedrizzi, Ginevra   54
Feng, Zixiang   364
Friedrich, Maik   293
Fuchs, Andrew   54

G
Garcia Lasheras, Raquel   181
Garcia, Lidia   181
Gluchshenko, Olga   293
Gu, Qiuli   306

H
Hao, Deng   73
Heggedahl, Timothy   126
Hiyama, Atsushi   383
Hu, Jun   397
Hurter, Christophe   181

I
Iglesias, Brais   181
Iliakis, Konstantinos   231
Imbert, Jean-Paul   277

J
Jadronova, Martina   181
Johnston, Samuel   126

K
Kalakou, Sofia   231
Kanno, Taro   383
Kebir, Sara   181
Kitagawa, Haruki   383
Kobayashi, Katsuomi   383
Künzel, Dominik   200

L
Lema, Florencia   181
Levantesi, Alfonso   181
Li, Hu   331
Li, Wei   445
Li, Wen-Chin   100
Liepe, Lisa   293
Lin, Chen   73
Lin, WeiZhen   413
Liu, Xinxiong   213
Liu, Yiqi   429
Lopes, Margarida   231
Lopez De Fruto, Patricia Maria   181
Lou, Yunyin   397
Luo, Jieyu   213

M
Majumdar, Neelakshi   14
Mallam, Steven   262
Manikath, Elizabeth   100
Mapar, Hossein   181
Maresca, Anna   126
Marsman, Laurie   181
Mcleod, James Lindsay Afonso de Brito   231
Metge, Adrien   54
Morgan, Justin   126
Mouratille, Damien   277
Muth, Kathleen   293

N
Nakanishi, Miwa   115
Nan, Li   73
Nazir, Salman   262
Nelson, Justin   126
Nöhren, Lennard   293

O
Ogawa, Ami   277
Ohtsubo, Yohsuke   383
Ono, Mako   115

P
Payre, William   345
Peng, GuoChao   413
Perillo, Andrés   54
Perello March, Jaume   163
Piotrowski, Pawel   100
Pozzi, Simone   243

R
Ren, Jingrui   318
Ruano, Sara   54
Rudolph, Florian   293

S
Samoili, Sofia   231
Sarıkaya, İbrahim   137
Schaper, Meilin   293
Schulte, Axel   200
Sicheng, Hua   73
Smeltink, Job   181
Smoker, Anthony   181
Su, JunJie   413

T
Takacs, Veronika Klara   243
Truong, Guillaume   181
Tyburzy, Lukas   293

U
Ücrak, Fuat   137

V
Vaiopoulos, Paris   54
van de Merwe, Koen   262
van Miltenburg, Maykel   181
Veyrie, Alexandre   181
Vicario, Anna Giulia   54, 181

W
Wang, Lili   147, 306
Wang, Yanqing   73, 318
Wu, Siyu   318

X
Xia, Chen   181
Xydis, Sotirios   231

Y
Yao, Xing   331
Yi, Yuxiao   429
Yoshino, Yuta   383
Yu, Xiaoqing   331

Z
Zhan, Zhenyu   445
Zhang, Ning   445
Zhang, Ruiqi   445

Zhang, Xiaolei   318
Zhao, Yue   413

Zhu, Mincong   147
Zon, Rolf   181